Essentials of

CONTEMPORARY MANAGEMENT

Fourth Canadian Edition

Gareth R. Jones
Texas A & M University

Jennifer M. George
Rice University

Jane W. Haddad
Seneca College of Applied Arts and Technology

Michael Rock, Ed.D.
Seneca College of Applied Arts and Technology (ret.)
University of Guelph

McGraw-Hill Ryerson
Connect. Learn. Succeed.

Essentials of Contemporary Management
Fourth Canadian Edition

ISBN-13: 978-0-07-105149-1

ISBN-10: 0-07-105149-X

1 2 3 4 5 6 7 8 9 0 DOW 1 9 8 7 6 5 4 3

Printed and bound in the United States of America

Editorial Director: *Rhondda McNabb*
Publisher: *Kim Brewster*
Marketing Manager: *Cathie Lefebvre*
Developmental Editors: *Lori McLellan and Becky Ranger*
Senior Editorial Associate: *Christine Lomas*
Supervising Editors: *Kara Stahl and Cathy Biribauer*
Copy Editor: *Kelli Howey*
Permissions Editor: *Derek Capitaine, www.mrmassociates.ca*
Production Coordinator: *Scott Morrison*
Cover and Interior Design: *Michelle Losier*
Page Layout: *Laserwords Private Limited*
Printer: *R. R. Donnelley*

Library and Archives Canada Cataloguing in Publication

Essentials of contemporary management / Gareth R. Jones . . [et al.]. — 4th Canadian ed.

First Canadian ed. by: Gareth R. Jones, Jennifer M. George, Nancy Langton; 2nd Canadian ed. by: Gareth R. Jones, Jennifer M. George, Nancy Langton and contributor, Jane Haddad.

Includes bibliographical references and index.

ISBN 978-0-07-105149-1

1. Management—Textbooks. I. Jones, Gareth R

HD31.E79 2013   658.4   C2012-904949-2

Jane W. Haddad received her Honours B.A. from Queen's University, Ontario, in 1984, followed by her M.A. from the Ontario Institute for Studies in Education at the University of Toronto in 1986. She has taught in the faculties of Sociology and Education at the University of Saskatchewan and the University of Regina, Saskatchewan, and in the Salem International University distance M.B.A. program. In addition to teaching Liberal Studies, Humanities, and Management theory for over 20 years, Jane is the coordinator of the post-graduate certificate program in Non-Profit Leadership and Management in the School of Business Management at Seneca College of Applied Arts and Technology, Toronto, Ontario. Professor Haddad coordinated a SSHRC-funded Community–University Research Alliance (CURA) grant at Seneca from 2000 to 2005 and currently sits on Seneca's Research Ethics Review Board. Professor Haddad's research interests include youth training and labour markets, barriers to accessing post-secondary education, social innovation, and social enterprise. She has presented several academic papers at Learned Society and other conferences across Canada and has published her work in journals such as *Canadian Women's Studies Journal* and *The College Quarterly*.

Michael Rock has recently retired as a full-time professor at Seneca College of Applied Arts and Technology. For many years, Professor Rock was an Adjunct Professor in the School of Management and Economics at the University of Guelph, where he currently teaches Ethics in Leadership in the distance education Leadership Studies M.A. program. Professor Rock holds a doctorate in Adult Education from Indiana University (1974) and is a licensed emotional intelligence coach and facilitator with Dr. Reuven Bar-On's Emotional Quotient-*Inventory*© (EQ-*i*©). Together with Dr. Bar-On, he has recently co-authored the Spiritual Quotient-*Inventory*© (SQ-*i*©), with the educational research version now available at www.sq-i.org. He has authored over 150 articles in human relations trade journals and magazines and twelve books, including *EQ Goes to Work* and *Ethics: To Live By, To Work By*, and is the co-author of *The 7 Pillars of Visionary Leadership*. Currently he is completing Ph.D. and D.Th. degrees in Spirituality in the Workplace and Theology at Saint Paul University and the University of Ottawa. He continues to provide executive retreats and presentations in the areas of emotional intelligence, spirituality, and ethics in the workplace, and leadership development.

Gareth Jones is a professor of Management in the Lowry Mays College and Graduate School of Business at Texas A&M University. He received his B.A. in Economics and Psychology and his Ph.D. in Management from the University of Lancaster. He specializes in strategic management and organizational theory and is well known for his research that applies transaction cost analysis to explain many forms of strategic and organizational behaviour. He is currently interested in strategy process, competitive advantage, and information technology issues. He is also investigating the relationships between ethics, trust, and organizational culture, and studying the role of affect in the strategic decision-making process. Professor Jones has published many articles in the leading journals of the field, including the *Academy of Management Review*, the *Journal of International Business Studies*, *Human Relations*, and the *Journal of Management*. Professor Jones has taken his academic knowledge and used it to craft leading textbooks in management and three other major areas in the management discipline; organizational behaviour, organizational theory, and strategic management. His books are widely recognized for their innovative, contemporary content and for the clarity with which they communicate complex, real-world issues to students.

Jennifer George is the Mary Gibbs Jones Professor of Management and Professor of Psychology in the Jesse H. Jones Graduate School of Business at Rice University. She received her B.A. in Psychology and Sociology from Wesleyan University and her M.B.A. in Finance and Ph.D. in Management and Organizational Behaviour from New York University. Professor George specializes in organizational behaviour and is well known for her research on mood and emotion in the workplace, their determinants, and their effects on various individual and group-level work outcomes. She is an award-winning author of many articles in leading peer-reviewed journals and has been on numerous editorial review boards. Professor George is a Fellow in the American Psychological Association, the American Psychological Society, and the Society for Industrial and Organizational Psychology, and a member of the Society for Organizational Behaviour. Professor George recently completed a six-year term as an associate editor for the *Journal of Applied Psychology*. She has also co-authored the widely used textbook *Understanding and Managing Organizational Behaviour*.

Brief Contents

Contents

CHAPTER 11

Managing Human Resources — 310

CHAPTER 12

Managing Communication and Conflict — 342

A manager is a person who makes other people's work meaningful.

When groups of people come together to pursue a common goal, often to satisfy their collective needs, various activities must be structured so that resources can be gathered and used to achieve the goal. The person or people who are assigned the task of keeping the whole group working toward the goal, deciding on timing and strategy and maintaining the structure of activities and relationships, are those who engage in *management*. The activities of managing are critical to any complex cooperative endeavour. Management is both the art and science of arranging and utilizing the physical and human factors of production toward a socially desirable outcome without interfering in nature's ability to regenerate itself. This book provides you, the student, with an introduction to sustainable management processes. This fourth Canadian edition is designed around the four main sets of activities that managers engage in to achieve organizational goals: Planning, Organizing, Leading and Controlling.

In **Part I, Chapter 1: Managers and Managing**, we discuss who managers are, the types and levels of managers found in organizations, the recent changes to management hierarchies, the managerial skills needed to perform their main responsibilities, and the roles they perform in planning, organizing, leading, and controlling.

Part II, Chapter 2: Managing the Organizational Environment, sets the management process in the environmental context of operating enterprises in Canada and the global economy. The economic, socio-cultural, legal-political and technological contexts, as well as the immediate agents in the organization's external environment, such as suppliers, customers, distributors and competitors, are analyzed for the threats and opportunities they present to managers trying to gain a sustainable competitive advantage. The awareness of differences in national cultures is important in being successful in the global economy. **Chapter 3: Managing Ethics, Social Responsibility and Diversity,** deals with the interrelatedness of doing what's right for stakeholders, including the environment, and doing what's good for business, in terms of utilizing the widest pool of talent available to enterprises in a multicultural and aging demographic context.

Part III, Chapter 4: Managing Decision Making and Sustainability addresses the fundamental challenge facing managers to make optimal and sustainable decisions. Decisions that promote the triple bottom line: People-Planet-Profit. Increasingly, this means utilizing and integrating Management Information Systems (MIS). **Chapter 5, Managing Planning and Strategy**, tackles the process of planning organizational goals, formulating strategies, and finding the best ways to implement and evaluate the success of those goals and strategies. Students will learn two common techniques for analyzing the environmental context that is vital to strategy formulation for a competitive advantage: SWOT and Porters' Five Forces model.

In **Part IV, Chapter 6: Managing Organizational Structure**, the elements of organizational design and structure are discussed. Students learn that ways of allocating authority and distributing control over decision making result in different organizational structures. The type of overall organizational structure depends on internal and external environmental factors, such as strategy, technology, human resources, and the degree of environmental change. **Chapter 7,**

Managing Innovation and Change, explores how fostering an innovative organizational culture is critical for success. When an organization's strategy and structure undergoes change, the culture must also adapt to regain competitiveness and sustainability. Two models of organizational change are presented.

Part V, Chapter 8: Motivation, discusses the means by which managers can motivate good work effort and performance from employees. Several need and process theories are discussed, and the importance of a total rewards strategy utilizing both intrinsic and extrinsic factors is highlighted. In **Chapter 9, Managing Leadership**, students will learn the importance of effective leadership in managing organizational performance. Trait, behavioural, and contingency theories are explored, and transformational and transactional leadership styles are compared. **Chapter 10, Managing Teams**, discusses the types of groups and teams found in contemporary organizations. Students will learn the elements of group dynamics, group decision making techniques, and what managers can do to create high-performing teams in their organizations. **Chapter 11, Managing Human Resources**, is focused on how managers can successfully recruit, select, develop, appraise, and compensate valued employees in the context of the Canadian legal and regulatory environment. **Chapter 12, Communication and Conflict**, deals with the changing technological impact on effective communication, conflict resolution, and negotiation techniques for managing information and people.

In **Part VI, Chapter 13: Organizational Control and Operations**, students will learn how managers monitor and measure the use of resources to make sure processes and products are up to standards throughout the entire value chain. Corporate governance practices are examined in light of recent economic crises. The types of controls that managers use impact the culture and structure of the organization and reflect either innovative or conservative practices.

Appendix A: Developing a Business Plan provides a template for students to apply the principles of management to the writing of a business plan for a new venture or new strategy for an existing organization.

New to this edition, is a **Focus on The Social Economy** box, which profiles a social enterprise that has both the function of creating economic value common to traditional for-profit businesses *and* creating social impact common to non-profit and charitable organizations. In each chapter, you will learn how a social enterprise can apply business management processes to help people and solve social problems that were once only the responsibility of governments. Social enterprises find innovative ways to deal with some of the fundamental concerns that the 'business-as-usual" mentality has created, including a growing gap between rich and poor and environmental degradation. The awareness that if we continue to operate solely on a "business-as-usual" basis, where profit maximization is the only measurement of success, we will fail all of the stakeholders in any enterprise: employees, customers, partners, suppliers, investors, communities, and nature. We have to embrace innovative and sustainable ways to foster an economy that enables us to clothe, feed, and care for ourselves and others, and enjoy life without interfering with nature's diversity or its ability to regenerate itself.

All of the material covered in *Essentials of Contemporary Management*, Fourth Canadian Edition, has a direct application to you as a student of organizational management as well as to any business or social enterprise you may own, manage, or work for in the future.

J. W. Haddad
November 2012

Guided Tour

Learning Tools

Learning Outcomes have been highlighted at the beginning of each chapter, identified throughout the text, and discussed in the **Summary and Review.**

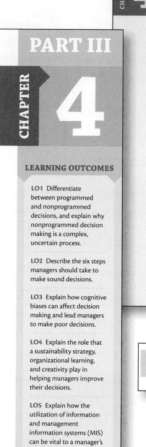

PART III

CHAPTER

4

LEARNING OUTCOMES

LO1 Differentiate between programmed and nonprogrammed decisions, and explain why nonprogrammed decision making is a complex, uncertain process.

LO2 Describe the six steps managers should take to make sound decisions.

LO3 Explain how cognitive biases can affect decision making and lead managers to make poor decisions.

LO4 Explain the role that a sustainability strategy, organizational learning, and creativity play in helping managers improve their decisions.

LO5 Explain how the utilization of information and management information systems (MIS) can be vital to a manager's decision-making processes.

CHAPTER 4

Summary and Review

LO1 The Nature of Managerial Decision Making *Programmed decisions* are routine decisions that are made so often that managers have developed decision rules to be followed automatically. *Nonprogrammed* decisions are made in response to situations that are unusual or unique; they are nonroutine decisions. The *classical model* of decision making assumes that decision makers have complete information, are able to process that information in an objective, rational manner, and make optimum decisions. March and Simon in the *administrative model* argue that managers are subject to *bounded rationality*, rarely have access to all the information they need to make optimum decisions, and consequently *satisfice* and rely on their *intuition* and *judgment* when making decisions.

LO2 Steps in the Decision-Making Process When making decisions, managers should take these six steps: *recognize the need for a decision, generate alternatives, assess alternatives, choose among alternatives, implement the chosen alternative,* and *evaluate and learn from feedback.*

LO3 Biases in Decision Making Managers are often fairly good decision makers. However, problems result when human judgment is adversely affected by the operation of cognitive biases. Cognitive biases are caused by systematic errors in the way decision-makers process information to make decisions. Sources of these errors include *prior hypothesis, representativeness, illusion of control,* and *escalating commitment.*

LO4 Improving Decision Making Managers can make better decisions when they examine their biases and spend appropriate amounts of time engaging in the process. But to make optimum decisions, managers should adopt a *sustainability strategy*—one that is transparent, engaging, and economically beneficial without leaving a large carbon footprint. They must become a *learning organization* and encourage *creativity* to ensure that new, innovative ideas are not overlooked.

LO5 Utilizing Information and Management Information Systems (MIS) Traditionally, managers used the organizational hierarchy as the main system for gathering the information they needed to coordinate and control the organization and make effective decisions. Today, managers use four types of computer-based information systems to provide them with the high-quality, timely, relevant, and relatively complete information they need to enable them to make effective decisions. Listed in ascending order of sophistication, they are *transaction-processing systems, operations information systems, decision support systems,* and *expert systems.*

LO1 Describe what management is, what managers do, and how managers use resources to achieve organizational goals.

Definitions of Key Terms are highlighted in each chapter and provided in the margins, and a list of these terms is provided at the end of each chapter and in the glossary at the end of the text, which includes page references.

nonprogrammed decision making Nonroutine decision making that occurs in response to unusual, unpredictable opportunities and threats.

classical model A prescriptive approach to decision making based on the idea that the decision maker can identify and evaluate all possible alternatives and their consequences and rationally choose the most suitable course of action.

optimum decision The most appropriate decision in light of what managers believe to be the most desirable future consequences for their organization.

Nonprogrammed decision making occurs when there are no ready-made decision rules that managers can apply to a situation. Nonprogrammed decision making is required for these *nonroutine* decisions. Nonprogrammed decisions are made in response to unusual or novel opportunities and threats. Rules do not exist because the situation is unexpected or uncertain and managers lack the information they would need to develop rules to cover it. Examples of nonprogrammed decision making include decisions to invest in a new kind of green technology, develop a new kind of product (as Jochen Zeitz did in the opening case), launch a new promotional campaign, ent... expand internationally, ... business. In the remaind... when we talk about dec... are referring to nonprog... making because it is the... the most problems for m...

Sometimes managers have to make ra... don't have the time for careful considera... involved. They must rely on their intu... respond to a pressing concern. For exa... chiefs, captains, and lieutenants manag... tling dangerous, out-of-control fires, th... rely on their expert intuition to make on-... that will protect the lives of the firefigh... lives of others, contain the fires, and pre...

Other times, managers do have the time available to make reasoned judgments but there are no established rules to guide their decisions, such as when deciding whether or not to proceed with a proposed merger. Regardless of the circumstances, nonprogrammed decisions can result in effective or ineffective decision making.

The *classical* and the *administrative* decision-making models reveal many of the assumptions, complexities, and pitfalls that affect decision making. These models help reveal the factors that managers and other decision makers must be aware of to improve the quality of their decision making. Keep in mind, however, that the classical and administrative models are just guides that can help managers understand the decision-making process. In real life, the process is typically not cut-and-dried, but these models can help guide a manager through it. We

KEY TERMS

administrative model	illusion of control	operations information
ambiguous information	information	system
bounded rationality	information distortion	optimum decision
classical model	information technology	organizational learning
cloud computing	innovation	prior hypothesis bias
creativity	intrapreneur	programmed decision making
data	intuition	real-time information
decision making	judgment	representativeness bias
decision support	learning organization	satisficing
system	management information	sustainability
escalating commitment	systems (MIS)	systematic errors
expert system	nonprogrammed decision	transaction-processing
heuristics	making	system

Figures and Tables are interspersed throughout the text to illustrate concepts and provide a visual framework for students.

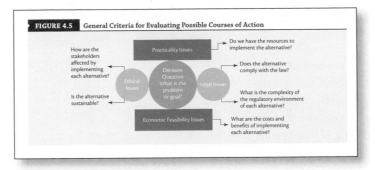

FIGURE 4.5   General Criteria for Evaluating Possible Courses of Action

Rich and Relevant Examples

An important feature of our book is the way we use real-world examples and stories about managers and companies to drive home the applied lessons to students. Moreover, unlike boxed material in other books, we integrate more applied and fewer types of boxes seamlessly into the text; they are an integral part of the learning experience, and not tacked on or isolated from the text itself. This is central to our pedagogical approach.

Each chapter begins with an **Opening Case**. These cases pose a real-world, chapter-related challenge and then discuss how companies or managers responded to that challenge, bringing to light the many issues surrounding the management process. At the end of the chapter, the **Wrap-Up to Opening Case** wraps up the opening case in light of the new information gleaned from the chapter. Students are provided with the answers to the questions raised in the opening case.

Tips for Managers distill the lessons that students can take from the chapter and apply to develop their management skills.

WRAP-UP TO ▸▸▸ OPENING CASE

Good Decision Making at PUMA

PUMA faced considerable threats in its task environment which led to a major decision by CEO Jochen Zeitz to reduce costs, increase sustainability in its operations, and launch a new product. After having read and understood the concepts in this chapter, you should be able to answer the following questions:

1. *What type of decision was made by Zeitz when PUMA launched into sport lifestyle fashions?*

   ANSWER: Decision making is made in response to either routine or unique situations. [...] decisions are made in response to routine situations where man[...] rules to guide behaviour. Most decision making that relates to the [...] of an organization is programmed decision making. Examples [...] making about how much inventory to hold, when to pay bills, [...]ers, and when to order materials and supplies. Nonprogrammed [...] required for nonroutine situations. Rules do not exist because [...] expected or uncertain and managers lack the information they [...]lop rules to cover it. Zeitz's decision to launch into sport lifestyle [...] a nonprogrammed decision made under conditions of risk and

[...]*and opportunities in the task environment that impact PUMA's*

[...]on making in response to threats occurs when events inside or out[...]on are adversely affecting organizational performance and manag[...]or ways to increase performance. In this case, PUMA was almost [...]kruptcy in the early 1990s when Zeitz made the nonprogrammed [...] a new "sport lifestyle" line of products instead of competing in [...]nce athletic shoe market. In responding to the threats, PUMA

Opening Case

Good Decision Making at PUMA

When Jochen Zeitz took over as CEO of PUMA AG in 1993 at the age of 30, the company was facing major threats.[1] PUMA AG, based in the small German sneaker-producing town of Herzogenaurach,[2] had lost money for the past eight years and PUMA North America was facing imminent bankruptcy.[3]

Facing tough decisions about how to turn around the company's fortunes, Zeitz decided that rather than trying to compete based on the performance capabilities of its athletic shoes and equipment, PUMA would focus more on style, colours, and lines of shoes produced in a sustainable manner. Essentially, Zeitz saw a potential opportunity in trying to start up a new division focused on experimental fashion and sport as lifestyle. Of course, Zeitz also made difficult decisions to respond to the threats the company was facing by, for example, dramatically reducing costs of production and taking back control over distribution of PUMA products in North America.[4] Another example is the decision to update its policies on sustainable production. In collaboration with Greenpeace, PUMA is engaged in a detoxification process of all of its operations. PUMA feels that an update of its sustainability policies must be based on sound decisions and has therefore started a dialogue with industry peers, experts, and the chemical industry to investigate which substances can be phased out with existing technology and where more research is needed.[5] PUMA continues to produce high-performance athletic shoes and gear for serious sport.[6]

Nonetheless, Zeitz's bold decision to pursue the world of fashion and style was a major contributor to PUMA becoming the fourth biggest athletic apparel company worldwide. Recognizing the importance of coming up with creative designs and sustainable products,

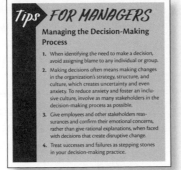

Tips ▸ FOR MANAGERS

Managing the Decision-Making Process

1. When identifying the need to make a decision, avoid assigning blame to any individual or group.

2. Making decisions often means making changes in the organization's strategy, structure, and culture, which creates uncertainty and even anxiety. To reduce anxiety and foster an inclusive culture, involve as many stakeholders in the decision-making process as possible.

3. Give employees and other stakeholders reassurances and confirm their emotional concerns, rather than give rational explanations, when faced with decisions that create disruptive change.

4. Treat successes and failures as stepping stones in your decision-making practice.

Experiential Learning Features

We have given considerable time and attention to developing state-of-the-art experiential end-of-chapter learning exercises that drive home the meaning of management to students. These exercises are grouped together at the end of each chapter in the section called **Management in Action.**

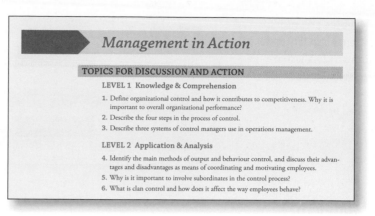

Management in Action

TOPICS FOR DISCUSSION AND ACTION

LEVEL 1 Knowledge & Comprehension

1. Define organizational control and how it contributes to competitiveness. Why it is important to overall organizational performance?
2. Describe the four steps in the process of control.
3. Describe three systems of control managers use in operations management.

LEVEL 2 Application & Analysis

4. Identify the main methods of output and behaviour control, and discuss their advantages and disadvantages as means of coordinating and motivating employees.
5. Why is it important to involve subordinates in the control process?
6. What is clan control and how does it affect the way employees behave?

TOPICS FOR DISCUSSION AND ACTION

LEVEL 1 Knowledge & Comprehension

1. Define organizational control and how it contributes to competitiveness. Why it is important to overall organizational performance?
2. Describe the four steps in the process of control.
3. Describe three systems of control managers use in operations management.

LEVEL 2 Application & Analysis

4. Identify the main methods of output and behaviour control, and discuss their advantages and disadvantages as means of coordinating and motivating employees.
5. Why is it important to involve subordinates in the control process?
6. What is clan control and how does it affect the way employees behave?

LEVEL 3 Synthesis & Evaluation

7. What types of controls would you expect to find most used in (a) a hospital, (b) the Armed Forces, and (c) a city police force? Why?
8. Watch the following video or a similar one on YouTube at www.youtube.com/watch?v=aOZhbOhEunY. Describe the culture at Google. What types of control measures are evident in these videos? What kinds of green initiatives make up the culture at Google?
9. Explain how *innovative* and *conservative* cultures control managerial action.

Topics for Discussion and Action are a set of chapter-related questions based on Bloom's three levels of developmental consideration: level 1 tests students' knowledge and comprehension; level 2 tests students' ability to apply concepts; and level 3 tests students' synthesis and evaluation skills.

Self-Reflection Exercises are unique exercises that ask students to internalize concepts from the chapter and apply them to their personal lives and situations at this moment, helping them to grasp the relevance of key chapter ideas and concepts.

SELF-REFLECTION EXERCISE

Your parents have indicated that they are expecting a big party for their 25th wedding anniversary and that you are in charge of planning it. Develop a timeline for carrying out the project, and then identify ways to monitor progress in planning for the party. How will you know that your plans have been successful? At what critical points do you need to examine your plans to make sure that everything is on track?

SMALL GROUP BREAKOUT EXERCISE

How Best to Control the Sales Force?

Form groups of three or four, and appoint one member as the spokesperson who will communicate your findings to the whole class when called on by the instructor. Then discuss the following scenario:

You are the regional sales manager of an organization that supplies high-quality windows and doors to building supply centres nationwide. Over the last three years, the rate of sales growth has slackened. There is increasing evidence that to make their jobs easier, salespeople are primarily servicing large customer accounts and ignoring small accounts.

Small Group Breakout Exercises are uniquely designed to allow instructors in large classes to utilize interactive experiential exercises in groups of three to four students. The instructor calls on students to form into small groups simply by turning to people around them. All students participate in the exercise in class, and a mechanism is provided for the different groups to share what they have learned with one another.

Business Planning Exercises provide professors with the opportunity to ask their students to write a business plan for a new venture or a strategic plan for an existing venture. At the end of every chapter, students can apply managerial and organizational concepts to the writing of a business plan by referring to Appendix A: Developing a Business Plan.

BUSINESS PLANNING EXERCISE

Your professor may ask you to write a business plan for a new venture or a strategic plan for an existing venture. At the end of every chapter, you will have an opportunity to apply managerial and organizational concepts to the exercise of writing a business plan. Refer to Appendix A.

You and your team realize that you must use a variety of control measures in your venture to monitor and evaluate the use of resources and make sure the goals of the organization are being met. In order to complete the financial plan component of your business plan, you know you must use output control techniques, including the financial ratios and equations in the text, to forecast the cash flow for one year and the break-even point. Angel investors or any bank will want to see the bottom-line numbers on your expenses and expected revenues to determine if their ROI will be worthwhile. For the financial plan, you must create a pro forma cash flow, income statement, opening balance sheet, and break-even analysis.

1. **Cash flow projections for year one:** At which points over the year will your expenses exceed your revenue? How will you make up the shortfall? Subtract all expenses in the cost of goods sold from all revenues to project a net gain or loss for one year. This is your Pro Forma Income Statement.
2. **Opening balance sheet:** Are the assets and liabilities equal to the shareholders' equity?
3. **Break-even analysis:** When will the revenues exceed the expenses of the venture?
4. Identify the assumptions you will need to make to complete the financial plan section of your business plan such as interest rates, taxation rates, and other details on which to base your financial projections. These should be clearly stated with reference to the specific line item on the spreadsheet.

MANAGING ETHICALLY EXERCISE

You are a manager of a group of 10 employees in their twenties. They are very innovative and are not accustomed to tight rules and regulations. Managers at the company want order and control on every front. Your team is fighting the rules and regulations, which is creating an ethical dilemma for you. They are being very productive and innovative but clearly not in the way top management wants things run. You have been asked to bring more order to your team. You really like your team and think they are effective but will leave if they are forced to conform. And the company needs their expertise and energy to remain competitive in the high-tech world. What would you do?

Managing Ethically Exercises present students with an ethical scenario or dilemma and ask them, either individually or in a group, to think about an issue from an ethical perspective in order to understand the issues facing practising managers.

Management Challenge Exercises present a realistic scenario in which a manager or organization faces some kind of challenge or opportunity and the student plays the role of a management consultant offering advice and recommending a course of action based on the chapter content.

MANAGEMENT CHALLENGE EXERCISE

Save the Children Project

Assume your professor has asked you to consult and manage the design of a special "Save the Children" innovative program that 10 teams of five students in your course will be working on. Save the Children Canada will be acting as final judge on the winning program submitted by different colleges and universities. You must manage 10 teams; because of the shortness of time for this request, the innovative program will need aspects designed by each team, as no one team can do it all. Hence, all 10 teams will have contributed to the finished product. Your professor will be grading you on how well you actually manage, motivate, and put into action controls to help each team function at optimal levels.

QUESTION

1. What is your plan to control the operations of the teams in such a way that they function optimally?

MANAGEMENT PORTFOLIO PROJECT

Answer the following questions about the organization you have chosen to follow:

1. What are the main types of control used by management to monitor and evaluate the performance of the organization and employees?
2. Are these methods of control appropriate, given the organization's strategy and culture?
3. What recommendations would you make with respect to the organizational control of this enterprise?

Management Portfolio Projects present an opportunity for students to follow and analyze an organization of their choice over the course of the semester. Each chapter includes an exercise that asks students to evaluate how the issues discussed in the chapter are dealt with by the organization they're following.

A **Video Management Case** and questions are included with every chapter to help students make the connections from chapter concepts to real-world applications. Videos are available on DVD and online through Connect.

VIDEO MANAGEMENT CASE ▄▀connect

Anne Mulcahy: How to Make Decisions

Since Anne Mulcahy became CEO of Xerox in 2001, she orchestrated what some have called the turnaround of the century.

1. Why is it so critical to make decisions sooner rather than later?
2. What biases should a manager like Anne Mulcahy avoid in making decisions?
3. How can managers make sure the tough decisions they make are ethical?

Each chapter also contains a **Management Case** dealing with current companies and engaging personalities, one to two pages in length, ending with questions for students to consider.

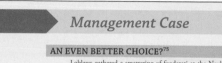

Management Case

AN EVEN BETTER CHOICE?[75]

Loblaws gathered a smattering of fooderati at the Neubacher Shor Contemporary Gallery in Toronto last month to officially launch its new "affordable luxury" line of President's Choice products. Dubbed "black label" for its distinct package design (although those words won't appear on the labels, thanks to a Johnnie Walker copyright) the new [...] from $1.99 to $21.99. Landing in 140 stores this October [...] 200 products ranging from an eight-year old cheddar and [...] bacon marmalade. But even the stylish launch party can't [...] onomic realities.

QUESTIONS

1. What type of decision did Loblaws make when it launched its black label line?
2. Identify the threats and opportunities in the task environment that impact Loblaws' decision.
3. How important is technology to the success of the decision?

A **New Continuing Case** at the end of each Part provides the students an opportunity to integrate and synthesize all the concepts and material learned in the previous sections to the management and organizational challenges of one particular small business. This running case feature helps keep continuity across the entire text and allows students to focus on problems faced by small businesses.

End of Part I: Continuing Case

CARROT TOPS: INTRODUCTION

The main theme of this book is that the management process—planning, organizing, leading, and controlling—is not confined to the top management, but rather is a process in which every manager must engage. Perhaps nowhere is this more apparent than in the typical small service business. Here the owner/operator usually has few staff to rely on. The success of the enterprise often depends on the effectiveness with which the manager structures activities and uses resources to achieve a goal. The activities of managing are critical to any complex cooperative endeavour. Management is both the art and science of arranging and utilizing the physical and human factors of production toward a desired outcome. This book provides the student with an introduction to the management process.

To help illustrate and emphasize the role of the front-line manager, throughout this book we will use a continuing or running case of a business based in Southern Ontario. Each segment will illustrate how the case's main players—owner/manager Mel Harvey and first-line manager Janet Khan—confront and solve management problems each day by applying the concepts and techniques presented in the book in each particular part: Part 1—Management; Part 2—The Environment of Management; Part 3—Planning and Decision Making; Part 4—Organizing; Part 5—Leading Individuals and Groups; and Part 6—Controlling. Here is some background information you'll need to answer the questions that arise in subsequent parts of this book.

CARROT TOPS: A PROFILE

After putting together a typical business plan to meet the requirements of a course on entrepreneurship, Mel Harvey started "Mel's General Store" in 2002. The business plan was about 20 pages long and outlined the usual array of topics: a profile of the organization; a profile of the industry; a profile of the product or service; marketing, organization, operating, and control systems plans; pro forma financial statements; and financial project tables and appendices. The one-page executive summary included a synopsis of the plan and covered "the business," "the market," "strategy," "competition," "management," and "financial details," including how the company intends to generate revenue, as well as a likely exit strategy. In this case, Mel was committed to supplying low-cost, basic groceries to the local community in which he lived in Southern Ontario. One day, he hoped to sell franchise licences.

QUESTIONS

Drawing on all segments of this case:

1. What kinds of activities does Mel have to consider in planning, organizing, leading, and controlling his enterprise?
2. What sets of skills will Mel use when planning, organizing, leading, and controlling?
3. Identify an example of an activity that Mel could undertake that illustrates each of Mintzberg's managerial roles.

Appendix A: Developing a Business Plan walks students through the steps of preparing a business plan and highlights organizational management issues. The appendix can be used with or without business planning software. Developing a Business Plan exercises are found at the end of each chapter and online through Connect.

APPENDIX

A

Developing a Business Plan

The Business Plan as an Exercise in the Processes of Management[1]

Writing a business plan may never be a more important exercise than in the context of today's rapidly changing environment. Even if you are not an entrepreneur and do not wish to develop a new original idea and bring it to market, developing a business plan is still a valuable exercise in practising the management processes. It provides a crucial foundation for managing an organization. In this section of the text, we will treat developing a business plan as an exercise in the management processes of planning, organizing, leading, and controlling. By doing the exercises at the end of each chapter, you will have the foundation to put together a plan that will help you develop as a manager. The experience you will gain is valid for profit and not-for-profit organizations as well as new and existing ventures. Writing a business plan gives you practice in thinking about managing activities such as:

McGraw-Hill Connect™ is a web-based assignment and assessment platform that gives students the means to better connect with their coursework, with their instructors, and with the important concepts that they will need to know for success now and in the future.

With Connect, instructors can deliver assignments, quizzes and tests online. Instructors can edit existing questions and author entirely new problems. Track individual student performance – by question, assignment or in relation to the class overall – with detailed grade reports. Integrate grade reports easily with Learning Management Systems (LMS) such as WebCT and Blackboard. And much more!

By choosing Connect, instructors are providing their students with a powerful tool for improving academic performance and truly mastering course material. Connect allows students to practice important skills at their own pace and on their own schedule. Importantly, students' assessment results and instructors' feedback are all saved online—so students can continually review their progress and plot their course to success.

Connect also provides 24/7 online access to an eBook—an online edition of the text—to aid them in successfully completing their work, wherever and whenever they choose.

Resources and Supplements

Instructor's Manual: Prepared by Jane Haddad, text author, the instructor's manual contains chapter overviews, lists of each chapter's learning objectives and key terms, detailed lecture outlines, lecture enhancers, and additional notes for end-of-chapter features.

Computerized Test Bank: Prepared by Jane Haddad, text author, the computerized test bank allows instructors to add and edit questions, save and reload multiple test versions, select questions based on difficulty level and learning objective, and use password protection. Questions test three levels of learning: (1) knowledge of key terms; (2) understanding of concepts and principles; and (3) application of principles.

Microsoft PowerPoint Presentations: Prepared by Sandra Wellman of Seneca College, the slideshows for each chapter are structured around the chapter learning objectives and include many of the figures and tables from the textbook. The presentations also include additional slides that support and expand the text discussions. All slides can be modified by the instructor.

Videos for all Chapters: Videos have been selected by Jane Haddad, text author, to accompany the Video Management Cases featured at the end of each chapter. The videos are available on DVD and can also be accessed on the student and instructor areas of Connect.

Management Asset Gallery—for Instructors and Students: The Management Asset Gallery is a one-stop-shop for a wealth of McGraw-Hill management assets, making it easier for instructors to locate specific materials to enhance their courses, and for students to supplement their knowledge (via the Student Asset Gallery). The Asset Galleries include non-text-specific management resources (Self-Assessments, Test Your Knowledge exercises, videos*, Manager's HotSeat resources, and additional group and individual exercises), along with supporting PowerPoint and instructor's manual materials.

The Manager's HotSeat is a resource within the Management Asset Gallery that allows students to watch over 14 real managers apply their years of experience to confront daily issues, such as ethics, diversity, teamwork, and the virtual workplace. Students are prompted for their feedback throughout each scenario and then submit a report critiquing the manager's choices, while defending their own. The Manager's HotSeat is ideal for group or classroom discussions.*

Business Plan Pro: The Business Plan Pro is available as a bundled option that includes more than 250 sample business plans and 400 case studies to give a wide variety of examples as students create their own plans. Students receive guidance to set up their own business by answering questions to guide the software customizing the plan. The student then enters the business's financial data to generate financial worksheets and statements.

New Business Mentor: For instructors who incorporate a business plan project into their class, the New Business Mentor software can be bundled upon request with student textbooks. The New Business Mentor includes sample business plans, resources to help students as they start a business, business planning and feasibility planning software, and the "mentor," who will walk you through each step of the business plan. Teaching notes are also available.

Superior Learning Solutions and Support

The McGraw-Hill Ryerson team is ready to help you assess and integrate any of our products, technology, and services into your course for optimal teaching and learning performance. Whether it's helping your students improve their grades, or putting your entire course online, the McGraw-Hill Ryerson team is here to help you do it. Contact your *i*Learning Sales Specialist today to learn how to maximize all of McGraw-Hill Ryerson's resources!

For more information on the latest technology and Learning Solutions offered by McGraw-Hill Ryerson and its partners, please visit us online: **www.mcgrawhill.ca/he/solutions**.

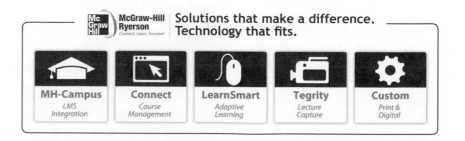

*The "Management in the Movies" videos are not licensed for distribution outside of the United States; however, adopting instructors are able to access the instructor notes.

Acknowledgements

I would like to thank all the people who were involved in reading early drafts of this manuscript and who provided insightful and constructive feedback. I have tried to address your concerns and implement your suggestions. Your input has made this a better book! I want to thank Michael Rock for his generosity in allowing me to use some of his material in this edition. I would like to acknowledge all the people at McGraw-Hill Ryerson who worked on the production of this edition. Without your direction and support, this edition would not have come off the press. And finally, I would like to thank my family for supporting and encouraging my work.

Jane W. Haddad

In the preparation of this edition, we have benefited greatly from the helpful critiques and suggestions of numerous professors across the country. They helped us identify new topics, as well as clarify information, rearrange and delete material, and suggested examples that students would identify with. Their assistance was invaluable, and we extend our many thanks to the following individuals:

Kerry Couet	*Concordia University College of Alberta*
Denise Fortier	*Williams School of Business, Bishop's University*
Robert Greene	*Niagara College Business School*
Timothy Hardie	*Lakehead University*
Brenda Lang	*Bissett School of Business, Mount Royal University*
Ed Leach	*Dalhousie University*
Michael Pearl	*Seneca College School of Business Management*
Kerry Rempel	*Okanagan College*
Vic de Witt	*Red River College*

PART I

CHAPTER 1

Managers and Managing

LEARNING OUTCOMES

LO1 Describe what management is, what managers do, and how managers use resources to achieve organizational goals.

LO2 Distinguish among planning, organizing, leading, and controlling, and explain how managers' abilities to handle each one affect organizational performance.

LO3 Differentiate among the types and levels of management, and understand the responsibilities of managers at different levels in the organizational hierarchy.

LO4 Discuss some major changes in management practices today and the use of advanced information technology (IT).

LO5 Distinguish among the kinds of managerial skills and roles that managers perform.

Management at Brick Brewing Co. Limited

Brick Brewing Co. Limited is Ontario's largest Canadian-owned and Canadian-based publicly held brewery. The company is a regional brewer of award-winning premium quality and value beers. The company, founded by Jim Brickman in 1984, was the first craft brewery to start up in Ontario, and is credited with pioneering the present-day craft brewing renaissance in Canada. Brick has complemented its J. R. Brickman Founder's Series and Waterloo Dark premium craft beers with other popular brands such as Laker, Red Cap, and Formosa Springs Draft.[1] In 2011, the company bought the Canadian rights to the Seagram Coolers brand from Corby Distilleries Limited.

Chief Financial Officer Jason Pratt—hired in 2008 by CEO and president George Croft—reports the cost of the transaction to be $7.3 million plus inventory on hand. Mr. Pratt is responsible for the timeliness and accuracy of all financial information that is provided to the Board and shareholders. He acts as corporate secretary for audit committee and Board meetings of the company, and is a key contributor to the company's overall strategy.[2]

Mr. Pratt graduated from McMaster University with an Honours Bachelor of Commerce degree and obtained his chartered accountant designation while working with Ernst & Young LLP. Before joining Brick Brewing in 2008, he held senior finance roles in companies operating in the telecommunications, food service, and brewing industries.

Upon Pratt's joining the company, CEO and President George Croft said that "He has a successful track record of developing and leading high-performance teams and brings an exemplary combination of business judgment, professional skills and integrity to Brick Brewing."[3]

Since 1984, Brick Brewing Co. Limited has supported thousands of cultural, charitable, and community organizations and events. From

backing amateur athletes and teams to participating in festival-style events across Ontario, Brick Brewing takes a partnership approach with each sponsorship relationship.

This commitment to the community and providing innovative products makes Brick Brewing Co. Limited a high-performing organization—one that provides goods and services that customers desire.

After reading and understanding the concepts in this chapter, you should be able to answer the following questions:

1. *What kinds of activities or tasks are involved in planning, organizing, leading, and controlling at Brick Brewing?*

2. *Characterize the type and level of management described in the case.*

3. *What skills does Jason Pratt bring to the Brick Brewing Co. as a top manager?*

4. *Which of Mintzberg's managerial roles are illustrated in this case by each manager?*

Overview

The actions of the top managers at Brick Brewing Co. Limited illustrate the many challenges managers face. Managing a company is a complex undertaking, and managers must possess the skills and knowledge needed to be effective. Making the right decision is difficult; even effective managers make mistakes. The most effective managers are the ones, like George Croft and Jason Pratt, who continually strive to find ways to improve their companies' performance.

In this chapter we look at what management is, what activities or functions are involved in the management process, the types and levels of managers we find in organizations, and the skills and roles that effective managers need to perform well. By the end of this chapter, you will have an appreciation of the role of managers in creating a high-performing organization.

> **LO1** Describe what management is, what managers do, and how managers use resources to achieve organizational goals.

What Is Management?

When you think of a manager, what kind of person comes to mind? Do you see someone who can determine the future prosperity of a large for-profit company? Or do you see the administrator of a not-for-profit organization such as a school, library, health care organization, or charity? Or do you think of the person in charge of your local McDonald's restaurant or Giant Tiger store? What do all these people have in common?

Management takes place in **organizations,** which are collections of people who work together and coordinate their actions to achieve a wide variety of goals and desired future outcomes.[4] Organizations provide jobs and employment. Outside of the public sector, most people in Canada are employed in small and medium sized organizations in the private sector or in the community or social sector. We categorize organizations based on their core purposes (see Figure 1.1). Organizations range from having a strictly social mission, such as a charitable nonprofit organization, funded by grants and donations, to a strictly commercial for-profit mission, with little regard for achieving socially useful outcomes. *Social enterprises, social ventures,* and *social purpose* businesses combine social and commercial missions to varying degrees and are collectively referred to as organizations in the **social economy.**[5] The concept of the social economy applies to all the organizations that have social objectives central to their mission and their practice, and either have explicit

economic objectives or generate some economic value through the services they provide and purchases that they undertake.[6] The social economy is often referred to as the third pillar of the economy; the other two being for-profit (FP) private enterprise and public sector (government) enterprise. Increasingly, a growing number of enterprising charities, not-for-profit organizations (NPO or NFP), co-operatives, and community organizations are creating businesses with economic as well as social and environmental returns. Public–private partnerships that mobilize private capital rather than relying on tax revenue will become more and more common in the effort to change the way society deals with social problems. The goal of social enterprise is to use market-mechanisms to produce or sell goods and services that provide a social or environmental benefit. Social enterprises often employ the clients they serve and thereby provide valuable experience to marginalized groups who can use the skills in the wider economy. Together, the diverse organizations in the social economy create the infrastructure that helps Canadian communities to grow and prosper. These organizations welcome newcomers, coach kids' sports, deliver meals on wheels, run food banks, day cares, and crisis hotlines, and provide countless other public-benefit services that allow people to be well and participate in civic life.

Chances are pretty good that you or someone you know works in the social sector of the economy. Canada's nonprofit and voluntary sector is the second largest in the world; the Netherlands is the largest; the United States is the fifth. There are an estimated 161 000 nonprofits and charities in Canada. The sector represents almost 8 percent of the GDP, a contribution larger than the automotive or manufacturing industries. Two million people are employed by organizations in the social sector.[7] This is why we have included a profile of an organization in the social economy in every chapter of this text.

Management is the planning, organizing, leading, and controlling of resources to achieve goals effectively and efficiently. **Resources** are assets such as people, machinery, raw materials, information, skills, and financial capital. A **manager** is a person responsible for supervising the use of a group's or organization's resources to achieve its goals.

organizations Collections of people who work together and coordinate their actions to achieve goals and desired future outcomes.

social economy A bridging concept for organizations that have social objectives central to their mission and their practice, and either have explicit economic objectives or generate some economic value through the services they provide and purchases that they undertake.

management The planning, organizing, leading, and controlling of resources to achieve organizational goals effectively and efficiently.

resources Assets such as people, machinery, raw materials, information, skills, and financial capital.

manager A person who is responsible for supervising the use of an organization's resources to achieve its goals.

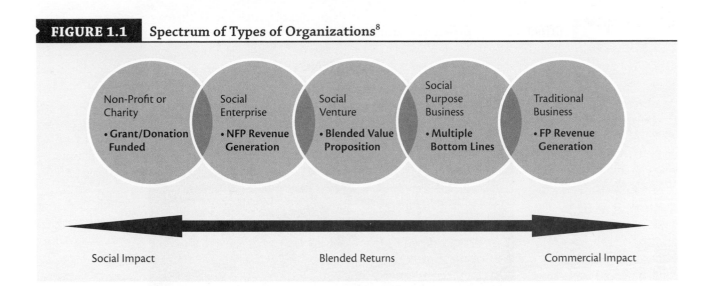

> **FIGURE 1.1**   Spectrum of Types of Organizations[8]

Achieving High Performance: A Manager's Goal

One of the most important goals of organizations and their members is to provide goods or services that customers value. As we saw in the opening case, by purchasing the rights to the Seagram Coolers brand, Brick Brewing Co. is "now able to satisfy a broader range of customers with a wider range of selection in taste and profile for those discerning drinkers."[9] The principal goal of doctors, nurses, and hospital administrators is to increase their hospital's ability to make sick people well; the principal goal of each McDonald's restaurant manager is to produce fast food that people want to eat and pay for so that they become loyal return customers. Phoenix Print Shop is a social enterprise in downtown Toronto with the principal goal to provide a training site for at-risk youth to gain employment skills and generate revenue that supports transitional housing for homeless youth. All of these examples illustrate how key serving the needs of customers is to the goals of managers.

Organizational performance is a measure of how efficiently and effectively managers use resources to satisfy customers and achieve organizational goals. Organizational performance increases in direct proportion to increases in effectiveness and efficiency (see Figure 1.2). What are efficiency and effectiveness?

Effectiveness is a measure of the appropriateness of the goals that managers have selected for the organization to pursue and of the degree to which the organization achieves those goals. Management expert

> **organizational performance** A measure of how efficiently and effectively a manager uses resources to satisfy customers and achieve organizational goals.
>
> **effectiveness** A measure of the appropriateness of the goals an organization is pursuing and of the degree to which the organization achieves those goals.
>
> **efficiency** A measure of how well or productively resources are used to achieve a goal.

Peter Drucker compared the two this way: efficiency is doing things right; effectiveness is doing the right thing.[10] Organizations are effective when managers choose appropriate goals and then achieve them. Some years ago, for example, managers at McDonald's decided on the goal of providing breakfast service to attract more customers. This goal was a smart choice because sales of breakfast food now account for more than 30 percent of McDonald's revenues and are still increasing—an important reason for its record profits in 2011.

Efficiency is a measure of how well or how productively resources are used to achieve a goal.[11] Organizations are efficient when managers minimize the amount of input resources (such as labour, raw materials, and component parts) or the amount of time needed to produce a given output of goods or services. For example, McDonald's developed a more efficient fat fryer that not only reduces (by 30 percent) the amount of oil used in cooking but also speeds up the cooking of french fries. A manager's responsibility is to ensure that an organization and its members perform, as efficiently as possible, all the activities needed to provide goods and services to customers. High-performing organizations such as Brick Brewing Co., McDonald's, Walmart, Intel, IKEA, and Habitat for Humanity are simultaneously efficient and effective.

Why Study Management?

Today, more students are competing for places in business courses than ever before; the number of people wishing to pursue

FIGURE 1.2 Effectiveness, Efficiency, and Performance in an Organization

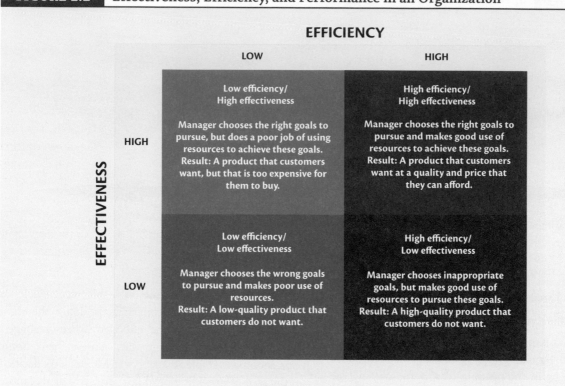

EFFICIENCY

	LOW	HIGH
HIGH	**Low efficiency/ High effectiveness** Manager chooses the right goals to pursue, but does a poor job of using resources to achieve these goals. Result: A product that customers want, but that is too expensive for them to buy.	**High efficiency/ High effectiveness** Manager chooses the right goals to pursue and makes good use of resources to achieve these goals. Result: A product that customers want at a quality and price that they can afford.
LOW	**Low efficiency/ Low effectiveness** Manager chooses the wrong goals to pursue and makes poor use of resources. Result: A low-quality product that customers do not want.	**High efficiency/ Low effectiveness** Manager chooses inappropriate goals, but makes good use of resources to pursue these goals. Result: A high-quality product that customers do not want.

EFFECTIVENESS

High-performing organizations are efficient *and* effective.

Master of Business Administration (MBA) degrees—today's passport to an advanced management position—either on campus or from online universities and colleges is at an all-time high. Why is the study of management currently so popular?[12]

First, in any society or culture resources are valuable and scarce, so the more efficient and effective use that organizations can make of those resources, the greater the relative well-being and prosperity of people in that society. Because managers are the people who decide how to use many of a society's most valuable resources—its skilled employees, raw materials like oil and land, computers and information systems, and financial assets—they directly impact the well-being of a society and the people in it. Understanding what managers do and how they do it is of central importance to understanding how a society creates wealth and takes care of its citizens.

Second, although most people are not managers, and many may never intend to become managers, almost all of us encounter managers because most people have jobs and bosses. Moreover, many people today are working in groups and teams and have to deal with coworkers. Studying management helps people to deal with their bosses and their coworkers. It reveals how to understand other people at work and make decisions and take actions that win the attention and support of the boss and coworkers. Management teaches people not yet in positions of authority how to lead coworkers, solve conflicts between them, achieve team goals, and so increase performance.

Third, in any society, people are in competition for a very important resource—a job that pays well and provides an interesting and satisfying career—and understanding management is one important path toward obtaining this objective. In general, jobs become more interesting the more complex or responsible they are. Any person who desires a motivating job that changes over time might therefore do well to develop management skills and become promotable. A person who has been working for several years and then returns to school for an MBA can usually, after earning the degree, find a more interesting, satisfying job and one that pays significantly more than the previous job. Moreover, salaries increase rapidly as people move up the organizational hierarchy, whether it is a school system, a large for-profit business organization, or a not-for-profit charitable or social enterprise.

Indeed, the salaries paid to top managers are enormous.[13] For example, the CEOs and other top executives or managers of companies such as Barrick Gold Corp., Onex Corp., Toronto Dominion Bank, Rogers Communications Inc., and Shoppers Drug Mart receive millions in actual salary each year. However, even more staggering is the fact that many top executives also receive stock or shares in the company they manage, as well as stock options that give them the right to sell these shares at a certain time in the future.[14] If the value of the stock goes up, then the managers keep the difference between the price they obtained the stock option for (say, $10) and what it is worth later (say, $33). By the time Michael Eisner resigned as CEO of Disney in 2005 he had received over $1 billion from selling his stock options. When Steve Jobs became CEO of Apple again in 1997 he accepted a salary of only $1 a year. However, he was also awarded stock options that, with the fast rise in Apple's stock price in the 2000s, were worth several billion dollars by the time he resigned and passed away in 2011. These incredible amounts of money provide some indication of both the responsibilities and the rewards that accompany the achievement of high management positions in major companies—and flow to anybody who successfully creates and manages a small business. Pay, however, is only one type of reward for high achievement. Managers also get great satisfaction from solving social problems. What is it that managers actually do to receive such rewards?[15]

Distinguish among planning, organizing, leading, and controlling, and explain how managers' ability to handle each one affects organizational performance.

LO2

Managerial Tasks and Functions

The job of management is to help an organization make the best use of its resources to achieve its goals. How do managers accomplish this objective? They do so by performing four essential managerial functions: planning, organizing, leading, and controlling (see Figure 1.3). Henri Fayol first outlined the nature of these managerial tasks in *General and Industrial Management,* published in 1916: a book that remains the classic statement of what managers must do to create a high-performing organization.[16]

Managers at all levels and in all departments— whether in small or large organizations, for-profit or not-for-profit organizations, or organizations that operate in one country or throughout the world—are responsible for performing these four functions, and we will look at each in turn. How well managers perform them determines how efficient and effective their organization is. Individuals who are not managers can also be involved in planning, organizing, leading, and controlling, so understanding these processes is important for everyone.

FIGURE 1.3 Four Functions of Management

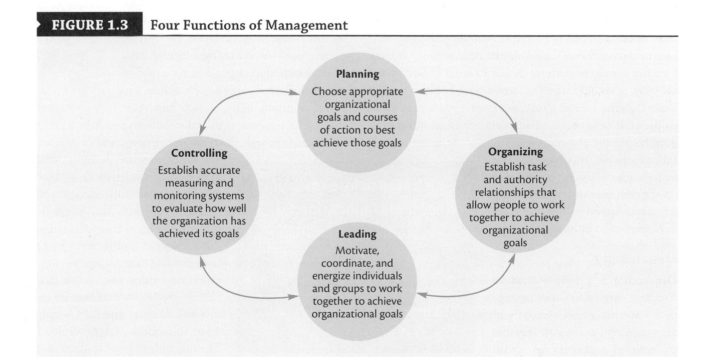

Planning

Planning is a process used to identify and select appropriate goals and courses of action. There are five steps in the planning process:

1. Deciding which goals the organization will pursue
2. Analyzing the organizational environment for threats and opportunities
3. Deciding what courses of action or strategy to adopt
4. Deciding how to allocate organizational resources to implement the plan
5. Evaluating whether the strategy achieved the goals

How well managers plan determines how effective and efficient their organization is—its performance level.[17]

The outcome of planning is a **strategy,** a cluster of decisions concerning what organizational goals to pursue, what actions to take, and how to use resources to achieve goals. For instance, Brick Brewing Co. follows a low-cost strategy with its popular Laker brand selling at the lowest legal price, but it also offers premium craft beers such as Red Baron Premium Blonde Lager, which won a gold medal at the Ontario Brewing Awards in 2011. The company offers award-winning quality and value beers. "It's easy to lose track of a simple foundation for customer satisfaction: Sell a quality product at a reasonable price," said George Croft, President and CEO of Brick Brewing Co. Limited. "I think there have been recent times when our beer industry lost sight of those two beacons." Planning is a difficult activity because, normally, it is not immediately clear which goals an organization should pursue or how best to pursue them. Choosing the right strategy is risky because managers commit organizational resources for activities that could either succeed or fail. Top managers at Brick Brewing created a successful management approach to the craft beer and specialty drink market, illustrating how important planning and strategy are to an organization's success. In Chapter 5, we focus on the planning process and on the strategies organizations can select to respond to opportunities or threats in an industry.

Organizing

Organizing is a process used to structure workplace relationships in a way that allows members of an organization to work together to achieve organizational goals.

Organizing involves grouping people into departments according to the kinds of job-specific tasks they perform. In organizing, managers also lay out the lines of authority and responsibility between different individuals and groups, and they decide how best to coordinate organizational resources, in particular human resources.

The outcome of organizing is the creation of an **organizational structure,** a formal system of task and reporting relationships that coordinates and motivates organizational members so they work together to achieve organizational goals. Organizational structure determines how an organization's resources can best be used to create goods and services.

We examine the organizing process in Chapter 6, where we consider the organizational structures that managers can use to coordinate and motivate people and utilize other resources.

Leading

An organization's *vision* is a short, succinct, and inspiring statement of what the organization intends to become and the goals it is seeking to achieve—its desired future state. In **leading,** managers articulate a clear organizational vision for the organization's members to accomplish, and they energize and enable employees so that everyone understands the part he or she plays in achieving organizational goals. Leadership depends on the use of power, influence, vision, persuasion, and communication skills for two important tasks: to coordinate the behaviours of individuals and groups so that their activities and efforts are in harmony, and to encourage employees to perform at a high level. Understanding how to manage and lead effectively is an important skill. You might be interested to know that CEOs have just a few short months to prove to investors that they are able to communicate a vision and carry it out. Recent studies suggest that investors and analysts give CEOs only 14 to 18 months to show results.[18] The outcome of good leadership is

> **"It's easy to lose track of a simple foundation for customer satisfaction: sell a quality product at a reasonable price."**
> *George Croft, President and CEO of Brick Brewing*

planning Identifying and selecting appropriate goals and courses of action; one of the four principal functions of management.

strategy A cluster of decisions about what goals to pursue, what actions to take, and how to use resources to achieve goals.

organizing Structuring workplace relationships so organizational members work together to achieve organizational goals; one of the four principal functions of management.

organizational structure A formal system of task and reporting relationships that coordinates and motivates organizational members so that they work together to achieve organizational goals.

leading Articulating a clear vision and energizing and empowering organizational members so that everyone understands his or her individual role in achieving organizational goals; one of the four principal functions of management.

a high level of motivation and commitment among organizational members. CEO and President of Brick Brewing Co. Limited George Croft's vision and leadership style resulted in a hardworking team of employees producing award-winning beverages.[19] He says, "I'm very proud of the hardworking team here who made these achievements possible and happier still that these awards affirm we are giving our beer drinkers products of extraordinary quality." "Our success at the Ontario Brewing Awards is a humbling accomplishment," he added.

We discuss the issues involved in managing and leading individuals and groups in Chapters 8 through 12.

Controlling

In **controlling,** the task of managers is to evaluate how well an organization is achieving its goals and take action to maintain or improve performance. For example, managers monitor the performance of individuals, departments, and the organization as a whole to see whether they are all meeting desired performance standards. If standards are not being met, managers take action to improve performance. Individuals working in groups also have the responsibility of controlling because they have to make sure the group achieves its goals and completes its actions. Brick Brewery's goal is to produce beer with a distinctive flavour; they achieve this through their "Craft Quality Assured" brewing method.[20]

The outcome of the control process is the ability to measure performance accurately and regulate organizational efficiency and effectiveness. In order to exercise control, managers must decide which goals to measure—perhaps goals pertaining to productivity, quality, or responsiveness to customers—and then they must design information and control systems that will provide the data they need to assess performance. These mechanisms provide feedback to managers, and managers provide feedback to employees. The controlling function also allows managers to evaluate how well they themselves are performing the other three functions of management—planning, organizing, and leading—and to take corrective action.

We cover the most important aspects of the control function in Chapter 13, where we outline the basic process of control and examine some control systems that managers can use to monitor and measure organizational performance.

The four managerial functions—planning, organizing, leading, and controlling—are essential to a manager's job. At all levels in a managerial hierarchy, and across all departments in an organization, effective management means making decisions and managing these four activities successfully.

Differentiate among the types and levels of management, and understand the responsibilities of managers at different levels in the organizational hierarchy. **LO3**

Types and Levels of Managers[21]

To perform the four managerial tasks effectively and efficiently, organizations group or differentiate their managers in two main ways—by level in hierarchy and by type of function. First, they differentiate managers according to their level or rank in the organization's hierarchy of authority. The three levels of managers are first-line managers, middle managers, and top managers—arranged in a hierarchy. Typically, first-line managers report to middle managers, and middle managers report to top managers.

Second, organizations group managers into different departments (or functions) according to their specific set of job-related skills, expertise, and experiences, such as a manager's engineering skills, marketing expertise, or sales experience. A **department,** such as the manufacturing, accounting, engineering, or sales department, is a group of managers and employees who work together because they possess similar skills and experience or use the same kind of knowledge, tools, or techniques to perform their jobs. Within each department are all three levels of management. Next, we examine the reasons why organizations use a hierarchy of managers and group them, by the jobs they perform, into departments.

Levels of Management

Organizations normally have three levels of management: first-line managers, middle managers, and top managers (see Figure 1.4.). Managers at each level have different but related responsibilities for utilizing organizational resources to increase efficiency and effectiveness.

As Figure 1.4 indicates, first-line, middle, and top managers differ from one another by virtue of their job-specific responsibilities, and are found in each of an organization's major departments.

First-Line Managers

At the base of the managerial hierarchy are **first-line managers** (often called supervisors). They are responsible for the daily supervision and coordination of

controlling Evaluating how well an organization is achieving its goals and taking action to maintain or improve performance; one of the four principal functions of management.

department A group of people who work together and possess similar skills or use the same knowledge, tools, or techniques to perform their jobs.

first-line managers Managers who are responsible for the daily supervision and coordination of nonmanagerial employees.

FIGURE 1.4   Management Hierarchy

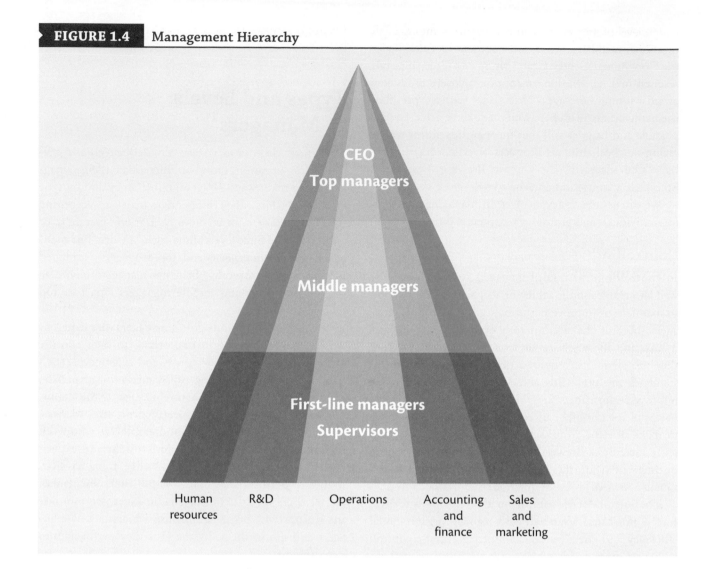

the nonmanagerial employees who perform many of the specific activities necessary to produce goods and services. First-line managers may be found in all departments of an organization.

Examples of first-line managers include the supervisor of a work team in the manufacturing department of a car plant, the head nurse in the obstetrics department of a hospital, and the chief mechanic overseeing a crew of mechanics in the service department of a new-car dealership. Functional area titles may include assistant manager of operations, or assistant sales manager.

Middle Managers

Middle managers supervise the first-line managers and have the responsibility of finding the best way to organize human and other resources to achieve organizational goals. To increase efficiency, middle managers try to find ways to help first-line managers and nonmanagerial employees make better use of resources in order to reduce manufacturing costs or improve the way services are provided to customers. To increase effectiveness, middle managers are responsible for evaluating whether the goals that the organization is pursuing are appropriate and for suggesting to top managers ways in which goals should be changed. A major part of the middle manager's job is to develop and fine-tune skills and know-how—manufacturing or marketing expertise, for example—that enable the organization to be efficient and effective. Middle managers also coordinate resources across departments and divisions. Middle managers make the thousands of specific decisions that go into the production of goods and services: Which first-line supervisors should be chosen for this particular project? Where can we find the highest quality resources? How should employees be organized to enable them to make the best use of resources?

middle managers
Managers who supervise first-line managers and are responsible for finding the best way to use resources to achieve organizational goals.

Middle managers perform an important role in organizations. For instance, behind a first-class sales team, look for the sales manager responsible for training, motivating, and rewarding assistant sales managers and salespeople. Behind a committed staff of secondary school teachers, look for the principal who energizes them to find ways to obtain the resources they need to do an outstanding and innovative job in the classroom. Functional area titles are human resources manager, operations manager, or sales manager.

Top Managers

In contrast to middle managers, **top managers** are responsible for the performance of all departments.[22] They have cross-departmental responsibilities and they are responsible for connecting the parts of the organization together. Top managers help carry out the organizational vision; they establish organizational goals, such as which goods and services the company should produce; they decide how the different departments should interact; and they monitor how well middle managers in each department use resources to achieve goals.[23] Top managers are ultimately responsible for the success or failure of an organization, and their performance is continually scrutinized by people inside and outside the organization, such as employees and investors.[24]

Top managers report to a company's chief executive officer (CEO)—for example, George Croft is the CEO as well as the president of Brick Brewing Co. Limited.

He hired Jason Pratt as the chief financial officer (CFO). The CEO and president are responsible for developing good working relationships among the top managers who head the various departments (manufacturing and marketing, for example) and who usually have the title vice-president or chief. A central concern of the CEO is the creation of a smoothly functioning **top-management team,** a group composed of the CEO, the president, and the department heads most responsible for helping to plan and achieve organizational goals.[25] The CEO also has the responsibility of setting the vision for the organization.

The relative importance of each of the four managerial functions—planning, organizing, leading, and controlling—to any particular manager depends on the manager's position in the managerial hierarchy.[26] As managers move up the hierarchy, they spend more time planning and organizing resources to maintain and improve organizational performance (see Figure 1.5). Top managers devote most of their time to planning and organizing, the functions that are so crucial to determining an organization's long-term performance. The lower a manager's position in the hierarchy, the more time he or she spends leading and controlling first-line managers or nonmanagerial employees.

top managers
Managers who establish organizational goals, decide how departments should interact, and monitor the performance of middle managers.

top-management team A group composed of the CEO, the president, and the heads of the most important departments.

> **FIGURE 1.5** **Relative Amounts of Time Managers Spend on the Four Managerial Functions**

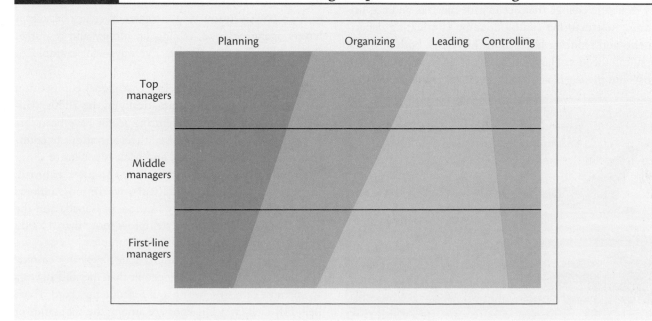

Recent Changes in Managerial Hierarchies

The tasks and responsibilities of managers at different levels have been changing dramatically in recent years. Increasingly, top managers are encouraging lower-level managers to look beyond the goals of their own departments and take a cross-departmental view to find new opportunities to improve organizational performance. Stiff competition for resources—both at home and abroad—has put increased pressure on all managers to improve efficiency, effectiveness, and organizational performance. Management information systems (MIS) give managers at all levels and in all areas access to more and better information and improve their ability to plan, organize, lead, and control. The latest technologies also provide employees with more job-related information and allows them to become more skilled, specialized, and productive.[27]

Restructuring and Outsourcing

To utilize cutting-edge technology to increase efficiency and effectiveness, CEOs and top-management teams have been restructuring organizations and outsourcing specific organizational activities to reduce the number of employees on the payroll and make more productive use of the remaining workforce.

Restructuring involves simplifying, shrinking, or downsizing an organization's operations to lower operating costs as many companies do in times of recession and/or dramatic change that occur with mergers and acquisitions. Restructuring can be done by eliminating departments and reducing levels in the hierarchy, both of which result in the loss of large numbers of jobs of top, middle, or first-line managers and nonmanagerial employees. While

Restructuring creates new occupations, such as Chief Twitter Officer at Southwest Airlines.

innovations in technology have reduced employment, they have also created many new positions and occupations that didn't exist just a few years ago. (Job titles such as Chief Twitter Officer at Southwest Airlines provide some interesting examples!) The ability of new technologies to increase efficiency has, however, increased the amount of downsizing in recent years. For example, new technologies make it possible for fewer employees to perform a given task because they increase each person's ability to process information and make decisions more quickly and accurately. Canadian companies are spending billions of dollars a year on MIS that improves efficiency and effectiveness and transforms communication processes. We discuss MIS and new technology's many dramatic effects on management in Chapter 4 and throughout this book.

Restructuring, however, can produce some powerful negative outcomes. It can reduce the morale of the remaining employees who are worried about their own job security. And top managers of many downsized organizations have realized they downsized too far when their employees complain they are overworked and when increasing numbers of customers complain about poor-quality service.[28] Dell faces this charge in the 2000s as it continues to reduce the number of its customer service reps and outsource their jobs to India to lower costs.

Outsourcing involves contracting with another company, usually in a low-cost country abroad, to have it perform a work activity the organization previously performed itself, such as manufacturing, marketing, or customer service. Outsourcing increases efficiency because it lowers operating costs, freeing up money and resources that can be used in more effective ways—for example, to develop new products.

The need to respond to low-cost global competition has speeded outsourcing dramatically in the 2000s. Millions of jobs in the manufacturing sector have been lost since 2000 as companies moved their operations to countries such as China, Taiwan, and Malaysia. Tens of thousands of high-paying jobs in IT have also moved abroad, to countries like India and Russia, where programmers work for one-third the salary of those in Canada and the United States. Dell currently employs more than 15 000 customer service reps in India, for example.[29]

Large for-profit organizations today typically employ 10 percent to 20 percent fewer people than they did 10 years ago because of restructuring and outsourcing. Ford, IBM, Bell, HP, Dell, and Du Pont are among the thousands of

restructuring
Downsizing an organization by eliminating the jobs of large numbers of top, middle, and first-line managers and nonmanagerial employees.

outsourcing
Contracting with another company, usually abroad, to have it perform an activity the organization previously performed itself.

organizations that have streamlined their operations to increase efficiency and effectiveness. The argument is that the managers and employees who have lost their jobs will find employment in new and growing companies where their skills and experience will be better utilized. For example, the millions of manufacturing jobs that have been sent overseas will be replaced by higher-paying jobs in the service sector that are made possible because of the growth in global trade. Many people, however, still struggle to find meaningful employment. Goodwill Industries, featured in our Focus on the Social Economy, is an organization devoted to helping people who have been marginalized from employment get back into the labour force.

Empowerment and Self-Managed Teams

The second principal way managers have sought to increase efficiency and effectiveness is by empowering lower-level employees and moving to self-managed teams. **Empowerment** is a management technique that involves giving employees more authority and responsibility over the way they perform their work activities—an approach used at Brick Brewing. The way in which John Deere, the

well-known manufacturer of tractors, empowered its employees illustrates how this technique can help raise performance. The employees who assemble Deere's vehicles possess detailed knowledge about how Deere products work. Deere's managers suddenly realized that these employees could become persuasive salespeople if they were given training. So groups of these employees were given intensive sales training and sent to visit Deere's customers and explain to them how to operate and service the company's new products. While speaking with customers, these newly empowered "salespeople" are also able to collect information that helps Deere develop new products that better meet customers' needs. The new sales jobs are only temporary; employees go on assignment but then return to the production line, where they use their new knowledge to find ways to improve efficiency and quality.

Information technology (IT) is being increasingly used to empower employees because it expands employees' job knowledge and increases the scope of their job responsibilities. Frequently, IT allows one employee to perform a task that was previously performed by many employees. As a

> **empowerment** The expansion of employees' knowledge, tasks, and decision-making responsibilities.

FOCUS ON ❯ *The Social Economy*

Goodwill Industries

Goodwill® inspires hope and self-confidence, helping people from all backgrounds and walks of life to feel successful, valuable, and dignified.

They help people earn a living, improve their lives, and strengthen their families and their communities.

The network of 165 independent, community-based Goodwills in the United States and Canada offers customized job training, employment placement, and other services to people who have disabilities, lack education or job experience, or face employment challenges.

In 2011, Goodwill helped more than 4 million people train for careers in industries such as banking, IT, and health care, to name a few—and get the support services they needed to be successful, such as English language training, additional education, or access to transportation and child care.

More than 189 000 people obtained meaningful employment in 2011 through their participation in Goodwill programs. These people went on to earn more than $2.95 billion in salaries and wages, and contributed to their communities as productive, tax-paying citizens.

Goodwill meets the diverse needs of people, including youth, seniors, veterans, immigrants, and people with disabilities, criminal backgrounds, and other specialized needs.

Goodwill has earned the trust and support of more than 79 million donors in the United States and Canada.

Local Goodwills are flexible and sustainable social enterprises that fund job training, employment placement services, and other community programs by selling donated clothes and household items at Goodwill stores and online.

Goodwills also generate revenue by contracting with businesses and government to provide a wide range of commercial services, including packaging and assembly, food service preparation, document imaging and shredding, and more.[30]

1. Research Goodwill Industries and find out how they help mitigate or buffer the forces of restructuring and outsourcing.

2. Describe the types and levels of managers found at Goodwill.

result, the employee has more autonomy and responsibility. At the Canadian construction company Ellis Don, a new technology platform called Edgebuilder has given the company the confidence to grant greater responsibilities to young employees that they may not have been given otherwise. To paraphrase the top management, it is much easier to decide to give someone authority for a project more complex than one they have ever handled when you have IT systems providing management with a transparent overview of how a job is progressing.[31]

Self-managed teams are groups of employees who are given responsibility for supervising their own activities and for monitoring the quality of the goods and services they provide. At WestJet, former CEO Clive Beddoe created an empowered self-managed workforce. He believes that his "management from the bottom" gives employees pride in fulfilling the company's overall objectives without interference from supervisors. "They are the ones making the decisions about what they're doing and how they're doing it," says Beddoe. Managerial hierarchies are changing.

> "**Management from the bottom gives employees pride in fulfilling the company's overall objectives without interference from supervisors.**"
>
> *Clive Beddoe*

LO5 Distinguish among the kinds of managerial skills and roles that managers perform.

Managerial Skills and Roles

Managerial Skills

To successfully perform their activities in planning, organizing, leading, and controlling, managers must have certain skills. Research has shown that formal education, training, and experience help managers acquire three principal types of skills: *conceptual, human,* and *technical.*[32] As you might expect, the level of these skills that a manager needs depends on his or her level in the managerial hierarchy (see Figure 1.6).

Conceptual Skills

Conceptual skills are demonstrated by the ability to analyze and diagnose a situation and to distinguish between cause and effect. Planning and organizing require a high level of conceptual skill. Top managers require the best conceptual skills because their primary responsibilities are planning and organizing.[33] Formal education and training are very important in helping managers develop conceptual skills. Business training at the undergraduate and graduate (MBA) levels provides many of the conceptual tools (theories and techniques in marketing, finance, and other areas) that managers need to perform their roles effectively. Conceptual skills allow managers to understand the big picture confronting an organization. The ability to focus on the big picture lets the manager see beyond the situation immediately at hand and consider choices while keeping the organization's long-term goals in mind.

Today, continuing management education and training, including training in advanced IT, are integral in building managerial skills because new theories and techniques are constantly being developed to improve organizational effectiveness, such as total quality management (TQM), benchmarking, Web-based

---

self-managed teams Groups of employees who supervise their own activities and monitor the quality of the goods and services they provide.

conceptual skills The ability to analyze and diagnose a situation and to distinguish between cause and effect.

► FIGURE 1.6 Conceptual, Human, and Technical Skills Used by the Three Levels of Management

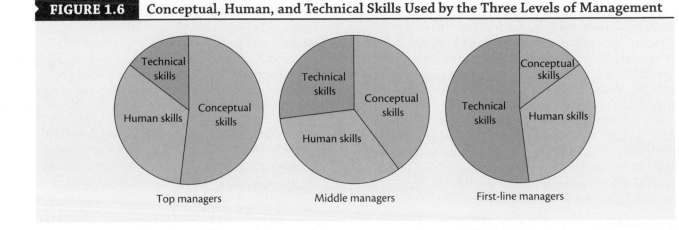

Top managers   Middle managers   First-line managers

organization, and business-to-business (B2B) networks. A quick scan through a magazine such as *Canadian Business* reveals a host of seminars on topics such as advanced marketing, finance, leadership, and human resources management that are offered to managers at many levels in the organization, from the most senior corporate executives to middle managers. Suncor, TELUS, BCE, and many other organizations designate a portion of each manager's personal budget to be used at the manager's discretion to attend management development programs.

In addition, organizations may wish to develop a particular manager's abilities in a specific skill area—perhaps to learn an advanced component of departmental skills, such as international bond trading, or to learn the skills necessary to implement total quality management. The organization thus pays for managers to attend specialized programs to develop these skills. Indeed, one signal that a manager is performing well is an organization's willingness to invest in that manager's skill development. Similarly, many nonmanagerial employees who are performing at a high level (because they have studied management) are often sent to intensive management training programs to develop their management skills and to prepare them for promotion to first-level management positions.

Human Skills

Human skills include the ability to understand, alter, lead, and control the behaviour of other individuals and groups. The ability to communicate and give feedback, to coordinate and motivate people, to give recognition, to mould individuals into a cohesive team, and to play politics effectively distinguishes effective managers from ineffective managers.

To manage interpersonal interactions effectively, each person in an organization needs to learn how to empathize with other people—to understand their viewpoints and the problems they face. One way to help managers understand their personal strengths and weaknesses is to have their superiors, peers, and subordinates provide feedback about their performance. Managers also need to be able to manage politics effectively so that they can deal with resistance from those who disagree with their goals. Effective managers use political strategies to influence others and gain support for their goals, while overcoming resistance or opposition. By all accounts, George Croft and Jason Pratt possess a high level of these human skills.

Like conceptual skills, human skills can be learned through education and training, and also can be developed through experience.[34]

Effective managers use human skills to understand and lead others.

Organizations increasingly utilize advanced programs in leadership skills and team leadership as they seek to capitalize on the advantages of self-managed teams.[35] To manage personal interactions effectively, each person in an organization needs to learn how to empathize with other people—to understand their viewpoints and the problems they face. One way to help managers understand their personal strengths and weaknesses is to have their superiors, peers, and subordinates provide feedback about their job performance. Thorough and direct feedback allows managers to develop their human skills.

Technical Skills

Technical skills are the job-specific knowledge and techniques that are required to perform an organizational role. Examples include a manager's specific manufacturing, accounting, marketing, and IT skills. Managers need a range of technical skills to be effective. The array of technical skills a person needs depends on his or her position in the organization. The manager of a restaurant, for example, may need cooking skills to fill in for an absent cook, accounting and bookkeeping skills to keep track of receipts and costs and to administer the payroll, and aesthetic skills to keep the restaurant looking attractive for customers.

Effective managers need all three kinds of skills—conceptual, human, and technical. The absence of even one type can lead to failure. One of the biggest problems that people who start small businesses confront, for example, is their lack of appropriate conceptual and human skills. Someone who has the technical skills to start a new business does not necessarily know how to manage the venture successfully. Similarly, one of the

human skills The ability to understand, alter, lead, and control the behaviour of other individuals and groups.

technical skills Job-specific knowledge and techniques that are required to perform an organizational role.

biggest problems that scientists or engineers who switch careers from research to management confront is their lack of effective human skills. Ambitious managers or prospective managers are constantly in search of the latest educational contributions to help them develop the conceptual, human, and technical skills they need to perform at a high level in today's changing and increasingly competitive global environment.

Managerial Roles

In the early 1970s, McGill University Professor Henry Mintzberg detailed 10 specific roles that effective managers undertake in their daily activities. A **role** is a set of specific tasks that a person is expected to perform because of the position he or she holds in an organization. Although the roles that Mintzberg described overlap with Fayol's model, they are useful because they focus on

> **role** The specific tasks that a person is expected to perform because of the position he or she holds in an organization.

what managers do in a typical hour, day, or week.[36] Below we discuss these roles.

Mintzberg examined all the specific tasks that managers need to perform as they plan, organize, lead, and control organizational resources, and he reduced them to three categories and 10 specific roles.[37] Managers assume each of these roles in order to influence the behaviour of individuals and groups inside and outside the organization. People inside the organization include other managers and employees. People outside the organization include stakeholders such as shareholders, customers, suppliers, the local community in which an organization is located, and any local or government agency that has an interest in the organization and what it does.[38] Mintzberg grouped the 10 roles into three broad categories: *interpersonal, informational,* and *decisional* (see Table 1.1). Managers often perform several of these roles simultaneously.

> **TABLE 1.1** Managerial Roles Identified by Mintzberg

Type of Role	Specific Role	Examples of Role Activities
INTERPERSONAL	Figurehead	Outline future organizational goals to employees at company meetings; open a new corporate headquarters building; state the organization's ethical guidelines and the principles of behaviour employees are to follow in their dealings with customers and suppliers.
	Leader	Provide an example for employees to follow; give direct commands and orders to subordinates; make decisions concerning the use of human and technical resources; mobilize employee support for specific organizational goals.
	Liaison	Coordinate the work of managers in different departments; establish alliances between different organizations to share resources to produce new goods and services.
INFORMATIONAL	Monitor	Evaluate the performance of managers in different functions and take corrective action to improve their performance; watch for changes occurring in the external and internal environment that may affect the organization in the future.
	Disseminator	Inform employees about changes taking place in the external and internal environment that will affect them and the organization; communicate to employees the organization's vision and purpose.
	Spokesperson	Launch a national advertising campaign to promote new goods and services; give a speech to inform the local community about the organization's future intentions.
DECISIONAL	Entrepreneur	Commit organizational resources to develop innovative goods and services; decide to expand internationally to obtain new customers for the organization's products.
	Disturbance handler	Move quickly to take corrective action to deal with unexpected problems facing the organization from the external environment (e.g., a crisis such as an oil spill), or from the internal environment (e.g., producing faulty goods or services).
	Resource allocator	Allocate organizational resources among different functions and departments of the organization; set budgets and salaries of middle and first-level managers.
	Negotiator	Work with suppliers, distributors, and labour unions to reach agreements about the quality and price of input, technical, and human resources; work with other organizations to establish agreements to pool resources to work on joint projects.

Interpersonal Roles

Managers assume interpersonal roles in order to coordinate and interact with organizational members and provide direction and supervision to employees and to the organization as a whole. A manager's first interpersonal role is to act as a *figurehead*—the person who symbolizes an organization or a department. Assuming the figurehead role, the chief executive officer determines the direction or mission of the organization and informs employees and other interested parties about what the organization is seeking to achieve. Managers at all levels act as figureheads and role models who establish the appropriate and inappropriate ways to behave in the organization.

A manager's role as a *leader* is to encourage subordinates to perform at a high level and to take steps to train, counsel, and mentor subordinates to help them reach their full potential. A manager's power to lead comes both from formal authority, due to his or her position in the organization's hierarchy, and from his or her personal qualities, including reputation, skills, and personality. The personal behaviour of a leader affects employee attitudes

In the role of negotiator, managers make agreements and contracts.

and behaviour; indeed, subordinates' desire to perform at a high level—and even whether they desire to arrive at work on time and not be absent often—depends on how satisfied they are with working for the organization.

In performing as a *liaison*, managers link and coordinate the activities of people and groups both inside and outside the organization. Inside the organization, managers are responsible for coordinating the activities of people in different departments to improve their ability to cooperate. Outside the organization, managers are responsible for forming linkages with suppliers, customers, or the organization's local community in order to obtain scarce resources. People outside an organization often come to equate the organization with the manager they are dealing with, or with the person they see on television or read about in the newspaper.

Informational Roles

Informational roles are closely associated with the tasks necessary to obtain and transmit information. First, a manager acts as a *monitor* and analyzes information from inside and outside the organization. With this information, a manager can effectively organize and control people and other resources.

Acting as a *disseminator,* the manager transmits information to other members of the organization to influence their work attitudes and behaviour. In the role of *spokesperson,* a manager uses information to promote the organization so that people both inside and outside the organization respond positively.

Decisional Roles

Decisional roles are closely associated with the methods that managers use to plan strategy and utilize resources. In the role of *entrepreneur,* a manager must decide

When dealing with people, a manager can act as a figurehead.

which projects or programs to initiate and how to invest resources to increase organizational performance.

As a **disturbance handler,** a manager assumes responsibility for handling an unexpected event or crisis that threatens the organization's access to resources. In this situation, a manager must also assume the roles of figurehead and leader to rally employees so that they can help secure the resources needed to avert the problem.

Under typical conditions, **resource allocator** is one of the important roles a manager plays—deciding how best to use people and other resources to increase organizational performance. While engaged as a resource allocator, the manager must also be a **negotiator,** reaching agreements with other managers or groups claiming the first right to resources, with the organization, and with outside groups such as shareholders or customers.

Tips > FOR MANAGERS

Tasks and Roles

Use Mintzberg's interpersonal roles to effectively promote diversity in your organization by:

1. Conveying that the effective management of diversity is a valued goal and objective (figurehead role),

2. Serve as a role model and institute policies and procedures to ensure that diverse organizational members are treated fairly (leader role), and

3. Enable diverse individuals and groups to coordinate their efforts and cooperate with each other both inside the organization and at the organization's boundaries (liaison role).

CHAPTER 1

Summary and Review

LO1 What Is Management? A manager is a person responsible for supervising the use of an organization's resources to meet its goals. An organization is a collection of people who work together and coordinate their actions to achieve a wide variety of goals. Management is the process of using organizational resources to achieve organizational goals effectively and efficiently through planning, organizing, leading, and controlling. An efficient organization makes the most productive use of its resources. An effective organization pursues appropriate goals and achieves these goals by using its resources to create the goods or services that customers want.

LO2 Managerial Tasks and Functions The four principal managerial functions are planning, organizing, leading, and controlling. Managers at all levels of the organization and in all departments perform these functions in varying degrees. Effective management means managing these activities successfully.

LO3 Types and Levels of Managers Managers are characterized by level and function. Functions typically include marketing, operations, human resources, accounting and finance, and research and development. Organizations typically have three levels of management. First-line managers are responsible for the day-to-day supervision of non-managerial employees. Middle managers are responsible for developing and utilizing organizational resources efficiently and effectively. Top managers have cross-departmental responsibilities. The top managers' job is to establish appropriate goals for the entire organization and to verify that department managers are using resources effectively and efficiently to achieve those goals.

LO4 Recent Changes in Managerial Hierarchies To increase efficiency and effectiveness, some organizations have altered their managerial hierarchies by restructuring, outsourcing, empowering their workforces, and using self-managed teams. Innovations in technology and global forces have accelerated the changes in management hierarchies.

LO5 Managerial Skills and Roles Three types of skills help managers perform their roles effectively: conceptual, human, and technical skills. According to Mintzberg, managers play 10 specific roles in their daily activities: figurehead, leader, liaison, monitor, disseminator, spokesperson, entrepreneur, disturbance handler, resource allocator, and negotiator.

KEY TERMS

conceptual skills	management	resources
controlling	manager	restructuring
department	middle managers	role
effectiveness	organizational performance	self-managed teams
efficiency	organizational structure	social economy
empowerment	organizations	strategy
first-line managers	organizing	technical skills
human skills	outsourcing	top managers
leading	planning	top-management team

WRAP-UP TO ▶▶▶ OPENING CASE

Management at Brick Brewing Co. Limited

In the opening case you were introduced to two top managers at Brick Brewing Co., Jason Pratt, CFO, and George Croft, CEO. After having read and understood the concepts in this chapter you should now be able to answer the following questions:

1. *What kinds of activities or tasks are involved in planning, organizing, leading, and controlling at Brick Brewing?*

ANSWER: Planning involves setting organizational goals and finding the best ways, or strategy, to achieve them. The top managers at Brick Brewing Company use several strategies concurrently to offer quality and value products to its customers. Purchasing the rights to Seagram Coolers strengthens their goal to provide specialty beverages. They are credited with founding the craft beer renaissance in Canada and have won awards for their premium craft beers, thereby differentiating themselves from other breweries. Brick Brewing also offers the lowest legally priced beer with its Laker brand, indicating a low-cost strategy can co-exist with a differentiation strategy.

Organizing involves putting people and allocating resources into jobs and grouping jobs together to coordinate tasks and achieve organizational goals. It involves creating lines of authority and establishing reporting relationships. In this case, Jason Pratt is responsible for the financial management of the company. In his capacity as CFO he allocated the funds necessary to purchase the Seagram Cooler brand from Corby. He reports directly to George Croft, CEO.

Leading involves creating and communicating a vision for the organization that motivates people to achieve organizational goals. George Croft and Jason Pratt created a high-performing team that won the company recognition at the Ontario Brewing Awards in 2011 for their premium beers, while also providing the cheap brand that is very popular among consumers. The vision: to sell a quality product at a reasonable price.

Controlling involves determining how well organizational goals have been achieved and taking corrective actions to improve performance. Brick Brewing achieves its goals by using quality assurance techniques to carefully monitor its brewing practices. This ensures a high level of performance.

2. *Characterize the type and level of management described in the case.*

ANSWER: Jason Pratt as chief financial officer (CFO) is a top manager at Brick Brewing Co. His functional or departmental area is finance. He would likely supervise middle and first-line managers in the finance department.

George Croft is the top manager as chief executive officer (CEO). Jason Pratt would be part of his top management team, as would other heads or vice-presidents of other functional areas or departments. The CEO is responsible for the overall well-being and operation of the whole organization. He or she sets the vision, organizational goals, and strategy.

3. *What skills does Jason Pratt bring to the Brick Brewing Co. as a top manager?*

ANSWER: All three sets of managerial skills are evident in this case on the part of Jason Pratt: conceptual skills are evident in the use of "business judgment and contribution to overall strategy"; human skills are evident in "developing and leading high-performance teams"; and technical skills are evident in his role as a professional chartered accountant and secretary to the audit committee of the Board.

4. *Which of Mintzberg's managerial roles are illustrated in this case by each manager?*

ANSWER: In performing interpersonal roles, Croft illustrated the specific managerial role of leading when he hired Pratt. Pratt acts as a leader in creating high-performance teams. Brick Brewing's top managers act in the role of a figurehead when they sponsor charitable events and as a liaison when they act in partnership with community organizations. Acting as a spokesperson, Pratt reported the acquisition of the Canadian rights to distribute the Seagram Coolers brands from Corby Distilleries by Brick Brewing Co. In performing decisional roles, the founder of the company acted as an entrepreneur when he started up the first craft brewery in Ontario in 1984. Subsequent managers have acted as entrepreneurs when introducing new brands such as Laker, Red Cap, and Formosa Springs Draft. In 2011, top managers acted in the role of entrepreneur when they struck a deal to purchase the Canadian distribution rights to Seagram Coolers.

Management in Action

TOPICS FOR DISCUSSION AND ACTION

LEVEL 1 Knowledge & Comprehension

1. Describe what management is and what managers do to achieve organizational goals.
2. Describe the difference between efficiency and effectiveness.
3. Describe the primary responsibilities of the three levels of management, and discuss the skills managers use in carrying out their roles and duties.

LEVEL 2 Application & Analysis

4. Ask a middle or top manager, perhaps someone you already know, to give examples of how he or she performs the management functions of planning, organizing, leading, and controlling. How much time does he or she spend in performing each function?

5. Like Mintzberg, try to find a cooperative manager who will allow you to follow him or her around for a day. List the types of roles the manager plays and how much time he or she spends performing them.

6. Search iTunes for a free podcast on how managers use their time in performing their roles. Write a brief report of your research.

LEVEL 3 Synthesis & Evaluation

7. Evaluate one (real) organization that you believe to be efficient and effective and one organization that you assess to be inefficient and ineffective in its use of resources. Give evidence to support your evaluation.

8. Put yourself in the position of a first-line manager of a retail store such as The Bay. What skills and roles would you use in your daily work? What role activities would you likely be involved in?

9. Explain how the managerial functions of planning, leading, organizing, and controlling differ in the three levels of management.

SELF-REFLECTION EXERCISE

In each chapter you will find a self-reflection feature, which gives you ideas on how to apply this material to your personal life. We do this to help reinforce the idea that management is not just for managers—all of us manage our lives and can apply many of the concepts in this book.

Think about where you hope to be in your life five years from now (i.e., your major goal). What is your competitive advantage for achieving your goal? What do you need to plan, organize, lead, and control to make sure that you reach your goal? Looking over Mintzberg's managerial roles (see Table 1.1), which roles do you perform in your daily life? Give examples.

SMALL GROUP BREAKOUT EXERCISE

Assume you and your teammates belong to a fusion rock band. The leader of the group wrote a proposal that will go before city council to get a licence to hold a concert. The band's leader calls a meeting to tell you that it has been accepted by the council with the strict condition that the band ensures that no laws are violated and the safety of all the concert-goers is maintained. Your group accepts the terms and now must figure out how to manage the event.

1. What set of skills did the leader mostly use in creating the proposal?

2. What must now be done to plan this event effectively and efficiently?

3. What kinds of resources must the band use in organizing the event?

4. Identify the managerial role the leader engaged in:

   a. when he or she called the meeting of the band

   b. when he or she met with the council

   c. when the group accepted the terms of the agreement

5. How could the leader of the band lead the group to put on a successful concert?

6. What kind of control measures could the group take to fulfill its agreement with the council?

BUSINESS PLANNING EXERCISE

Your professor may ask you to write a business plan for a new venture or a strategic plan for an existing venture. At the end of every chapter, you will have an opportunity to apply managerial and organizational concepts to the exercise of writing a business plan. Refer to Appendix A.

You and two partners are thinking about writing a business plan for a large restaurant in your local community. Each of you can invest $25 000 in the venture, and with a solid business plan you hope to secure an additional investment of $450 000 in the form of a bank loan. You and your partners have little experience in the food industry beyond serving meals or eating in restaurants. But after reading this chapter, you know a little bit more about how you will manage it.

1. Decide what activities and tasks the three levels of management should be responsible for in the restaurant.

2. How should you and your partners go about (a) planning, (b) organizing, (c) leading, and (d) controlling resources effectively in opening the new restaurant?

MANAGING ETHICALLY EXERCISE

Recently, six global pharmaceutical companies admitted that they had conspired to artificially raise the prices of vitamins on a global basis. This involved a Swiss firm, a German firm, and four others. The decision to inflate the prices came from senior managers in each company through a joint decision. This unethical action resulted in passing on unfair expenses to the customers. In several meetings around the world, they worked out the details that went undiscovered for many years. Once they were caught, there was jail for some and continuing prosecution for others; all were fired.

The result of this situation was that each company agreed to create a special position of ethics officer to oversee behaviour in the organization. Why are some people unethical, while others would not even consider doing what is described above? Is ethics an internal force in each individual, or can you educate people in ethics, or can people be made to be ethical? How do you define "unethical" in this case? Do you think it is possible for businesses to be ethical? What was the gain for the managers?

MANAGEMENT CHALLENGE EXERCISE

Planning for the Unthinkable[39]

By now, many people have seen the movie *Titanic* and know what an incredible tragedy it all turned out to be.[40] "On April 15, 1912, at 2:10 AM, the mighty ship of dreams, *The R.M.S. Titanic* foundered, bringing with it some 1523 souls into the cold sea."[41] The sinking of the *Titanic* turned out to be the "most infamous disaster of the twentieth century." Each of us asks, "But how could that be? This was a time of optimism, of new materials, of adventure, of safety."

Could the disaster be attributed to bad management practices? Mark Kozak-Holland, in his "Plan for the Unthinkable," writes, "... prestige overtook safety as the primary principle in *Titanic*'s design, the ship many thought invincible had a fate that was inevitable. Worse still, the bad guys got away with it."

The business case put forward at the time was that the building of such a ship as the *Titanic* would be a two-year payback project, quite a feat in those days. However, there was a very serious glitch: a competitive frenzy to get the ship out on the water. Executives overrode the architects' plans for "safety, performance, stability, security, maintainability, and the environment to ensure the ship delivered its functions." In practice, this meant that operating the *Titanic* put everyone at risk. The ship's performance, therefore, was severely compromised. Pride got in the way as well. The architects gave in to the executives' demands to get the ship afloat and have the "ultimate passenger experience" because of their overconfidence in the ship's design. "The lifeboats were viewed as an added safety feature, useful if *Titanic* had to rescue another ship in distress." Planning for testing was also compromised because of time and investment pressures. The net result was the perception that the *Titanic* was invincible. Reputations, corporate and personal, were at stake. Testing was sporadic and inadequate at best. However, management philosophy literally was "full-steam ahead"!

Think now what kind of a manager you would be as the planning was being done to get the *Titanic* ready to sail.

1. What suggestions would you have made for planning and controlling? Refer to www.gma.org/space1/titanic.html

MANAGEMENT PORTFOLIO PROJECT

You may be asked to follow and analyze an organization over the semester to help you build your management skills. Each chapter will have an exercise that asks you to evaluate how the issues in the chapter are dealt with by your organization. Choose a large, well-known, publicly traded Canadian company that is easy to research through company websites, newspapers, the Canadian Securities Administrators' website, SEDAR.com, and company annual reports. Cite all your sources of information using an appropriate method.

Answer the following questions about the organization you have chosen to follow:

1. Give a brief profile of the organization. How large is it in terms of number of employees, annual revenues, profits, location of facilities, and so on? What kind of products or services does it provide?

2. Give a brief profile of the industry in which it operates. Under what industrial classification does it fall? How many competitors are active? What is their target market?

3. Identify the top management team. Who is the CEO, and what is his or her background? Give examples of the activities of the CEO that illustrate how he or she engages in the management processes of planning, organizing, leading, and controlling.

VIDEO MANAGEMENT CASE

Whole Foods Market[42]

John Mackey, co-founder and CEO of Whole Foods Market, has a vision and a mission that pays attention to all stakeholders.

1. Describe the responsibility John Mackey feels toward each of the following:
   a. customers
   b. community

    c. employees

    d. investors

2. How has competition from other food retailers affected John Mackey and Whole Foods Market?

Management Case

Secrets of Canada's Best Bosses[43]

Paul Seed, president of London, Ont.-based StarTech.com Ltd., didn't stop to measure employee engagement at his fast-growing firm until 2002. When he finally did—using internal resources—he was stunned to learn just how dissatisfied the employees at his computer hardware distribution firm were. That taught him a lesson: "When you're running a company that started in the basement and grew to 153 employees, you have to change your style as you grow," says Seed. "We didn't update our communication style to suit the size of the company."

After a few years of tracking engagement internally, Seed was confident things had improved and enrolled in the BSME program in 2005. To his surprise, StarTech failed to make the 50 Best list. Clearly, employees weren't nearly as engaged as he'd thought. After poring over employee feedback, Seed noticed two particularly glaring complaints, both of which reflected badly on his leadership team's people-management approach: first, poor communication from management; and second, a lack of involvement in how the company makes decisions.

Seed was determined to make changes that would stick. To bridge the communication gap, he quickly placed a much stronger emphasis on management/employee dialogue. Perhaps too quickly; the sudden about-face raised the eyebrows of more cynical employees. "Everyone was a bit skeptical at first," Seed admits. But he stuck to it. He encouraged senior managers to keep initiating conversations with front-line workers, to share news of developments and to act on any concerns. After about a year, even the wariest employees were hard-pressed to question management's commitment to communication.

To get employees involved in the decision-making process, Seed gathered staff at corporate headquarters for a weekend to discuss the firm's progress and goals. Called the StarTech One Team conference, it was meant to give all staff an understanding of the firm's achievements and goals while creating an opportunity for them to contribute to the company's strategic direction. It was a hit. Since its debut in 2005, the now-annual conference has expanded to include entertainment; it is now as much a social team-building affair as a strategic one. It has also grown in size—today, the firm flies in employees from its U.S. and U.K. offices, too. The cost of hosting the conference is between $50 000 and $60 000, not including the time-and-a-half pay and day-in-lieu each staffer is granted for working on a weekend. "It costs," Seed reasons, "but employees get a chance not only to talk to everyone but to see where the firm is going."

These actions are clearly resonating with staff. StarTech finally made the BSME ranking, in 45th place, in 2009 and occupies 36th place this year. The benefits of boasting a dedicated, determined workforce aren't lost on Seed. "You can never underestimate the power of employee engagement and the difference it makes in moving from a good company to a great company," he says. Although StarTech does not disclose its financials, the CEO directly credits engagement initiatives with revenue growth ranging from 10 percent to 25 percent in 2005 through 2008, 5 percent at the height of the recession in 2009, and 35 percent last year [2010].

1. What changes to managerial hierarchies are illustrated in this case?
2. How does Seed empower the employees at StarTech?
3. What kinds of managerial skills are illustrated in this case?

McGraw Hill connect™

Connect allows you to practise important concepts at your own pace and on your own schedule, with 24/7 online access to an eBook, practice quizzes, video cases, interactive exercises, study tools, and more.

End of Part I: Continuing Case

CARROT TOPS: INTRODUCTION

The main theme of this book is that the management process—planning, organizing, leading, and controlling—is not confined to the top management, but rather is a process in which every manager must engage. Perhaps nowhere is this more apparent than in the typical small service business. Here the owner/operator usually has few staff to rely on. The success of the enterprise often depends on the effectiveness with which the manager structures activities and uses resources to achieve a goal. The activities of managing are critical to any complex cooperative endeavour. Management is both the art and science of arranging and utilizing the physical and human factors of production toward a desired outcome. This book provides the student with an introduction to the management process.

To help illustrate and emphasize the role of the front-line manager, throughout this book we will use a continuing or running case of a business based in Southern Ontario. Each segment will illustrate how the case's main players—owner/manager Mel Harvey and first-line manager Janet Khan—confront and solve management problems each day by applying the concepts and techniques presented in the book in each particular part: Part I—Management; Part II—The Environment of Management; Part III—Planning and Decision Making; Part IV—Organizing; Part V—Leading Individuals and Groups; and Part VI—Controlling. Here is some background information you'll need to answer the questions that arise in subsequent parts of this book.

CARROT TOPS: A PROFILE

After putting together a typical business plan to meet the requirements of a course on entrepreneurship, Mel Harvey started "Mel's General Store" in 2002. The business plan was about 20 pages long and outlined the usual array of topics: a profile of the organization; a profile of the industry; a profile of the product or service; marketing, organization, operating, and control systems plans; pro forma financial statements; and financial project tables and appendices. The one-page executive summary included a synopsis of the plan and covered "the business," "the market," "strategy," "competition," "management," and "financial details," including how the company intends to generate revenue, as well as a likely exit strategy. In this case, Mel was committed to supplying low-cost, basic groceries to the local community in which he lived in Southern Ontario. One day, he hoped to sell franchise licences.

Drawing on all segments of this case:

1. What kinds of activities does Mel have to consider in planning, organizing, leading, and controlling his enterprise?

2. What sets of skills will Mel use when planning, organizing, leading, and controlling?

3. Identify an example of an activity that Mel could undertake that illustrates each of Mintzberg's managerial roles.

PART II

Managing the Organizational Environment

LEARNING OUTCOMES

LO1 Explain why the ability to perceive, interpret, and respond appropriately to the organizational environment is crucial for managerial success.

LO2 Identify the main forces in an organization's task and general environments and the challenges these forces present to managers.

LO3 Discuss how national cultures differ and why it is important that managers be sensitive to the political and social systems of nations around the world.

LO4 Explain the ways managers can minimize threats and uncertainty from forces in the external environment.

LO5 Evaluate the major challenges managers face in gaining a competitive advantage in the global economy.

Opening Case

IKEA Is on Top of the Furniture World[1]

IKEA is the largest furniture chain in the world; in 2011, the Swedish company operated more than 300 stores in 35 countries, employing over 130 000 people. In 2008, IKEA sales had soared to more than $31 billion, or over 20 percent of the global furniture market, but to its managers and employees this is just the tip of the iceberg. They believe IKEA is poised for massive growth throughout the world in the coming decade because it can provide what the average customer wants: well-designed and well-made contemporary furniture at an affordable price. IKEA's ability to provide customers with affordable furniture is very much the result of its approach to globalization, to the way it treats its global employees and operates its global store empire. In a nutshell, IKEA's global approach revolves around simplicity, attention to detail, cost-consciousness, and responsiveness in every aspect of its operations and behaviour.

IKEA's global approach derives from the personal values and beliefs of its founder, Ingvar Kamprad, about how companies should treat their employees and customers. Kamprad, who is in his early 80s, was born in Smaland, a poor Swedish province whose citizens are well known for being entrepreneurial, frugal, and hardworking. Kamprad definitely absorbed these values, for when he entered the furniture business he made them the core of his management approach. He teaches store managers and employees his values; his beliefs about the need to operate in a no-frills, cost-conscious way; and his view that they are all in business "together," by which he means that every person who works in his global empire plays an essential role and has an obligation to everyone else.

What does Kamprad's approach mean in practice? It means that all IKEA's members fly coach class on business trips, stay in inexpensive

hotels, and keep travel expenses to a minimum. It also means that IKEA stores operate on the simplest set of rules and procedures possible and that employees are expected to cooperate to solve problems and get the job done. Many famous stories exist about the frugal Kamprad, such as that he always flies coach class, and that when he takes a Coke can from the mini-bar in a hotel room he replaces it with one bought in a store—despite the fact that he is a multibillionaire ranked in the top 20 on the *Forbes* list of the world's richest people!

IKEA's employees see what his global approach means as soon as they are recruited to work in a store in one of the many countries in which the company operates. They start learning about IKEA's global corporate culture by performing jobs at the bottom of the ladder, and they are quickly trained to perform all the various jobs involved in store operations. During this process they internalize IKEA's global values and norms, which centre on the importance the company

attaches to their taking the initiative and responsibility for solving problems and for focusing on the customer. Employees are rotated between departments and sometimes stores, and rapid promotion is possible for those who demonstrate the enthusiasm and togetherness that signifies they have bought into IKEA's global culture.

Most of IKEA's top managers rose from its ranks, and the company holds "breaking the bureaucracy weeks" in which they are required to work in stores and warehouses for a week each year to make sure they and all employees stay committed to IKEA's global values. No matter which country they operate in, all employees wear informal clothes to work at IKEA—Kamprad has always worn an open-neck shirt—and there are no marks of status such as executive dining rooms or private parking places. Employees believe that if they buy into IKEA's work values, behave in ways that keep its growing global operations streamlined and efficient, and focus on being one step ahead of potential problems, they will share in its success. Promotion, training, above-average pay, a generous store bonus system, and the personal well-being that comes from working in a company where people feel valued are some of the rewards that Kamprad pioneered to build and strengthen IKEA's global approach.

After reading and understanding the concepts in this chapter, you should be able to answer the following questions:

1. *Explain how the forces in the external organizational environment affected IKEA's global operations.*

2. *Discuss how national culture has impacted management decisions at IKEA.*

3. *Evaluate how managers at IKEA handle environmental change and uncertainty.*

4. *Explain how IKEA embraced the challenges of being competitive in the global economy.*

Overview

In recent years there has been a marked shift toward a more open global environment in which capital flows more freely as people and companies search for new opportunities to create profit and wealth. This has hastened the process of globalization. **Globalization** is the set of specific and general forces that work together to integrate and connect economic, political, and social systems across countries, cultures, or geographic regions so that nations become increasingly interdependent and similar. Top managers of a global company like IKEA are always operating in an environment where they are competing with other companies for scarce and valuable resources. The process of globalization has been furthered by declining barriers to international trade and investment and declining barriers of distance and culture.

Although the global economy and internal environments of organizations influence each other, we leave detailed discussion of how to manage the internal environment until Parts 3 and 4. In this chapter, we explore the nature of the external forces—the forces and conditions that operate beyond an organization's boundaries but affect a manager's

globalization The set of specific and general forces that work together to integrate and connect economic, political, and social systems across countries, cultures, or geographic regions so that nations become increasingly interdependent and similar.

organizational environment The set of forces and conditions that can affect the way an organization operates.

ability to acquire and utilize resources in detail. The two components—task and general—create opportunities and threats managers must deal with and thus affect the way organizations plan, organize, lead, and control. We conclude with a study of ways that managers can adjust and respond to forces in the organization's environment. By the end of the chapter, you will understand the steps managers must take to ensure that organizations adequately address and appropriately respond to the external environment.

Explain why the ability to perceive, interpret, and respond appropriately to the organizational environment is crucial for managerial success.   **LO1**

What Is the Organizational Environment?

The **organizational environment** is a set of forces and conditions, such as globalization, technology, and competition, that can affect the way the organization operates and the way managers engage in planning and organizing.[2] These forces change over time and thus present managers with *opportunities* and *threats*. Changes in the organizational environment, such as the development of efficient new production technology, the availability of lower-cost components, or the opening of new global markets, create opportunities for

| **FIGURE 2.1** | Forces in the Organizational Environment |

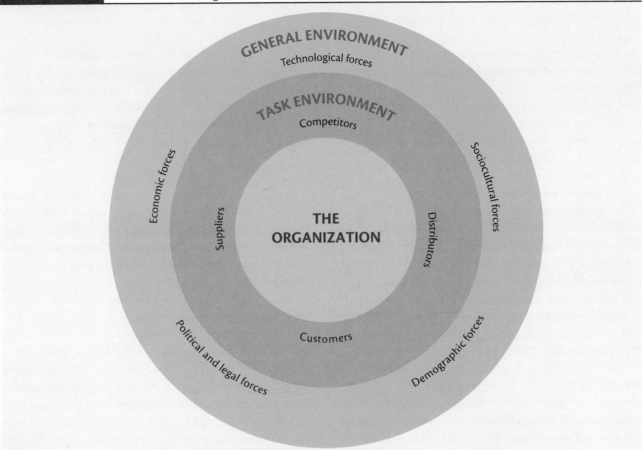

managers to make and sell more products, obtain more resources and capital, and thereby strengthen their organization. In contrast, the rise of new global competitors, a global economic recession, or an oil shortage poses threats that can devastate an organization if managers are unable to sell its products and revenues and profits plunge. The quality of managers' understanding of forces in the global environment and their ability to respond appropriately to those forces, such as IKEA's managers' ability to make and sell the furniture products customers around the world want to buy, are critical factors affecting organizational performance.

The organizational environment can be divided into the internal environment and the external environment. The **internal environment** consists of forces operating within an organization and stemming from the organization's structure and culture, including the strategy, human resources, and technology capabilities. The **external environment** consists of forces operating outside an organization that affect how an organization functions. We generally divide the organization's external environment into two major categories: the task environment and the general environment. All of these environments are shown in Figure 2.1. All the persons, groups, and institutions that are directly affected by the internal and external environments are known as the **stakeholders** of the organization.

Identify the main forces in an organization's task and general environments and the challenges these forces present to managers.   **LO2**

The Task and General Environments

The **task environment** is a set of external forces and conditions that start with suppliers, distributors, customers, and competitors and affect an organization's ability to obtain inputs, or raw materials, and dispose of its outputs, or finished products. The task environment contains the forces that have the most *immediate* and *direct* effect on managers because they pressure and influence managers on a daily basis and thus have considerable impact on short-term decision making. When managers turn on the radio or television, arrive at their offices, open their mail, or look at their computer screens, they are likely to learn about problems facing them because of changing conditions in their organization's task environment.

The **general environment** is a wide-ranging set of external factors—including economic, technological, socio-cultural, demographic, political and legal, and global forces—that affect the organization and its task environment directly or indirectly. For the individual manager, opportunities and threats resulting from changes in the general environment are often more difficult to identify and respond to than are events in the task environment. However, changes in these forces can have major impacts on managers and their organizations.

The ability of managers to perceive, interpret, and respond to forces in the organizational environment is critical to an organization's performance. The implication is clear: Managers must constantly analyze forces in the general environment because these forces affect ongoing decision making and planning.

The Task Environment

The *task* or *specific* environment includes several groups, organizations, and persons that the organization deals with directly in its daily operations and that have an immediate effect on the operations and performance levels of the organization. Forces in the task environment result from the actions of suppliers, distributors, customers, and competitors (see Figure 2.1). These four groups affect a manager's ability to obtain resources and distribute outputs on a daily, weekly, or monthly basis and thus have a significant impact on short-term decision making. We discuss each of these factors in turn.

Suppliers

Suppliers are the individuals and organizations that provide an organization with the input resources (such as raw materials, component parts, or employees) that it needs to produce goods and services. In return, the supplier receives compensation for those goods and services. An important aspect of a manager's job is to ensure a reliable supply of input resources. IKEA has more than 2000 suppliers that manufacture over 12 000 products in more

general environment The economic, technological, socio-cultural, demographic, political and legal, and global forces that affect an organization and its task environment.

suppliers Individuals and organizations that provide an organization with the input resources that it needs to produce goods and services.

than 50 countries. The company developed its own software, Electronic Commerce for IKEA Suppliers (ECIS), to coordinate the global supply chain efficiently.

Finding the overseas suppliers that offer the lowest-priced and highest-quality products is an important task facing the managers of global organizations. Since these suppliers are located in thousands of cities in many countries around the world, finding them is a difficult business. Often, global companies use the services of overseas intermediaries or brokers, located near these suppliers, to find the one that best meets their input requirements. Li & Fung, now run by brothers Victor and William Fung, is one of the brokers that has helped hundreds of global companies to locate suitable overseas suppliers, especially suppliers in mainland China.[3]

In the 2000s, however, managing global companies' supply chains became a more complicated task. To reduce costs, overseas suppliers were increasingly *specializing* in just one part of the task of producing a product. For example, in the past, a company such as Target might have negotiated with an overseas supplier to manufacture one million units of some particular shirt at a certain cost per unit. But with specialization, Target might find it can reduce the costs of producing the shirt even further by splitting apart the operations involved in its production and having *different* overseas suppliers, often in *different* countries, perform each operation. For example, to get the lowest cost per unit, rather than negotiating with a single overseas supplier over the price of making a particular shirt, Target might first negotiate with a yarn manufacturer in Vietnam to make the yarn; then ship the yarn to a Chinese supplier to weave it into cloth; and then ship the cloth to several different factories in Malaysia and the Philippines to cut the fabric and sew the shirts. Then, another overseas company might take responsibility for packaging and shipping the shirts to wherever in the world they are required. Because a company such as Target has thousands of different clothing products under production, and they change all the time, the problems of managing such a supply chain to get the full cost savings from global expansion are clearly difficult and costly.

Li & Fung capitalized on this opportunity. Realizing that many global companies do not have the time or expertise to find such specialized low-price suppliers, its founders moved quickly to provide such a service. Li & Fung employs 3600 agents who travel across 37 countries to locate new suppliers and inspect existing suppliers to

Managing a global supply chain poses a significant challenge to managing effectively and efficiently.

find new ways to help its global clients get lower prices or higher-quality products. Global companies are happy to outsource their supply chain management to Li & Fung because they realize significant cost savings. Even though they pay a hefty fee to Li & Fung, they avoid the costs of employing their own agents. As the complexity of supply chain management continues to increase, more and more companies like Li & Fung are appearing.

Changes in the nature, number, or types of suppliers lead to opportunities and threats that managers must respond to if their organizations are to prosper. Often, when managers do not respond to a threat, they put their organization at a competitive disadvantage. For example, rapid growth in the first decade of the 21st century posed a serious challenge for IKEA: "We can't increase by more than 20 stores a year because supply is the bottleneck," said Lennart Dahlgren, country manager for Russia. Since Russia is a source of timber, IKEA aims to turn it into a major supplier of finished products.[4]

Distributors

Distributors are organizations that help other organizations sell their goods or services to customers. The decisions that managers make about how to distribute products to customers can have important effects on organizational performance. For many years, Apple Computer refused to let others sell its computers, which meant that customers had to buy directly from Apple. Thus, potential customers who shopped at large computer stores with a variety of products were less likely to buy an Apple computer, since it would not be sold there.

The changing nature of distributors and distribution methods can also bring opportunities and threats for managers. If distributors are so large and powerful that they can control customers' access to a particular organization's goods and services, they can threaten the organization by demanding that it reduce the prices of its goods and services.[5] For example, before Chapters was taken over by Indigo Books & Music, publishers complained that Chapters had used its market share to force them into dropping their wholesale prices to the book retailer. Because Chapters was the largest distributor of books to customers in Canada, publishers felt compelled to comply with Chapters' demands.

In contrast, the power of a distributor may be weakened if there are too many options for manufacturers and wholesalers. Selling directly to customers on the Internet with B2B and B2C can significantly reduce the demand for distributors' services by eliminating their role as intermediaries.

Customers

Customers are the individuals and groups that buy the goods and services an organization produces. Changes in the numbers and types of customers or changes in customers' tastes and needs result in opportunities and threats. For example, when IKEA tried to enter the Japanese market, it was a disaster because consumers wanted high-quality products made of quality materials, not low-cost products made of recycled particle board. IKEA customizes its products for particular national markets: "Americans prefer to store most of their clothes folded, and Italians like to hang." The result was a wardrobe that features deeper drawers for U.S. customers.[6]

Competitors

One of the most important forces that an organization confronts in its task environment is competitors. **Competitors** are organizations that produce goods and services that are similar to a particular organization's goods and services. In other words, competitors are organizations that are vying for the same customers. Statistics Canada indicates that 40 percent of successful businesses identified more than 20 competitors each. "Think of the *benefit* of your product and service and then consider who else can provide that same *benefit* to your customers. There is only so much money in a consumer or business budget, and a family or company must decide how best to spend it. Your competition is every company that is in some way vying for those same 'benefit' dollars."[7]

Rivalry between competitors can be the most threatening force that managers must deal with. A high level of rivalry often results in price competition, and

distributors Organizations that help other organizations sell their goods or services to customers.

customers Individuals and groups that buy the goods and services that an organization produces.

competitors Organizations that produce goods and services that are similar to a particular organization's goods and services.

FIGURE 2.2 Barriers to Entry and Competition

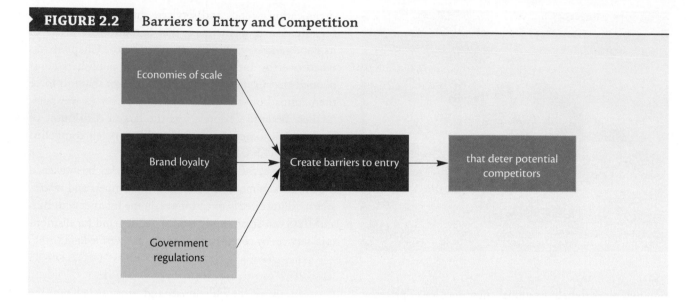

falling prices reduce access to resources and cause profits to decrease. Telecommunications giants TELUS and Shaw Media have tremendous rivalry in Western Canada. IKEA is relentless at cost-cutting. The retailer aims to lower prices across its entire offering by an average of 2 percent to 3 percent each year. It goes deeper when it wants to hit rivals in certain segments. "We look at the competition, take their price, and then slash it in half," says Mark McCaslin, manager of IKEA Long Island, in Hicksville, N.Y.[8]

Barriers to Entry

The rivalry among existing competitors is a major threat, and so is the possibility that new competitors will enter the task environment. In general, the potential for new competitors to enter a task environment (and thus boost the level of competition) depends on barriers to entry.[9] **Barriers to entry** are factors that make it difficult and costly for an organization to enter a particular task environment or industry.[10] The higher the barriers to entry, the smaller is the number of competitors in an organization's task environment and thus the lower the threat of competition. With fewer competitors, it is easier to obtain customers and keep prices high. Airlines are the classic example of an industry with barriers to entry. Montreal-based Air Canada operated as a near monopoly because of the high cost of establishing an airline for many years in Canada. In 2001 alone, Royal Airlines and CanJet were swallowed up by Canada 3000, and Roots Air was bought out by Air Canada after only one month

of operation. Canada 3000 then went out of operation at the end of 2001. In mid-March 2005, Jetsgo also met its demise. "High fuel prices, brutal fare wars, and safety concerns all weighed on Jetsgo."[11] Competitors such as WestJet and Porter Airlines have since appeared and have gained market share.

Barriers to entry result from two main sources: economies of scale and brand loyalty (see Figure 2.2). **Economies of scale** are the cost advantages associated with large operations. Economies of scale result from factors such as being able to manufacture products in large quantities or buy inputs in bulk, or being more effective than competitors at making use of organizational resources by fully utilizing employees' skills and knowledge. If organizations already in the task environment are large and enjoy significant economies of scale, then their costs are lower than the costs of potential entrants will be, and newcomers will find it very expensive to enter the industry. U.S. giant Target is trying to compete with IKEA.

Brand loyalty is customers' preference for the products of organizations that currently exist in the task environment. If established organizations enjoy significant brand loyalty, then a new entrant will find it extremely difficult and costly to obtain a share of the market. Newcomers must bear the huge advertising costs for building customer awareness of the good or service they intend to provide.[12] IKEA has created a global brand cult among customers that has been documented in Business School case studies and endless customer comments. Examples: "IKEA makes me free to become what I want to be" (from Romania). Or this: "Half my house is from IKEA—and the nearest store is six hours away" (the United States). Or this: "Every time, it's trendy for less money" (Germany).[13]

barriers to entry
Factors that make it difficult and costly for an organization to enter a particular task environment or industry.

economies of scale
Cost advantages associated with large operations.

brand loyalty Customers' preference for the products of organizations that currently exist in the task environment.

In some cases, *government regulations* function as a barrier to entry by creating monopolies. For example, the government of Nova Scotia launched a community-based initiative to promote renewable wind energy in 2011, but restricted the type of wind turbine to only one of the two approved by Nova Scotia Power Inc. This prohibited free market competition by creating a monopoly.

Many industries that were deregulated, such as air transport, trucking, utilities, and telecommunications, experienced a high level of new entry after deregulation; this forced existing companies in those industries to operate more efficiently or risk being put out of business. At the national and global level, administrative barriers are government policies that create a barrier to entry and limit imports of goods by overseas companies. Japan is well known for the many ways in which it attempts to restrict the entry of overseas competitors or lessen their impact on Japanese firms. For example, why do Dutch companies export tulip bulbs to almost every country in the world except Japan? Japanese customs inspectors insist on checking every tulip bulb by cutting the stems vertically down the middle, and even Japanese ingenuity cannot put them back together.[14]

In summary, high barriers to entry create a task environment that is highly threatening and causes difficulty for managers trying to gain access to customers and other resources an organization needs. Conversely, low barriers to entry result in a task environment where competitive pressures are more moderate and managers have greater opportunities to acquire customers and other resources for their organizations to be effective.

The General Environment

Managers not only must concern themselves with finding suppliers and customers, but also must pay attention to the larger environment around them. Economic, technological, demographic, socio-cultural, and political and legal forces in an organization's general environment can have profound effects on the organization's task environment, effects that may be ignored by some managers. For example, technology in the telecommunications industry has made it possible for companies to offer their customers a variety of products. In the past, consumers simply chose the cheapest long-distance package or the best telephone system, but now they are looking at enhanced communication products—such as texting, cell phone apps, Internet access, and face-time—that are offered as part of the package. Telephone providers who failed to expand their range of offerings quickly have had difficulty keeping customers.

Managers have to constantly analyze the forces impacting the general environment in order to manage effectively. Their decisions and planning will have long-term effects.

Below we examine each of the major forces in the general environment in turn, exploring their impact on managers and on the organization's task environment and examining how managers can deal with them.

Economic Forces

Economic forces affect the general health and well-being of a nation or the regional economy of an organization. They include interest rates, inflation, unemployment, and economic growth. Economic forces produce many opportunities and threats for managers. Low levels of unemployment and falling interest rates mean a change in the customer base: more people have more money to spend, and as a result organizations have an opportunity to sell more goods and services. Good economic times affect supplies: Resources become easier to acquire, and organizations have an opportunity to flourish.

In contrast, worsening macroeconomic conditions pose a threat because they limit managers' ability to gain access to the resources their organization needs. Profit-oriented organizations such as retail stores and hotels have fewer customers for their goods and services during economic downturns. Not-for-profit organizations such as charities and colleges receive fewer donations during economic downturns. Even a moderate deterioration in national or regional economic conditions can seriously affect performance.

> **economic forces**
> Interest rates, inflation, unemployment, economic growth, and other factors that affect the general health and well-being of a nation or the regional economy of an organization.

The Occupy movement included protests in Vancouver.

Lululemon's innovative fabric helped the company gain a competitive advantage.

Poor economic conditions make the environment more complex and managers' jobs more difficult and demanding. Managers may need to reduce the number of individuals in their departments and increase the motivation of remaining employees, and managers and workers alike may need to identify ways to gain and use resources more efficiently. Recent debt crises in the euro zone, specifically with Greece, illustrate how important it is for managers to realize the effects that economic forces have on their organizations, and they pay close attention to changes in the national and regional economies in order to respond appropriately.

But when a global economic crisis occurs, as it did in October 2008, dire consequences result for managers, especially in the financial industry. That global financial crisis demonstrated that too much risk-taking and not enough oversight and governance of economic forces can severely derail economic growth. The credit crunch, precipitated by the largest housing bubble in U.S. history, saw many innovative financial products derived from mortgage-backed securities. When the value of the products collapsed as the bubble broke and houses were foreclosed on, several investment banks in the United States collapsed. The trading of these debt instruments led to the worst economic collapse and the largest intervention in the market by governments since the stock market crash of 1929 and the Great Depression.

> In two tumultuous weeks the Federal Reserve and the Treasury between them nationalized the country's two mortgage giants, Fannie Mae and Freddie Mac; took over AIG, the world's largest insurance company; in effect extended government deposit insurance to $3.4 trillion in money-market funds; temporarily banned short-selling in over 900 mostly financial stocks; and, most dramatic of all, pledged to take up to $700 billion of toxic mortgage-backed assets on to its books.[15]

While the unregulated financial instruments called into question banking systems around the world, Canada's banks, which had relatively little exposure to the new and complicated debt products, were ranked the world's most sound with a score of 6.8.[16] Canada inched ahead of the banks in five other countries—Sweden, Luxembourg, Australia, Denmark, and the Netherlands—all of which received a score of 6.7 percent. The United States was ranked 40th, with a score of 6.1 out of 7.[17]

Technological Forces

Technology is the combination of skills and equipment that managers use in the design, production, and distribution of goods and services. **Technological forces** are outcomes of changes in the technology that managers use to design, produce, or distribute goods and services. Technological forces have increased greatly since the Second World War because the overall pace of technological change has sped up so much.[18] Computers have become increasingly faster and smaller. Transportation speed has increased. Distribution centres are able to track goods in ways that were unthinkable even 10 years ago with technologies such as radio-frequency identification (RFID) systems.

Technological forces can have profound implications for managers and organizations. Technological change can make established products obsolete overnight—for example, typewriters, black-and-white televisions, and bound sets of encyclopaedias—forcing managers to find new products to make. Although technological change can threaten an organization, it also can create a host of new opportunities for designing, making, or distributing new and better kinds of goods and services. Brand powerhouse Lululemon gained a competitive advantage in the global economy based on the use of innovative high-tech fabrics. Managers must move quickly to respond to such changes if their organizations are to survive and prosper.

Changes in information technology also are changing the very nature of work itself within organizations, and the manager's job. Telecommuting, texting, and face-to-face video streaming are now everyday activities that provide opportunities for managers to supervise and coordinate employees working from home or other locations. Even students engage in telecommuting, communicating with classmates and instructors via email or Facebook, and completing assignments at home. This has changed the way instructors do their jobs.

technology The combination of skills and equipment that managers use in the design, production, and distribution of goods and services.

technological forces Outcomes of changes in the technology that managers use to design, produce, or distribute goods and services.

demographic forces
Outcomes of changes in, or changing attitudes toward, the characteristics of a population, such as age, gender, ethnic origin, race, sexual orientation, and social class.

Demographic Forces

Demographic forces are outcomes of changes in, or changing attitudes toward, the characteristics of a population, such as age, gender, ethnic origin, race, sexual orientation, and social class. In 2006, with regard to the aging population, the Auditor General of Canada stated: "The demographic die is cast: there is little we can do to reverse or even slow the aging of Canada's population over the coming decades. But it is certainly within our power to plan better for it. And better planning begins with better information concerning the long-term fiscal implications of the coming demographic shift."[19] Like the other forces in the general environment, demographic forces present managers with opportunities and threats and can have major implications for organizations. "A projection from the Urban Futures Institute sees Canada requiring nearly 20.6 million people in the labour force in 2017, a 14-percent increase from 2006. Overall, the female workforce will grow by 15 percent while the male contingent grows by 13 percent."[20] The dramatic increase in the number of working women has focused public concern on issues such as equal pay for equal work and sexual harassment at work. One issue in particular that managers will have to address more and more is the lack of women in top positions. This concern is important because managers are responsible for attracting and making full use of the talents of female employees. In 2010, 36.8 percent of women in the labour force occupied management positions. In that same year, only about 32 percent of the senior (corporate) management occupations were held by women in Canada.[21] Research shows that performance levels are higher in companies where women are well represented in senior positions and where women serve on boards of directors.[22] Needless to say, managers must factor these kinds of circumstances into their decision making.

Changes in the age distribution of a population are another example of a demographic force that affects managers and organizations. Currently, most industrialized nations are experiencing the aging of their populations as a consequence of falling birth and death rates and the aging of the baby

The aging population leads to both opportunities and threats.

> **"The demographic die is cast: there is little we can do to reverse or even slow the aging of Canada's population over the coming decades. But it is certainly within our power to plan better for it."**
>
> *Auditor General of Canada*

boom generation, whereas many emerging nations are experiencing a bulge in their youth populations. In Germany, for example, the percentage of the population over age 65 was 20.4 percent in 2010; it was 14.1 percent in Canada, 22 percent in Japan, and 12.9 percent in the United States.[23] The largest proportional youth populations projected by the CIA are in Pakistan, Afghanistan, Saudi Arabia, Yemen, and Iraq.[24] The aging of the population in developed nations is increasing opportunities for organizations that cater to older people. The recreation and home health care industries, for example, are seeing an upswing in demand for their services.

The aging of the population also has several implications for the workplace. Most significant are a relative decline in the number of young people joining the workforce and an increase in active employees willing to postpone retirement past the retirement age of 67. These changes suggest that organizations will need to find ways to motivate older employees and use their skills and knowledge, an issue that many industrialized societies have yet to tackle.

Socio-cultural Forces

Socio-cultural forces are pressures emanating from the social structure of a country or society or from the national culture. Pressures from both sources can either constrain or facilitate the way organizations operate and managers behave. **Social structure** is the arrangement of relationships between individuals and groups in a society. Societies differ substantially in social structure. In societies that have a high degree of social stratification, there are many distinctions among individuals and groups. Caste systems in India and Tibet and the recognition of numerous social classes in Great Britain and France produce a multilayered social structure in each of those countries. In contrast, social stratification is lower in relatively egalitarian New Zealand and in Canada, where the social structure reveals few distinctions among people. Most top managers in France come from the upper classes of French society, but top managers in Canada come from all strata of society.

Societies also differ in the extent to which they emphasize the individual over the group. For example, the United States emphasizes the primacy of the individual, and Japan emphasizes the primacy of the group. This difference may dictate the methods managers need to use to motivate and lead employees. **National culture** is the set of values that a society considers important and the norms of behaviour that are approved or sanctioned in that society. Societies differ substantially in the values and norms that they emphasize. For example, in the United States individualism is highly valued, and in Korea and Japan individuals are expected to conform to group expectations.[25] National culture, discussed at length later in this chapter, also affects the way managers motivate and coordinate employees and the way organizations do business. Ethics, an important aspect of national culture, is discussed in detail in Chapter 3.

Social structure and national culture not only differ across societies but also change within societies over time. In Canada, attitudes toward the roles of women, love, sex, sexual orientation, and

Cultural variations affect the way managers conduct business.

marriage changed in every past decade. Many people in Asian countries such as Hong Kong, Singapore, Korea, and Japan think that the younger generation is far more individualistic and "American-like" than previous generations. Currently, throughout much of Eastern Europe, new values that emphasize individualism and entrepreneurship are replacing communist values based on collectivism and obedience to the state. The pace of change is accelerating.

Individual managers and organizations must be responsive to changes in, and differences among, the social structures and national cultures of all the countries in which they operate. In today's increasingly integrated global economy, managers are likely to interact with people from several countries, and many managers live and work abroad. Effective managers are sensitive to differences between societies and adjust their behaviours accordingly.

Managers and organizations also must respond to social changes within a society. In the last few decades, for example, Canadians have become increasingly interested in their personal health and fitness. Managers who recognized this trend early and exploited the opportunities that resulted from it were able to reap significant gains for their organizations. PepsiCo used the opportunity presented by the fitness trend and took market share from archrival Coca-Cola by being the first to introduce diet colas and fruit-based soft drinks. Quaker Oats made Gatorade the most popular sports drink and brought out a whole host of low-fat food products. The health trend, however, did not offer opportunities to all companies; to some it posed a threat. Tobacco companies came under intense pressure due to consumers' greater awareness of negative health impacts from smoking. Laura Secord and other manufacturers of candy have been threatened by customers' desires for low-fat, healthy foods. The rage for "low-carb" foods in the 2000s led to a huge increase in demand for meat and hurt bread and pasta companies.

socio-cultural forces Pressures emanating from the social structure of a country or society or from the national culture.

social structure The arrangement of relationships between individuals and groups in a society.

national culture The set of values that a society considers important and the norms of behaviour that are approved or sanctioned in that society.

Political and Legal Forces

Political and legal forces are outcomes of changes in laws and regulations. They result from political and legal developments that take place within a nation, within a world region, or across the world and significantly affect managers and organizations everywhere. Political processes shape a nation's laws and the international laws that govern the relationships among nations. Laws constrain the operations of organizations and managers and thus create both opportunities and threats.[26] For example, in much of the industrialized world, there has been a strong trend toward deregulation of industries previously controlled by the state and privatization of organizations once owned by the state.

Deregulation and privatization are just two examples of political and legal forces that can create challenges for organizations and managers. Others include increased emphasis on safety in the workplace and on environmental protection and the preservation of endangered species. Successful managers carefully monitor changes in laws and regulations in order to take advantage of the opportunities they create and counter the threats they pose in an organization's task environment.

The Competition Act of 1986 provides more legislation that affects how companies may operate. Under this Act, the Bureau of Competition Policy acts to maintain and encourage competition in Canada. For example, when companies merge, they face intense scrutiny from the bureau to make sure there is no unfair competitive advantage to customers, employees, and other stakeholders. Even though Ellis Jacob, CEO of Cineplex Galaxy LP, had the "deal of a lifetime" with a $500-million purchase of rival movie theatre exhibition chain Famous Players from Viacom Inc., he had to sell theatres to meet the demands of regulators: "The federal Competition Bureau sought to maintain competition in pricing and choice by making it a condition of the deal that Cineplex sell 35 theatres in 17 cities across Canada, which would have brought in about 11 percent of the companies' combined revenue of $874 million."[27]

Global Forces

Global forces are outcomes of changes in international relationships, changes in nations' economic, political, and legal systems, and changes in technology. Perhaps the most important global force affecting managers and organizations is the increasing economic integration of countries around the world.[28] Developments such as the North American Free Trade Agreement (NAFTA), the free-trade agreements enforced by the World Trade Organization (WTO), and the growth of the European Union (EU) have led to a lowering of barriers to the free flow of goods and services between nations.[29]

Falling trade barriers have created enormous opportunities for organizations in one country to sell goods and services in other countries. But by allowing foreign companies to compete for an organization's domestic customers, falling trade barriers also pose a serious threat because they increase competition in the task environment. After NAFTA was signed, one of the major challenges facing Canadian managers was how to compete successfully against American companies moving into this country. Zellers and The Bay, for instance, faced strong challenges from Target and Walmart as well as smaller boutique operations. Target acquired Zellers as part of its international expansion strategy into Canada. Rona must now compete with American giants Home Depot and Lowes.

In essence, as a result of falling trade barriers, managers view the global environment as open—that is, as an environment in which companies are free to buy goods and services from, and sell goods and services to, whichever companies and countries they choose. They also are free to compete against each other to attract customers around the world. They must establish an international network of operations and subsidiaries to build global competitive advantage. Coca-Cola and PepsiCo, for example, have competed aggressively for 20 years to develop the strongest global soft-drink empire, just as Toyota and Honda have built hundreds of car plants around the

political and legal forces Outcomes of changes in laws and regulations, such as the deregulation of industries, the privatization of organizations, and increased emphasis on environmental protection.

global forces Outcomes of changes in international relationships; changes in nations' economic, political, and legal systems; and changes in technology, such as falling trade barriers, the growth of representative democracies, and reliable and instantaneous communication.

People, money, resources, and power flow between nations in the global economy.

world to provide the vehicles that global customers like. Some products are subject to "regional content" rules that specify a percentage of component parts must be made or assembled in the trade agreement member nations in order for the product to qualify for no tariffs to be levied. This is the case under NAFTA. IKEA must comply with the regional content rules on furniture production in order to trade its goods tariff-free within the member nations of the United States, Mexico, and Canada.[30]

But what drives or spurs globalization? What makes people and companies like Bombardier, Nestlé, Toyota, or Microsoft want to venture into an uncertain global environment that puts into motion the complex set of forces that result in globalization? The answer is that the path of globalization is shaped by the ebb and flow of *capital* (valuable wealth-generating assets) as it moves through companies, countries, and world regions seeking its most highly valued use—that is, the investment through which capital can earn the greatest returns (wealth). Managers, employees, and companies like IKEA and Bombardier are motivated to try to profit or benefit by using their skills to make products customers around the world want to buy. Four principal forms of capital flow between countries:

- *Human capital:* the flow of people around the world through immigration, migration, and emigration.
- *Financial capital:* the flow of money capital across world markets through overseas investment, credit, lending, and aid.
- *Resource capital:* the flow of natural resources and semi-finished products between companies and countries such as metals, minerals, lumber, energy, food products, microprocessors, and auto parts.
- *Political capital:* the flow of power and influence around the world using diplomacy, persuasion, aggression, and force of arms to protect a country's or world region or political bloc's access to the other forms of capital.

Most of the changes associated with globalization are the result of these four capital flows and the interactions among them, as nations compete on the world stage to protect and increase their standards of living and to further the political goals and social causes that are espoused by their societies' cultures. In a positive sense the faster the flow, the more capital is being utilized where it can create the most value, in the sense of people moving to where their skills earn them more money, or investors switching to the stocks or bonds that give them higher dividends or interest, or companies finding lower-cost sources of inputs. In a negative sense, however, a fast flow of capital also means that individual countries or world regions can find themselves in trouble when companies and investors

move their capital to invest it in more productive ways in other countries or world regions, often those with lower labour costs or rapidly expanding markets. When capital leaves a country, the result is higher unemployment, recession, and a lower standard of living for its people.

While declining barriers to trade have increased the pace of globalization, nations still differ widely from each other because they have distinct cultural values and norms that managers must appreciate if they are to compete successfully across countries.

Discuss how national cultures differ and why it is important that managers be sensitive to the political and social systems of nations around the world. **LO3**

The Impact of National Culture

The result of globalization is that nations and peoples become increasingly *interdependent* because the same forces affect them in similar ways. The fates of peoples in different countries become interlinked as the world's markets and businesses become increasingly interconnected. And, as nations become more interdependent, they become more similar to one another in the sense that people develop a similar liking for products as diverse as cell phones, iPods, blue jeans, Coke, Manchester United, curry, green tea, maple syrup, Japanese cars, and Colombian coffee. One outcome of globalization is that the world is becoming a "global village": products, services, or people can become well known throughout the world—something IKEA, with its range of furniture designed to appeal to customers around the world, is taking advantage of, as we described at the beginning of the chapter.

National culture includes the values, norms, knowledge, beliefs, moral principles, laws, customs, and other practices that unite the citizens of a country.[31] National culture shapes individual behaviour by specifying appropriate and inappropriate behaviour and interaction with others. People learn national culture in their everyday lives by interacting with those around them. This learning starts at an early age and continues throughout their lives.

The basic building blocks of national culture are values and norms. **Values** are ideas about what a society believes to be good, right, desirable, or beautiful. They provide the basic underpinnings for notions of individual freedom, democracy, truth, justice, honesty, loyalty, social obligation, collective responsibility, the appropriate roles for men and women, love, sex, marriage, and so on. Values are more than merely abstract concepts; they are invested with considerable emotional

values Ideas about what a society believes to be good, right, desirable, or beautiful.

significance. People argue, fight, and even die over values such as freedom.

Although deeply embedded in society, values are not static; however, change in a country's values is likely to be slow and painful. For example, the value systems of many formerly communist states, such as Russia, are undergoing significant changes as those countries move away from a value system that emphasizes the state and toward one that emphasizes individual freedom. Social turmoil often results when countries undergo major changes in their values.

Differences among national cultures have important implications for managers. Management practices that are effective in Canada might not work in Japan, Hungary, or Mexico. For example, pay-for-performance systems used in Canada, which emphasize the performance of individuals alone, are less suitable in Japan, where individual performance is valued only when in pursuit of group goals.

To be an effective global manager, according to research done by McGill University professors Karl Moore and Henry Mintzberg, the most important characteristics are to be able to understand, empathize, and work with multiple cultures.[32] As we shall see in our discussion of diversity in Chapter 3, businesses increasingly face customers and clients who are culturally different. Doing business internationally necessitates an understanding of these differences. "For example, business in Latin America is based very much on relationships of personal trust: One gets to know a Mexican or Argentinean boss before one presents him with a formal contract. In France, one deals directly with the powerful patron at the top. In Germany, on the other hand, written rules and procedures are all-important: A foreign manager seeking to speak to a German CEO will immediately be directed to the appropriate department head. In contrast to Germany's strict written rules, the Japanese operate on strict *unwritten* rules, known as *kata*. Job security is considered in America to produce a mediocre employee, but in Japan, the *lack* of job security will do the same. The French admire intellectual prowess and the Americans short-term success; Australians are often wary of both."[33]

The research of Geert Hofstede provides us with a framework for understanding how national cultures differ (see Figure 2.3). As a psychologist for IBM, Hofstede collected data on employee values and norms from more than 100 000 IBM employees in 64 countries. Based on his research, Hofstede developed five dimensions along which national cultures can be placed. The first dimension, which Hofstede labelled "individualism versus collectivism," has a long history in human thought. **Individualism** is a worldview that values individual freedom and self-expression and adherence to the principle that people should be judged by their individual achievements rather than by their social background. In Western countries, individualism usually includes admiration for personal success, a strong belief in individual rights, and high regard for individual entrepreneurs.[34]

In contrast, **collectivism** is a worldview that values subordination of the individual to the goals of the group and adherence to the principle that people should be judged by their contribution

individualism A worldview that values individual freedom and self-expression and adherence to the principle that people should be judged by their individual achievements rather than by their social background.

collectivism A worldview that values subordination of the individual to the goals of the group and adherence to the principle that people should be judged by their contribution to the group.

> **FIGURE 2.3**   **Hofstede's Cultural Dimensions**[35]

Cultural Dimension	Meaning	Examples of Nations
Power distance (PD)	The degree to which the least powerful people accept the unequal distribution of power. A high PD score indicates a tolerance and acceptance of inequality.	High PD: Argentina Low PD: USA
Individualism (IDV) versus collectivism	Individualistic countries have a lower reliance on the community or society and a stronger reliance on immediate family in providing well-being. Countries that have a low IDV score show strong group cohesion and loyalty and respect among members of the group.	High IDV: USA Low IDV: Japan
Masculinity (MAS) versus femininity	The degree to which the nation values "assertiveness" (which Hofstede called masculinity) over "caring" (which he called femininity).	High MAS: Austria Low MAS: Denmark
Uncertainty avoidance index (UAI)	The degree to which the nation is anxious and uncomfortable with uncertain and unknown situations. A low UAI score indicates a greater acceptance of uncertainty.	High UAI: Greece Low UAI: UK
Long-term orientation (LTO) versus short-term focus	The degree to which the nation values traditions and customs. A high LTO score indicates a strong adherence to social norms and obligations.	High LTO: Japan Low LTO: USA

to the group. Collectivism was widespread in communist countries but has become less prevalent since the collapse of communism in most of those countries. Japan is a non-communist country where collectivism is highly valued.

Collectivism in Japan traces its roots to the fusion of Confucian, Buddhist, and Shinto thought that occurred during the Tokugawa period in Japanese history (1600–1870s).[36] One of the central values that emerged during this period was strong attachment to the group—whether a village, a work group, or a company. Strong identification with the group is said to create pressures for collective action in Japan, as well as strong pressure for conformity to group norms and a relative lack of individualism.[37]

Managers must realize that organizations and organizational members reflect their national culture's emphasis on individualism or collectivism. Indeed, one of the major reasons why Japanese and American management practices differ is that Japanese culture values collectivism and U.S. culture values individualism.

Nations such as Japan, which ranks very high in the world's multinational corporations according to *Fortune 500,* has very low levels of diversity, and consequently, "only natives can scale the heights within Japanese companies, which dramatically reduces the interest of ambitious young foreigners, cutting off Japanese multinationals from a critical source of new ideas and making it difficult for them to truly understand foreign markets and develop a cadre of global managers."[38] (See the Management Case at the end of this chapter.) On the other hand, nations that are not the largest players in the global economy but have a great deal of diversity produce great global managers. According to Moore and Mintzberg, these countries include Canada, Switzerland, Belgium, Singapore, Norway, Sweden, the Netherlands, Denmark, Australia, and Finland.[39]

By **power distance** Hofstede meant the degree to which societies accept the idea that inequalities in the power and well-being of their citizens are due to differences in individuals' physical and intellectual capabilities and heritage. This concept also encompasses the degree to which societies accept the economic and social differences in wealth, status, and well-being that result from differences in individual capabilities.

Societies in which inequalities are allowed to persist or grow over time have *high power distance.* In high-power-distance

societies, workers who are professionally successful amass wealth and pass it on to their children, and, as a result, inequalities may grow over time. In such societies, the gap between rich and poor, with all the attendant political and social consequences, grows very large. In contrast, in societies with *low power distance,* large inequalities between citizens are not allowed to develop. In low-power-distance countries, the government uses taxation and social welfare programs to reduce inequality and improve the welfare of the least fortunate. These societies are more attuned to preventing a large gap between rich and poor and minimizing discord between different classes of citizens.

Western countries such as the United States, Germany, the Netherlands, and the United Kingdom have relatively low power distance and high individualism. Economically poor Latin American countries such as Guatemala and Panama, and Asian countries such as Malaysia and the Philippines, have high power distance and low individualism.[40] These findings suggest that the cultural values of richer countries emphasize protecting the rights of individuals and, at the same time, provide a fair chance of success to every member of society. In Canada, efforts are made to uphold the values of equality of opportunity by a variety of community organizations. As our Focus on the Social Economy case illustrates, EthniCity Catering in Calgary helps improve the welfare of newcomers by celebrating their cultural differences.

Societies that have an **achievement orientation** value assertiveness, performance, success, competition, and results. Societies that have a **nurturing orientation** value the quality of life, warm personal relationships, and services and care for the weak. Japan and the United States tend to be achievement-oriented; the Netherlands, Sweden, and Denmark are more nurturing-oriented.

Societies as well as individuals differ in their tolerance for uncertainty and risk. Societies low on **uncertainty avoidance** (such as the United States and Hong Kong) are easygoing, value diversity, and tolerate differences in personal beliefs and actions. Societies high on uncertainty avoidance (such as Japan and France) are more rigid and skeptical about people whose behaviours or beliefs differ from the norm. In these societies, conformity to the values of the social and work groups to which a person belongs is the norm, and structured situations are preferred because they provide a sense of security.

The last dimension that Hofstede described is orientation toward life and work.[41] A national culture with a **long-term orientation** rests on values such as thrift (saving) and persistence in achieving goals. A national culture with a **short-term orientation** is concerned with maintaining personal stability or happiness and living for the present. Societies with a long-term orientation include Taiwan and

power distance The degree to which societies accept the idea of inequalities in the power and well-being of their citizens are due to differences in individuals' physical and intellectual capabilities and heritage.

achievement orientation A worldview that values assertiveness, performance, success, and competition.

nurturing orientation A worldview that values the quality of life, warm personal friendships, and services and care for the weak.

uncertainty avoidance The degree to which societies are willing to tolerate uncertainty and risk.

long-term orientation A worldview that values thrift and persistence in achieving goals.

short-term orientation A worldview that values personal stability or happiness and living for the present.

FOCUS ON ▶ *The Social Economy*

EthniCity Catering

EthniCity Catering offers workplace training and employment to immigrant women in transition, and serves a menu of authentic, multi-ethnic dishes to Calgary customers. EthniCity is a training business and social enterprise of the Centre for Newcomers Society of Calgary, one of the largest immigrant-serving agencies in Alberta. Customers of EthniCity's catering receive delicious meals and snacks, prepared from recipes which EthniCity's program participants have contributed. Participants come from the Mediterranean, East Asia, South Asia, and other regions. Participants in the EthniCity training program acquire work experience, develop their workplace-essential skills, including communication and self-confidence, and practise communicating in English on the job. They make connections beyond their own language community, break the "first-job" barrier, and move on to further employment or training on the basis of a wider network of community connections.[42]

1. Visit the website of EthniCity Catering and describe how the organization tries to provide a fair chance of success to every member of society.
2. Which of Hofstede's dimensions does this organization illustrate and why?

Hong Kong, well known for their high rate of per capita savings. The United States and France have a short-term orientation, and their citizens tend to spend more and save less.

A culturally diverse management team can be a source of strength in the global marketplace. Organizations that employ managers from a variety of cultures better appreciate how national cultures differ than do organizations with culturally similar management teams, and they tailor their management systems and behaviours to the differences. Arcelor Mittal (India) and Lenovo (China) are good examples of top global companies with international management teams and are poised to become role models for all global companies.[43]

LO4 Explain the ways managers can minimize threats and uncertainty from forces in the external environment.

Managing the External Environment

As previously discussed, an important task for managers is to understand how forces in the task and general environments create opportunities for, and threats to, their organizations. To analyze the importance of opportunities and threats in the external environment, managers must measure (1) the level of complexity in the environment and (2) the rate at which the environment is changing. With this information, they can plan better and choose the best goals and courses of action.

The complexity of the external environment depends on the number and potential impact of the forces that managers must respond to in the task and general environments. A force that seems likely to have a significant negative impact is a potential threat to which managers must devote a high level of organizational resources. A force likely to have a marginal impact poses little threat to an organization and requires only a minor commitment of managerial time and attention. A force likely to make a significant positive impact warrants a considerable commitment of managerial time and effort to take advantage of the opportunity. When Starbucks went to Vienna, the company had to think carefully about its no-smoking policy, since it would be the only coffee shop in the city to ban smoking.

In general, the larger an organization is, the greater is the number of environmental forces that managers must respond to. Consider Tim Hortons. Each year it must consider, to take just one example, the environmental issue of its coffee cups when it announces its "Roll Up the Rim" contest. For some people, as in Edmonton, it is a chance to win an SUV; for environmentalists, however, these cups represent a serious biodegradable hazard; they also litter the environment.[44] "I don't think it's socially responsible to have a promotion which creates massive waste," said Ronald Colman, executive director of GPI Atlantic, a non-profit group that researches environmental and quality-of-life issues.[45] A study in Nova Scotia showed Tim Hortons and McDonald's alone account for one-third of all litter in that province. Thus, managers have to ensure that the organization's practices do not clash with socio-cultural trends, such as environmental sustainability, while responding to customers' preferences and marketing strategies. The movement toward more sustainable decision-making practices is discussed in Chapter 4.

environmental change
The degree to which forces in the task and general environments change and evolve over time.

Environmental change is the degree to which forces in the task and general environments change and evolve over time. Change is problematic for an organization and its managers because the consequences of change can be difficult to predict.[46] Managers can try to forecast or simply guess about future conditions in the task environment, such as where and how strong the new competition may be. But, confronted with a complex and changing task environment, managers cannot be sure that decisions and actions taken today will be suitable in the future. This uncertainty makes their jobs especially challenging. It also makes it vitally important for managers to understand the forces that shape the external environment.

An understanding of the external environment is necessary so that managers can anticipate how the task environment might look in the future and decide on the actions to pursue if the organization is to prosper. McDonald's is a good example of how adaptive an organization must be to remain successful. With the aging population, and the emphasis on low-fat foods, McDonald's began changing its menu by including salads and wraps that had fewer fats and carbohydrates. It is also aware of people with food allergies and other food sensitivities and has made adjustments accordingly.[47] Sony Corporation is a good example of how an organization failed to adapt to changes in the organizational environment. Companies in Korea, Taiwan, and China began to innovate new technologies like digital LCD screens and flash memory that made Sony's technologies obsolete. Companies such as Apple and Nokia came out with the iPod, smartphones, and tablet computers that better fit customer needs than Sony's "old-generation" products such as the Walkman.

Reducing the Impact of Environmental Forces

Finding ways to reduce the number and potential impact of forces in the external environment is the job of all managers in an organization.

- The principal task of the CEO and the top-management team is to devise strategies that will allow an organization to take advantage of opportunities and counter threats in its general and task environments (see Chapter 5 for a discussion of this vital topic).

- Middle managers in an organization's departments collect relevant information about the task environment, such as (1) the future intentions of the organization's competitors, (2) the identity of new customers for the organization's products, and (3) the identity of new suppliers of crucial or low-cost inputs.

- First-line managers find ways to use resources more efficiently to hold costs down or to get close to customers and learn what they want.

Managers at all three levels and in all functional areas are responsible for reducing the negative impact of environmental forces as they evolve over time (see Figures 2.4 and 2.5).

> **FIGURE 2.4** **Responsibilities for Managing the Forces in the Organization's Environment**

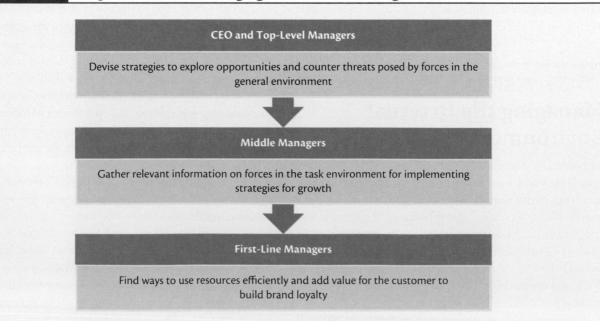

> **FIGURE 2.5**   Managing Forces in the Organizational Environment

Functional Area Managers	Role in Managing the Forces in the Organizational Environment
Sales and Service	Ensure customer satisfaction and brand loyalty
Research and Development	Deal with technological forces
Marketing and Strategy	Deal with pressures from competitors
Accounting and Finance	**Handle economic forces**
Legal and Public Relations	Deal with political and legal forces
Operations and Materials Management	Deal with pressures from suppliers

Managers as Agents of Change

It is important to note that although much of the change that takes place in the external environment is independent of a particular organization—for example, basic advances in biotechnology or plastics—a significant amount of environmental change is the direct consequence of actions taken by managers within organizations.[48] An organization is an open system: It takes in inputs from the environment and converts them into goods and services that are sent back to the environment. Thus, change in the environment is a two-way process. Often, however, the choices that managers make about which products to produce and even about how to compete with other organizations affect the system as a whole. Our ability to predict and control the course of events is determined by the rate of change in the environment and the complexity of the environment (see Figure 2.6).

Many decisions managers make in response to the forces in the environment are made under conditions of **uncertainty** and risk. As we will see in Chapter 4, it is very difficult to know all the possible outcomes of adopting a particular alternative or strategy. The more complex and dynamic the environment, the greater are the uncertainty and risk. Strategies and organizational structures must be somewhat flexible to be able to accommodate change. However, when managers act under conditions of **certainty,** there is less risk and

uncertainty The state of environmental forces that is so dynamic that managers cannot predict the probable outcomes of a course of action.

certainty The state of environmental forces that is stable enough to predict possible outcomes of decisions.

| **FIGURE 2.6** | **Uncertainty in the Environment and Managerial Action** |

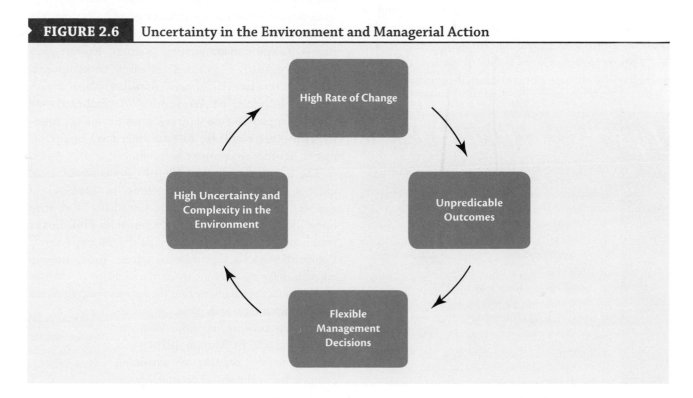

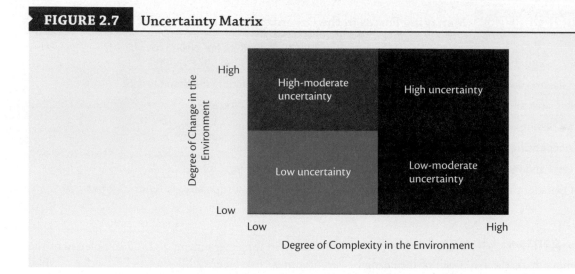

> **FIGURE 2.7** **Uncertainty Matrix**

more complete knowledge of the possible outcomes of their decisions (see Figure 2.7). Managers must minimize threats from changes in the task and general environmental forces while capitalizing on the opportunities they present. They do this by adopting flexible organizational structures and culture. Managers of a global company like IKEA, who have a global supply chain network of over 2000 companies in over 50 nations, necessarily operate under conditions of uncertainty and risk. Managing these risks is made easier with a decentralized organizational structure based on geographical region, which empowered divisional managers so that products could be customized to meet the demand of different cultures and populations. The cultural norm in Japan of companies providing "life-long" employment was a threat to Sony Corp's ability to manage the forces in the rapidly changing organizational environment.

Tips FOR MANAGERS

Managing the External Environment

Reduce uncertainty and risk associated with a high degree of change in the demographic characteristics of the population by:

1. Recognizing the ethical and legal requirement to treat human resources in a fair and equitable manner.

2. Establishing human resources policies that do not discriminate against any organizational member.

3. Taking advantage of the talents of a diverse workforce made up of several national cultures.

4. Creating a flexible organizational structure and culture.

Evaluate the major challenges managers face in gaining a competitive advantage in the global economy.

LO5

Challenges for Management in a Global Environment

Canadian firms are less likely to operate only within their own borders these days. The rise of **global organizations**—organizations that operate and compete in more than one country—has put severe pressure on many organizations to improve their performance and to identify better ways to use their resources. The successes of Indian metals industry giant Arcelor Mittal, German chemical companies Schering and Hoechst, Italian furniture manufacturer Natuzzi, Korean electronics company Samsung, Swedish contemporary furniture retailer IKEA, and Brazilian plane maker Empresa Brasileira de Aeronautica SA (Embraer)—all global companies—are putting pressure on organizations in other countries to raise their level of performance in order to compete successfully.

The list of the top 100 Global Companies of 1998 did not include any Canadian firms. In 2011, 11 of the 500 Global Companies were Canadian. More than three times as many Canadian companies rank in the world top five in their industry as did 20 years ago.[49] Bombardier is a Canadian global success. Today, managers who make no attempt to learn and adapt to changes in the global environment find themselves reacting rather than innovating, and their organizations often become uncompetitive and fail.[50] Research In Motion (RIM) succumbed to the pressure of remaining competitive in the global economy when

global organizations
Organizations that operate and compete in more than one country.

its market share for BlackBerry hand-held devices dropped off in 2012.

Three major challenges stand out for Canadian managers in today's global economy: building a competitive advantage, maintaining ethical standards, and utilizing new kinds of information systems and technologies.

Building a Competitive Advantage

If managers and organizations are to reach and remain at the top of the competitive environment, they must build a **competitive advantage,** which is the ability of one organization to outperform other organizations because it produces desired goods or services more efficiently and effectively than its competitors. The four building blocks of competitive advantage are superior *efficiency, quality, innovation,* and *responsiveness to customers* (see Figure 2.8).

Increasing Efficiency

Organizations increase their efficiency when they reduce the quantity of resources (such as people and raw materials) they use to produce goods or services. In today's competitive environment, organizations are constantly seeking new ways to use their resources to improve efficiency. Many organizations are training their workers in new skills and techniques to increase their ability to perform many new and different tasks. Designers at IKEA work closely with in-house production teams to find the least costly materials and suppliers. They aim to cut the cost of all their products by 2 percent to 3 percent per year. No product goes on

competitive advantage
The ability of one organization to outperform other organizations because it produces desired goods or services more efficiently and effectively than competitors do.

the floor of IKEA without being affordable. Most large items are flat packed in boxes allowing customers to take the merchandise home with them, saving IKEA millions of dollars in shipping costs.

New technological solutions to project management are another way companies can increase efficiency. EllisDon, one of Canada's largest construction companies, developed a software platform technology to help it deal with the "mountains of documents—forms, correspondence, quotes, contracts, schedules, purchase orders, architectural drawings, drawing revisions, photographs, meeting minutes, payroll time sheets, permits, safety inspection reports, and anything else one could think of with respect to building structures in a way that involved clients, consultants, and innumerable subtrades."[51] The result was that the company grew by 50 percent without having to increase staff.

In addition to training staff and introducing new technologies, companies can sometimes work together to increase efficiency. Creating alliances and partnerships, where two companies with their own relative strengths cooperate to produce results that neither could have achieved alone, can result in positive synergies and cost savings. (These kinds of network structures and B2B relationships are discussed in more detail in Chapter 6.)

Spin Master, a Canadian toy company, has achieved efficiencies through creating alliances in all aspects of its operations, from designing new products to manufacturing and retailing. The flexibility of outsourcing everything has allowed Spin Master to concentrate on what it does best—bringing products to market faster than any of the big companies, such as Hasbro and Mattel, could ever do. Take, for example, the deal to manufacture and market Catch-a-Bubble. "Six months after the first meeting in Hong Kong, Spin Master shipped 7 million units and invoiced $15 million."[52] Gaining a competitive advantage in the global economy demands that organizations achieve efficiencies in order to provide affordable merchandise to their customers.

Increasing Quality

The challenge from global organizations such as Korean electronics manufacturers, Mexican agricultural producers, and European marketing and financial firms has also increased pressure on companies to improve the quality of goods and services delivered. One major thrust to improve quality has been to introduce quality-enhancing techniques known as *total quality management* (TQM). Employees involved in TQM are often organized into

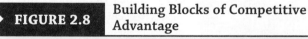

FIGURE 2.8 Building Blocks of Competitive Advantage

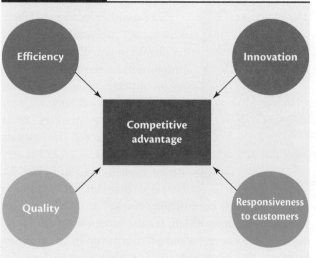

Efficiency is a key component of IKEA's competitive strength.

quality control teams and are given the responsibility of continually finding new and better ways to perform their jobs; including reducing the environmental footprint by utilizing recycled materials and by-products of production processes. They also are given the responsibility for monitoring and evaluating the quality of the goods they produce. Rigorous testing of products for durability as well as function and design is one of IKEA's trademarks.

Increasing Innovation

Innovation—the process of creating new goods and services that customers want, or developing better ways to produce or provide goods and services—poses a special challenge. Managers must create an organizational culture in which people are encouraged to be innovative. Typically, innovation takes place in small groups or teams; management passes on control of work activities to team members and creates an organizational culture that rewards risk-taking. Understanding and managing innovation and creating a work setting that encourages risk-taking are among the most difficult managerial tasks. Dr. Michael Rachlis, an associate professor at the University of Toronto's department of health care, points out how the Sault Ste. Marie Group Health Centre in Ontario assigned a home-care nurse to visit every heart-failure patient. This innovative practice reduced re-admissions by 70 percent.[53] IKEA's "design culture," along with its drive to be socially responsible and competitive, creates the kind of work setting that fosters innovation. As the president of IKEA Sweden said, "Designing beautiful-but-expensive products is

easy, designing beautiful products that are inexpensive and functional is a huge challenge."[54]

Research In Motion (RIM) was particularly good at innovation. Founded in 1984 and headquartered in Waterloo, Ontario, RIM is a leading designer, manufacturer, and marketer of innovative wireless solutions for the worldwide mobile communications market. It first developed in 1999 the BlackBerry device that had the new capability of sending wireless email. One of the strengths of the BlackBerry brand was its secure messaging system, used most notably in organizing the popular protests that toppled many political despots in Arab nations in 2011. Barak Obama and the U.S. government used the BlackBerry exclusively because of its top-notch security. In 2012, however, RIM lost market share to Apple's iPhone and Google's Android when both received U.S. government approval for use. For 13 years, RIM enjoyed a near monopoly in the mobile communications market based on its innovative technology.

Increasing Responsiveness to Customers

Organizations use their products and services to compete for customers, so training employees to be responsive to customers' needs is vital for all organizations, and particularly for service organizations. Retail stores, banks, and restaurants, for example, depend entirely on their employees to give high-quality service at a reasonable cost.[55] As Canada and other countries move toward a more service-based economy (in part because of the loss of manufacturing jobs to China, Malaysia, and other countries with low labour costs), managing behaviour in service organizations is becoming increasingly important. For example, IKEA offers quality supervised child care for customers while they shop.

Take another example: Harry Rosen, a high-end menswear retailer. In today's global economy, innovations in the fashion industry are quickly replicated at lower costs by knock-off manufacturers in emerging markets. It is not enough to sell uniqueness at premium prices. CEO Larry Rosen explains, "Quality for the customer becomes less a question of what you sell than of how you sell it. When you get to a price point at Rosen, it's the experience you're buying. We don't perceive ourselves as being in the clothing business. We don't just sell suits and sport jackets. It's

> **"Designing beautiful-but-expensive products is easy, designing beautiful products that are inexpensive and functional is a huge challenge."**
>
> *Jeanette Söderberg, President, IKEA Sweden*

innovation The process of creating new goods and services or developing better ways to produce or provide goods and services.

a relationship-based business. My business is to get to know you, to have you build a relationship with one of my highly trained associates. I want to be your clothier for life. The whole key to our business is loyal clients. I strongly believe we have a corporate culture that has a love of quality and a love of clients. And building customer relationships is a managed process."[56]

Maintaining Ethical Standards

While mobilizing organizational resources, all managers are under considerable pressure to increase the level at which their organizations perform. For example, top managers receive pressure from shareholders to increase the performance of the entire organization in order to boost stock prices, improve profits, or raise dividends. In turn, top managers may then pressure middle managers to find new ways to use organizational resources to increase efficiency or quality in order to attract new customers, earn more revenues, and reduce the ecological footprint of their activities.

Pressure to improve performance can be healthy for an organization because it causes managers to question the organization's operations and encourages them to find new and better ways to plan, organize, lead, and control. However, too much pressure to perform can be harmful.[57] It may induce managers to behave unethically in dealings with individuals and groups both inside and outside the organization.[58] For example, a purchasing manager for a large retail chain might buy inferior clothing as a cost-cutting measure. Or to secure a large foreign contract, a sales manager in a large company might offer bribes to foreign officials. Or overzealous stockbrokers might trade in credit default swaps and other securities derivatives to make a fast buck without due consideration of the risk of total financial collapse, as almost happened in the crisis of 2008. Codes of ethical conduct are a useful tool for managers to train and control the behaviour of employees and partners. IKEA has a supplier code of conduct which requires suppliers to meet minimum standards with respect to the environment and social and working conditions for employees, including prohibiting the use of child labour.

When managers act unethically, some individuals or groups may obtain short-term gains, but in the long run the organization and people inside and outside the organization will pay. In Chapter 3, we discuss the nature of ethics and the importance of managers and all members of an organization behaving ethically as they pursue organizational goals.

Utilizing New Information Systems and Technologies

Another important challenge facing managers is the pressure to increase performance through new information systems and technologies.[59] The importance of information systems and new technologies to managers in acquiring and utilizing information is discussed in great detail in Chapter 4. Coordinating the production of more than 12 000 products from 50 countries and 2000 suppliers would not be possible in today's global economy without IKEA's own software, Electronic Commerce for IKEA Suppliers (ECIS).

Summary and Review

LO1 What Is the Organizational Environment? The organizational environment is the set of forces and conditions that affect a manager's ability to acquire and use resources. The organizational environment has two components: the internal environment and the external environment. The external environment can be divided into the task environment and the general environment. Failure of managers to perceive, interpret, and respond to forces in the organizational environment can lead to failure when competing in the global economy.

LO2 The Task and General Environments The task environment is the set of forces and conditions that originate with suppliers, distributors, customers, and competitors and that influence managers on a daily basis. The general environment includes wider-ranging economic, technological, demographic, socio-cultural, political and legal, and global forces that affect an organization and its task environment.

LO3 The Impact of National Culture Managers find the cultural dimensions depicted by Hofstede useful in understanding how cultures differ along five dimensions: power distance (PD), individualism (IDV) versus collectivism, masculinity (MAS) versus femininity, uncertainty avoidance index (UAI), and long-term orientation (LTO) versus short-term focus. Managerial practices that work in one culture may not work in another. Managers must be culturally sensitive to create successful global companies.

LO4 Managing the External Environment Two factors affect the nature of the opportunities and threats that organizations face: (1) the level of complexity in the environment and (2) the rate of change in the environment. Managers must learn how to analyze the forces in the environment in order to respond effectively to opportunities and threats. Managers at all three levels and in all functional areas are responsible for reducing the negative impact and embracing the new opportunities posed by environmental forces as they evolve over time.

LO5 Challenges for Management in a Global Environment Today's competitive global environment presents three main challenges to managers: Building a competitive advantage by increasing efficiency, quality, innovation, and responsiveness to customers; behaving ethically toward stakeholders inside and outside the organization; and utilizing new information systems and technologies.

KEY TERMS

achievement orientation	external environment	power distance
barriers to entry	general environment	short-term orientation
brand loyalty	global forces	social structure
certainty	global organizations	socio-cultural forces
collectivism	globalization	stakeholders
competitive advantage	individualism	suppliers
competitors	innovation	task environment
customers	internal environment	technological forces
demographic forces	long-term orientation	technology
distributors	national culture	uncertainty
economic forces	nurturing orientation	uncertainty avoidance
economies of scale	organizational environment	values
environmental change	political and legal forces	

WRAP-UP TO »» OPENING CASE

IKEA Is on Top of the Furniture World

In the opening case you were introduced to the IKEA concept. After having read and understood the concepts in this chapter, you should be able to answer the following questions:

1. *Explain how the forces in the external organizational environment affected IKEA's global operations.*

ANSWER: The external organizational environment includes forces in the task and general environments. The task environment is made up of forces that present immediate opportunities and threats for managers in acquiring and utilizing resources, while the forces in the organization's general environment pose problems and promises that have a longer-term effect and have a great impact on management planning and decision making. Forces in the task environment result from the actions of suppliers, distributors, customers, and competitors. Forces in the general environment result from technological, demographic, economic, legal and political, and global trends. IKEA, as a global company, deals with more than 2000 suppliers of goods manufactured in over 50 nations, producing more than 12 000 products. Suppliers must abide by the IKEA code of conduct if they want to provide the company with goods. This code includes rules for using sustainable materials and providing good working conditions for labour. IKEA is such a large customer for its suppliers that they comply with its rules in order to maintain their contracts. Many companies compete for IKEA's business, thus minimizing the power they exert on the company. IKEA has built brand loyalty among its customers all over the world by providing a unique shopping experience for low cost, modern furniture and household fixtures that they can usually take home and assemble themselves. Competitors are firms that sell similar products and services. While IKEA provides a unique experience for customers, companies like U.S. giant Target Corp. are offering similar style low-cost furniture, and could pose a threat to IKEA by luring away its customers with a low-cost strategy.

To minimize the problem of coordinating the great number of suppliers, IKEA developed its own software to manage its supply chain. As the population age rises in developed countries like Canada, IKEA must capitalize on the opportunity for growth by providing goods desired by older people. Catering to the needs of parents by providing quality child care while parents shop has proved to be good for business. During times of recession, customers seek value-based products such as the ones sold by IKEA. The company's low-cost strategy of selling affordable goods that make living better is a strategy that can weather fluctuations in economic conditions. When IKEA locates its stores in nations, it must abide by its laws governing trade and commerce. While trade barriers are declining, international trade agreements, such as NAFTA, stipulate a minimal amount of member-nation content or assembly that IKEA must meet to sell its goods tariff-free in the member nations. IKEA has taken advantage of the global economy by locating stores in over 40 nations. The challenge for its global operations is to customize products to meet the needs of different national cultures.

2. *Discuss how national culture has impacted management decisions at IKEA.*

ANSWER: National cultures have impacted the decisions IKEA managers make in terms of coordinating the supply of products with the demand for products. Americans like to fold their clothes, while Italians like to hang theirs. This difference in national cultural norms resulted in changes to the design of wardrobes for each nation. The kind of low-cost offerings IKEA provides does not appeal to cultures such as the Japanese culture, which values high-quality, high-cost products. Thus, the demand for IKEA products in Japan was minimal, resulting in failure in that country.

3. *Evaluate how managers at IKEA handle environmental change and uncertainty.*

ANSWER: Environmental change occurs when the forces in the task and general environments change. An understanding of the external environment is necessary so that managers can anticipate how the task environment might look in the future and decide on the actions to pursue if the organization is to prosper. If the changes in the forces in the external environment can be easily predicted, managers can make decisions with more certainty and less risk. If the changes are complicated and happen quickly, managers are less likely to be able to predict future outcomes of decisions. To minimize uncertainty, companies adopt flexible organizational structures, work processes, and cultures. IKEA has a geographical organizational structure that allows divisional managers to analyze the forces in the environment and create strategy, such as customizing products, to meet the specific needs of the national culture. Work teams that consist of designers and producers try to find environmentally sustainable inputs and more efficient ways to produce affordable, portable products.

4. *Explain how IKEA embraced the challenges of being competitive in the global economy.*

ANSWER: The challenges for managers in the global economy to be competitive include creating an advantage by developing four building blocks, managing ethically and utilizing information technology systems to make management decisions. The four building blocks of a competitive advantage are 1) increasing efficiencies, 2) focusing on quality, 3) being responsive to customers, and 4) adopting a culture of innovation. IKEA looks for ways to reduce the costs of its products by 2 percent to 3 percent per year, while using sustainable and recycled materials that do not diminish quality. IKEA creates affordable products that customers can take home and assemble themselves with some basic tools the company provides. Designers continually aim to create appealing household furnishings that can be flat packed and easily transported. The network of more than 2000 global suppliers must adhere to a code of conduct. The entire supply chain is coordinated by IKEA's own software technology. IKEA is a successful company in the competitive global economy.

Management in Action

TOPICS FOR DISCUSSION AND ACTION

LEVEL 1 Knowledge & Comprehension

1. Identify and describe the forces found in an organization's task and general environments.
2. Describe the implications that differences in national cultures have for managers.
3. Describe what each level of manager can do to reduce the impact of the forces in the organizational environment.

LEVEL 2 Application & Analysis

4. Ask the manager of an organization to discuss the types and strengths of forces in the organization's task environment. What are the current opportunities and threats resulting from competitors, customers, and suppliers?
5. Scan the environmental forces affecting local businesses by reading the business section of today's newspaper or listening to a business podcast. Explain the impact of the forces on the ability of local businesses to acquire and use resources.
6. Go to the library and gather information that allows you to compare and contrast the political, economic, demographic, and cultural systems of the United States, Mexico, and Canada. How might the similarities and differences affect the management of an enterprise such as Walmart, which does business in all three countries?

LEVEL 3 Synthesis & Evaluation

7. Illustrate how each force in the organization's task environment can pose an opportunity and a threat for a manager of a Tim Hortons restaurant wishing to expand into the United States.
8. Put yourself in the position of a first-line manager of a retailer such as Giant Tiger. What suggestions would you make to your boss on how to use the four building blocks to gain a competitive advantage?
9. Which organization is likely to face the most complex task environment: a biotechnology company trying to develop a cure for cancer, or a large retailer such as Target or The Bay? Explain why this is the case with reference to each force in the organization's task environment.

SELF-REFLECTION EXERCISE

You are considering organizing an event to raise funds for a special cause (e.g., children living in poverty, breast cancer research, literacy, or something of your choice). Think about who you might invite to this event (i.e., your "customers"—those who will buy tickets to the event). What type of event might appeal to them? What suppliers might you approach for help in organizing the event? What legal issues might you face in setting up this event? After considering all these issues, how difficult is the environment you face in holding this event?

SMALL GROUP BREAKOUT EXERCISE

Assume you and your teammates run a management consultancy company. Two of your clients, a multinational pharmaceutical company and a home construction company, are concerned about changing demographic trends in Canada. The population is aging because of declining birth rates, declining death rates, and the aging of the baby boom generation.

1. What might be some of the implications (opportunities and threats) of this demographic trend for your clients?

BUSINESS PLANNING EXERCISE

Your professor may ask you to write a business plan for a new venture or a strategic plan for an existing venture. At the end of every chapter, you will have an opportunity to apply managerial and organizational concepts to the exercise of writing a business plan. Refer to Appendix A.

After reading this chapter, you start to realize you have to analyze the forces in the organizational environment to determine the impact of the opportunities and threats from the forces in the task and general environment for your business plan. This analysis will form an important part of the Profile of the Industry (Section 4, Appendix A).

1. Who are your customers? Research the characteristics of your target market. For example, what is their demographic profile and size of population in your community (age, income, amount of disposable income spent on eating out, etc.)?

2. Who are your competitors? Research the numbers and the strengths and weaknesses of your competitors. What degree of threat do they pose?

3. Where will you obtain all the inputs you will need to run your business? For the restaurant example, who will supply the food, kitchen equipment, tables, cutlery, etc.?

4. What kind of legal and political factors do you need to address? Which types of licences are needed, and where can you obtain them?

5. Are there any significant socio-cultural forces in your community that might present an opportunity or a threat that should be discussed in your business plan?

6. Illustrate how the building blocks of competitive advantage could be used to help your restaurant succeed.

MANAGING ETHICALLY EXERCISE

You are a manager for a drug company that has developed a pill to cure river blindness, a common disease in Africa. It was a quick and easy solution, but there were no buyers because the people afflicted or who could be afflicted are too poor to buy the pills. Should you shelve the pills and wait until the market can pay the price? What other alternatives might you have?

MANAGEMENT CHALLENGE EXERCISE

How to Enter the Copying Business

You have decided to open a small printing and copying business in a college town of 100,000 people. Your business will compete with companies like FedEx Kinko's. You know that over 50% of small businesses fail in their first year, so to increase your chances of success, you have decided to do a detailed analysis of the task environment of the copying business to discover what opportunities and threats you will likely encounter.

1. Decide what you must know about (a) your future customers, (b) your future competitors, and (c) other critical forces in the task environment if you are to be successful.

2. Evaluate the main barriers to entry into the copying business.

3. Based on this analysis, list some of the steps you would take to help your new copying business succeed.

MANAGEMENT PORTFOLIO PROJECT

Answer the following questions about the organization you have chosen to follow:

1. Describe the main forces in the task environment that are affecting the organization.

2. Describe the main forces in the general environment that are affecting the organization.

3. Try to determine whether the organization's task and general environments are relatively stable or changing rapidly.

4. Explain how these environmental forces affect the job of an individual manager within this organization. How do these forces determine the opportunities and threats that managers must confront?

5. How does the organization utilize the four building blocks of a competitive advantage?

VIDEO MANAGEMENT CASE   connect

Cirque Du Soleil[60]

Guy Laliberté, founder of Cirque Du Soleil, created an international success with more than 600 employees from over 25 countries.

1. How did global forces affect the company?

2. What are the challenges that Cirque faces as a global company?

Management Case

A *Gaijin* Works to Turn Around Sony

Sony, the Japanese electronics maker, used to be renowned for using its innovation and engineering prowess to turn out blockbuster new products such as the Walkman and Trinitron TV. In the 1990s product engineers at Sony turned out an average of four new product ideas every day. Why? A large part of the answer was Sony's culture, called the "Sony Way," which emphasized communication, cooperation, and harmony between groups of engineers across the company to foster innovation and change. Engineers were given considerable freedom to pursue their own ideas, and the managers of different product groups championed their own innovations, but problems arose with Sony's approach in the 2000s.

Companies in Korea, Taiwan, and China began to innovate new technologies like digital LCD screens and flash memory that made Sony's technologies obsolete. Companies such as Apple and Nokia came out with the iPod, smartphones, and tablet computers that better fit customer needs than Sony's "old-generation" products such as the Walkman. One reason why Sony experienced major problems responding to these changes was that its culture had changed with its success. The top managers of its many divisions had become used to acting as if they had control of a fiefdom, and, protected by the Japanese tradition of lifetime employment, they worked to promote their own division's interests, not their company's. This competition had increased Sony's bureaucracy and slowed its decision making, making it much harder for Sony to take advantage of its pipeline of new product innovations. At the same time, its research was becoming enormously expensive, as divisions demanded more and more funds to create innovative new products.

Sensing this was a crucial turning point in their company's history, Sony's Japanese top managers turned to a *gaijin,* or non-Japanese, executive to lead their company. Their choice was Sir Howard Stringer, a Welshman, who headed Sony's North American operations and had been instrumental in cutting costs and increasing the profits of Sony's U.S. division. Stringer cannot speak Japanese, but luckily for him many of Sony's top executives speak English.

While he was in command, he faced the problem of reducing costs in Japan, where many Japanese companies have a policy of lifetime employment. He made it clear that layoffs would be forthcoming, as Sony must reduce its high operating costs. He has also made it clear that the politicking going on between Sony's different product groups must stop and that managers must prioritize new products, investing only in those that have the highest chance of success, for Sony must reduce its huge R&D budget. Indeed, he wanted to make engineering, not management, the focus once again at Sony and eliminate the tall, bloated hierarchy that has developed over time—by, for example, downsizing corporate headquarters. In Stringer's own words, the culture or "business of Sony has been management, not making products." However, he has to accomplish this in Japan, which has a national culture known for its collectivist, long-term orientation and for its distrust of *gaijin* or overseas values. And these same values operate inside Sony, so Stringer had to be hard-headed and push Sony to make the best use of its resources. Stringer demonstrated his hard-headed approach in 2009, when after Sony's losses increased, he replaced his top management team and streamlined the management hierarchy to speed decision making.

In his effort to revamp the company, Stringer confronted difficult, challenging cultural differences while bringing his cost-cutting expertise to bear on Sony's deteriorating situation. Sony was still struggling to regain its former leadership position. When Stringer stepped down in April 2012, replaced by Mr. Kazuo Hirai, the company's television division was losing $80 on each set it sold.[61]

1. Evaluate how the forces in the organizational environment impacted Sony.

2. How were the actions of management influenced by environmental change in this case?

3. How did the new manager use the building blocks of a competitive advantage to try to turn around the operations at Sony?

McGraw Hill connect

Connect allows you to practise important concepts at your own pace and on your own schedule, with 24/7 online access to an eBook, practice quizzes, video cases, interactive exercises, study tools, and more.

Managing Ethics, Social Responsibility, and Diversity

Opening Case

Mountain Equipment Co-op: Doing Things Right

Ranked one of the 100 top Canadian employers in 2011, Mountain Equipment Co-op (MEC) also celebrated its 40th birthday in the same year. The idea for the co-op came to be when four climbers from Vancouver voiced their frustration with always having to cross the border to the United States to get quality but affordable outdoor gear.

The group incorporated as a co-operative in 1971 to manufacture and sell quality outdoor gear at affordable prices. MEC allows anyone to join by paying a membership fee. Members can purchase goods, vote on how the co-op is governed, and further the co-op's mission. Because voting is based on one vote per member, no single member can hold more influence over the co-op than any other, and all members enjoy the same rights and privileges. There are no shareholders, as in publicly traded corporations, and after paying the salaries of the 1500 employees working in 14 stores across the country, the suppliers in Canada and from 12 other countries, and the operating costs, any profits left are distributed back to the members. However, like all co-ops, its reason for existence is not to make profit, but to provide benefits to its members.[1]

Operations are conducted in an environmentally and socially sustainable manner. MEC sources all materials and products, such as organically grown cotton, from ethical suppliers, and developed alternatives to problematic compounds like PVC. Their partners and affiliates adhere to codes of conduct that ensure safe working conditions for employees in factories, legal working hours, and reasonable pay for work done. MEC monitors and reports on its performance in sustainable practices. This type of reporting shows where MEC is meeting goals

and where there is further work to do. For example, the goal to improve factory workers' lives by having 100 percent of contract manufacturers' factories monitored for fair labour practices fell short in 2010, when only 93 percent were audited. While all of its activities have an ecological footprint, MEC is committed to the goal of reducing impact by "greening" all its practices and operations, including reducing carbon emissions, energy, and water use. MEC donated $2.5 million through the Community Involvement Program, which invests in grants and partnerships to support organizations working on conservation and recreational access.

While the organization has grown from six founding members to more than 3.5 million, the vision to create a democratically run organization providing quality, affordable, and sustainable outdoor gear has not changed. That's not the only thing that hasn't changed—it cost $5 to become a member in 1971, and 40 years later, it's still only $5!

After reading and understanding the concepts in this chapter, you should be able to answer the following questions:

1. *Who are the stakeholders in this organization? How does this differ from a traditional corporation?*

2. *Which model of ethics underlies MEC's decisions?*

3. *How would you describe MEC's approach to social responsibility?*

Overview

While a strong code of ethics can influence the way employees behave, what causes people to behave unethically in the first place? Moreover, how do managers and employees determine what is ethical or unethical? In this chapter, we examine the nature of the obligations and responsibilities of managers and the companies they work for toward the people and society that are affected by their actions. In other words, we explore what it means to behave ethically and in a socially responsible way toward the individuals and groups in their organizational environment.

We then focus on how to manage diversity to ensure that everyone an organization employs is fairly and equitably treated. Managers' ability and desire to behave ethically and to manage diversity effectively are central concerns in today's complex business environment. Increasingly, if managers ignore these issues or fail to act appropriately, their organizations are unlikely to prosper in the future.

We also discuss workplace harassment, which is both unethical and illegal, and a behaviour that managers and organizations must confront and respond to in a serious manner. By the end of the chapter, you will appreciate why ethics, social responsibility, and diversity are issues that make a manager's job both more challenging and more complex.

> **LO1**   Describe the concept of ethics and making ethical decisions.

What Are Ethics?

The opening case on Mountain Equipment Co-op highlights ethical concerns to which managers need to pay attention. **Ethics** are moral principles or beliefs about what is right or wrong. These beliefs guide individuals in their dealings with other individuals and groups who have a concern in a particular situation and provide a basis for deciding if a behaviour is right and proper.[2] At the same time, ethics also indicate what inappropriate behaviour is and how a person should behave to avoid doing harm to another person. Ethics help people determine moral responses to situations in which the best course of action is unclear.

Managers often experience an **ethical dilemma** when they confront a situation that requires them to choose between two courses of action, especially if each decision is likely to serve the interests of one particular stakeholder group to the detriment of another or one's

> **ethics** Moral principles or beliefs about what is right or wrong.
>
> **ethical dilemma** The quandary people find themselves in when they have to decide if they should act in a way that might help another person or group even though doing so might go against their own self-interest.

self-interest.[3] People often know they are confronting an ethical dilemma when their moral scruples come into play and cause them to hesitate, debate, and reflect upon the "rightness" or "goodness" of a course of action. Moral scruples are thoughts and feelings that tell a person what is right or wrong; they are a part of a person's ethics. The essential problem in dealing with ethical issues, and thus solving moral dilemmas, is that there are no absolute or indisputable rules or principles that can be developed to decide if an action is ethical or unethical. Put simply, different people or groups may dispute which actions are ethical or unethical depending on their own personal self-interest and specific attitudes, beliefs, and values. Sometimes, making a decision is easy because some obvious standard, value, or norm of behaviour applies. In other cases, managers have trouble deciding what to do. How, therefore, are we and companies and their managers and employees to decide what is ethical and so act appropriately toward other people and groups?

Making Ethical Decisions

The first answer to this question is that society as a whole, using the political and legal process, can lobby for and pass laws that specify what people can and cannot do. Many different kinds of laws exist to govern business—for example, laws against fraud and deception and laws governing how companies can treat their employees and customers. Laws also specify what sanctions or punishments will follow if those laws are broken. Different groups in society lobby for which laws should be passed based on their own personal interests and beliefs with regard to what is right or wrong. The group that can summon the most support is able to pass the laws that most closely align with its interests and beliefs. Once a law is passed, a decision about what the appropriate behaviour is with regard to a person or situation is taken from the personally determined ethical realm to the societally determined legal realm. If you do not conform to the law you can be prosecuted, and if you are found guilty of breaking the law you can be punished. You have little say in the matter; your fate is in the hands of the court and its lawyers.

In studying the relationship between ethics and law, it is important to understand that *neither laws nor ethics are fixed principles,* cast in stone, which do not change over time. Ethical beliefs alter and change as time passes, and as they do so, laws change to reflect the changing ethical beliefs of a society. For example, it was seen as ethical, and it was legal, to acquire and possess slaves in ancient Rome and Greece and in the United

States until the late 19th century. Ethical views regarding whether slavery was morally right or appropriate changed, however. Slavery was made illegal in the United States when those in power decided that slavery degraded the very meaning of being human. In denying freedom to others, we risk losing it ourselves, just as stealing from others opens the door for them to steal from us in return.

There are many types of behaviour—such as murder, theft, slavery, rape, driving while intoxicated—that most, if not all, people currently believe are unacceptable and unethical and should therefore be illegal. There are also, however, many other kinds of actions and behaviours whose ethical nature is open to dispute. Some people might believe that a particular behaviour—for example, smoking tobacco or gambling—is unethical and so should be made illegal. Others might argue that it is up to the individual or a group to decide if such behaviours are ethical or not and thus whether a particular behaviour should remain legal.

As ethical beliefs change over time, some people may begin to question whether existing laws that make specific behaviours illegal are still appropriate today. They might argue that although a specific behaviour is deemed illegal, this does not make it unethical and thus the law should be changed. In Canada, possession of marijuana (cannabis) was criminalized in 1923. To justify this law, it is commonly argued that smoking marijuana leads people to try more dangerous drugs. Once the habit of taking drugs has been acquired, people can get hooked on them. More powerful drugs such as the murderous heroin are fearfully addictive, and most people cannot stop using them without help from others. Thus, the argument is that the use of marijuana, because it might lead to further harm, is an unethical practice. Worldwide research has documented that the criminalization of marijuana has failed to solve the problem for which it was ostensibly created.

Moreover, it has been documented that the use of marijuana has many medical benefits for people with certain illnesses. For example, for cancer sufferers who are undergoing chemotherapy and for those with AIDS who are on potent medications, marijuana offers relief from many of the treatment's side effects, such as nausea and lack of appetite. Medical marijuana is available in Canada with a doctor's prescription. About 10 000 people have prescriptions, and about 3400 licences have been issued by Health Canada to grow the plants, two-thirds of them in Ontario and British Columbia.[4] Nevertheless, in Canada there has been a widespread movement to decriminalize marijuana. While not making the drug legal, decriminalization removes the threat of prosecution even for uses that are not medically related. An ethical debate is currently raging over this issue in many countries.

The important point to note is that while ethical beliefs lead to the development of laws and regulations to prevent certain behaviours or encourage others, laws themselves can and do change or even disappear as ethical beliefs change. In Britain in 1830 there were over 350 different crimes for which a person could be executed, including sheep stealing. Today there are none; capital punishment and the death penalty are no longer legal in Britain. Thus, both ethical and legal rules are relative: no absolute or unvarying standards exist to determine how we should behave, and people are caught up in moral dilemmas all the time. Because of this we have to make ethical choices.

The previous discussion highlights an important issue in understanding the relationship between ethics, law, and business. Throughout the 2000s many scandals have plagued major companies such as Enron, Nortel Networks, WorldCom, Hollinger Inc., and others. Managers, such as Canadian-born Conrad Black of Hollinger Inc., are often convicted of breaking the law and using illegal means to defraud investors.

Illustrate how ethics helps managers determine the right way to behave when dealing with different stakeholder groups.   **LO2**

Ethics and Stakeholders

The individuals and groups that have an interest, claim, or stake in an organization and in what it does are known as **organizational stakeholders**.[5] Organizational stakeholders include shareholders, managers, nonmanagerial employees, customers, suppliers, the local community in which an organization operates, and even citizens of the country in which an organization operates. To survive and prosper, an organization must effectively satisfy the often competing needs of its stakeholders.[6] Shareholders want dividends, managers and employees want salaries and stable employment, and customers want high-quality products at reasonable prices. If stakeholders do not receive these benefits, they may withdraw their support for the organization: shareholders will sell their stock, managers and workers will seek jobs in other organizations, and customers will take their business elsewhere. Since stakeholders can directly benefit or be harmed by its actions, the ethics of a company and its managers are important to them. Who are a company's major stakeholders? What do they contribute to a company, and what do they claim in return? Below we examine the claims of

organizational stakeholders Shareholders, employees, customers, suppliers, and others who have an interest, claim, or stake in an organization and in what it does.

these stakeholders—shareholders; managers; employees; suppliers and distributors; customers; and community, society, and nation.

Shareholders

Shareholders have a claim on a company because when they buy its stock or shares they become its owners. Whenever the founder of a company decides to publicly incorporate the business to raise capital, shares of the stock of that company are issued. This stock grants its buyers ownership of a certain percentage of the company and the right to receive any future stock dividends. For example, in December 2004 Microsoft decided to pay the owners of its 5 billion shares a record dividend payout of $32 billion! Bill Gates received $3.3 billion in dividends based on his shareholding, and he donated this money to the Bill and Melinda Gates Foundation, to which he has reportedly donated over $30 billion to date, with the promise of much more to come; so has Warren Buffett, who committed in 2006 to donate at least $30 billion to the Gates Foundation over the next decade. The two richest people in the world have decided to give away a large part of their wealth to serve global ethical causes—in particular, to address global health concerns such as malnutrition, malaria, tuberculosis, and AIDS.

Shareholders are interested in the way a company operates because they want to maximize the return on their investment. Thus, they watch the company and its managers closely to ensure that management is working diligently to increase the company's profitability.[7] Increasingly, shareholders are also concerned about the social impact of the businesses they invest in. Members of MEC recognize that, unlike shareholders in traditional corporations whose primary concern is for maximizing short-term private profit, they benefit just as much from creating sustainable, balanced growth.

Shareholders also want to ensure that managers are behaving ethically and not risking investors' capital by engaging in actions that could hurt the company's reputation. Adopting transparent accountability measures and making their performance public has enhanced MEC's reputation with the public.

Managers

Managers are a vital stakeholder group because they are responsible for using a company's financial capital and human resources to increase its performance and thus its stock price.[8] Managers have a claim on an organization because they bring to it their skills, expertise, and experience. They have the right to expect a good return or reward by investing their human capital to improve a company's performance. Such rewards include good salaries and benefits, the prospect of promotion and a career, and stock options and bonuses tied to company performance.

Managers are the stakeholder group that bears the responsibility to decide which goals an organization should pursue to most benefit stakeholders and how to make the most efficient use of resources to achieve those goals. In making such decisions, managers are frequently in the position of having to juggle the interests of different stakeholders, including themselves.[9] These decisions are sometimes very difficult and challenge managers to uphold ethical values because in some cases decisions that benefit some stakeholder groups (managers and shareholders) harm other groups (individual workers and local communities).

Layoff decisions are always difficult, as they not only take a heavy toll on workers, their families, and local communities but also mean the loss of the contributions of valued employees to an organization. Whenever decisions such as these are made—benefiting some groups at the expense of others—ethics come into play.

As we discussed in Chapter 1, managers must be motivated and given incentives to work hard in the interests of shareholders. Their behaviour must also be scrutinized to ensure they do not behave illegally or unethically, pursuing goals that threaten shareholders' and the company's interests.[10] Unfortunately, we have seen in the 2000s how easy it is for top managers to find ways to ruthlessly pursue their self-interest at the expense of shareholders and employees because laws and regulations were not strong enough to force them to behave ethically. As a result of his unethical actions, in 2007, Canadian-born Conrad Black was convicted of fraud and sentenced to a lengthy jail term. His appeal in 2011 was denied, but he was released in 2012 after having served his sentence.

In a nutshell, the problem has been that in many companies corrupt managers focus not on building the

Managers who act ethically tend to be honest and reliable.

company's capital, shareholders' wealth, and the well-being of society, but on maximizing their own *personal* capital and wealth. In an effort to prevent future scandals, governments have begun to rework the rules governing a company's relationship with its auditor, as well as regulations concerning stock options, and increase the power of outside directors to scrutinize a CEO. The goal is to turn many actions that were previously classified as only unethical into illegal behaviour in the near future. For example, companies are now forced to reveal to shareholders the value of the stock options they give their top executives and directors, and when they give them these options, and this shows how much such payments reduce company profits. Managers and directors can now be prosecuted if they disguise or try to hide these payments. U.S. CEOs now get paid about 600 times what the average worker earns, compared to about 40 times in 1980—a staggering increase. The richest Canadian CEOs earn 189 times what the average Canadian makes.[11]

Is it ethical for top managers to receive such vast amounts of money from their companies? Do they really earn it? Remember, this money could have gone to shareholders in the form of dividends. It also could have gone to reduce the huge salary gap between those at the top and those at the bottom of the hierarchy. Many people argue that the growing disparity between the rewards given to CEOs and to other employees is unethical and should be regulated. CEO pay has become too high because CEOs are the people who set and control one another's salaries and bonuses! They can do this because they sit on the boards of other companies, as outside directors, and thus can control the salaries and stock options paid to other CEOs. Others argue that because top managers play an important role in building a company's capital and wealth, they deserve a significant share of its profits.

Employees

A company's employees are the hundreds of thousands of people who work in its various departments and functions, such as research, sales, and manufacturing. Employees expect that they will receive rewards consistent with their performance. One principal way that a company can act ethically toward employees and meet their expectations is by creating an occupational structure that fairly and equitably rewards employees for their contributions. Companies, for example, need to develop recruitment, training, performance appraisal, and reward systems that do not discriminate against employees and that employees believe are fair. MEC adheres to the principles of the International Labour Organization (ILO) and is a member of the Fair Labor Association (FLA).

Tips ▶ FOR MANAGERS

Championing Ethical Behaviour

1. When trying to produce the greatest good for the greatest number of people, use the utilitarian model to make ethical decisions.

2. Use the moral rights model to make ethical decisions that protect the rights of stakeholders.

3. The justice model of ethical decision making can be used by managers to allocate benefits to stakeholders in an equitable manner.

Suppliers and Distributors

No company operates alone. Every company is in a network of relationships with other companies that supply it with the inputs (e.g., raw materials, components, contract labour, and clients) that it needs to operate. It also depends on intermediaries such as wholesalers and retailers to distribute its products to the final customer. Suppliers expect to be paid fairly and promptly for their inputs; distributors expect to receive quality products at agreed-upon prices.

Once again, many ethical issues arise in the way companies contract and interact with their suppliers and distributors. Important issues concerning how and when payments are to be made or product quality specifications are governed by the terms of the legal contracts a company signs with its suppliers and distributors. Many other issues are dependent on business ethics. For example, numerous products sold in Canadian stores have been outsourced to countries that do not have Canadian regulations and laws to protect the workers who make these products. All companies must take an ethical position on the way they obtain and make the products they sell. Commonly, this stance is published on a company's website. MEC illustrates the importance and challenges of ethical sourcing.

Customers

Customers are often regarded as the most critical stakeholder group since if a company cannot attract them to buy its products, it cannot stay in business. Thus, managers and employees must work to increase efficiency and effectiveness in order to create loyal customers and attract new ones. They do so by selling customers quality products at a fair price and providing good after-sales service. They can also strive to improve their products over time and provide guarantees to customers about the integrity of their products.

Many laws exist that protect customers from companies that attempt to provide dangerous or shoddy products. Laws exist that allow customers to sue a company whose product causes them injury or harm, such as a defective tire or vehicle. Other laws force companies to clearly disclose the interest rates they charge on purchases—an important hidden cost that customers frequently do not factor into their purchase decisions. Every year thousands of companies are prosecuted for breaking these laws, so "buyers beware" is an important rule customers must follow when buying goods and services.

Community, Society, and Nation

The effects of the decisions made by companies and their managers permeate all aspects of the communities, societies, and nations in which they operate. *Community* refers to physical locations like towns or cities or to social milieus like ethnic neighbourhoods in which companies are located. A community provides a company with the physical and social infrastructure that allows it to operate; its utilities and labour force; the homes in which its managers and employees live; the schools, colleges, and hospitals that service their needs; and so on.

Through the salaries, wages, and taxes it pays, a company contributes to the economy of the town or region and often determines whether the community prospers or declines. Similarly, a company affects the prosperity of a society and a nation and, to the degree that a company is involved in global trade, all the countries it operates in and thus the prosperity of the global economy.

Although the individual effects of the way each McDonald's restaurant operates might be small, for instance, the combined effects of the way all McDonald's and other fast-food companies do business are enormous. In the United States alone, over 500 000 people work in the fast-food industry, and many thousands of suppliers like farmers, paper cup manufacturers, builders, and so on depend on it for their livelihood. Small wonder, then, that the ethics of the fast-food business are scrutinized closely. Responding to protests about chickens raised in cages where they cannot move their wings, McDonald's—the largest egg buyer in the United States—issued new ethical guidelines concerning cage size and related matters that its egg suppliers must abide by if they are to retain its business. What ethical rules does McDonald's use to decide its stance toward minimum cage sizes?

Business ethics are also important because the failure of companies can have catastrophic effects on a community; a general decline in business activity affects a whole nation.

ethical decisions Decisions that reasonable or typical stakeholders would find acceptable because they aid stakeholders, the organization, or society.

unethical decisions Decisions that a manager would prefer to disguise or hide from other people because they enable a company or a particular individual to gain at the expense of society or other stakeholders.

utilitarian model An ethical decision is a decision that produces the greatest good for the greatest number of people.

The decision of a large company to pull out of a community, for example, can seriously threaten the community's future. Some companies may attempt to improve their profits by engaging in actions that, although not illegal, can hurt communities and nations. One of these actions is pollution. As we have seen, companies like Mountain Equipment Co-op strive to reduce the pollution in their manufacturing operations from CO_2 emissions. So how do managers and companies make **ethical decisions**—that is, decisions that reasonable or typical stakeholders would find acceptable because they aid stakeholders, the organization, or society? And, similarly, how do they avoid making **unethical decisions**—decisions that a manager might disguise or hide from others because they enable a company or individual to gain at the expense of society or other stakeholders?

Philosophers have debated for centuries about the specific criteria that should be used to determine whether decisions are ethical or unethical. When making business decisions, managers must take the claims of all stakeholders into consideration.[12] To help themselves and employees make ethical decisions and behave in ways that benefit their stakeholders, managers can use three sets of principles to analyze the effects of their business decisions on stakeholders: the *utilitarian, moral rights,* and *justice models*. See Table 3.1.[13]

Utilitarian Model

The **utilitarian model** is that an ethical decision is a decision that produces the greatest good for the greatest number of people. To decide which is the most ethical course of business action, managers should first consider how different possible courses of business action would benefit or harm different stakeholders. They should then choose the course of action that provides the most benefits—or, conversely, the one that does the least harm—to stakeholders.[14]

The ethical dilemma for managers involves how to measure the benefits and harms that will be done to each stakeholder group. Moreover, how do we evaluate the rights of different stakeholder groups, and the relative importance of each group, in coming to a decision? Since shareholders are the owners of the company, shouldn't their claims be held above those of employees? For example, managers might be faced with a choice of using global outsourcing to reduce costs and lower prices to customers or continuing with high-cost production

TABLE 3.1	Utilitarian, Moral Rights, and Justice Models of Ethics	
Model	**Managerial Implications**	**Problems for Managers**
Utilitarian Model An ethical decision is a decision that produces the greatest good for the greatest number of people.	Managers should compare and contrast alternative courses of action based on the benefits and costs of those alternatives for different organizational stakeholder groups. They should choose the course of action that provides the most benefits to stakeholders. For example, managers should locate a new manufacturing plant at the place that will most benefit its stakeholders.	How do managers decide on the relative importance of each stakeholder group? How are managers to measure precisely the benefits and harms to each stakeholder group? For example, how do managers choose among the interests of shareholders, employees, and customers?
Moral Rights Model An ethical decision is a decision that best maintains and protects the fundamental rights and privileges of the people affected by it. For example, ethical decisions protect people's rights to freedom, life and safety, privacy, free speech, and freedom of conscience.	Managers should compare and contrast alternative courses of action based on the effect of those alternatives on stakeholders' rights. They should choose the course of action that best protects stakeholders' rights. For example, decisions that would involve significant harm to the safety or health of employees or customers are unethical.	If a decision will protect the rights of some stakeholders and hurt the rights of others, how do managers choose which stakeholder rights to protect? For example, in deciding whether it is ethical to snoop on an employee, does an employee's right to privacy outweigh an organization's right to protect its property or the safety of other employees?
Justice Model An ethical decision is a decision that distributes benefits and harms among stakeholders in a fair, equitable, or impartial way.	Managers should compare and contrast alternative courses of action based on the degree to which the action will promote a fair distribution of outcomes. For example, employees who are similar in their level of skill, performance, or responsibility should receive the same kind of pay. The allocation of outcomes should not be based on arbitrary differences such as gender, race, or religion.	Managers must learn not to discriminate between people because of observable differences in their appearance or behaviour. Managers must also learn how to use fair procedures to determine how to distribute outcomes to organizational members. For example, managers must not give people they like bigger raises than they give to people they do not like or bend the rules to help their favourites.

at home. A decision to use global outsourcing benefits shareholders and customers but will result in major lay-offs that will harm employees and the communities in which they live. Typically, in a capitalist society such as Canada or the United States, the interests of shareholders are put above those of employees, so production will move abroad. This is commonly regarded as being an ethical choice because in the long run the alternative, home production, might cause the business to collapse and go bankrupt, in which case greater harm will be done to all stakeholders.

Moral Rights Model

Under the **moral rights model**, an ethical decision is a decision that best maintains and protects the fundamental or inalienable rights and privileges of the people affected

by it. For example, ethical decisions protect people's rights to freedom, life and safety, property, privacy, free speech, and freedom of conscience. The adage "Do unto others as you would have them do unto you" is a moral rights principle that managers should use to decide which rights to uphold. Customers must also consider the rights of the companies and people who create the products they wish to consume.

From a moral rights perspective, managers should compare and contrast different courses of business action on the basis of how each course will affect the rights of the company's different stakeholders. Managers should then choose the course of action that best protects and upholds the rights of *all* the stakeholders. For

moral rights model
An ethical decision is one that best maintains and protects the fundamental or inalienable rights and privileges of the people affected by it.

example, decisions that might result in significant harm to the safety or health of employees or customers would clearly be unethical choices.

The ethical dilemma for managers is that decisions that will protect the rights of some stakeholders often will hurt the rights of others. How should they choose which group to protect? For example, in deciding whether it is ethical to snoop on employees, or search them when they leave work to prevent theft, does an employee's right to privacy outweigh an organization's right to protect its property? Suppose a coworker is having personal problems and is coming in late and leaving early, placing you in the position of being forced to pick up the person's workload. Do you tell your boss even though you know this will probably get that person fired?

Justice Model

The **justice model** is that an ethical decision is a decision that distributes benefits and harms among people and groups in a fair, equitable, or impartial way. Managers should compare and contrast alternative courses of action based on the degree to which they will result in a fair or equitable distribution of outcomes for stakeholders. For example, employees who are similar in their level of skill, performance, or responsibility should receive the same kind of pay. The allocation of outcomes should not be based on differences such as gender, race, or religion.

The ethical dilemma for managers is to determine the fair rules and procedures for distributing outcomes to stakeholders. Managers must not give people they like bigger raises than they give to people they do not like, for example, or bend the rules to help their favourites. On the other hand, if employees want managers to act fairly toward them, then employees need to act fairly toward their companies and work hard and be loyal. Similarly, customers need to act fairly toward a company if they expect it to be fair to them—something people who illegally copy digital media should consider.

In theory, each model offers a different and complementary way of determining whether a decision or behaviour is ethical, and all three models should be used to sort out the ethics of a particular course of action. Ethical issues are seldom clear-cut, however, and the interests of different stakeholders often conflict, so it is often extremely difficult for a decision maker to use these models to identify the most ethical course of action. That is why many

experts on ethics propose the following practical guide to determine whether a decision or behaviour is ethical.[15]

A decision is probably acceptable on ethical grounds if a person can answer "yes" to each of these questions:

1. Does my decision fall within the accepted values or standards that typically apply in the organizational environment?

2. Am I willing to see the decision communicated to all individuals and groups affected by it—for example, by having it reported in newspapers or on television?

3. Would the people with whom I have a significant personal relationship, such as family members, friends, or even managers in other organizations, approve of the decision?

Asking these three practical questions to analyze a business decision helps ensure that managers are taking into account the interests of all stakeholders.

A major responsibility of managers is to protect and nurture the resources under their control. Any organizational stakeholders—managers, workers, shareholders, suppliers—who advance their own interests by behaving unethically toward other stakeholders, either by taking resources or by denying resources to others, waste collective resources. If other individuals or groups copy the behaviour of the unethical stakeholder ("If he can do it, we can do it, too"), the rate at which collective resources are misused increases, and eventually there are few resources available to produce goods and services. Unethical behaviour that goes unpunished creates incentives for people to put their unbridled self-interests above the rights of others.[16] When this happens, the benefits that people reap from joining together in organizations disappear very quickly. This is why many organizations help managers and employees make ethical decisions by developing codes of ethics.

Codes of Ethics

Codes of ethics are formal standards and rules, based on beliefs about right or wrong, that managers can use to make appropriate decisions in the best interests of their stakeholders.[17] Ethical standards embody views about abstractions such as justice, freedom, equity, and equality. An organization's code of ethics derives from three main sources in the organizational environment: (1) *societal ethics,* governing how everyone deals with each other on issues such as fairness, justice, poverty, and the rights of the individual; (2) *professional ethics,* governing how members of the profession make decisions when the way they should behave is not clear-cut; and (3) the *individual*

justice model An ethical decision is a decision that distributes benefits and harms among people and groups in a fair, equitable, or impartial way.

codes of ethics Formal standards and rules, based on beliefs about right or wrong, that managers can use to make appropriate decisions in the best interests of their stakeholders.

| **FIGURE 3.1** | Sources of an Organization's Code of Ethics |

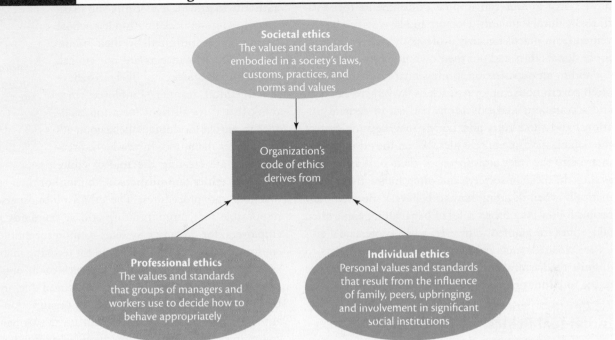

ethics, or personal standards for interacting with others, of the organization's top managers (see Figure 3.1).

Societal Ethics

Societal ethics are standards that govern how members of a society deal with each other in matters involving issues such as fairness, justice, poverty, and the rights of the individual. Societal ethics emanate from a society's laws, customs, and practices, and from the unwritten attitudes, values, and norms that influence how people interact with each other. People in a particular country may automatically behave ethically because they have internalized values and norms that specify how they should behave in certain situations. Not all values and norms are internalized, however. The typical ways of doing business in a society and laws governing the use of bribery and corruption are the result of decisions made and enforced by people with the power to determine what is appropriate.

Societal ethics vary among societies. For example, ethical standards accepted in Canada are not accepted in all other countries. In many economically poor countries bribery is standard practice to get things done, such as getting a telephone installed or a contract awarded.

In Canada and many other Western countries, bribery is considered unethical and often illegal.

Societal ethics control self-interested behaviour by individuals and organizations—behaviour threatening to society's collective interests. Laws spelling out what is good or appropriate business practice provide benefits to everybody. Free and fair competition among organizations is possible only when laws and rules level the playing field and define what behaviour is acceptable or unacceptable in certain situations. For example, it is ethical for a manager to compete with managers in other companies by producing a higher-quality or lower-priced product, but it is not ethical (or legal) to do so by spreading false claims about competitors' products, bribing stores to exclude competitors' products, or blowing up competitors' factories.

Professional Ethics

Professional ethics are standards that govern how members of a profession, managers or workers, make decisions when the way in which they should behave is not clear-cut.[18] Medical ethics govern the way doctors and nurses are to treat patients. Doctors are expected to perform only necessary medical procedures and to act in the patient's interest and not in their own. The ethics of scientific research require scientists to conduct their experiments and present their findings in ways that ensure the

societal ethics
Standards that govern how members of a society deal with each other on issues such as fairness, justice, poverty, and the rights of the individual.

professional ethics
Standards that govern how members of a profession make decisions when the way they should behave is not clear-cut.

validity of their conclusions. Like society at large, most professional groups can impose punishments for violations of ethical standards. Doctors and lawyers can be prevented from practising their professions if they disregard professional ethics and put their own interests first.

Within an organization, professional rules and norms often govern how employees such as lawyers, researchers, and accountants make decisions and act in certain situations, and these rules and norms may become part of the organization's code of ethics. When they do, workers internalize the rules and norms of their profession (just as they do those of society) and often follow them automatically when deciding how to behave.[19] Because most people follow established rules of behaviour, people often take ethics for granted. However, when professional ethics are violated, such as when scientists fabricate data to disguise the harmful effects of products, ethical issues rise to the forefront of attention.

Individual Ethics

Individual ethics are personal values and attitudes that govern how individuals interact with other people.[20] Sources of individual ethics include the influence of one's family, peers, and upbringing in general, and an individual's personality and experience. The experiences gained over a lifetime—through membership in significant social institutions such as schools and religions, for example—also contribute to the development of the personal standards and values that a person applies to decide what is right or wrong and whether to perform certain actions or make certain decisions. Many decisions or behaviours that one person finds unethical, such as using animals for cosmetics testing, may be acceptable to another person because of differences in their personalities, values, and attitudes.

Managers can emphasize the importance of ethical behaviour and social responsibility by ensuring that ethical values and norms are a central component of organizational culture. An organization's code of ethics guides decision making when ethical questions arise, but managers can go one step farther by ensuring that important ethical values and norms are key features of an organization's culture. For example, MEC's charter, which governs everything it does as an organization, has this to say on stewardship: "We act to preserve and restore wild places. We do so actively, consistently, and generously." Ethical values and norms such as these that are part of an organization's culture help organizational members resist self-interested action and recognize that they are part of something bigger than themselves.[21]

The role of managers in developing ethical values and standards in other employees is very important.

Employees naturally look to those in authority to provide leadership, and managers become ethical role models whose behaviour is scrutinized by their subordinates. If top managers are not ethical, their subordinates are not likely to behave in an ethical manner. Employees may think that if it's all right for a top manager to engage in dubious behaviour, it's all right for them, too. Increasingly, organizations are creating the role of ethics officer, or **ethics ombudsperson**, to monitor their ethical practices and procedures. The ethics ombudsperson is responsible for communicating ethical standards to all employees, for designing systems to monitor employees' conformity to those standards, and for teaching managers and nonmanagerial employees at all levels of the organization how to respond appropriately to ethical dilemmas.[22] Because the ethics ombudsperson has organization-wide authority, organizational members in any department can communicate instances of unethical behaviour by their managers or coworkers without fear of retribution. This arrangement makes it easier for everyone to behave ethically. In addition, the ethics ombudsperson can provide guidance when organizational members are uncertain about whether an action is ethical. Some organizations have an organization-wide ethics committee to provide guidance on ethical issues and help write and update the company code of ethics.

Ethical control systems such as codes of ethics and regular training programs help employees and managers learn an organization's values. However, only a third of Canadian businesses provide managers with such training, and it is generally less than one hour a year.[23] Moreover, strong codes of ethics and good governance practices still do not guarantee ethical behaviour. Enron and Arthur Andersen, the accounting company that certified and audited Enron's fraudulent accounts, both had codes of ethics. Even companies that are recognized and rewarded for good governance can be ethically deceptive, as is illustrated by the case of Satyam.

The Case of Satyam

- Employs 53 000 people, operates in 66 countries

- Won 2008 global award for excellence in corporate governance by World Council for Corporate Governance (WCFCG)

- Became official IT services provider for the FIFA World Cups 2010 and 2014

- Ramalinga Raju, Satyam's founder and chairman, won Ernst & Young's 2007 entrepreneur of the year award

individual ethics
Personal standards that govern how individuals interact with other people.

ethics ombudsperson
An ethics officer who monitors an organization's practices and procedures to ensure that they are ethical.

In 2008, Satyam, India's fourth largest software development company, was awarded the global award for excellence in corporate governance by the World Council for Corporate Governance (WCFCG). In 2009, it was the subject of the largest scandal in the global economy since Enron's bankruptcy in 2001.[24] Ramalinga Raju, the founder and chairman of Satyam, in a statement sent to the stock exchange, admitted to "inflating profits" and the shares of the company immediately plunged by 82 percent. He said "[w]hat started as a marginal gap between actual operating profits and the one reflected in the books of accounts continued to grow over the years . . . It was like riding a tiger, not knowing how to get off without being eaten."

> "What started as a marginal gap between actual operating profits and the one reflected in the books of accounts continued to grow over the years . . . It was like riding a tiger, not knowing how to get off without being eaten."
>
> *Ramalinga Raju*

organizational stakeholders and society at large. An example of this approach occurred when media mogul Conrad Black defrauded the shareholders of Hollinger Inc. by using corporate funds for personal use.

A **defensive approach** indicates at least a commitment to ethical behaviour. Managers adopting this approach do all they can to ensure that their employees behave legally and do not harm others. But when making ethical choices, these managers put the claims and interests of their shareholders first, at the expense of other stakeholders.

Some economists believe that managers in a capitalist society should always put shareholders' claims first. They suggest that if such choices are unacceptable or are considered unethical to other members of society, then

---

LO3 Evaluate four approaches to corporate social responsibility.

Social Responsibility

There are many reasons why it is important for managers and organizations to act ethically and do everything possible to avoid harming stakeholders. However, what about the other side of the coin? What responsibility do managers have to provide benefits to their stakeholders and to adopt courses of action that enhance the well-being of society at large? The term **social responsibility** refers to a manager's duty or obligation to make decisions that nurture, protect, enhance, and promote the welfare and well-being of stakeholders and society as a whole. Many kinds of decisions signal an organization's interest in being socially responsible (see Table 3.2).

Approaches to Social Responsibility by Traditional Businesses

The strength of traditional for-profit businesses' commitment to social responsibility ranges from low to high (see Figure 3.2).[25] At the low end of the range is an **obstructionist approach**. Obstructionist managers choose not to behave in a socially responsible way. Instead, they behave unethically and illegally and do all they can to prevent knowledge of their behaviour from reaching other

social responsibility
A manager's duty or obligation to make decisions that promote the well-being of stakeholders and society as a whole.

obstructionist approach Disregard for social responsibility; willingness to engage in and cover up unethical and illegal behaviour.

defensive approach
Minimal commitment to social responsibility; willingness to do what the law requires and no more.

TABLE 3.2	Examples of Socially Responsible Behaviour

Managers are being socially responsible and showing their support for their stakeholders when they:

- Provide severance payments to help laid-off workers make ends meet until they can find another job;
- Provide workers with opportunities to enhance their skills and acquire additional education so they can remain productive and do not become obsolete because of changes in technology;
- Allow employees to take time off when they need to and provide extended health care and pension benefits to employees;
- Contribute to charities or support various civic-minded activities in the cities or towns in which they are located;
- Decide to keep open a factory whose closure would devastate the local community;
- Decide to keep a company's operations in Canada to protect the jobs of Canadian workers rather than outsource and move abroad;
- Decide to spend money to improve a new factory so that it will not pollute the environment;
- Procure ethically sourced inputs;
- Decline to invest in countries that have poor human rights records;
- Choose to help poor countries develop an economic base to improve living standards.

FIGURE 3.2 Approaches to Social Responsibility by Traditional Businesses

Obstructionist approach   Defensive approach   Accommodative approach   Proactive approach

Low social responsibility   Social Responsibility   High social responsibility

---

accommodative approach Moderate commitment to social responsibility; willingness to do more than the law requires, if asked.

proactive approach Strong commitment to social responsibility; eagerness to do more than the law requires and to use organizational resources to promote the interests of all organizational stakeholders.

society must pass laws and create rules and regulations to govern the choices managers make.[26] From a defensive point of view, it is not managers' responsibility to make socially responsible choices; their job is to abide by the rules that have been legally established. Milton Friedman said: "There is one and only one social responsibility of business—to use its resources and engage in activities designed to increase its profits, so long as it stays within the rules of the game, which is to say, engages in open and free competition without deception or fraud."[27]

But increasingly, going beyond what is legislated may be the only way to do any business at all. Indian mining giant Vedanta Resources was told by the Supreme Court of India that its application to mine bauxite in the pristine Nyuamgiri hills in one of India's poorest states would be turned down by the Supreme Court unless it participated in a joint venture with the state-owned Orissa Mining Corporation to spend 100 million rupees (US$2.4 million) a year, or 5 percent of its operating profits, whichever is greater, on fighting poverty and protecting wildlife and the tribal people.[28]

An **accommodative approach** is an acknowledgment of the need to support social responsibility. Accommodative managers agree that organizational members ought to behave legally and ethically, and they try to weigh the interests of different stakeholders against one another so that the claims of one group of shareholders are seen in relation to the claims of other stakeholders. Managers adopting this approach want to make choices that are reasonable in the eyes of society and want to do the right thing when called on to do so. Walmart Canada has been criticized for its policy of doing business with third-party suppliers—such as Hampton Industries, Sutton Creations, Global Gold, Stretch-O-Rama, Cherry Stix, and By Design—that import goods from Myanmar, which engages in forced labour, including that of children. In defence of the company's actions, Walmart Canada spokesman Andrew Pelletier noted, "We have a policy we are looking at, of monitoring vendors sourcing from other countries."[29] The company started with a defensive approach, focusing on not doing anything illegal, but has moved to a more accommodative and, since 2005, perhaps a proactive style. Even the ex-president of the famous environmental group the Sierra Club is now "working with the enemy." *Fast Company* magazine writes, "Once the youngest president of the Sierra Club, Adam Werbach used to call Wal-Mart toxic. Now the company is his biggest client."[30] Since 2005, Walmart has set goals to become the world's largest and environmentally sustainable retail company by reducing its ecological footprint and increasing the number of environmentally friendly products it sells and, after some nasty legal battles, promoting better labour practices and working conditions.[31]

Managers taking a **proactive approach** actively embrace the need to behave in socially responsible ways, go out of their way to learn about the needs of different stakeholder groups, and are willing to use organizational resources to promote the interests of shareholders as well as other stakeholders. David Suzuki said of Walmart Canada: "Wal-Mart's commitment to sustainability acts as an inspiration and incentive to other corporations to follow suit. The company has enormous influence on corporate thinking and I am delighted with the priorities it has selected."[32]

Why Be Socially Responsible?

There are several advantages to social responsibility by managers and organizations. First, employees and society benefit directly because organizations (rather than the government) bear some of the costs of helping employees. Second, it has been said that if all organizations in a society were socially responsible, the quality of life as a whole would be higher.[33] Indeed, several management experts have argued that the way organizations behave toward their employees determines many of a society's values and norms and the ethics of its citizens. Experts point to Japan, Sweden, Germany, the Netherlands, and Switzerland as countries where organizations are socially responsible and where, as a result, crime and unemployment rates are relatively low, the literacy rate is relatively high, and socio-cultural values promote harmony among different groups of people. Other reasons for being socially responsible are that it is the right thing to do and that companies that act responsibly toward their stakeholders benefit from increasing business and see their profits rise.[34] The most pressing reason to practise business in a socially responsible manner is the recognition that the Earth cannot support unsustainable practices that focus on short-term profit making. The World Business Council for Sustainable Development put it this way, "Business cannot function if ecosystems and the services they deliver—like water, biodiversity, fibre, food and climate—are degraded or out of balance."[35]

Jason Mogus, president of Communicopia, finds that being socially responsible is a competitive advantage: "The times that we are in right now are tough times for a lot of high-tech firms, and the ones that are thriving are the ones that really did build community connections and have strong customer and employee loyalty," says Mogus. "If everyone's just there for the stock price and it goes underwater, then what you have is a staff of not very motivated workers."[36]

Given these advantages, why would anyone quarrel over organizations and their managers pursuing social responsibility? One response is that a commitment to social responsibility could benefit some stakeholders and not others. For instance, some shareholders might think they are being harmed financially when organizational resources are used for socially responsible courses of action. Some people, like Freidman, as noted earlier, argue that business has only one kind of responsibility: to use its resources for activities that increase its profits and thus reward its shareholders.[37] See Figure 3.3.

How should managers decide which social issues they will respond to, and to what extent their organizations should trade profits for social gain? With impact investing managers don't view investing in social missions

as a trade-off to profit making. **Impact investing** involves investing in solving social or environmental challenges, while generating a return of principal capital or a better-than-market financial return. There is a recognition that societies cannot rely solely on community and government agencies to solve social problems.

Organizations surveyed in 2011 by the Global Impact Investing Network (GIIN) and J.P. Morgan believed that impact investing was in its infancy, but most also expected that 5 percent to 10 percent of their overall portfolios will be allocated to impact investments in 10 years' time.[38] The increasingly popular view is that firms need not sacrifice financial return in exchange for social impact. A **social audit** allows managers to consider both the organizational and the social effects of particular decisions. The audit ranks various courses of action according to both their profitability and their social benefits. The GIIN has compiled a list of 399 metrics that can be used in a social audit to report impacts which range from indicators that describe the organization's environmental footprint to indicators that describe the performance and reach of the organization's product and services. Using these metrics, an organization's social and environmental impacts can be rated, much like Standard & Poor's rates a company's credit risk. This allows investors to make decisions based on standardized, comparable data and will open up access to much-needed capital to social entrepreneurs and social enterprises.

Evidence suggests that in the long run, managers who behave in a socially responsible way will most benefit all organizational stakeholders (including shareholders). It appears that socially responsible companies, in comparison with less responsible competitors, are less risky investments, tend to be somewhat more profitable, have a more loyal and committed workforce, and have a better **reputation**—the esteem that organizations gain when they behave ethically. These qualities encourage stakeholders (including customers and suppliers) to establish long-term business relationships with the companies.[39] Thus, there are many reasons to believe that, over time, strong support

impact investing
Investments that seek to solve social or environmental problems and generate financial returns to the investor.

social audit A tool that allows managers to analyze the profitability and social returns of socially responsible actions.

reputation The esteem or high repute that individuals or organizations gain when they behave ethically

> "Business cannot function if ecosystems and the services they deliver—like water, biodiversity, fibre, food and climate—are degraded or out of balance."
>
> *World Business Council for Sustainable Development*

FIGURE 3.3 Why Be Socially Responsible?

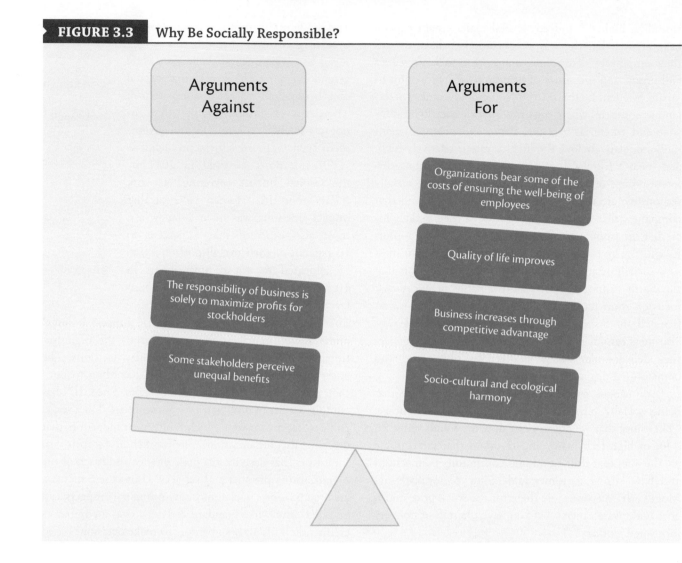

of impact investing brings the most benefits to organizational stakeholders (including shareholders) and society at large.

LO4 Appreciate diversity, and explain why the effective management of diverse employees is both an ethical issue and a business imperative.

Diversity

One of the most important issues in management to emerge over the past 30 years has been the increasing diversity of the workforce. **Diversity** is dissimilarity—differences—among people due to age, gender, race, ethnicity, religion, sexual orientation, socio-economic background, capabilities or disabilities, position, status, seniority, parental status, and so on. Managing diversity raises important ethical and social responsibility issues. Managers

diversity Differences among people in age, gender, race, ethnicity, ability, and sexual orientation.

must treat their employees fairly and consistently regardless of the dissimilarities in their characteristics. Failure to do so can lead to charges of discrimination, conflict among groups and individuals, and disgruntled stakeholders. High-performing organizations manage diversity well.

Gardenswartz and Roe explain the complexity of diversity in a model that involves four layers. See Figure 3.4. The model illustrates the organizational factors that affect individuals, such as seniority and status, as well as the external and internal dimensions that influence diversity. The most immediate layer of factors that create diversity relate to one's age, gender, ability, ethnicity, race, and sexual orientation.

Diversity in Canada

Canada has become a truly diverse country, although this might not be apparent to everyone. More than 200 different ethnic origins were reported in the 2006

FIGURE 3.4 Sources of Diversity in the Workforce[40]

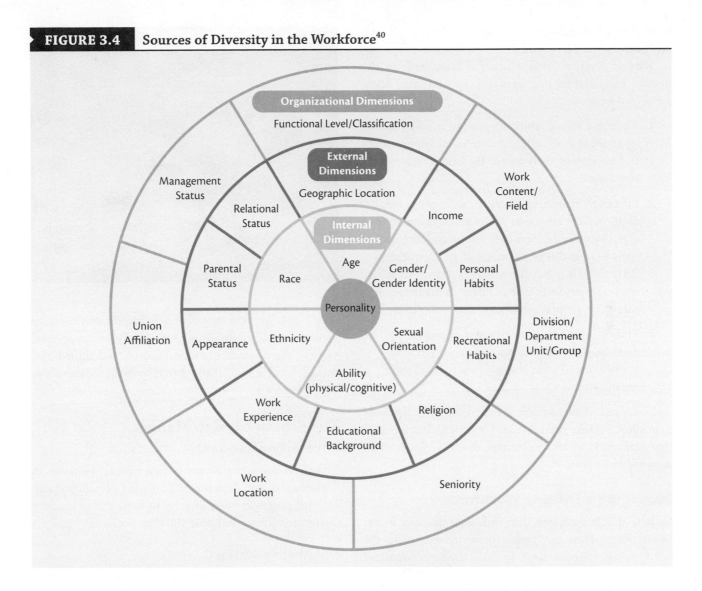

Census. The Aboriginal birth rate is 1.5 times that of non-Aboriginals. An estimated 5 068 100 individuals were members of the visible minority population. They represented 16.2 percent of the total population in 2006, up from 13.4 percent in 2001.[41] The numbers of the visible minority population vary widely across the country. The largest number of people identifying themselves as visible minorities is found in Ontario with almost 3 million, or 23 percent, of the population. British Columbia, with just over one million, represents about one-quarter of its population. Next highest is Alberta with approximately 14 percent of its population identifying themselves as visible minority, followed by Manitoba with almost 10 percent; Quebec has about 9 percent; Northwest Territories have 5.5 percent; Nova Scotia and Yukon both have approximately 4 percent; and, finally, Newfoundland and Labrador, New Brunswick, Prince Edward Island, and Nunavut all have

2 percent or less of the population identifying themselves as visible minorities.

Markham, Ontario has the largest population of visible minorities in Canada: 65 percent. "In what's known as the census metropolitan area of Toronto, 42.9 percent of the population identified themselves as a visible minority. A total of 27.8 percent of the visible minority population was born in Canada. The largest visible minority population was South Asian (684 070), followed by Chinese (486 325) and black (352 220)."[42] Canada accepts about 250 000 immigrants a year. In 2017, visible minorities will be the majority in Canada.

It is still a struggle for many highly skilled immigrants to find adequate and well-paying jobs in Canada. "Recent immigrant men holding a degree earned only 48 cents for each dollar their university-educated, Canadian-born counterparts did. Some 30 percent of male immigrants with a university degree worked in jobs that required no more than a high-school education—more than twice the rate of those born in Canada."[43]

Why is diversity such a pressing issue both in the popular press and for managers and organizations? There are several reasons:

1. There is a strong ethical imperative in many societies to see that all people receive equal opportunities and are treated fairly and justly. Unfair treatment is also illegal.

2. Effectively managing diversity can improve organizational effectiveness. When managers manage diversity well, they not only encourage other managers to treat diverse members of an organization fairly and justly but also realize that diversity is an important resource that can help an organization gain a competitive advantage.

3. Embracing diversity encourages employee participation and thus encourages differences of opinions or ideas that are beneficial to the organization.

In the rest of this section, we examine why effectively managing diversity makes sense. Then we look at the steps that managers can take to manage diversity effectively in their organizations.

Managing a Diverse Workforce

So how should managers deal with such diversity in the labour force? How can underrepresented groups in the labour force increase their participation? The Calgary, Alberta, Economic Development Report suggest breaking down barriers by changing attitudes and stereotypes: "[I]ncreasingly depends upon thoughtful consideration as to how to address the barriers to more fulsome participation. For example, attitudes and beliefs about older workers currently impact employability. Older workers can be perceived to be less productive, less flexible, and less skilled than recent graduates and have more health issues. Hence both employer perceptions and worker perceptions would need to be modified in order to attract and retain older workers."[44]

Age diversity presents managers with unique challenges. Older workers are staying longer in the labour force and retiring later at the same time that **Generation Y** is entering the labour force.

Generation Y Also known as *millennials;* people born between 1981 and 1992.

distributive justice
A moral principle calling for the distribution of pay raises, promotions, and other organizational resources to be based on meaningful contributions that individuals have made and not on personal characteristics over which they have no control.

overt discrimination
Knowingly and willingly denying diverse individuals access to opportunities and outcomes in an organization.

Attaining distributive and procedural justice is a management challenge.

A challenge for managers is to gain respect and commitment from this group of stakeholders. Table 3.3 presents some of the myths about Generation Y and the positive strategies managers can adopt to help integrate them into the labour force.

The Ethical Need to Manage Diversity Effectively

Effectively managing diversity is an ethical obligation in Canadian society. Two moral principles provide managers with guidance when they try to meet this obligation: distributive justice and procedural justice.

Distributive Justice

The principle of **distributive justice** dictates that the distribution of pay raises, promotions, job titles, interesting job assignments, office space, and other organizational resources among members of an organization are fair. The distribution of these outcomes should be based on the meaningful contributions that individuals have made to the organization (such as time, effort, education, skills, abilities, and performance levels) and not on irrelevant personal characteristics over which individuals have no control (such as gender, race, or age).[45] Managers have an obligation to ensure that distributive justice exists in their organizations. This does not mean that all members of an organization receive identical or similar outcomes; rather, it means that members who receive more outcomes than others have made much greater or more significant contributions to the organization.

Is distributive justice common in organizations in corporate Canada? Probably the best way to answer this question is to say that things are getting better. Fifty years ago, **overt discrimination** (knowingly and willingly

TABLE 3.3	Perceptions of Generation Y and Management Strategies to Deal with Them[46]	
Perceptions	**Why?**	**Positive Strategies**
Disrespectful and vocal if dissatisfied	Gen Ys were raised in a less authoritarian manner. Parents and teachers were addressed by their first names, family decisions were made collectively, and they have always been encouraged to express their feelings and opinions. They will question everything.	1. Engage Gen Ys—explain how and why things are done. 2. Provide opportunities for employees to voice opinions and share ideas and concerns. 3. Their respect will be earned by engaging and listening to them.
Lack a strong work ethic	There is not the same pressure to succeed as they are entering a workforce in which they are being sought out. They value the work-life balance.	1. Find out how they define work ethic, and share your expectations. 2. Determine what motivates them. 3. Challenge them.
Not loyal	Gen Ys saw their parents and grandparents downsized after years of loyal service. They are prepared to change jobs as new opportunities arise.	Gen Ys will stay with a company: 1. That engages in meaningful work that makes a difference. 2. Where coworkers share their values. 3. That meets their personal goals. 4. That has a strong sense of social corporate responsibility.
High maintenance	Gen Ys have been raised with high expectations of success and achievement. This generation tends to be more tech savvy, and better educated than any previous generation.	They expect: 1. Constant learning experiences. 2. New challenges. 3. Open lines of communication.
Technologically dependent	Gen Ys were raised in the computer age. They can instantly access, collect, and share information.	1. Use technology in new and innovative ways. 2. Young people need stimulation to stay engaged.
Sense of entitlement	Due to the ease of information access, Gen Ys are aware of what jobs should pay and are likely to question the effort-reward equation. Be prepared to discuss salary.	Gen Ys will work for the organization that has: 1. The greater sense of corporate responsibility. 2. Provides professional development. 3. Provides opportunities and supports work-life balance.
Supportive relationships	Many Gen Ys had a full schedule of sports, music, and special-interest lessons. Coaches and teachers have always played a key role in terms of providing guidance and feedback.	Before a job begins: 1. Clearly outline the parameters. 2. Give them space to tackle the task. 3. Provide constant feedback. 4. Debrief once the task is completed.

denying diverse individuals access to opportunities and outcomes in an organization) against women, people with disabilities, and minorities was not uncommon; today, organizations are inching closer toward the ideal of distributive justice. Statistics comparing the treatment of women and minorities with the treatment of white men suggest that most managers would need to take a proactive approach in order to achieve distributive justice in their organizations. For instance, Calgary-based Enbridge Inc., Canada's largest gas utility, takes a proactive approach to distributive justice by supporting the career development of women employees through the woman@enbridge program. "The program provides peer coaching, mentorship opportunities, and leadership training in an effort to increase the representation of women in senior management positions, encourage their participation on company boards, and retain women employees."[47]

In many countries, managers have not only an ethical obligation to strive to achieve distributive justice in their organizations but also a legal obligation to treat all employees fairly. Managers risk being sued by employees who feel that they are not being fairly treated.

Procedural Justice

The principle of **procedural justice** requires managers to use fair procedures to determine how to distribute outcomes to organizational members.[48] This principle applies to typical procedures such as appraising subordinates' performance, deciding who should receive a raise or a promotion, and deciding whom to lay off when an organization is forced to downsize.

Procedural justice exists, for example, when managers (1) carefully appraise a subordinate's performance; (2) take into account any environmental obstacles to high performance beyond the subordinate's control, such as lack of supplies, machine breakdowns, or dwindling customer demand for a product; and (3) ignore irrelevant personal characteristics, such as the subordinate's age or ethnicity. Like distributive justice, procedural justice is necessary not only to ensure ethical conduct but also to avoid costly lawsuits. A variety of legislative acts affect diversity management in Canada. This is discussed in detail in Chapter 11, Managing Human Resources.

A significant challenge for managers in Canada today is to ensure that the principles of distributive and procedural justice are maintained to avoid discrimination. People with disabilities often find it difficult to gain meaningful employment. Our featured organization in our Focus on the Social Economy case, Just-Work, tries to remedy that.

> **procedural justice**
> A moral principle calling for the use of fair procedures to determine how to distribute outcomes to organizational members.

Each year a significant number of immigrants come to Canada but cannot find suitable employment because their credentials are not recognized. The process to have their experience and education recognized is onerous and lengthy; many end up being underemployed, even when companies are in need of their services. Organizations like UMA Foundation are working with governments at all levels to try to speed up the process of recognizing international accreditation that would help integrate skilled new immigrants into the Canadian economy.[49]

Effectively Managing Diversity Makes Good Business Sense

Though organizations are forced to follow the law, the diversity of organizational members can be a source of competitive advantage in more than a legal sense, as it helps an organization provide customers with better goods and services.[50] In fact, Cirque du Soleil, headquartered in Montreal, Quebec, has made diversity part of its global brand. Its international cast of performers, gymnasts, and artists has given the Canadian company a reputation for unique and quality entertainment experiences in every corner of the world. Cirque du Soleil's competitive advantage is its embodiment of diverse cultures.[51] The variety of points of view and approaches to problems and opportunities that diverse employees provide can improve managerial decision making. Just as the workforce is becoming

---

FOCUS ON ❯ *The Social Economy*

JustWork Economic Initiative

JustWork Economic Initiative is a Vancouver-based nonprofit organization whose mission is to foster dignified, gainful work opportunities for individuals who face major barriers to work. As of 2008, 70 percent of their employees had a permanent physical or mental disability. They develop and support social enterprises which provide flexible employment to their employees and quality goods and services to their customers.

JustWork currently has three social enterprises, of which one of them is JustRenos. The others are Just-Catering and JustPotters.

JustRenos started in Vancouver in June 2009. After running one crew a few days a week for the first eight months, in 2010 they operated two full-time crews. The enterprise is led by a licensed carpenter with more than 20 years of experience and veteran crew leaders with decades of additional industry experience. The work includes decks and fences, complete interior renovations, as well as building maintenance.

Between 2007 and 2010, JustWork (through all its social enterprises) has gone from employing just 14 people with barriers to employment to 33, and from $33 000 in annual revenues to $407 000.[52]

1. Go to the JustWork website. Which model of justice does this organization use in its programs?

2. Why are social enterprises like these necessary in our society? Who benefits and why?

increasingly diverse, so too are the customers who buy an organization's goods or services.

Diverse members of an organization are likely to be attuned to what goods and services diverse segments of the market want and do not want. Major car companies, for example, are increasingly assigning women to their design teams to ensure that the needs and desires of female customers (a growing segment of the market) are taken into account in new car design.

Effectively managing diversity makes good business sense for another reason. More and more, consumer and civil rights organizations are demanding that companies think about diversity issues from a variety of angles. For instance, Toronto-based Royal Bank of Canada found its efforts to acquire North Carolina–based Centura Banks Inc. under attack by Inner City Press/Community on the Move (ICP), a U.S. civil rights group. In April 2001, the group asked American and Canadian regulators to delay approval of the acquisition to allow further investigation of alleged abusive lending practices carried out by Centura. "Centura's normal interest rate lending disproportionately denies and excludes credit applications from people of colour," said Matthew Lee, ICP executive director.[53] ICP alleged that in two American cities, Centura denied applications for home purchase from Black people three times more frequently than applications from White people. The group wanted Royal Bank to guarantee that it would end the alleged unfair lending practices.

Women wearing the hijab, the traditional head cover of Muslim women, face discrimination when they look for jobs in Canada. A recent study found that 40 percent of the time when visibly Muslim women asked if jobs were available, they were either told there were not or were not given a chance to apply for a job.

In the province of Quebec, a debate on the reasonable accommodation of how religious and ethnic minorities should be integrated into the province was front and centre in 2007 when the premier of the province initiated hearings into the issue. The state commission quickly revealed sentiments that polarized the population on whether Muslim religious symbols, including wearing the hijab, should be allowed in public service. Christian symbols and practices were not part of the debate, leading the Muslim minority to charge the government with overt racism toward non-dominant cultures and calling into question the view of Canada as tolerant of cultural diversity.[54]

In 2009, Canada's largest supermarket chain, Loblaw, purchased the Asian food retailer T&T Supermarket Inc. to take advantage of the growing ethnic food business. T&T serves South Asian and Chinese families in

Muslim women face discrimination in the workplace.

Ontario, Alberta, and British Columbia. In 2008, this segment of the market spent 23 percent more than the average on groceries and accounted for about one-third of grocery spending in Vancouver and Toronto. Allan Leighton, president of Loblaw, said, "The ethnic market opportunity in Canada is vast. Today we have a relatively small share. Our objective is to be the #1 player. T&T gives us the platform to build to this objective."[55]

Being aware of diversity issues extends beyond employees to include the issues of suppliers, clients, and customers. Nestlé Canada recently announced that it was planning to do away with its nut-free products because trying to keep the production area free of nut products seemed more costly than it was beneficial. Nestlé Canada was soon deluged with protests from Canadian families who had relied upon such products as Kit Kat, Mirage, Coffee Crisp, and Aero chocolate bars and Smarties. Between 1 and 2 percent of all Canadians, and perhaps as many as 8 percent of children, are allergic to peanuts and other nuts, which is why the protest was so vocal. Within a month, Nestlé Canada announced that it would go back to producing these candies in a nut-free facility to cater to its consumers with this particular disability. Nestlé's initial decision factored in "a growing public demand for chocolate with nuts, as well as the need to protect jobs at its Toronto plant."[56] Nestlé senior vice-president Graham Lute still wants to expand Nestlé's manufacturing in Canada but says, "We'll just execute it in a different way, but not as attractive a way as it would have been before, from a sheer business point of view."[57] In other words, the attention to this particular diversity issue has caused the company to rethink part of its business strategy.

Increasing Diversity Awareness

It is natural to see other people from your own point of view because your feelings, thoughts, attitudes, and experiences guide how you perceive and interact with others. The ability to appreciate diversity, however, requires people to become aware of other perspectives and the various attitudes and experiences of others. Many diversity awareness programs in organizations strive to increase managers' and employees' awareness of (1) their own attitudes, biases, and stereotypes and (2) the differing perspectives of diverse managers, subordinates, coworkers, and customers. Diversity awareness programs often have these goals[58]:

1. Providing organizational members with accurate information about diversity

2. Uncovering personal biases and stereotypes

3. Assessing personal beliefs, attitudes, and values and learning about other points of view

4. Overturning inaccurate stereotypes and beliefs about different groups

5. Developing an atmosphere in which people feel free to share their differing perspectives

6. Improving understanding of others who are different from oneself

Many managers use a varied approach to increase diversity awareness and skills in their organizations: Films and printed materials are supplemented by experiential exercises to uncover any hidden **bias** (the systematic tendency to use information about others in ways that result in inaccurate perceptions) or **stereotype** (simplistic and often inaccurate belief about the typical characteristics of particular groups of people). Sometimes simply providing a forum for people to learn about and discuss their differing attitudes, values, and experiences can be a powerful means for increasing awareness. Also useful are role-playing exercises in which people act out problems that result from lack of awareness and then indicate the increased

bias The systematic tendency to use information about others in ways that result in inaccurate perceptions.

stereotype Simplistic and often inaccurate beliefs about the typical characteristics of particular groups of people.

understanding that comes from appreciating others' viewpoints. Accurate information and training experiences can debunk stereotypes. Group exercises, role plays, and diversity-related experiences can help organizational members develop the skills they need to work effectively with a variety of people.

Managers sometimes hire outside consultants to provide diversity training. For instance, Trevor Wilson, president of Toronto-based Omnibus Consulting, has presented employment equity programs to such clients as IBM Canada Ltd., Molson Inc., and National Grocers Co. Ltd.[59] Some organizations have their own in-house diversity experts, such as Maureen Geddes at Union Gas, based in Chatham, Ontario.

The Importance of Top-Management Commitment to Diversity

When top management is truly committed to diversity, top managers embrace diversity through their actions and example, spread the message that diversity can be a source of competitive advantage, deal effectively with diverse employees, and are willing to commit organizational resources to managing diversity. That last step alone is not enough. If top managers commit resources to diversity (such as providing money for training programs) but as individuals do not value diversity, any steps they take are likely to fail.

Some organizations recruit and hire women for first-level and middle-management positions, but after being promoted into middle management, some of these female managers quit to start their own businesses. A major reason for their departure is their belief that they will not be promoted into top-management positions because of a lack of commitment to diversity among members of the top-management team. As Professor David Sharp of the Richard Ivey School of Business notes, "It seems that some Canadian women entrepreneurs are neither born nor made. They are pushed."[60] Enbridge is an example of an organization that has been very proactive in making sure women will not leave, through its efforts to aggressively promote women to upper-management positions.

By now, it should be clear that managers can take a variety of steps to manage diversity effectively. Many of the companies, such as Enbridge, Air Canada, and others, that are recognized for exceptional diversity and inclusive programs and their managers continue to develop and experiment with new diversity initiatives to meet this ethical and business challenge.[61] Although some steps prove unsuccessful, it is clear that managers must make a long-term commitment to diversity. Training sessions oriented toward the short term are doomed to failure: Participants quickly slip back into their old ways of doing things. The effective management of diversity, like the management of the organization as a whole, is an ongoing process: It never stops and never ends. The main reasons for managing diversity are to improve productivity and remain competitive, to form better work relationships among employees, to enhance social responsibility, and to address legal concerns.

> **LO5** Identify instances of workplace harassment, and discuss how to prevent its occurrence.

Harassment in the Workplace

Harassment in the workplace can take many forms. It refers to any behaviour directed toward an employee that is known to be or ought to be known to be offensive and unwelcome. According to Service Canada, "[i]t comprises objectionable conduct, comment or display made on either a one time or continuous basis that demeans, belittles, or causes personal humiliation or embarrassment to an employee of the department. It includes harassment within the meaning of the Canadian Human Rights Act, which is based on any of the prohibited grounds of discrimination listed in that Act."[62] Abuse of authority and sexual harassment are two common forms of **workplace harassment**, which we will discuss here. Abuse of authority occurs when the legitimate power vested in a position is used improperly to influence the behaviour of an employee. Threats that intimidate and coerce employee behaviour are examples of abuse of authority, as is blackmail. When "an individual improperly uses the power and authority inherent in his or her position to endanger an employee's job, undermine the performance of that job, threaten the economic livelihood of the employee, or in any way interfere with or influence the career of the employee," they are committing an abuse of authority.[63] Bullying is a form of abuse of authority when committed by a boss. "Over 72 percent of bullies are bosses, some are co-workers, and a minority of employees bullies higherups. A bully is equally likely to be a man or a woman."[64]

Sexual harassment is defined by the Supreme Court of Canada as unwelcome behaviour of a sexual nature in the workplace that negatively affects the work environment or leads to adverse job-related consequences for the employee. Sexual harassment is prevalent in many organizations today. Several women in the RCMP came forward recently to disclose they were the victims of sexual harassment and gender abuse for many years. They charge that

the culture of the organization, traditionally male dominated, supported and tacitly encouraged abuse of its female officers. In 2012, the women launched a class action suit against the RCMP for failing to protect them. And although in 1987 the Supreme Court ruled that employers will be held responsible for harassment by their employees and that the employers should promote a workplace free of harassment, one is left to wonder if the Supreme Court of Canada's regulations have any teeth. One RCMP officer was convicted of sexual harassment in 2012 after confessing to a number of abuses, but instead of being fired or directed to mandatory counselling, the offender was simply transferred from Ontario to British Columbia to serve at another branch of the RCMP.[65] Many were outraged at what was perceived as a reward rather than a punishment.

Although women are the most frequent victims of sexual harassment—particularly those in male-dominated occupations, or those who occupy positions stereotypically associated with certain gender relationships (such as a female secretary reporting to a male boss)—men can be victims, too. Several male employees at Jenny Craig in the United States said that they were subject to lewd and inappropriate comments from female coworkers and managers.[66]

Sexual harassment seriously damages the victims as well as the reputation of the organization. It is not only unethical but also illegal. Beyond the negative publicity, sexual harassment can cost organizations large amounts of money. Managers have an ethical obligation to ensure that they, their coworkers, and their subordinates never engage in sexual harassment, even unintentionally.

Forms of Sexual Harassment

There are two basic forms of sexual harassment: *quid pro quo sexual harassment* and *hostile work environment sexual harassment*. **Quid pro quo sexual harassment** occurs when a harasser asks or forces an employee to perform sexual favours to keep a job, receive a promotion or raise, obtain some other work-related opportunity, or avoid receiving negative consequences such as demotion or dismissal.[67] This "Sleep with me, honey, or you're fired" form of harassment is the more extreme form and leaves no doubt in anyone's mind that sexual harassment has taken place.[68] A study conducted by York University in 1999 found that

workplace harassment Any behaviour directed toward an employee that is known to be or ought to be known to be offensive and unwelcome.

sexual harassment Unwelcome behaviour of a sexual nature in the workplace that negatively affects the work environment or leads to adverse job-related consequences for the employee.

quid pro quo sexual harassment Asking or forcing an employee to perform sexual favours in exchange for some reward or to avoid negative consequences.

3 percent of working Canadian women reported having experienced quid pro quo sexual harassment.[69]

Hostile work environment sexual harassment is more subtle. It occurs when organizational members are faced with an intimidating, hostile, or offensive work environment because of their gender.[70] Lewd jokes, sexually oriented comments, displays of pornography, displays or distribution of sexually oriented objects, and sexually oriented remarks about someone's physical appearance are examples of hostile work environment sexual harassment. About 45 percent of working Canadian women reported this form of harassment in the recent study at York University. Barbara Orser, a researcher with the Conference Board of Canada, noted that "sexual harassment is more likely to occur in workplace environments that tolerate bullying, intimidation, yelling, innuendo, and other forms of discourteous behaviour."[71]

A hostile work environment interferes with organizational members' ability to perform their jobs effectively and has been deemed illegal by the courts. Managers who engage in hostile work environment harassment or allow others to do so risk costly lawsuits for their organizations, as was the experience of Magna International Inc. based in Aurora, Ontario.[72] Sexual harassment is against the law. "Sexual harassment in the workplace is an abuse of power in working relationships. Like other forms of sexual violence, sexual harassment both reflects and reinforces the inequality between men and women in our society. No employee is safe if sexual harassment is ignored! Organizations are responsible to address and investigate all complaints of sexual harassment."[73]

Steps Managers Can Take to Eradicate Workplace Harassment

Managers have an ethical obligation to eradicate workplace harassment in their organizations. There are many ways to accomplish this objective. Here are four initial steps that managers can take to deal with the problem.[74]

1. *Develop and clearly communicate a workplace harassment policy endorsed by top management.* This policy should include prohibitions against both general workplace and sexual harassment. It should contain: (1) examples of types of behaviour that are unacceptable, (2) a procedure for employees to use to report instances of harassment, (3) a discussion of the disciplinary actions that will be taken when harassment has taken place, and (4) a commitment to educate and train organizational members about sexual harassment.

2. *Use a fair complaint procedure to investigate charges of workplace harassment.* Such a procedure should (1) be managed by a neutral third party, (2) ensure that complaints are dealt with promptly and thoroughly, (3) protect and fairly treat victims, and (4) ensure that alleged harassers are fairly treated.

3. *When it has been determined that workplace harassment has taken place, take corrective actions as soon as possible.* These actions can vary depending on the severity of the harassment. When harassment is extensive, prolonged over a period of time, of a quid pro quo nature, or severely objectionable in some other manner, corrective action may include firing the harasser.

4. *Provide workplace harassment education and training to organizational members, including managers.* Managers at Du Pont, for example, developed Du Pont's "A Matter of Respect" program to help educate employees about workplace harassment and prevent it from happening.

Barbara Orser, a researcher with the Conference Board of Canada, noted that most large Canadian organizations have harassment policies on paper. However, many lack a clear resolution process.

Summary and Review

LO1 What Are Ethics? Ethics are moral principles or beliefs about what is right or wrong. These beliefs guide people in their dealings with other individuals and groups that have an interest in the situation at hand (stakeholders) and provide a basis for deciding whether a behaviour is right and proper. Many organizations have a formal code of ethics derived mainly from societal ethics, professional ethics, and the individual ethics of the organization's top managers.

LO2 Ethics and Stakeholders Managers can apply ethical standards to help themselves determine the proper way to behave toward organizational stakeholders—the people and communities that are affected by business actions. Managers can use three models of ethics in promoting ethical decision making: *moral rights, utilitarian,* and *justice models.* Promoting ethical and socially responsible behaviour is a major managerial challenge. Written codes of ethics help guide employee behaviour and help managers make good decisions.

LO3 Social Responsibility Managers of traditional, for-profit businesses generally take one of four approaches to the issue of socially responsible behaviour: *obstructionist, defensive, accommodative,* or *proactive.* Proactive approaches benefit organizational stakeholders and create a competitive advantage by promoting sustainable practices that are popular and ecologically friendly.

LO4 Diversity Diversity refers to differences among people due to age, gender, race, ethnicity, religion, sexual orientation, socio-economic background, position status, and capabilities or disabilities. Effectively managing diversity is an ethical obligation that makes good business sense. Diversity can be managed effectively if top management is committed to principles of *distributive and procedural justice,* values diversity as a source of competitive advantage, and is willing to devote organizational resources to increasing employees' diversity awareness and diversity skills. The primary reasons for managing diversity are to improve productivity and remain competitive, to form better work relationships among employees, to enhance social responsibility, and to address legal concerns.

LO5 Harassment in the Workplace Workplace harassment is any conduct that is known or ought to be reasonably known to be offensive and unwelcome. It can take the form of abuse of authority, bullying, and sexual harassment. Steps that managers can take to halt harassment include developing and communicating a workplace harassment policy endorsed by top management, using fair complaint procedures; ensuring prompt corrective action when harassment occurs; and training and educating organizational members on workplace harassment.

KEY TERMS

accommodative approach	hostile work environment sexual harassment	professional ethics
bias	impact investing	quid pro quo sexual harassment
codes of ethics	individual ethics	reputation
defensive approach	justice model	sexual harassment
distributive justice	moral rights model	social audit
diversity	obstructionist approach	social responsibility
ethical decisions	organizational stakeholders	societal ethics
ethical dilemma		stereotype
ethics	overt discrimination	unethical decisions
ethics ombudsperson	proactive approach	utilitarian model
Generation Y	procedural justice	workplace harassment

WRAP-UP TO OPENING CASE

Mountain Equipment Co-op: Doing Things Right

Mountain Equipment Co-op (MEC) is a model company that strives to do the right thing when it comes to balancing stakeholder needs and social responsibility. After having read and understood the concepts in this chapter, you should be able to answer the following questions:

1. *Who are the stakeholders in this organization? How does this differ from a traditional corporation?*

   ANSWER: Organizational stakeholders are shareholders, employees, customers, suppliers, and others who have an interest, claim, or stake in an organization and in what it does. In this case there are no shareholders that one would find in a typical, traditional business corporation whose interests would be maximization of the value of the shares they own and payment of profits in the form of dividends. MEC is structured as a co-operative enterprise; MEC's 3.5 million members benefit by using the services of the company and in determining how the organization should operate. Each member has only one vote, unlike shareholders in a traditional publicly traded corporation who have one vote per share owned. This prevents one person from holding all the power and decision making. Members are the customers and are key stakeholders in MEC. The other stakeholders include the suppliers/manufacturers in Canada and 12 other nations, 1500 employees in 14 stores across Canada, and the communities in which they sell and locate facilities. MEC obtains all materials from ethical sources and adheres to fair labour practices. It contributes about 1 percent of its annual sales to community programs that invest in conservation and recreational services. Striving to reduce its environmental footprint, MEC sets goals for waste, water, and CO_2 reductions and conducts a social audit to determine its performance on social responsibility.

2. *Which model of ethics underlies MEC's decisions?*

   ANSWER: The three models of ethics used by managers are the utilitarian, moral rights, and justice models. The utilitarian model suggests that ethical decisions produce the greatest good for the greatest number of people. Incorporating as a co-operative allows no one member to have more power than any other. The moral rights model holds that an ethical decision is one that best maintains and protects the fundamental or inalienable rights and privileges of the people affected by it. Each member of MEC enjoys the same rights and privileges as any other. The justice model of ethics argues that decisions should be based on the degree to which they will result in a fair or equitable distribution of outcomes for stakeholders. MEC ensures that suppliers adhere to fair labour practices and use sustainable inputs such as organic cotton. Any surplus that remains after paying employees, suppliers, and operating costs is distributed back to the members. It can be argued that MEC uses all three models of ethics in its decision making.

3. *How would you describe MEC's approach to social responsibility?*

ANSWER: There are four approaches to social responsibility: obstructionist, defensive, accommodative, and proactive. The obstructionist approach is illustrated by managers who are willing to engage in and cover up unethical and illegal behaviour. The defensive approach is taken by managers who do nothing more toward enhancing the well-being of society than obeying the law. The accommodative approach is taken by managers who will comply with requests from stakeholders to act socially responsible ways, by supporting a charity, for example, but does not actively seek ways to enhance social well-being. The proactive approach goes beyond compliance with the law and requests from stakeholders to do the right thing. Managers taking this approach actively seek out ways they can make better decisions that are sustainable and balanced. MEC critically examines every aspect of its operations with a view to improving its environmental performance and makes the results transparent by publicly reporting them. They have codes of conduct for ethical sourcing, fair labour practices, and goals to green all aspects of their operations. They actively seek out ways to help communities and groups conserve and preserve wildlife. All of which enhances their mission to build quality gear and minimize their environmental impact. This illustrates the proactive approach to social responsibility.

Management in Action

TOPICS FOR DISCUSSION AND ACTION

LEVEL 1 Knowledge & Comprehension

1. Describe the concept of ethics and the three different models of ethics.

2. Outline the four approaches to social responsibility.

3. Define diversity, workplace harassment, and sexual harassment.

LEVEL 2 Application & Analysis

4. Ask a manager to describe an instance of ethical behaviour and an instance of unethical behaviour that she or he observed. What caused these behaviours, and what were the outcomes?

5. Search business magazines such as *Report on Business* or *Canadian Business* or a business podcast for one example of ethical behaviour and one example of unethical behaviour. What caused these behaviours, and what were the outcomes?

6. Discuss an occasion when you may have been stereotyped and as a result treated unfairly. What caused these behaviours, and what were the outcomes?

LEVEL 3 Synthesis & Evaluation

7. Compare and contrast the principles of distributive and procedural justice. What should managers do to support these principles in their organizations?

8. Develop a list of standards for ethical behaviour that you can incorporate into your own personal code of ethics.

9. Design a program to manage diversity in a university.

SELF-REFLECTION EXERCISE

Read the following examples of ethical dilemmas. Analyze the situation and the stakeholder involvement using the three models of ethics. What would you do?

1. You are an employee at a small children's clothing store. There is a sale coming up, and your boss asks you to mark up the prices by the equivalent amount of the discount so that customers still pay the same price even though they think they are getting a deal.

2. A good friend of yours who has dark skin and an Arab name applied for a job at an ice cream parlour and was told that the vacancy had been filled. Not knowing of her experience, you, with fair skin and an Anglo-Saxon name, applied later the same day and got the position.

SMALL GROUP BREAKOUT EXERCISE

Discuss the following scenario with your teammates, and answer the questions below. A very important division meeting at XYZ Company was scheduled in conflict with a religious holiday of a minority religious group. This holiday is one of the most important and solemn holidays for this religion. An employee approached his manager and explained that he would be unable to attend the meeting due to the religious holiday. The manager responded by telling the employee that he should not expect to succeed in this company if he did not attend mandatory meetings such as this one.

1. In what ways, if any, were biases, stereotypes, or overt discrimination involved in this situation?

2. What could you or the person who was treated unfairly have done to improve matters and immediately rectify the injustice?

3. If you had authority over the decision maker (for example, you were his or her manager or supervisor), what steps would you take to ensure that the decision maker no longer treated diverse individuals unfairly?

BUSINESS PLANNING EXERCISE

Your professor may ask you to write a business plan for a new venture or a strategic plan for an existing venture. At the end of every chapter, you will have an opportunity to apply managerial and organizational concepts to the exercise of writing a business plan. Refer to Appendix A.

After reading this chapter, you and your group should discuss who the stakeholders are in your new venture, how competing interests should be balanced, and what set of values and professional ethics should be incorporated into your business plan.

1. Write a values statement and a code of ethics that you can incorporate into your vision and mission statements.

MANAGING ETHICALLY EXERCISE

The state of California is having an energy crisis. You are a manager at BC Hydro. You have discovered that it is possible to anticipate periods of severe power shortage and plan for them by letting your reservoirs rise overnight and then opening them to create hydro-electricity. Electricity can thus be produced inexpensively but sold for a premium. Your research of the law suggests that this behaviour would be consistent with what is allowed under the rules of the electricity marketplace. Is the idea good business, or is this unethical behaviour?

MANAGEMENT CHALLENGE EXERCISE

Expensive Lesson In Using Discipline[75]

Rather than shrieking with delight, Christine Pynaker's heart sank upon receiving a bouquet of flowers and a gold necklace. Yet again, Wayne Brazeau, 25 years her senior, was after her. For more than three years, Brazeau had showered Pynaker with gifts, including flowers, jewellery—even an airline ticket to visit her parents in Spain—accompanied by romantic cards and emails.

Pynaker's attempts at rebuffing Brazeau, who, like her, was employed as an international representative for the International Brotherhood of Electrical Workers (IBEW), were futile. Although she accepted many of the presents, she also told Brazeau that his conduct was offensive. Finally, after more than three years, Pynaker flatly told Brazeau that he was too old; that no relationship could ever materialize between them; and that she regarded his behaviour as sexual harassment.

Brazeau, properly, immediately ceased directing any attention toward Pynaker. But, improperly, he also ceased being as supportive of her as he had been in the past. Over the next several years, Brazeau was episodically hostile to Pynaker: failing to provide her with the materials and information required to effectively do her work; making disparaging remarks about her sex life; and accusing a male colleague of flirting with her.

Believing that Brazeau was retaliating for her earlier rebuff, Pynaker lodged a complaint of sexual harassment with her employer.

1. You are the manager. What would you do?
2. What other alternative actions could Pynaker have taken?

MANAGEMENT PORTFOLIO PROJECT

Answer the following questions about the organization you have chosen to follow:

1. Briefly describe all the stakeholders. How does the company satisfy all the different needs and interests of each group?
2. Does the company have a formal code of ethics? How has it dealt with ethical dilemmas in the past (look at historical news reports).
3. How does the company approach social responsibility? Which model does it use?
4. How does the company approach managing diversity?

VIDEO MANAGEMENT CASE connect

Bakery with a Conscience

Dancing Deer is an inner-city Boston baking company that is exceptional in its commitment to employees and the community.

1. What values provide the foundation for Dancing Deer? How do these values benefit the company?

2. How does Dancing Deer meet the expectations of its various stakeholders?

3. How does Trish Carter illustrate a commitment to a diverse workforce?

Management Case

Is It Right to Use Child Labour?

In recent years, the number of Canadian and U.S. companies that buy their inputs from low-cost foreign suppliers has been growing, and concern about the ethics associated with employing young children in factories has been increasing. In Pakistan, children as young as six years work long hours in deplorable conditions to make rugs and carpets for export to Western countries. Many children in poor countries throughout Africa, Asia, and South America work in similar conditions.

Opinions about the ethics of child labour vary widely. Some believe that the practice is totally reprehensible and should be outlawed on a global level. Another view, championed by *The Economist* magazine (www.economist.com), is that while nobody wants to see children working in factories, citizens of rich countries need to recognize that in poor countries a child is often the family's only breadwinner. Thus, denying children employment would cause whole families to suffer, and correcting one wrong (child labour) might produce a greater wrong (poverty). Instead, *The Economist* favours regulating the conditions under which children are employed and hope that over time, as poor countries become richer, the need for child employment will disappear.

Many Canadian and U.S. retailers buy their clothing from low-cost foreign suppliers, and managers in these companies have had to take their own ethical stance on child labour. In Chapter 1, we discussed how Mountain Equipment Co-op (www.mec.ca) was facing demands from some of its members to discontinue manufacturing clothing in China. Walmart Canada (www.walmart.com) has been criticized for its policy of doing business with third-party suppliers—such as Hampton Industries, Sutton Creations, Global Gold, Stretch-O-Rama, Cherry Stix, and By Design—that import goods from Myanmar (Burma), which engages in forced labour, including that of children. In defence of the company's actions, Walmart Canada spokesman Andrew Pelletier noted, "We have a policy we are looking at, of monitoring vendors sourcing from other countries. . . . For other corporations, our expectation is that they would take their direction from the Canadian government, that's what we would recommend they would do."

At present, the Canadian government, unlike the U.S. government, does not have regulations governing the use of child labour in foreign countries by Canadian companies.

1. Should Canada develop regulations governing the use of child labour in foreign countries by Canadian companies?

2. You are the manager of a company considering setting up a factory in a foreign country that allows child labour. What would be the benefits to your company for deciding not to use child labour?

3. You are the manager of a company considering setting up a factory in a foreign country that allows child labour. Should you simply rely on the laws of that country when deciding what to do about child labour? Why, or why not?

Mc Graw Hill **connect**

Connect allows you to practise important concepts at your own pace and on your own schedule, with 24/7 online access to an eBook, practice quizzes, video cases, interactive exercises, study tools, and more.

End of Part II: Continuing Case

CARROT TOPS: CREATING AND SUSTAINING A COMPETITIVE ADVANTAGE

As the population grew, so too did the competition. Pretty soon it was apparent that Mac's Milk and Shoppers Drug Mart were able to offer customers a wider selection of lower-priced products than Mel's store. Mel had to find a new way to manage his small business if it was going to survive. He began brainstorming new strategies. He researched trends in the food industry. There might be a niche for supplying specialty products, he thought, such as organic and gourmet foods, which were more profitable to sell. He would no longer be competing against giants like Shoppers. He changed the name of his store to Carrot Tops and stocked it with a wide variety of gourmet Canadian food products. He began to offer fine foods, local cheeses, fresh bread, and organic fruits and vegetables. Finding a reliable source of products from local farmers and producers could be a stumbling block to his success, but he did have Janet Khan to head up produce procurement and logistics.

His plan worked. Customers loved his new upscale supermarket concept. The premium products he had chosen to stock sold quickly. Realizing that he needed to capitalize on his success to protect his growing business, Mel continually expanded the variety of premium organic foods and drinks he sold. Taking advantage of the popularity of the name Carrot Tops, he began to offer his own store-label products. Today, over 80 percent of the products Carrot Tops sells sport its own label. Every product adheres to sustainable environmental production practices.

To compete in the premium-quality segment of the supermarket business and keep customers buying high-priced organic products, Carrot Tops needed to provide excellent customer service. Mel provided training and support. The store employees feel valued by Mel and provide excellent customer service and develop personal relationships with customers, who are often on first-name terms. Mel feels really good about the approach Carrot Tops is taking toward its stakeholders. He is considering formalizing a Code of Ethics to guide new employees and introduce them to the culture of the organization.

Drawing on all segments of this case:

1. Identify the stakeholders and their issues in this case.

2. What threats and opportunities exist in the task and general environments for Carrot Tops? Recommend how Mel should deal with them.

3. How does Mel use the building blocks of a competitive advantage?

4. How would you characterize the Carrot Tops approach to ethics and social responsibility?

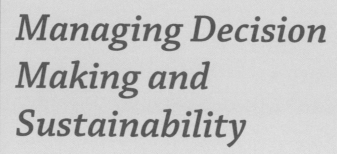

Managing Decision Making and Sustainability

LEARNING OUTCOMES

LO1 Differentiate between programmed and nonprogrammed decisions, and explain why nonprogrammed decision making is a complex, uncertain process.

LO2 Describe the six steps managers should take to make sound decisions.

LO3 Explain how cognitive biases can affect decision making and lead managers to make poor decisions.

LO4 Explain the role that a sustainability strategy, organizational learning, and creativity play in helping managers improve their decisions.

LO5 Explain how the utilization of information and management information systems (MIS) can be vital to a manager's decision-making processes.

Opening Case

Good Decision Making at PUMA

When Jochen Zeitz took over as CEO of PUMA AG in 1993 at the age of 30, the company was facing major threats.[1] PUMA AG, based in the small German sneaker-producing town of Herzogenaurach,[2] had lost money for the past eight years and PUMA North America was facing imminent bankruptcy.[3]

Facing tough decisions about how to turn around the company's fortunes, Zeitz decided that rather than trying to compete based on the performance capabilities of its athletic shoes and equipment, PUMA would focus more on style, colours, and lines of shoes produced in a sustainable manner. Essentially, Zeitz saw a potential opportunity in trying to start up a new division focused on experimental fashion and sport as lifestyle. Of course, Zeitz also made difficult decisions to respond to the threats the company was facing by, for example, dramatically reducing costs of production and taking back control over distribution of PUMA products in North America.[4] Another example is the decision to update its policies on sustainable production. In collaboration with Greenpeace, PUMA is engaged in a detoxification process of all of its operations. PUMA feels that an update of its sustainability policies must be based on sound decisions and has therefore started a dialogue with industry peers, experts, and the chemical industry to investigate which substances can be phased out with existing technology and where more research is needed.[5] PUMA continues to produce high-performance athletic shoes and gear for serious sport.[6]

Nonetheless, Zeitz's bold decision to pursue the world of fashion and style was a major contributor to PUMA becoming the fourth biggest athletic apparel company worldwide. Recognizing the importance of coming up with creative designs and sustainable products,

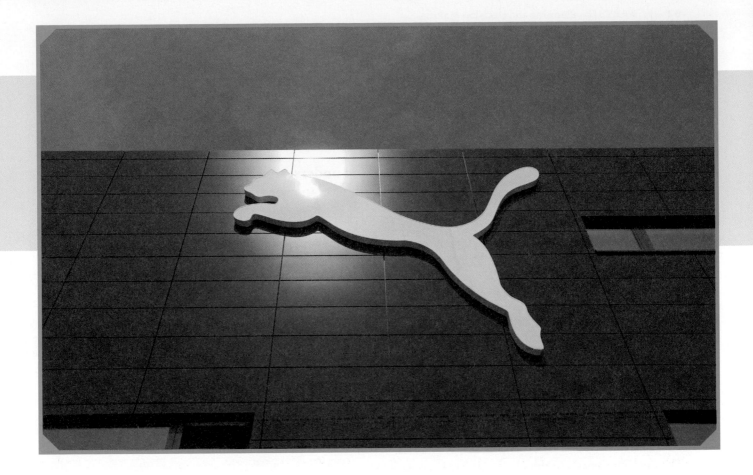

he decided to create a new division called "sport life-style" led by Antonio Bertone, then a 21-year-old skateboarder.[7] The division was tasked to create experimental fashion products. In 1998, Bertone partnered with German fashion designer Jil Sander to turn PUMA's traditional 1960s-style cleated soccer shoe into a trendy fashion sneaker using funky colours and suede. At first, this new experimental product line received a lot of skepticism from industry experts and retailers alike; famed soccer player Pelé had worn PUMA cleats, and it was unthinkable to many that PUMA would succeed in the world of fashion. As Zeitz indicates, "It took a while—and from my perspective, a lot of energy—to protect this new little child [the lifestyle group] of PUMA from getting killed . . . Eventually, it became the entire company."[8]

Customers loved the more ecologically friendly, retro look and edgy colours of the new line of sneakers, which are now sold in a variety of venues ranging from Foot Locker to high-end stores like Barneys to upscale department stores. PUMA has its own showcase boutique in the meatpacking district of Manhattan and 74 stores around the world.[9]

Zeitz continues to pursue new opportunities at PUMA—reinventing traditional products to combine performance with style—and continues to partner with creative thinkers such as Zuly Bet, born in Mali and now a Paris fashion designer, and Yasuhiro Mihara of Japan to create new products.[10]

Former skateboarder Bertone is now based in Boston as PUMA's global director of brand management. Now a top manager, Bertone continues to make decisions to seize opportunities for creative and innovative product lines such as the limited-edition line called Thrift (products made from vintage clothing) and Mongolian Shoe BBQ (shoes that can be customized online).[11]

Zeitz continues to make decisions in response to opportunities and, in the process, has expanded PUMA's range of products in far-reaching directions.[12] Clearly, the decisions Zeitz and other managers make at PUMA are key contributors to the success of PUMA today.[13] And while much uncertainty and ambiguity surrounded these decisions at the time they were made, and they were sometimes met with skepticism, they have propelled PUMA to be a powerhouse of innovation and sustainability.[14]

After reading and understanding the concepts in this chapter, you should be able to answer the following questions:

1. *What type of decision was made by Zeitz when PUMA launched into sport lifestyle fashions?*

2. *Identify the threats and opportunities in the task environment that impact PUMA's decision.*

3. *How does PUMA foster sustainability and promote creativity and innovation? Why is this good decision making?*

Overview

The opening scenario in this chapter allows us to see how decision making can have a profound influence on organizational effectiveness. The decisions that managers make at all levels in companies large and small can have a dramatic impact on the growth and prosperity of these companies and the well-being of their employees, customers, and other stakeholders. Yet such decisions can be very difficult to make because they are fraught with uncertainty.

In this chapter we examine how managers make decisions and explore how individual, group, and organizational factors affect the quality of the decisions they make and thus determine organizational performance. We discuss the nature of managerial decision making and examine some models of the decision-making process that help reveal the complexities of successful decision making. Then we outline the main steps of the decision-making process; in addition, we explore the biases that may cause capable managers to make poor decisions both as individuals and as a group. We then examine how managers can promote sustainability, organizational learning, and creativity to improve the quality of their decision making. Finally, we look at how management information systems (MIS) are changing the way managers utilize technology in decision making. By the end of this chapter, you will understand the crucial role that decision making plays in creating a high-performing organization.

decision making The process by which managers respond to opportunities and threats by analyzing options and making determinations about specific organizational goals and courses of action.

Differentiate between programmed and nonprogrammed decisions, and explain why nonprogrammed decision making is a complex, uncertain process.   **LO1**

The Nature of Managerial Decision Making

Every time a manager acts to plan, organize, direct, or control organizational activities, he or she makes a stream of decisions. In opening a new restaurant, for example, managers have to decide where to locate it, what kinds of food to provide to customers, what kinds of people to employ, and so on. Decision making is a basic part of every task in which a managers perform.

As we discussed in Chapter 2, one of the main tasks facing a manager is to manage the organizational environment. Forces in the external environment give rise to many opportunities and threats for managers and their organizations. In addition, inside an organization managers must address many opportunities and threats that may arise during the course of utilizing organizational resources. To deal with these opportunities and threats, managers must make decisions—that is, they must select one solution from a set of alternatives. **Decision making** is the process by which managers respond to the opportunities and threats that confront them by analyzing the options and making determinations, or *decisions,* about specific organizational goals and courses of action. Good decisions result in the selection of appropriate goals and courses of action that increase organizational performance; bad decisions result in lower performance.

Decision making in response to opportunities occurs when managers search for ways to improve organizational performance to benefit customers, employees, and other stakeholder groups. In the opening case, Jochen Zeitz turned around PUMA's fortunes by the decisions he made in response to opportunities, and he continues to engage in decision making in response to opportunities to this day. *Decision making in response to threats* occurs when events inside or outside the organization are adversely affecting organizational performance and managers are searching for ways to increase performance.[15] When Zeitz become CEO of PUMA, high production costs and an ineffective distribution system were threats that prompted Zeitz to make a number of decisions to improve the performance and viability of the company.[16] Decision making is central to being a manager, and whenever managers engage in planning, organizing, leading, and controlling—their four principal functions—they are constantly making decisions.

Managers are always searching for ways to make better decisions to improve organizational performance. At the same time, they do their best to avoid costly mistakes that will hurt organizational performance. Examples of spectacularly good decisions include Liz Claiborne's decision in the 1980s to focus on producing clothes for the growing number of women entering the workforce—a decision that contributed to making her company one of the largest clothing manufacturers. Also, Bill Gates's decision to buy a computer operating system for $50 000 from a small company in Seattle and sell it to IBM for the new IBM personal computer turned Gates and Microsoft, respectively, into the richest man and richest software company in the United States. Examples of spectacularly bad decisions include the decision by managers at NASA and Morton Thiokol to launch the *Challenger* space shuttle—a decision that resulted in the deaths of six astronauts in 1986. Also, the decision by Richard Branson to invest $20 million in designing an MP3 player called the Virgin Pulse backfired when the product bombed against Apple's iPod and iTunes, and the investment had to be written off.[17]

Programmed and Nonprogrammed Decision Making

Regardless of the specific decision that a manager is responsible for, the decision-making process is either programmed or nonprogrammed.[18]

Programmed Decision Making

Programmed decision making is a routine, virtually automatic process. Programmed decisions are decisions that have been made so many times in the past that managers have been able to develop rules or guidelines to be applied when certain situations inevitably occur. Programmed decision making takes place when a school principal asks the school board to hire a new teacher whenever student enrolment increases by 40 students; when a manufacturing supervisor hires new workers whenever existing workers' overtime increases by more than 10 percent; and when an office manager orders basic office supplies, such as paper and pens, whenever the inventory of supplies on hand drops below a certain level. Furthermore, in the last example, the office manager probably orders the same amount of supplies each time. The decision-making process involved in such a routine, repetitive task is an example of programmed decision making.

This decision making is called *programmed* because an office manager, for example, does not need to repeatedly make new judgments about what should be done. He or she can rely on long-established decision rules such as these:

- *Rule 1.* When the storage shelves are three-quarters empty, order more paper.
- *Rule 2.* When ordering paper, order enough to fill the shelves.

Managers can develop rules and guidelines to regulate all routine organizational activities. For example, rules can specify how a worker should perform a certain task, and rules can specify the quality standards that raw materials must meet to be acceptable. Most decision making that relates to the day-to-day running of an organization is programmed decision making. Examples include decision making about how much inventory to hold, when to pay bills, when to bill customers, and when to order materials and supplies. Programmed decision making occurs when managers have the information they need to create rules that will guide decision making. There is little ambiguity involved in assessing when the stockroom is empty or counting the number of new students in class.

Nonprogrammed Decision Making

Suppose, however, managers are not at all certain that a course of action will lead to a desired outcome. Or, in even more ambiguous terms, suppose managers are not even clear about what they are really trying to achieve. Obviously, rules cannot be developed to predict uncertain events.

> **programmed decision making** Routine, virtually automatic decision making that follows established rules or guidelines.

nonprogrammed decision making Nonroutine decision making that occurs in response to unusual, unpredictable opportunities and threats.

classical model A prescriptive approach to decision making based on the idea that the decision maker can identify and evaluate all possible alternatives and their consequences and rationally choose the most suitable course of action.

optimum decision The most appropriate decision in light of what managers believe to be the most desirable future consequences for their organization.

Nonprogrammed decision making occurs when there are no ready-made decision rules that managers can apply to a situation. Nonprogrammed decision making is required for these *nonroutine* decisions. Nonprogrammed decisions are made in response to unusual or novel opportunities and threats. Rules do not exist because the situation is unexpected or uncertain and managers lack the information they would need to develop rules to cover it. Examples of nonprogrammed decision making include decisions to invest in a new kind of green technology, develop a new kind of product (as Jochen Zeitz did in the opening case), launch a new promotional campaign, enter a new market, expand internationally, or start a new business. In the remainder of this chapter, when we talk about decision making, we are referring to nonprogrammed decision making because it is the kind that causes the most problems for managers.

Sometimes managers have to make rapid decisions and don't have the time for careful consideration of the issues involved. They must rely on their intuition to quickly respond to a pressing concern. For example, when fire chiefs, captains, and lieutenants manage firefighters battling dangerous, out-of-control fires, they often need to rely on their expert intuition to make on-the-spot decisions that will protect the lives of the firefighters and save the lives of others, contain the fires, and preserve property—decisions made in emergency situations entailing high uncertainty, high risk, and rapidly changing conditions.[19]

Other times, managers do have the time available to make reasoned judgments but there are no established rules to guide their decisions, such as when deciding whether or not to proceed with a proposed merger. Regardless of the circumstances, nonprogrammed decisions can result in effective or ineffective decision making.

The *classical* and the *administrative* decision-making models reveal many of the assumptions, complexities, and pitfalls that affect decision making. These models help reveal the factors that managers and other decision makers must be aware of to improve the quality of their decision making. Keep in mind, however, that the classical and administrative models are just guides that can help managers understand the decision-making process. In real life, the process is typically not cut-and-dried, but these models can help guide a manager through it. We compare and contrast them below.

The Classical Model

One of the earliest models of decision making, the **classical model** (also referred to as the *rational model*) is prescriptive, which means that it specifies how decisions *should* be made. Managers using the rational model make a series of simplifying assumptions about the nature of the decision-making process (see Figure 4.1). The idea behind this model is that once managers recognize the need to make a decision, they should be able to make a complete list of *all* alternatives. For each alternative they should be able to list all consequences, and they can then make the best choice. In other words, the classical model assumes that managers have access to *all* the information they need to make the **optimum decision,** which is the most appropriate decision possible in light

---

FIGURE 4.1 The Classical Model of Decision Making

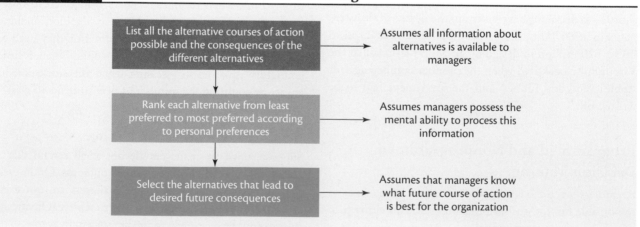

administrative model An approach to decision making that explains why decision making is an inherently uncertain and risky process and why managers usually make satisfactory rather than optimum decisions.

bounded rationality Cognitive limitations that constrain one's ability to interpret, process, and act on information.

ambiguous information Information that can be interpreted in multiple and often conflicting ways.

satisficing Searching for and choosing acceptable, or satisfactory, ways to respond to problems and opportunities, rather than trying to make the best decision.

of what they believe to be the most desirable future consequences for their organization. Furthermore, the rational model assumes that managers can easily list their own preferences for each alternative and rank them from least to most preferred in order to make the optimum decision.

The Administrative Model

James March and Herbert Simon disagreed with the underlying assumptions of the classical model of decision making. In contrast, they proposed that managers in the real world do not have access to all the information they need to make a decision. Moreover, they pointed out that even if all information were readily available, many managers would lack the mental or psychological ability to absorb and evaluate it correctly. As a result, March and Simon developed the **administrative model** of decision making to explain why decision making is always an inherently uncertain and risky process—and why managers can rarely make decisions in the manner prescribed by the classical model. Simon, who trained as a political scientist, questioned the mainstream economists' view of the economic manager as "a lightning-quick calculator of costs and benefits."[20] Instead, the manager had to also deal with constraints before making a decision. The administrative model is based on three important concepts: *bounded rationality, incomplete information,* and *satisficing.* See Figure 4.2.

Bounded Rationality

March and Simon pointed out that human decision-making capabilities are bounded by people's cognitive limitations that constrain their ability to interpret, process, and act on information.[21] They argued that the limitations of human intelligence constrain the ability of decision makers to determine the optimum decision. March and Simon coined the term **bounded rationality** to describe the situation in which the number of alternatives a manager must identify is so great and the amount of information so vast that it is difficult for the manager to even come close to evaluating it all before making a decision.[22]

FIGURE 4.2 The Administrative Model of Decision Making

Recognizes that decision makers:
- Have incomplete and imperfect information
- Are constrained by bounded rationality
- Tend to satisfice

Incomplete Information

Even if managers did have an unlimited ability to evaluate information, they still would not be able to arrive at the optimum decision because they would have incomplete information. Information is incomplete because the full range of decision-making alternatives is unknowable in most situations, and the consequences associated with known alternatives are uncertain.[23] There are three reasons why information is incomplete:

1. Because of risk and uncertainty, the probabilities of alternative outcomes cannot be determined, and future outcomes are *unknown.*

2. Another reason why information may be incomplete is that much of the information that managers have at their disposal is **ambiguous information.** Its meaning is not clear—it can be interpreted in multiple and often conflicting ways.[24]

3. Time constraints and the cost of searching for alternative solutions to problems can be prohibitive.

Satisficing

March and Simon argue that managers do not attempt to discover every alternative when faced with bounded rationality, an uncertain future, unquantifiable risks, considerable ambiguity, time constraints, and high information costs. Rather, they use a strategy known as **satisficing,** exploring a limited sample of possible alternatives.[25] Consider the situation confronting a Ford Motor Company purchasing manager who has one month to choose a supplier (out of thousands) for a small engine part. Given the time

> Simon questioned the mainstream economists' view of the economic manager as "a lightning-quick calculator of costs and benefits."

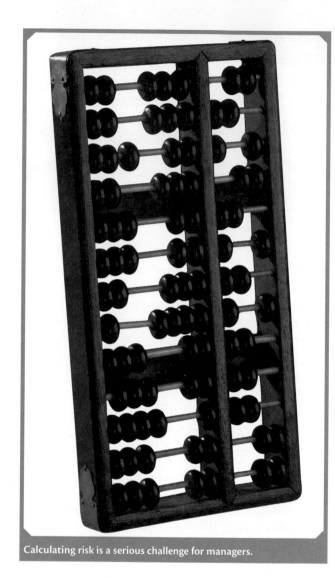

Calculating risk is a serious challenge for managers.

available, the purchasing manager cannot contact all potential suppliers and ask each for its terms (price, delivery schedules, and so on). Moreover, even if the time were available, the costs of obtaining the information, including the manager's own time, would be prohibitive. When managers satisfice, they search for and choose acceptable, or satisfactory, ways to respond to problems and opportunities, rather than trying to make the best decision.[26] For instance, the purchasing manager for Ford Canada would likely engage in a limited search to identify supplies. This might involve asking a limited number of suppliers for their terms, trusting that they are representative of suppliers in general, and making a choice from that set. Although this course of action is reasonable from the point of view of the purchasing manager, it may mean that a potentially superior supplier is overlooked.

March and Simon pointed out that managerial decision making often is more art than science. In the real world,

managers must rely on their intuition and judgment to make what seems to them to be the best decision in the face of uncertainty and ambiguity.[27] **Intuition** is a person's ability to make sound decisions based on past experience and immediate feelings about the information at hand. **Judgment** is a person's ability to develop a sound opinion because of the way he or she evaluates the importance of the information available in a particular context. Managerial decision making is often fast-paced, as managers use their experience and judgment to make crucial decisions under conditions of incomplete information. Although there is nothing wrong with this approach, decision makers should be aware that human judgment is often flawed. As a result, even the best managers sometimes end up making very poor decisions.[28] Cognitive biases that lead to poor decision outcomes are discussed a little later in this chapter. Next we turn to the steps managers can follow in making optimum decisions.

intuition Ability to make sound decisions based on past experience and immediate feelings about the information at hand.

judgment Ability to develop a sound opinion based on one's evaluation of the importance of the information at hand.

Describe the six steps managers should take to make sound decisions.

LO2

Steps in the Decision-Making Process

The conditions for an optimum decision rarely exist. To help managers make the best decision possible, researchers have developed a step-by-step model of the decision-making process and the issues and problems that managers confront at each step. There are six steps that managers should consciously follow to make a good decision (see Figure 4.3).[29] We introduce this model by examining a case where a manager at a mid-sized company had to make a nonprogrammed decision. Linda must make a decision as to what type of vehicles she should purchase for her sales team. The existing fleet of Ford Escorts is old, inefficient, and the employees no longer feel safe in them while on the road.

Step 1: Recognize the Need for a Decision

The first step in the decision-making process is to recognize the need for a decision. Managers face decisions that arise both internally and as a consequence of changes in the external environment.[30] An organization possesses a set of skills, competencies, and resources in its employees and in departments such as marketing, manufacturing, and research and development. Managers who actively

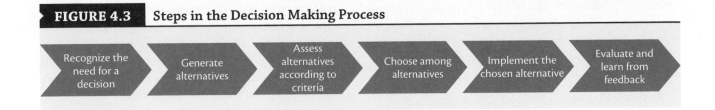

FIGURE 4.3 Steps in the Decision Making Process

Recognize the need for a decision → Generate alternatives → Assess alternatives according to criteria → Choose among alternatives → Implement the chosen alternative → Evaluate and learn from feedback

pursue opportunities to use these competencies create the need to make decisions. Managers thus can be proactive or reactive in recognizing the need to make a decision, but the important issue is that they must recognize this need and respond in a timely and appropriate way.[31]

Once a decision maker recognizes the need to make a decision, he or she will need to diagnose the issue or problem in order to determine all the factors underlying the problem. In our scenario, Linda appreciates that many of the company's customers are located in rural areas that are not supported by publicly accessible transportation such as airplanes, buses, and trains, and so purchasing vehicles appears to be her only option for reaching them. She recognizes the problem and formulates the following decision question: What type of vehicle should she purchase? Recognizing the need to make a decision is an important part of the process that generally involves two steps: stating the problem and formulating the decision question. The identification of the problem involves analyzing the current state of affairs and what the future state of affairs should be. It does not suggest a solution. See Figure 4.4.

In our example, the current situation for Linda is that the fleet of cars that her salesforce uses is no longer dependable. The desired future state or goal is to have a reliable fleet of vehicles that will meet the travel needs of the sales team. The question that flows from this problem is what type of vehicles should Linda purchase?

Step 2: Generate Alternatives

Having recognized the need to make a decision, a manager must generate a set of feasible alternative courses of action to take in response to the opportunity or threat. The failure to properly generate and consider different alternatives is one reason why managers sometimes make bad decisions.[32] In our example, the manager comes up with three alternatives: Ford Escort, Toyota Corolla, and Suburu Legacy.

Linda believes these alternatives, once examined and assessed according to the criteria that are important to the decision (Step 3), will meet her original expectations and solve the problem of the aging fleet. Should none of these alternatives end up meeting expectations, Linda would have to begin again with the entire process.

Step 3: Assess Alternatives

Once managers have listed a set of alternatives, they must evaluate the advantages and disadvantages of each one.[33] The key to a good assessment of the alternatives is being able to define the opportunity or threat exactly, and then specifying the criteria that *should* influence the selection of alternative ways of responding to the problem or opportunity.

One reason for bad decisions is that managers often fail to specify the criteria that are important in reaching

FIGURE 4.4 Tools to Help Assess the Accuracy of the Problem Statement and Decision Question

- Make sure the current state of the situation is stated clearly and that it does not reflect the symptom of the problem.
- At this point, you are not asking why there is a problem on which a decision has to be made. But you should be asking: Who does the problem affect? What does the problem affect? When does the problem affect? And how and where is it a problem?
- Ask yourself what the desired future state would look like. What is the goal of the project? Where do you want to be?
- Make sure you focus on only one problem.
- Make sure the problem statement does not suggest a solution or assign any blame.
- The decision question follows from the combined statement of the current situation and the desired future state, or problem statement.
- The decision question avoids asking "Why" but can be formulated as "What" or "How" questions.

a decision.[34] Moreover, the relative importance assigned to the criteria is something that must be clearly thought through. In general, successful managers use four criteria to evaluate the pros and cons of alternative courses of action (see Figure 4.5):

1. *Practicality.* Managers must decide whether they have the capabilities and resources to implement the alternative, and they must be sure that the alternative will not threaten the ability to reach other organizational goals. At first glance an alternative might seem to be economically superior to other alternatives, but if managers realize that it is likely to threaten other important projects, they might decide that it is not practical after all.

2. *Economic feasibility.* Managers must decide whether the alternatives make sense economically and fit the organization's performance goals. Typically, managers perform a cost-benefit analysis of the various alternatives to determine which one is likely to have the best financial payoff.

3. *Ethicalness.* Managers must ensure that a possible course of action is ethical and that it will not unnecessarily harm any stakeholder group. Many of the decisions that managers make may help some organizational stakeholders and harm others (see Chapter 3).

4. *Legality.* Managers must ensure that a possible course of action is legal and will not violate any domestic and international laws or government regulations.

Very often, a manager must consider these four criteria simultaneously. Some of the worst managerial decisions can be traced to poor assessment of the alternatives, such as the decision to launch the *Challenger* space shuttle mentioned earlier. In that case, the desire of NASA and Morton Thiokol managers to demonstrate to the public the success of the U.S. space program in order to ensure future funding (*economic feasibility*) conflicted with the need to ensure the safety of the astronauts (*ethicalness*). Managers deemed the economic criterion more important and decided to launch the space shuttle even though there were unanswered questions about safety. Tragically, some of the same decision-making problems that resulted in the *Challenger* tragedy led to the demise of the *Columbia* space shuttle in 2003, 17 years later, killing all seven astronauts on board.[35] In both the *Challenger* and the *Columbia* disasters, safety questions were raised before the shuttles were launched; safety concerns took second place to budgets, economic feasibility, and schedules; top decision makers seemed to ignore or downplay the inputs of those with relevant technical expertise; and speaking up was discouraged.[36] Rather than making safety a top priority, decision makers seemed overly concerned with keeping on schedule and within budget.[37]

In order to arrive at a reasonable decision about which car to purchase, Linda consulted with her team and made a list of the features and criteria that were important to make the best decision. The new vehicle had to have the following features to meet the needs of the salesforce:

Have all-wheel drive (AWD)

Have the full automatic package

Be fuel efficient

Be equipped with automatic braking system (ABS)

Be reasonably priced

Maintain good value over time

> **FIGURE 4.5**   **General Criteria for Evaluating Possible Courses of Action**

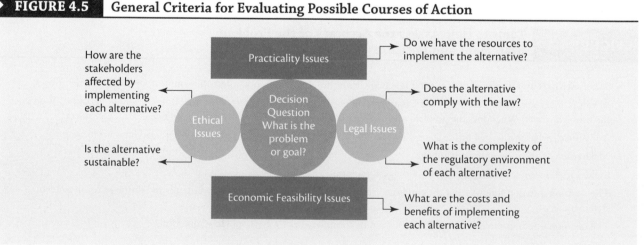

Be easy and convenient to service, with a good warranty policy

Be manufactured by a reputable and reliable company

Linda then categorized the requirements into the categories of criteria. While she recognized that some of the requirements could fall into more than one category, she decided to combine the ethical and legal concerns into one. The most important criteria in deciding which type of vehicles to purchase was difficult to decide. Linda knew the company must allocate a substantial budget for the fleet and it was important that safety concerns as well as efficiency costs must be balanced. She gave the practical concerns a weight of 50 percent and the economic feasibility concerns a value of 20 percent, and assigned a relative value or weight of 30 percent to the ethical and legal aspects. See Figure 4.6.

Next, Linda began to research how the alternatives measured up to the criteria in order to arrive at a score out of 10 points. She displayed her analysis in a decision preference matrix (see Figure 4.7):

- The Subaru Legacy had AW drive, the Toyota Corolla and the Ford Focus did not, and therefore out of a possible score of 10, she rated the Subaru Legacy 10, the Ford Focus 0, and the Corolla 0.

| **FIGURE 4.6** | **Weighted Decision Criteria** |

Criteria	Weight
Practicality—50%	
AWD	20%
Fully loaded	15%
Fuel efficient	10%
ABS	5%
Economic Feasibility—20%	
5-year residual value	11%
On-the-road price	9%
Ethical and Legal Criteria—30%	
Service record/warranty	11%
Dealer reputation	10%
Dealer accessibility	9%
Total	100%

- All cars could be bought fully loaded, although the Subaru Legacy had a few extras such as heated side mirrors and windshield wipers, as well as heated front seats, and the Focus had lower quality finishings, so she gave Subaru 10, Corolla 9, and Focus 7.

- The Corolla had slightly better fuel efficiency over Subaru and the Focus, thus a score of 10 for Corolla, 8 for Subaru, and 6 for Focus.

- All cars had ABS and seemed to have the same rating from most reviewers; thus all cars scored a 10 out of 10.

- For cost, most reviewers mentioned that both Corolla and Subaru held their values very well; but Corolla had a slight edge for resale, thus a score of 10 for Corolla and 9 for Subaru. Ford Focus had the lowest five-year residual value and thus scored 5.

- When Linda priced the cars, Focus was the cheapest. Corolla was cheaper than Subaru but in fairness was not quite as big or as powerful as Legacy. However, Ford was more amenable when it came to trade-in values for the fleet of old cars—thus 9 for Corolla, 8 for Subaru, and 10 for Ford.

- From experience and fact gathering, Linda was confident that the service record of Corolla was slightly superior to those of Ford and Subaru in terms of price and customer service—thus 10 for Corolla, 8 for Subaru, and 8 for Ford.

- The Japanese manufacturers have a very enviable reputation relative to North American manufacturers, but Toyota sells many more cars than does Subaru—therefore 10 for Corolla, 8 for Subaru, and 6 for Ford.

- Both Toyota and Subaru dealerships are within 5 km from Linda's office, and both are relatively easy to get to for the salespeople, therefore both received a score of 9 out of 10; but Ford has a dealership just 2.5 km from the office, thus gets a score of 10.

Step 4: Choose Among Alternatives

Once the set of alternative solutions has been carefully evaluated, the next task is to rank the various alternatives (using the criteria discussed in the previous section) and make a decision. When ranking alternatives, managers must be sure that all of the available information is brought to bear on the problem or issue at hand. Identifying all relevant information for a decision does not mean that the manager has complete information. In most instances, information is incomplete. Perhaps more serious than the existence of incomplete information is the often-documented tendency of managers to ignore

> **FIGURE 4.7** | Decision Preference Matrix

	Weight	Corolla Score (1-10)	Weighted score	Subaru Score (1-10)	Weighted score	Ford Focus Score (1-10)	Weighted score
Practicality—50%							
AW drive	20%	0	0	10	200	0	0
Fully loaded	15%	9	135	10	150	7	105
Fuel efficient	10%	10	100	8	80	6	60
ABS	5%	10	50	10	50	10	50
Practicality Subtotal	**50**		**285**		**480**		**215**
Economic Feasibility—20%							
5-year residual value	11%	10	110	9	99	5	55
On-the-road price	9%	9	81	8	72	10	90
Economic Feasibility Subtotal	**20**		**191**		**171**		**145**
Ethical and Legal Criteria—30%							
Service record/warranty	11%	10	110	8	88	8	88
Dealer reputation	10%	10	100	8	80	6	60
Dealer accessibility	9%	9	81	9	81	10	90
Ethical and Legal Criteria Subtotal	**30**		**291**		**249**		**238**
Totals	**100%**		**767**		**900**		**598**

Managers make good decisions when they further the direction of their organization's mission and goals.

critical information even when it is available. We discuss this tendency in detail below when we examine the operation of cognitive biases.

In our example, Linda's research leads her to the Subaru Legacy as the highest-ranking alternative car for her salespeople. She takes her research and results to her manager so that the decision can be acted upon.

Step 5: Implement the Chosen Alternative

Once a decision has been made and an alternative has been selected, the alternative must be implemented and many subsequent and related decisions must be made. After a course of action has been decided—as with PUMA's launch of sport lifestyle apparel—thousands of subsequent decisions are necessary to implement it. These decisions would involve recruiting designers, obtaining ethically sourced materials, finding high-quality manufacturers, and signing contracts with retail stores to sell the new line.

Although the need to make further decisions may seem obvious, many managers make the initial decision and then fail to act on it.[38] This is the same as not making a decision at all. To ensure that a decision is implemented, top managers must let middle managers participate in decisions, and then give them the responsibility to make the follow-up decisions necessary to achieve the goal. They must give middle managers enough resources to achieve the goal, and they must hold the middle managers accountable for their performance. Linda's manager is very impressed with the thoroughness of her decision-making process and is prepared to support the implementation of the outcome. Linda is given the budget she requested, and she goes ahead and purchases the new Subarus for her team.

Step 6: Evaluate and Learn from Feedback

The final step in the decision-making process is learning from feedback. Managers who do not evaluate the results of their decisions do not learn from experience; instead they stagnate and are likely to make the same mistakes again and again.[39] To avoid this problem, managers must establish a formal procedure for learning from the results of past decisions. The procedure should include these steps:

1. Compare what actually happened to what was expected to happen as a result of the decision.

2. Explore why any expectations for the decision were not met.

The Subaru Legacy ranks highest according to the weighted criteria used in the decision-making process.

> **Tips FOR MANAGERS**
>
> **Managing the Decision-Making Process**
>
> 1. When identifying the need to make a decision, avoid assigning blame to any individual or group.
>
> 2. Making decisions often means making changes in the organization's strategy, structure, and culture, which creates uncertainty and even anxiety. To reduce anxiety and foster an inclusive culture, involve as many stakeholders in the decision-making process as possible.
>
> 3. Give employees and other stakeholders reassurances and confirm their emotional concerns, rather than give rational explanations, when faced with decisions that create disruptive change.
>
> 4. Treat successes and failures as stepping stones in your decision-making practice.

3. Develop guidelines that will help in future decision making.

Individuals who always strive to learn from past mistakes and successes are likely to continuously improve their decision making. A significant amount of learning can take place when the outcomes of decisions are evaluated, and this assessment can produce enormous benefits. In our example, Linda seeks feedback from the salespeople who have been driving the new Subarus for a number of months to determine if her choice of vehicle is meeting their needs and has solved the initial problem of which type of vehicle to purchase.

> Explain how cognitive biases can affect decision making and lead managers to make poor decisions.
>
> **LO3**

Biases in Decision Making

In the 1970s, two psychologists, Daniel Kahneman and Amos Tversky, suggested that because all decision makers are subject to bounded rationality, they tend to use **heuristics,** which are rules of thumb that simplify the process of making decisions.[40] Kahneman and Tversky argued that rules of thumb are often useful because they help decision makers make sense of complex, uncertain, and ambiguous information. Sometimes, however, the use of heuristics can lead to systematic errors in the way decision makers process information about alternatives and make decisions. **Systematic errors** are

heuristics Rules of thumb that simplify decision making.

systematic errors Errors that people make over and over again and that result in poor decision making.

errors that people make over and over again and that result in poor decision making.[41] Four sources of bias that can negatively affect the way managers make decisions are *prior hypothesis, representativeness, illusion of control,* and *escalating commitment* (see Figure 4.8).

Prior Hypothesis Bias

Decision makers who have strong prior beliefs about the relationship between two variables tend to make decisions based on those beliefs *even when presented with evidence that their beliefs are wrong.* In doing so, they are falling victim to **prior hypothesis bias.** Moreover, decision makers tend to seek and use information that is consistent with their prior beliefs and to ignore information that contradicts those beliefs. Sony Corp. associated product innovation with providing life-long employment. The belief is that stable teams have the opportunity to develop state of the art technology. Sticking with that hypothesis caused Sony to be overtaken by Apple and others who developed innovative new technologies like digital LCD screens and flash memory that made Sony's technologies obsolete. Faced with the crisis of falling profits, Sony only recently changed its life-long employment strategy to reduce its bureaucracy and cut costs by downsizing. A CEO who has a strong prior belief that a certain strategy makes sense might continue to pursue that strategy, despite evidence that it is inappropriate or failing.

prior hypothesis bias A cognitive bias resulting from the tendency to base decisions on strong prior beliefs even if evidence shows that those beliefs are wrong.

representativeness bias A cognitive bias resulting from the tendency to generalize inappropriately from a small sample or from a single vivid case or episode.

illusion of control A source of cognitive bias resulting from the tendency to overestimate one's own ability to control activities and events.

Another example of this bias occurred with the decision of Ken Olsen, founder of Digital Equipment Corporation, to stay with mainframe computers in the 1980s and not allow his engineers to spend the company's resources on creating new kinds of personal computers because of his belief that "personal computers are just toys." It was a decision that cost Olsen his job as CEO and almost ruined his company.

Representativeness Bias

Many decision makers inappropriately generalize from a small sample or even from a single vivid case or episode. An interesting example of the **representativeness bias** occurred as Walmart began to expand internationally. Walmart managers assumed that the model that worked so well in the United States would work in every country. They were wrong. The efficient layout of stores, while suitable for the individualistic culture of the United States, proved to discourage shoppers in Asia, who consider shopping a more social event. This led to Walmart having to re-think its decisions when expanding internationally.

Illusion of Control

Other errors in decision making result from the **illusion of control,** the tendency of decision makers to overestimate their ability to control activities and events. Top-level managers seem to be particularly prone to this bias. Having worked their way to the top of an organization,

FIGURE 4.8 Cognitive Biases in Decision Making

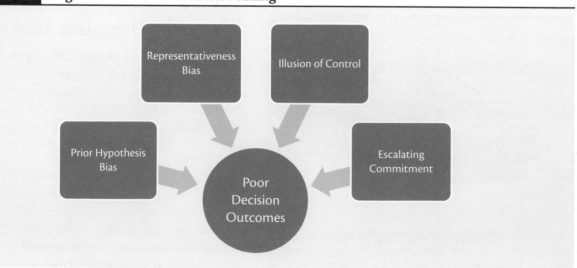

Virgin CEO Richard Branson has made both good decisions and poor decisions.

bias the analysis of decision makers and lead to **escalating commitment.** They decide to increase their investment of time and money in a course of action and ignore evidence that it is illegal, unethical, uneconomical, or impractical (refer to Figure 4.4). Often, the more appropriate decision would be to "cut and run." Escalating commitment bias can cause organizational and financial crises.[45] A Stanford University study on the decisions made by financial analysts found that in cases where company earnings forecasts were proving to be wrong, the analysts were reluctant to adjust their estimates to reflect new data. "The more their forecast differed from consensus, the more stubborn they became and the more they escalated their commitment to their erroneous forecast."[46]

> **escalating commitment**
> A source of cognitive bias resulting from the tendency to commit additional resources to a project even if evidence shows that the project is failing.

When managers work as a team to make decisions and solve problems, their choices of alternatives are less likely to fall victim to the biases and errors discussed previously. They are able to draw on the combined skills, competencies, and accumulated knowledge of group members and thereby improve their ability to generate feasible alternatives and make good decisions. Group decision making also allows managers to process more information and to correct one another's errors. And in the implementation phase, all managers affected by the decisions agree to cooperate. When a group of managers makes a decision (as opposed to one top manager making a decision and imposing it on subordinate managers), the probability that the decision will be implemented successfully increases. Group decision making techniques are discussed in Chapter 10, Managing Teams.

they tend to have an exaggerated sense of their own worth and are overconfident about their ability to succeed and to control events.[42] The illusion of control causes managers to overestimate the odds of a favourable outcome and, consequently, to make inappropriate decisions. For example, Richard Branson launched the Virgin Pulse MP3 player to compete with Apple's iPod against the advice of his management team, who argued that very high numbers would have to be sold to make the $20 million investment work. After it bombed, Branson said, "Ignoring my managers' advice and losing millions trying to take down the iPod reminded me: the CEO is not always right."[43]

Escalating Commitment

Having already committed significant resources to a course of action, some managers commit more resources to the project *even if they receive feedback that the project is failing.*[44] Feelings of personal responsibility for a project apparently

Explain the role that a sustainability strategy, organizational learning, and creativity play in helping managers improve their decisions. **LO4**

Improving Decision Making

How can managers avoid the negative effects of cognitive biases and improve their decision-making and problem-solving abilities? They must uncover their biases and use their time wisely, but the quality of decision making ultimately depends on innovative responses to opportunities and threats in the environment. Managers can increase their ability to make good nonprogrammed decisions by adopting a *sustainability strategy,* becoming a *learning organization* that promotes individual and group creativity, and utilizing *management information systems (MIS)* effectively.

Uncover Biases and Manage Time Wisely

Individual managers as well as whole companies often have difficulty identifying their own biases and assumptions and seeking help from networks outside of their firms such as from consulting and marketing firms to help them uncover their biases.[47] More and more, openness and transparency in revealing and sharing decision-making challenges are becoming popular among progressive companies. For example, PUMA is engaging in frank and candid discussions of its sourcing decisions with its stakeholders and networks in an effort to examine the criteria it uses to assess and evaluate the ethicality of alternative courses of action and if any cognitive biases and heuristics were used to arrive at the chosen options.

Often managers fail to allocate enough time, let alone other resources, to the decision-making process. The development of time-management skills is essential. Experts suggest it can be helpful to managers to recall two recent decisions, one that turned out well and one that turned out poorly, and analyze the decision process. Examine how much time was spent on each of the six steps in the decision-making process to see if it was sufficient.[48] Make sure enough and uninterrupted time is devoted to important activities in the decision-making process.

Adopt a Sustainability Strategy

Sustainability is a way to make decisions that meet the needs of the current generation without sacrificing the future generation's ability to do so. It serves the core competencies of the business to create, innovate, and enter new markets in responsible ways. A **sustainability** strategy has four elements: it protects the environment, promotes social responsibility, respects different cultures, and has an economic benefit. Sustainability has to have the support of the top management of the organization but also has to engage the employees. Everyone must internalize the individual responsibility for the good of the whole. Eva's Phoenix Print Shop, featured in Focus on the Social Economy, does just that.

One way that employees are encouraged to engage in sustainable strategies at Saatchi & Saatchi is to have them embark on their own personal projects inside and outside the office. This might mean making the decision to park as far away from the door of the shopping mall as possible, to get a little walk in for exercise while shopping. Or it might mean deciding to bicycle to work rather than driving. Such forms of engagement create sustainable practices and make for good decision making in every area of life.

sustainability
Decisions that protect the environment, promote social responsibility, respect cultural differences, and provide an economic benefit.

organizational learning The process through which managers seek to improve employees' desire and ability to understand and manage the organization and its task environment.

learning organization
An organization in which managers try to maximize the ability of individuals and groups to think and behave creatively and thus maximize the potential for organizational learning to take place.

Making sustainable decisions becomes particularly important when managers consider the choice of source of their inputs. Chef Robert Clark of Vancouver's C Restaurant promotes sustainable fishing practices in British Columbia through the Ocean Wise program at the Vancouver Aquarium. Part of the program includes purchasing direct from fishers who use organic means of growing, selective harvesting, and exclusive production techniques that support and maintain the diverse marine ecosystem.[49] Compass Group Canada and Sea Choice Canada expanded the Ocean Wise program nationwide to include new purchasing standards, internal compliance mechanisms, and chef and public education and awareness. "As the Canadian leader in food and support services, we are proud to embrace a sustainable seafood policy that will support the health of our oceans. Our purchasing shift can make a significant impact and it is clearly the right thing for us to do,"[50] says Jack MacDonald, CEO of Compass Group Canada.

Many universities and colleges are making the decision to not purchase eggs from caged hens because caging severely limits the ability of the hens to engage many of their natural behaviours such as wing stretching, walking, dust bathing, standing on solid ground, or laying eggs in a nest. The European Union banned the practice of caged hens in 2012. More than 300 universities and colleges in North America, including the University of Guelph, the University of British Columbia, Langara College, and the BC Institute of Technology, have already stopped purchasing eggs from suppliers that cage their hens.[51]

Firms also need to become more transparent about their efforts to create a sustainability strategy. The organizations that are open about their challenges with sustainability issues, such as MEC, the organization featured in the opening case in Chapter 3, are gaining respect and market share.

Consumers still have trouble identifying the leaders in sustainability.[52] A recent study by IMC2 on how effectively S&P 100 companies are communicating their sustainability efforts found that financial, media, and entertainment companies had the worst practices and policies related to communicating with the outside world about their sustainability issues, while the automotive and forestry industries were the best.[53]

Become a Learning Organization

Organizational learning is the process through which managers seek to improve employees' desire and ability to understand and manage the organization and its task environment so that employees can make decisions that constantly raise organizational effectiveness.[54] A **learning organization** is one in which managers do everything possible to maximize the ability of individuals and groups to think and

FOCUS ON ▶ *The Social Economy*

Eva's Phoenix Print Shop

Eva's Phoenix Print Shop is arguably one of the most successful social purpose enterprises in Toronto, having achieved an enviable balance of its blended value proposition: sustainable business results, remarkable social outcomes, and environmental responsibility.

Eva's Phoenix Print Shop was opened in 2002 and exists within an equally innovative and successful organization serving homeless and at-risk youth. Eva's Initiatives for Homeless Youth is a registered Canadian charity operating three shelters that house 114 youth aged 16-24 every night. Its first shelter, Eva's Place, opened in 1994, posthumously honouring Eva Smith, a tireless community outreach worker and school counsellor who fought to improve the future for homeless and at-risk youth. Eva's Satellite opened its doors in 1998, followed by Eva's Phoenix in 2000, where Eva's Phoenix Print Shop is located.

The Eva's Phoenix Print Shop is a socially and environmentally responsible commercial printer that supports the award-winning print training program for youth who are homeless or at risk of homelessness. Print services are competitively priced and on-time delivery is guaranteed. The Print Shop is powered with green electricity, and is Forestry Stewardship Council (FSC) certified. Some customers include Ontario Insurance Adjusters Association, TD Bank, Toronto Hydro, and Porter Airline. Recent congratulations were given to the Phoenix Print Shop on being selected as one of the print suppliers for the Toronto Organizing Committee for the 2015 Pan American and Parapan American Games.

The Print Shop recruits participants from shelters and employment programs across Toronto. Once they pass an initial screening, they go through a three-month training program to learn the basics of the print business including the operation of equipment and machinery. Upon completion of the print training program, the trainees apply for work with the support of Print Shop staff, accessing a broad network of employer-contacts that Eva's has established over the years in the print industry. The Print Shop offers three graduates per year, a 3 month placement in the commercial print shop, and hires other graduates when business volume allows.

Phoenix Print Shop has had significant success over the years. Since 2002, 140 youth have graduated, most (55%) connect to full-time jobs at an average wage of $12 per hour. Many (14%) return to school, some with the assistance of a bursary from Eva's Phoenix Print Shop. Others have started their own businesses or part-time jobs. More than half of all the youth who have joined the Print Shop have improved their housing, moving out of a shelter or marginal housing into independent or better accommodation. In 2007 the Phoenix Print Shop received a Toronto Community Foundation Vital Ideas Award for experience, expertise and ingenuity in providing practical solutions to challenging social issues.

Since 2002, the Print Shop has evolved its business model through several phases. In the early years, the business focused on "low-hanging fruit", pursuing print jobs from its "friends" in the non-profit sector. It soon found that this market niche was not sustainable, and has applied its efforts to developing substantial contracts with corporations and institutions that can offer regular business. While these relationships took several years to build, they are now the mainstay of the Print Shop's business, helping sales grow by 320% from 2006 to 2011. The enterprise's Business Cost Recovery (the ratio of sales to business costs) has risen from 48% in 2004 to 104% in 2011 – the Toronto Enterprise Fund considers that a social purpose enterprise is sustainable when it attains 100% Business Cost Recovery. The Print Shop's network of contacts in the industry has been crucial to their business achievements as well as their success with participants. Many of these contacts sit on a 12-person Advisory Board that provides strategic direction and helps with sales leads. Much of the Print Shop's equipment has been donated through these connections, as well as creative solutions, such as the loan of two Heidelberg presses.[55]

1. Describe how Eva's Print Shop has adopted the elements of improved decision making.

---

creativity A decision maker's ability to discover original and novel ideas that lead to feasible alternative courses of action.

behave creatively and thus maximize the potential for organizational learning to take place. At the heart of organizational learning is **creativity,** the ability of a decision maker to discover original ideas that lead to feasible alternative courses of action. Encouraging creativity among managers is such a pressing organizational concern that many organizations hire outside experts to help them develop programs to train their managers in the art of creative thinking and problem solving.

Promote Individual Creativity

Research suggests that individuals are most likely to be creative when certain conditions are met. First, people must be given the opportunity and freedom to generate new ideas. Creativity declines when managers look over the shoulders of talented employees and try to "hurry up" a creative solution. How would you feel if your boss said you had one week to come up with a new product idea to beat the competition? Creativity results when individuals have an opportunity to experiment, to take risks, and to make mistakes and learn from them. Companies that have a lot of innovation foster intrapreneurship through their formal structure and expectations. An **intrapreneur** is a manager, scientist, or researcher who works inside an organization and notices opportunities to develop new or improved products and better ways to make them. For instance, in one recent year, 3M launched more than 200 new products, many of which came from employee intrapreneurs.[56] Highly innovative companies such as Google, Apple, and Facebook are well known for the wide degree of freedom they give their managers and employees to experiment and develop innovative goods and services.[57] **Innovation,** discussed in more detail in Chapter 7, is the implementation of creative ideas. Companies try to foster promotion to the ranks of top management. Organizations must

> **intrapreneur** A manager, scientist, or researcher who works inside an organization and notices opportunities to develop new or improved products and better ways to make them.
>
> **innovation** The implementation of creative ideas in an organization.

reward intrapreneurs equitably if they wish to prevent them from leaving and becoming outside entrepreneurs who might form a competitive new venture. Nevertheless, intrapreneurs frequently do so.

Sometimes a manager misses a good opportunity because of decision-making biases, as discussed earlier in this chapter, and sometimes it happens because they do not share their concerns about an idea with others and simply reject it outright.

Sharing challenges and getting feedback from a wide variety of channels, including other firms through networking, can help managers make sure they do not miss out on a good idea—as did Hewlett-Packard when it decided not to develop one of its employees' ideas. The result: Steve Wozniak went off with his device to co-found Apple Computer. Other examples of poor decisions are shown in Figure 4.9.

Managers seek to improve employees' desire and ability to understand and manage the organization and its task environment so that employees can make decisions that continuously raise organizational effectiveness. Managers must take steps to promote organizational learning and creativity to improve the quality of decision making. Employees who believe that they are working on important, vital issues will be motivated to put forth the high levels of effort that creativity demands.

FIGURE 4.9 | **Some of the Biggest Mistakes Managers Have Ever Made**

Alexander Graham Bell invented the telephone in 1876, but he had a hard time attracting backers. U.S. President Rutherford B. Hayes used a prototype telephone and remarked, "That's an amazing invention, but who would ever want to use one of them?" Bell approached Western Union Telegraph Company and offered to sell them the patents. Their decision: They had no use for an electrical toy.

- A young inventor, Chester Carlson, took his idea to 20 corporations, all of which turned him down. He finally got a small New York company named Haloid Co. to purchase the rights to his electrostatic paper-copying process. Haloid became Xerox Corporation, and Carlson's process made both Xerox and Carlson very rich.

- In 1962 four musicians played for executives of Decca Recording Company. One executive later explained that his company just did not like the group's sound, noting that guitar groups were on their way out. Four other record companies turned them down. The Decision Making Hall of Fame will have a special place for Decca, which turned down the Beatles.

- The decision of Ken Olsen, founder of Digital Equipment Corporation, to stay with mainframe computers in the 1980s and not allow his engineers to spend the company's resources on creating new kinds of personal computers because of his belief that "personal computers are just toys" was a decision that cost Olsen his job as CEO and almost ruined his company.

- Hewlett-Packard decided not to develop a product created by an employee. Steve Wozniak went off with his device to co-found Apple Computer.

- Monster.com approached *The Globe and Mail* to collaborate on online job advertising, but was turned down. *The Globe and Mail* lost huge revenues from job advertisement as a result of large numbers of firms moving from print to online.

- BlackBerry maker Research In Motion (RIM) CEOs took days to communicate to the public the apology for the power outage in 2011 that caused loyal users around the world to switch to the iPhone or Android.

Despite the importance of fostering creativity in organizations, in a recent survey of 500 CEOs only 6 percent felt that they were doing a great job at managing their creative people. John MacDonald, co-founder of MacDonald Dettwiler & Associates Ltd. (MDA), based in Richmond, BC, suggests that "managing creative people is a bit like riding herd on a thousand prima donnas. They are all highly individual people who don't follow the herd, so managing them is a challenge."[58]

> **"Managing creative people is a bit like riding herd on a thousand prima donnas. They are all highly individual people who don't follow the herd."**
>
> *John MacDonald, co-founder of MacDonald Dettwiler & Associates Ltd. (MDA)*

LO5 Explain how the utilization of information and management information systems (MIS) can be vital to a manager's decision-making processes.

Utilizing Information and Management Information Systems (MIS)

In order for managers to generate and assess alternatives in making a decision, they need access to data and information both from inside the organization and from external stakeholders. When deciding how to price a seat sale, for example, the WestJet marketing manager needs information about how consumers will react to different prices. They need information about unit costs so as not to set the price below the costs of flying. They also need data about how many people (and what class of flyer—business or economy) are likely to fly on any given day. WestJet also needs information about competitors' prices, since its pricing strategy should be consistent with its competitive strategy. Some of this information can come from outside the organization (e.g., from consumer surveys) and some from inside the organization (information about flight costs from operations). As this example suggests, managers' ability to make effective decisions rests on their ability to acquire and process information.

Information is not the same as data.[59] **Data** are raw, un-summarized, and unanalyzed facts such as volume of sales, level of costs, or number of customers. **Information** is data that are organized in a meaningful fashion such as in a graph showing the change in sales volume or

data Raw, unsummarized, and unanalyzed facts.

information Data that are organized in a meaningful fashion.

information technology The means by which information is acquired, organized, stored, manipulated, and transmitted.

costs over time. The distinction between data and information is important because one of the uses of information technology is to help managers transform data into information in order to make better managerial decisions. **Information technology (IT)** is the means by which information is acquired, organized, stored, manipulated, and transmitted. Rapid advances in the power of information technology— specifically, through the use of computers—are having a fundamental impact on information systems and on managers and their organizations.[60]

Attributes of Useful Information

When we evaluated the classical decision-making process earlier in this chapter, we noted that it is often difficult for individuals to have access to all possible information needed to make a decision. While information is still collected from individuals, much information is now accessed through information technology (websites, databases, and the like). Regardless of how it is acquired, individuals need to decide whether the information is useful. Four factors determine the usefulness of information: *quality, timeliness, completeness,* and *relevance* (see Figure 4.10).

FIGURE 4.10   **Factors Affecting the Usefulness of Information**

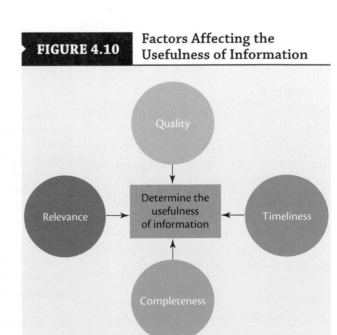

Quality

Accuracy and reliability determine the quality of information.[61] The greater the accuracy and reliability, the higher is the quality of information. For an information system to work well, the information that it provides must be of high quality. If managers conclude that the quality of information provided by their information system is low, they are likely to lose confidence in the system and stop using it. Alternatively, if managers base decisions on low-quality information, poor and even disastrous decision making can result. For example, the partial meltdown of the nuclear reactor at Three Mile Island in Pennsylvania during the 1970s was the result of poor information caused by an information system malfunction. The information system indicated to engineers controlling the reactor that there was enough water in the reactor core to cool the nuclear pile, although this was, in fact, not the case. The consequences included the partial meltdown of the reactor and the release of radioactive gas into the atmosphere.

Timeliness

Information that is timely is available when it is needed for managerial action, not after the decision has been made. In today's rapidly changing world, the need for timely information often means that information must be available on a real-time basis.[62] Following Twitter feeds can yield up-to-the-minute information from individuals and organizations. **Real-time information** is information that reflects current conditions. In an industry that experiences rapid changes, real-time information may need to be updated frequently. Airlines use real-time information on the number of flight bookings and competitors' prices to adjust their prices on an hour-to-hour basis to maximize their revenues.

Completeness

Information that is complete gives managers all the information they need to exercise control, achieve coordination, or make an effective decision. We have already noted that because of uncertainty, ambiguity, and time and cost constraints, managers have to make do with incomplete information.[63] One of the functions of information systems is to increase the completeness of the information that managers have at their disposal.

Relevance

Information that is relevant is useful and suits a manager's particular needs and circumstances. Irrelevant information is useless and

may actually hurt the performance of a busy manager who has to spend valuable time determining whether information is relevant. Given the massive amounts of information that managers are now exposed to and the limited information-processing capabilities of humans, the people who design information systems need to make sure that managers receive only relevant information.

Management Information Systems (MIS)

Computer-based information gathering and processing systems are central to the operation of most organizations today. **Management information systems (MIS)** are electronic systems of interconnected components designed to collect, process, store, and disseminate information to facilitate management decision making, planning, and control. They are designed specifically to help managers make efficient and effective decisions when planning, leading, organizing, and controlling. Four types of management information systems are discussed below after mentioning the one that preceded them all: the organizational hierarchy.

Four types of computer-based management information systems can be particularly helpful in providing managers with the information they need to make decisions and to coordinate and control organizational resources: transaction-processing systems, operations information systems, decision support systems, and expert systems. In Figure 4.11, these systems are arranged along a continuum according to their increasing usefulness in providing managers with the information they need to make nonprogrammed decisions.

Traditionally, managers have used the organizational hierarchy as a system for gathering the information they need to achieve coordination and control and make decisions (see Chapter 6 for a discussion of organizational structure and hierarchy). Although the organizational hierarchy is a useful information system, several drawbacks are associated with it. First, in organizations with many layers of managers, it can take a long time for information to travel up the hierarchy and for decisions to travel back down. This slow pace can reduce the timeliness and usefulness of information and prevent an organization from responding quickly to changing market conditions.[64] Second, information can be distorted as it moves from one layer of management to another. **Information distortion,** changes in meaning that occur as information passes through a series of senders

real-time information Frequently updated information that reflects current conditions.

management information systems (MIS) Electronic systems of interconnected components designed to collect, process, store, and disseminate information to facilitate management decision making, planning, and control.

information distortion Changes in meaning that occur as information passes through a series of senders and receivers.

> **FIGURE 4.11**   Four Computer-Based Management Information Systems

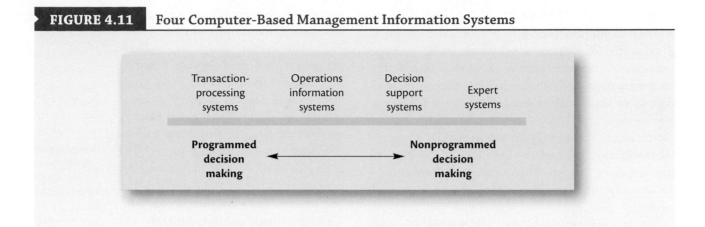

Transaction-processing systems · Operations information systems · Decision support systems · Expert systems

Programmed decision making ← → **Nonprogrammed decision making**

and receivers, reduces the quality of information.[65] Third, because managers have only a limited span of control, as an organization grows larger its hierarchy lengthens; this tall structure can make the hierarchy a very expensive information system. The popular idea that companies with tall management hierarchies are bureaucratic and unresponsive to the needs of their customers arises from the inability of tall hierarchies to effectively process data and provide managers with timely, complete, relevant, and high-quality information. Until modern computer-based information systems came along, however, the management hierarchy was the best information system available.

Transaction-Processing Systems

A **transaction-processing system** is a system designed to handle large volumes of routine, recurring transactions. Transaction-processing systems began to appear in the early 1960s with the advent of commercially available mainframe computers. They were the first type of computer-based management information system adopted by many organizations, and today they are commonplace. Bank managers use a transaction-processing system to record deposits into, and payments out of, bank accounts. Supermarket managers use a transaction-processing system to record the sale of items and to track inventory levels. More generally, most managers in large organizations use a transaction-processing system to handle tasks such as payroll preparation and payment, customer billing, and payment of suppliers.

Operations Information Systems

Many types of management information systems followed hard on the heels of transaction-processing systems in the 1960s. An **operations information system** is a system that gathers comprehensive data, organizes it, and summarizes it in a form that is of value to managers.

Whereas a transaction-processing system processes routine transactions, an operations information system provides managers with information that they can use in their non-routine coordinating, controlling, and decision-making tasks. Most operations information systems are coupled with a transaction-processing system. An operations information system typically accesses data gathered by a transaction-processing system, processes those data into useful information, and organizes that information into a form accessible to managers. Managers often use an operations information system to obtain sales, inventory, accounting, and other performance-related information. For example, the information that T. J. Rodgers at Cypress Semiconductor gets on individual employee goals and performance is provided by an operations information system.

FedEx uses an operations information system to track the performance of its 1500 or so ground stations. Each ground station is evaluated according to four criteria: delivery (the goal is to deliver 100 percent of all packages by noon the day after they were picked up), productivity (measured by the number of packages shipped per employee-hour), controllable cost, and station profitability. Each ground station also has specific delivery, efficiency, cost, and profitability targets that it must attain. Every month FedEx's operations information system is used to gather information on these four criteria and summarize it for top managers, who are then able to compare the performance of each station against its previously established targets. The system quickly alerts senior managers to underperforming ground stations, so they can intervene selectively to help solve any problems that may have given rise to the poor performance.[66]

transaction-processing system A management information system designed to handle large volumes of routine, recurring transactions.

operations information system A management information system that gathers, organizes, and summarizes comprehensive data in a form that managers can use in their non-routine coordinating, controlling, and decision-making tasks.

Decision Support Systems

A **decision support system** is an interactive computer-based system that provides models that help managers make better nonprogrammed decisions.[67] Recall that nonprogrammed decisions are decisions that are relatively unusual or novel, such as decisions to invest in new productive capacity, develop a new product, launch a new promotional campaign, enter a new market, or expand internationally. Although an operations information system organizes important information for managers, a decision support system gives managers a model-building capability and so provides them with the ability to manipulate information in a variety of ways. Managers might use a decision support system to help them decide whether to cut prices for a product. The decision support system might contain models of how customers and competitors would respond to a price cut. Managers could run these models and use the results as an *aid* to decision making.

The stress on the word *aid* is important, for in the final analysis a decision support system is not meant to make decisions for managers. Rather, its function is to provide valuable information that managers can use to improve the quality of their decision making.

Expert Systems and Artificial Intelligence

Expert systems are the most advanced management information systems available. An **expert system** is a system that employs human knowledge captured in a computer to solve problems that ordinarily require human expertise.[68] Expert systems are a variant of artificial intelligence.[69] Mimicking human expertise (and intelligence) requires a computer that can at a minimum (1) recognize, formulate,

Cloud computing allows organizations to connect and synchronize the data managers need to make good decisions.

and solve a problem; (2) explain the solution; and (3) learn from experience.

In the recent past, the software designed to manage information had to be purchased by individual firms which were granted licences to use the closely guarded programs. In the last decade, many of the kinds of service applications that were once distributed privately, at a very large expense to individuals and companies, have become available on the Internet for a fraction of the cost. Companies such as IBM, Amazon, and Apple now offer **cloud computing:** Web-based services including everything from managing supply chains and human resources, to data storage and digital content creation. Almost all software can be offered as a service that can be merged and intertwined with other applications, effectively being tailored to a firm's specific needs. These cloud computing Web services allow online offerings to connect and synchronize the data managers need to make good decisions.

According to a study by *The Economist*,[70] two clumps of services are emerging: integrated suites of applications, such as Google Apps and Zoho, which offer many applications including word processing, project management, customer relationship management (CRM), and platforms similar to operating systems used today, providing consumer services such as the social network Facebook. The competition is so fierce in cloud computing that some suggest the platform war will rival that of the epic fights between Microsoft and Apple. The annual compound growth in cloud computing has been about 30 percent over the last decade.

As a result of this growth, data centres are becoming "factories of computing services on an industrial scale; software is increasingly being delivered as an online service; and wireless networks connect more and more devices to such offerings," making large IT departments in firms obsolete.[71] Moreover, the increase in data centres will have an enormous ecological imprint on the environment. According to $E = MC^2$, a marketing firm that helps companies figure out their carbon footprint and how to offset it, energy consumption tied to data centres doubled in the first five years of this century.[72] The Environmental Protection Agency (EPA) estimates that it already accounts for 2 percent of the world's carbon emissions, an impact equivalent to air travel.

decision support system An interactive computer-based management information system with model-building capability that managers can use when they must make nonroutine decisions.

expert system A management information system that employs human knowledge captured in a computer to solve problems that ordinarily require human expertise.

cloud computing Web-based services including everything from managing supply chains and human resources, to data storage and digital content creation.

Summary and Review

LO1 The Nature of Managerial Decision Making   *Programmed decisions* are routine decisions that are made so often that managers have developed decision rules to be followed automatically. *Nonprogrammed* decisions are made in response to situations that are unusual or unique; they are nonroutine decisions. The *classical model* of decision making assumes that decision makers have complete information, are able to process that information in an objective, rational manner, and make optimum decisions. March and Simon in the *administrative model* argue that managers are subject to *bounded rationality*, rarely have access to all the information they need to make optimum decisions, and consequently *satisfice* and rely on their *intuition* and *judgment* when making decisions.

LO2 Steps in the Decision-Making Process   When making decisions, managers should take these six steps: *recognize the need for a decision, generate alternatives, assess alternatives, choose among alternatives, implement the chosen alternative,* and *evaluate and learn from feedback.*

LO3 Biases in Decision Making   Managers are often fairly good decision makers. However, problems result when human judgment is adversely affected by the operation of cognitive biases. Cognitive biases are caused by systematic errors in the way decision-makers process information to make decisions. Sources of these errors include *prior hypothesis, representativeness, illusion of control,* and *escalating commitment.*

LO4 Improving Decision Making   Managers can make better decisions when they examine their biases and spend appropriate amounts of time engaging in the process. But to make optimum decisions, managers should adopt a *sustainability strategy*—one that is transparent, engaging, and economically beneficial without leaving a large carbon footprint. They must become a *learning organization* and encourage *creativity* to ensure that new, innovative ideas are not overlooked.

LO5 Utilizing Information and Management Information Systems (MIS)   Traditionally, managers used the organizational hierarchy as the main system for gathering the information they needed to coordinate and control the organization and make effective decisions. Today, managers use four types of computer-based information systems to provide them with the high-quality, timely, relevant, and relatively complete information they need to enable them to make effective decisions. Listed in ascending order of sophistication, they are *transaction-processing systems, operations information systems, decision support systems,* and *expert systems.*

KEY TERMS

administrative model

ambiguous information

bounded rationality

classical model

cloud computing

creativity

data

decision making

decision support
system

escalating commitment

expert system

heuristics

illusion of control

information

information distortion

information technology

innovation

intrapreneur

intuition

judgment

learning organization

management information
systems (MIS)

nonprogrammed decision
making

operations information
system

optimum decision

organizational learning

prior hypothesis bias

programmed decision making

real-time information

representativeness bias

satisficing

sustainability

systematic errors

transaction-processing
system

WRAP-UP TO **OPENING CASE**

Good Decision Making at PUMA

PUMA faced considerable threats in its task environment which led to a major decision by CEO Jochen Zeitz to reduce costs, increase sustainability in its operations, and launch a new product. After having read and understood the concepts in this chapter, you should be able to answer the following questions:

1. *What type of decision was made by Zeitz when PUMA launched into sport lifestyle fashions?*

   ANSWER: Decision making is made in response to either routine or unique situations. Programmed decisions are made in response to routine situations where managers can establish rules to guide behaviour. Most decision making that relates to the day-to-day running of an organization is programmed decision making. Examples include decision making about how much inventory to hold, when to pay bills, when to bill customers, and when to order materials and supplies. Nonprogrammed decision making is required for nonroutine situations. Rules do not exist because the situation is unexpected or uncertain and managers lack the information they would need to develop rules to cover it. Zeitz's decision to launch into sport lifestyle gear and apparel is a nonprogrammed decision made under conditions of risk and uncertainty.

2. *Identify the threats and opportunities in the task environment that impact PUMA's decision.*

   ANSWER: Decision making in response to threats occurs when events inside or outside the organization are adversely affecting organizational performance and managers are searching for ways to increase performance. In this case, PUMA was almost on the brink of bankruptcy in the early 1990s when Zeitz made the nonprogrammed decision to launch a new "sport lifestyle" line of products instead of competing in the high-performance athletic shoe market. In responding to the threats, PUMA decreased costs, took over distribution of PUMA North America, and adopted a sustainable operations strategy. The bold move appealed to consumers and turned around the fortunes of the company. PUMA is the fourth largest athletic apparel company in the world.

Decision making in response to opportunities occurs when managers search for ways to improve organizational performance to benefit customers, employees, and other stakeholder groups. In this case, Zeitz's decision to focus on lifestyle and fashion products appealed to the younger demographic in the market. Hiring a 21-year-old skateboarder and partnering with well respected fashion designers from Europe and Japan were decisions that paid off for shareholders. PUMA also took advantage of the growing trend among young people to buy products that are made in a sustainable manner, thus reducing the degradation of the environment. PUMA's decisions improved its organizational performance and benefited customers, the environment, and other stakeholders.

3. *How does PUMA foster sustainability and promote creativity and innovation? Why is this good decision making?*

ANSWER: Sustainability involves making decisions that meet the needs of the current generation without sacrificing the future generation's ability to do so. A sustainability strategy protects the environment, promotes social responsibility, respects different cultures, and has an economic benefit to the enterprise. PUMA collaborated with Greenpeace to embark on the "detoxification" of its operations. It collaborated with the chemical industry to determine how to phase out toxic materials in the production of its goods while lowering production costs. Thus PUMA is promoting social responsibility toward the environment while creating an economic benefit to the company.

Creativity is the ability to discover original ideas that lead to feasible alternative courses of action. Zeitz recognized the importance of coming up with creative designs that combined performance with style and hired a young skateboarder, Bertone, to head up the sport lifestyle division. As head of the division, the young manager partnered with experts and designers to create trendy products using sustainable materials. Bertone was able to implement new creative ideas including a limited-edition line called Thrift (products made from vintage clothing) and Mongolian Shoe BBQ (shoes that can be customized online). Zeitz and other managers like Bertone foster innovation at PUMA.

The decisions Zeitz made at PUMA illustrate good decision making in the face of a highly competitive industry. In responding to those threats, Zeitz sought opportunities to create a high-performing organization by fostering creativity, innovation, and adopting a sustainability strategy in making the decision to change the direction of the company. It is a good decision because all the stakeholders benefit.

Management in Action

TOPICS FOR DISCUSSION AND ACTION

LEVEL 1   Knowledge & Comprehension

1. Define and describe the two types of decisions.

2. Describe the six steps that managers should take to make the best decisions.

3. Describe the difference between data and information. What are the characteristics of useful information?

LEVEL 2 Application & Analysis

4. Ask a manager to recall the best and the worst business decisions he or she ever made. Try to determine why these decisions were so good or so bad.

5. Ask a manager to describe the main kinds of information systems that he or she uses on a routine basis at work.

6. Listen to the podcast "Sustainability—The Only Strategy" from Harvard Business Ideacast 111, September 11, 2008, and describe how managers use the "TEN" cycle to promote sustainability, creativity, and organizational learning.

LEVEL 3 Synthesis & Evaluation

7. Compare and contrast the assumptions underlying the classical and administrative models of decision making.

8. You are a first-line manager of a grocery store that has a home delivery service. You tell your boss that you have found a cheaper supplier of insurance for the drivers with the same amount of coverage. Your boss continues to use the more expensive insurer. What decision-making bias is your boss suffering from?

9. When a manager is asked to judge an alternative in terms of a cost-benefit analysis, which criterion are they weighting most highly?

SELF-REFLECTION EXERCISE

How Do You Make Decisions?

Pick a decision that you have made recently that has had important consequences for you. This decision may be your decision concerning which university to attend, which program to select, which part-time job to take, or even whether or not to take a part-time job. Using the material in this chapter, analyze the way in which you made the decision:

1. Identify the criteria you used, either consciously or unconsciously, to guide your decision making.

2. List the alternatives that you considered. Were these all the possible alternatives? Did you unconsciously (or consciously) ignore some important alternatives?

3. How much information did you have about each alternative? Did you base the decision on complete or incomplete information?

4. Try to remember how you reached a decision. Did you sit down and consciously think through the implications of each alternative, or did you make a decision on the basis of intuition? Did you use any rules of thumb to help you make the decision?

5. Do you think that your choice of decision alternative was shaped by any of the cognitive biases discussed in this chapter?

6. Do you think in retrospect that you made a reasonable decision? What, if anything, might you do to improve your ability to make good decisions in the future?

SMALL GROUP BREAKOUT EXERCISE

What Type of Computer Should We Buy?

Form groups of three or four people, and appoint one member as the spokesperson who will communicate your findings to the whole class when called on by the instructor. Then discuss the following scenario:

Assume your group is charged with solving the problem of replacing the obsolete desktop computer monitors for the human resources department. You must purchase seven new monitors, but are struggling over the decision of what brand to buy. Apply the steps in the decision-making process.

1. State the decision question.

2. Brainstorm the brands of computer monitors available.

3. a. List the factors that are important in making the decision, and fit them into the four categories of criteria.

   b. Assign a value or weight to each of the criteria categories and subfactors.

   c. Discuss the advantages and disadvantages of each of the brands in terms of the decision criteria and assign them a score out of 10 (0 is low).

   d. Make a decision preference matrix (see Figure 4.7) to display the weighted scores.

4. Which brand will you choose, and why?

5. How will you go about implementing your decision?

6. How will you know if you made a good decision?

BUSINESS PLANNING EXERCISE

Your professor may ask you to write a business plan for a new venture or a strategic plan for an existing venture. At the end of every chapter, you will have an opportunity to apply managerial and organizational concepts to the exercise of writing a business plan. Refer to Appendix A.

You and your teammates want to make the best decision possible about the type of restaurant on which you will be writing the business plan. You have to keep several important factors in mind when making this decision—for example, your business plan must demonstrate to investors that the venture is worth their while. You decide to use the six-step decision-making model to help you make a choice that is likely to succeed.

Step 1: Recognize the need to make a decision as to the type of restaurant you should develop your business plan on.

Step 2: Generate alternatives.

Make a list of all of your options and place these in the columns across the top of a table as column headings.

Step 3: Assess the alternatives using a decision preference matrix (see Figure 4.7).

1. Make a list of all the factors that are important to the decision; that is, the criteria that fall under the four categories outlined in the text. Place these in rows on the left-hand side of the table. Put all the factors that are important to the decision under the appropriate category of criteria as a subheading.

2. Next, weight the four categories of criteria by working out their relative importance to the decision. For example, you might believe the category of Economic Feasibility

should carry the most weight (say 50 percent), followed by Practical Issues (30 percent), and Legal and Ethical Criteria (10 percent each).

3. Assign each decision variable a score based on information you gathered through research. Show these as numbers from, say, 0 to 10, where 0 means that the factor is absolutely unimportant or has the least beneficial outcome in the final decision, and 10 means that it is very important or has the most favourable outcome. (It is perfectly acceptable to have factors with the same level of importance.) For example: Your research may suggest that a restaurant with entertainment may require more complicated permits and licences to operate than a restaurant that serves only breakfast. Under the criteria of Legal Issues, the breakfast option scores higher than the nightclub, say, 10 to 2, in terms of licensing because it is less legally complicated. However, when considering Economic Feasibility, the nightclub has greater potential to earn revenue than does the breakfast option and thus would have a greater score, say 9 to 1.

4. Create another column for the weighted scores. Working down the columns of options, multiply the score on each decision variable by the value assigned to its relative importance. In our example, under Legal Issues, the nightclub option's weighted score is $2 \times 10 = 20$ for licensing, whereas the breakfast option has a weighted score of $10 \times 10 = 100$. Under Economic Feasibility, the nightclub scores $9 \times 50 = 450$, while the breakfast option scores $1 \times 50 = 50$ for potential to generate revenue.

5. Finally, add up these weighted scores for each of your options.
   Step 4: Choose among the alternatives.
   The option that scores the highest is the one you will choose for your business plan.
   Step 5: Implement the alternative.

Now that you have decided which type of restaurant, you must create an action plan to manage the project of writing the business plan. You might consider using a Gantt chart to manage the tasks and timelines in completing the business plan project.

Step 6: Evaluate and learn from feedback.

You will know if you made a good decision when you present your business plan to an investor (or your professor) and it is favourably received.

MANAGING ETHICALLY EXERCISE

Managers Struggle with Ethical Decisions[73]

It is hard to do the right thing as a manager—especially when you are not sure what the "right thing" is. Sometimes you must balance your own sense of ethics with organizational pressures.

Take the case of employees at a cabinet manufacturing company. A number of them routinely work on their own projects on company time. The manager is aware of this. But there is a labour crunch in the booming construction sector, and she is concerned about retaining staff. So she turns a blind eye. The organization tacitly supports the manager's decision not to stop the practice because labour is hard to find. Nevertheless, the manager is uncomfortable. The decision does not sit right, and she has noticed that allowing the practice has affected other workers. People are taking longer lunches and breaks and talking on the phone during company time. Productivity is starting to slide. How do you think the manager should deal with this situation?

MANAGEMENT CHALLENGE EXERCISE

George Stroumboulopoulos of CBC's *The Hour* initiated a campaign called "One Million Acts of Green,"[74] which is an attempt to get Canadians to engage in something that will prevent greenhouse gas emissions. The act "can be as simple as switching to compact fluorescent lightbulbs, starting a recycling program, or walking to work."

1. As a manager, what decisions could you make that will promote sustainability?

MANAGEMENT PORTFOLIO PROJECT

Answer the following questions about the organization you have chosen to follow:

1. Try to find some evidence that managers at the organization made a few poor decisions over the past decade.

2. If poor decisions were made, what role, if any, did decision-making biases play?

3. Evaluate the approach to sustainability taken by this organization.

4. What kinds of MIS are used in this company? How do they increase efficiency and performance?

VIDEO MANAGEMENT CASE   connect

Anne Mulcahy: How to Make Decisions

Since Anne Mulcahy became CEO of Xerox in 2001, she orchestrated what some have called the turnaround of the century.

1. Why is it so critical to make decisions sooner rather than later?

2. What biases should a manager like Anne Mulcahy avoid in making decisions?

3. How can managers make sure the tough decisions they make are ethical?

Management Case

AN EVEN BETTER CHOICE?[75]

Loblaws gathered a smattering of fooderati at the Neubacher Shor Contemporary Gallery in Toronto last month to officially launch its new "affordable luxury" line of President's Choice products. Dubbed "black label" for its distinct package design (although those words won't appear on the labels, thanks to a Johnnie Walker copyright) the new look items will range in price from $1.99 to $21.99. Landing in 140 stores this October [2011], it includes more than 200 products ranging from an eight-year old cheddar and gingerspiced chocolate sauce to bacon marmalade. But even the stylish launch party can't erase the memory of certain economic realities.

The Canadian grocery market is highly competitive, and with consumers evermore conscious of every dollar spent, Loblaws, Sobey's, Walmart and more are continuously battling to lower prices to keep warm bodies in the store. In his second-quarter earnings call in July, in which the company's food sales were flat, Loblaws executive chairman

Galen Weston said, "Unpredictable and competitively intense market conditions continue to put retail sales at risk."

According to the Nielsen Co., the house food brands created for retailers such as PC, Sobey's Our Compliments or Walmart's Great Value, also known as private labels, are an $11.4-billion annual market in Canada. It's into this fray that Loblaws last year decided to develop and launch its own line of fine foods to win over consumers who might buy the bulk of their groceries at Loblaws then head off to a gourmet food store for a handful of indulgences. The idea is to make Loblaws a one-stop shop for food snobs, where they can pick up both toothpaste and truffle oil. But in this era of austerity, where private-label goods are considered a bang-for-your-buck value proposition, and where cheaper increasingly means better, can the mighty President's Choice get people to pay for luxury? Will bacon marmalade be Loblaws' next Decadent cookie, or is this gourmet gambit too risky a bet?

While a first in Canada, the idea of a major grocery chain getting into classy cheese and exotic oils is not a new one. In the U.K. and Europe, no strangers to recent financial hardships, supermarket heavyweights like Tesco and Carrefour successfully offered high-quality foods (known as "super-premium") at the lower prices associated with private-label brands. It boils down to applying the proven private-label model—develop products and establish relationships with suppliers to cut out the cost of middleman brands and take a bigger cut of the profit margins—to increasingly high-end products.

Ian Gordon, vice-president of Loblaw Brands, says the new black-label line aims to fill a gap in the Loblaws offerings, adding the third tier to what many private-label producers refer to as a "good, better, best" portfolio of goods. There's No Name, President's Choice, of which Blue Menu is the healthier option, and now black label. "There is a 15% to 20% range at the top in the fine-foods area that we do not have an offering in for the consumer," says Gordon. "It's a niche we haven't tried to talk to before now."

In a typical year, a Loblaws product developer might work on up to 50 new items. Hougham is largely credited, along with vice president of product development Maria Charvat, with getting all 213 new black-label products to market in about nine months. It helped that the bulk of the new line are single-ingredient foods like olive oils, chocolates, cheese and pastas, as opposed to something like lasagna, but unearthing tasty products and reliable suppliers that fit the company's vision on such a tight timeline is still a Herculean task.

. . .

Because the new products will only be available in 140 stores initially, don't expect to see Galen Weston Jr. on TV shilling for PC black-label mulling spice anytime soon. There are no plans for a national marketing campaign. Instead, a more targeted digital effort aims to tell the story behind the products and serve up ideas on how to use them. What would you put umami paste in? Exactly. A recipe app for smartphones and the iPad and BlackBerry PlayBook tablets will help answer the question.

While it is a limited rollout, the company is banking on the black-label line's potential. Company officials are certainly confident enough that plans for a Phase II of black label are already in motion. Seeing as Tesco is raking in sales with its upscale Finest line in the U.K., particularly in ready-made meals, and France's Carrefour Group has opened an entire gourmet store in Belgium specializing in meals, perhaps it's no big secret what Canadians can expect next.

There's obviously no guarantee this experiment won't end up a Memories of Market Miscalculations. But if international trends are anything to go by, and in the private-label game they typically are, Loblaws' foray into the finer things bodes well for the PC brand in differentiating from Walmart and other race-to-the-bargain-basement competitors while drawing back those consumers whose wallets have wandered higher up the food chain.

1. What type of decision did Loblaws make when it launched its black label line?

2. Identify the threats and opportunities in the task environment that impact Loblaws' decision.

3. How important is technology to the success of the decision?

Mc Graw Hill connect™

Connect allows you to practise important concepts at your own pace and on your own schedule, with 24/7 online access to an eBook, practice quizzes, video cases, interactive exercises, study tools, and more.

Managing Planning and Strategy

Opening Case

Amazon: Taking Over the Online World

The rapid pace at which the world is changing is forcing the managers of all kinds of companies to develop new strategies to protect their competitive advantage. If they don't, they will be overtaken by agile competitors that respond faster to changing customer needs. Nowhere is this truer than in the cut-throat mobile computing business.

Billionaire founder Jeff Bezos incorporated Amazon.com, Inc. in 1994 and opened its Internet store in July 1995 with the aim to provide "earth's biggest selection."[1] His strategy was to offer an unlimited selection of books and, where possible, to have them shipped directly from distributors to customers. The company grew to mammoth proportions, taking much of the book retailing business with it. Circuit City, Borders, and others succumbed to the cut-throat competition and closed up shop, unable to match the variety of online goods and delivery service. Amazon then launched an online TV and movie store in 2006, the Kindle e-book store in 2007, and the MP3 digital music store in 2008. In 2011, Amazon aimed its sights on Netflix with an instant video streaming service that's free for members. It also now offers customers an online auction service.

Today, Amazon aims to provide "earth's biggest selection" by selling everything from diapers to digital televisions online. Best Buy had to cut the square footage of its big-box stores as Amazon commoditized whole product categories that it sells. Walmart has not been able to match the reliability of its shipping network. Companies like Zappos and Diapers.com that could match Amazon in price, selection, and customer service have all been acquired by Bezos. Amazon is growing in leaps and bounds, while the competition is lagging.

One of the biggest growth areas Amazon has experienced is in developing its own hardware e-readers and providing cloud computing services. The latest e-reader, the Kindle Fire device, not only entices people to buy their books from Amazon, but also makes it easier for them to use Amazon.com as their primary e-commerce site for the huge range of consumer goods it provides. Kindle Fire owners can watch newly released films, scroll through magazines, and access their music collection on Amazon's cloud computing servers, adding more clout to one of the world's fastest-growing retail operations.

Bezos's strategy to compete with Apple's iPad is two-pronged. First, it offers apps based on Google's Android system that direct users to Amazon's own content and optimizes the shopping experience by doing away with the clutter on the main website. The browser, called Amazon Silk, will make it easier for customers to browse and shop online because it allows free storage of data, music, and movies on its vast cloud computing servers instead of these items being stored only by the browser in the device. So although the device has only 8 gigabytes of memory (the best iPad has a maximum of 64), owners of the Kindle Fire get to store as many books, songs, movies, and personal documents on Amazon's cloud servers as they like. The second prong is the price. The Kindle Fire retails for significantly less than the iPad or RIM's PlayBook. Bezos is able to undercut the competition because he expects customers to make additional purchases of things like toys, toasters, and tires.

So although margins may be small on the device itself, Bezos is banking that the tablet will funnel users into the company's e-commerce and cloud computing domains. The company also generates revenue from membership fees for preferential delivery services. And, if that wasn't enough to strengthen its competitive position, Amazon published 122 books in physical and e-book form in the fall of 2011, placing it in direct competition with the suppliers it once relied on.[2] Amazon's already-thin profit margins could face a significant threat if Apple were to take a bigger share of the tablet e-commerce market and get into cloud computing. And Apple aims to do just that. Apple launched iCloud, an online communications, media storage, and backup service in October 2011 to replace MobileMe, a collection of Web-based products that failed to create much revenue for the company.[3]

On the rivalry between Amazon and Apple, Bezos says that "Everything we do is driven by seeing opportunity rather than being worried about defending. . . . Both companies like to invent, both companies like to pioneer, both companies start with the customer and work backwards. There's a like-mindedness. . . . Are two companies like Amazon and Apple occasionally going to step on each other's toes? Yes."[4]

After reading and understanding the concepts in this chapter, you should be able to answer the following questions:

1. *What was the vision for Amazon.com and how has it changed?*

2. *Describe the corporate-level strategy employed by Amazon.*

3. *What business-level strategies has Amazon pursued?*

4. *Apply Porter's Five Forces model to the tablet computer industry.*

Overview

As the opening case suggests, in a fast-changing competitive environment such as mobile computing, managers must continually evaluate how well products are meeting customer needs and engage in thorough, systematic planning to find new strategies to better meet those needs. This chapter explores the manager's role both as planner and as strategist. We first discuss what planning is, who does it, why it's important for high performance, and what qualities make effective plans. We then discuss the five main steps in the planning process: a) determining and communicating an organization's vision, mission, and goals; b) analyzing the forces in the organizational environment; c) formulating strategy at the corporate, business, and functional level; d) implementing strategy; and, finally, e) evaluating the success of the strategy in achieving the mission and goals of the organization. By the end of this chapter, you will understand the vital role managers carry out when they plan, develop, and implement strategies to create a high-performing organization.

Describe what planning is, who does it, types of plans, why it is important, and what qualities make plans effective. **LO1**

An Overview of the Planning Process

Planning, as we noted in Chapter 1, is a process that managers use to identify and select suitable goals and courses of action for an organization.[5] It is one of the four principal managerial functions. The organizational plan that results from the planning process details the goals of the organization and specifies how managers intend to attain those goals. The cluster of decisions and actions that managers take to help an organization attain its goals is its **strategy.** Thus, planning is both a goal-making and a strategy-making process.

Essentially, to perform the planning task, managers (1) establish and discover where an organization is *at the present time;* (2) determine where it should be in the

planning Identifying and selecting suitable goals and courses of action; one of the four principal functions of management.

strategy A cluster of decisions about what goals to pursue, what actions to take, and how to use resources to achieve goals.

FIGURE 5.1   **Steps in the Planning Process**

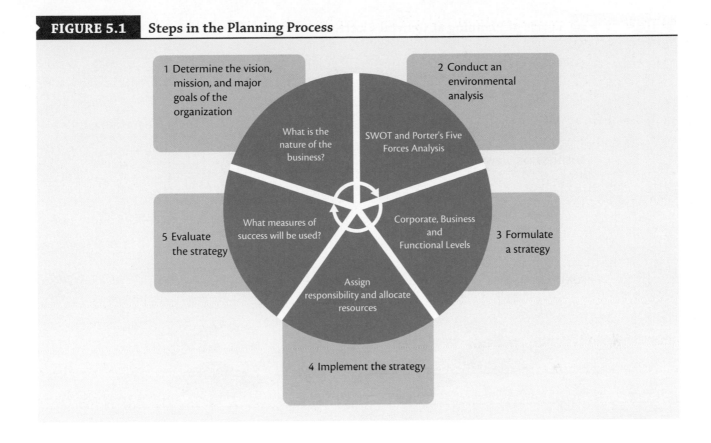

future, its *desired future state;* and (3) decide how to *move it forward* to reach that future state. When managers plan, they must forecast what may happen in the future in order to decide what to do in the present. The better their predictions, the more effective will be the strategies they formulate to take advantage of future opportunities and counter emerging competitive threats in the environment. As previous chapters noted, however, the external environment is uncertain and complex, and managers typically must deal with incomplete information and bounded rationality. This is why planning and strategy making is such a difficult and risky activity, and if managers' predictions are wrong and strategies fail, organizational performance falls. See Figure 5.1 for an overview of the planning process.

Who Plans?

In large organizations, planning usually takes place at three levels of management: corporate, business or division, and department or functional.[6] GE has three main levels of management: corporate level, business level, and functional level (see Figure 5.2). At the corporate level are CEO and Chairman Jeffrey Immelt, three other top managers, and

division A business unit that has its own set of managers and functions or departments and competes in a distinct industry.

divisional managers Managers who control the various divisions of an organization.

their corporate support staff. Below the corporate level is the business level. At the business level are the different divisions of the company. A **division** is a business unit that competes in a distinct industry; GE has more than 150 divisions, including GE Capital, GE Aircraft Engines, GE Lighting, GE Motors and Industrial Systems, GE Plastics, and NBC. Each division has its own set of **divisional managers.** In turn, each division has its own set of functions or departments—manufacturing, marketing, human resources, research and development (R&D), and so on. Thus, GE Aircraft Engines has its own marketing function, as do GE Lighting, GE Motors, and NBC.

Even though corporate-level planning is the responsibility of top managers, lower-level managers can be and usually are given the opportunity to become involved in the process. At GE and many other companies, divisional and functional managers are encouraged to submit proposals for new business ventures to the CEO and top managers, who evaluate the proposals and decide whether to fund them.[7] Corporate-level managers are also responsible for approving business- and functional-level plans to ensure that they are consistent with the corporate plan.

> **FIGURE 5.2** Levels of Planning at General Electric

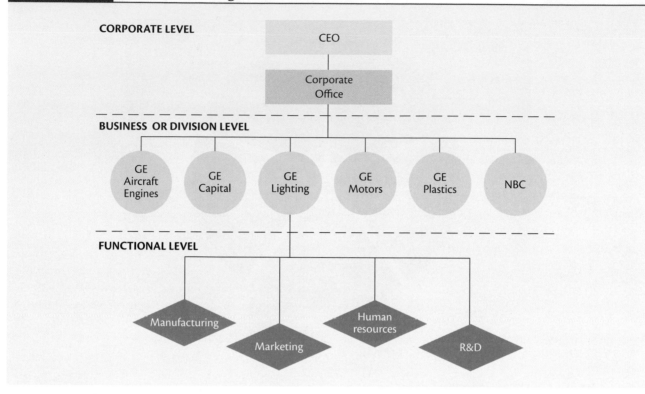

An important issue in planning is ensuring *consistency* in planning across the three levels. Functional goals and strategies should be consistent with divisional goals and strategies, which, in turn, should be consistent with corporate goals and strategies, and vice versa. Once complete, each function's plan is normally linked to its division's business-level plan, which, in turn, is linked to the corporate plan. Although many organizations are smaller and less complex than GE, most do their planning as GE does and have written plans to guide managerial decision making.

Time Horizons of Plans

Plans differ in their **time horizons,** or intended durations. Managers usually distinguish among long-term plans with a horizon of five years or more, intermediate-term plans with a horizon between one and five years, and short-term plans with a horizon of one year or less.[8] Typically, corporate- and business-level goals and strategies require long- and intermediate-term plans, and functional-level goals and strategies require intermediate- and short-term plans.

Although most organizations operate with planning horizons of five years or more, it would be inaccurate to infer from this that they undertake major planning exercises only once every five years and then "lock in" a specific set of goals and strategies for that period. Most organizations

time horizon The intended duration of a plan.

have an annual planning cycle, which is usually linked to their annual financial budget (even though a major planning effort may be undertaken only every few years).

Although a corporate- or business-level plan may extend over five years (or more), it is typically treated as a *rolling plan,* a plan that is updated and amended every year to take into account changing conditions in the external environment. Thus, the time horizon for an organization's 2015 corporate plan might be 2020, but it might be reviewed and amended in 2016, 2017, 2018, and 2019. The use of rolling plans is essential because of the high rate of change in the environment and the difficulty of predicting competitive conditions five years in the future. Rolling plans allow managers to make any mid-course corrections that environmental changes warrant or to change the thrust of the plan altogether if it no longer seems appropriate. The use of rolling plans allows managers to plan flexibly, without losing sight of the need to plan for the long term.

Standing Plans and Single-Use Plans

Another distinction often made between plans is whether they are standing or single-use plans. Managers create standing and single-use plans to help achieve an organization's specific goals. *Standing plans* are used in situations where programmed decision making is appropriate. When the same situations occur repeatedly, managers develop

standard operating procedures (SOPs) Written instructions describing the exact series of actions that should be followed in a specific situation.

policy A general guide to action.

rule A formal, written guide to action.

policies, rules, and **standard operating procedures (SOPs)** to control the way employees perform their tasks. A **policy** is a general guide to action; a **rule** is a formal, written guide to action; and an SOP is a written instruction describing the exact series of actions that should be followed in a specific situation. For example, an organization may have a standing plan about the ethical behaviour of employees. This plan includes a policy that all employees are expected to behave ethically in their dealings with suppliers and customers; a rule that requires employees to report any gift worth more than $10 that is received from a supplier or customer; and an SOP that obliges the recipient of the gift to make the disclosure in writing within 30 days.

In contrast, *single-use plans* are developed to handle nonprogrammed decision making in unusual or one-of-a-kind situations. Examples of single-use plans include *programs* (integrated sets of plans for achieving certain goals) and *projects* (specific action plans created to complete various aspects of a program). One of NASA's major programs was to reach the moon, and one project in this program was to develop a lunar module capable of landing on the moon and returning to Earth. Refer to Figure 5.3 for the levels of managers responsible for various types of plans.

Why Planning Is Important

Almost all managers engage in planning, and all *should* do so because planning helps predict future opportunities and threats. The absence of a plan often results in hesitation, false steps, and mistaken changes of direction that can hurt an organization or even lead to disaster. Planning is important for four main reasons:

1. *It is a useful way of getting managers to take part in decision making* about the appropriate goals and strategies for an organization.

2. *It is necessary to give the organization a sense of direction and purpose.*[9] By stating which organizational goals and strategies are important, a plan keeps managers on track so that they use the resources under their control efficiently and effectively.

3. *A plan helps coordinate managers of the different functions and divisions of an organization to ensure that they all pull in the same direction and work to achieve its future desired state.* Without a good plan, it is possible that the members of the manufacturing function will produce more products than the members of the sales function can sell, resulting in a mass of unsold inventory. This happened to high-flying Internet router supplier Cisco Systems in the early 2000s when manufacturing, which previously had been able to sell all the routers it produced, found it had over $2 billion of inventory that the sales force could not sell; customers now wanted new kinds of optical routers that Cisco had not planned to develop—even though sales had told manufacturing that customer needs were changing.

4. *A plan can be used as a device for controlling managers within an organization.* A good plan specifies not only which goals and strategies the organization is committed to but also who is responsible for putting the strategies into action to attain the

▶ FIGURE 5.3 Level of Manager Responsible for Types of Plans

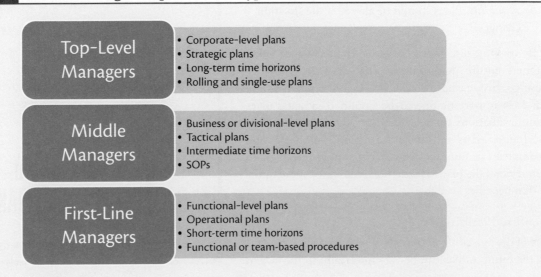

Top-Level Managers
- Corporate-level plans
- Strategic plans
- Long-term time horizons
- Rolling and single-use plans

Middle Managers
- Business or divisional-level plans
- Tactical plans
- Intermediate time horizons
- SOPs

First-Line Managers
- Functional-level plans
- Operational plans
- Short-term time horizons
- Functional or team-based procedures

A group of managers meet to plot their company's strategy. Their ability to assess opportunities and challenges and to forecast the future doesn't just depend on brilliance. Tools such as SWOT analysis can significantly bolster the accuracy of their predictions.

goals. When managers know that they will be held accountable for attaining a goal, they are motivated to do their best to make sure the goal is achieved.

Effective Plans

Effective plans have four qualities[10]:

1. *Unity.* Only one central guiding plan should be put into operation at any one time.

2. *Continuity.* Planning does not just happen once. Rather, plans are built, refined, and modified so that all levels—corporate, business, and functional— fit together into one broad framework.

3. *Accuracy.* Managers need to make every attempt to collect and use all available information at their disposal in the planning process.

4. *Flexibility.* Plans should be altered if the situation changes.

By making sure that plans have these characteristics, planners ensure that multiple goals and plans do not cause confusion and disorder. Managers must recognize that it is important not to be bound to a static plan, because situations change. They must also recognize that uncertainty exists and that information is almost always incomplete, so one does the best planning possible and then reviews the plans as situations change or more information becomes available.

Scenario Planning

One of the most difficult aspects of making plans is predicting the future, which can be very uncertain. In the face of uncertainty, one of the most widely used planning techniques is scenario planning. **Scenario planning** (also known as *contingency planning*) is the generation of multiple forecasts of future conditions followed by an analysis of how to respond effectively to each of those conditions.

Scenario planning generates "multiple futures"—or scenarios of the future— based on different assumptions about conditions that *might prevail* in the future, and then develops different plans that detail what a company *should do* in the event that any of these scenarios actually occur. Managers use scenario planning to generate different future scenarios of conditions in the environment. They then develop responses to the opportunities and threats facing the different scenarios and create a set of plans based on these responses. The great strength of scenario planning is its ability not only to anticipate the challenges of an uncertain future but also to educate managers to think about the future—to think strategically.[11]

Paul J. H. Schoemaker with George Day, in a *Business-Week* article titled "Peripheral Vision: Detecting the Weak

scenario planning The generation of multiple forecasts of future conditions followed by an analysis of how to respond effectively to each of those conditions; also called *contingency planning.*

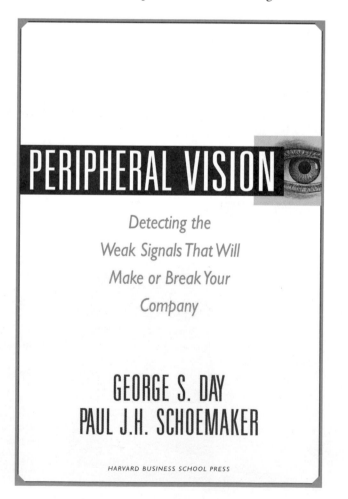

PERIPHERAL VISION

Detecting the
Weak Signals That Will
Make or Break Your
Company

GEORGE S. DAY
PAUL J.H. SCHOEMAKER

HARVARD BUSINESS SCHOOL PRESS

Signals That Will Make or Break Your Company,"[12] points out the following:

> Traditional forecasting and budgeting systems produce linear projections insufficient for risky, uncertain times. What's needed is scenario planning, where companies stress-test their strategies and processes against a wide range of future scenarios to identify their vulnerabilities. Thus informed, the companies can adjust them to be more responsive and resilient. But scenario planning often takes a backseat to more immediate concerns: developing new products, fighting an aggressive competitor, meeting earnings targets. So when large-scale external events hit, their impact is seismic.[13]

Crisis Management

In many cases, managers cannot predict the conditions that might give rise to a contingency plan. In cases where unpredictable and unforeseeable conditions prevail, usually a disaster that can seriously damage the organization is in the making. The degree to which the organization can recover from such a crisis largely hinges on how transparent and open the top managers are with the stakeholders. **Crisis management plans** are formulated to deal with possible future crises.[14] Management crisis software can help formulate a response that minimizes the potential damage to reputation and consumer confidence that comes along with a disaster. Several companies have faced crises that had to be managed for damage control. See Figure 5.4.

In two Toronto-based cases, two very different approaches to crisis management were used, resulting in two very different outcomes. In the late 2000s, Maple Leaf Foods recalled its entire stock of 220 meat products from one of its plants that was shut down after being found to be the source of food-borne bacteria called *Listeria monocytogenes*. The listeriosis outbreak caused several deaths and illnesses. How did CEO Michael McCain handle the crisis? In an effort to protect the company and its customers, he gave press releases, media interviews, and posted up-to-date information on the efforts the company was making to get rid of the bacteria. His highly apparent candour about the situation won him praise from the public. Communication was the key to Maple Leaf's crisis management

crisis management plans Formulated to deal with possible future crises.

Tips FOR MANAGERS

Planning

1. Vision matters because it serves as a source of inspiration and motivation for the stakeholders of the organization. Craft the vision statement so that it reflects what the organization is striving to achieve. For example, the vision of a food bank may be "to end hunger."

2. Operationalize the vision by breaking it down into a mission—a statement of purpose of the organization. For example, the mission of the food bank may be "feeding hungry people in our community."

3. Further break down the mission into a series of cascading relating goals and objectives. For example, the goal may be "to have enough resources to feed those who need the food bank's services for six months." A related objective may be "keeping a one-week supply of food, having enough staff and volunteers to meet unexpected increases in demand, and increasing funding levels by 10 percent above the previous year's budget."

4. If each objective is met, then the broad goal of "having enough resources" is likely to be achieved and the organization is fulfilling its mission.

> **FIGURE 5.4** **Notable Corporate Responses to Crisis Management[15]**

1.	Johnson & Johnson's response to the case of tampered Tylenol is widely cited as the gold standard response to a crisis. In 1982, in Chicago, seven people died after taking extra-strength Tylenol that had been laced with cyanide. The company yanked the product off the shelves across the United States. It would ultimately introduce three-way, tamper-proof pill bottles. Within a year, Tylenol had regained its market share.
2.	U.S.-based toy giant Mattel issued an extraordinary apology to China in September 2007 over the recall of millions of Chinese-made toys, taking the blame for design flaws and saying it had recalled more lead-tainted toys than justified. Mattel ordered three high-profile recalls in the summer of 2007 involving more than 21 million Chinese-made toys, including Barbie doll accessories and toy cars due to concerns about lead paint and tiny magnets that could be swallowed.
3.	In March 2007, the president of Canadian pet food company Menu Foods apologized to pet owners amid a recall of products found to contain Chinese-supplied wheat gluten laced with poisonous melamine. Company shares dropped following deaths of cats and dogs. Executives were asked to take pay cuts, and the company downsized its workforce after millions of packages of pet food were recalled and dozens of lawsuits were launched. The recall cost Menu Foods an estimated $55 million.

Effective planning and controlling are key challenges for managers.

strategy. What could have ruined the business turned out to be a short-lived crisis with a quick recovery.

On the other hand, the blast at the Sunrise Propane plant in North York, Ontario, which caused the deaths of two people and the evacuation of some 12 000 residents, was handled quite differently. The company kept a very low profile "in order to avoid prejudicing themselves, or to create problems for themselves later if there are legal proceedings."[16] Similarly, ex-CEOs of RIM Jim Balsillie and Mike Lazaridis were criticized for failing to address their loyal users quickly after a power outage in 2011 created a worldwide blackout for BlackBerry users. These example illustrate two very different approaches to managing crises.

LO2 Describe planning as a five-step process.

Five Steps in the Planning Process

In most organizations, planning is a five-step process (refer to Figure 5.1). The first step is *determining the organization's vision, mission, and goals.*

A **vision statement** reveals the big picture of the organization, its dream for the future.

A **mission statement** is a broad declaration of an organization's overriding purpose; this statement is intended to identify an organization's products and customers, as well as to distinguish the organization in some way from its competitors. A **goal** is a desired future outcome that an organization strives to achieve within a specified timeframe. Generally, the goals are set based on the vision and mission of the organization. Once the mission and goals

are agreed upon and formally stated in the corporate plan, they guide the next steps by defining which strategies are appropriate and which are inappropriate.[17]

The second step involves analyzing the forces in the organizational environment to determine where the opportunities lie and how to counter any threats. Managers use several techniques to *analyze the current situation,* two of which, SWOT and Porter's Five Forces analysis, we examine in this chapter. The third step is *formulating strategy.* Managers analyze the organization's current situation and then conceive and develop the strategies necessary to attain the organization's mission and goals. The fourth step is *implementing strategy.* Managers decide how to allocate the resources and responsibilities required to implement the chosen strategies among individuals and groups within the organization.[18] The last step is *evaluation.* How does a manager know if the strategy was successful? In subsequent sections of this chapter, we look in detail at the specifics of each of these steps.

Step 1: Defining the Vision

Vision differs from other forms of organizational direction setting in several ways:

> A vision has clear and compelling imagery that offers an innovative way to improve, which recognizes and draws on traditions, and connects to actions that people can take to realize change. Vision taps people's emotions and energy. Properly articulated, a vision creates the enthusiasm that people have for sporting events and other leisure time activities, bringing that energy and commitment to the workplace.[19]

The organization's vision is generally set by the CEO. When Bill Gates founded Microsoft, his vision was "a computer on every desk, in every home, and in every office." Steve Ballmer, Microsoft's current CEO, sees this vision as insufficient in today's high-tech world and has developed a new vision: "Empower people anytime, anywhere, on any device."[20] Amazon's vision is "to be earth's most customer centric company; to build a place where people can come to find and discover anything they might want to buy online."[21]

Setting the Mission

The organization's mission is supposed to flow from the vision for the organization.

vision statement
A broad declaration of the big picture of the organization and/or a statement of its dreams for the future.

mission statement
A broad declaration of an organization's purpose that identifies the organization's products and customers and distinguishes the organization from its competitors.

goal A desired future outcome that an organization strives to achieve within a specified timeframe.

To determine an organization's mission, managers must first define its business so that they can identify what kind of value they will provide to customers. To define the business, managers must ask three questions[22]: (1) Who are our customers? (2) What customer needs are being satisfied? and (3) How are we satisfying customer needs? These questions identify the customer needs that the organization satisfies and the way the organization satisfies those needs. Answering these questions helps managers identify not only what customer needs they are satisfying now but what needs they should try to satisfy in the future and who their true competitors are. All of this information helps managers determine the mission and then establish appropriate goals. Amazon's mission as published in their 2010 Annual Report is "We seek to be earth's most customer-centric company for three primary customer sets: consumers, sellers, and enterprises. In addition, we generate revenue through other marketing and promotional services, such as online advertising, and co-branded credit card agreements."[23] The mission statements of Montreal based Gildan Activewear Inc.; TELUS; and TD Group are presented in Figure 5.5.

Establishing Major Goals

Once the business is defined, managers must establish a set of primary goals to which the organization is committed. Developing these goals gives the organization a sense of direction or purpose. Thus, as we showed in this chapter's opening case, the CEO of Amazon is committed to serving its customers in this very challenging environment. Just after going public in 1997, Bezos stated this in a letter to investors: "Our goal remains to continue to solidify and extend our brand and customer base. This requires sustained investment in systems and infrastructure to support outstanding customer convenience, selection, and service while we grow." He has published the same letter to investors in every year since. The best statements of organizational goals are ambitious—that is, they stretch the organization and require that all its members work to improve its performance.[24] The role of **strategic leadership,** the ability of the CEO and top managers to convey a compelling vision of what they want to achieve to their subordinates, is important here. If subordinates buy into the vision, and model their behaviours on the leader, they develop a willingness to undertake the hard, stressful work that is necessary for creative, risk-taking strategy making.[25] Many popular books such as *Built to Last* provide lucid accounts of strategic leaders establishing "big, hairy, audacious goals (BHAGs)" that serve as rallying points for their subordinates.[26] Other elements of effective goals are represented by the acronym "SMART + C."[27] See Figure 5.6. To be effective, goals should be specific, not vague; be measurable—that is, quantifiable whenever possible; be attainable; be realistic; fall within an appropriate timeframe; and be communicated to all stakeholders.

The period in which a goal is expected to be achieved should be stated. Time constraints are important because they emphasize that a goal must be reached within a reasonable period; they inject a sense of urgency into goal attainment and act as a motivator.

The issue of how to design reward systems to motivate managers and other organizational employees is discussed in Chapter 8. The evaluation of whether goals were

> **strategic leadership**
> The ability of the CEO and top managers to convey a compelling vision of what they want the organization to achieve to their subordinates.

FIGURE 5.5 **Three Mission Statements**

COMPANY	MISSION STATEMENT
TD Bank Group	We will be the Best Run, Customer focused, Integrated Financial Institution with a Unique and Inclusive Employee Culture.
TELUS	To unleash the power of the Internet to deliver the best solutions to Canadians at home, in the workplace and on the move.
Gildan Activewear	Gildan Activewear is dedicated to being the lowest-cost manufacturer and leading marketer of branded basic activewear to wholesale channels of distribution both in North America and internationally. To attain this goal, we will deliver the best in quality, service, and price to our customers and, ultimately, to the end-users of our activewear products.

FIGURE 5.6 **Qualities of Good Goal Formulation: Make Them SMART + C**

- **S**pecific
- **M**easurable
- **A**ssignable (Achievable, Attainable, Action-oriented, Acceptable, Agreed-upon, Accountable)
- **R**ealistic (Relevant, Result-oriented)
- **T**ime-related (Timely, Time-bound, Tangible, Traceable)
- + Communicated

---

achieved is part of the control process, which we discuss in-depth in Chapter 13.

LO3 Explain how managers use diagnostic techniques to evaluate the opportunities and threats in the organization's environment.

Step 2: Analyzing the Environment

Strategy formulation includes analyzing an organization's current situation and then developing strategies to accomplish the organization's mission and achieve its goals.[28] Strategy formulation begins with managers analyzing the factors within an organization and outside—in the task and general environments—that affect or may affect the organization's ability to meet its current and future goals. Several techniques can be used to analyze the organization's environment, including *PESTEL, TOWES, SWOT analysis,* and the *Five Forces model.* The last two are discussed in this section. Once the environmental forces are analyzed for opportunities and threats, decisions about how to best accomplish the organization's vision, mission, and goals can be made. These decisions translate into strategies that managers pursue at the corporate, business, and functional levels.

SWOT Analysis

SWOT analysis is the first step in strategy formulation at any level. It is a planning exercise in which managers identify organizational strengths (S) and weaknesses (W), and environmental opportunities (O) and threats (T). Based on a SWOT analysis, managers at the different levels of the organization select corporate-, business-, and functional-level strategies to best position the organization to achieve its mission and goals (see Figure 5.7).

The first step in SWOT analysis is to identify an organization's strengths and weaknesses that characterize the present state of the organization *relative to its competition,* and then consider how the strengths will be maintained and the weaknesses overcome to gain a competitive advantage. Take, for example, the company in our opening case, Amazon. See Figure 5.8. Amazon.com is a pioneer in e-commerce. It sells products ranging from books, music, and movies to toys, electronics, and automotive. It developed technologies and procedures that are commonplace with online retailers today, including one-click shopping, email verification notices to clients, and comparison shopping tools. These strengths positioned the company to excel in online retailing. In 1997, when Amazon.com went public, sales grew by 838 percent and customer accounts increased by 738 percent.[29] At that time, the company established long-term relationships with strategic partners that would promote Amazon's business interests, including America Online, Yahoo!, Excite, Netscape, GeoCities, AltaVista, @ Home, and Prodigy.

Identifying the strengths of an organization involves an analysis of the things it does well. CEO Bezos was confident that

Diagnosing threats and opportunities are key to a manager's success.

strategy formulation Analysis of an organization's current situation followed by the development of strategies to accomplish the organization's mission and achieve its goals.

SWOT analysis A planning exercise in which managers identify organizational strengths (S) and weaknesses (W), and environmental opportunities (O) and threats (T) relative to the competition.

FIGURE 5.7   **Environmental Assessment and Strategy Formulation**

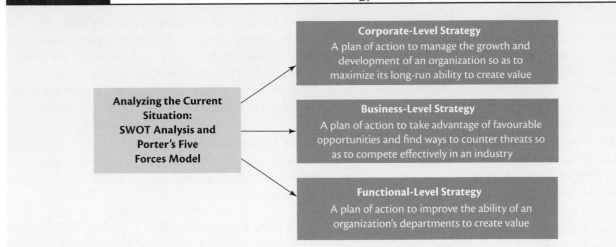

FIGURE 5.8   SWOT of Amazon.com

Strengths	Weaknesses
• continuous, fast growth mainly through acquisitions of competitors • partnerships with Internet companies to promote its business • strong personalized customer service: including email notifications, recommendations to clients, award-winning books section and other programs that help clients decide what products to purchase • developed technologies that are commonplace to e-commerce today • client convenience in online shopping: widest range of online products • reliable, trustworthy, reputable e-commerce site	• cluttered, unattractive website • employee morale is questionable • secretive corporate culture • thin profit margins increases reliance on establishing a mass client base
Opportunities	**Threats**
• expand its e-commerce product lines • promote and expand its cloud computing services • grow its hardware e-reader tablet business • promote the fee-for-membership model of revenue generation • increase clients through innovative Web-related content, commerce and communication services for changing lifestyles • continue to foster its reputation and increase its status among competitors • increase acquisitions of competitive online retailers	• competitors like Apple, RIM, and Samsung may take a larger share of the e-commerce market • innovative tablet products that compete with the Kindle Fire such as BlackBerry PlayBook • Apple's iCloud cloud computing services may take market share away from Amazon's cloud computing services • legal and political threats include having to collect and pay sales taxes in many U.S. states • growth is limited to Internet users, which in many areas of the world is limited • competitors have greater brand recognition, more resources, longer histories, and a greater number of customers

e-commerce was the way of the future and that focusing on customer satisfaction in making the online shopping experience convenient would pay off. When conducting a SWOT on a competitor, the manager looks at the internal organizational forces such as the strategy, resources (assets and people), management competencies, organizational structure, capacity and capabilities, location, trademarks and patents, length of time in business, and source of competitive advantage. When identifying weaknesses, managers look at the internal organizational forces that are done poorly, such as gaps in capabilities, lack of competitive strength, financials (debt to equity, ROI), reputation, level of employee morale, and lack of management competencies. Opportunities are found in the external organizational environment. Opportunities are chances for increasing market share and growth. Managers look for things in the organizational environment that present such opportunities. Threats are things in the external environment that hinder profitability and growth, such as shifts in market demand and legal and political changes. See Table 5.1 for a list of elements managers look at in a SWOT analysis of a competitor. Table 5.2 illustrates the kind of questions that may be asked.

When managers are able to identify potential opportunities and threats in their environments that affect the organization at the present and may affect it in the future, they can then consider how to take advantage of the opportunities for growth and overcome any threats. For Amazon, this analysis led to a shift in corporate-level strategy to capitalize on the growing market for hand-held mobile electronic devices. It got into the business of designing and building its own hardware to compete in the lucrative and highly competitive tablet market. Its latest generation of e-reader, the Kindle Fire, steers customers toward using Amazon.com for all of their online shopping needs.

The Five Forces Model

Michael **Porter's Five Forces model** is a widely used technique for analyzing the potential profitability of entering and competing in a particular industry (see Figure 5.9). It helps managers isolate particular forces in the external environment that are potential threats. Porter identified five factors (the first four are also discussed

> **Porter's Five Forces model** A technique managers use to analyze the potential profitability of entering and competing in a particular industry.

TABLE 5.1   Elements Managers Look for in a SWOT Analysis of a Competitor

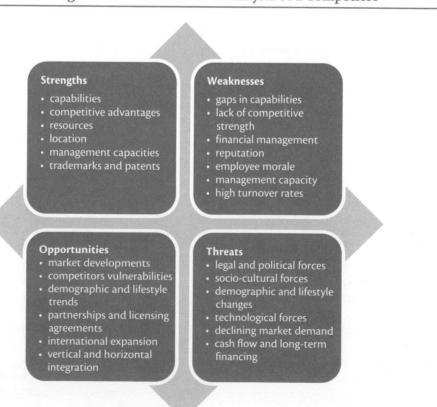

Strengths
- capabilities
- competitive advantages
- resources
- location
- management capacities
- trademarks and patents

Weaknesses
- gaps in capabilities
- lack of competitive strength
- financial management
- reputation
- employee morale
- management capacity
- high turnover rates

Opportunities
- market developments
- competitors vulnerabilities
- demographic and lifestyle trends
- partnerships and licensing agreements
- international expansion
- vertical and horizontal integration

Threats
- legal and political forces
- socio-cultural forces
- demographic and lifestyle changes
- technological forces
- declining market demand
- cash flow and long-term financing

| **TABLE 5.2** | Questions Managers Ask in a SWOT Analysis | | | |

Potential Strengths	Potential Opportunities	Potential Weaknesses	Potential Threats
Well-developed strategy?	Expand core business(es)?	Poorly developed strategy?	Attacks on core business(es)?
Strong product lines?	Exploit new market segments?	Obsolete, narrow product lines?	Increase in domestic competition?
Broad market coverage?	Widen product range?	Rising manufacturing costs?	Increase in foreign competition?
Manufacturing competence?	Extend cost or differentiation advantage?	Decline in R&D innovations?	Change in consumer tastes?
Good marketing skills?	Diversify into new growth businesses?	Poor marketing plan?	Fall in barriers to entry?
Good materials management systems?	Expand into foreign markets?	Poor materials management systems?	Rise in new or substitute products?
R&D skills and leadership?	Apply R&D skills in new areas?	Loss of customer goodwill?	Increase in industry rivalry?
Human resource competencies?	Enter new related businesses?	Inadequate human resources?	New forms of industry competition?
Brand-name reputation?	Vertically integrate forward?	Loss of brand name?	Potential for takeover?
Cost of differentiation advantage?	Vertically integrate backward?	Growth without direction?	Changes in demographic factors?
Appropriate management style?	Overcome barriers to entry?	Loss of corporate direction?	Changes in economic factors?
Appropriate organizational structure?	Reduce rivalry among competitors?	Infighting among divisions?	Downturn in economy?
Appropriate control systems?	Apply brand-name capital in new areas?	Loss of corporate control?	Rising labour costs?
Ability to manage strategic change?	Seek fast market growth?	Inappropriate organizational structure and control systems?	Slower market growth?
Others?	Others?	High conflict and politics?	Others?
		Others?	

in Chapter 2) that are major threats because they affect how much profit organizations that compete within the same industry can expect to make:

- *The level of rivalry among organizations in an industry.* The degree of rivalry is the extent of the competition—the amount that companies compete against one another for customers. For example, by lowering the prices of their products or by increasing advertising, the lower is the level of industry profits. Low prices mean less profit. Amazon's Kindle Fire sells at about one-third the cost of Apple's iPad, leaving Amazon with very thin profit margins. The degree to which firms vigorously compete with one another used to be conceptualized in terms of the entire operation of one firm against another. Recently, as Peter Drucker predicted,[30] firms have begun to swallow their pride and cooperate in specific areas while maintaining fierce competition in others. Automobile manufacturers

> "Are two companies like Amazon and Apple occasionally going to step on each other's toes? Yes."
>
> *Jeff Bezos, CEO, Amazon*

and airlines have long since adopted these networked strategic alliances to achieve economies of scale by collaborating on vehicle platforms and sharing check-in facilities, but recently industries such as media and courier companies have increased their cooperation, coined **co-opetition** by professors at Yale University.[31] In a 10-year deal, the German-owned parcel-delivery company DHL would pay rival American UPS to carry its packages in the United States, Canada, and Mexico to reduce its losses in North America while taking advantage of UPS's excess capacity. "When this deal is finalized, nothing will change the fact that we are a rabid competitor of DHL," says a UPS executive.[32]

co-opetition Arrangements in which firms compete vigorously with one another, while also cooperating in specific areas to achieve economies of scale.

- *The potential for entry into an industry.* This refers to how easy it is for another firm to enter the industry. The easier it is for companies to enter an

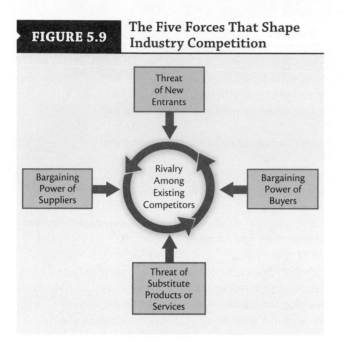

FIGURE 5.9	The Five Forces That Shape Industry Competition

industry—because, for example, barriers to entry are low (see Chapter 2)—the more likely it is for industry prices and therefore industry profits to be low. For example, there are huge barriers to entry in the oil and aerospace industries because of the large investment of capital needed to start up and operate. Moreover, brand loyalty, such as that enjoyed by Amazon's competitor, Apple, protects profits. Industries that rely on the "difficulty of change," such as Microsoft's Windows operating system and drug companies that enjoy long-term patents on proprietary drugs, make it harder for new firms to compete, create large barriers to entry, and thus enjoy a stronger potential for profits.

- *The power of suppliers.* If there are only a few suppliers of an important input, then (as discussed in Chapter 2) suppliers can drive up the price of that input, and expensive inputs result in lower profits for the producer. Samsung is Apple's most important supplier in the smartphone and tablet-computer markets. Samsung components, which include all the product's application processors, account for 16 percent of the value of an iPhone. This much reliance on one supplier has Apple searching for ways to diversify its supply chain.[33] The airline industry suffers from threats posed by the suppliers of expensive fuel. As jet fuel prices increase, airlines have little choice but to pay the higher prices.

- *The power of customers.* The bargaining power of your customers is affected by their size and how much revenue they generate for your company. If only a few large customers are available to buy an industry's output, they can bargain to drive down the price of that output. As a result, producers make lower profits. For example, Walmart, as the largest retailer in the global economy, has a huge impact on firms that supply it with goods to sell. If Walmart refuses to carry a company's products, it would be unlikely for the company to become successful in the global economy. Walmart is such a large customer, it purchases so much inventory and accounts for such a large proportion of a supplier's revenue, that most companies will do anything to protect their business with them.

- *The threat of substitute products.* Often, the output of one industry is a substitute for the output of another industry (e.g., plastic may be a substitute for steel in some applications). Companies that produce a product with a known substitute cannot demand high prices for their products, and this constraint keeps their profits low. On the other hand, industries that have few, if any, substitutes can command very high profits as long as there remains a demand for the product. For example, there is no widespread substitute for oil. If gasoline prices go too high, people may switch to hybrid or electric vehicles, or pay the high price because they cannot easily find a substitute for gasoline powered cars. With clothing, on the other hand, if the price of designer clothing goes up, people have the option of buying many cheaper no-name brands. When a substitute for their product exists, companies cannot demand very high prices for it or customers will switch to the substitute, and this constraint keeps their profits low.

Porter argued that when managers analyze opportunities and threats, they should pay particular attention to these five forces because they are likely to affect the levels of profitability. See Figure 5.10. It is the job of managers at the corporate, business, and functional levels to formulate strategies to counter these threats so that an organization can respond to both its task and general environments, perform at a high level, and generate high returns and social impact. The Focus on the Social Economy feature illustrates how the Prince George Native Friendship Centre generates high social impact.

Differentiate among corporate-level, business-level, and functional-level strategies.

LO4

Step 3: Developing Strategy

Once the environmental forces are analyzed for opportunities and threats, decisions about how to best accomplish the organization's vision, mission, and goals can be made.

FIGURE 5.10	Porter's Five Forces Competitive Analysis Summary
Threat	**Outcome**
Level of rivalry	Increased competition results in lower profits
Potential for entry	Easy entry leads to lower prices and profits
Power of suppliers	If there are only a few suppliers of important items, supply costs rise
Power of customers	If there are only a few large buyers, they can bargain down prices
Substitutes	More available substitutes tend to drive prices and profits lower

These decisions translate into strategies that managers pursue at the corporate, business, and functional levels.

Corporate-Level Strategy

Corporate-level strategy is a plan of action concerning which industries and countries an organization should invest its resources in to achieve its mission and goals. In developing a corporate-level strategy, managers ask: How should the growth and development of the company be managed in order to increase its ability to create value for its customers (and thus increase performance) over the long run? Managers of most organizations have the goal to grow their enterprises and actively seek out new opportunities to use the organization's resources to create more goods and services for customers. Seeking out new opportunities occurs when companies and their strategies are able to adapt to changing circumstances due to changing forces in the task or general environment. For example, customers may no longer be buying the kinds of goods and services a company is producing (manual typewriters, eight-track tapes, black-and-white televisions), or other organizations may have entered the market and attracted customers away (this happened to Intel in the 2000s after AMD began to produce more powerful chips). Top managers aim to find the best strategies to help the organization respond to these changes and improve performance. **Corporate-level plans** contain decisions relating to the organization's mission and goals, overall or grand strategy, and structure that facilitate growth.

The principal corporate-level strategies that managers use to help a company grow, to keep it on top of its industry, and to help it retrench and reorganize in order to stop its decline are *concentration on a*

corporate-level plans Top management's decisions relating to the organization's mission, overall strategy, and structure.

FOCUS ON ❯ *The Social Economy*

Prince George Native Friendship Centre

The Prince George Native Friendship Centre (PGNFC) is a social service agency whose mission is to "facilitate individual, family and community growth through the power of friendship." PGNFC has four meeting rooms which can be rented out and used for community events. Their social enterprise is their Gathering Place Hospitality and Catering Services, based out of their Smokehouse Kitchen, which operates an employment training program. Offsite catering customers have included Meals on Wheels, a residential shelter, and a soup bus program.

Started in 1998, the Smokehouse Kitchen Training Program provides Aboriginal participants with the practical knowledge, skills, and experience required to acquire entry-level employment in the food industry or to access post-secondary education in a related field. Two dozen participants are trained each year in a full commercial kitchen with a restaurant and catering department that cater events ranging from box-lunch drop-off to full-service in-house catering. Participants also receive job placements for work experience. The program provides participants with the necessary information, tools, and support they need when exploring, seeking, securing, or re-entering the Food Service and Hospitality Industry. In addition, [their] participants receive employment assistant services that include career planning, job skills, interest, job leads, and skills development. Over the years the Smokehouse Kitchen Program participant completion rate is averaging around 70 percent. The majority of participants that complete the Smokehouse Kitchen Program go on to employment in the food service industry.[34]

1. Research the PGNFC on the Web. Identify the organization's vision and mission.

2. Perform a SWOT analysis on PGNFC. What strategies would you recommend the organization pursue to gain a competitive advantage?

single business; diversification; vertical integration; and international expansion. These four strategies are all based on one idea: An organization benefits from pursuing a strategy only when it helps *further increase the value of the organization's goods and services for customers.* To increase the value of goods and services, a **corporate-level strategy** must help a company, or one of its divisions, either (1) lower the costs of developing and making products, or (2) increase product differentiation so that more customers want to buy the products even at high or premium prices. Both of these outcomes strengthen a company's competitive advantage and increase its performance.

> "[S]trengthen those [internal] capabilities because that is what you know as an organization, that is what you are good at."
>
> *Micheal Sabia, CEO, BCE*

Concentration on a Single Business

Most organizations begin their growth and development with a corporate-level strategy aimed at concentrating resources in one business or industry in order to develop a strong competitive position within that industry. Tom Peters, in his best-selling book *In Search of Excellence,* pointed out that excellent companies "stick to the knitting"; that is, they focus on what they do best and keep doing it.[35] Under intense competition from Rogers Communication, CEO of BCE Michael Sabia explained his singleness of purpose and strategy this way: "The perspective is now don't diversify away from Bell—reposition Bell, fix Bell, transform Bell, add to Bell, strengthen those capabilities because that is what you know as an organization, that is what you are good at."[36]

Sometimes, concentration on a single business becomes an appropriate corporate-level strategy when managers see the need to reduce the sizes of their organizations in order to increase performance. Managers may decide to get out of certain industries, for example, when particular divisions lose their competitive advantage. Managers may sell off those divisions, lay off workers, and concentrate remaining organizational resources in another market or business to try to improve performance. This happened to electronics maker Hitachi when customers were increasingly switching from bulky CRT monitors to newer, flat LCD monitors. Hitachi announced it would close its three CRT factories in Japan, Singapore, and Malaysia and would use its resources to invest in the new LCD technology.[37]

In contrast, when organizations are performing effectively, they often decide to enter new industries in which they can use their resources to create more value. Thus they begin to pursue vertical integration or diversification.

Diversification

Diversification is the strategy of expanding operations into a new business or industry and producing new goods or services.[38] Examples of diversification include PepsiCo's diversification into the snack-food business with the purchase of Frito-Lay, Time-Warner's diversification into Internet services with the acquisition of AOL, and Quebecor Media Inc.'s move into broadcasting with its acquisition of Vidéotron ltée. There are two main kinds of diversification: related and unrelated.

RELATED DIVERSIFICATION **Related diversification** is the strategy of entering a new business or industry to create a competitive advantage in one or more of an organization's existing divisions or businesses. Related diversification can add value to an organization's products if managers can find ways for its various divisions or business units to share their valuable skills or resources so that synergy is created.[39] **Synergy** is obtained when the value created by two cooperating divisions is greater than the value that would be created if the two divisions operated separately. When Metro Inc. bought A&P they realized cost savings from procurement synergies as well as distribution efficiencies. The merger of Molson Inc. with Adolph Coors Company to create

BCE made a strategic decision to build on its strengths in order to compete rather than diversify.

Molson-Coors adopted a globally integrated operations system to achieve synergy.

Molson Coors Brewing Co. is another case in point: the company is now one of the largest brewers in the world, with leading positions in three of the world's largest and most profitable beer markets. By converting existing applications and systems to a globally integrated solution, the brewer was able to reduce application maintenance costs and gain operational synergy.[40]

In pursuing related diversification, managers often seek to find new businesses where they can use the existing skills and resources in their departments to create synergies, add value to the new business, and hence improve the competitive position of the company. Alternatively, managers may acquire a company in a new industry because they believe that some of the skills and resources of the *acquired* company might improve the efficiency of one or more of their existing divisions. If successful, such skill transfers can help an organization lower its costs or better differentiate its products because they create synergies between divisions.

UNRELATED DIVERSIFICATION Managers pursue **unrelated diversification** when they enter new industries or buy companies in new industries that are not related in any way to their current businesses or industries. One of the main reasons for pursuing unrelated diversification is that sometimes managers can buy a poorly performing company, transfer their management skills to that company, turn its business around, and increase its performance, all of which creates value.

Another reason for pursuing unrelated diversification is that buying businesses in different industries lets managers use a *portfolio strategy*, which is dividing financial resources among divisions to increase financial returns or spread risks among different businesses, much as individual investors do with their own portfolios. For instance, managers may transfer funds from a rich division (a "cash cow") to a new and promising division (a "star") and, by allocating money appropriately between divisions, create value. Toronto-based Brascan Corporation is one of the last large Canadian conglomerates that continues to pursue a diversified strategy in three industries: real estate (Toronto-based Brookfield Properties), financial services (Toronto-based Brascan Financial), and power generation (Masson-Angers, Quebec-based Brascan Power).[41] Also, the company owns Toronto-based Noranda Inc., a mining subsidiary, and Toronto-based Nexfor Inc., a paperboard company. Though used as a popular explanation in the 1980s for unrelated diversification, portfolio strategy started running into increasing criticism in the 1990s.[42]

Today, many companies and their managers are abandoning the strategy of unrelated diversification because there is evidence that too much diversification can cause managers to lose control of their organizations' core business so that they end up reducing value rather than creating it.[43] Since the 1990s, there has been a trend among many diversified companies to sell off unrelated divisions and concentrate organizational resources on their core business and related diversification.[44] For instance, Toronto-based George Weston Ltd., the food processing and supermarket giant, sold the Blacks Harbour, New Brunswick–based Connors Bros., a fish processing operation, so that it could acquire Bestfoods Baking Co. Chairman Galen Weston explained that the move allowed the company to concentrate on its core business; that is, "to go forward in the baking and the supermarket business."[45] The company did not feel that it held a competitive advantage in the fish processing industry. With the acquisition of Bestfoods Baking, George Weston inherited one of the nation's largest and most efficient DSD (direct-store-delivery) systems. The company's product line includes such grain-based food products as sweet baked goods, doughnuts, soft cookies, breakfast bars, soft breadsticks, pizza crusts, English muffins, rolls, pan bread, pita bread, and pasta.[46]

Vertical Integration

When an organization is doing well in its business, managers often see new opportunities to create value by either producing their own inputs or distributing their own outputs. Managers at E.&J. Gallo Winery, for example, realized that they could lower Gallo's costs if they produced their own wine bottles rather than buying them

unrelated diversification

Entering a new industry or buying a company in a new industry that is not related in any way to an organization's current businesses or industries.

from a glass company. As a result, Gallo established a new division to produce glass bottles. Similarly, Starbucks began roasting its own coffee beans and had three roasting plants by the late 1990s. By investing in this type of backward vertical integration, Starbucks could better control the quality of the beans by discarding batches that were not up to par.[47]

Vertical integration is the corporate-level strategy through which an organization becomes involved in producing its own inputs (backward vertical integration) or distributing and selling its own outputs (forward vertical integration).[48] A steel company that supplies its iron ore needs from company-owned iron ore mines is using backward vertical integration. When Steve Jobs announced in 2001 that Apple Computer would open 25 retail stores to sell Macintosh machines directly to consumers, he showed that Apple was engaging in forward vertical integration. Starbucks uses a forward vertical integration strategy through a mail order and Internet distribution service.[49]

Figure 5.11 illustrates the four main stages in a typical raw-materials-to-consumer value chain; value is added at each stage. Typically, the primary operations of an organization take place in one of these stages. For a company based in the assembly stage, backward integration would involve establishing a new division in intermediate manufacturing or raw-material production, and forward integration would involve establishing a new division to distribute its products to wholesalers or to sell directly to customers. A division at one stage receives the product made by the division in the previous stage, transforms it in some way—adding value—and then transfers the output at a higher price to the division at the next stage in the chain.

A major reason why managers pursue vertical integration is that it allows them either to add value to their products by making them special or unique or to lower the costs of value creation. For example, SunOpta Inc. lowered its costs by adopting a vertically integrated strategy by acquiring firms up and down their supply chain. The headquarters is located in a red brick farmhouse north of Toronto. Executives plant a tree each time they complete an acquisition. If you look around the property, you will notice a "mall forest" of saplings that illustrates the company's acquisitions in reaching their goal of "sourcing, processing and distribution of natural and organic food products integrated from seed through packaged products."[50]

Coca-Cola and PepsiCo, in a case of forward vertical integration to build brand loyalty and enhance the differentiated appeal of their colas, decided to buy up their major bottlers to increase control over marketing and promotion efforts—which the bottlers had been handling.[51] An example of using forward vertical integration to lower costs is Panasonic Electric's decision to open company-owned stores to sell its own products and thus keep the profit that independent retailers otherwise would earn.[52]

Although vertical integration can strengthen an organization's competitive advantage and increase its performance, it can also reduce an organization's flexibility to respond to changing environmental conditions and create threats that must be countered by changing the organization's strategy. For example, IBM used to produce most of the components it used to make its own mainframe computers. While this made sense in the 1970s when IBM enjoyed a major competitive advantage, it became

vertical integration
A strategy that allows an organization to create value by producing its own inputs or distributing and selling its own outputs.

FIGURE 5.11 **Stages in a Vertical Value Chain**

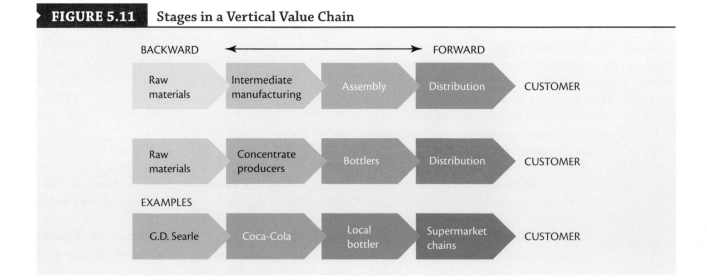

a major handicap for the company in the 1990s when the increasing use of organization-wide networks of PCs meant slumping demand for mainframes. IBM had lost its competitive advantage and found itself with an excess-capacity problem in its component operations. Closing down this capacity, and exiting the computer components industry, cost IBM more than $5 billion.[53]

Thus, when considering vertical integration as a strategy to add value, managers must be careful because sometimes it may reduce a company's ability to create value when the environment changes. This is why so many companies now outsource the production of component parts to other companies and, like IBM, have exited the components industry—by vertically *disintegrating* backward. IBM, however, found a profitable new opportunity for forward vertical integration in the 1990s: It entered the IT consulting services industry to provide advice to large companies about how to install and manage their computer hardware and software.[54] Providing IT services has been a major source of IBM's profitability in the 2000s.

International Expansion

As if planning whether or not to vertically integrate, diversify, or concentrate on the core business were not a difficult enough task, corporate-level managers also must decide on the appropriate way to compete internationally.

A basic question confronts the managers of any organization that competes in more than one national market: To what extent should the organization customize features of its products and marketing campaign to different national conditions?[55] When managers decide that their organization should sell the same standardized product in each national market in which it competes and use the same basic marketing approach, they adopt a **global strategy.**[56] Such companies undertake very little, if any, customization to suit the specific needs of customers in different countries. Such is the case with Tim Hortons. Its corporate strategy of expanding into the United States involved little if any customization. It has adopted a global strategy based on a global brand. But if managers decide to customize products and marketing strategies to specific national conditions, they adopt a **multi-domestic strategy.** McDonald's had to customize its food products for the global market. When McDonald's went to India, it had to sell chicken burgers and mutton burgers rather than beef burgers. IKEA customizes its products for particular national markets. "Americans prefer to store most of their clothes folded, and

Differences in national cultures lead managers to create multi-domestic strategies.

Italians like to hang." The result was a wardrobe that features deeper drawers for U.S. customers.[57]

Both global and multi-domestic strategies have advantages and disadvantages. The major advantage of a global strategy is the significant cost savings associated with not having to customize products and marketing approaches to different national conditions. The major disadvantage of pursuing a global strategy is that by ignoring national differences, managers may leave themselves vulnerable to local competitors that do differentiate their products to suit local tastes.

The advantages and disadvantages of a multi-domestic strategy are the opposite of those of a global strategy. The major advantage of a multi-domestic strategy is that by customizing product offerings and marketing approaches to local conditions, managers may be able to gain market share or charge higher prices for their products. The major disadvantage is that customization raises production costs and puts the multi-domestic company at a price disadvantage because the company often has to charge prices higher than the prices charged by competitors pursuing a global strategy. Obviously, the choice between these two strategies calls for trade-offs.

Business-Level Strategy

Managers at the corporate level make strategic decisions about whether to grow their business through international expansion, vertical integration, diversification, or concentrating on a single industry. Once an opportunity has been identified in a particular market or industry, managers must develop business-level decisions and strategies to gain a competitive advantage.

global strategy Selling the same standardized product and using the same basic marketing approach in each national market.

multi-domestic strategy Customizing products and marketing strategies to specific national conditions.

Michael Porter, the researcher who developed the Five Forces model discussed earlier, also formulated a theory of how managers can select a **business-level strategy** and a **business-level plan** to gain a competitive advantage in a particular market or industry.[58] According to Porter, managers must choose between the two basic ways of increasing the value of an organization's products: higher quality or lower costs. Porter also argues that managers must choose between serving the whole market or serving just one segment or part of a market. Given those choices, managers choose to pursue one of four business-level strategies: *cost-leadership, differentiation,* and *focused low-cost or focused differentiation* (see Table 5.3).

Cost-Leadership Strategy

With a **cost-leadership strategy,** managers try to gain a competitive advantage by focusing the energy of all the organization's departments or functions on driving the organization's costs down below the costs of its rivals. This strategy means manufacturing managers must search for new ways to reduce production costs, R&D managers must focus on developing new products that can be manufactured more cheaply, and marketing managers must find ways to lower the costs of attracting customers. According to Porter, organizations following a low-cost strategy can sell a product for less than their rivals and still make a profit because more customers will be attracted to their lower costs. Thus, organizations that pursue a low-cost strategy hope to enjoy a competitive advantage based on their low prices. Amazon sells the Kindle Fire device for about a third of the cost of an Apple iPad, thus adopting a cost-leadership strategy.

Differentiation Strategy

With a **differentiation strategy,** managers try to gain a competitive advantage by focusing all the energies of the organization's departments or functions on distinguishing the organization's products from those of competitors in one or more important dimensions, such as product design, quality, or after-sales service and support. For instance, Canada's oldest confectionary, Ganong Bros. Ltd., based in St. Stephen, New Brunswick, is a small player in the Canadian chocolate market. It differentiates itself from bigger chocolate makers by focusing on innovative products. In the 1890s the company was one of the first, if not the

| TABLE 5.3 | Porter's Business-Level Strategies |

Strategy	Number of Market Segments Served	
	Many	Few
Cost-leadership	√	
Focused low-cost		√
Differentation	√	
Focused differentiation		√

first, Canadian confectioner to produce a lollipop. In 1910, the family owners/managers began experimenting by sprinkling nuts into their own brand of milk chocolate, and shaping the product into long narrow pieces. They created the first chocolate nut bar in the world, which they began mass producing and selling.[59] Best Buy Co. Inc. aims to woo shoppers with more personalized service. Best Buy's customer-centric strategy allowed the company to differentiate its offerings from those of gargantuan Wal-Mart Stores, Inc., as well as rivals Target, Dell, and Amazon.

Often, the process of making products unique and different is expensive. This strategy, for example, often requires managers to increase spending on product design or R&D to make the product stand out, and costs rise as a result. However, organizations that successfully pursue a differentiation strategy may be able to charge a *premium price* for their products, a price usually much higher than the price charged by a low-cost organization. The premium price allows organizations pursuing a differentiation strategy to recoup their higher costs. Coca-Cola, PepsiCo, and Procter & Gamble are some of the many well-known companies that pursue a strategy of differentiation. They spend enormous amounts of money on advertising to differentiate, and create a unique image for, their products. Also, differentiation makes industry entry difficult because new companies have no brand name to help them compete and customers don't perceive other products to be close substitutes, so this also allows for premium pricing and results in high profits.

"Stuck in the Middle"

According to Porter's theory, managers cannot simultaneously pursue both a cost-leadership strategy and a differentiation strategy. Porter

business-level strategy A plan that indicates how a division intends to compete against its rivals in an industry.

business-level plan Divisional managers' decisions relating to divisions' long-term goals, overall strategy, and structure.

cost-leadership strategy Driving the organization's costs down below the costs of its rivals.

differentiation strategy Distinguishing an organization's products from the products of competitors in dimensions such as product design, quality, or after-sales service.

identified a simple correlation: Differentiation raises costs and thus necessitates premium pricing to recoup those high costs. According to Porter, managers must choose between a cost-leadership strategy and a differentiation strategy. He says that managers and organizations that have not made this choice are "stuck in the middle." According to Porter, organizations stuck in the middle tend to have lower levels of performance than do those that pursue a low-cost or a differentiation strategy. To avoid being stuck in the middle, top managers must instruct departmental managers to take actions that will result in either low cost or differentiation in formulating functional level strategies.

However, exceptions to this rule can be found. In many organizations, managers have been able to drive costs down below those of rivals and simultaneously differentiate their products from those offered by rivals.[60] For example, Toyota's production system is reportedly the most efficient in the world. This efficiency gives Toyota a low-cost strategy vis-à-vis its rivals in the global car industry. At the same time, Toyota has differentiated its cars from those of rivals on the basis of superior design and quality. This superiority allows the company to charge a premium price for many of its popular models.[61] Thus, Toyota seems to be simultaneously pursuing both a low-cost and a differentiated business-level strategy. Brick Brewing Company Limited follows a cost-leadership strategy with its lowest priced brand, Laker, while simultaneously brewing award-winning premium priced brands. These examples suggest that although Porter's ideas may be valid in most cases, very well-managed companies, such as Toyota and Brick Brewery, have both low-cost and differentiated products.

Brick Brewing offers both Laker, a low-cost brand, and expensive premium lagers, showing that low-cost and differentiation strategies can be used successfully by the same firm.

Focused Low-Cost and Focused Differentiation Strategies

Both the differentiation strategy and the cost-leadership strategy are aimed at serving most or all segments of the market. Porter identified two other business-level strategies that aim to serve the needs of customers in only one or a few market segments.[62] A company pursuing a **focused low-cost strategy** serves one or a few segments of the overall market and aims to be the lowest-cost company serving that segment. In the last decade the global soft-drink environment has undergone a major change because of Gerald Pencer, a Canadian entrepreneur who came up with a new strategy for competing against powerful differentiators in the soft drink industry—Coke and Pepsi. Pencer's strategy was to produce a high-quality, low-priced cola, manufactured and bottled by the Cott Corporation, of which he was CEO at the time, but to sell it as the private-label house brand of major retail stores such as Walmart (Sam's Cola brand) and supermarket chains such as Kroger's (Big K brand), thus bypassing the bottlers. Pencer could implement his *focused low-cost* strategy and charge a low price for his soft drinks because he did not need to spend any money on advertising (the retail stores did that) and because Cott's soft drinks are distributed by the store chains and retailers using their efficient national distribution systems, such as the nationwide trucking system developed by giant retailer Walmart. Retailers are willing to do this because Cott's low-cost soft drinks allow them to make much more profit than they receive from selling Coke or Pepsi. At the same time, the products build their store-brand image. By 2004, Cott was the world's largest supplier of retailer-branded carbonated soft drinks.[63] It has manufacturing facilities in Canada, the United States, and the United Kingdom, and a syrup-concentrate production plant in Columbus, Georgia, which supply most of the private-label grocery store, drugstore, mass-merchandising, and convenience store chains in these countries. However, note that while Cott is the leading supplier of retailer-branded sodas, it is still focusing on its low-cost strategy. It makes no attempt to compete with Coke and Pepsi, which pursue differentiation strategies and whose brand-name soft drinks dominate the global market.

By contrast, a company pursuing a **focused differentiation strategy** serves just one or a few segments of the market and aims to be the most differentiated company serving that segment. BMW, for example, pursues a

Cott Corporation offers a focused low-cost strategy.

focused differentiation strategy, producing cars exclusively for higher-income customers. By contrast, Toyota pursues a differentiation strategy and produces cars that appeal to consumers in almost *all* segments of the car market, from basic transportation (Toyota Corolla) through the middle of the market (Toyota Camry) to the high-income end of the market (Lexus).

As these examples suggest, companies pursuing either of these focused strategies have chosen to specialize in some way—by directing their efforts at a particular kind of customer (such as serving the needs of babies or affluent customers) or even the needs of customers in a specific geographical region (customers on the East Coast or the West Coast).

Functional-Level Strategy

A **functional-level strategy** is a plan of action to improve the ability of an organization's departments to create value that is consistent with the business-level and corporate-level strategies. It is concerned with the actions that **functional managers** of individual departments (such as manufacturing or marketing **functions**) can take to add value to an organization's goods and services and thereby increase the value customers receive.

There are two ways in which departments can add value to an organization's products:

1. Departmental managers can lower the costs of creating value so that an organization can attract customers by keeping its prices lower than its competitors' prices.

2. Departmental managers can add value to a product by finding ways to differentiate it from the products of other companies.

For instance, the marketing and sales departments at Molson-Coors create value by building brand loyalty and finding more effective ways to attract customers. General Electric's Lighting division's strategy to drive costs down might translate into a **functional-level plan** for the manufacturing department to "reduce production costs by 20 percent over three years." The functional-level strategy to accomplish this might include (1) investing in state-of-the-art production facilities and (2) developing an electronic global business-to-business network to reduce the cost of inputs and inventory-holding costs. Each organizational function has an important role to play in lowering costs or adding value to a product (see Table 5.4).

Gaining a Competitive Advantage

In trying to add value or lower the costs of creating value, all managers should pay attention to the four goals of building a competitive advantage[64]:

1. *To attain superior efficiency.* Efficiency is a measure of the amount of inputs required to produce a given amount of outputs. The fewer the inputs required to produce a given output, the higher is the efficiency and the lower the cost of outputs.

2. *To attain superior quality.* Here, quality means producing goods and services that are reliable—they do the job they were designed for and do it well.[65] Providing high-quality products creates a brand-name reputation for an organization's products. In turn, this enhanced reputation allows the organization to charge a higher price.

3. *To attain superior innovation.* Anything new or unusual about the way in which an organization operates or the goods and services it produces is the result of innovation. Innovation leads to advances in the kinds of products, production processes, management systems, organizational structures, and strategies that an organization develops. Successful innovation gives an organization something unique that its rivals lack. This uniqueness may enhance the value added and thereby allow the organization to differentiate itself

functional-level strategy A plan that indicates how a function intends to achieve its goals.

functional managers Managers who supervise the various functions—such as manufacturing, accounting, and sales—within a division.

functions Units or departments in which people have the same skills or use the same resources to perform their jobs.

functional-level plan Functional managers' decisions relating to the goals that they propose to pursue to help the division reach its business-level goals.

> **TABLE 5.4**   Examples of Functional-level Strategies

Department or Functional Area	Ways to Lower the Cost of Creating Value (Low-Cost Advantage)	Ways to Add Value (Differentiation Advantage)
Sales and marketing	• Find new customers • Find low-cost advertising methods	• Promote brand-name awareness and loyalty • Tailor products to suit customers' needs
Materials management	• Use just-in-time inventory system/computerized warehousing • Develop long-term relationships with suppliers and customers	• Develop long-term relationships with suppliers to provide high-quality inputs • Reduce shipping time to customers
Research and development	• Improve efficiency of machinery and equipment • Design products that can be made more cheaply	• Create new products • Improve existing products
Manufacturing	• Develop skills in low-cost manufacturing	• Increase product equity and reliability
Human resource management	• Reduce turnover and absenteeism • Raise employee skills	• Hire highly skilled employees • Develop innovative training programs

from its rivals and attract customers who will pay a premium price for its product.

4. *To attain superior responsiveness to customers.* An organization that is responsive to customers tries to satisfy their needs and give them exactly what they want. An organization that treats customers better than its rivals treats them provides a valuable service for which customers may be willing to pay a higher price.

The important issue to remember here is that all of these techniques can help an organization achieve a competitive advantage by lowering the costs of creating value or by adding value above and beyond that offered by rivals.

> **LO5**   Describe how managers implement strategy and evaluate its success.

Steps 4 and 5: Implementing and Evaluating Strategy

Strategy Implementation

After conducting a SWOT analysis and analyzing the forces in the organization's industry using Porter's Five Forces model, managers formulate appropriate strategies at the corporate, business, and functional level that support the organization's vision, mission, and goals. The next step in the planning process, implementation, now confronts managers with the challenge of how to put those strategies into action. Strategy implementation is a five-step process in itself:

1. Allocating responsibility for implementation to the appropriate individuals or groups.

2. Drafting detailed action plans that specify how a strategy is to be implemented.

3. Establishing a timetable for implementation that includes precise, measurable goals linked to the attainment of the action plan. A **Gantt chart** can be used to manage the project.[66] A Gantt chart is a graphic bar chart managers use to schedule tasks in a project showing what tasks need to be done, who will do them, and by what timeframe they will be completed.

4. Allocating appropriate resources to the responsible individuals or groups.

5. Holding specific individuals or groups responsible for reaching corporate, divisional, and functional goals.

The planning process goes beyond the mere identification of strategies; it also includes actions taken to ensure that the organization actually implements its strategies.

Evaluating Strategy

The last step in the process of planning is evaluating whether or not the strategy

Gantt chart A graphic bar chart managers use to schedule tasks in a project showing what tasks need to be done, who will do them, and by what timeframe.

has been successful in achieving the major goals set out in step one. How do managers know when they are successful? In evaluating the success of a strategy, managers must monitor progress, evaluate performance levels, and make corrective adjustments if there is a substantial gap between the goal and the actual performance. This is essentially the *controlling process* more fully discussed in Chapter 13. Managers monitor and measure actual performance levels and compare the results with the initial goal for a particular strategy. For example, following a corporate-level strategy of international expansion, the CIBC decided to enter the U.S. retail banking market by putting branches in grocery stores. But after about a decade of losses amounting to hundreds of millions of dollars, the strategy was abandoned. CIBC largely pulled out of the United States after this strategy failed. Instead, CIBC bought a stake in a troubled Irish bank. Looking overseas to expand internationally may be, in part, because of its disastrous venture into the United States.[67]

Campbell's Soup Company did an about-face after it lost its competitive advantage to General Mills when the latter began offering a more health-conscious line of soup in the early 2000s. Campbell's responded to this threat by realigning its products to meet the changing nutrition needs of consumers. Among the changes, it reduced the amount of sodium in soups. By 2011, sales were sluggish and incoming CEO Denise Morrison reversed the low-sodium strategy to try to regain market share. Premium Select Harvest soups had sodium levels raised to 650 milligrams from 480 milligrams a serving.[68] When goals are unmet, strategy must be rethought in such a way as to stay true to the vision and mission of the organization.

It should be noted that the plan for implementing a strategy may require radical redesign of the *structure* of the organization, the adoption of a program for changing the *culture* of the organization, and the development of new *control systems.* We address the first two issues in the next two chapters and discuss the issues of control in Chapter 13.

Summary and Review

LO1 An Overview of the Planning Process Planning is setting goals and finding the best strategy to achieve them. This is done by management at all three levels of the organization: top-level managers are responsible for long-term strategic planning and strategizing, middle-level for intermediate planning, and first-line for functional-level planning. Planning serves to give direction and purpose to the organization, it coordinates different functions and divisions, and it allows managers to control the use of resources. *Scenario or contingency planning* is managers forecasting what may happen in the future and then gathering resources to meet these anticipated needs, opportunities, and threats. *Crisis management* occurs when unanticipated and unplanned contingencies arise.

LO2 Five Steps in the Planning Process

1. Determining an organization's vision, mission, and goals
2. Analyzing the forces in the organizational environment
3. Formulating strategy
4. Implementing strategy
5. Evaluating strategy

LO3 Step Two in the Planning Process This step involves conducting an analysis of the organizational environment to evaluate how the internal and external forces impact the organization by creating opportunities and threats. *SWOT analysis* examines the internal strengths and weaknesses of the organization, while *Porter's Five Forces* model analyzes the potential for profitability within a particular industry by looking at the degree of competitive rivalry, the ease of entry, the power of buyers, the power of suppliers, and the threat of substitute products. Managers use these techniques to evaluate what strategy would gain them a competitive advantage.

LO4 Step Three in the Planning Process: Developing Strategy At the *corporate level,* organizations use strategies such as concentration on a single business, diversification, vertical integration, and international expansion to help increase the value of the goods and services provided to customers. At the *business or divisional level,* managers are responsible for developing a low-cost or differentiation strategy, either for the whole market or for a particular segment of it (focus strategy). At the *functional level,* departmental managers try to add value to the product or service by differentiation or increasing efficiencies by reducing costs. All managers attempt to gain a competitive advantage by increasing quality, responsiveness to customers, and efficiencies and innovations.

LO5 Steps Four and Five in the Planning Process: Implementing and Evaluating Strategy These steps require managers to allocate responsibilities to individuals or groups, draft detailed action plans that specify how a strategy is to be implemented, establish a timetable for implementation that includes specific measurable goals, allocate necessary resources, and hold the individuals or groups accountable for reaching goals. Managers monitor the progress of goal achievement and make corrective adjustments when strategies fail to accomplish the organization's mission and goals.

KEY TERMS

business-level plan	functional managers	rule
business-level strategy	functional-level plan	scenario planning
co-opetition	functional-level strategy	standard operating
corporate-level plans	functions	procedures (SOPs)
corporate-level strategy	Gantt chart	strategic leadership
cost-leadership strategy	global strategy	strategy
crisis management plans	goal	strategy formulation
differentiation strategy	mission statement	SWOT analysis
diversification	multi-domestic strategy	synergy
division	planning	time horizon
divisional managers	policy	unrelated diversification
focused differentiation strategy	Porter's Five Forces model	vertical integration
focused low-cost strategy	related diversification	vision statement

WRAP-UP TO ▶▶▶ OPENING CASE

Amazon: Taking Over the Online World

The rapid pace at which the world is changing is forcing the managers of all kinds of companies to develop new strategies to protect their competitive advantage. If they don't, they will be overtaken by agile competitors that respond faster to changing customer needs. Nowhere is this truer than in the cut-throat mobile computing business in which Amazon competes. After having read and understood the concepts in this chapter you should now be able to answer the following questions:

1. *What was the vision for Amazon.com and how has it changed?*

ANSWER: Amazon.com began with the vision of offering the world's biggest selection of books over the Internet. Since 1995, the vision has expanded to include all kinds of products, not just books, for sale over the Internet. Amazon's vision is "to be earth's most customer centric company; to build a place where people can come to find and discover anything they might want to buy online."

2. *Describe the corporate-level strategy employed by Amazon.*

ANSWER: Amazon has positioned itself as an industry leader in e-commerce mainly through acquisitions of other online retailers. This is a diversification strategy. The diversification is related because the acquisitions are in the same online retailing industry. Examples include Zappos and Diapers.com. Through related diversification, Amazon.com became the world's largest online retailer.

The company is also pursuing other diversification strategies that at first appear to be unrelated to their core business of online retailing, however, upon closer analysis, will strengthen it. Amazon developed a tablet computer, the Kindle Fire, that will compete with Apple's iPad. Investing in the design and production of computer hardware appears unrelated to the core business of online retailing, however, the innovative browser, called Amazon Silk and run on a modified Google Android operating system, will make it easier for customers to browse and shop online (at Amazon.com) because it allows free storage of data, music, and movies on its vast cloud computing servers instead of being stored only by the browser in the device, thus adding value and convenience to customers.

Amazon's foray into the publishing business is an example of a vertical integration strategy. Where once it relied on publishers to produce the books it sells online, it now publishes many books itself. This is an example of backward vertical integration that cuts out the producer and thus increases the profits for the company.

3.   *What business-level strategies has Amazon pursued?*

ANSWER: Amazon has pursued a corporate-level strategy of acquiring any firms that could rival its e-commerce business and has propelled itself to the world's largest online retailer as a result. It now competes with eBay by offering an online auction site. Apple's iCloud competes with Amazon's cloud computing services.

In the hand-held computer business, its main competitors are Apple, RIM, and others run on Google's Android operating system. It competes on two fronts in this business: differentiation through design and cost leadership. Providing access to unlimited cloud computing with the Kindle Fire tablet gives Amazon a competitive advantage over Apple and the others. That kind of capacity cannot be substituted on a hand-held device. The power of a vast system of servers in a warehouse in Seattle cannot be outdone by the limited capacity of an individual hand-held device. These design features set the Kindle Fire apart from its competitors. And while the iPad sells for around $500, the Kindle Fire sells for $200. At this price point, Amazon is betting that more customers will purchase its tablet over the more expensive devices. Rather than focusing on higher-income tablet consumers, as Apple does, Amazon appeals to the entire market of tablet users. Thus, it is simultaneously pursuing a differentiation and cost-leadership strategy in the computer tablet industry.

4.   *Apply Porter's Five Forces model to the tablet computer industry.*

ANSWER: Porter's Five Forces model, when applied to the tablet industry in which Amazon competes, illustrates the threats the company faces in trying to gain a competitive advantage:

a.   *The degree of rivalry* among the competition is cut-throat. Apple, RIM, and Google offer different operating systems for tablet computing. Each is trying to gain market share. Amazon's Kindle Fire undercuts the competition by offering a lower price for its product. Apple has more resources to promote its iPad brand. The high level of rivalry drives down the profit margins in the industry.

b.   *The ease of entry* into the tablet industry is complicated by the limited number of operating systems on which the devices run. Amazon took Google's open Android system and modified it to suit their new browser, Amazon Silk. RIM has developed a new operating system, the BBX. There is an enormous amount of capital invested in each innovation, making the barriers to entering this industry very large. This accounts for the small number of firms competing for the overall market, making the potential for profitability larger than if there were low barriers to entry. Amazon must compete against the significant brand loyalty, another barrier to entry, that Apple and RIM's BlackBerry command.

c.   *The power of suppliers* in this case could potentially drive up the costs of firms competing in the tablet industry if the inputs they provide are rare or difficult to obtain. A metal used by Apple in its iPad, called Coltan, is mined in the Democratic Republic of Congo, where miners are shutting down due to ongoing violence in the North East provinces. This will drive up the cost to Apple.

d. *The power of customers* is minimal in this case. The tablet market relies on many consumers purchasing directly from the producer or through large networks of distributors. No single large customer, such as Walmart, has a corner on the tablet market, and therefore the power of customers to demand lower prices is minimal.

e. *The threat of substitute products* is considerable in the tablet market. Amazon was able to produce and sell a tablet with access to cloud computing storage at a fraction of the cost of similar Web-enabled hand-held computing devices. RIM launched its tablet computer on its own proprietary operating system. Amazon and RIM products are both potential substitutes to Apple's iPad, with the possibility of breaking its monopoly in the tablet market. Innovations in operating systems may further threaten product sales in this industry, taking away market share and profits from the existing players. Pressure to drive down the prices of their products to avoid customers switching to the substitutes will likely increase.

Management in Action

TOPICS FOR DISCUSSION AND ACTION

LEVEL 1 Knowledge & Comprehension

1. Describe the five steps in the planning process. Explain how they are related.

2 Discuss who plans, the time horizons of plans, the difference between standing and single-use plans, and why planning is important. What are the qualities of effective plans?

3. Describe scenario planning. How can scenario planning help managers predict the future?

LEVEL 2 Application & Analysis

4. Ask a manager to identify the corporate-, business-, and functional-level strategies used by his or her organization.

5. Watch the video on Porter Airlines at www.youtube.com/watch?v=xnhExEZvJNI. Identify the airline's mission. What type of business-level strategy is it pursuing? Give evidence to support your answer.

6. Go to the website of Bombardier. Identify the vision, mission, and major goals for the company. What corporate-level strategy is it engaged in? What is the business-level strategy of its largest division?

LEVEL 3 Synthesis & Evaluation

7. Research a well-known company that you can easily find information about. What is the main industry that the company competes in? Apply Porter's Five Forces model to this industry to determine its profitability.

8. Present an argument for having lower-level managers participate in the company's strategic planning process. What might happen if they were to have no input?

9. Research two firms in the same industry, and perform a competitive SWOT analysis. What type of corporate-, business-, and functional-level strategies would you recommend for the firms, and why?

SELF-REFLECTION EXERCISE

Think ahead to five years from now to consider what it is that you might like to be doing with your life. Develop your own vision and mission statements. Establish a set of goals that will help you achieve your vision and mission.

Develop a SWOT analysis for considering what you want to be doing in five years. What are your strengths and weaknesses? What are the opportunities and threats in carrying out this plan?

Develop a five-year plan that maps out the steps you need to take in order to get to where you want to be in your life at that time.

SMALL GROUP BREAKOUT EXERCISE

Form groups of three or four, and appoint one member as the spokesperson who will communicate your findings to the class when called on by the instructor. Then discuss the following scenario:

You are a team of management consultants hired by a grocery store chain to plan the feasibility of opening a store in your community. You must answer all the questions below and report back to your clients.

1. List the major supermarket chains in your city, and identify their strengths and weaknesses relative to one another. What opportunities and threats exist for each chain?
2. What business-level strategies are these supermarkets currently pursuing?
3. What kind of supermarket strategy would do best against the competition?
4. What would you recommend to your clients, and why?

BUSINESS PLANNING EXERCISE

Your professor may ask you to write a business plan for a new venture or a strategic plan for an existing venture. At the end of every chapter, you will have an opportunity to apply managerial and organizational concepts to the exercise of writing a business plan. Refer to Appendix A.

In Chapter 4, your team made a decision on what type of venture you will write a business plan on. Now the planning must begin. You must create a Profile of the Organization and Industry. Using the planning tools in this chapter, do the following:

1. Write the vision and mission statements for your venture.
2. Formulate two major goals for the business. These could relate to revenue within the first year or market share or number of customers served.
3. Find out the NAICS code for your industry. Research the trends in the industry.
4. Analyze the competitive environment by applying Porter's Five Forces model to the industry. What threats exist for your venture, and how will you minimize the risks?
5. Conduct a SWOT analysis of your venture relative to one direct competitor.
6. What strategy will your venture pursue to gain a competitive advantage over your rival?

MANAGING ETHICALLY EXERCISE

A major department store has received repeated criticism for selling clothes that are produced at low cost in developing countries. The CEO of the department store knows that suppliers are paying 5 percent better than the going rate of wages in these countries and feels that this is fair enough. Working conditions at suppliers' factories are no worse than at other factories in those countries. The CEO has come to you to check her assumptions that as long as the suppliers are buying from manufacturing plants that have better-than-average working conditions for the country where the company is located, nothing further needs to be done. What would you advise her? How would you justify your advice?

MANAGEMENT CHALLENGE EXERCISE

Beyond the Green Door

The Green Door is a vegetarian restaurant in Ottawa with an "eye and palette . . . focused on nourishment drawn from the local, organic, seasonal, natural, wholesome, comforting and colourful."[69] The restaurant is situated directly across from Saint Paul University[70] (part of the University of Ottawa and home to about 1000 undergraduate and graduate students in such disciplines as spirituality, philosophy, human sciences, pastoral counselling, and conflict studies). OttawaPlus.ca considers The Green Door the "heaven for vegetarians" and an Ottawa institution.[71]

1. Name some vegetarian restaurants in the city where you live. Do a SWOT analysis as to their strengths and weaknesses.

2. Look up reviews of The Green Door on the Internet. If The Green Door wanted to expand, what kind of business-level strategy should it pursue?

MANAGEMENT PORTFOLIO PROJECT

Answer the following questions about the organization you have chosen to follow:

1. Identify the vision, mission, and major goals of the organization.

2. What is the corporate-level strategy of the company?

3. What is the business-level strategy of the company?

4. Have the strategies supported the vision and mission? How so?

5. Has there been a significant shift in strategy over the past decade? If yes, describe it, and try to determine why the organization made the changes.

6. How successful is the organization's planning process?

VIDEO MANAGEMENT CASE

Panera Bread Company

Panera Bread Co. combines some of the best aspects of fast-food and sit-down venues.

1. How do Panera Bread's corporate vision and strategy lead to a competitive advantage in the restaurant industry?

2. How does Panera achieve responsiveness to customers?

3. How does its corporate culture help make Panera Bread a high-performing company?

Management Case

Stirring Up Campbell Soup

Campbell Soup Co., one of the oldest and best-known global food companies, saw demand for its major product, condensed soup, plummet by 30 percent during the early

2000s as customers switched from high-salt, processed soups to healthier low-fat, low-salt varieties. Campbell's profits and stock price plunged as its condensed soup business collapsed, and in 2001 its directors brought in a new CEO, Douglas Conant, to help the troubled company. Conant decided it was necessary to develop a three-year turnaround plan to help the company strengthen its market position against aggressive competitors such as General Mills, whose Progresso Soup division had attracted away many of Campbell's customers with its innovative new lines of healthier soup.

One of Conant's first actions was to analyze the competitive environment which identified the growth of the organic and health-food segment of the food market and the increasing number of other kinds of convenience foods as a threat to Campbell's core soup business. It also revealed three growth opportunities: (1) the growing market for health and sports drinks, in which Campbell already was a competitor with its V8 juice; (2) the growing market for quality bread and cookies, in which Campbell competed with its Pepperidge Farm brand; and (3) chocolate products, where Campbell's Godiva brand had enjoyed increasing sales throughout the 1990s. Campbell's emerged as a leader in the low-carb, health-conscious, and luxury-food market segments.

With the analysis of the environment complete, Conant turned his attention to his organization's resources and capabilities. His internal analysis of Campbell identified a number of major problems. These included staffing levels that were too high relative to its competitors and high costs associated with manufacturing its soups because of the use of outdated machinery.

Also, Conant noted that Campbell had a very conservative culture in which people seemed to be afraid to take risks—something that was a real problem in an industry where customer tastes are always changing and new products must be developed constantly. At the same time, the analysis identified a huge positive: Campbell enjoyed huge economies of scale because of the enormous quantity of food products that it makes, and it also had a first-rate R&D division capable of developing exciting new food products.

Using this information, Conant and his managers decided that Campbell needed to use its product development skills to revitalize its core products and modify or reinvent them in ways that would appeal to increasingly health-conscious and busy consumers. Moreover, it needed to expand its franchise in the health- and sports-, snack-, and luxury-food segments of the market. Also, to increase sales, Campbell's needed to tap into new food outlets, such as corporate cafeterias, college dining halls, and other mass eateries, to expand consumers' access to its foods. Finally, Conant decided to decentralize authority to managers at lower levels in the organization and make them responsible for developing new soup, bread, and chocolate products that met customers' changing needs. In this way he hoped to revitalize Campbell's slow-moving culture and speed the flow of improved and new products to the market.

Conant put his new plan into action, sales of new soup products increased, and he began to put more emphasis on sales of soup at outlets such as 7–11 and Subway and less on supermarket sales.[72] By 2004, analysts felt that he had made a significant difference in Campbell's performance but that there was still a lot to do, as Campbell's operating margins were still shrinking. Conant decided Campbell should produce more products to meet the needs of the "low-carb diet," such as new kinds of low-carb bread and cookies. He also decided to shrink the company's operations to lower costs. His goal was to raise profit margins to the level of his major competitors Kraft and General Mills by 2007 using a new three-year plan.[73]

By 2006 Conant had substantially achieved his goals: Sales of soup had recovered and the Pepperidge Farm and Godiva divisions were earning record sales and profits (sales of Goldfish crackers had increased by 100 percent!).[74] Campbell's stock price soared, and Conant and employees at all levels received bonuses that rewarded their intense efforts to turn around the company. However, Conant immediately set in motion a new round of analysis to find new opportunities for developing new kinds of products for new customers.[75]

On the threat side, it was clear that customers wanted more nutritious food and snack products, so he set into motion research to make Campbell's food products more appealing to health-conscious customers. One major opportunity was to reformulate a number of its soups to reduce sodium content, and it introduced new kinds of low-salt soup in 2007. Another opportunity was to develop nutritious luxury soups that would command premium prices.[76] Both these initiatives worked well. On the other hand, pursuing his new goal of making Campbell's foods more nutritious led Conant to question if its highly profitable Godiva chocolate brand was still a good fit for the company. He decided it had become a weakness, and in 2008 he sold it for $850 million.[77] He then used some of the proceeds of this sale to build new company strengths. For example, he invested in R&D to develop the skills needed to customize Campbell's brands to the needs of customers in countries such as India and China, a move that spearheaded global expansion. Under Conant, Campbell's share value rose and it raised its dividend each year. In the second decade of the 2000s, and after yet another examination of the forces in the rapidly changing environment, Campbell's Soup company did an "about-face."

By 2011, sales were sluggish and incoming CEO Denise Morrison reversed the low-sodium strategy to try to regain market share. Premium Select Harvest soups will have sodium levels raised to 650 milligrams from 480 milligrams a serving.[78] And, while international expansion plans continued, it seems the loyal baby boomer demographic base in North America still wanted the salty taste of their childhood!

1. Conduct a SWOT analysis on Campbell's Soup company.

2. Use Porter's Five Forces to analyze the global food industry in which Campbell's competes.

McGraw Hill connect™

Connect allows you to practise important concepts at your own pace and on your own schedule, with 24/7 online access to an eBook, practice quizzes, video cases, interactive exercises, study tools, and more.

End of Part III: Continuing Case

CARROT TOPS: BUILDING A COMPETITIVE ADVANTAGE

As the population grew, so too did the competition. Pretty soon it was apparent that Mac's Milk and Shoppers Drug Mart were able to offer customers a wider selection of lower-priced products than Mel's store. Mel had to find a new way to manage his small business if it was going to survive. He began brainstorming new strategies. He researched trends in the food industry. There might be a niche for supplying specialty products, he thought, such as organic and gourmet foods, which were more profitable to sell. He would no longer be competing against giants like Shoppers. He changed the name of his store to Carrot Tops and stocked it with a wide variety of gourmet Canadian food products. He began to offer fine foods, local cheeses, fresh bread, organic fruits and vegetables. Finding a reliable source of products from local farmers and producers could be a stumbling block to his success, but he did have Janet Khan to head up produce procurement and logistics.

His plan worked. Customers loved his new upscale supermarket concept. The premium products he had chosen to stock sold quickly. Realizing that he needed to capitalize on his success to protect his growing business, Mel continually expanded the variety of premium organic foods and drinks he sold. Taking advantage of the popularity of the name Carrot Tops, he began to offer his own store-label products. Today, more than 80 percent of the products Carrot Tops sells sport its own label. Every product adheres to sustainable environmental production practices.

To compete in the premium-quality segment of the supermarket business and keep customers buying high-priced organic products, Carrot Tops needed to provide excellent customer service. Mel provided training and support. The store employees feel valued by Mel and provide excellent customer service and develop personal relationships with customers, who are often on first-name terms. Mel feels really good about the approach Carrot Tops is taking toward its stakeholders. He is considering formalizing a Code of Ethics to guide new employees and introduce them to the culture of the organization.

Drawing on all segments of this case:

1. Identify the stakeholders and their issues in this case.

2. What threats and opportunities exist in the task and general environments for Carrot Tops? Recommend how Mel should deal with them.

3. How does Mel use the building blocks of a competitive advantage?

4. How would you characterize the Carrot Tops approach to ethics and social responsibility?

PART IV

Managing Organizational Structure

LEARNING OUTCOMES

LO1 Identify the elements involved in designing organizational structures.

LO2 Explain how managers group tasks into jobs that are motivating and satisfying for employees.

LO3 Describe how managers can group jobs into functional, divisional, network, and hybrid structures.

LO4 Explain the ways that managers allocate authority and coordinate activities.

LO5 Evaluate the factors that managers consider when deciding on a formal or flexible overall structure.

Opening Case

Samsung Reorganizes for the 21st Century

From a humble beginning as a noodle maker in 1938 in Korea, Samsung has grown to become Asia's largest conglomerate, comprising 83 individual networked companies held under an umbrella company called Everland, with products ranging from transistor radios to insurance and credit card services. Similar to General Electric in the United States, the Samsung Group conglomerate is in dozens of unrelated industries. The largest company within the network, Samsung Electronics Co. Ltd. is a leader in electronics technology, making more televisions, memory chips, and LCD flat screens than any other company in the world. Within Samsung Electronics, there are two main product groups with 10 operating divisions: Digital Media and Communications, and Device Solutions.

In 2010, Samsung reorganized the Electronics Company structure to give more autonomy to each business division by eliminating the Global Business Manager (GBS) layer responsible for overseeing the major product divisions.[1] The reorganization replaces the "two business group structure with 7 independent companies under a single corporate entity."[2] Prior to the change, business units did not control their own budgets—they didn't even have their own balance sheets and income statements.[3] The change gave the business divisions independence to act as stand-alone companies with their own President and CFO. Each product division head now reports directly to the newly created executive position—the COO for all divisions. The new COO, who happens to be the heir apparent to the empire, would help expedite decision making, improve efficiency, and mediate between business units. This model is used by many multinational corporations. The management hierarchy went from three to two levels, making decision making faster as well as the speed to market of new products.

In terms of sales Samsung Electronics galloped to the front of the pack, yet now the company wants to diversify away from consumer electronics before the low profit margins, falling prices, and fast product cycles take the company's profits down.[4] Believing that green technologies will drive future growth, Chairperson Lee Kun-hee told his executives in 2011 that, "The majority of our products today will be gone in ten years."[5] The company plans to invest $20 billion over the next decade in five new industries: solar panels, LED lighting, electric vehicle batteries, medical devices, and biotech drugs. To be successful in these new endeavours, Samsung realizes it has to partner with start-ups in each industry. For example, in electric vehicle battery production they have joined up with German car parts supplier Bosch. The partnership company, called SB LiMotive, already has Chrysler and BMW as its customers.

These new businesses move Samsung away from the electronic products, for which there are ready substitutes, toward green technology and health care products that it believes will be in high demand in the 21st century. A new structure for a new strategy.

After reading and understanding the concepts in this chapter, you should be able to answer the following questions:

1. *How would you characterize Samsung Electronics' organizational structure?*

2. *How did the changes to Samsung's organizational structure affect the hierarchy of authority and span of control?*

3. *How is Samsung's strategy related to its structure?*

Overview

In Part 4, we examine how managers can organize human and other resources to create high-performing organizations. To organize, managers must design a structure that makes the best use of resources to produce the goods and services customers want. They must consider how rapidly the organization's environment is changing, and the strategy and culture of the organization such that the organizational structure is closely aligned. Managers design organizational structures to fit the factors or circumstances that are affecting the company the most, and causing them the most uncertainty.[6] Thus, there is no one best way to design an organization: Design reflects each organization's specific situation, and researchers have argued that in some situations stable, mechanistic structures may be most appropriate while in others flexible, organic structures might be the most effective. As noted in Chapter 5, an organization's design and structure must be closely aligned with its strategy. The strategy depends on the nature of the business and the competitive and environmental landscape. Strategy is successful when the leaders and management teams recognize the opportunities and threats in the environment and organize the resources effectively to compete in such a market. Leaders need to make decisions on how best to adapt and change to remain competitive. The family-owned and controlled Samsung Group of companies has done just that. Our opening case illustrates how a powerhouse company like Samsung Electronics changed its organizational structure to better fit with its strategy for the 21st century.

By the end of this chapter, you will be familiar not only with various organizational structures but also with various factors that determine the organizational design choices that managers make. Then, in Chapter 7, we examine issues surrounding the organization's culture and what it takes for an organization to achieve innovation and change.

LO1 Identify the elements involved in designing organizational structures.

Designing Organizational Structure

Organizing is the process by which managers establish the structure of working relationships among employees to allow them to achieve organizational goals efficiently and effectively. **Organizational structure** is the formal system of task and reporting relationships that determines how employees use resources to reach organizational goals.[7] **Organizational design** is the process by which managers make specific organizing choices that result in

the construction of a particular organizational structure.[8] The questions managers ask and the criteria that provide the answers are outlined in Table 6.1. As the opening case illustrates, a company's organizational design and structure is closely aligned with its strategy and culture.

In general, managers design organizational structures with four important elements in mind:

1. How to group tasks into individual jobs that are interesting and motivating for employees

2. How to group jobs into departments and divisions as organizations grow

3. How to allocate authority among functional areas and divisions to ensure coordination and integration

4. Whether to pursue a more formal or flexible structure

The ability to make the right kinds of organizing choices is often what differentiates effective from ineffective managers and creates a high-performing organization.

> **organizational structure** A formal system of both task and reporting relationships that coordinates and motivates organizational members so that they work together to reach organizational goals.
>
> **organizational design** The process by which managers make specific organizing choices that result in a particular kind of organizational structure.
>
> **job design** The process by which managers decide how to divide tasks into specific jobs.

Explain how managers group tasks into jobs that are motivating and satisfying for employees. **LO2**

Grouping Tasks into Jobs: Job Design

The first step in organizational design is **job design**, the process by which managers decide how to divide into specific jobs the tasks that have to be performed to provide customers with goods and services. Managers at McDonald's, for example, have decided how best to divide the tasks required to provide customers with fast, cheap food in each McDonald's restaurant. After experimenting with different job arrangements, McDonald's managers decided on a basic division of labour among chefs and food servers. Managers allocated all the tasks involved in actually cooking the food (putting oil in the fat fryers, opening packages of frozen french fries, putting beef patties on the grill, making salads, and so on) to the job of chef. They allocated all the tasks involved in giving the food to customers (such as greeting customers, taking orders, putting fries and burgers into bags, adding salt, pepper, and napkins, and taking money) to food servers. In addition, they created other

> **TABLE 6.1**   Organizational Design Questions and Answers

Questions to Consider	Design Options	Criteria
How should tasks be grouped into jobs?	• Job design: creating an initial division of labour • Job enlargement: increasing the number of tasks • Job simplification: reducing the number of tasks • Job enrichment: adding responsibility and control	• Based on the most efficient way to produce the product/service and serve the customer.
How should jobs be grouped into units?	• Functional structure: departments such as Operations, Finance, HR, Sales, and Marketing • Divisional structures: product, geographic, market • Matrix product team and hybrid structures • Strategic alliances and network structures • Outsourcing	• Based on matching the organization's environment, HR, technology and strategy with the organization's size and resources.
How should authority be distributed so that the organization can coordinate and control its activities?	• Hierarchy of authority: tall or flat • Centralized or decentralized control over decision making	• Based on the minimum chain of command principle, which states that the managerial hierarchy should have the fewest levels necessary to use organizational resources efficiently and effectively.
Should the overall organizational structure be formal or flexible?	• Mechanistic structures: formal, stable, and rigid • Organic structures: fluid, dynamic, and flexible	• Depends on the degree of change in the organizational environment, the use of industrial or new technology, the use of skilled or unskilled labour, and the type of strategy (low cost or differentiation).

jobs—the job of dealing with drive-through customers, the job of keeping the restaurant clean, and the job of overseeing employees and responding to unexpected events. The result of the job design process is a **division of labour** among employees, one that McDonald's managers have discovered through experience is most efficient.

Establishing an appropriate division of labour among employees is a critical part of the organizing process, one that is vital to increasing efficiency and effectiveness. At McDonald's, the tasks associated with chef and food server were split into different jobs because managers found that, for the kind of food McDonald's serves, this approach was most efficient. It is efficient because when each employee is given fewer tasks to perform (so that each job becomes more specialized), employees become more productive at performing the tasks that constitute each job.

> "The majority of our products today will be gone in ten years."
>
> *Lee Kun-hee, Chairperson, Samsung Group*

division of labour The overall result of job design among employees in an organization.

At Subway sandwich shops, however, managers chose a different kind of job design. At Subway, there is no division of labour among the people who make the sandwiches, wrap the sandwiches, give them to customers, and take the money. The roles of chef and food server are combined into one. This different division of tasks and jobs is efficient for Subway and not for McDonald's because Subway serves a limited menu of mostly submarine-style sandwiches that are prepared to order. Subway's production system is far simpler than McDonald's, because McDonald's menu is much more varied and its chefs must cook many different kinds of foods. At Subway, the roles of chef and server are combined into one, making the job "larger" than the jobs of McDonald's more specialized food servers. The idea behind job enlargement is that increasing the range of tasks performed by the worker will reduce boredom.

Managers of every organization must analyze the range of tasks to be performed and then create jobs that best allow the organization to give customers the goods and services they want. In deciding how to assign tasks to individual jobs, however, managers must be careful not to go too far with **job simplification**—the process of reducing the number of tasks that each employee performs.[9] Too much job simplification may reduce efficiency rather than increase it if workers find their simplified jobs boring and monotonous, become de-motivated and unhappy, and as a result perform at a low level.

job simplification
Reducing the number of tasks that each worker performs.

job enlargement
Increasing the number of different tasks in a given job by changing the division of labour.

job enrichment
Increasing the degree of responsibility a worker has over his or her job.

of doing the job, (2) encouraging employees to develop new skills, (3) allowing employees to decide how to do the work and giving them the responsibility for deciding how to respond to unexpected situations, and (4) allowing employees to monitor and measure their own performance.[11] The idea behind job enrichment is that increasing employees' responsibility increases their involvement in their jobs and thus increases their interest in the quality of the goods they make or the services they provide.

Job Enlargement and Job Enrichment

Researchers have looked at ways to create a division of labour and design individual jobs to encourage employees to perform at a higher level and be more satisfied with their work. Based on this research, they have proposed job enlargement and job enrichment as better ways than job simplification to group tasks into jobs.

Job enlargement increases the *number of different tasks* in a given job by changing the division of labour.[10] For example, because Subway food servers make the food as well as serve it, their jobs are "larger" than the jobs of McDonald's food servers. The idea behind job enlargement is that increasing the range of tasks performed by an employee will reduce boredom and fatigue and may increase motivation to perform at a high level—increasing both the quantity and the quality of goods and services provided.

Job enrichment increases the *degree of responsibility* a worker has over his or her job by, for example, (1) empowering employees to experiment to find new or better ways

In general, managers who make design choices that increase job enrichment and job involvement are likely to increase the degree to which workers behave flexibly rather than rigidly or mechanically. Narrow, specialized jobs are likely to lead people to behave in predictable ways; employees who perform a variety of tasks and who are allowed and encouraged to discover new and better ways to perform their jobs are likely to act flexibly and creatively. Thus, managers who enlarge and enrich jobs create a flexible organizational structure, and those who simplify jobs create a more formal structure. If employees are also grouped into self-managed work teams, the organization is likely to be flexible because team members provide support to each other and can learn from one another.

The Job Characteristics Model

J. R. Hackman and G. R. Oldham's job characteristics model is an influential model of job design that explains in detail how managers can make jobs more interesting and motivating.[12] Hackman and Oldham's model (see Figure 6.1) also describes the likely personal and organizational outcomes that will result from enriched and enlarged jobs.

FIGURE 6.1 The Job Characteristics Model

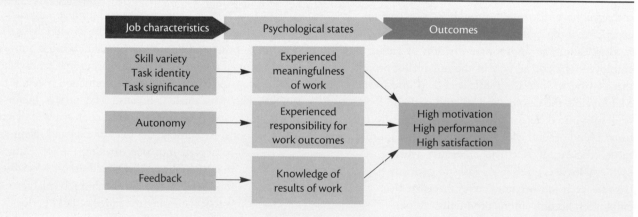

According to Hackman and Oldham, every job has five characteristics that determine how motivating the job is. These characteristics determine how employees react to their work and lead to outcomes such as high performance and satisfaction and low absenteeism and turnover:

- *Skill variety:* The extent to which a job requires that an employee use a wide range of different skills, abilities, or knowledge. Example: The skill variety required by the job of a research scientist is higher than that called for by the job of a McDonald's food server.

- *Task identity:* The extent to which a job requires that a worker perform all the tasks necessary to complete the job from the beginning to the end of the production process. Example: A craftsworker who takes a piece of wood and transforms it into a custom-made desk has higher task identity than does a worker who performs only one of the numerous operations required to assemble a flat-screen TV.

- *Task significance:* The degree to which a worker feels his or her job is meaningful because of its effect on people inside the organization, such as coworkers, or on people outside the organization, such as customers. Example: A teacher who sees the effect of his or her efforts in a well-educated and well-adjusted student enjoys high task significance compared to a dishwasher who monotonously washes dishes as they come to the kitchen.

- *Autonomy:* The degree to which a job gives an employee the freedom and discretion needed to schedule different tasks and decide how to carry them out. Example: Salespeople who have to plan their schedules and decide how to allocate their time among different customers have relatively high autonomy compared to assembly-line workers, whose actions are determined by the speed of the production line.

- *Feedback:* The extent to which actually doing a job provides a worker with clear and direct information about how well he or she has performed the job. Example: An air traffic controller whose mistakes may result in a midair collision receives immediate feedback on job performance; a person who compiles statistics for a business magazine often has little idea of when he or she makes a mistake or does a particularly good job.

Hackman and Oldham argue that these five job characteristics affect an employee's motivation because they affect three critical psychological states (refer to Figure 6.1). The more employees feel that their work is *meaningful* and that they are *responsible for work outcomes and responsible for knowing how those outcomes affect others,* the more motivating work becomes and the more likely employees are to be satisfied and to perform at a high level. Moreover, employees who have jobs that are highly motivating are called on to use their skills more and to perform more tasks, and they are given more responsibility for doing the job. All of the foregoing are characteristic of jobs and employees in flexible structures where authority is decentralized and where employees commonly work with others and must learn new skills to complete the range of tasks for which their group is responsible.

Describe how managers can group jobs into functional, divisional, network, and hybrid structures.   **LO3**

Grouping Jobs into Functional, Divisional, Network, and Hybrid Structures

Once managers have decided which tasks to allocate to which jobs, they face the next organizing decision: how to group jobs together into units to best match the needs of the organization's environment, strategy, technology, and human resources. Typically, managers first decide to group jobs into departments and they design a *functional structure* to use organizational resources effectively. As an organization grows and becomes more difficult to control, managers must choose a more complex organizational design, such as a divisional structure, matrix, product team structure, network, or hybrid structure. The different ways in which managers can design organizational structure are discussed next. Selecting and designing an organizational structure to increase efficiency and effectiveness is a significant challenge. As noted in Chapter 5, managers reap the rewards of a well-thought-out strategy only if they choose the right type of structure to implement the strategy.

Functional Structure

A function is a group of people, working together, who possess similar skills or use the same kind of knowledge, tools, or techniques to perform their jobs. Manufacturing, sales, and research and development are often organized

Pier 1 Imports uses a functional structure.

into functional departments. A **functional structure** is an organizational structure composed of all the departments that an organization requires to produce its goods or services. Pier 1 Imports, a home furnishings company, uses a functional structure to supply its customers with a range of goods from around the world to satisfy their desires for new and innovative products. Figure 6.2 shows the functional structure that Pier 1 Imports uses.

Pier 1's main functions are finance and administration, merchandising (purchasing the goods), stores (managing the retail outlets), logistics (managing product distribution), marketing, human resources, and real estate. Each job inside a function exists because it helps the function perform the activities necessary for high organizational performance. Thus, within the logistics department are all the jobs necessary to distribute and transport products efficiently to stores. Inside the marketing department are all the jobs (such as promotion, photography, and visual communication) that are necessary to increase the appeal of Pier 1's products to customers.

There are several advantages to grouping jobs according to function. See Figure 6.3.

> **functional structure**
> An organizational structure composed of all the departments that an organization requires to produce its goods or services.

FIGURE 6.2 The Functional Structure of Pier 1 Imports

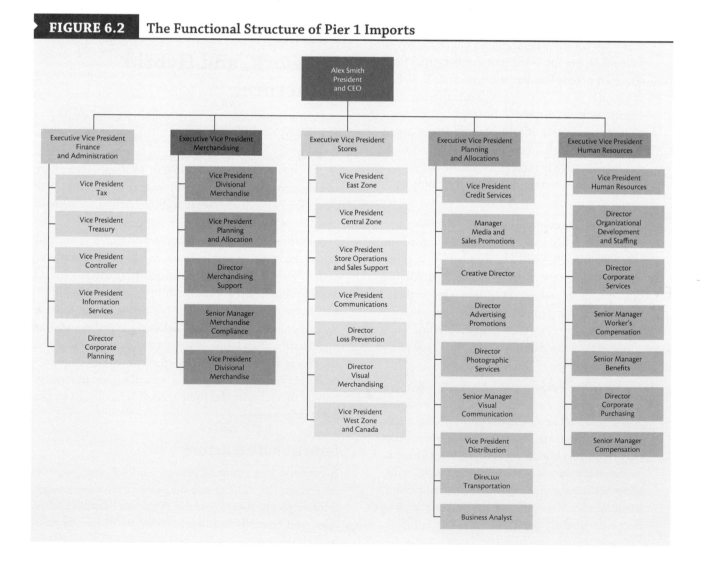

FIGURE 6.3 **The Advantages and Disadvantages of Functional Structures**

Functional Structure	Advantages for Managers	Disadvantages for Managers
Grouping similar jobs together	• People learn from each other and cooperation is encouraged • Control is easier as is employee performance evaluation • Targeted environmental scanning allows managers to develop better strategy and minimize risk	• Difficulty in communicating across functions as organizations grow • Organizational goals take second place to departmental goals • Organizational effectiveness and efficiency can be compromised

• First, when people who perform similar jobs are grouped together, they can learn from watching one another. Thus they become more specialized and can perform at a higher level. The tasks associated with one job often are related to the tasks associated with another job, which encourages cooperation within a function. In Pier 1's planning department, for example, the person designing the photography program for an ad campaign works closely with the person responsible for designing store layouts and with visual communication experts. As a result, Pier 1 is able to develop a strong, focused marketing campaign to differentiate its products.

• Second, when people who perform similar jobs are grouped together, managers can monitor and evaluate their performance more easily.[13] Imagine if marketing experts, purchasing experts, and real-estate experts were grouped together in one function and supervised by a manager from merchandising. Obviously, the merchandising manager would not have the expertise to evaluate all these different people appropriately. However, a functional structure allows workers to evaluate how well coworkers are performing their jobs, and if some workers are performing poorly, more experienced workers can help them develop new skills.

• Finally, managers like functional structure because it allows them to create the set of functions they need for scanning and monitoring the competitive environment and obtain information about the way it is changing.[14] With the right set of functions in place, managers are then in a good position to develop a strategy that allows the organization to respond to its changing situation. Employees in the marketing group can specialize in monitoring new marketing developments that will allow Pier 1 to better target its customers. Employees in merchandising can monitor all potential suppliers of home furnishings both at home and abroad to find the goods most likely to appeal to Pier 1's customers and manage Pier 1's global outsourcing supply chain.

As an organization grows and its strategy changes to produce a wider range of goods and services for different kinds of customers, several problems can make a functional structure less efficient and effective.[15] See Figure 6.3.

• First, managers in different functions may find it more difficult to communicate and coordinate with one another when they are responsible for several different kinds of products, especially as the organization grows both domestically and internationally.

• Second, functional managers may become so preoccupied with supervising their own specific departments and achieving their departmental goals that they lose sight of organizational goals. If that happens, organizational effectiveness will suffer because managers will be viewing issues and problems facing the organization only from their own, relatively narrow, departmental perspectives.[16] Both of these problems can reduce efficiency and effectiveness.

Small businesses often adopt a very simple structure where the owner is the general manager responsible for the

Tips **FOR MANAGERS**

Choosing a Divisional Structure

1. As the manager of a small business, you often end up performing all the functions in-house, but this may not be the most efficient and effective way of organizing.

2. The decision to "make-or-buy" depends on relative costs. Sometimes an outside firm can perform the function both better and cheaper because of greater specialization, superior technology, or some other advantage.

3. Decisions to contract out noncore functions must be made in relation to the capabilities and competencies of your staff.

4. Form (structure) and function (strategy) have to fit well together, but be flexible to accommodate unpredictable changes in the organization's environment.

activities of all the functions. Take for example the enterprise of a restaurant. It is not uncommon for a head chef to manage the "back of the house," or the food purchasing and hiring/supervision of the kitchen staff, while another manager operates the "front of the house" including supervising the wait staff and bartender/sommelier. The manager may decide to contract out the noncore functions that are necessary to the operation of the restaurant but not central to its mission, like payroll and accounting.

Divisional Structures: Product, Geographic, and Market

As the problems associated with growth and diversification increase over time, managers must search for new ways to organize their activities to overcome the problems linked with a functional structure. Most managers of large organizations choose a **divisional structure** and create a series of business units to produce a specific kind of product for a specific kind of customer. Each division is a collection of functions or departments that work together to produce the product. The goal behind the change to a divisional structure is to create smaller, more manageable units within the organization. There are three forms of divisional structure (see Figure 6.4.).[17]

When managers organize divisions according to the type of good or service they provide, they adopt a *product* structure. When managers organize divisions according to

divisional structure An organizational structure composed of separate business units within which are the functions that work together to produce a specific product for a specific customer.

> **FIGURE 6.4** Product, Geographic, and Market Structures

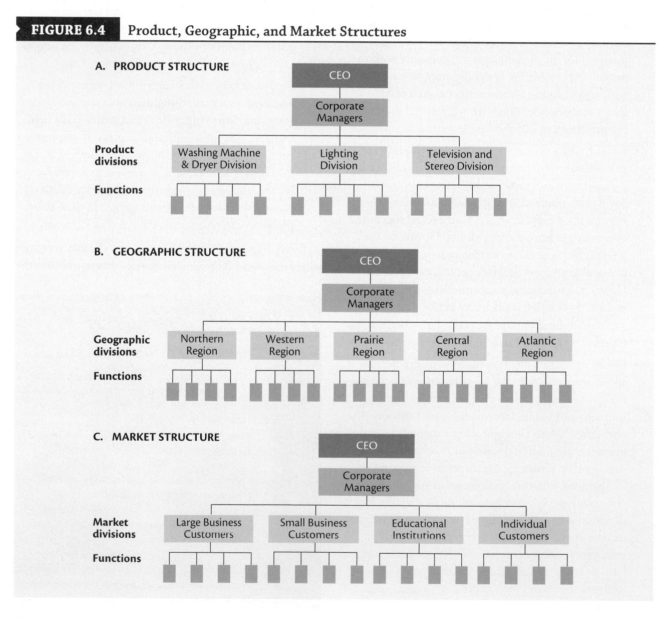

the area of the country or world they operate in, they adopt a *geographic* structure. When managers organize divisions according to the types of customers they focus on, they adopt a *market* structure.

Product Structure

Imagine the problems that managers at Pier 1 would encounter if they decided to diversify into producing and selling cars, fast food, and health insurance—in addition to home furnishings—and tried to use their existing set of functional managers to oversee the production of all four kinds of products. No manager would have the necessary skills or abilities to oversee those four products. No individual marketing manager, for example, could effectively market cars, fast food, health insurance, and home furnishings at the same time. To perform a functional activity successfully, managers must have experience in specific markets or industries. Consequently, if managers decide to diversify into new industries or to expand their range of products, they commonly design a product structure to organize their operations. Using a **product structure** (see Figure 6.4A), managers place each distinct product line or business in its own self-contained division and give divisional managers the responsibility for devising an appropriate business-level strategy to allow the division to compete effectively in its industry or market.[18] Each division is self-contained because it has a complete set of all the functions—marketing, R&D, finance, and so on—that it needs to produce or provide goods or services efficiently and effectively. Functional managers report to divisional managers, and divisional managers report to top or corporate managers.

Small businesses can also organize along product lines within, for example, the same store. A shoe store may sell children's as well as men's and women's shoes in the same location. As the company grows, it may be appropriate for individual managers to oversee each product category, thus gaining from the same advantages as a product divisional structure.

Grouping functions into divisions focused on particular products or services has several advantages for managers at all levels in the organization. First, a product structure allows functional managers to specialize in only one product area, so they are able to build expertise and fine-tune their skills in this particular area. Second, each division's managers can become experts in their industry; this expertise helps them choose and develop a business-level strategy to differentiate their products or lower their costs while meeting the needs of customers.

> **product structure** An organizational structure in which each product line or business is handled by a self-contained division.
>
> **geographic structure** An organizational structure in which each region of a country or area of the world is served by a self-contained division.

Third, a product structure frees corporate managers from the need to supervise each division's day-to-day operations directly; this latitude allows corporate managers to create the best corporate-level strategy to maximize the organization's future growth and ability to create value. Corporate managers are likely to make fewer mistakes about which businesses to diversify into or how best to expand internationally, for example, because they are able to take an organization-wide view.[19] Corporate managers also are likely to better evaluate how well divisional managers are doing, and they can intervene and take corrective action as needed.

The extra layer of management, the divisional management layer, can improve the use of organizational resources. Moreover, a product structure puts divisional managers close to their customers and lets them respond quickly and appropriately to the changing task environment.

Geographic Structure

When organizations expand rapidly both at home and abroad, functional structures can create special problems because managers in one central location may find it increasingly difficult to deal with the different problems and issues that may arise in each region of a country or area of the world. In these cases, a **geographic structure**, in which divisions are broken down by geographical location, is often chosen (see Figure 6.4B). To achieve the corporate mission of providing next-day mail service, Fred Smith, chair, president, and CEO of Federal Express, "with transportation in his blood,"[20] chose a geographic structure and divided up operations by creating a division in each region. Large retailers often use a

Global companies pose organizational design challenges.

FIGURE 6.5 Global Geographic and Global Product Structures

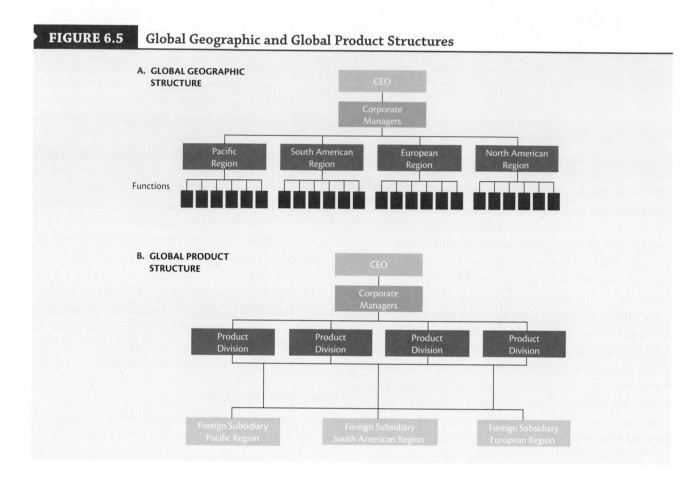

geographic structure. Since the needs of retail customers differ by region—for example, umbrellas in Vancouver and down-filled parkas in the Prairies and the East—a geographic structure gives regional retail managers the flexibility they need to choose products that best meet the needs of regional customers.

In adopting a *global geographic structure,* such as shown in Figure 6.5A, managers locate different divisions in each of the world regions where the organization operates. Managers are most likely to do this when they pursue a multi-domestic strategy, because customer needs vary widely by country or world region. For example, if products that appeal to Canadian customers do not sell in Europe, the Pacific Rim, or South America, then managers must customize the products to meet the needs of customers in those different world regions; a global geographic structure with global divisions will allow them to do this.

In contrast, to the degree that customers abroad are willing to buy the same kind of product, or slight variations thereof, managers are more likely to pursue a global strategy. In this case they are more likely to use a global product structure. In a *global product structure,* each product division, not the country and regional managers,

takes responsibility for deciding where to manufacture its products and how to market them in countries worldwide (see Figure 6.5B). Product division managers manage their own global value chains and decide where to establish foreign subsidiaries to distribute and sell their products to customers in foreign countries. As we noted at the beginning of this chapter, an organization's strategy is a major determinant of its structure both at home and abroad.

Market Structure

Sometimes, the pressing issue managers face is how to group functions according to the type of customer buying the product, in order to tailor the organization's products to each customer's unique demands. TELUS, based in Burnaby, BC, is structured around six customer-focused business units: Consumer Solutions, focused on households and individuals; Business Solutions, focused on small- to medium-sized businesses and entrepreneurs; Client Solutions, focused on large organizations in Canada; Partner Solutions, focused on Canadian and global carriers into and within Canada; Wireless Solutions, focused on people and businesses on the go; and TELUS Québec, a TELUS company for the Quebec marketplace.

FOCUS ON ❯ *The Social Economy*

Common Thread Co-operative

Common Thread is a cooperative of Canadian organizations that have sewing programs and enterprises. The cooperative provides brokering and production coordination for their members and other producers. The co-op's members are social enterprises—businesses that have a primary social purpose, such as creating employment for a specific group such as newcomers to Canada or Aboriginal communities. Common Thread members include the following organizations:

- The Kettle Friendship Society provides a variety of flexible work settings for its members who are recovering from mental illness.

- Coast Mental Health started Sewing With Heart in 2003 as a way to provide work opportunities and skill development for people recovering from mental illness.

- Progressive Intercultural Community Services (PICS) operates a 12-week sewing program exclusively for women that teaches cutting and tailoring.

- EMBERS (Eastside Movement for Business & Economic Renewal Society) is based in Vancouver's Downtown Eastside where it provides programs and services that increase the sustainability of small business in the community.[21]

As members of the apex or umbrella organization Common Thread, the members participate in its governance on a one-vote-per-member basis. Any profits generated by Common Thread from helping members sell their products are redistributed back to members according to their use of the cooperative's services.

1. How does the tier structure of cooperatives such as Common Thread differ from traditional businesses organized by market divisions?

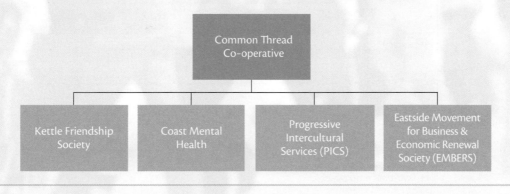

To satisfy the needs of diverse customers, TELUS adopts a **market structure** (also called a *customer structure*), which groups divisions according to the particular kinds of customers they serve (see Figure 6.4C). A market structure allows managers to be both responsive to the needs of their customers and able to act flexibly to make decisions in response to customers' changing needs.

In the case of tier-structured cooperative organizations, the customers are the owners and members. As the Focus on the Social Economy illustrates, organizations structured as cooperatives that are involved in providing similar services often have an apex or umbrella co-op that coordinates and supports member organizations. They do this by either acting as a broker to market member-produced goods or by acting as a purchasing agent, allowing the member organizations to achieve economies of scale in procuring the inputs they need for their businesses. The Canadian cooperative Arctic Co-operatives Ltd. (ACL) is organized with this tiered structure. ACL is owned by 31 community-based cooperative businesses located in Nunavut and the Northwest Territories. These 31 organizations are its customers as well as its member/owners. The ACL provides financing, purchasing of goods and services needed by the member co-ops, and the marketing of Aboriginal art produced by the Inuit, Métis, and Dene owners of the member businesses. As with cooperatives

market structure An organizational structure in which each kind of customer is served by a self-contained division; also called *customer structure.*

in general, each owner/member has one voting share that allows them to participate in the governance of ACL. Surplus revenues are distributed among the 31 owner/members based on their use of ACL's services. Between 1986 and 2007, the redistributed funds paid to the 31 members from ACL totalled $34.6 million.[22]

Matrix and Product Team Designs

Moving to a product, market, or geographic divisional structure means managers can respond more quickly and flexibly to the particular set of circumstances they confront. However, when information technology or customer needs are changing rapidly and the environment is very uncertain even a divisional structure may not provide managers with enough flexibility to respond

to the environment quickly. To operate effectively under these conditions, managers must design the most flexible organizational structure available: a *matrix structure* or a *product team structure* (see Figure 6.6).

Matrix Structure

In a **matrix structure**, managers group people and resources in two ways simultaneously: by function and by product.[23] Employees are grouped into *functions* to allow them to learn from one another and become more skilled and productive. Employees are also grouped into *product teams*, in which members of different functions work together to develop a specific product. The result

> **matrix structure** An organizational structure that simultaneously groups people and resources by function and by product.

> **FIGURE 6.6**   **Matrix and Product Team Structures**

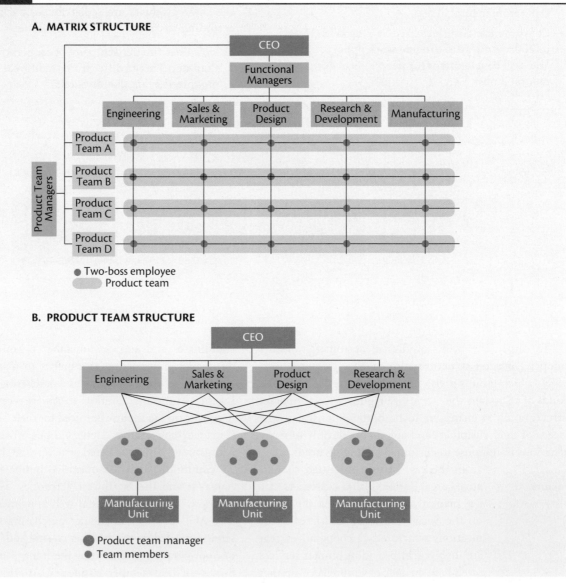

is a complex network of reporting relationships among product teams and functions that make the matrix structure very flexible (see Figure 6.6A). Each person in a product team reports to two managers: (1) a functional manager, who assigns individuals to a team and evaluates their performance from a functional point of view, and (2) the manager of the product team, who evaluates their performance on the team. Thus, team members are known as *two-boss employees*.

The functional employees assigned to product teams change over time as the specific skills that the team needs change. At the beginning of the product development process, for example, engineers and R&D specialists are assigned to a product team because their skills are needed to develop new products. When a provisional design has been established, marketing experts are assigned to the team to gauge how customers will respond to the new product. Manufacturing personnel join when it is time to find the most efficient way to produce the product. As their specific jobs are completed, team members leave and are reassigned to new teams. In this way, the matrix structure makes the most use of human resources.

To keep the matrix structure flexible:

* Product teams are empowered and team members are responsible for making most of the important decisions involved in product development.[24]

* The product team manager acts as a facilitator, controlling the financial resources and trying to keep the project on time and within budget.

* The functional managers try to ensure that the product is the best that it can be in order to make the most of its differentiated appeal.

High-tech companies have been using matrix structures successfully for many years. These companies operate in environments where new product developments happen monthly or yearly and the need to innovate quickly is vital to the organization's survival. The matrix structure provides enough flexibility for managers to keep pace with a changing and increasingly complex environment. For this reason, matrixes also have been designed by managers who want to control international operations as they move abroad and face problems of coordinating their domestic and foreign divisions.[25] Virtual teams, discussed in Chapter 10, are becoming increasingly common as a way of organizing product and service matrixes in global companies.

Product Team Structure

The dual reporting relationships that are at the heart of a matrix structure have always been difficult for managers and employees to deal with. Often, the functional manager and the product manager make conflicting demands on team members, who do not know which manager to satisfy first. Also, functional and product team managers may come into conflict over precisely who is in charge of which team members and for how long. To avoid these problems, managers have devised a way of organizing people and resources that still allows an organization to be flexible but makes its structure easier to operate: a product team structure.

The **product team structure** differs from a matrix structure in two ways: (1) it does away with dual reporting relationships for employees, and (2) functional employees are permanently assigned to a cross-functional team that is empowered to bring a new or redesigned product to market. A **cross-functional team** is a group of individuals brought together from different departments to perform organizational tasks. When individuals are grouped into cross-departmental teams, the artificial boundaries between departments disappear, and a narrow focus on departmental goals is replaced with a general interest in working together to achieve organizational goals. The results of such changes have been dramatic: For example, Chrysler Canada's use of cross-functional teams has reduced the time it takes to retool for a new product from months to just weeks.

Members of a cross-functional team report only to the product team manager or to one of his or her direct subordinates. The functional managers have only an informal, advisory relationship with members of the product teams. These managers counsel and help cross-functional team members, share knowledge among teams, and provide new technological developments that can help improve each team's performance (see Figure 6.6B).[26]

Organizations sometimes change their divisional strategy because of market changes and changes in the organizational environment. Even though organizations in the past were generally organized as functional bureaucracies of manufacturing, sales, and R&D, which were coordinated and controlled at the top, today organizations use a complex mix of these structures.

For example, AT&T is split into three companies on the basis of product but continues to use the mix of markets, products, regions, and functions and processes. Its Network Services Division is structured according to processes such as provisioning, maintenance, leadership, and human resource management.[27] These organizational structures are referred to as *hybrid structures*.

product team structure
An organizational structure in which employees are permanently assigned to a cross-functional team and report only to the product team manager or to one of his or her direct subordinates.

cross-functional team
A group of individuals from different departments brought together to perform organizational tasks.

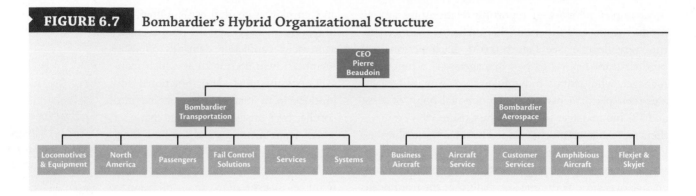

FIGURE 6.7 Bombardier's Hybrid Organizational Structure

Hybrid Structures

A large organization that has many divisions and simultaneously uses many different structures has a **hybrid structure**. Most large organizations use product division structures and create self-contained divisions; then, each division's managers select the structure that best meets the needs of the particular environment, strategy, and so on. Thus, one product division may choose to operate with a functional structure, a second may choose a geographic structure to provide support and product customization for different regions, and a third may choose a product team structure because of the nature of the division's products or the desire to be more responsive to customers' needs. Bombardier, award-winning supplier of light rail, business, and commercial aircraft, has two main product groups, transportation and areospace, and a hybrid mixture of functional and geographically organized divisions within each group. See Figure 6.7.

Strategic Alliances and Network Structures

Recently, increasing globalization and the use of new IT have brought about two innovations in organizational architecture that are sweeping through North American and European companies: strategic alliances and business-to-business (B2B) network structures. A **strategic alliance** is a formal agreement that commits two or more companies to exchange or share their resources in order to produce and market a product.

Most commonly, strategic alliances are formed because the companies share similar interests and believe they can benefit from cooperating. For example, Japanese car companies such as Toyota and Honda have formed many strategic alliances with particular suppliers of inputs such as car axles, gearboxes, and air-conditioning systems. Over time, these car companies work closely with their suppliers to improve the efficiency and effectiveness of the inputs so that the final product—the car produced—is of higher quality and very often can be produced at lower cost. Toyota and Honda have also established alliances

with suppliers throughout Canada, the United States, and Mexico because both companies now build several models of cars in these countries. Samsung and Bosch are collaborating to produce batteries for electric vehicles for BMW.

The growing sophistication of IT with global intranets and teleconferencing has made it much easier to manage strategic alliances and allow managers to share information and cooperate. One outcome of this has been the growth of strategic alliances into a network structure. A **network structure** is a series of global strategic alliances that an organization creates with suppliers, manufacturers, and/or distributors to produce and market a product. Network structures allow an organization to manage its global value chain in order to find new ways to reduce costs and increase the quality of products—without incurring the high costs of operating a complex organizational structure (such as the costs of employing many managers). Many of the 83 companies in the Samsung Group supply inputs to other product divisions. For example, micro-processing chips are used in household appliances and microwaves.

More and more Canadian, American, and European organizations are relying on global network structures to gain access to low-cost foreign sources of inputs. This approach allows managers to keep costs low. As discussed in Chapter 4, PUMA is a company that has used this approach extensively. Nike, the most profitable shoe manufacturer in the world, also uses a network structure to produce and market shoes. As noted in Chapter 5, many successful companies today are trying to pursue simultaneously a low-cost and a differentiation strategy. Nike CEO Philip Knight decided early that to do this at Nike he needed an organizational architecture that would allow his company to focus on some functions, such as design, and to leave others, such as manufacturing, to other organizations.

---

hybrid structure The structure of a large organization that has many divisions and simultaneously uses many different organizational structures.

strategic alliance a formal agreement that commits two or more companies to exchange or share their resources in order to produce and market a product.

network structure A series of strategic alliances that an organization creates with suppliers, manufacturers, and/or distributors to produce and market a product.

Nike's network structure allows it to remain competitive by keeping up with fashion trends and keeping costs low.

By far the largest function at Nike's Oregon headquarters is the design function, composed of talented designers who pioneered innovations in sports shoe design such as the air pump and Air Jordans that Nike introduced so successfully. Designers use computer-aided design (CAD) to design Nike shoes, and they electronically store all new product information, including manufacturing instructions. When the designers have finished their work, they electronically transmit all the blueprints for the new products to a network of Southeast Asian suppliers and manufacturers with which Nike has formed strategic alliances.[28] Instructions for the design of a new sole may be sent to a supplier in Taiwan, and instructions for the leather uppers to a supplier in Malaysia. The suppliers produce the shoe parts and send them for final assembly to a manufacturer in China with which Nike has established another strategic alliance. From China the shoes are shipped to distributors throughout the world. Ninety-nine percent of the 120 million pairs of shoes that Nike makes each year are made in Southeast Asia.

This network structure gives Nike two important advantages. First, Nike is able to respond to changes in sports shoe fashion very quickly. Using its global IT system, Nike literally can change the instructions it gives each of its suppliers overnight, so that within a few weeks its foreign manufacturers are producing new kinds of shoes.[29] Any alliance partners that fail to perform up to Nike's standards are replaced with new partners.

Second, Nike's costs are very low because wages in Southeast Asia are a fraction of what they are in the United States, and this difference gives Nike a low-cost advantage. Also, Nike's ability to use foreign manufacturers to produce all its shoes abroad allows Knight to keep the organization's U.S. structure flat and flexible. Nike is able to use a relatively inexpensive functional structure to organize its activities. However, sports shoe manufacturers' attempts to keep their costs low have led to many charges that Nike and others are supporting sweatshops that harm foreign workers.

Nike was one of the first to experience a backlash when critics revealed how workers in these countries were being treated. Indonesian workers were stitching together shoes in hot, noisy factories for only 80 cents a day, or about $18 a month.[30] Workers in Vietnam and China fared better; they could earn $1.60 a day. In all cases, however, critics charged that at least $3 a day was needed to maintain an adequate living standard.

These facts generated an outcry in North America, where Nike was roundly attacked for its labour practices; a backlash against sales of Nike products forced Phil Knight, Nike's billionaire owner, to re-evaluate Nike's labour practices. Nike announced that henceforth all the factories producing its shoes and clothes would be independently monitored and inspected. After its competitor Reebok, which also had been criticized for similar labour practices, announced that it was raising wages in Indonesia by 20 percent, Nike raised them by 25 percent to $23 a month.[31] Small though this may seem, it was a huge increase to workers in these countries.

In Europe, another sportswear company, Adidas, had largely escaped such criticism. But in 1999 it was reported that in El Salvador, a Taiwan-based Adidas subcontractor was employing girls as young as 14 in its factories and making them work for more than 70 hours a week. They were allowed to go to the restroom only twice a day, and if they stayed longer than three minutes, they lost a day's wages.[32] Adidas moved swiftly to avoid the public relations nightmare that Nike had experienced. Adidas announced that henceforth its subcontractors would be required to abide by more strict labour standards.

What happened in the sports shoe industry has happened throughout the clothing industry as well as other industries like electronics and toys in the 2000s. Companies such as Walmart, Target, The Gap, Sony, and Mattel have all been forced to re-evaluate the ethics of their labour practices and to promise to keep a constant watch on subcontractors in the future. Ethical sourcing practices are being adopted in all industries which rely on global supply chains and network organizational structures.

The ability of managers to develop networks to produce or provide the goods and services customers want, rather than creating a complex organizational structure to do so, has led many researchers and consultants to popularize the idea of a **boundaryless organization** composed of people who are linked by computers, computer-aided design systems, and video teleconferencing, and who rarely, if ever, see one another face

boundaryless organization An organization whose members are linked by computers, computer-aided design systems, and video teleconferencing, and who rarely, if ever, see one another face to face.

to face. People are used when their services are needed, much as in a matrix structure, but they are not formal members of an organization. They are functional experts who form an alliance with an organization, fulfill their contractual obligations, and then move on to the next project.

Large consulting companies such as Accenture utilize their global consultants in this way. Consultants are connected by laptops to an organization's knowledge management system, its company-specific information system that systematizes the knowledge of its employees and provides them with access to other employees who have the expertise to solve the problems that they encounter as they perform their jobs. iGEN Knowledge Solutions Inc., based in New Westminster, BC, operates as a boundaryless organization to bring technical solutions to its business clients. Associates work from home offices connected by wireless technologies and the Internet and collaborate to solve client problems. The virtual model allows fast cycle times for idea implementation, service delivery, and product development. The model makes it easy to set up operations in different regions of the world without large overhead costs.

The use of outsourcing and the development of network structures is increasing rapidly as organizations recognize the many opportunities they offer to reduce costs and increase organizational flexibility. The push to lower costs has led to the development of electronic **business-to-business (B2B) networks,** in which most or all of the companies in an industry (e.g., car makers) use the same software platform to link to each other and establish industry specifications and standards. Then, these companies jointly list the quantity and specifications of the inputs they require and invite bids from the thousands of potential suppliers around the world. Suppliers also use the same software platform so that electronic bidding, auctions, and transactions are possible between buyers and sellers around the world. Canada's Mediagrif has B2B networks in nine areas: electronics components, wines and spirits, computer equipment, telecommunications equipment, automotive aftermarket parts, truck parts, government e-tendering (which includes the MERX electronic tendering system used by the federal government of Canada), medical equipment, and IT parts and equipment.[33] The idea is that high-volume, standardized transactions can help drive down costs at the industry level.

The use of outsourcing is increasing rapidly as organizations recognize the many opportunities that the approaches offer to reduce costs and increase organizational flexibility. Canadian Pacific Railway (CPR) outsources the maintenance of applications for which it does not need to develop in-house expertise. For example, it

has outsourced the maintenance of some of its legacy applications to RIS and also outsources its mainframe infrastructure to IBM. When CPR did the work itself in-house everything was not running smoothly. Allen Borak, vice-president for information services at CPR in Calgary, said, "I would say that part of our business wasn't well managed." The decision to outsource has left CPR free to concentrate on what it does best.[34] Stephen Libman, president of Libman Chimo Travel in Montreal, has a similar story. He has gained 90 percent of his time back after he outsourced to another Montreal company, Eternitee Systems Inc., Libman's desktop hardware and software and its network for a fixed monthly fee. Libman says he spends about the same amount of money on technology as before but has gained his time back.[35]

Companies that specialize in outsourced work, such as EDS Corporation—which manages the information systems of large organizations such as Xerox, Eastman Kodak, and even the Central Bank of Canada[36]—are major beneficiaries of this new approach. While many companies use outsourcing, not all have been successful at implementing it. Managers should be aware of the following concerns when considering its use: (1) choosing the wrong activities to outsource, (2) choosing the wrong vendor, (3) writing a poor contract, (4) failing to consider personnel issues, (5) losing control over the activity, (6) ignoring the hidden costs, and (7) failing to develop an exit strategy (for either moving to another vendor or deciding to bring the activity back in-house).[37] A review of 91 outsourcing activities found that writing a poor contract and losing control of the activity were the most likely reasons for an outsourcing venture to fail. Designing organizational structure is becoming an increasingly complex management function. To maximize efficiency and effectiveness, managers must carefully assess the relative benefits of having their own organization perform a functional activity versus forming an alliance with another organization to perform the activity.

connect

Learn more about outsourcing in Connect.

Explain the ways that managers allocate authority and coordinate activities.

LO4

Linking and Coordinating Functions and Divisions

The more complex the structure a company uses to group its activities, the greater are the problems of *linking and coordinating* its different functions and divisions. Coordination becomes a problem because each function or division develops a different orientation toward the other groups that affects the way it interacts with them. Each function or division comes to view the problems facing the company from its own particular perspective; for example, they may develop different views about the major goals, problems, or issues facing a company.

At the functional level, the manufacturing function typically has a very short-term view; its major goal is to keep costs under control and get the product out the factory door on time. By contrast, the product development function has a long-term viewpoint because developing a new product is a relatively slow process and high product quality is seen as more important than low costs. Such differences in viewpoint may make manufacturing and product development managers reluctant to cooperate and coordinate their activities to meet company goals. At the divisional level, in a company with a product structure employees may become concerned more with making *their* division's products a success than with the profitability of the entire company. They may refuse, or simply not see the need, to cooperate and share information or knowledge with other divisions.

Allocating Authority

Having discussed how managers divide organizational activities into jobs, functions, and divisions to increase efficiency and effectiveness, we now look at how they put the parts back together by designing the hierarchy of authority.[38] **Authority** is the power to hold people accountable for their actions and to make decisions concerning the use of organizational resources. The **hierarchy of authority** is an organization's *chain of command*—the relative authority that each manager has—extending from the CEO at the top, down through the middle managers and first-line managers, to the nonmanagerial employees who actually make goods or provide services. Every manager, at every level of the hierarchy, supervises one or more subordinates. The term **span of control** refers to the number of subordinates who report directly to a manager.

Figure 6.8 shows a simplified picture of the hierarchy of authority and the span of control of managers in McDonald's in 2011. At the top of the hierarchy is

authority The power to hold people accountable for their actions and to make decisions concerning the use of organizational resources.

hierarchy of authority An organization's chain of command, specifying the relative authority of each manager.

span of control The number of subordinates who report directly to a manager.

line manager Someone in the direct line or chain of command who has formal authority over people and resources at lower levels

staff manager Someone responsible for managing a specialist function, such as finance or marketing.

Jim Skinner, CEO and vice chairman of McDonald's board of directors, who took control in 2004.[39] Skinner is the manager who has ultimate responsibility for McDonald's performance, and he has the authority to decide how to use organizational resources to benefit McDonald's stakeholders.[40] Don Thompson is next in line; he is president and COO and is responsible for overseeing all of McDonald's U.S. restaurant operations. Thompson reports directly to Skinner, as does chief financial officer Peter Bensen. Unlike the other managers, Bensen is not a **line manager,** someone in the direct line or chain of command who has formal authority over people and resources. Rather, Bensen is a **staff manager,** responsible for one of McDonald's specialist functions, finance. Worldwide chief restaurant officer Jeff Stratton is responsible for overseeing all functional aspects of McDonald's overseas operations, which are headed by the presidents of world regions: Europe; Canada and Latin America; and Asia/Pacific, Middle East, and Africa. Of special mention is Janice Fields, who is president of McDonald's U.S. operations and reports to Donald Thompson.

Managers at each level of the hierarchy confer on managers at the next level down the authority to make decisions about how to use organizational resources. Accepting this authority, those lower-level managers then become responsible for their decisions and are accountable for how well they make those decisions. Managers who make the right decisions are typically promoted, and organizations motivate managers with the prospects of promotion and increased responsibility within the chain of command.

Below Fields are the other main levels or layers in the McDonald's American chain of command—executive vice presidents of its West, Central, and East regions, regional managers, and supervisors. A hierarchy is also evident in each company-owned McDonald's restaurant. At the top is the store manager; at lower levels are the first assistant, shift managers, and crew personnel. McDonald's managers have decided that this hierarchy of authority best allows the company to pursue its business-level strategy of providing fast food at reasonable prices.

Tall and Flat Organizations

As an organization grows in size (normally measured by the number of its managers and employees), its hierarchy

> **FIGURE 6.8** Simplified Hierarchy of Authority and Span of Control at McDonald's Corporation

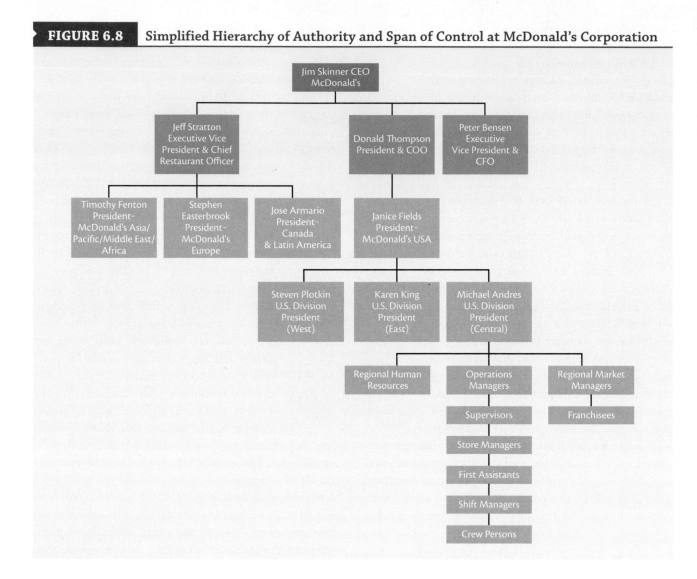

of authority normally lengthens, making the organizational structure taller. A *tall* organization has many levels of authority relative to company size; a *flat* organization has fewer levels relative to company size (see Figure 6.9).[41] As a hierarchy becomes taller, problems may result that make the organization's structure less flexible and slow managers' response to changes in the organizational environment.

For instance, communication problems may arise. When an organization has many levels in the hierarchy, it can take a long time for the decisions and orders of upper-level managers to reach managers farther down in the hierarchy, and it can take a long time for top managers to learn how well their decisions worked out. Feeling out of touch, top managers may want to verify that lower-level managers are following orders and may require written confirmation from them. Middle managers, who know they will be held strictly accountable for

their actions, start devoting more time to the process of making decisions in order to improve their chances of being right. They might even try to avoid responsibility by making top managers decide what actions to take.

Another communication problem that can result is the distortion of commands and messages being transmitted up and down the hierarchy, which causes managers at different levels to interpret differently what is happening. Distortion of orders and messages can be accidental, occurring because different managers interpret messages from their own narrow functional perspectives. Or it can be intentional, when managers low in the hierarchy decide to interpret information to increase their own personal advantage.

Another problem with tall hierarchies is that usually they indicate an organization is employing too many managers, and managers are expensive. Managerial salaries, benefits, offices, and secretaries are a huge expense for

FIGURE 6.9 Flat and Tall Organizations

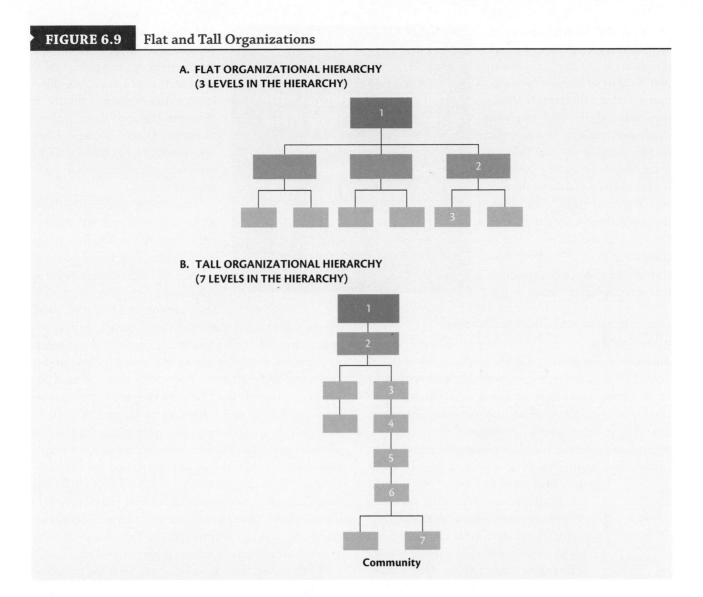

A. FLAT ORGANIZATIONAL HIERARCHY
(3 LEVELS IN THE HIERARCHY)

B. TALL ORGANIZATIONAL HIERARCHY
(7 LEVELS IN THE HIERARCHY)

Community

organizations. Large companies such as IBM and General Motors pay their managers billions of dollars a year. Throughout the early 2000s, hundreds of thousands of middle managers were laid off as companies tried to reduce costs by restructuring and downsizing their workforces. In the economic downturn in 2008, many companies announced layoffs to reduce operating costs.

The Minimum Chain of Command

To ward off the problems that result when an organization becomes too tall and employs too many managers, top managers need to work out whether they are employing the right number of middle and first-line managers, and to see whether they can redesign their organizational structure to reduce the number of managers. Top managers might well follow a basic organizing principle—the principle of the **minimum chain of command**—which states that top managers should always construct a

hierarchy with the fewest levels of authority necessary to efficiently and effectively use organizational resources.

Effective managers constantly scrutinize their hierarchies to see whether the number of levels can be reduced—for example, by eliminating one level and giving the responsibilities of managers at that level to managers above and empowering employees below. One organization that is trying to empower staff is Ducks Unlimited Canada of Stonewall, Manitoba, a private non-profit charitable organization founded by sportsmen that is devoted to preserving wetlands and associated waterfowl habitats.[42] The company recently went through a reorganization, flattening its management structure. The 330 staff members have been divided into groups to focus on different areas critical to the future of the organization. They

minimum chain of command The idea that top managers should always construct a hierarchy with the fewest levels of authority necessary to efficiently and effectively use organizational resources.

are examining such issues as performance, development, and job classification. Gary Goodwin, past director of human resources, explains that "the reorganization was essentially to help empower employees, making it easier for people working in the field to make decisions quickly without having to go up and down the proverbial power ladder."[43] This practice has become more common in Canada and the United States as companies that are battling low-cost foreign competitors search for new ways to reduce costs.

> "[T]he reorganization was essentially to help empower employees, making it easier for people working in the field to make decisions quickly without having to go up and down the proverbial power ladder."
>
> *Gary Goodwin,*
> *Ducks Unlimited*

Centralization and Decentralization of Authority

Another way in which managers can keep the organizational hierarchy flat is by **decentralizing authority**—that is, by giving lower-level managers and nonmanagerial employees the right to make important decisions about how to use organizational resources.[44] If managers at higher levels give lower-level employees the responsibility to make important decisions and only manage by exception, then the problems of slow and distorted communication noted previously are kept to a minimum. Moreover, fewer managers are needed because their role is not to make decisions but to act as coach and facilitator and to help other employees make the best decisions. In addition, when decision making is done at the low

decentralizing authority Giving lower-level managers and nonmanagerial employees the right to make important decisions about how to use organizational resources.

level in the organization and near the customer, employees are better able to recognize and respond to customer needs. Samsung Electronics decentralized authority to divisional managers when it eliminated the Global Business Manager function and created a COO position to whom all division presidents report.

Decentralizing authority allows an organization and its employees to behave flexibly even as the organization grows and becomes taller. This is why managers are so interested in empowering employees, creating self-managed work teams, establishing cross-functional teams, and establishing liaisons among groups, teams, and departments to increase communication and coordination among functions and division. These *integrating mechanisms* are design innovations that help keep the organizational structure flexible and responsive to changes in the task and general environments, complex technologies, and complex strategies. The greater the complexity of an organization's structure, the greater is the need for coordination among people, functions, and divisions to make the organizational structure work efficiently and effectively.[45] Thus, when managers choose to adopt a divisional, matrix, or product team structure, they must use integrating mechanisms to achieve organizational goals.

While more organizations are taking steps to decentralize authority, too much decentralization has certain disadvantages:

1. If divisions, functions, or teams are given too much decision-making authority, they may begin to pursue their own goals at the expense of organizational goals. Managers in engineering design or R&D, for example, may become so focused on making the best possible product that they fail to realize that the best product may be so expensive that few people will be willing or able to buy it.

2. Also, with too much decentralization, lack of communication among functions or among divisions may prevent possible synergies among them from ever materializing, and organizational performance suffers.

Top managers have to look for the balance between centralization and decentralization of authority that best meets the organization's needs. If managers are in a stable

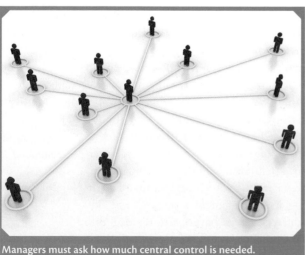

Managers must ask how much central control is needed.

environment, using well-understood technology, and producing staple kinds of products (such as cereal, canned soup, books, or televisions), there is no pressing need to decentralize authority, and managers at the top can maintain control of much of the organizational decision making.[46] However, in uncertain, changing environments where high-tech companies are producing state-of-the-art products, top managers must empower employees and allow teams to make important strategic decisions so that the organization can keep up with the changes taking place.

Loblaws chose to centralize its management structure after years of decentralized regional offices created their own dysfunctional fiefdoms. T&T, the Asian-focused supermarket chain that Loblaws acquired in 2009, was being run separately out of two offices—one in British Columbia and one in Ontario. Non-food merchandising was consolidated in 2010, strengthening the centralized operation and giving Loblaws more clout as the largest retailer in Canada.[47]

> **LO5** Evaluate the factors that managers consider when deciding on a formal or flexible overall structure.

Choosing a Formal or Flexible Overall Structure

Earlier in this chapter, we discussed the choices managers make in deciding how tasks should be organized into jobs and jobs should be grouped into functions, divisions, and departments so as to coordinate the use of resources efficiently and effectively. We discussed the creation of authority relations and principles managers can use to determine the appropriate hierarchy of authority. So how do managers determine how formal or flexible they want the organization to be?

Burns and Stalker proposed two basic ways in which managers can organize and control an organization's activities to respond to characteristics of its external environment: They can use a formal *mechanistic structure* or a flexible *organic structure*.[48] Figure 6.10 illustrates the differences between these two types of structures. After describing these two structures, we discuss what factors managers consider when choosing between them.

> **mechanistic structure**
> An organizational structure in which authority is centralized at the top of the hierarchy, tasks and roles are clearly specified, and employees are closely supervised.

Mechanistic Structures

When the environment around an organization is stable, managers tend to choose a mechanistic structure to organize and control activities and make employee behaviour predictable. In a **mechanistic structure**, authority is centralized at the top of the managerial hierarchy, and the vertical hierarchy of authority is the main means used to control subordinates' behaviour. Tasks and roles are clearly specified, subordinates are closely supervised, and the emphasis is on strict discipline and order. Everyone knows his or her place, and there is a place for everyone. A mechanistic structure provides the most efficient way to operate in a stable environment because it allows managers to obtain inputs at the lowest cost, giving an organization the most control over its conversion processes and enabling the most efficient production of goods and services with the smallest expenditure of resources. This explains McDonald's mechanistic structure.

Organic Structures

In contrast, when the environment is changing rapidly it is difficult to obtain access to resources. Managers need to organize their activities in a way that allows them to

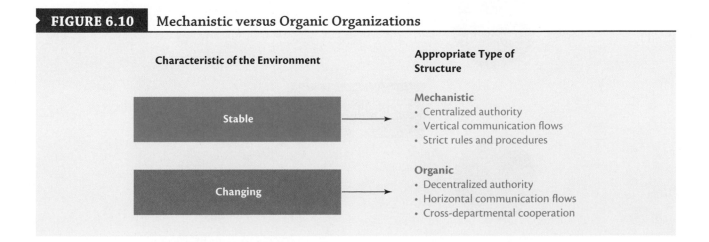

> **FIGURE 6.10**   **Mechanistic versus Organic Organizations**

Characteristic of the Environment

Appropriate Type of Structure

Stable →

Mechanistic
- Centralized authority
- Vertical communication flows
- Strict rules and procedures

Changing →

Organic
- Decentralized authority
- Horizontal communication flows
- Cross-departmental cooperation

cooperate, to act quickly to obtain resources (such as new types of wood to produce new kinds of furniture), and to respond effectively to the unexpected. In an **organic structure**, authority is decentralized to middle and first-line managers to encourage them to take responsibility and act quickly to pursue scarce resources. Departments are encouraged to take a cross-departmental or functional perspective, and authority rests with the individuals and departments best positioned to control the current problems the organization is facing. Control in an organic structure is much looser than it is in a mechanistic structure, and reliance on shared norms to guide organizational activities is greater.

Managers in an organic structure can react more quickly to a changing environment than can managers in a mechanistic structure. However, an organic structure is generally more expensive to operate, so it is used only when needed—when the organizational environment is unstable and rapidly changing. Organic structures may also work more effectively if managers establish semi-structures that govern "the pace, timing, and rhythm of organizational activities and processes." In other words, introducing a bit of structure while preserving most of the flexibility of the organic structure may reduce operating costs.[49]

Factors Affecting Choice of Overall Organizational Structure

Organizational structures need to fit the factors or circumstances that affect the company the most and cause them the most uncertainty.[50] Thus, there is no "best" way to design an organization: Design reflects each organization's

specific situation. Four factors are important determinants of organizational structure: the nature of the *organizational environment*, the type of *strategy* the organization pursues, the *technology* the organization uses, and the characteristics of the organization's *human resources* (see Figure 6.11).[51]

The Organizational Environment

In general, the more quickly the external environment is changing and the greater the uncertainty within it, the greater are the problems a manager faces in trying to gain access to scarce resources. In this situation, to speed decision making and communication and make it easier to obtain resources, managers typically make organizing choices that bring flexibility to the organizational structure.[52] They are likely to decentralize authority and empower lower-level employees to make important operating decisions.

In contrast, if the external environment is stable, if resources are readily available, and if uncertainty is low, then less coordination and communication among people and functions is needed to obtain resources, and managers can make organizing choices that bring more formality to the organizational structure. Managers in this situation prefer to make decisions within a clearly defined hierarchy of authority and use extensive rules, standard operating procedures, and restrictive norms to guide and govern employees' activities—a more mechanistic form of organizing.

As we discussed in Chapter 2, change is rapid in today's marketplace, and increasing competition both at home

organic structure
An organizational structure in which authority is decentralized to middle and first-line managers and tasks and roles are left ambiguous to encourage employees to cooperate and respond quickly to the unexpected.

> **FIGURE 6.11** **Factors Affecting Overall Organizational Structure**

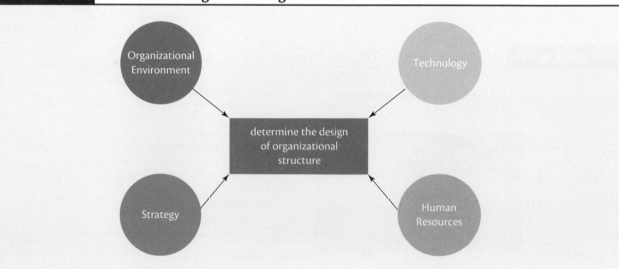

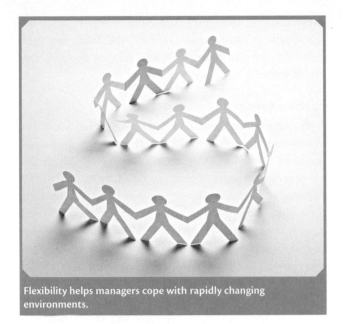

Flexibility helps managers cope with rapidly changing environments.

and abroad is putting greater pressure on managers to attract customers and increase efficiency and effectiveness. Thus, there has been growing interest in finding ways to structure organizations—such as through empowerment and self-managed teams—to allow people and departments to behave flexibly. A case in point is media executive Kathleen Dore, president of television and radio at Canwest Mediaworks Inc., and her unique empowerment management style. In a world dominated by men, she has become a role model for other women. She uses a term, "force multiplier," which focuses on "using your skills, abilities, and experience as a magnet which pulls others toward you and makes them want to engage in the undertaking you're about."[53]

Strategy

As discussed in Chapter 5, once managers decide on a strategy, they must choose the right means to implement it. Different strategies often call for the use of different organizational structures. For example, a differentiation strategy aimed at increasing the value customers perceive in an organization's goods and services usually succeeds best in a flexible structure. Flexibility assists a differentiation strategy because managers can develop new or innovative products quickly—an activity that requires extensive cooperation among functions or departments. In contrast, a low-cost strategy that is aimed at driving down costs in all functions usually fares best in a more formal structure, which gives managers greater control over the expenditures and actions of the organization's various departments.[54]

In addition, at the corporate level, when managers decide to expand the scope of organizational activities by,

for example, vertical integration or diversification, they need to design a flexible structure to provide sufficient coordination among the different business divisions.[55] As discussed in Chapter 5, many companies have been divesting businesses because managers have been unable to create a competitive advantage to keep them up to speed in fast-changing industries. By moving to a more flexible structure, such as a product division structure, divisional managers gain more control over their different businesses.

Finally, expanding internationally and operating in many different countries challenges managers to create organizational structures that allow organizations to be flexible on a global level.[56]

Technology

Recall that *technology* is the combination of skills, knowledge, tools, machines, computers, and equipment that are used in the design, production, and distribution of goods and services. As a rule, the more complicated the technology that an organization uses, the more difficult it is for managers and employees to impose strict control on technology or to regulate it efficiently.[57] Thus, the more complicated the technology, the greater is the need for a flexible structure to enhance managers' and employees' ability to respond to unexpected situations and give them the freedom to work out new solutions to the problems they encounter. In contrast, the more routine the technology, the more appropriate a formal structure is because tasks are simple and the steps needed to produce goods and services have been worked out in advance.

The nature of an organization's technology is an important determinant of its structure. Today, there is a growing use of computer-controlled production, and a movement toward using self-managed teams (groups of employees who are given the responsibility for supervising their own activities and for monitoring the quality of the goods and service they provide) to promote innovation, increase quality, and reduce costs. As a result, many companies are trying to make their structures more flexible to take advantage of the value-creating benefits of complex technology. What makes a technology routine or complicated? One researcher who investigated this issue, Charles Perrow, argued that two factors determine how complicated or nonroutine technology is: task variety and task analyzability.[58] *Task variety* is the number of new or unexpected problems or situations that a person or function encounters in performing tasks or jobs. *Task analyzability* is the degree to which programmed solutions are available to people or functions to solve the problems they encounter. Nonroutine or complicated technologies

Assembling fine-dining dinner plates requires motivated and skilled staff, while serving fast food is very routine.

are characterized by high task variety and low task analyzability; this means that many varied problems occur and that solving these problems requires significant nonprogrammed decision making. In contrast, routine technologies are characterized by low task variety and high task analyzability; this means that the problems encountered do not vary much and are easily resolved through programmed decision making.

Examples of nonroutine technology are found in the work of scientists in an R&D laboratory who develop new products or discover new drugs, and they are seen in the planning exercises an organization's top-management team uses to chart the organization's future strategy. Examples of routine technology include typical mass-production or assembly operations, where workers perform the same task repeatedly and where managers have already identified the programmed solutions necessary to

perform a task efficiently. Similarly, in service organizations such as fast-food restaurants, the tasks that crew members perform in making and serving fast food are very routine.

Human Resources

A final important factor affecting an organization's choice of structure and culture is the characteristics of the human resources it employs. In general, the more highly skilled an organization's workforce and the more people are required to work together in groups or teams to perform their tasks, the more likely the organization is to use a flexible, decentralized structure. Highly skilled employees or those who have internalized strong professional values and norms of behaviour as part of their training usually desire freedom and autonomy and dislike close supervision. Accountants, for example, have learned the need to report company accounts honestly and impartially, and doctors and nurses have absorbed the obligation to give patients the best care possible without being watched over by a supervisor.

Flexible structures, characterized by decentralized authority and empowered employees, are well suited to the needs of highly skilled people. Similarly, when people work in teams, they must be allowed to interact freely, which also is possible in a flexible organizational structure. Thus, when designing an organizational structure and culture, managers must pay close attention to the needs of the workforce and to the complexity and kind of work employees perform.

In summary, an *organization's external environment, strategy, technology,* and *human resources* are the factors to be considered by managers seeking to design the best structure and culture for an organization. The greater the level of uncertainty in an organization's environment, the more complex its strategy and technology, and the more highly qualified and skilled its workforce, the more likely managers will design a structure and culture that are flexible, can change quickly, and allow employees to be innovative in their responses to problems, customer needs, and so on. The more stable an organization's environment, the less complex and better understood its strategy or technology, and the less skilled its workforce, the more likely managers will design an organizational structure that is formal and controlling and a culture whose values and norms prescribe how employees should act in particular situations.

Summary and Review

LO1   Designing Organizational Structure   Organizational structure is the formal system of both task and reporting relationships that determines how employees use resources to achieve organizational goals. The way organizational structures work depends on how tasks are grouped into individual jobs; how jobs are grouped into functions and divisions; how coordination and allocating authority are accomplished; and whether the structure is formal or flexible.

LO2   Grouping Tasks into Jobs: Job Design   Job design is the initial process by which managers group tasks into jobs. To create more interesting jobs, and to get workers to act flexibly, managers can enlarge and enrich jobs. Hackman and Oldman's job characteristics model provides a tool managers can use to measure how motivating or satisfying a particular job is.

LO3   Grouping Jobs into Functional, Divisional, Network, and Hybrid Structures   Managers can choose from many kinds of organizational structures to make the best use of organizational resources. Depending on the specific organizing problems they face, managers can choose from functional, divisional (based on product, geography, or market segment), matrix, product team, network, and hybrid structures which combine several forms of organizing.

LO4   Linking and Coordinating Functions and Divisions   No matter which structure managers choose, they must decide how to distribute authority in the organization, how many levels to have in the hierarchy of authority, and what balance to strike between centralization and decentralization to keep the number of levels in the hierarchy to a minimum. As organizations grow, managers must increase integration mechanisms to ensure coordination among functions and divisions.

LO5   Choosing a Formal or Flexible Overall Structure   Overall organizational structure is determined by four main factors: the external environment, strategy, technology, and human resources. In general, the higher the level of uncertainty associated with these factors, the more appropriate a flexible, adaptable structure is as opposed to a formal, rigid one.

KEY TERMS

authority	hierarchy of authority	minimum chain of command
boundaryless organization	hybrid structure	network structure
business-to-business (B2B) networks	job design	organic structure
	job enlargement	organizational design
cross-functional team	job enrichment	organizational structure
decentralizing authority	job simplification	product structure
division of labour	line manager	product team structure
divisional structure	market structure	span of control
functional structure	matrix structure	staff manager
geographic structure	mechanistic structure	strategic alliance

WRAP-UP TO — OPENING CASE

Samsung Reorganizes for the 21st Century

As noted in Chapter 5, an organization's design and structure must be closely aligned with its strategy. The strategy depends on the nature of the business and the competitive and environmental landscape. Strategy is successful when the leaders and management teams recognize the opportunities and threats in the environment and organize the resources effectively to compete in such a market. Leaders need to make decisions on how best to adapt and change to remain competitive. The family-owned and controlled Samsung Group of companies has done just that. After having read and understood the concepts in this chapter, you should be able to answer the following questions:

1. *How would you characterize Samsung Electronics' organizational structure?*

ANSWER: After its reorganization, Samsung Electronics is using a global product structure common to many multinational organizations. This is a form of divisional structure, where autonomous business units are set up to produce a specific product for a specific customer. Each division is self-contained with its own president and CFO. Product division managers manage their own budgets and global value chains and decide where to establish foreign subsidiaries to distribute and sell their products to customers in foreign countries.

2. *How did the changes to Samsung's organizational structure affect the hierarchy of authority and span of control?*

ANSWER: The hierarchy of authority is the organization's chain of command. Samsung Electronics' change in organizational structure has reduced the levels in the hierarchy of authority by eliminating one level of management. The span of control refers to the number of subordinates who report directly to a manager. In this case, the president and chief financial officer of each global product division now reports directly to the newly created position of chief operating officer (COO).

3. *How is Samsung's strategy related to its structure?*

ANSWER: Samsung has pursued a corporate-level strategy of unrelated diversification resulting in 83 different companies in several industrial sectors including financial services and electronics. Its global operations were overseen by individual Global Business Management (GBM) divisions creating a top-heavy hierarchy of authority, which slowed down decision making, speed to market, and customer responsiveness. Samsung Electronics reorganized to a *global product structure,* where each product division manager takes responsibility for deciding where to manufacture its products and how to market them in countries worldwide. Removing one level of management, by eliminating the GBM, allowed each product to be managed in its own self-contained division and give divisional managers the responsibility for devising an appropriate business-level strategy to allow it to compete effectively in its industry or market. Decision time was reduced, divisional managers could focus on developing strategies that focus on their particular customers, and the time it takes to get new products to market became faster. The global product structure is a more efficient way of organizing resources.

By adopting a global product divisional structure, Samsung will be better positioned to compete in the five new industries over the next 10 years. To compete in the new industries, Samsung is using strategic alliances and networks of strategic alliances which take advantage of expertise and knowledge sharing through cooperation between two or more companies. For example, it has partnered with Bosch, a car parts supplier, to help develop electric vehicle batteries. Of the 83 companies under the Samsung Group umbrella, several provide inputs to each others' business products. Thus, we can say that Samsung's new strategy lends itself to a series of strategic alliances resulting in a global network structure.

Management in Action

TOPICS FOR DISCUSSION AND ACTION

LEVEL 1 Knowledge & Comprehension

1. When and under what conditions might a manager change from a functional structure to (a) a product, (b) a geographic, or (c) a market structure?

2. How do matrix structures and product team structures differ? Why is the product team structure more widely used?

3. Using the job characteristics model as a guide, discuss how a manager might enlarge or enrich a salesperson's or secretary's job to make it more motivating.

LEVEL 2 Application & Analysis

4. Google's organizational structure has been described as being similar to the "Brownian motion," the way that molecules of food colouring move through water in a bottle. View the following video on YouTube, and describe Google's organizational structure: www.youtube.com/watch?v=Q1qoDY-gjKY&eurl=andy-grove-describes-googles-organizational-structure-as-brownian-motion/

5. Find and interview a manager and identify the kind of organizational structure that his or her organization uses to coordinate people and resources. Discuss the distribution of authority. Does the manager think that decentralizing authority and empowering employees is appropriate?

6. Research the organizational structure of Branson's Virgin Group Investments Ltd. Would you characterize the Branson empire as mechanistic or organic in overall structure?

LEVEL 3 Synthesis & Evaluation

7. Compare the pros and cons of using a network structure to perform organizational activities and performing all activities in-house (within one organizational hierarchy).

8. Would a flexible or a more formal structure be appropriate for these organizations: (a) a large department store, (b) a big accounting firm, (c) a biotechnology company? Explain your reasoning.

9. When and under what circumstances would it be appropriate for a manager to consider outsourcing some of its activities? What are the risks?

SELF-REFLECTION EXERCISE

Choose an organization for which you have worked. How did the structure of your job and the organization affect your job satisfaction? Did the tasks within your job make sense? In what ways could they be better organized? What structural changes would you make to this organization? Would you consider making this a taller or flatter organization? How would the changes you have proposed improve responsiveness to customers and your job satisfaction?

SMALL GROUP BREAKOUT EXERCISE

Bob's Appliances

Form groups of three or four, and appoint one member as the spokesperson who will communicate your findings to the whole class when called on by the instructor. Then discuss the following scenario:

Bob's Appliances sells and services household appliances such as washing machines, dishwashers, stoves, and refrigerators. Over the years, the company has developed a good reputation for the quality of its customer service, and many local builders are customers at the store. Recently, some new appliance retailers, including Best Buy, have opened stores that also sell numerous appliances. In addition to appliances, however, to attract more customers these stores carry a complete range of consumer electronics products, including television sets, stereos, and computers. Bob Lange, the owner of Bob's Appliances, has decided that to stay in business he must widen his product range and compete directly with the chains.

In 2007, he decided to build a new 1800-square-metre store and service centre, and he is now hiring new employees to sell and service the new line of consumer electronics. Because of his company's increased size, Lange is not sure of the best way to organize the employees. Currently, he uses a functional structure; employees are divided into sales, purchasing and accounting, and repair. Bob is wondering whether selling and servicing consumer electronics is so different from selling and servicing appliances that he should

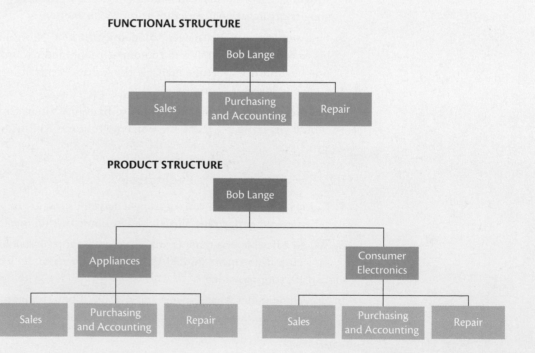

move to a product structure (see the figure) and create separate sets of functions for each of his two lines of business.[59]

You are a member of a team of local consultants that Bob has called in to advise him as he makes this crucial choice. Which structure would you recommend? Why?

BUSINESS PLANNING EXERCISE

Your professor may ask you to write a business plan for a new venture or a strategic plan for an existing venture. At the end of every chapter, you will have an opportunity to apply managerial and organizational concepts to the exercise of writing a business plan. Refer to Appendix A.

After reading this chapter, begin to think about how your new venture should be designed and structured to achieve your mission and goals. You need to think about the following questions for your business plan:

1. How should you design the jobs that need to be done?

2. How should you best group jobs and processes together?

3. Describe your venture in terms of:

   a. Centralized versus decentralized decision making

   b. Span of control

4. Create and draw organizational charts for Year One and Year Three of your venture.

   a. How might they change as the business grows?

   b. Is a tall, mechanistic structure or a flat, organic structure more suited to your venture in the first year? Why?

MANAGING ETHICALLY EXERCISE

In many businesses—such as chicken-processing plants, small engineering companies, furniture makers, warehouses, and offices—unskilled workers perform the same repetitive tasks for many hours a day, day in and day out, and often for years if they stay at the same job. Boredom is common, as is the development of physical ailments such as skin problems, muscle fatigue, and carpal tunnel syndrome. Is it ethical for managers to allow workers to perform repetitive tasks for long periods of time? What kinds of standards would you use to settle this issue? To what degree should job redesign be used to change such a situation and enrich jobs if it also would raise costs and make a company less competitive? How could organizational structure be redesigned to make this problem less prevalent?

MANAGEMENT CHALLENGE EXERCISE

Speeding Up Website Design

You have been hired by a website design, production, and hosting company whose new animated website designs are attracting a lot of attention and a lot of customers. Currently, employees are organized into different functions such as hardware, software design, graphic art, and website hosting, as well as functions such as marketing and human resources. Each function takes its turn to work on a new project from initial customer request to final online website hosting.

The problem the company is experiencing is that it typically takes one year from the initial idea stage to the time that the website is up and running; the company wants to shorten this time by half to protect and expand its market niche. In talking to other managers, you discover that they believe the company's current functional structure is the source of the problem—it is not allowing employees to develop websites fast enough to satisfy customers' demands. They want you to design a better one.

1. Discuss ways in which you can improve how the current functional structure operates so that it speeds website development.

2. Discuss the pros and cons of moving to a (a) multidivisional, (b) matrix, or (c) product team structure to reduce website development time.

3. Which of these structures do you think is most appropriate, and why?

MANAGEMENT PORTFOLIO PROJECT

Answer the following questions about the organization you have chosen to follow:

1. Describe the organizational structure of the firm.

2. Does the enterprise have centralized or decentralized control over decision making?

3. How many levels are present in the hierarchy of authority? Is the structure tall or flat?

4. Is the structure suitable for the strategy, technology, human resources, and organizational environment in which the firm operates? If not, suggest ways in which it could better align its structure to support its mission.

VIDEO MANAGEMENT CASE connect

General Motors Global Research Network

GM's top managers realized that the organization was too self-contained and that to increase its competitiveness they needed to change the company's business model.

1. How does technology influence organizational structure at GM? What other factors should managers at GM consider when selecting a structure?

2. What organizational structures do you equate with GM's old model of research? Which structures do you equate with the new model?

3. What must GM managers consider as they move from the old structure to the new structure?

Management Case

Canada Pension Plan Bids to Buy Reorganized Yahoo!

The Canada Pension Plan Investment Board partnered with Microsoft to offer to purchase Yahoo! only weeks after the CEO, Carol Bartz, was fired.[60]

During her short reign as CEO, Bartz undertook a major overhaul of the company's management and streamlined its structure. In her blog post on Yahoo!'s official site, Bartz commented that there's "plenty that has bogged this company down" and that the new organizational structure will make the company "a lot faster on its feet."[61] Prior to the changes, the company was organized on a "matrix management" system where executives collaborated on new products and projects. The decentralized product groups each had their own functions, including engineering for each world region. That led to slow decision making and little accountability. Bartz said in her blog post that "you'd be amazed at how complicated some things are here."

Bartz began to centralize decision making and accountability. She removed managers and appointed one person to be head of all products. She also consolidated international operations under one manager—it used to be three separate global regional divisions. North American operations got a new chief. UBS Securities analyst Ben Schachter said the "simpler org chart leads to more of a focus on the company's core businesses." However, another analyst, Jeffrey Lindsa, from Sanford Bernstein, suggested that too much centralization might thwart innovation in product development and that he preferred a structure that focused on key strategic products like search ads. Still others see the reorganization as a vast improvement over the matrix system that led to slow decision making and little accountability.

With the new organizational structure, Bartz anticipated a recovery from the decline in market share to Google and Facebook—but it didn't happen. Bartz was fired over the telephone by the Chair of the Board in September 2011. Yahoo! reported second-quarter revenue in July that fell short of estimates as Bartz's overhaul of the U.S. sales force made it harder to close deals and slowed growth in display advertising. And while some of the company's troubles pre-dated the reshuffle, "The slowdown in their display business is simply from her inability to keep the display team together over the last 18 months," said Ross Sandler, an analyst at RBC Capital Markets in New York.[62]

The company considered bids from the likes of Microsoft in partnership with CPP, but Google and others also tendered an offer. In 2008, Yahoo! declined an offer from Microsoft of $44.6 billion. Since then, share values have dwindled by 44 percent and now the company could be bought for around half the price.

1. In what specific ways has Yahoo's ex-CEO Carol Bartz changed the company's organizational structure?

2. Why did she make these changes? In what ways does she expect the new structure to benefit Yahoo's strategy and performance?

McGraw Hill connect™

Connect allows you to practise important concepts at your own pace and on your own schedule, with 24/7 online access to an eBook, practice quizzes, video cases, interactive exercises, study tools, and more.

LEARNING OUTCOMES

LO1 Understand the role of innovation and entrepreneurship in fostering a motivating organizational culture.

LO2 Explain the role of managers in influencing a culture of innovation in an organization.

LO3 Understand how organizational change relates to an organization's culture.

LO4 Explain the processes involved in managing organizational change.

LO5 Evaluate the challenges managers face in balancing innovation, high performance culture, and organizational change.

Opening Case

Ford's Culture Shift

HOW CAN MANAGERS CHANGE HOSTILE ORGANIZATIONAL CULTURES?

Ford posted a record loss of $13.3 billion in 2006, after which William Ford III, who had been CEO for the last five years, decided he was not the right person to turn around the company's fortunes.[1] In fact, he was a part of the problem because it turned out that over the years Ford had developed a corporate culture based on empire-building, in which top managers had emulated Ford; they strived to build their own empires, and to protect those empires they would never admit that mistakes had occurred. Finally, Ford's board of directors realized they needed an outsider to change Ford's culture—and the way it was being controlled—and they recruited Alan Mulally, CEO of Boeing in 2006, to become Ford's new CEO.

After arriving Mulally went to hundreds of meetings to meet his new managers, and at one executive meeting he became confused why one top division manager, who obviously did not know the answer to one of Mulally's questions concerning the performance of his car division, had rambled on for several minutes trying to disguise his ignorance. Mulally turned around to his second-in-command Mark Fields and asked him why the manager had done that. Fields explained that "at Ford you never admit when you don't know something."[2]

It turned out that over the years Ford had developed a tall hierarchy composed of managers whose main goal was to protect their turf and avoid any direct blame for its plunging car sales. So, when asked why car sales were falling, they did not admit to bad design and poor quality issues in their divisions; instead, they hid in the details. They brought thick notebooks and binders to meetings, listing the high prices of components and high labour costs to explain why their own particular car models were not selling well or even why they had to be sold at a

loss. Mulally wanted to know why Ford's top executives had this inward-looking, destructive mindset.

He soon realized that the problem was the values and norms in Ford's culture that had created a situation in which the managers of its different divisions and functions thought that the best way to maintain their jobs, salaries, and status was to hoard information and not share it. Thus, values and norms of secrecy and ambiguity, and of emphasizing status and rank to protect information, had developed. Ford's culture allowed managers to hide the extent of the problems they were facing and how badly they were performing. The old Ford culture—keep your mouth shut and mind your own business—had to change if improvements were to be had. What could Mulally do?

He issued a direct order that the managers of every division should share with every other Ford division a detailed statement of the costs they incurred to build each of its vehicles. He insisted that each of Ford's divisional presidents should attend a weekly—rather than a monthly—meeting to discuss openly and share

the problems all the company's divisions faced. He also told them that they should bring a different subordinate with them to each meeting so that every manager in the hierarchy would learn of the problems that had been kept hidden.[3] Essentially, Mulally's goal was to demolish the dysfunctional inbred values and norms of Ford's culture that had focused managers' attention on their own empires at the expense of the whole company. No longer would they be allowed to protect their own careers at the expense of customers.

Mulally's goal was to create new values and norms—that it is all right to admit mistakes, share information about all aspects of model design and costs, and of course find ways to speed development and reduce costs. He also wanted to emphasize norms of cooperation within and across divisions to improve performance. When Mulally arrived he found that no two models shared even the most basic components, such as side mirrors or the hinges that hold up the hood—something that drives up costs. Not anymore. Mulally standardized the thin metal support bars used to prop up the hoods on every Ford car. He also sold off Jaguar and Land Rover, which were unprofitable lines. Now, all problems are addressed through interdivisional openness and cooperation.

How could this situation have gone unchanged in a major car company that has been experiencing increased competition since the mid-1970s? The answer is that the norms and values of an organization's culture are very hard to change, and despite Ford's major problems, no CEO had been able to change the mindset of the top managers in the company. Ford had even become more hierarchical and bureaucratic over time as its problems increased because poor performance led managers to become even more defensive and concerned to defend their fiefdoms or empires.[4] In the five years since Mulally took the reins at Ford, and despite the worst economic climate in decades (Ford was the only automotive manufacturer not to take any federal bailout money in 2008–09), Ford has made a huge turnaround: It is now a profitable company, sales have increased by 20 percent, nearly double the rest of the industry, and it has gained in market share against competitors. Mulally was successful at changing people's mindsets and pulling them together to achieve a common goal. Speaking of his workforce, Mulally said, "They know why they're coming in in the morning. They know what success looks like."[5]

After reading and understanding the concepts in this chapter, you should be able to answer the following questions:

1. *Was the old organizational culture at Ford adaptive or inert?*

2. *How did Ford know it was necessary to make a change?*

3. *What are the driving and restraining forces to change in this case?*

Overview

Over a decade ago, Harvard professors John Kotter and James Heskett showed, through empirical research at more than 200 companies such as Hewlett-Packard, Xerox, and Nissan, how the culture of a corporation powerfully influences its economic performance, for better or for worse. Their thesis is that adaptive cultures—not necessarily strong ones on certain dimensions—are more likely to survive. Different cultures in organizations will be shaped by the different ways that managers interact with their employees. If, as we saw in Chapter 6, organizational structure provides an organization with a skeleton, organizational culture provides the muscles, sinews, nerves, and sensations that allow managers to regulate and govern the organization's activities. Organizational culture affects the ability of the organization to engage in innovation and change when it is necessary to adapt to new environments. As the opening case illustrates, cultures are difficult to change, but, like at Ford, those that adapt can turn the company's fortunes around.

In this chapter, we look at the role that entrepreneurship plays in creating organizational innovation and how managers can foster an innovative climate that is motivating for employees. We define organizational culture and examine how it is learned by organizational members. This continues our discussion from the previous chapter about how managers organize human and other resources to create high-performing organizations. We examine why culture can inspire employees to achieve great goals and why it can also lead to organizational failure. Next, we will look at how to manage change successfully in the face of a strong culture by overcoming resistance to change. By the end of this chapter, you will understand how an innovative culture helps convey meaning and purpose to employees. You will also understand the vital role that change plays in building competitive advantage and creating a high-performing organization.

Innovation and Entrepreneurship

The intensity of competition today, particularly from agile, small companies, has made it increasingly important for large, established organizations to promote and encourage a culture of intrapreneurship to raise the level of **innovation,** the implementation of creative ideas in an organization. As we discussed in Chapter 1, managers are responsible for supervising the use of human and other resources to achieve effective and efficient organizational goals. **Entrepreneurs,** by contrast, are the people who notice opportunities and take responsibility for mobilizing the resources necessary to produce new and improved goods and services.

Essentially, entrepreneurs bring about change to companies and industries because they see new and improved ways to use resources to create products customers will want to buy. At the same time, entrepreneurs who start new business ventures are responsible for all the initial planning, organizing, leading, and controlling necessary to make their idea a reality. Thus, entrepreneurs are an important source of creativity in the organizational world. If their idea is viable and entrepreneurs do attract customers, then their business grows and then they need to hire managers who will take responsibility for organizing and controlling all the specific functional activities—such as marketing, accounting, and manufacturing—necessary for a growing organization to be successful.

Typically, entrepreneurs assume the substantial risk associated with starting new businesses (many new businesses fail), and they receive all the returns or profits associated with the new business venture. These people are the Ted Rogerses (founder of Rogers Communications Inc.) of the world who make vast fortunes when their businesses succeed. Or they are among the millions of people who start new business ventures only to lose their money when their businesses fail. Despite the fact that an estimated 80 percent of small businesses fail in the first three to five years, by some estimates 38 percent of men and 50 percent of women in today's workforce want to start their own companies.[6]

Social entrepreneurs are individuals who pursue initiatives and opportunities to address social problems and needs in order to improve society and well-being, such as reducing poverty, increasing literacy, protecting the natural environment, or reducing substance abuse.[7] Their motivation is not primarily private profit maximization. Rather, social entrepreneurs are motivated by the desire to help others. Social entrepreneurs seek to mobilize resources to solve social problems through creative solutions.[8] Social entrepreneurs create enterprises with social missions. A pioneer social entrepreneur, Muhammad Yunus, founder of the Grameen Bank that provides micro credit to poor rural people to start businesses, has said, "We can think about a social business as a selfless business whose purpose is to bring an end to a social problem. In this kind of business, the company makes a profit—but no one takes the profit. Because the company is dedicated entirely to the social cause, the whole idea of making personal profit is removed from the business. The owner can take back over a period of time only the amount invested."[9] While social entrepreneurs often face challenges in raising funds to support their initiatives, their options are increasing as more and more investors look for innovative ways to achieve a sustainable social impact. The term **social innovation** refers to finding new ways of solving social problems such as poverty, homelessness, and food security. The Focus on the Social Economy box discusses a good example of social innovation.

Entrepreneurship does not just end once a new business is founded. Entrepreneurship carries on inside an organization over time, and many people throughout an organization take responsibility for developing innovative goods and services. For example, managers, scientists, or researchers employed by existing companies engage in entrepreneurial activity when they develop new or improved products. To distinguish these individuals from entrepreneurs who found their own businesses, employees of existing organizations who notice opportunities for product or service improvements and are responsible for managing the development process are known as intrapreneurs. In general, then, **entrepreneurship** is the mobilization of resources to take advantage of an opportunity to provide customers with new or improved goods and services; intrapreneurs engage in entrepreneurship within an existing company.

innovation The implementation of creative ideas in an organization.

entrepreneurs People who notice opportunities and take responsibility for mobilizing the resources necessary to produce new and improved goods and services.

social entrepreneurs Individuals who pursue initiatives and opportunities and mobilize resources to address social problems and needs in order to improve society and well-being through creative solutions.

social innovation Developing new ways of solving social problems.

entrepreneurship The mobilization of resources to take advantage of an opportunity to provide customers with new or improved goods and services.

FOCUS ON ▶ *The Social Economy*

The Centre for Social Innovation (CSI) Toronto

"The Centre for Social Innovation is a social enterprise with a mission to catalyze social innovation in Toronto and around the world. We believe that society is facing unprecedented economic, environmental, social and cultural challenges. We also believe that new innovations are the key to turning these challenges into opportunities to improve our communities and our planet."[10]

The Centre began in 2003, when the founders determined that the social mission sector faced capacity and resource challenges. As a result, too many organizations were working out of isolated and substandard facilities. Some of the questions they tried to address were, How can we improve access to office facilities, lower the cost of administration and let organizations focus on their social missions? and How can we best become a catalyst for social change? Today, the CSI has three locations and rents space to over 350 nonprofits, charities, and groups working for the public benefit and social change.[11]

1. Go to the CSI website. What is their definition of social innovation?

> **product champion**
> A manager who takes "ownership" of a project and provides the leadership and vision that take a product from the idea stage to the final customer.

An interesting relationship exists between entrepreneurs and intrapreneurs. Many intrapreneurs become dissatisfied when their superiors decide not to support or to fund new product ideas and development efforts that the intrapreneurs think will succeed. Organizations with rigid, inflexible organizational cultures do not support the kind of creative risk taking that is necessary to foster innovation. What do intrapreneurs do who feel that they are getting nowhere? Very often intrapreneurs decide to leave their employers and start their own organizations to take advantage of their new product ideas. In other words, intrapreneurs become entrepreneurs and found companies that may compete with the companies they left.

Many of the world's most successful organizations have been started by frustrated intrapreneurs who became entrepreneurs. William Hewlett and David Packard left Fairchild Semiconductor, an early industry leader, when managers of that company would not support Hewlett and Packard's ideas; their company soon outperformed Fairchild. Compaq Computer was founded by Rod Canion and some of his colleagues, who left Texas Instruments (TI) when managers there would not support Canion's idea that TI should develop its own personal computer. To prevent the departure of talented people, organizations need to take steps to promote a culture that encourages internal entrepreneurship and innovation.

As we discussed in Chapter 4, a learning organization encourages all employees to identify opportunities and solve problems, thus enabling the organization to continuously experiment, improve, and increase its ability to provide customers with new and improved goods and services. The higher the level of intrapreneurship, the higher will be the level of creativity, learning, and *innovation,* the implementation of creative ideas in an organization. How can organizations promote innovation and intrapreneurship? See Figure 7.1.

Product Champions

One way to promote intrapreneurship is to encourage individuals to assume the role of a **product champion,** a manager who takes ownership of a project and provides the leadership and vision that take a product from the idea stage to the final customer. 3M Canada, a company well known for its attempts to promote intrapreneurship, encourages all its managers to become product champions and identify new product ideas. A product champion becomes responsible for developing a business plan for

> "We can think about a social business as a selfless business whose purpose is to bring an end to a social problem."
>
> *Muhammad Yunus, 2006 Nobel Peace Prize winner and social entrepreneur*

FIGURE 7.1   The Process of Innovation

Product Champion
• Takes ownership of the new idea

+

Skunkworks
• Top-level managers sponsor and support the development of new products

=

Innovation
• Implementation of creative ideas in an organization including rewarding intrapreneurs

the product. Armed with this business plan, the champion appears before 3M Canada's product development committee, a team of senior 3M Canada managers who probe the strengths and weaknesses of the plan to decide whether it should be funded. If the plan is accepted, the product champion assumes responsibility for product development.

Skunkworks

The idea behind the product champion role is that employees who feel ownership for a project are inclined to act like outside entrepreneurs and go to great lengths to make the project succeed. Using skunkworks and new venture divisions can also strengthen this feeling of ownership. A **skunkworks** is a group of intrapreneurs who are deliberately separated from the normal operation of an organization—for example, from the normal chain of command—to encourage them to devote all their attention to developing new products. The idea is that if these people are isolated, they will become so intensely involved in a project that development time will be relatively brief and the quality of the final product will be enhanced. The term *skunkworks* was coined at the Lockheed Corporation, which formed a team of design engineers to develop special aircraft such as the U2 spy plane. The secrecy with which this unit functioned and speculation about its goals led others to refer to it as "the skunkworks." Bombardier's small-bodied regional jet, called the "C" series, was similarly developed.

Rewards for Innovation

To encourage managers to bear the uncertainty and risk associated with the hard work of entrepreneurship, it is necessary to link performance to rewards. Increasingly,

companies are rewarding intrapreneurs on the basis of the outcome of the product development process. Intrapreneurs are granted large bonuses if their projects succeed, or they are granted stock options that can make them millionaires if the product sells well. Both Microsoft and Google, for example, have made hundreds of their employees multimillionaires as a result of the stock options they were granted as part of their reward packages. In addition to receiving money, successful intrapreneurs can expect to receive promotion to the ranks of top management. Most of 3M Canada's top managers, for example, reached the executive suite because they had a track record of successful entrepreneurship. Organizations must reward intrapreneurs equitably if they wish to prevent them from leaving and becoming outside entrepreneurs who might form a competitive new venture. Nevertheless, intrapreneurs frequently do so.

Explain the role of managers in influencing a culture of innovation in an organization.   **LO2**

The Role of Managers in Influencing Culture

Organizational culture is the shared set of beliefs, expectations, values, norms, and work routines that influences how members of an organization relate to one another and work together to achieve organizational goals. It refers to a system of shared meaning held by organizational members that distinguishes the organization from other organizations.[12] Culture is the "glue" that keeps organizational members together and guides their behaviour. New employees learn the organizational culture from their managers and other employees.

Culture can be viewed as something that both helps employees make sense of the organization and guides employee behaviour. In essence, culture defines the rules of the game. Every organization develops a core

skunkworks A group of intrapreneurs who are deliberately separated from the normal operation of an organization to encourage them to devote all their attention to developing new products.

organizational culture The shared set of beliefs, expectations, values, norms, and work routines that influence how members of an organization relate to one another and work together to achieve organizational goals.

values Stable, long-lasting beliefs about what is important.

norms Unwritten rules or guidelines for appropriate behaviour in particular situations.

creativity A person's ability to discover original and novel ideas that lead to innovation.

artifacts Aspects of an organization's culture that one sees, hears, and feels.

beliefs The understandings of how objects and ideas relate to each other.

assumptions The taken-for-granted notions of how something should be in an organization.

set of assumptions, understandings, and implicit rules that govern day-to-day behaviour in the workplace.[13]

Organizational culture can control how individuals and groups in an organization behave because employees internalize organizational values and norms, and then let these values and norms guide their decisions and actions. **Values** are stable, long-lasting beliefs about what is important. **Norms** are unwritten rules or guidelines that prescribe appropriate behaviour in particular situations. Norms emerge from values.[14]

Just as people in society at large generally behave in accordance with socially acceptable values and norms, such as lining up at the checkout counters in supermarkets, so are individuals in an organizational setting mindful of the force of organizational values and norms. When a strong and cohesive set of organizational values and norms is in place, employees focus on thinking about what is best for the organization in the long run—all their decisions and actions become oriented toward helping the organization perform well. For example, a teacher spends personal time after school coaching and counselling students; an R&D scientist works 80 hours a week, evenings, and weekends to help speed up a late project; a salesclerk at a department store runs after a customer who left a credit card at the cash register. Strong organizational cultures based on these kinds of values and norms support **creativity**—a person's ability to discover original and novel ideas that lead to innovation and intrapreneurship.

Levels of Culture

Culture exists at two levels in an organization: the visible level and the invisible level. We see culture through its **artifacts**—what you see, hear, and feel when you are within an organization. For instance, organizations have different dress policies, different ways of organizing office space, and different ideas of what should be displayed on company walls. The things you see reveal the organization's culture, or, as Burke suggests, "the 'artefacts' . . . are manifestations or surface levels of culture, but not the essence of the culture."[15]

> "[T]he 'artefacts' . . . are manifestations or surface levels of culture, but not the essence of the culture."
>
> *WW Burke*

At the invisible level of culture are the values, beliefs, and assumptions that make up the organizational culture. **Beliefs** are the understandings of how objects and ideas relate to each other. **Assumptions** are the taken-for-granted notions of how something should be. Because of basic assumptions that are held by organizational members, it can be difficult to introduce change and adapt to new competitive environments.

The values and assumptions of an organization are not easily observed and can be elusive, intangible, implicit, and taken for granted. Thus, we look to organizational artifacts (i.e., the things we can observe) to help us uncover the values and assumptions. For instance, managers' and employees' behaviour often reveals the organization's values and assumptions. When employees continue talking to each other in front of a waiting customer, they signal that employees are more important than customers to this organization.

Creating a Strong Organizational Culture

Culture is created and sustained in three ways[16]:

1. The founders and/or senior managers of the organization hire and keep only employees who think and feel the way they do.

2. The management indoctrinates and socializes these employees to their way of thinking and feeling.

3. Top managers serve as role models. By observing their behaviour, employees identify with them and internalize their beliefs, values, and assumptions.

In an organization, values and norms make it clear to organizational members what goals they should pursue and how they should behave to reach those goals. Thus, values and norms perform the same function as formal goals, written rules, or direct supervision. Research shows that having a strong culture usually pays off, except in times of a changing environment.[17] Those companies with stronger cultures tend to have better returns on investment, higher net income growth, and larger increases in share price than firms with weaker cultures. However, strong culture can be a liability when the environment is changing because organizations have greater difficulty adapting to change.

Managers can influence the kinds of values and norms that develop in an organization. Some managers might cultivate values and norms that let subordinates know they are welcome to perform their roles in innovative and creative ways. Employees are thus encouraged to be entrepreneurial and are willing to experiment and go out on a limb even if there is a significant chance of failure. At organizations such as Lucent Technologies and 3M Canada, top managers encourage employees to adopt such values in order to support organizational commitment to innovation as a source of competitive advantage.

Other managers, however, might cultivate values and norms that let employees know that they should always be conservative and cautious in their dealings with others. Thus, these employees should always consult with their superiors before making important decisions and should always put their actions in writing so they can be held accountable for whatever happens. In any setting where caution is needed—nuclear power stations, large oil refineries, chemical plants, financial institutions, and insurance companies—a conservative, cautious approach to making decisions might be highly appropriate.[18] When used inappropriately, however, caution may stifle employees' ability to innovate or communicate.

Adaptive Cultures Versus Inert Cultures

Many researchers and managers believe that employees of some organizations go out of their way to help the organization because it has a strong and cohesive organizational culture—an *adaptive culture* that encourages positive attitudes and behaviours that foster creativity and innovation. Adaptive cultures, such as that at WestJet and 3M Canada, are cultures whose values and norms help an organization to build momentum and to grow and change as needed to achieve its goals and be effective. By contrast, *inert cultures* are those that lead to values and

norms that fail to motivate or inspire employees; they lead to stagnation and often failure over time. What leads to an adaptive or inert culture?

Researchers have found that organizations with strong adaptive cultures, like 3M Canada, WestJet, Google, and IBM, invest in their employees. They demonstrate their commitment to their members by, for example, emphasizing the long-term nature of the employment relationship and trying to avoid layoffs. These companies develop long-term career paths for their employees and invest heavily in training and development to increase employees' value to the organization. In these ways, terminal and instrumental values pertaining to the worth of human resources encourage the development of supportive work attitudes and behaviours.

In adaptive cultures employees often receive rewards linked directly to their performance and to the performance of the company as a whole. Sometimes, employee stock ownership plans (ESOPs) are developed in which workers as a group are allowed to buy a significant percentage of their company's stock. Workers who are owners of the company have additional incentive to develop skills that allow them to perform highly and search actively for ways to improve quality, efficiency, and performance. At Shaw Media Inc., for example, employees are able to buy Shaw stock at a steep discount; this allows them to build a sizable stake in the company over time.

Some organizations, however, develop cultures with values that do not include protecting and increasing the worth of their human resources as a major goal. Their employment practices are based on short-term employment according to the needs of the organization and on minimal investment in employees who perform simple, routine tasks. Moreover, employees are not often rewarded based on their performance and thus have little incentive to improve their skills or otherwise invest in the organization to help it to achieve goals. If a company has an inert culture, poor working relationships frequently develop between the organization and its employees, and instrumental values of noncooperation, laziness, and loafing and work norms of output restriction are common.

Moreover, an adaptive culture develops an emphasis on entrepreneurship and respect for the employee and allows the use of organizational structures, such as the cross-functional team structure, that empower employees to make decisions and motivate them to succeed. By contrast, in an inert culture, employees are content to be told what to do and have little incentive or motivation to perform beyond minimum work requirements. As

Innovation thrives at Google.

The Nokia Way promotes innovative cultural norms and values.

you might expect, the emphasis is on close supervision and hierarchical authority, which result in a culture that makes it difficult to adapt to a changing environment.

Nokia was the world's largest wireless phone maker until in 2012 Samsung overtook it in terms of volume of sales and global market share, forcing the company to lay off 10 000 jobs and close a number of plants, including one in Canada. Nevertheless, Nokia, headquartered in Finland, is a good example of a company in which managers have strived to create an adaptive culture.[19] Nokia's outgoing president, Matti Alahuhta, believes that Nokia's cultural values are based on the Finnish character: Finns are down-to-earth, rational, straightforward people. They are also very friendly and democratic people who do not believe in a rigid hierarchy based either on a person's authority or on social class. Nokia's culture reflects these values because innovation and decision making are pushed right down to the bottom line, to teams of employees who take up the challenge of developing the ever-smaller and more sophisticated phones for which the company is known. Bureaucracy is kept to a minimum at Nokia; its adaptive culture is based on informal and personal relationships and norms of cooperation and teamwork.

To help strengthen its culture, Nokia has built a futuristic open-plan steel and glass building just outside Helsinki. Here, in an open environment, its research and development people can work together to innovate new kinds of wireless phones. More than one out of every three of Nokia's 60 000 employees work in research; what keeps these people together and focused is Nokia's company mission to produce phones that are better, cheaper, smaller, and easier to use than competitors' phones.[20] This is the "Nokia Way," a system of cultural values and norms that can't be written down but is always present

in the values that cement people together and in the language and stories that its members use to orient themselves to the company.

Another company with an adaptive culture is Merck & Co., one of the largest producers of prescription drugs in the world. Much of Merck's success can be attributed to its ability to attract the very best research scientists, who come because its adaptive culture nurtures scientists and emphasizes values and norms of innovation. Scientists are given great freedom to pursue intriguing ideas even if the commercial payoff is questionable. Moreover, researchers are inspired to think of their work as a quest to alleviate human disease and suffering worldwide, and Merck has a reputation as an ethical company whose values put people above profits.

Although the experience of Nokia and Merck suggests that organizational culture can give rise to managerial actions that ultimately benefit the organization, this is not always the case. The cultures of some organizations become dysfunctional, encouraging managerial actions that harm the organization and discouraging actions that might lead to an improvement in performance.[21] For example, Ford Motor Company almost went bankrupt in the early 2000s. The newly appointed CEO in 2006, Alan Mulally, set out to find the source of the problem and put the blame on the organizational culture developed by generations of Ford family members as CEOs. Mulally deduced that the culture based on fear and blame encouraged managers to fight over and protect their turf—an inert culture. Managers were afraid to rock the boat or make suggestions since they could not predict what would happen to them.

An aerial view of the cafeteria at Nokia's headquarters in Espoo, Finland. The open architecture of the building reflects the company's culture, which is based on informal and personal relationships and norms of cooperation and teamwork.

Mulally was appointed to change the company's culture. He found it very hard to do so, as his senior managers were so used to the old values and norms. By demanding transparency and regular communication among divisions and departments, he went about the slow process of changing values and norms to emphasize cooperation, teamwork, and respect for others. Clearly, managers can influence the way their organizational culture develops over time, often in a short period of time.

Learning Organizational Culture

Managers deliberately cultivate and develop the organizational values and norms that are best suited to their task and general environments, strategy, or technology. Organizational culture is transmitted to and shared with organizational members through the values of the founder, the process of socialization, ceremonies and rites, and stories and language (see Figure 7.2).

Values of the Founder

One manager who has a very important impact on the kind of organizational culture that emerges in an organization is the founder. An organization's founder and his or her personal values and beliefs have a substantial influence on the values, norms, and standards of behaviour that develop over time within the organization.[22] Founders set the stage for the way cultural values and norms develop because they hire other managers to help them run their organizations. It is reasonable to assume that founders select managers who share their vision of the organization's goals and what it should be doing. In any case, new managers quickly learn from the founder what values and norms are appropriate in the organization and thus what is desired of them. Subordinates imitate the style of the founder and, in turn, transmit his

or her values and norms to their subordinates. Gradually over time, the founder's values and norms permeate the organization.[23]

A founder who requires a great display of respect from subordinates and insists on such things as formal job titles and formal modes of dress encourages subordinates to act this way toward their subordinates. Often, a founder's personal values affect an organization's competitive advantage. Frank Stronach, founder of Magna Corporation, based in Aurora, Ontario, believes that his employees should show a "strong sense of ownership and entrepreneurial energy." He practises this belief by diverting 10 percent of pre-tax profit to profit-sharing programs for his employees. Similarly, managers' salaries are deliberately set "below industry standards" so that managers will earn more through profit-sharing bonuses. To further emphasize managerial responsibility, Magna's managers are given considerable autonomy over buying, selling, and hiring. Through these policies of profit-sharing and empowerment, Stronach has developed a workforce that has made Magna one of the largest and most profitable companies in the country.

Another success story in "living the dreams" and upholding the values of the founder is the innovative Canadian company Cirque du Soleil. Every travelling Cirque du Soleil show has its own creative director who makes sure the production stays true to the vision and passion of its co-founder Guy Laliberté.[24]

Socialization

Over time, organizational members learn from each other which values are important in an organization and the norms that specify appropriate and inappropriate behaviours. Eventually, organizational members behave in accordance with the organization's values and

> **FIGURE 7.2** **Factors in Learning Organizational Culture**

New members of an organization learn the culture through participation in events.

TABLE 7.1   Organizational Rites

Type of Rite	Example of Rite	Purpose of Rite
Rite of passage	Induction and basic training	Learn and internalize norms and values
Rite of integration	Office Christmas party	Build common norms and values
Rite of enhancement	Presentation of annual award	Motivate commitment to norms

organizational socialization The process by which newcomers learn an organization's values and norms and acquire the work behaviours necessary to perform jobs effectively.

norms—often without realizing they are doing so. **Organizational socialization** is the process by which newcomers learn an organization's values and norms and acquire the work behaviours necessary to perform jobs effectively.[25] As a result of their socialization experiences, organizational members internalize an organization's values and norms and behave to fit in with them, not only because they think they have to but also because they think that these values and norms describe the right and proper way to behave.[26]

Most organizations have some kind of socialization program to help new employees "learn the ropes"—the values, norms, and culture of their organization. The military, for example, is well known for the rigorous socialization process it uses to turn raw recruits into trained soldiers. Many organizations put new recruits through a rigorous training program to provide them with the knowledge they need not only to perform well in their jobs but also to represent the company to its clients. Thus, through the organizational socialization program, the founder and top managers of an organization can transmit to employees the cultural values and norms that shape the behaviours of organizational members.

Ceremonies and Rites

Another way in which managers can try to create or influence an organizational culture is by developing organizational ceremonies and rites—formal events that recognize incidents of importance to the organization as a whole and to specific employees.[27] The most common rites that organizations use to transmit cultural norms and values to their members are rites of passage, of integration, and of enhancement (see Table 7.1).[28]

Rites of passage determine how individuals enter, advance within, or leave the organization. At Cirque du Soleil, an annual training event is held at the Montreal headquarters studio for all new recruits, who come from all over the world. For many, it is a major adjustment on two cultural fronts: first, it is a new country for most; and second, to fully integrate the values of the organization, the athletes must shift their focus from a world of competition to a world of expression. The socialization programs developed by all organizations are rites of passage. Likewise, the ways in which an organization prepares people for promotion or retirement are rites of passage.

Sometimes, rites of passage can get out of hand. Fraternities, sororities, sports teams, and even the military have been known to use hazing to initiate members. Activities can include "sleep deprivation, public nudity and childish pranks or, at worst, extreme drunkenness, gross racial slurs, even beatings."[29] The videotaped hazing rituals at CFB Petawawa caused the Airborne Regiment to be disbanded. While the goal of the hazing might have been to desensitize new recruits to the brutality of war, many Canadians felt that the practice had gone too far. In Australia, a court held an organization liable for assault after a teenager, who was wrapped in cling film during a hazing ritual, prosecuted a company and two of its directors for assault under workplace safety laws.

Rites of integration, such as office parties, company cookouts, and shared announcements of organizational successes, build as well as reinforce common bonds among organizational members. WestJet, based out of Calgary, is well known for its efforts to develop ceremonies and rituals to bond employees to the organization by showing them that they are valued members. WestJet holds large profit-sharing parties twice annually, one in the fall and another in the spring, to literally give cheques to workers. "One of the hallmarks of our culture is celebrating success," president and CEO Gregg Saretsky explains. "I can't think of a better way to celebrate success than actually physically handing out checks . . . We have

WestJet celebrates success with fun staff parties.

a big party. Live music, an open bar. We have fun. Everybody is standing shoulder to shoulder and it's very much kind of a festival atmosphere."[30]

Rites of enhancement, such as awards dinners, newspaper releases, and employee promotions, let organizations publicly recognize and reward employees' contributions and thus strengthen their commitment to organizational values. By bonding members within the organization, rites of enhancement help promote group cohesiveness.

Stories and Language

Stories and language also communicate organizational culture. At WestJet, you never hear people using the word "passengers," only travelling "guests." Stories (whether fact or fiction) about organizational heroes and villains and their actions provide important clues about values and norms. Such stories can reveal the kinds of behaviours that are valued by the organization and the kinds of practices that are frowned on.[31] Stories about Steve Jobs, the person (hero) who made Apple Computers the company it is today, shed light on many aspects of the company's corporate culture. Stories also about Bill Newnham, founder of Seneca College in Toronto, speak volumes about his spirit and how this spirit lives on in the organizational culture of the college.[32] Language—through slogans, symbols, and jargon—is used to help employees come to know expectations while bonding with one another.

The concept of organizational language encompasses not only spoken language but also how people dress, the offices they occupy, the cars they drive, and the degree of formality they use when they address one another. IBM Canada, long known for its dark-blue suits, introduced less formal clothing in the 1990s so that customers would feel more comfortable when interacting with the company.[33] When employees "speak" and understand the language of their organization's culture, they know how to behave in the organization and what attitudes are expected of them.

Material Symbols

The organization's layout is a material symbol, and so are the size of offices; whether individuals wear uniforms or have a dress code; and the kinds of cars that top executives are given.[34] Material symbols convey to employees who is important, how much distance there is between top management and employees, and what kinds of behaviour are appropriate. For example, at Toronto-based Willow Manufacturing, an industrial machining firm, everyone from the CEO down wears the same type of uniform. This is typical of industrial environments, especially in Asia, where conformity to group norms is important to the production process. It is not so common in high-tech design firms, where conformity to a dress code is less likely to be part of the culture of the organization.

Midlevel workers at WestJet sit in cubicles that are positioned close to large windows, providing plenty of natural light and a view of aircraft landing and taking off at Calgary International, where the picturesque Rocky Mountains are visible in the background. Senior executives' modern but modest offices are, on the other hand, at the building's interior with no window view. Similarly, at Husky Injection Molding Systems, based in Bolton, Ontario, employees and management share the parking lot, dining room, and even washrooms, conveying the sense of an egalitarian workplace.

At Husky, employees and management share the parking lot, dining room, and even washrooms, conveying the sense of an egalitarian workplace.

LO3 Understand how organizational change relates to an organization's culture.

Organizational Change and Culture

Organizational change can affect practically all aspects of organizational functioning, including organizational structure, strategies, control systems, groups and teams, as well as the human resource management system and critical organizational processes such as communication, motivation, and leadership. **Organizational change** is the movement of an organization away from its present state and toward some desired future state to increase its efficiency and effectiveness. Organizational change can bring alterations in the ways managers carry out the critical tasks of planning, organizing, leading, and controlling and the ways they perform their managerial roles. Thus, all changes in the organization need to be carried out within the context of examining the organization's culture, and while adaptive and innovative cultures facilitate the initiation and development of new ideas, implementing the change is often meet with resistance.

There are two ways for organizational change to come about. It is either induced or imposed. **Induced change** refers to planned new institutional arrangements in terms of strategy, technology, human resources, and organizational structure in response to changes in the task and general organizational environments made to gain a competitive advantage. **Imposed change** can be viewed as new institutional arrangements set out by changes in legislation and law that force change in order to comply with the new rules. For example, when the City of

"Casserole" protestors in Vancouver support the student resistance to increases in tuition rates in Quebec.

Changes in policies often meet with resistance

Toronto legislated a ban on smoking in restaurants, all organizations had to accept that change and implement alternative strategies that targeted smokers, even though it had been imposed rather than induced.

Even induced change that comes from within the organization is risky and challenging. In a recent online survey,[35] 600 global leaders were interviewed about change and business transformation. Fifty-eight percent of the respondents said that over the past five years, half or fewer of their change initiatives had been successful. For the United States, the participant experience was worse, with 75 percent stating that half or fewer of their change initiatives had been successful. The most frequently cited barrier was winning over the hearts and minds of employees at all levels (51 percent). Management buy-in (31 percent) and cultural issues (27 percent) were featured as major barriers. Organizations that want to move in a new direction, such as mergers, acquisitions, divestitures, or global expansions, must alter structures, policies, behaviours, and beliefs in order to get from "how we've always done it" to how things will be done in the future. Thus, all changes in the organization need to be carried out within the context of examining and changing the organization's culture.

Moreover, the necessity to become an **e-business**—that is, using the Internet and intranet applications to communicate with employees, suppliers, customers, and other stakeholders—is one of the greatest challenges facing business today. Transforming a traditional "bricks and mortar" company into a "clicks and mortar" company demands vast changes in the organization's

organizational change
The movement of an organization away from its present state and toward some desired future state to increase its efficiency and effectiveness.

induced change
Planned new institutional arrangements made to gain a competitive advantage.

imposed change
New institutional arrangements made to comply with regulations.

e-business Connecting suppliers, customers, employees, and other stakeholders using the internet and intranet applications to facilitate commerce.

structural changes
Any change in the design and management of an organization.

technological changes
Changes that relate to an organization's operational processes.

product changes A change in the products and services offered by the organization.

cultural changes A shift in the shared set of beliefs, expectations, values, norms, and work routines that influence how members of an organization relate to one another and work together to achieve organizational goals.

culture, as it fundamentally changes the way it views, serves, and satisfies customers. As we saw in the opening case on Ford Motor Company, changes in any organizational activities often result in resistance.

While it is difficult to analyze organizational change that is imposed from outside, in the next part of this chapter we look at the dimensions of organizational change when organizational change is induced from within. Figure 7.3 outlines the types of change we find in organizations when the changes are induced or planned. Organizational change can affect practically all aspects of organizational functioning, including organizational structure, critical operational processes involving technology, new product development, and changes in the cultural norms and values of the organization. **Structural changes** in an organization involve any changes in the way the organization is designed, planned, and controlled including how authority is allocated and how departments and activities are integrated and coordinated. Bombardier changed its structure when it created a skunkworks for the "C" series jet. **Technological changes** occur when operational processes are redesigned to be more efficient. Point of sale technology allows organizations in retail and food services to track sales and order inventory in one transaction. **Product changes** occur when new ideas are developed and innovation occurs—that is, creative ideas

are implemented resulting in new products or services. The "C" series regional jet is a new product from Bombardier. **Cultural changes** are shifts in the shared set of beliefs, expectations, values, norms, and work routines that influence how members of an organization relate to one another and work together to achieve organizational goals. Training and development play a critical role in moving people's beliefs and attitudes from the way things have always been done to the new desired state. Organizational change can bring alterations in the ways managers carry out all the critical tasks in planning, organizing, leading, and controlling and the ways they perform their managerial roles.

Explain the processes involved in managing organizational change. **LO4**

Managing Organizational Change

The need to constantly search for ways to improve efficiency and effectiveness makes it vital that managers develop the skills necessary to manage change effectively. The movement of an organization away from its present state and toward some desired future state to increase its efficiency and effectiveness needs to be managed well if it is to be successful. Several experts have proposed a model that managers can follow to introduce change successfully while effectively managing conflict and politics.[36] Figure 7.4 outlines the steps that managers must take to manage change effectively.

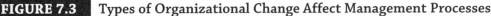

FIGURE 7.3 Types of Organizational Change Affect Management Processes

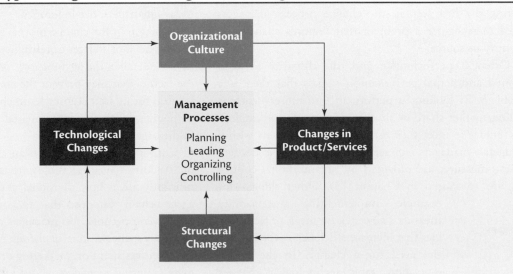

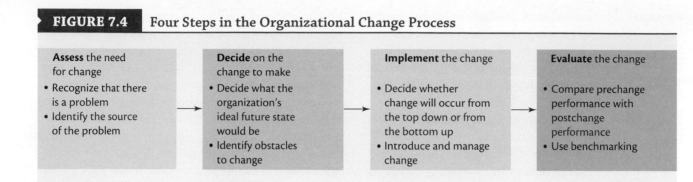

FIGURE 7.4   Four Steps in the Organizational Change Process

Assess the need for change	**Decide** on the change to make	**Implement** the change	**Evaluate** the change
• Recognize that there is a problem • Identify the source of the problem	• Decide what the organization's ideal future state would be • Identify obstacles to change	• Decide whether change will occur from the top down or from the bottom up • Introduce and manage change	• Compare prechange performance with postchange performance • Use benchmarking

Assessing the Need for Change

Deciding how to change an organization is a complex matter, not least because change disrupts the status quo and poses a threat, prompting employees to resist attempts to alter work relationships and procedures. Organizational learning, the process through which managers try to increase organizational members' abilities to understand and appropriately respond to changing conditions, can be an important impetus for change and can help all members of an organization, including managers, effectively make decisions about needed changes.

Assessing the need for change calls for two important activities: *recognizing that there is a problem* and *identifying its source.* Sometimes the need for change is obvious, such as when an organization's performance is suffering, as was the case with Ford. Often, however, managers have trouble determining that something is going wrong because problems develop gradually; organizational performance may slip for a number of years before it becomes obvious. Even if there is no problem with current performance, implementing a new idea or innovation will require changes in structure, strategy, and control processes—and therein lies the problem. Thus, during the first step in the change process, managers need to recognize a problem that requires change and identify its source.

Often, a **performance gap,** the disparity between desired and actual performance, signals that there is a problem. By looking at performance measures—such as falling market share or profits, rising costs, or employees' failure to meet their established goals or stay within budgets—managers can see whether change is needed. These measures are provided by organizational control systems (discussed in Chapter 13). Other things—for example, implementing sustainability measures, new creative ideas, or technologies that increase efficiencies—precipitate the need for a change. In the era of e-business, rapid technological changes

are forcing traditional land-based, bricks-and-mortar business to radically change operations to compete with low cost competitors.

Deciding on the Change to Make

Once managers have identified the source of the problem, they must decide what they think the organization's ideal future state would be. In other words, they must decide where they would like their organization to be in the future—what kinds of goods and services it should be offering, what its business-level strategy should be, how the organizational structure should be changed, and so on. During this step, managers also must engage in planning how they are going to attain the organization's ideal future state. Companies transforming to e-business create customer value by using networked computing to improve internal communications among employees and external communications with customers, suppliers, and strategic partners. Ideally, the hybrid "clicks and mortar" company will serve customers better through customized products, lower turnaround times, and lower costs. But changing from a "bricks and mortar" to a "clicks and mortar" organization presents significant challenges to today's managers. See Figure 7.5.[37]

This step in the change process also includes identifying obstacles or sources of resistance to change (discussed in more detail in the next section). Managers must analyze the factors that may prevent the company from reaching its ideal future state. Obstacles to change are found at the corporate, divisional, departmental, and individual levels of the organization.

Corporate-level changes in an organization's strategy or structure—even seemingly trivial changes—may significantly affect how divisional and departmental managers behave. Suppose that to compete with low-cost foreign competitors, top managers decide to increase the resources spent on state-of-the-art machinery and reduce the resources spent on marketing or R&D. The power of manufacturing managers would increase, and the power

performance gap
A disparity between desired and actual performance levels.

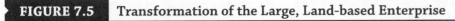

> **FIGURE 7.5**   Transformation of the Large, Land-based Enterprise

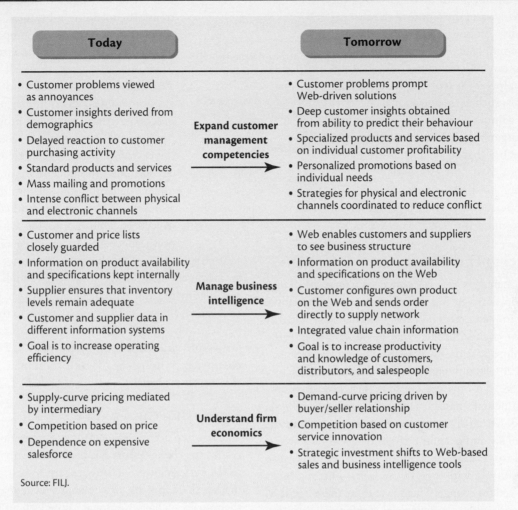

of marketing and R&D managers would fall. This decision would alter the balance of power among departments and might lead to increased politics and conflict as departments start fighting to retain their status in the organization. An organization's present strategy and structure are powerful obstacles to change.

Whether a company's culture is adaptive or inert facilitates or obstructs change. Organizations with entrepreneurial, flexible cultures, such as high-tech companies, are much easier to change than are organizations with more rigid cultures such as those sometimes found in large bureaucratic organizations—for example the RCMP or, as the opening case illustrated, Ford.

The same obstacles to change exist at the divisional and departmental levels as well. Division managers may differ in their attitudes toward the changes that top managers propose and will resist those changes if their interests and power seem threatened. Managers at all levels usually fight to protect their power and control over resources. Given that departments have different goals and time horizons, they may also react differently to the changes that other managers propose. When top managers are trying to reduce costs, for example, sales managers may resist attempts to cut back on sales expenditures if they believe that problems stem from the manufacturing managers' inefficiencies.

At the individual level, too, people are often resistant to change because change brings uncertainty, and uncertainty brings stress. For example, older individuals may resist the introduction of e-business technology because they are uncertain about their abilities to learn it and effectively use it.

These obstacles make organizational change a slow process. Managers must recognize these potential obstacles to change and take them into consideration. Some obstacles can be overcome by improving communication and integrating mechanisms so that all organizational members are aware of both the need for change and the nature of the changes being made. Empowering employees and inviting them to take part in the planning for change also can help overcome resistance and reduce employees' fears. Emphasizing big-picture goals, such as organizational effectiveness, and gaining a competitive advantage can make organizational members who resist a change realize that the change is ultimately in everyone's best interests because it will increase organizational performance. The larger and more complex an organization is, the more complex is the change process.

Introducing the Change

Generally, managers can introduce and manage change from the top down or from the bottom up.[38] **Top-down change** is implemented quickly: top managers identify the need for change, decide what to do, and then move quickly to introduce the changes throughout the organization. For example, top managers may decide to restructure and downsize the organization and then give divisional and departmental managers specific goals to achieve. With top-down change, the emphasis is on making the changes quickly and dealing with problems as they arise.

Bottom-up change is typically more gradual. Top managers consult with middle and first-line managers about the need for change. Then, over time, these low-level managers work with nonmanagerial employees to develop a detailed plan for change. A major advantage of bottom-up change is that it can reduce uncertainty and resistance to change. The emphasis in bottom-up change is on participation and on keeping people informed about what is going on, thus minimizing resistance from employees.

top-down change
Change that is introduced quickly throughout an organization by upper-level managers.

bottom-up change
Change that is introduced gradually and involves managers and employees at all levels of an organization.

benchmarking
Comparing performance on specific dimensions with the performance of high-performing organizations.

For example, to understand the changes a traditional land-based business must make to transform to doing e-business, we can look at how a strictly dot-com company operates. Born out of a website, the virtual business must outsource everything. It depends on Web-enabled networks of third-party suppliers, warehouses, distributors, and payment processors that together provide reliable products or services when, where, and how the customer needs them. A common strategy has been to concentrate on unmet customer demand for customized products at lower costs than traditional companies have been able to provide with their high overhead costs. An example of this is TD Waterhouse, an online discount brokerage firm aimed at customers who do not want to pay high commission fees for advice from a financial adviser. An account with such a firm allows the customer to trade in the stock market relatively cheaply and quickly. E-business companies are simply facilitators and intermediaries. They facilitate commerce by using the Web to coordinate suppliers on the customer's behalf.

Evaluating the Change

The last step in the change process is to evaluate how successful the change effort has been in improving organizational performance.[39] Using measures such as changes in market share, profits, or the ability of managers to meet their goals, managers compare how well an organization is performing after the change with how well it was performing before.

Managers also can use **benchmarking,** comparing their performance on specific dimensions with the performance of high-performing organizations to decide how successful the change effort has been. For example, when Xerox was doing poorly in the 1980s, it benchmarked the efficiency of its distribution operations against those of L.L. Bean, the efficiency of its central computer operations against those of John Deere, and its marketing abilities against those of Procter & Gamble. Those companies are renowned for their skills in those different areas, and by studying how they performed, Xerox was able to dramatically increase its own performance.

Managing organizational change is key to an organization's performance. In responding to the threats and opportunities in the environment, managers must be alert to the need to align new strategies and structures. Innovation and change is more successful in organizations with entrepreneurial and adaptive cultures. High-performing

Tips ▶ FOR MANAGERS

Introducing Change

1. Explaining the "reasons" for the change, the need for the change, the logic behind the change, the benefits of the change, or other seemingly rational approaches may fail.

2. Logical explanations often fail because they are viewed as "uncaring" and people feel their emotional concerns are unheard.

3. Respond to the affected people by confirming their emotional concerns.

organizations are those whose managers are attuned to the need to continually modify the way they operate and adopt techniques to foster innovative, adaptive organizational cultures and organizational learning, such as empowered work groups and teams, and benchmarking, to remain competitive in a global world.

LO5 Evaluate the challenges managers face in balancing innovation, high performance culture, and organizational change.

Models of Organizational Change

Interestingly enough, there is a fundamental tension or need to balance two opposing forces that influences the way organizations change. Organizations and their managers need to be able to control their activities and make their operations routine and predictable. At the same time, however, organizations have to be responsive to the need for innovation and change, and managers and employees have to "think on their feet" and realize when they need to depart from routines to be responsive to unpredictable events. Employees need to feel that they have the autonomy to depart from routines as necessary to increase innovation without being punished by rigid rules and regulations. It is for this reason that many researchers believe that the highest-performing

organizations are those that are constantly changing—and thus become experienced at doing so—in their search to become more efficient and effective. The need to constantly search for ways to improve efficiency and effectiveness makes it vital that managers develop the skills necessary to manage change effectively. In this section we examine two models of organizational change: Lewin's three-stage model and Ralph Stacey's complexity theory. Finally, we end our discussion with how managers deal with change in a unionized organizational setting.

Lewin's Three-Stage Model of Change

Kurt Lewin identified a three-step process that organizations could use to manage change successfully: *unfreeze* the status quo, *move* to a new state, and *refreeze* the new change to make it permanent.[40]

Organizations in their ordinary state reflect the status quo. To move toward a new state, unfreezing is necessary. Unfreezing, the process by which an organization overcomes the resistance to change, can occur in one of three ways, as shown in Figure 7.6. **Driving forces,** which direct behaviour away from the status quo, can be increased. **Restraining forces,** which hinder movement from the existing equilibrium, can be decreased. One can also combine the first two approaches.

> **driving forces**
> Forces that direct behaviour away from the status quo.
>
> **restraining forces**
> Forces that prevent movement away from the status quo.

FIGURE 7.6 Lewin's Model of Change

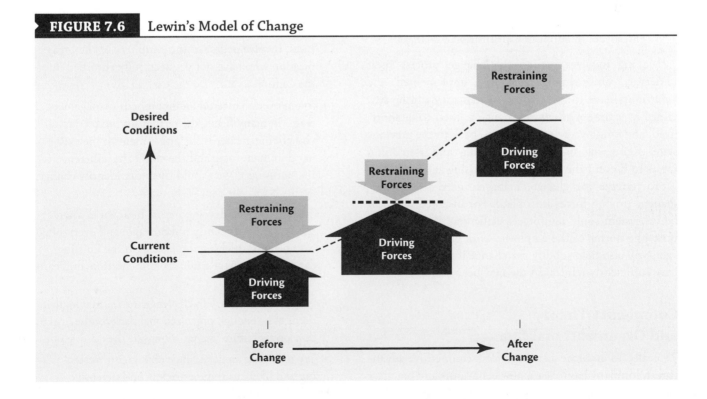

Individuals generally resist change for two primary reasons:

1. *Fear.* People fear the unknown. The perception that change can lead to a loss of power and privilege can hold weight, especially when resources and budgets need to be reallocated. There can be winners and losers in the change process.

2. *Doubt.* If people doubt the legitimacy of the change, or perceive it not to be in the best interests of the organization, they are likely to act as a restraining force against the change.

Managers can take steps to break down that resistance:

1. They can communicate the desired outcome or future state clearly and seek input from others.

2. They can increase the driving forces by promising new rewards or benefits if employees work toward the change.

3. Managers can also remove some of the restraining forces. For instance, if employees fear change because they do not know how to use the new technology, training could be given to reduce that fear.

4. When resistance to change is extremely high, managers may have to work on both the driving forces and the restraining forces for unfreezing to be successful.

5. As a last resort, managers may use their formal power to withhold rewards in order to persuade employees to adopt new institutional changes.

Moving involves getting the change process itself underway. Once change has been implemented, the behaviours have to be refrozen so that they can be sustained over time. Otherwise, change is likely to be short-lived, and employees are likely to go back to the previous state. Refreezing balances the driving and restraining forces to prevent the old state from arising again.

To refreeze the change, managers need to put permanent driving forces into place. For instance, the new bonus system could reinforce specific new changes. Over time, the norms of the employee work groups and managers will also help solidify the change if senior managers have sufficiently reinforced the new behaviour.

Complexity Theory and Organizational Change

Typically, to embrace a strategy for a competitive advantage, a company has to learn new behaviours and practices until they become second nature. The new behaviours and cultural practices must be refrozen to match the new strategy. This alignment positions the firm to take advantage of internal strengths and counter any external threats. However, Ralph Stacey suggests that too much "fit" can prevent an organization from making the necessary changes that would allow it to compete in a dynamic organizational environment. **Complexity theory** suggests that organizations respond best to fundamental change if they are poised on the "edge of chaos"; that is, not perfectly aligned with their environments. To achieve this state, managers have to do the following:

complexity theory
Organizations respond best to change if they are not perfectly aligned with their environment.

- Increase the channels of communication to promote informal and spontaneous self-organization—people coming together because they are motivated to find new ways of doing things, not because their department has detailed them to attend a particular committee.

- Not dictate agendas or set specific objectives but identify problems or pose paradoxes for groups to resolve. For example, how can we be both a successful innovator and a low-cost producer? Set rules and establish the constraints for the debate; do not try to predict outcomes.

- Rotate people regularly so that they do not get stale and can both disseminate their own expertise and gain insights from other parts of the business. Bring in outsiders with different backgrounds and cultures. Involve people at the periphery of the organization who have not yet been fully absorbed into the culture.

- Avoid overreliance on an incumbent management team. In many firms, the farther up the hierarchy you go, the greater is the attachment to the existing dominant logic and the closer the adherence to the status quo. We should therefore identify change agents below the top.

- Tolerate parallel developments. In a world where the future is inherently unknowable and everything is to play for, sticking too closely to the knitting can be disastrous. Permit experimentation and learn from failure.

- Avoid excessive "fit." To challenge the status quo, there needs to be enough organizational slack for the firm to develop the future "recipe" alongside the existing one.

- Try to reduce anxiety. Since change is threatening and likely to induce anxiety and defensive behaviour, fear needs to be reduced by offering realistic terms: for example, continued employment in return for total flexibility.[41]

Complexity theory suggests that fixed notions such as mission statements, developing core competencies, and leadership may be suitable for firms operating in a stable environment but have little relevance to those confronting the necessities for fundamental change to remain competitive today. Complexity theory focuses more on processes and organizational dynamics that question the traditional notion that strategy can be planned and programmed.

Managing Change in a Unionized Environment

When managers work in a unionized environment, they may have some other considerations to face. Two consultants who have worked with a number of Canadian organizations in recent years note four essential elements for managing change in a unionized environment.[42]

- *An effective system for resolving day-to-day issues.* Employees should have alternatives to the formal grievance process so that they feel they can be heard easily. If the workplace is open to hearing workers' issues, this will underscore a commitment to participation and empowerment.

- *A jointly administered business education process.* Because union leaders and their members become uneasy about the effects of change on jobs,

How can organizations remain competitive in a dynamic environment?

education can help employees understand the need for change. Making them more aware of company performance helps them better understand the decisions the company makes.

- *A jointly developed strategic vision for the organization.* Giving union members the opportunity to be involved in setting the vision lets them focus on how change can be made, rather than whether it should be made. The vision "should describe performance expectations, work design, organizational structure, the supply chain, governance, pay and rewards, technology, education and training, operating processes, employee involvement, employment security, and union-management roles and relations."[43]

- *A nontraditional, problem-solving method of negotiating collective agreements.* Managers need to create an atmosphere of tolerance and willingness to listen. Expanding the traditional scope of bargaining to include complex issues such as strategic plans is also helpful. Management resists bargaining over these issues, but when managers do bargain, it communicates a commitment to working jointly with unionized employees.

In summary, managers face several challenges in balancing innovation, creating high performance culture, and implementing organizational change successfully. Innovation—implementing new creative ideas to gain a competitive advantage—happens in companies whose organizational culture is based on norms and values which support individual creativity and organizational learning and risk taking. Managers must appropriately reward individual intrapreneurs for new ideas, even if in the end they do not come to market. Employees and managers who feel empowered to work on new solutions, without risk of repercussion, create an adaptive organizational culture that can better cope with organizational change. Changes in any aspect of an organization's operations, strategy, or structure may result in resistance from employees and managers who would rather maintain the status quo than give up any power or privilege. Managers must adopt techniques to overcome resistance. The challenge is for managers to balance the need for smooth predictable operations with the need to respond quickly to changes in the environment to maintain or gain a competitive advantage. Companies who are ever-ready for change as it arises are more likely to have innovative, adaptive organizational cultures and be high performing organizations.

Summary and Review

LO1 Innovation and Entrepreneurship   Innovation is the implementation of creative ideas within an organization. Employees are more motivated to innovate when the organizational culture is supportive and flexible. Managers can promote innovation by creating product champions, creating skunkworks, and rewarding employees for taking risks.

LO2 The Role of Managers in Influencing Culture   Organizational culture is the set of values, norms, standards of behaviour, and common expectations that guide how individuals and groups in an organization interact with each other and work to achieve organizational goals. Culture guides individuals and groups through shared values, norms, standards of behaviour, and expectations. Organizational culture is transmitted to employees through the values of the founder, the process of socialization, organizational ceremonies and rites, and stories and language. The way managers perform their management functions influences the kind of culture—either adaptive or inert—that develops in an organization.

LO3 Organizational Change and Culture   Organizational change is the movement of an organization away from its present state and toward some desired future state to increase its efficiency and effectiveness. When organizational change is either induced from inside the organization or imposed from outside, changes in the culture—shared values, norms, and behaviours—of the organization are necessary in order to be successful.

LO4 Managing Organizational Change   Managing organizational change is one of managers' most important and difficult tasks. Four steps in the organizational change process are assessing the need for change, deciding on the change to make, introducing the change, and evaluating how successful the change effort has been.

LO5 Models of Organizational Change   A central challenge for managers is to balance the need for predictable stable work patterns with the need to respond to changes in the environment by innovating and changing strategy and structure. Kurt Lewin suggests a three-step process to manage change: (1) the status quo is unfrozen, (2) the organization moves to the desired state, and (3) the changes are refrozen to make them permanent. Complexity theory suggests that to effectively deal with change, managers must create flexible systems that teeter on the "edge of chaos" rather than rigid, permanent structures. To manage change in a unionized environment it is important to resolve day-to-day issues, provide education about the change, work together on developing a vision for the organization, and establish new, cooperative problem-solving arrangements. A high performance culture based on norms and values that support innovation and risk taking is better adapted to organizational change.

KEY TERMS

artifacts	creativity	imposed change
assumptions	cultural changes	induced change
beliefs	driving forces	innovation
benchmarking	e-business	norms
bottom-up change	entrepreneurs	organizational change
complexity theory	entrepreneurship	organizational culture

organizational socialization	restraining forces	structural changes
performance gap	skunkworks	technological changes
product champion	social entrepreneurs	top-down change
product changes	social innovation	values

>>>> *WRAP-UP TO* >>>>   (**OPENING CASE**)

Ford's Culture Shift

HOW CAN MANAGERS CHANGE HOSTILE ORGANIZATIONAL CULTURES?

Ford's board of directors realized they needed an outsider to change Ford's culture and they recruited Alan Mulally in 2006 to become Ford's new CEO. After arriving at Ford he soon realized the problem was the values and norms in Ford's culture that had created a situation in which the managers of its different divisions and functions believed that the best way to maintain their jobs, salaries, and status was to hoard information and not share it. After having read and understood the concepts in this chapter, you should be able to answer the following questions:

1. *Was the old organizational culture at Ford adaptive or inert?*

ANSWER: An adaptive culture is strong and cohesive based on values and norms that emphasize entrepreneurship and respect for the employee and allow the use of organizational structures, such as the cross-functional team structure, that empower employees to make decisions and motivate them to succeed. By contrast, in an inert culture, employees are content to be told what to do and have little incentive or motivation to perform beyond minimum work requirements. In an inert culture, the emphasis is on close supervision and hierarchical authority, which result in a culture that makes it difficult to adapt to a changing environment. Ford had an inert culture before Alan Mulally took over as CEO. Ford had developed a tall hierarchy composed of managers whose main goal was to protect their turf and avoid any direct blame for its plunging car sales. The culture encouraged hoarding information vital to the success of the whole organization. It had a "keep your mouth shut and mind your own business" culture that was slow to respond to changes in the market conditions. The old culture at Ford was an inert organizational culture.

2. *How did Ford know it was necessary to make a change?*

ANSWER: Assessing the need for change calls for two important activities: *recognizing that there is a problem* and *identifying its source.* In this case, slumping sales under the reign of William Ford III, who had been CEO for the last five years, was the biggest indicator that something was terribly wrong with the company and that change was needed. He also recognized that he was not the person to implement those changes. In fact, the culture that he helped build at Ford was a major part of the problem. To discover the source of the problems, managers need to look both within and outside the organization. Looking within the organization, the new CEO Mulally quickly realized the problem was the values and norms in Ford's culture that had created a situation in which the managers of its different divisions and functions thought that the best way to maintain their jobs, salaries, and status was to hoard information and not share it. He issued a direct order that the managers of every division should share with every other Ford division a detailed statement of the costs they incurred to build each of its vehicles. Essentially, Mulally's goal was to demolish the dysfunctional inbred values and norms of Ford's culture that had focused managers' attention on their own empires at the expense of the whole company. He wanted to create new values and norms that it is all right to admit mistakes, share information about all aspects of model design and costs, and of course find ways to speed development and reduce costs. Mulally standardized parts across all vehicle lines, which reduced production costs significantly. Outside of the company the competitive landscape was changing, and car lines like Jaguar and Land Rover became unprofitable and were sold off to concentrate on core brands.

3. *What are the driving and restraining forces to change in this case?*

ANSWER: Organizations with entrepreneurial, flexible cultures are much easier to change than are organizations with more rigid cultures, like Ford. To get an organization to change, managers must find a way to increase the forces for change, reduce resistance to change, or do both simultaneously. The norms and values of an organization's culture are very hard to change; and despite Ford's major problems no CEO had successfully forced its managers to change the way they operated inside the company. Ford's board of directors acted as a force for change when they realized they needed an outsider to change Ford's culture and they recruited Alan Mulally in 2006 to become Ford's new CEO. Mulally believed Ford's problems could be solved if he could get its managers to adopt new cultural values and norms of openness and collaboration. The resistance to change came from the managers who had a secretive culture and hoarded information vital to the organization as a whole in order to not be blamed for falling sales. Resistance to change often comes from managers at all levels who fight to protect their power and control over resources. Mulally was able to change the mindset of managers and employees to turn around the company's fortunes. He did this by emphasizing group or shared goals such as organizational efficiency and effectiveness. This allayed fear and helped Mulally overcome resistance to changing the norms and values. Mulally moved quickly to implement top-down style changes to communication and reporting.

Management in Action

TOPICS FOR DISCUSSION AND ACTION

LEVEL 1 Knowledge & Comprehension

1. What is organizational culture? How does it guide behaviour in organizations? How is corporate culture created and maintained?

2. Explain how members of an organization learn corporate culture.

3. Describe the four steps in managing organizational change.

LEVEL 2 Application & Analysis

4. View some videos on YouTube about Google and evaluate its organizational culture. What kinds of green initiatives make up the culture at Google? How does this company entrench its culture?

5. Interview some employees of an organization; ask them about their organization's values, norms, socialization practices, ceremonies and rites, and special language and stories. Referring to this information, describe the organization's culture.

6. Interview a manager about a change effort that he or she was involved in. What issues were involved? What problems were encountered? What was the outcome of the change process?

LEVEL 3 Synthesis & Evaluation

7. Analyze the difficulties managers face when trying to introduce organizational change. How might they overcome some of these difficulties?

8. Do some research on the Internet and listen to some podcasts on Pixar. Describe how the co-founder Ed Catmull fosters a creative culture at Pixar. How will the culture be maintained when he leaves the company?

9. Discuss and evaluate the importance of complexity theory in change management.

SELF-REFLECTION EXERCISE

Think of something that you would like to change in your personal life. It could be your study habits, your fitness and nutrition, the way you interact with others, or anything else that is of interest to you. What values and assumptions have encouraged the behaviour that currently exists (i.e., the one you want to change)?

What driving and restraining forces can you address in order to make the desired change?

SMALL GROUP BREAKOUT EXERCISE

Reducing Resistance to Advances in Information Technology

Form groups of three or four, and appoint one member as the spokesperson who will communicate your findings to the whole class when called on by the instructor. Then discuss the following scenario:

You are a member of a team of managers in charge of information and communications in a large consumer products corporation. Your company has already introduced many advances in information technology. Managers and employees have access to voice mail, email, the Internet, your company's own intranet, and groupware.

Many employees use the new technology, but the resistance of some is causing communication problems. For example, all managers have email addresses and computers in their offices, but some refuse to turn their computers on, let alone send and receive email. These managers feel that they should be able to communicate as they have always done—in person, over the phone, or in writing. Thus, when managers who are unaware of their preferences send them email messages, those messages are never retrieved.

Moreover, the resistant managers never read company news sent by email. Another example of the resistance that your company is encountering concerns the use of groupware. Members of some work groups do not want to share information with others electronically.

Although you do not want to force people to use the technology, you want them at least to try it and give it a chance. You are meeting today to develop strategies for reducing resistance to the new technologies.

1. One resistant group of employees is made up of top managers. Some of them seem computer-phobic. They have never used, and do not want to start using, personal computers (PCs) for any purpose, including communication. What steps will you take to get these managers to give their PCs a chance?

2. A second group of resistant employees consists of middle managers. Some middle managers resist using your company's intranet. Although these middle managers do not resist the technology per se and use their PCs for multiple purposes, including communication, they seem to distrust the intranet as a viable way to communicate and get things done. What steps will you take to get these middle managers to take advantage of the intranet?

3. A third group of resistant employees is made up of members of groups and teams that do not want to use the groupware that has been provided to them. You think that the groupware could improve their communication and performance, but they seem to think otherwise. What steps will you take to get these members of groups and teams to start using groupware?

BUSINESS PLANNING EXERCISE

Your professor may ask you to write a business plan for a new venture or a strategic plan for an existing venture. At the end of every chapter, you will have an opportunity to apply managerial and organizational concepts to the exercise of writing a business plan. Refer to Appendix A.

The culture of your organization is reflected in every aspect of the operation—from the art that hangs on the walls, to how open and transparent the management is with the stakeholders. In planning your business, you aim to embed your values and principles in the norms and material symbols of the organization. Think about these issues and what to include in the organizational plan component of your business plan.

1. Develop a set of values and principles or philosophy that you want your venture to follow.

2. Describe the organizational culture you want to foster.

3. How will you teach the managers and staff to internalize these norms and values?

MANAGING ETHICALLY EXERCISE

Some organizations, such as Arthur Andersen and Enron, seem to have developed norms and values that caused their members to behave in unethical ways. When and why might a strong norm that encourages high performance become one that can cause people to act unethically? How can organizations prevent their values and norms becoming "too strong"?

MANAGEMENT CHALLENGE EXERCISE

The Personal Touch[44]

You have been called in to help with a five-year-old plastics company. This company has grown enormously since its inception and been very successful financially. It has expanded rapidly and now has over 100 employees. The company has come to realize that while it has a very "hands-on" culture as far as technical expertise goes, this approach to working with employees alienated some of the newer employees. As a matter of fact, the company recently lost three of its best employees. In exit interviews, they said they found the company had become very "impersonal" and they did not want to work in such an organization.

1. What would be some suggestions you could make to create a more "personal" corporate culture?

2. How would you go about helping managers develop a team performance culture as well?

MANAGEMENT PORTFOLIO PROJECT

Answer the following questions about the organization you have chosen to follow:

1. Describe the organizational culture of the firm you are following.

2. How does this organization socialize its managers into its cultural values?

3. Has the organization undergone a significant change in the last decade? Describe the driving and restraining forces that operated in this change.

4. If the organization was to experience a significant change in the future, what steps could be taken to ensure that the change takes hold?

VIDEO MANAGEMENT CASE   connect

HR's Role in a Business Transformation

John Sicard, COO of Kinaxis in Ottawa, talks about the role HR plays when business is undergoing a major transformation, including getting employees involved and overcoming their resistance to change. Kinaxis helps organizations deal with complex supply chain management.

1. Why did Kinaxis undergo a major transformation?

2. How did Sicard couple the business transformation with a cultural transformation?

3. How did the employees react to the organizational changes?

4. What was the role of HR in the successful transformation?

Management Case

WestJet's Value Proposition[45]

Spend a day at WestJet's headquarters and you'll never hear the word "passenger," even though the LCC transports 15 million per year. The word "employee" sometimes slips into a conversation but generally is not used to describe the nearly 7,900 people employed by the carrier. Here in this western Canadian city known for rodeos, "WestJeters/owners" work for an airline that serves "guests" traveling aboard a fleet of 91 737NGs (configured with single-class cabins staffed by crew with a reputation for friendliness) throughout Canada, to leisure destinations in the US and increasingly to hotspots in the Caribbean and Mexico.

The language is not the only thing one notices that indicates the nearly 15-year-old carrier is somewhat different from the typical airline. The 18-month-old, C$120 million, 350,000-sq.-ft. headquarter building's first floor features a Starbucks and a full-scale food court, both populated by mingling employees throughout the day, with a big, animated crowd gathering at lunchtime. Midlevel workers sitting in cubicles are positioned close to large windows, providing plenty of natural light and a view of aircraft landing and taking off at Calgary International, where the picturesque Rocky Mountains are visible in the background. Senior executives' modern but modest offices are at the building's interior with no window view.

"There's no us and them," President and CEO Gregg Saretsky tells *ATW* during a wide-ranging interview in his office, which features two glass walls that allow any passing employee to look in. "We don't have reserved parking . . . If I'm the first one in, I'll get a nice spot. If I'm in later, I'll be parked way out there . . . I think if you go to our US, our Canadian competitors, you'll find that all of the executives have close-in parking and they have a corporate dining room [WS executives regularly eat meals in the first-floor eatery] . . . I think [corporate] leadership in North America has earned a quite-deserved reputation for elitism."

He points out that 85% of WestJet's completely nonunionized workforce own stock in the company through an employee share purchase plan. A "WestJeter" can dedicate up to 20% of his or her pay to purchasing stock and the airline will "match dollar for dollar," Saretsky notes. "That's unheard of in this business."

WS holds large profit-sharing parties twice annually, one in the fall and another in the spring, to literally give checks to workers. "One of the hallmarks of our culture is celebrating success," he explains. "I can't think of a better way to celebrate success than actually physically handing out checks . . . We have a big party. Live music, an open bar. We have fun. Everybody is standing shoulder to shoulder and it's very much kind of a festival atmosphere."

Profitable Growth   The company has had much to celebrate in the more than 14 years since Calgary entrepreneurs led by Clive Beddoe founded a western Canadian regional carrier modeled after Southwest Airlines that operated three 737-200s on a five-city network. Today, WS operates about 420 flights daily to 71 cities (double the 35 it served as recently as 2006) including 31 in Canada, 17 in the Caribbean (including Bermuda), 13 in the continental US (including five in Florida), four in Hawaii and six in Mexico. It enjoys a 37% share of the Canadian domestic market. Onboard it offers live television and pay-per-view movies on most flights (headsets may be purchased or passengers can bring their own) as well as buy-on-board sandwiches and snacks.

"Our strategy is built primarily around two things: our guest experience and our low costs."

Reliably high levels of growth and profitability, coupled with very positive brand awareness among Canadians and a management-worker relationship that is surely the envy of many airlines worldwide, have been the norm for WestJet, which flew through the global recession largely undamaged.

"At a time when a lot of airlines were furloughing employees and parking aircraft, the morale of their workforces plummeting, we continued to grow with a low cost structure that has allowed growth even at a time when revenues are underperforming," Saretsky says. "WestJeters have yet to have any furloughs. Knock on wood as I say that, but 14 years of growth results in employees feeling pretty good about the place where they work . . . We had double-digit [capacity] growth for the whole period [during the downturn] except for 2009, when growth was [2.6%]. That stands in stark contrast to most of our competitors, who actually shrank."

He says he understands that much of what has made WS successful was "learned a long time ago" by the founders, observing, "The track record speaks for itself. I don't want to be the CEO that messes a good thing up. On the other hand, I do have 25 years of experience and I do think I can help bring about change here in an effective way."

1. How would you characterize the organizational culture at WestJet?

2. How do WestJeters learn the organizational culture?

3. What makes Saretsky so sure he can bring about change in an effective way?

connect

Connect allows you to practise important concepts at your own pace and on your own schedule, with 24/7 online access to an eBook, practice quizzes, video cases, interactive exercises, study tools, and more.

End of Part IV: Continuing Case

CARROT TOPS: ORGANIZATIONAL CULTURE AND STRUCTURE

As the CEO, Mel oversees the outsourcing of the production of his brand-name labels and manages the store employees while Janet sources organic produce and runs the delivery drivers. Both need their people to perform at a high level, but approach employee motivation very differently. Mel's approach was to decentralize authority, empowering salespeople to take responsibility for meeting customer needs. Mel created a store environment in which employees were treated as individuals and felt valued as people. Rather than forcing employees to follow strict operating rules, Mel gave them autonomy to make decisions and provide personalized customer service. The result is that employees feel they "own" their supermarket. Janet, on the other hand, has been accused of "micro-managing" the drivers. For example, even though she doesn't know the city as well as the drivers, she insists on controlling the scheduling of deliveries. This practice results in few deliveries being made on time: drivers find nobody home because they arrive early or arrive late. Drivers feel frustrated with the complicated rules and the endless paperwork they have to fill out for Janet.

Drawing on all segments of this case:

1. Draw an organizational chart for Carrot Tops and describe the hierarchy of authority.

2. Would you describe Carrot Tops as an organic or a mechanistic structure?

3. Characterize the culture of store employees and of the drivers.

4. What can Janet do to motivate the drivers and create an entrepreneurial culture?

PART V

Managing Motivation

LEARNING OUTCOMES

LO1 Describe the nature of motivation and how it leads to the attainment of intrinsic and extrinsic outcomes.

LO2 Explain how need theories of motivation help managers determine the needs of employees and provide outcomes that satisfy them.

LO3 Describe how process theories of motivation help managers explain high and low performance levels.

LO4 Identify the motivation lessons that managers can learn from learning theories of motivation.

LO5 Explain how managers use reward systems to increase employee motivation.

Opening Case

Motivation at Enterprise Rent-A-Car

HOW CAN MANAGERS MOTIVATE EMPLOYEES AT ALL LEVELS TO PROVIDE EXCELLENT CUSTOMER SERVICE?

Enterprise Rent-A-Car was founded by Jack Taylor in 1957 in St. Louis, Missouri, as a very small auto leasing business with a fleet of seven cars.[1] Today, it is an internationally recognized brand with more than 6000 neighbourhood and airport locations in the United States, Canada, the U.K., Ireland, and Germany. With over $12.6 billion in revenue and more than 68 000 employees, Enterprise and its subsidiaries, Alamo and National, operate with more than 1 million cars and trucks, making them the largest car rental service provider in the world measured by revenue, employees, and fleet.[2] One of the biggest employers of new college graduates, Enterprise typically hires over 8000 entry-level employees each year and was ranked the number one Top Entry Level Employer in 2011.[3]

A privately held company, Enterprise is very much a family business. In its entire history, Enterprise has had only two CEOs, founder Jack Taylor, who is now retired but still quite involved in the company, and his son Andrew Taylor, who became president in 1980 and CEO in 1994.[4] Nonetheless, Enterprise's policy of promoting from within ensures that all employees who perform well have the opportunity to advance in the company.[5]

One of the keys to Enterprise's success is the way it motivates its employees to provide excellent customer service.[6] Practically all entry-level hires participate in Enterprise's Management Training Program.[7] As part of the program, new hires learn all aspects of the company's business and how to provide excellent customer service. Management

trainees first have a four-day training session focused primarily on Enterprise's culture. They are then assigned to a branch office for around 8 to 12 months where they learn all aspects of the business, from negotiating with body shops to helping customers to washing cars. As part of this training, they learn how important high-quality customer service is to Enterprise and how they can personally provide great service, increasing their confidence levels.[8]

All those who do well in the program are promoted after about a year to the position of management assistant. Management assistants who do well are promoted to become assistant branch managers with responsibility for mentoring and supervising employees. Assistant managers who do well can be promoted to become branch managers who are responsible for managing a branch's employees and provision of customer service, rental car fleet, and financial performance. Branch managers with about five years of experience in the position often move on to take up management positions at headquarters or assume the

position of area manager overseeing all the branches in a certain geographic region.[9] By training all new hires in all aspects of the business including the provision of excellent customer service, by providing them with valuable experience with increasing levels of responsibility and empowerment, and by providing all new hires who perform well with the opportunity to advance in the company, Enterprise has a highly motivated workforce. As Patrick Farrell, vice president of corporate communications, indicated, "What's unique about our company is that everyone came up through the same system, from the CEOs on down . . . 100% of our operations personnel started as management trainees."[10]

In addition to motivating high performance and excellent customer service through training and promotional opportunities, Enterprise also uses financial incentives to motivate employees. Essentially, each branch is considered a profit centre and the managers overseeing the branch and in charge of all aspects of its functioning have the autonomy and responsibility for the branch's profitability almost as if the branch was their own small business or franchise.[11] All branch employees at the rank of assistant manager and higher earn incentive compensation whereby their monthly pay depends upon the profitability of their branch. Managers at higher levels, such as area managers, have their monthly pay linked to the profitability of the region they oversee. Thus, managers at all levels know that their pay is linked to the profitability of the parts of Enterprise for which they are responsible. And they have the autonomy to make decisions ranging from buying and selling cars to even opening new branches.[12]

Another way in which Enterprise motivates its employees is through its philanthropic activities and initiatives to protect the natural environment.[13] For example, the Enterprise Rent-A-Car Foundation has committed $50 million to plant 50 million trees over a 50-year period in public forests. The Foundation also focuses on supporting and giving back to the communities in which Enterprise operates.[14] Of all rental car companies, Enterprise has the biggest fleet of fuel-efficient cars.[15] All in all, the multiple ways in which Enterprise motivates its employees and satisfies its customers have contributed to its ongoing success story.[16]

After reading and understanding the concepts in this chapter, you should be able to answer the following questions:

1. *Apply Hertzberg's motivator-hygiene theory to this case.*

2. *Apply Vroom's expectancy theory to this case.*

3. *How does Enterprise Rent-A-Car use a total reward strategy to motivate employee performance?*

Overview

Even with the best strategy in place and an appropriate organizational architecture, an organization will be effective only if its members are motivated to perform at a high level. Jack and Andrew Taylor of Enterprise Rent-A-Car clearly realize this. One reason why leading is such an important managerial activity is that it entails ensuring that each member of an organization is motivated to perform highly and help the organization achieve its goals. When managers are effective, the outcome of the leading process is a highly motivated workforce. A key challenge for managers of organizations both large and small is to encourage employees to perform at a high level.

In this chapter, we describe what motivation is, where it comes from, and why managers need to promote high levels of it for an organization to be effective and achieve its goals. In Figure 8.1 we list some of the important theories of motivation that we discuss in this chapter.

Each of the theories found in Figure 8.1 provides managers with important insights about how to motivate organizational members. The theories are complementary in that each focuses on a somewhat different aspect of motivation. *Need theories* of motivation help managers understand how human needs motivate us to act to satisfy them either extrinsically or intrinsically. *Process theories* help managers explain why people act the way they do and thus help managers understand the roots of high and low performance levels among employees. *Learning theories* help managers see the link between giving rewards for high performance behaviour and the repetition of that behaviour among employees. Considering all of the theories together helps managers gain a rich understanding of the many issues and problems involved in encouraging high levels of motivation throughout an organization. We end this chapter with a discussion of a *total reward strategy* as a motivation tool. By the end of this chapter, you will understand what it takes to have a highly motivated workforce.

FIGURE 8.1   Important Theories of Motivation

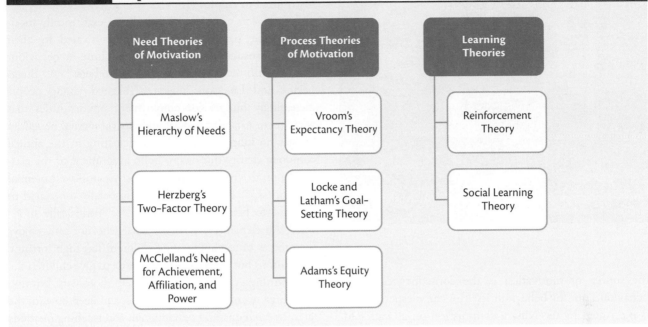

LO1 Describe the nature of motivation and how it leads to the attainment of intrinsic and extrinsic outcomes.

The Nature of Motivation

The term **motivation** refers to the psychological forces that determine the *direction* of a person's behaviour in an organization, a person's level of *effort,* and a person's level of *persistence* in the face of obstacles.[17] The *direction of a person's behaviour* refers to the many possible behaviours that a person could engage in. For example, employees at Enterprise Rent-A-Car know that they should do whatever is required to provide high-quality customer service such as giving customers rides to pick up and drop off rental cars. *Effort* refers to how hard people work. Employees at Enterprise Rent-A-Car exert high levels of effort to provide superior customer service. *Persistence* refers to whether, when faced with roadblocks and obstacles, people keep trying or give up. Branch managers at Enterprise Rent-A-Car persistently seek to improve the profitability of their branches while maintaining very high levels of customer service.

Motivation is central to management because it explains *why* people behave the way they do in organizations. Motivation also explains why a waiter is polite or rude and why a kindergarten teacher really tries to get

motivation Psychological forces that determine the direction of a person's behaviour in an organization, a person's level of effort, and a person's level of persistence.

intrinsically motivated behaviour Behaviour that is performed for its own sake.

extrinsically motivated behaviour Behaviour that is performed to acquire material or social rewards or to avoid punishment.

children to enjoy learning or just goes through the motions. It explains why some managers truly put their organizations' best interests first, whereas others are more concerned with maximizing their salaries and why—more generally—some workers put forth twice as much effort as others.

Motivation can come from *intrinsic* or *extrinsic* sources. **Intrinsically motivated behaviour** is behaviour that is performed for its own sake; the source of motivation is actually performing the behaviour, and motivation comes from doing the work itself. Many managers are intrinsically motivated; they derive a sense of accomplishment and achievement from helping the organization to achieve its goals and gain competitive advantages. Jobs that are interesting and challenging are more likely to lead to intrinsic motivation than are jobs that are boring or do not make use of a person's skills and abilities. An elementary school teacher who really enjoys teaching children, a computer programmer who loves solving programming problems, and a commercial photographer who relishes taking creative photographs are all intrinsically motivated. For these individuals, motivation comes from performing their jobs, whether it be teaching children, finding bugs in computer programs, or taking pictures.

Extrinsically motivated behaviour is behaviour that is performed to acquire material or social rewards or to avoid punishment;

An elementary school teacher gets satisfaction from helping students learn to read.

the source of motivation is the consequences of the behaviour, not the behaviour itself. A car salesperson who is motivated by receiving a commission on all cars sold, a lawyer who is motivated by the high salary and status that go along with the job, and a factory worker who is motivated by the opportunity to earn a secure income are all extrinsically motivated. Their motivation comes from the consequences they receive as a result of their work behaviours.

People can be intrinsically motivated, extrinsically motivated, or both intrinsically and extrinsically motivated.[18] A top manager who derives a sense of accomplishment and achievement from managing a large corporation and strives to reach year-end targets to obtain a hefty bonus is both intrinsically and extrinsically motivated. Similarly, a nurse who enjoys helping and taking care of patients and is motivated by having a secure job with good benefits is both intrinsically and extrinsically motivated. At Enterprise Rent-A-Car, employees are both extrinsically motivated, because of opportunities for promotions and having their pay linked to the performance of their branches or units, and intrinsically motivated, because they get a sense of satisfaction out of serving customers and learning new things.

Whether workers are intrinsically motivated, extrinsically motivated, or both depends on a wide variety of factors: (1) workers' own personal characteristics (such as their personalities, abilities, values, attitudes, and needs), (2) the nature of their jobs (such as whether they are interesting and challenging), and (3) the nature of the organization (such as its structure, its culture, its control systems, its human resource management

system, and the ways in which rewards such as pay are distributed to employees).

In addition to being intrinsically or extrinsically motivated, some people are prosocially motivated by their work.[19] **Prosocially motivated behaviour** is behaviour that is performed to benefit or help others.[20] As Bugg-Levine and Emerson suggest, "Talented young people increasingly hunger for employment opportunities that allow them to address social and environmental benefit, a hunger no longer satiated by participating in the annual corporate charity run or pro bono assignment or the classic nonprofit approach that ignores the positive potential of business."[21] Behaviour can be prosocially motivated in addition to being extrinsically and/or intrinsically motivated. An elementary school teacher who not only enjoys the process of teaching young children (has high intrinsic motivation) but also has a strong desire to give children the best learning experience possible, help those with learning disabilities overcome their challenges, and keep up with the latest research on child development and teaching methods in an effort to continually improve the effectiveness of his teaching has high prosocial motivation in addition to high intrinsic motivation. A surgeon who specializes in organ transplants and enjoys the challenge of performing complex operations, has a strong desire to help her patients regain their health and extend their lives through successful organ transplants, and also is motivated by the relatively high income she earns has high intrinsic, prosocial, and extrinsic motivation. A social entrepreneur who creates a business that employs people marginalized from mainstream society, as illustrated in the Focus on the Social Economy segment, is motivated by all three principles. Recent preliminary research suggests that when workers have high prosocial motivation, also having high intrinsic motivation can be especially beneficial for job performance.[22]

Regardless of whether people are intrinsically, extrinsically, or prosocially motivated, they join and are motivated to work in organizations to obtain certain outcomes. An **outcome** is anything a person gets from a job or organization. Some outcomes, such as autonomy, responsibility, a feeling of accomplishment, and the pleasure of doing interesting or enjoyable work, result in intrinsically motivated behaviour. Outcomes such as improving the lives or well-being of other people and doing good by helping others result in prosocially motivated behaviour. Other outcomes, such as pay, job security, benefits, and vacation time, result in extrinsically motivated behaviour.

Organizations hire people to obtain important *inputs*. An **input** is anything a

prosocially motivated behaviour Behaviour that is performed to benefit or help others.

outcome Anything a person gets from a job or organization.

input Anything a person contributes to his or her job or organization.

person contributes to his or her job or organization, such as time, effort, education, experience, skills, knowledge, and actual work behaviours. Inputs such as these are necessary for an organization to achieve its goals. Managers strive to motivate members of an organization to contribute inputs—through their behaviour, effort, and persistence—that help the organization achieve its goals. They do this by making sure that members of an organization obtain the outcomes they desire when they make valuable contributions to the organization. Managers use outcomes to motivate people to contribute their inputs to the organization. Giving people outcomes when they contribute inputs and perform well aligns the interests of employees with the goals of the organization as a whole because when employees do what is good for the organization, they personally benefit.

This alignment between employees and organizational goals as a whole can be described by the motivation equation shown in Figure 8.2. Managers aim to ensure that people are motivated to contribute important inputs to the organization, that these inputs are put to good use or

> "Talented young people increasingly hunger for employment opportunities that allow them to address social and environmental benefit..."
>
> *Bugg-Levine and Emerson,*
> *Impact Investing*

focused in the direction of high performance, and that high performance results in employees obtaining the outcomes they desire.

Each of the theories of motivation we discuss in this chapter focuses on one or more aspects of the motivation equation in Figure 8.2. Together, the theories provide a comprehensive set of guidelines for managers to follow to promote high levels of employee motivation. Effective managers tend to follow many of these guidelines, whereas ineffective managers often fail to follow them and seem to have trouble motivating organizational members.

Explain how need theories of motivation help managers determine the needs of employees and provide outcomes that satisfy them. **LO2**

Need Theories of Motivation

A **need** is a requirement or necessity for survival and well-being. The basic premise of need theories is that people are motivated to obtain outcomes at work

need A requirement or necessity for survival and well-being.

FOCUS ON ❯ *The Social Economy*

Inspirations Studio, Toronto

Inspirations Studio is an art-based incubator and social enterprise initiative that utilizes a self-employment model that focuses on building women's capacity to supplement their income and enhance their livelihoods through arts/crafts training, production and business development. The participants are low-income women who have been impacted by poverty, homelessness, trauma, and displacement. Located on Queen West, Inspirations Studio offers individual or small group instruction in art, primarily ceramics, painting/print making, and jewellery making.

Inspirations Studio members sell their art through retail businesses, community art fairs and community businesses, and the Inspirations Studio website. Inspirations Studio has a website with photographs showcasing its members' work. The studio sells on consignment at three stores in downtown Toronto and through sales held during festivals and at organizations such as the Canadian Broadcasting Corporation, the United Way, the Ontario Institute for Studies in Education, Alterna Savings Credit Union, Metro Hall, the Centre for Addiction and Mental Health, and through other trade sales.[23]

Inspirations Studio is an integral part of Sistering, a multi-service women's organization that offers practical and emotional support to women through programs that enable them to take greater control over their lives.

1. Would you describe the motivation of the low-income women that Inspirations Studio serves as intrinsic or extrinsic and why?

2. How would you describe the motivation of the people who run Inspirations Studio?

> **FIGURE 8.2** The Motivation Equation

INPUTS FROM ORGANIZATIONAL MEMBERS	PERFORMANCE	OUTCOMES RECEIVED BY ORGANIZATIONAL MEMBERS
Time Effort Education Experience Skills Knowledge Work behaviours	Contributes to organizational efficiency, organizational effectiveness, and the attainment of organizational goals	Pay Job security Benefits Vacation time Job satisfaction Autonomy Responsibility A feeling of accomplishment The pleasure of doing interesting work

that will satisfy their needs. **Need theories** suggest that in order to motivate a person to contribute valuable inputs to a job and perform at a high level, a manager must determine what needs the person is trying to satisfy at work and ensure that the person receives outcomes that help satisfy those needs when the person performs at a high level and helps the organization achieve its goals.

There are several need theories. We discuss three needs theories below: Abraham Maslow's *hierarchy of needs,* Frederick Herzberg's *two-factor* or *motivator-hygiene theory,* and David McClelland's need for *achievement, affiliation,* and *power.* These theories describe needs that people try to satisfy at work. In doing so, the theories provide managers with insights about what outcomes will motivate members of an organization to perform at a high level and contribute inputs to help the organization achieve its goals.

Maslow's Hierarchy of Needs

Psychologist Abraham Maslow proposed that everyone aims to satisfy five basic kinds of needs: physiological needs, safety needs, belongingness needs, esteem needs, and self-actualization needs (see Figure 8.3).[24] He suggested that these needs constitute a **hierarchy of needs,** with the most basic or compelling needs—physiological and safety needs—at the bottom. Maslow argued that these lowest-level needs must be met or almost completely met before a person will be motivated to satisfy needs higher up in the hierarchy, such as self-esteem needs. Once a need is satisfied, he proposed, it no longer is a source of motivation, and needs in the next level become motivators, driving people to take action to fulfill them.

Although Maslow's theory identifies needs that are likely to be important sources of motivation for many

people, research does not support his contention that there is a needs hierarchy or his notion that only one level of needs is motivational at a time.[25] Nevertheless, a key conclusion can be drawn from Maslow's theory: People differ in what needs they are trying to satisfy at work. To have a motivated workforce that achieves goals, managers must determine which needs employees are trying to satisfy in organizations and then make sure that individuals receive outcomes that will satisfy their needs when they perform at a high level and contribute to organizational effectiveness. By doing this, managers align the interests of individual members with the interests of the organization as a whole. By doing what is good for the organization (that is, performing at a high level), employees receive outcomes that satisfy their needs.

In an increasingly global economy, it is also important for managers to realize that citizens of different countries might differ in the needs they try to satisfy through work.[26] Some research suggests, for example, that people in Greece and Japan are especially motivated by safety needs and that people in Sweden, Norway, and Denmark are motivated by belongingness needs.[27] In poor countries with lower standards of living, physiological and safety needs are likely to be the prime motivators of behaviour. As countries become wealthier and have higher standards of living, it is likely that needs related to personal growth and accomplishment (such as esteem and self-actualization) become important as motivators of behaviour.

need theories Theories of motivation that focus on what needs people are trying to satisfy at work and what outcomes will satisfy those needs.

Maslow's hierarchy of needs An arrangement of five basic needs that, according to Maslow, motivate behaviour. Maslow proposed that the lowest level of unmet needs is the prime motivator and that only one level of needs is motivational at a time.

> **FIGURE 8.3** Maslow's Hierarchy of Needs

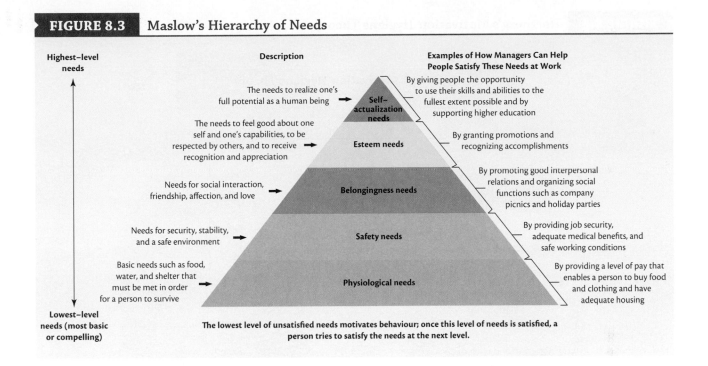

Highest–level needs

Description

Examples of How Managers Can Help People Satisfy These Needs at Work

The needs to realize one's full potential as a human being → Self–actualization needs — By giving people the opportunity to use their skills and abilities to the fullest extent possible and by supporting higher education

The needs to feel good about one self and one's capabilities, to be respected by others, and to receive recognition and appreciation → Esteem needs — By granting promotions and recognizing accomplishments

Needs for social interaction, friendship, affection, and love → Belongingness needs — By promoting good interpersonal relations and organizing social functions such as company picnics and holiday parties

Needs for security, stability, and a safe environment → Safety needs — By providing job security, adequate medical benefits, and safe working conditions

Basic needs such as food, water, and shelter that must be met in order for a person to survive → Physiological needs — By providing a level of pay that enables a person to buy food and clothing and have adequate housing

Lowest–level needs (most basic or compelling)

The lowest level of unsatisfied needs motivates behaviour; once this level of needs is satisfied, a person tries to satisfy the needs at the next level.

Herzberg's Motivator-Hygiene Theory

Adopting an approach different from Maslow's, Frederick Herzberg focuses on two factors: (1) outcomes that can lead to high levels of motivation and job satisfaction and (2) outcomes that can prevent people from being dissatisfied. According to **Herzberg's motivator-hygiene theory,** also known as the *two-factor theory,* people have two sets of needs or requirements: motivator needs and hygiene needs.[28] *Motivator needs* are related to the nature of the work itself and how challenging it is. Outcomes such as interesting work, autonomy, responsibility, being able to grow and develop on the job, and a sense of accomplishment and achievement help satisfy motivator needs. In order to have a highly motivated and satisfied workforce, Herzberg suggested, managers should take steps to ensure that employees' motivator needs are being met.

Hygiene needs are related to the physical and psychological context in which the work is performed. Hygiene needs are satisfied by outcomes such as pleasant and comfortable working conditions, fair pay, job security, good relationships with coworkers, and effective supervision. According to Herzberg, when hygiene needs are not met, workers will be dissatisfied, and when hygiene needs are met, workers are not dissatisfied. Satisfying hygiene needs, however, does not result in high levels of motivation or even high levels of job satisfaction. For motivation and job satisfaction to be high, motivator needs must be met.

Herzberg measures dissatisfaction and satisfaction on two different continuums because the factors causing each are different. According to Herzberg, the opposite of satisfaction is not dissatisfaction but, rather, *no* satisfaction. Similarly, the opposite of dissatisfaction is *no* dissatisfaction. Hygiene factors must be adequate for employees to feel no dissatisfaction, while jobs must be sufficiently empowered in order for employees to feel satisfaction. This is illustrated in Figure 8.4.

Many research studies have tested Herzberg's propositions, and, by and large, the theory fails to receive support.[29] Nevertheless, Herzberg's formulations have contributed to our understanding of motivation in at least two ways. First, Herzberg helped researchers and managers focus attention on the important distinction between intrinsic motivation (related to motivator needs) and extrinsic motivation (related to hygiene needs), covered earlier in the chapter. Second, his theory prompted researchers and managers to study how jobs can be designed or redesigned so that they are intrinsically motivating. Recall from Chapter 6 how the job characteristics model can help managers design jobs that are more interesting and motivating.

Hackman and Oldham's job characteristics model outlines five core job dimensions that when incorporated into the design of a job can lead to positive personal and organizational outcomes. Jobs that require the employee to do a

> **Herzberg's motivator-hygiene theory** A need theory that distinguishes between motivator needs (related to the nature of the work itself) and hygiene needs (related to the physical and psychological context in which the work is performed). Herzberg proposed that motivator needs must be met in order for motivation and job satisfaction to be high. This theory is also known as the *two-factor theory.*

> **FIGURE 8.4** Herzberg's Motivation-Hygiene Theory

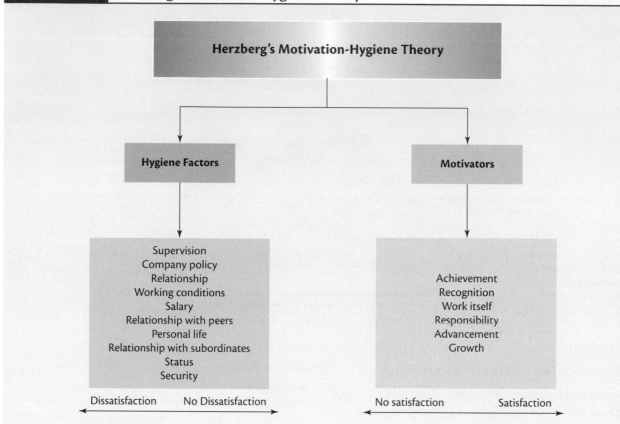

broad range of tasks instead of a narrow range of tasks have a high level of *skill variety*. *Task identity* is the degree to which one associates oneself with the work or profession. The extent that one controls the entire process of production or simply a small part of it determines the task identity. Jobs that involve conceptualizing the product and executing the tasks involved in its production have high levels of task identity. *Task significance* is the degree to which the job is socially relevant and important. The above three core job dimensions have the potential to create a sense of meaningfulness for employees and generally result in positive personal and organizational outcomes. When *autonomy* is built into a job, employees direct their own work. The results of the work activity are known to the employee from the degree of *feedback* they get from doing the work itself. The degree of feedback can be high or low. See Table 8.1 for examples.

The degree to which the core job characteristics should be built into the design of the job depends on the state of the employee's

need for achievement
The extent to which an individual has a strong desire to perform challenging tasks well and to meet personal standards for excellence.

need for affiliation
The extent to which an individual is concerned about establishing and maintaining good interpersonal relations, being liked, and having the people around him or her get along with each other.

need for growth—that is, the desire and ability to take on responsibility and challenging goals. Employees with a strong growth need will be motivated to perform well when the job design has high levels of the core job characteristics, while an employee who has a low need for growth, perhaps due to stress and burnout, will not be motivated to perform well if given additional responsibility.

McClelland's Need for Achievement, Affiliation, and Power

Psychologist David McClelland has extensively researched the needs for achievement, affiliation, and power.[30] The **need for achievement** is the extent to which an individual has a strong desire to perform challenging tasks well and to meet personal standards for excellence. People with a high need for achievement often set clear goals for themselves and like to receive performance feedback. The **need for affiliation** is the extent to which an individual is concerned about

TABLE 8.1	Job Characteristics Model Examples	
Job Characteristics	**Example of High Levels**	**Example of Low Levels**
Skill Variety	A worker at Subway sandwiches who bakes the buns, makes the customer's sandwich, and processes the payment for the order	A worker at McDonald's who grills hamburgers for the entire shift
Task Identity	A seamstress or tailor who designs a suit, creates the pattern, selects the cloth, and sews the garment	A worker in a textile factory who operates a machine that cuts cloth
Task Significance	A firefighter who rescues people and property from devastation	A cashier at a coffee shop
Autonomy	An electrician who decides which jobs to do, when to do them, and how best to fix any problems that arise	An automotive assembly-line worker
Feedback	A chef who cooks and tastes the dish and adjusts the seasonings	A kitchen hand who peels potatoes but has no role in preparing a dish with them and tasting it

establishing and maintaining good interpersonal relations, being liked, and having the people around him or her get along with each other. The **need for power** is the extent to which an individual desires to control or influence others.[31]

While each of these needs is present in each of us to some degree, their importance in the workplace depends upon the position one occupies. For example, research suggests that high needs for achievement and for power are assets for first-line and middle managers and that a high need for power is especially important for upper managers.[32] One study found that U.S. presidents with a relatively high need for power tended to be especially effective during their terms of office.[33] A high need for affiliation may not always be desirable in managers and other leaders because it might lead them to try too hard to be liked by others (including subordinates) rather than doing all they can to ensure that performance is as high as it can and should be. Although most research on these needs has been done in the United States, some studies suggest that the findings may be applicable to people in other countries as well, such as India and New Zealand.[34]

Other Needs

Clearly, more needs motivate employees than those described by these theories. For example, more and more employees are feeling the need for work–life balance and time to take care of their loved ones while also being highly motivated at work. Interestingly enough, recent research suggests that being exposed to nature (even just by being able to

see some trees from your office window) has many beneficial effects and that a lack of such exposure can actually impair well-being and performance.[35] Thus, having some time during the day when one can at least see nature may be another important need.

Managers of successful companies often strive to ensure that as many of their valued employees' needs as possible are satisfied in the workplace.

Describe how process theories of motivation help managers explain high and low performance levels. **LO3**

Process Theories of Motivation

Process theories explain the processes by which employee behaviour can be aroused and then directed. Within the process theories, we cover *expectancy theory, equity theory,* and *goal-setting theory.*

Expectancy Theory

Victor H. Vroom believed that employees consciously decide whether or not to perform at high levels at work. This decision solely depended on the employee's motivation level, which in turn depends on three interrelated factors of expectancy, instrumentality, and valence. **Expectancy theory,** formulated by Vroom in the 1960s, states that motivation will be high when employees believe that high levels of effort will lead

need for power
The extent to which an individual desires to control or influence others.

process theories
Theories that explain the processes by which employee behaviour can be aroused and then directed.

expectancy theory
The theory that motivation will be high when employees believe that high levels of effort will lead to high performance and that high performance will lead to the attainment of desired outcomes.

to high performance and that high performance will lead to receiving desired outcomes. Expectancy theory is one of the most popular theories of work motivation because it focuses on all three parts of the motivation equation: inputs, performance, and outcomes. Expectancy theory identifies three major factors that determine a person's motivation: *expectancy*, *instrumentality*, and *valence* (see Figure 8.5).[36]

Expectancy

Expectancy is a person's perception about the extent to which effort (an input) will result in a certain level of performance. A person's level of expectancy determines whether he or she believes that a high level of effort will result in a high level of performance. People are motivated to put forth a lot of effort on their jobs only if they think that their effort will pay off in high performance— that is, if they have a high expectancy. Think about how motivated you would be to study for a test if you thought that no matter how hard you tried, you would get only a D. Think about how motivated a marketing manager would be who thought that no matter how hard he or she worked, there was no way to increase sales of an unpopular product. In these cases, expectancy is low, so overall motivation is also low.

Members of an organization are motivated to put forth a high level of effort

expectancy In expectancy theory, a perception about the extent to which effort will result in a certain level of performance.

Irving Oil provides leadership training to increase expectancy levels.

only if they think that doing so leads to high performance.[37] In other words, in order for people's motivation to be high, expectancy must be high. In trying to influence levels of expectancy, managers need to make sure that their skilled subordinates believe that if they do try hard, they actually can succeed. In addition to expressing confidence in subordinates, another way for managers to boost subordinates' expectancy levels and motivation is by providing training so that people have all the expertise they need for high performance. Irving Oil is a family-owned and privately held regional energy processing, transporting, and marketing company headquartered in Saint John, New Brunswick. Managers eagerly look

---

FIGURE 8.5 **Expectancy, Instrumentality, and Valence**

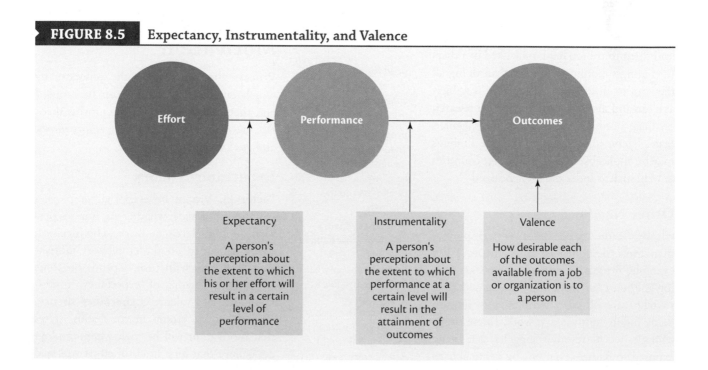

forward to leadership training through a variety of programs that instill lifelong learning and development of the individual, including undergraduate and graduate business programs in partnership with New Brunswick universities, and leadership discussion forums focused on world issues and current events.[38]

The training increases the organizational member's expectancy by improving his or her ability to perform well. At Enterprise Rent-A-Car in the opening case, the Management Training Program helps new hires develop high levels of expectancy, and these high levels of expectancy are maintained as experienced employees are given more responsibility and autonomy to ensure that their branches are profitable and provide excellent customer service.

Instrumentality

Expectancy captures a person's perceptions about the relationship between effort and performance. **Instrumentality,** the second major concept in expectancy theory, is a person's perception about the extent to which performance at a certain level will result in receiving outcomes or rewards (refer to Figure 8.5). According to expectancy theory, employees will be motivated to perform at a high level only if they think that high performance will lead to (or is *instrumental* for attaining) outcomes such as pay, job security, interesting job assignments, bonuses, or a feeling of accomplishment. In other words, instrumentalities must be high for motivation to be high—people must perceive that because of their high performance they will receive outcomes.[39]

Managers promote high levels of instrumentality when they clearly link performance to desired outcomes and communicate this. By making sure that rewards are given to organizational members based on their performance, managers promote high instrumentality and motivation. When rewards are linked to performance in this way, high performers receive more than low performers. In the case of Cognos Inc., the Ottawa-based software company (now a subsidiary of IBM), when employees realized there would be more feedback, more recognition, and more help in meeting their personal goals, they were more motivated to stay with the company. They see the link between performance and reward. Andrew Taylor, from Enterprise Rent-A-Car, raises levels of instrumentality and motivation for employees by linking opportunities for promotion and pay to performance.

Valence

Although all members of an organization must have high expectancies and instrumentalities,

expectancy theory acknowledges that people differ in their preferences for outcomes or rewards. For many people, pay is the most important outcome of working. For others, a feeling of accomplishment or enjoying one's work is more important. The term **valence** refers to how desirable each of the outcomes available from a job or organization is to a person. To motivate organizational members, managers need to determine which outcomes have high valence for them—are highly desired—and make sure that those outcomes are provided when members perform at a high level. From the opening case, it appears that not only pay but also autonomy, responsibility, commitment to environmental sustainability and opportunities for promotions are highly desirable outcomes for many employees at Enterprise Rent-A-Car.

Bringing It All Together

According to expectancy theory, high motivation results from high levels of expectancy, instrumentality, and valence (see Figure 8.6). If any one of these factors is low, motivation is likely to be low. No matter how tightly desired outcomes are linked to performance, if a person thinks that it is practically impossible for him or her to perform at a high level, then motivation to perform at a high level will be exceedingly low. Similarly, if a person does not think that outcomes are linked to high performance, or if a person does not desire the outcomes that are linked to high performance, then motivation to perform at a high level will be low. Managers of successful companies try to ensure that employees' levels of expectancy, instrumentality, and valence are high so that they will be highly motivated (see Figure 8.7).

Equity Theory

Equity theory is a theory of motivation that concentrates on people's perceptions of the fairness of their work *outcomes* relative to, or in proportion to, their work *inputs*. Equity theory complements need and expectancy theories by focusing on how people perceive the relationship between the outcomes they receive from their jobs and organizations and the inputs they contribute. Equity theory was formulated in the 1960s by J. Stacy Adams, who stressed that what is important in determining motivation is the *relative* rather than the *absolute* levels of outcomes a person receives and inputs a person contributes. Specifically, motivation is influenced by the comparison of one's own outcome–input

instrumentality In expectancy theory, a perception about the extent to which performance will result in the attainment of outcomes.

valence In expectancy theory, how desirable each of the outcomes available from a job of organization is to a person.

equity theory A theory of motivation that focuses on people's perceptions of the fairness of their work outcomes relative to their work inputs.

FIGURE 8.6 Expectancy Theory

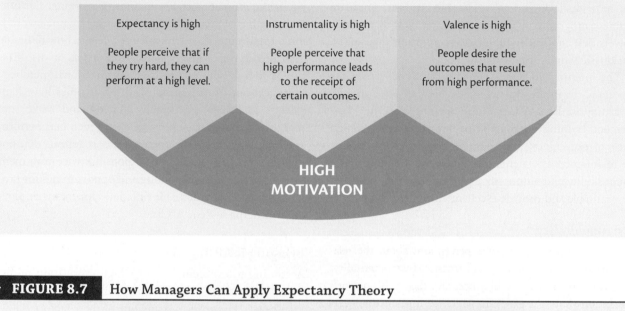

FIGURE 8.7 How Managers Can Apply Expectancy Theory

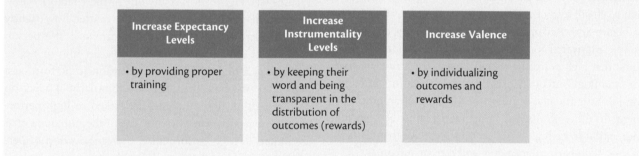

ratio with the outcome–input ratio of a referent.[40] The *referent* could be another person or a group of people who are perceived to be similar to oneself; the referent also could be oneself in a previous job or one's expectations about what outcome–input ratios should be. In a comparison of one's own outcome–input ratio to a referent's ratio, one's *perceptions* of outcomes and inputs (not any objective indicator of them) are key.

Equity

Equity exists when a person perceives his or her own outcome/input ratio to be equal to a referent's outcome/input ratio. Under conditions of equity (see Table 8.2), if a referent receives more outcomes than you receive, the referent contributes proportionally more inputs to the organization, so his or her outcome/input ratio still equals your outcome/input ratio. Maria Lau and Claudia King, for example, both work in a shoe store in a large mall. Lau is paid more per hour

equity The justice, impartiality, and fairness to which all organizational members are entitled.

than King but also contributes more inputs, including being responsible for some of the store's bookkeeping, closing the store, and periodically depositing cash in the bank. When King compares her outcome/input ratio to Lau's (her referents), she perceives the ratios to be equitable because Lau's higher level of pay (an outcome) is proportional to her higher level of inputs (bookkeeping, closing the store, and going to the bank).

Similarly, under conditions of equity, if you receive more outcomes than a referent, then your inputs are perceived to be proportionally higher. Continuing with our example, when Lau compares her outcome–input ratio to King's (her referent's) ratio, she perceives them to be equitable because her higher level of pay is proportional to her higher level of inputs.

When equity exists, people are motivated to continue contributing their current levels of inputs to their organizations to receive their current levels of outcomes. If people wish to increase their outcomes under conditions of equity, they are motivated to increase their inputs.

Managers must promote a perception of fairness and equity.

Inequity

Inequity, lack of fairness, exists when a person's outcome/input ratio is not perceived to be equal to a referent's. Inequity creates pressure or tension inside people and motivates them to restore equity by bringing the two ratios back into balance.

There are two types of inequity: underpayment inequity and overpayment inequity (see Table 8.2). **Underpayment inequity** exists when a person's own outcome/input ratio is perceived to be *less* than that of a referent: In comparing yourself to a referent, you think that you are *not* receiving the outcomes you should be receiving, given your inputs. **Overpayment inequity** exists when a person perceives that his or her own outcome/input ratio is *greater* than that of a referent: in comparing yourself to a referent, you think that you are receiving *more* outcomes than you should be, given your inputs.

Ways to Restore Equity

According to equity theory, both underpayment inequity and overpayment inequity create tension that motivates most people to restore equity by bringing the ratios back into balance.[41] See Figure 8.8. When people experience *underpayment* inequity, they may be motivated to lower their inputs by reducing their working hours, putting forth less effort on the job, or being absent, or they may be motivated to increase their outcomes by asking for a raise or a promotion. Take an employee like Mary Campbell, a financial analyst at a large corporation. She noticed that she was working longer hours and getting more work accomplished than a coworker who had the same position, yet they both received the exact same pay and other outcomes. To restore equity, Campbell decided to stop coming in early and staying late. Alternatively, she could have tried to restore equity by trying to increase her outcomes by, for example, asking her boss for a raise.

When people experience *underpayment* inequity and other means of equity restoration fail, they can change their perceptions of their own or the referent's inputs or outcomes. For example, they may realize that their referent is really working on more difficult projects than they are or that they really take more time off from work than their referent does. Alternatively, if people who feel that they are underpaid have other employment

inequity Lack of fairness.

underpayment inequity Inequity that exists when a person perceives that his or her own outcome/input ratio is less than the ratio of a referent.

overpayment inequity Inequity that exists when a person perceives that his or her own outcome/input ratio is greater than the ratio of a referent.

▶ TABLE 8.2	Equity Theory			
Condition	**Person**		**Referent**	**Example**
Equity	$\frac{\text{Outcomes}}{\text{Inputs}}$	=	$\frac{\text{Outcomes}}{\text{Inputs}}$	An engineer perceives that he contributes more inputs (time and effort), and receives proportionally more outcomes (a higher salary and choice job assignments) than his referent does.
Underpayment inequity	$\frac{\text{Outcomes}}{\text{Inputs}}$	< (less than)	$\frac{\text{Outcomes}}{\text{Inputs}}$	An engineer perceives that he contributes more inputs but receives the same outcomes as his referent.
Overpayment inequity	$\frac{\text{Outcomes}}{\text{Inputs}}$	> (greater than)	$\frac{\text{Outcomes}}{\text{Inputs}}$	An engineer perceives that he contributes the same inputs but receives more outcomes than his referent.

> **FIGURE 8.8** Possible Actions Taken to Restore Equity

Actions Taken to Restore Equity

Underpayment Inequity	Overpayment Inequity	Equity
• Reduce inputs • Increase outcomes • Change the referent • Quit the job	• Change the perception of one's own or the referent's inputs and outcomes • Change the referent	• Continue contributing current levels of inputs to receive current levels of outcomes • No changes are made to inputs or outcomes

options, they may leave the organization. As an example, John Steinberg, an assistant principal in a high school, experienced underpayment inequity when he realized that all of the other assistant principals of high schools in his school district had received promotions to the position of principal even though they had been in their jobs for a shorter time than he had been. Steinberg's performance had always been appraised as being high, so after his repeated requests for a promotion went unheeded, he found a job as a principal in a different school district.

When people experience *overpayment* inequity, they may try to restore equity by changing their perceptions of their own or their referents' inputs or outcomes. Equity can be restored when people "realize" that they are contributing more inputs than they originally thought. Equity also can be restored by perceiving the referent's inputs to be lower or the referent's outcomes to be higher than one originally thought. When equity is restored in this way, actual inputs and outcomes are unchanged and the person being overpaid takes no real action. What has changed is how people think about or view their own or the referent's inputs and outcomes. For example, employee Susan Martineau experienced overpayment inequity when she realized that she was being paid $2 an hour more than a coworker who had the same job as hers in a record store and who contributed the same amount of inputs. Martineau restored equity by changing her perceptions of her inputs. She "realized" that she worked harder than her coworker and solved more problems that came up in the store.

Experiencing either overpayment or underpayment inequity, you might decide that your referent is not appropriate because, for example, the referent is too different from yourself. Choosing a more appropriate referent may bring the ratios back into balance. Angela Martinez, a middle manager in the engineering department of a chemical company, experienced overpayment inequity when she realized that she was being paid quite a bit more than her friend, who was a middle manager in the marketing department of the same company. After thinking about the discrepancy for a while, Martinez decided that engineering and marketing were so different that she should not be comparing her job to her friend's job even though they were both middle managers. Martinez restored equity by changing her referent; she picked a middle manager in the engineering department as a new referent.

Tough economic times and increased global competition have resulted in some workers putting in longer and longer working hours (i.e., increasing their inputs) without any kind of increase in their outcomes. For those whose referents are not experiencing a similar change, perceptions of inequity are likely.

Motivation is highest when as many people as possible in an organization perceive that they are being equitably treated, that is, their outcomes and inputs are in balance. Top contributors and performers are motivated to continue contributing a high level of inputs because they are receiving the outcomes they deserve. Mediocre contributors and performers realize that if they want to increase their outcomes, they have to increase their inputs. Managers of effective organizations, like Jack and Andrew Taylor at Enterprise Rent-A-Car, realize the importance of equity for motivation and performance and continually strive to ensure that employees believe they are being equitably treated.

Goal-Setting Theory

Goal-setting theory focuses on motivating workers to contribute their inputs to their jobs and organizations; in this way it is similar to expectancy theory and equity theory. But goal-setting theory takes this focus a step further by considering as well how managers can ensure that organizational members focus their inputs in the direction of high performance and the achievement of organizational goals.

Ed Locke and Gary Latham, the leading researchers on goal-setting theory, suggest that the goals that organizational members strive to achieve determine their motivation and subsequent performance. A *goal* is what a person is trying to accomplish through his or her efforts and behaviours.[42] Just as you may have a goal to get a good grade in this course, members of an organization have goals that they strive to meet. For example, salespeople at Harry Rosen strive to meet sales goals, while top managers pursue market share and profitability goals.

Goal-setting theory suggests that in order to result in high motivation and performance, goals must be *specific and difficult*.[43] Specific goals are often quantitative—a salesperson's goal to sell $200 worth of merchandise each day, a scientist's goal to finish a project in one year, a CEO's goal to reduce debt by 40 percent and increase revenues by 20 percent, a restaurant manager's goal to serve 150 customers each evening. In contrast to specific goals, vague goals such as "doing your best" or "selling as much as you can" do not have much motivational force. Difficult goals are ones that are hard but not impossible to attain. In contrast to difficult goals, easy goals are those that practically everyone can attain, and moderate goals are goals that about one-half of the people can attain. Both easy and moderate goals have less motivational power than difficult goals.

Regardless of whether specific difficult goals are set by managers, workers, or managers and workers together, they lead to high levels of motivation and performance. When managers set goals for their subordinates, it is important that their subordinates accept the goals or agree to work toward them and also that they are committed to them or really want to attain them. Some managers find that having subordinates participate in the actual setting of goals boosts their acceptance of and commitment to the goals. It is also important for organizational members to receive *feedback* about how they are doing; feedback can often be provided by the performance appraisal and feedback component of an organization's human resource management system (see Chapter 11).

goal-setting theory
A theory that focuses on identifying the types of goals that are most effective in producing high levels of motivation and performance and explaining why goals have these effects.

Specific, difficult goals affect motivation in two ways. First, they motivate people to contribute more inputs to their jobs. Specific, difficult goals cause people to put forth high levels of effort, for example. Just as you would study harder if you were trying to get an A in a course instead of a C, so too will a salesperson work harder to reach a $200 sales goal instead of a $100 sales goal. Specific, difficult goals also cause people to be more persistent than easy, moderate, or vague goals when they run into difficulties. Salespeople who are told to sell as much as possible might stop trying on a slow day, whereas having a specific, difficult goal to reach causes them to keep trying.

A second way in which specific, difficult goals affect motivation is by helping people focus their inputs in the right direction. These goals let people know what they should be focusing their attention on, be it increasing the quality of customer service or sales or lowering new product development times. The fact that the goals are specific and difficult also frequently causes people to develop *action plans* for reaching them.[44] Action plans can include the strategies to attain the goals and timetables or schedules for the completion of different activities crucial to goal attainment. Like the goals themselves, action plans also help ensure that efforts are focused in the right direction and that people do not get sidetracked along the way.

Although specific, difficult goals have been found to increase motivation and performance in a wide variety of jobs and organizations both in Canada and abroad, recent research suggests that they may detract from performance under certain conditions. When people are performing complicated and very challenging tasks that require them to focus on a considerable amount of learning, specific, difficult goals may actually impair performance.[45]

Goals must be challenging to be motivating.

Striving to reach such goals may direct some of a person's attention away from learning about the task and toward trying to figure out how to achieve the goal. Once a person has learned the task and it no longer seems complicated or difficult, then the assignment of specific, difficult goals is likely to have its usual effects. Additionally, for work that is very creative and uncertain, specific, difficult goals may be detrimental.

LO4 Identify the motivation lessons that managers can learn from learning theories of motivation.

Learning Theories

The basic premise of **learning theories** as applied to organizations is that managers can increase employee motivation and performance by the ways they link the outcomes that employees receive to the performance of desired behaviours and the attainment of goals. Thus, learning theory focuses on the linkage between performance and outcomes in the motivation equation (refer back to Figure 8.2).

learning theories
Theories that focus on increasing employee motivation and performance by linking the outcomes that employees receive to the performance of desired behaviours and the attainment of goals.

learning A relatively permanent change in knowledge or behaviour that results from practice or experience.

operant conditioning theory The theory that people learn to perform behaviours that lead to desired consequences and learn not to perform behaviours that lead to undesired consequences.

reinforcer Any stimulus that causes a given behaviour to be repeated.

positive reinforcement Giving people outcomes they desire when they perform organizationally functional behaviours.

Learning can be defined as a relatively permanent change in a person's knowledge or behaviour that results from practice or experience.[46] Learning takes place in organizations when people learn to perform certain behaviours to receive certain outcomes. For example, a person learns to perform at a higher level than in the past or to come to work earlier because he or she is motivated to obtain the outcomes that result from these behaviours, such as a pay raise or praise from a supervisor. In the opening case, Enterprise Rent-A-Car's emphasis on training ensures that new hires learn how to provide excellent customer service and perform all the tasks necessary for successful branch operations.

Of the different learning theories, operant conditioning or *reinforcement theory* and *social learning theory* provide the most guidance to managers in their efforts to have a highly motivated workforce. According to **operant conditioning theory,** developed by psychologist B. F. Skinner, people learn to perform behaviours that lead to desired consequences and learn not to perform behaviours that lead to undesired consequences.[47]

Hence, it is a motivation theory that looks at the relationship between behaviour and its consequences. Skinner's theory suggests that people will be motivated to perform at a high level and attain their work goals to the extent that high performance and goal attainment allow them to obtain outcomes they desire. Similarly, people avoid performing behaviours that lead to outcomes they do not desire. By linking the performance of *specific behaviours* to the attainment of *specific outcomes,* managers can motivate organizational members to perform in ways that help an organization achieve its goals.

Operant conditioning theory provides four tools that managers can use to motivate high performance and prevent workers from engaging in absenteeism and other behaviours that detract from organizational effectiveness. These tools are positive reinforcement, negative reinforcement, extinction, and punishment.[48]

Positive reinforcement and punishment involve presenting a stimulus or reinforcer, while negative reinforcement and extinction involve removing the *stimulus* or *reinforcer.* A **reinforcer** is any stimulus that causes a behaviour to be repeated. See Table 8.3. Managers use these four techniques to modify the dysfunctional workplace behaviours of employees such as absenteeism, and lack of punctuality.

Positive Reinforcement

Positive reinforcement gives people outcomes they desire when they perform well. These outcomes, called *positive reinforcers,* include any outcome that a person desires, such as good pay, praise, or a promotion. Performing well might include producing high-quality goods and services, providing high-quality customer service, and meeting deadlines. By linking positive reinforcers to positive performance, managers motivate people to perform the desired behaviours. For instance, managers at Brandon's

People respond poorly to punishment and coercion.

> **TABLE 8.3** Four Operant Conditioning Techniques

Action	Type of Stimulus	
	Positive	**Negative**
Present the Reinforcer or Stimulus	**Positive reinforcement**—increases the desired behaviour. Give a reward when desired actions are exhibited.	**Punishment**—decreases the undesired behaviour. Take something of value away when the undesired action is exhibited.
	For example: Jon arrives at work early (desired action) and is given praise (positive stimulus) by his manager.	**For example:** Sarah arrives at work late consistently (undesired action) and is made to stay late (negative stimulus) by her manager to make up the time.
Remove the Reinforcer or Stimulus	**Extinction**—decreases the undesired behaviour. Ignore the undesired behaviour when it occurs to stop it from being repeated.	**Negative reinforcement**—increases the desired behaviour. Remove the unpleasant consequence or punishment when the desired behaviour is exhibited.
	For example: Ash constantly asks inappropriate questions at staff meetings. Rather than acknowledging Ash (positive stimulus is removed) and giving her a platform to be heard, her manager ignores her raised hand.	**For example:** When Sarah arrives at work on time (desired action), her manager does not demand that she work late (negative stimulus is removed).

hog slaughterhouse offer a variety of incentives to encourage workers to show up for their shifts. To be eligible for a truck raffle, held every three months, employees have to show up for every one of their shifts during that period. Employees get bonuses on top of their regular wage for perfect attendance during shorter periods. The incentive program has paid off. Before the rewards, 12 percent of the employees skipped work each day. Since the rewards, absenteeism has dropped to about 7 to 8 percent.

Negative Reinforcement

Negative reinforcement also can be used to encourage members of an organization to perform desired or organizationally functional behaviours. Managers using negative reinforcement actually eliminate or remove undesired outcomes once the desired behaviour is performed. These undesired outcomes, called *negative reinforcers,* can include unpleasant assignments, a manager's constant nagging or criticism, or the ever-present threat of termination. When negative reinforcement is used, people are motivated to perform behaviours because they want to avoid or stop receiving undesired outcomes. For example, when a salesperson exceeds the sales quota, his or her manager cancels the pep-talk meetings. In this case, the reinforcer or negative stimulus is removed (the pep-talk lecture) because the salesperson has performed the desired behaviour (booked more than expected sales).

Whenever possible, managers should try to use positive reinforcement. Negative reinforcement can make for a very unpleasant work environment and even a negative culture in an organization. No one likes to be nagged, threatened, or exposed to other kinds of negative outcomes. The use of negative reinforcement sometimes causes subordinates to resent managers and try to get back at them.

Even managers who use positive reinforcement (and refrain from using negative reinforcement) can get into trouble if they are not careful to identify the right behaviours to reinforce—behaviours that are truly functional for the organization. Doing this is not always as straightforward as it might seem. First, it is crucial for managers to choose behaviours over which subordinates have control; in other words, subordinates must have the freedom and opportunity to perform the behaviours that are being reinforced. Second, it is crucial that these behaviours contribute to organizational effectiveness.

Extinction

Sometimes members of an organization are motivated to perform behaviours that actually detract from organizational effectiveness. According to the theory, all behaviour is controlled or determined by its consequences. One way for managers to curtail the performance of dysfunctional behaviours is to eliminate whatever is reinforcing them. This process is called **extinction.**

negative reinforcement Eliminating or removing undesired outcomes once people have performed organizationally functional behaviours.

extinction Stopping the performance of dysfunctional behaviours by eliminating whatever is reinforcing them.

Suppose a manager has a subordinate who frequently stops by the office to chat—sometimes about work-related matters but at other times about various topics ranging from politics to last night's football game. The manager and the subordinate share certain interests and views, so these conversations can get quite involved, and both seem to enjoy them. The manager, however, realizes that these frequent and sometimes lengthy conversations are actually causing him to stay at work later in the evenings to make up for the time he loses during the day. The manager also realizes that he is actually reinforcing his subordinate's behaviour by acting interested in the topics the subordinate brings up and responding at length to them. To extinguish this behaviour, the manager stops acting interested in these non–work-related conversations and keeps responses polite and friendly but brief. No longer being reinforced with a pleasant conversation, the subordinate eventually ceases to be motivated to interrupt the manager during working hours to discuss non-work issues.

Punishment

Sometimes managers cannot rely on extinction to eliminate dysfunctional behaviours because they do not have control over whatever is reinforcing the behaviour or because they cannot afford the time needed for extinction

Non-productive workplace behaviours go the way of the dinosaur when extinction is used as a reinforcement technique.

to work. When employees are performing dangerous behaviours or those that are illegal or unethical, the behaviours need to be stopped immediately. Sexual harassment, for example, is an organizationally dysfunctional behaviour that cannot be tolerated. In such cases managers often rely on **punishment,** administering undesired or negative consequences to subordinates when they perform the dysfunctional behaviours. Punishments used by organizations range from verbal reprimands to pay cuts, temporary suspensions, demotions, and terminations. Punishment, however, can have unintended side effects—resentment, loss of self-respect, a desire for retaliation, and so on— and should be used only when absolutely necessary.

To avoid the unintended side effects of punishment, managers should keep in mind these guidelines:

- Downplay the emotional element involved in punishment. Make it clear that you are punishing a person's performance of a dysfunctional behaviour, not the person him- or herself.

- Try to punish dysfunctional behaviours as soon after they occur as possible, and make sure the negative consequence is a source of punishment for the individuals involved. Be certain that organizational members know exactly why they are being punished.

- Try to avoid punishing someone in front of others, for this can hurt a person's self-respect and lower esteem in the eyes of coworkers as well as make coworkers feel uncomfortable.[49] Even so, making organizational members aware that an individual who has committed a serious infraction has been punished can sometimes be effective in preventing future infractions and teaching all members of the organization that certain behaviours are unacceptable. For example, when organizational members are informed that a manager who has sexually harassed subordinates has been punished, they learn or are reminded of the fact that sexual harassment is not tolerated in the organization.

Managers and students alike often confuse negative reinforcement and punishment. To avoid such confusion, keep in mind the two major differences between them. First, negative reinforcement is used to promote the performance of functional behaviours in organizations; punishment is used to stop the performance of dysfunctional behaviours. Second, negative reinforcement entails the *removal* of a negative consequence when functional

punishment
Administering an undesired or negative consequence when dysfunctional behaviour occurs.

behaviours are performed while punishment entails the *administration* of negative consequences when dysfunctional behaviours are performed.

Social Learning Theory

Social learning theory proposes that motivation results not only from direct experience of rewards and punishments but also from a person's thoughts and beliefs. Social learning theory extends operant conditioning's contribution to managers' understanding of motivation by explaining (1) how people can be motivated by observing other people perform a behaviour and be reinforced for doing so *(vicarious learning)*, (2) how people can be motivated to control their behaviour themselves *(self-reinforcement)*, and (3) how people's beliefs about their ability to successfully perform a behaviour affect motivation *(self-efficacy)*.[50] We look briefly at each of these motivators.

Vicarious Learning

Vicarious learning, often called *observational learning,* occurs when a person (the learner) becomes motivated to perform a behaviour by watching another person (the model) perform the behaviour and be positively reinforced for doing so. Vicarious learning is a powerful source of motivation on many jobs in which people learn to perform functional behaviours by watching others. Salespeople learn how to be helpful to customers, medical school students learn how to treat patients, law clerks learn how to practise law, and nonmanagers learn how to be managers, in part, by observing experienced members of an organization perform these behaviours properly and be reinforced for them. In general, people are more likely to be motivated to imitate the behaviour of models that are highly competent, are (to some extent) experts in the behaviour, have high status, receive attractive reinforcers, and are friendly or approachable.[51]

To promote vicarious learning, managers should strive to have the learner meet the following conditions:

- The learner observes the model performing the behaviour.
- The learner accurately perceives the model's behaviour.
- The learner remembers the behaviour.
- The learner has the skills and abilities needed to perform the behaviour.
- The learner sees or knows that the model is positively reinforced for the behaviour.[52] One of the ways in which aspiring physicians learn is by watching skilled physicians treat patients.

Self-Reinforcement

Although managers are often the providers of reinforcement in organizations, sometimes people motivate themselves through self-reinforcement. People can control their own behaviour by setting goals for themselves and then reinforcing themselves when they achieve the goals.[53] **Self-reinforcers** are any desired or attractive outcomes or rewards that people can give to themselves for good performance, such as a feeling of accomplishment, going to a movie, having dinner out, buying a new CD, or taking time out for a golf game. When members of an organization control their own behaviour through self-reinforcement, managers do not need to spend as much time as they ordinarily would trying to motivate and control behaviour through the administration of consequences because subordinates are controlling and motivating themselves. In fact, this self-control is often referred to as the *self-management of behaviour.*

When employees are highly skilled and are responsible for creating new goods and services, managers typically rely on self-control and self-management of behaviour, as is the case at Google. Employees at Google are given the flexibility and autonomy to experiment, take risks, and sometimes fail as they work on new projects. They are encouraged to learn from their failures and apply what they learn to subsequent projects.[54] Google's engineers are given one day a week to work on their own projects that they are highly involved with, and new products such as Google News often emerge from these projects.[55]

Self-Efficacy

Self-efficacy is a person's belief about his or her ability to perform a behaviour successfully.[56] Even with all the most attractive consequences or reinforcers hinging on high performance, people are not going to be motivated if they do not think that they can actually perform at a high level. Similarly, when people control their own behaviour, they are likely to set for themselves difficult goals that will lead to outstanding accomplishments only if they think that they have the capability to reach those goals. Thus, self-efficacy influences motivation both when managers provide reinforcement and when workers themselves provide it.[57] The greater the self-efficacy, the greater is the

social learning theory A theory that takes into account how learning and motivation are influenced by people's thoughts and beliefs and their observations of other people's behaviour.

vicarious learning Learning that occurs when the learner becomes motivated to perform a behaviour by watching another person perform it and be reinforced for doing so; also called *observational learning.*

self-reinforcer Any desired or attractive outcome or reward that a person gives to himself or herself for good performance.

self-efficacy A person's belief about his or her ability to perform a behaviour successfully.

motivation and performance. In the opening case, managers at Enterprise Rent-A-Car boost self-efficacy by providing employees with training, increasing their levels of autonomy and responsibility as they gain experience with the company, and expressing confidence in their ability to manage their own units. Such verbal persuasion, as well as a person's own past performance and accomplishments and the accomplishments of other people, plays a role in determining a person's self-efficacy.

LO5 Explain how managers use reward systems to increase employee motivation.

Total Reward Strategy

Research by Gallup shows that in world-class organizations the ratio of engaged to actively disengaged employees is about 10:1. In average organizations, the ratio of engaged to actively disengaged employees is less than 2:1.[58] How can managers use rewards to motivate employees?

A **total reward strategy** encompasses both intrinsically and extrinsically motivating factors such as giving positive reinforcement, recognition, opportunities for advancement and personal growth, responsibility, adequate training to raise expectancy levels, and individualized benefits such as flexible hours for work–life balance. We save our discussion of training and benefits for Chapter 11. Here we focus on the basic principle that managers must recognize that reward systems must be tailored to individual needs if they are to be motivating.

When it comes to employees' perceptions of fair rewards, the top concern is neither total pay nor increases in salary. It is access to career development opportunities. A recent survey reveals the top five concerns in reward fairness are[59]:

1. career development opportunities

2. merit increases

3. base pay amounts

4. non-financial recognition

5. employee development and training

One thing that motivation theories help managers understand is that people are motivated by the outcomes they receive for their efforts. These outcomes can be either intrinsically motivating or extrinsically motivating. A total reward strategy encompasses both of these elements. Receiving non-financial recognition for a job well done is one of the top five concerns in fairness and

one of the simplest forms of engaging an employee. It makes people feel good to have their efforts appreciated by managers. **Employee recognition programs** are based on the principle of giving personal attention to employee performance, and expressing interest, approval, and appreciation for a job well done. When employees are recognized by managers for the important contributions they make to the organization, they are more likely to be motivated toward high levels of performance.

total reward strategy
A total reward strategy encompasses both intrinsically and extrinsically motivating factors.

employee recognition programs Management expressions of interest, approval and appreciation for a job well done by individuals or groups of employees.

Pay and Motivation

Managers can also use pay to motivate employees to perform at a high level and attain their work goals. Pay is used to motivate entry-level workers, first-line and middle managers, and even top managers such as CEOs. Pay is an extrinsic motivator, and is only one part of a total rewards strategy. How compensation and benefit structures and levels are determined is discussed in Chapter 11. Here we focus on how pay can be used to motivate people to perform behaviours that help an organization achieve its goals, and how it can be used to motivate people to join and remain with an organization.

As illustrated in Figure 8.9, pay is an important extrinsic motivating factor addressed by both *need* and *process theories*.

- **Need theories:** Physiological needs are satisfied through earning wages needed to purchase food, clothing, and shelter. Pay levels must be adequate to avoid feeling dissatisfaction but do not contribute to one's level of satisfaction, according to Herzberg.

- **Expectancy theory:** Instrumentality, the linkage between performance and outcomes such as pay, must be high for motivation to be high. Pay is also an outcome that has a positive valence.

- **Goal-setting theory:** Outcomes such as pay should be linked to the attainment of goals.

- **Equity theory:** Outcomes such as pay should be distributed in proportion to the level of inputs.

- **Learning theories:** The distribution of pay and other rewards should depend on the performance of desirable workplace behaviours.

As these theories suggest, to promote high motivation, managers should base the distribution of pay on performance levels so that high performers receive more pay than do low performers (other things being equal).[60]

> **FIGURE 8.9**   How Pay Motivates

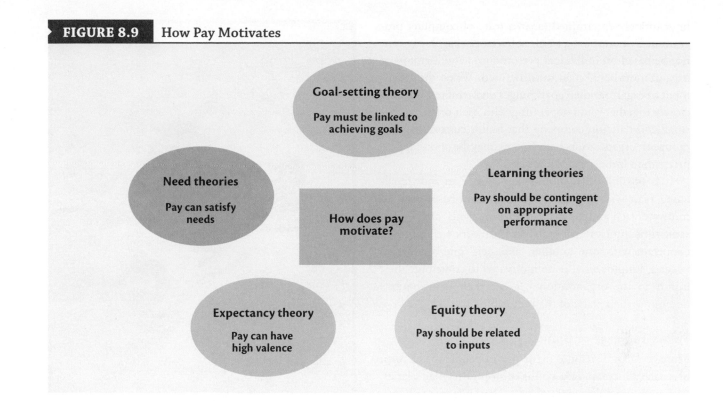

Goal-setting theory

Pay must be linked to achieving goals

Need theories

Pay can satisfy needs

Learning theories

Pay should be contingent on appropriate performance

How does pay motivate?

Expectancy theory

Pay can have high valence

Equity theory

Pay should be related to inputs

merit pay plan A compensation plan that bases pay on performance.

It should be remembered that pay is, however, only *one* part of a total reward strategy.

In deciding whether to pay for performance, managers also have to determine whether to use salary increases or bonuses. Thus some pay-for-performance programs (particularly those that use bonuses) are *variable-pay programs* or **merit pay plans,** where earnings go up and down annually based on performance.[61] Thus, there is no guarantee that an individual will earn as much this year as the last.

The number of employees affected by variable-pay plans has been rising in Canada. Keri Humber, a senior compensation consultant with Hewitt Associates, remarked, "In this economy, especially, employers must continue to ensure their corporate pay strategies are properly executed. . . . In order to remain competitive and continue to attract quality talent, organizations will need to look beyond base salary for ways to reward and motivate their employees. . . . Variable pay plans are one alternative."[62]

> "*. . . In order to remain competitive and continue to attract quality talent, organizations will need to look beyond base salary for ways to reward and motivate their employees.*"
>
> *Keri Humber, Hewitt Associates*

These programs are more common among nonunionized workers[63]; Prem Benimadhu from the Conference Board of Canada notes, "Canadian unions have been very allergic to variable compensation."[64] In addition to wage uncertainty, employees may object to pay for performance if they feel that factors out of their control might affect the extent to which bonuses are possible.

Basing Variable Pay Plans on Individual, Group, or Organizational Performance

Managers can base merit pay on individual, group, or organizational performance. Perhaps this is why a recent survey on reward fairness found that variable pay, such as bonuses and incentives, was not among the top five concerns (listed above). When individual performance (such as the dollar value of merchandise a salesperson sells, the number of loudspeakers a factory worker assembles, and a lawyer's billable hours) can be accurately determined, individual motivation is likely to be highest when pay is based on individual performance.[65] When members of an organization work closely together and individual performance cannot be accurately determined (as in a team of computer programmers developing a single software package), pay cannot be based on individual performance, and a group- or organization-based plan must be used. When the attainment of organizational goals hinges on members' working closely together and cooperating with each other (as in a small construction company that builds custom homes), group or organization-based plans may be more appropriate than individual-based plans.[66]

It is possible to combine elements of an individual-based plan with a group or organization-based plan to motivate each individual to perform highly and, at the same time, motivate all individuals to work well together, cooperate with one another, and help one another as needed. Employees also are motivated to contribute their inputs to the organization because their contributions determine their share of the bonus fund.

Salary Increase or Bonus?

Managers can distribute merit pay to people in the form of a salary increase or a bonus on top of regular salaries. Although the dollar amount of a salary increase or bonus might be identical, bonuses tend to have more motivational impact for at least three reasons. First, salary levels are typically based on performance levels, cost-of-living increases, and so forth from the day people start working in an organization, which means that the absolute level of the salary is based largely on factors unrelated to *current* performance. A 5 percent merit increase in salary, for example, may seem relatively small in comparison to one's total salary. Second, a current salary increase may be affected by other factors in addition to performance, such as cost-of-living increases or across-the-board market adjustments. Third, because organizations rarely reduce salaries, salary levels tend to vary less than performance levels do. Related to this point is the fact that bonuses give managers more flexibility in distributing outcomes. If an organization is doing well, bonuses can be relatively high to reward employees for their contributions. However, unlike salary increases, bonus levels can be reduced when an organization's performance lags. All in all, bonus plans have more motivational impact than salary increases because the amount of the bonus can be directly and exclusively based on performance.[67]

Consistent with the lessons from motivation theories, bonuses can be linked directly to performance and vary from year to year and employee to employee. In addition to receiving pay raises and bonuses, high-level managers and executives are sometimes granted employee stock options. **Employee stock options** are financial instruments that entitle the bearer to buy shares of an

Pay is only one aspect of a total rewards strategy.

organization's stock at a certain price during a certain period of time or under certain conditions.[68] For example, in addition to salaries, stock options are sometimes used to attract high-level managers. The exercise price is the stock price at which the bearer can buy the stock, and the vesting conditions specify when the bearer can actually buy the stock at the exercise price. The option's exercise price is generally set equal to the market price of the stock on the date it is granted, and the vesting conditions might specify that the manager has to have worked at the organization for 12 months or perhaps met some performance target (increase in profits) before being able to exercise the option. In high-technology firms and start-ups, options are sometimes used in a similar fashion for employees at various levels in the organization.[69]

From a motivation standpoint, stock options are used not so much to reward past individual performance but, rather, to motivate employees to work in the future for the good of the company as a whole. This is true because stock options issued at current stock prices have value in the future only if an organization does

employee stock options Financial instruments that entitle the bearer to buy shares of an organization's stock at a certain price during a certain period of time or under certain conditions.

well and its stock price appreciates; thus, giving employees stock options should encourage them to help the organization improve its performance over time.[70] At high-technology start-ups and dot-coms, stock options have often motivated potential employees to leave promising jobs in larger companies and work for the start-ups. In the late 1990s and early 2000s, many dot-commers were devastated to learn not only that their stock options were worthless, because their companies went out of business or were doing poorly, but also that they were unemployed. Unfortunately, stock options have also led to unethical behaviour; for example, sometimes individuals seek to artificially inflate the value of a company's stock to increase the value of stock options.

Examples of Merit Pay Plans

Managers can choose among several merit pay plans, depending on the work that employees perform and other considerations. Using *piece-rate pay,* an individual-based merit plan, managers base employees' pay on the number of units each employee produces, whether televisions, computer components, or welded auto parts. Advances in information technology are currently simplifying the administration of piece-rate pay in a variety of industries. For example, farmers typically allocated piece-rate pay to farm workers through a laborious, time-consuming process. Now, they can rely on metal buttons the size of a dime that farm workers clip to their shirts or put in their pockets. Made by Dallas Semiconductor Corporation, these buttons are customized for use in farming by Agricultural Data Systems, based in Laguna Niguel, California.[71] Each button contains a semiconductor linked to payroll computers by a wand-like probe in the field.[72] The wand relays the number of boxes of fruit or vegetables that each worker picks as well as the type and quality of the produce picked, the location it was picked in, and the time and the date. The buttons are activated by touching them with the probe; hence, they are called Touch Memory Buttons. Managers generally find that the buttons save time, improve accuracy, and provide valuable information about their crops and yields.[73]

Using *commission pay,* another individual-based merit pay plan, managers base pay on a percentage of sales. Managers at the successful real-estate company Re/Max International Inc. use commission pay for their agents, who are paid a percentage of their sales. Some department stores use commission pay for their salespeople.

Examples of organizational-based merit pay plans include the Scanlon plan and profit sharing. The *Scanlon plan* (developed by Joseph Scanlon, a union leader in a US steel and tin plant in the 1920s) focuses on reducing expenses or cutting costs; members of an organization are motivated to come up with and implement cost-cutting strategies because a percentage of the cost savings achieved during a specified time is distributed to the employees.[74] Under *profit sharing,* employees receive a share of an organization's profits. Approximately 16 percent of the employees in medium or large firms receive profit sharing, and about 25 percent of small firms give their employees a share of the profits.[75] Regardless of the specific kind of plan that is used, managers should always strive to link pay to the performance of behaviours that help an organization achieve its goals.

Japanese managers in large corporations have long shunned merit pay plans in favour of plans that reward seniority. However, more and more Japanese companies are adopting merit-based pay due to its motivational benefits; among such companies are SiteDesign,[76] Tokio Marine and Fire Insurance, and Hissho Iwai, a trading organization.[77]

Summary and Review

LO1 The Nature of Motivation Motivation encompasses the psychological forces within a person that determine the direction of his or her behaviour in an organization, level of effort, and level of persistence in the face of obstacles. Managers strive to motivate employees to contribute their inputs to an organization, to focus these inputs in the direction of high performance, and to ensure that people receive the outcomes they desire when they perform at a high level. People are motivated to work hard *extrinsically* to acquire material rewards or avoid punishment, *intrinsically* for its own sake, and *prosocially* to help others.

LO2 Need Theories of Motivation *Need theories* suggest that to motivate their workforces, managers should determine what needs people are trying to satisfy in organizations and then ensure that people receive outcomes that satisfy these needs when they perform at a high level and contribute to organizational effectiveness. Managers can design jobs with five core dimensions in mind to make them more interesting and motivating.

LO3 Process Theories of Motivation *Process theories* help managers explain why people act the way they do and thus help managers understand the roots of high and low performance levels among employees.

LO4 Learning Theories *Learning theories* help managers see the link between giving rewards for high performance behaviour and the repetition of that behaviour among employees.

LO5 Total Reward Strategy Each of the motivation theories discussed in this chapter alludes to the importance of pay and suggests that pay should be based on performance. Pay is only one part of a *total reward strategy,* which includes both extrinsic elements such as pay and intrinsic elements such as providing opportunities for growth and development and non-financial recognition.

KEY TERMS

employee recognition
   programs
employee stock options
equity
equity theory
expectancy
expectancy theory
extinction

extrinsically motivated
   behaviour
goal-setting theory
Herzberg's motivator-
   hygiene theory
inequity
input
instrumentality

intrinsically motivated
   behaviour
learning
learning theories
Maslow's hierarchy of needs
merit pay plan
motivation
need

need for achievement

need for affiliation

need for power

need theories

negative reinforcement

operant conditioning
   theory

outcome

overpayment inequity

positive reinforcement

process theories

prosocially motivated
   behaviour

punishment

reinforcer

self-efficacy

self-reinforcer

social learning theory

total reward strategy

underpayment
   inequity

valence

vicarious learning

WRAP-UP TO OPENING CASE

Motivation at Enterprise Rent-A-Car

HOW CAN MANAGERS MOTIVATE EMPLOYEES AT ALL LEVELS TO PROVIDE EXCELLENT CUSTOMER SERVICE?

Enterprise Rent-A-Car is an internationally recognized brand with more than 6000 neighbourhood and airport locations in the United States, Canada, the U.K., Ireland, and Germany. With over $12.6 billion in revenue and more than 68 000 employees, Enterprise and its subsidiaries, Alamo and National, operate with more than 1 million cars and trucks, making them the largest car rental service provider in the world measured by revenue, employees, and fleet.[78] After having read and understood the concepts in this chapter, you should be able to answer the following questions:

1. *Apply Herzberg's motivator-hygiene theory to this case.*

ANSWER: Frederick Herzberg focuses on two factors: outcomes that can lead to high levels of motivation and job satisfaction, and outcomes that can prevent people from being dissatisfied. According to Herzberg's motivator-hygiene theory, people have two sets of needs or requirements: motivator needs and hygiene needs. *Motivator needs* are related to the nature of the work itself and how challenging it is. Outcomes such as interesting work and responsibility help to satisfy motivator needs. To have a highly motivated and satisfied workforce, managers should take steps to ensure that employees' motivator needs are being met. At Enterprise Rent-A-Car, managers ensure that employees experience a great deal of autonomy, responsibility, and empowerment in making day-to-day operating decisions and creating superior customer service. Moreover, they provide ample opportunities for growth and development—all factors that lead to high motivation and employee satisfaction.

Hygiene needs are related to the physical and psychological context in which the work is performed. Hygiene needs are satisfied by outcomes such as pleasant working conditions, adequate pay, and job security. When hygiene needs are not met, workers are dissatisfied. Managers at Enterprise use financial incentives based on pay for performance to keep all branch employees at the rank of assistant manager and higher to keep them from feeling dissatisfaction. Moreover, policies such as their environmental and philanthropic initiatives contribute to employees experiencing no dissatisfaction at Enterprise. However, satisfying hygiene needs alone does not result in high levels of motivation or job satisfaction. For motivation and job satisfaction to be high, motivator needs must also be met.

2. *Apply Vroom's expectancy theory to this case.*

ANSWER: Expectancy theory posits that motivation will be high when workers believe that high levels of effort will lead to high performance and high performance will lead to the attainment of desired outcomes. A person's level of expectancy determines whether he or she believes that a high level of effort will result in a high level of performance. Managers can strengthen employees' levels of expectancy by providing training so that they have the expertise they need for high performance. Managers at Enterprise give extensive training in customer service to an employee which strengthens confidence and expectancy levels. Employees will be motivated to perform at a high level only if they think that high performance will lead to desirable outcomes. This is referred to as one's perception of instrumentality and it must be high if employees are to be motivated to perform well. At Enterprise, employees observe that if they perform well after some time, they will be promoted to the position of management assistant, then assistant branch manager, branch manager, and then management positions at corporate headquarters. All managers in the organization started as management trainees. With this type of promotion system, employees have strong levels of instrumentality. They believe they will be promoted (receive the outcome) if they put in the effort. Promotion is valued highly by employees at Enterprise and thus the valence or desirability placed on the outcome is high. High motivation results from high levels of expectancy, instrumentality, and valence. Enterprise provides strong links among all three elements, resulting in a highly motivated workforce.

3. *How does Enterprise Rent-A-Car use a total reward strategy to motivate employee performance?*

ANSWER: A total reward strategy motivates employees by encompassing both intrinsically and extrinsically motivating factors as outcomes for high performance. Intrinsically motivating factors such as receiving recognition for a job well done and extrinsically motivating factors such as variable pay or merit pay for performance are two examples of how Enterprise uses a total reward strategy to motivate high performance among employees.

Management in Action

TOPICS FOR DISCUSSION AND ACTION

LEVEL 1 Knowledge & Comprehension

1. Define motivation, and describe how it is related to behaviours that concern managers in organizations.

2. What are the qualities of organizational goals that make them motivating?

3. Discuss how each theory of motivation treats pay as a part of a total reward strategy.

LEVEL 2 Application & Analysis

4. From the point of view of expectancy theory, evaluate what managers should do to have a highly motivated workforce.

5. From the point of view of equity theory, assess what managers should do to have a highly motivated workforce.

6. Describe Maslow's hierarchy of needs *or* Herzberg's two-factor theory *or* McClelland's need theory and suggest what managers could do to apply them in the workplace.

LEVEL 3 Synthesis & Evaluation

7. How can managers use social learning theory to develop a highly motivated work team?

8. Discuss why two people with similar abilities may have very different expectancies for performing at a high level. What steps could a manager take to influence people's levels of expectancy, instrumentality, and valence?

9. Under what circumstances should a manager use each of the techniques in operant conditioning theory? Which technique is the best for long-term changes in behaviour?

SELF-REFLECTION EXERCISE

The following is a typical situation that students often face: you are in a team with six other management students, and you have a major case analysis due in four weeks. This assignment will count for 25 percent of your course mark. *You are the team's leader.*

The problem: Several of your team members are having difficulty getting motivated to start work on the project.

The task: Identify ways you could motivate your team members by using the following theories of motivation as studied in this chapter:

1. Need theories

2. Expectancy theory

3. Goal setting

4. Operant conditioning or reinforcement theory

5. Equity theory

SMALL GROUP BREAKOUT EXERCISE

Form groups of three or four, and appoint one member as the spokesperson who will communicate your findings to the whole class when called on by the instructor. Then discuss the following scenario:

Assume you are the manager of a small company that hired five employees, two of them at minimum wage. One of these employees, Khan, tends to slack off when you are not around to directly supervise his work. When you are around, he puts out more work effort to avoid being disciplined, but he just does not seem motivated. Jack is the company clown. He spends most of the day telling jokes and making the other employees laugh. Jack is almost always late for work. The last time he was late you reprimanded him in front of all the other staff, and Jack felt very uncomfortable but made a joke out of it anyway. Lately, Khan has been taking a lot of sick time. Something is not right.

1. What can you do to motivate high performance from Khan and Jack?
2. Identify the behaviours you would like to see Khan increase and Jack decrease.
3. Design a program using operant conditioning theory to:
    a. Increase the frequency of the functional behaviours you want the employees to exhibit, and
    b. Decrease the frequency of the undesirable behaviours.

BUSINESS PLANNING EXERCISE

Your professor may ask you to write a business plan for a new venture or a strategic plan for an existing venture. At the end of every chapter, you will have an opportunity to apply managerial and organizational concepts to the exercise of writing a business plan. Refer to Appendix A.

You and your business plan writing team find yourselves in a typical situation. The business plan is due in four weeks, and several of the team members are having difficulty getting motivated to finish the work that needs to be done for the project.

Identify ways you could motivate your team members by using the following theories of motivation as studied in this chapter:

- Maslow's hierarchy of needs
- Herzberg's motivator-hygiene theory
- Expectancy theory
- Goal-setting theory
- Learning theory

MANAGING ETHICALLY EXERCISE

You are the new CEO of a pharmaceutical company that has a reputation for compensating managers well but not employees. Top and middle managers get a 15 percent across-the-board increase, while the employees receive a 4 percent increase annually. The justification is that managers take the risks, make the decisions, and figure out the strategies. But, in fact, for years the company has been using teams to make many of the most crucial decisions for the company. And everyone has input into strategic planning. Employees also have to work extra-long hours during the busiest seasons with no overtime pay. You find that employee morale is very low. While they seem motivated because they have a passion for the work, developing drugs to help cure major diseases, many are threatening to leave if they are not rewarded more fairly. What would you do?

MANAGEMENT CHALLENGE EXERCISE

Handing Over the Reins

Recently a former colleague at a company of 100 employees called you in. You know this company very well because you worked there for seven years before becoming a motivational consultant. It is a family-owned business. Your former colleague is the daughter of the founder who is very reluctant to hand over the reins of management completely to his daughter. He knows he must, but he keeps saying that he needs that "little extra push"! Your former colleague believes that you have the "motivational key" for this transfer of power.

1. Using the motivational theories from this chapter, what theory or theories would you utilize to try to work this current challenge?

2. What motivational plan are you reasonably comfortable with that you can present to your former colleague?

MANAGEMENT PORTFOLIO PROJECT

Answer the following questions about the organization you have chosen to follow:

1. What evidence can you find on the types of motivation theories that are at work in this organization? For example, if it has an "employee of the month" award, what needs does this fulfill?

2. What kinds of things does the management do to increase the expectancy levels of employees? What about levels of instrumentality?

3. What practices does the management engage in to ensure there is a perception of equity within the organization? Do the outcomes appear to be distributed fairly?

VIDEO MANAGEMENT CASE connect

Johnson & Johnson

Johnson & Johnson (J&J) is a family-oriented health care and personal products company with about 330 operating units and more than 150,000 employees around the world. The company is well known for "the Credo," a set of value statements introduced in 1938 to help J&J's executives and employees make better decisions.

1. Why does Johnson & Johnson place so much importance on "the Credo"?

2. How does Johnson & Johnson ensure that managers understand and apply "the Credo" in their daily decisions and actions?

Management Case

Canada's Next Mega-Brand: How Lululemon Motivates Customers and Shareholders

Chip Wilson began his small boutique-style retail store selling well fitting yoga outfits in Vancouver in 1998. By 2011, he was the 15th richest Canadian for the effort.[79] Customers and shareholders alike are motivated by Lululemon, Canada's next megabrand.

What is behind this athletic wear success? Looking in from the outside one sees just another sports apparel store, but on the inside Lululemon offers something much more enticing than a new look: "the potential to transform into the best imaginable version of themselves."[80] For shoppers, the event has been likened to a "spiritual awakening" creating an almost cult-like following to the brand. Lulu doesn't sell work-out clothes so much as it sells memberships to a popular club—complete with uniform. The club promotes an ethic of self-betterment through exercise, positive thinking, and clothes that are comfortable and flattering for all ages and body shapes. Lululemon sends its employees to local yoga and fitness classes, wearing the latest fashion, of course. They host free in-store work-out sessions and community events. This puts the buyer and seller on the same side working toward common goals. The retail space is transformed into a low-pressure place for personal development. A shopper, referred to as a guest, goes into the store and talks to an employee, called an educator, about her passions and pursuits and they work together to choose the ideal outfit. The final purchase represents an investment in her personal betterment, her ideas and goals, overshadowing the commercial transaction. To cement the process, Lululemon stores keep goal-setting sheets under the counter to give out to guests to help them plan their journey toward personal achievement. The educators will even teach guests how to do yoga poses in the store, making them feel confident and associating feeling good with the brand. The culture at Lululemon is summed up in their manifesto. The code of conduct to live by is internalized by educators and guests alike. For example, one of the lines in the manifesto is "Friends are more important that money."[81]

Guests are not the only ones feeling inner satisfaction and fulfillment. Lululemon is just as popular on the stock market as it is in the mall. Lulu's share price has catapulted by 2000 percent in just two years. While stocks like Apple and Google trade at around 15 times their future earnings, Lululemon traded around 45 times

Chip Wilson, founder of Lululemon, saw how to exploit the yoga boom years before others.

projected earnings in 2011, 57 times in 2012,[82] and still investors can't get enough. Most analysts are still bullish, even though it is questionable as to whether the boutique, salon-style retail strategy can survive the journey to high-volume megabranding.[83]

1. What kind of motivation do Lulu shoppers exhibit?
2. Apply expectancy theory to the experience of shopping at Lululemon.
3. How does Lululemon use goal setting theory to motivate?

McGraw Hill connect™

Connect allows you to practise important concepts at your own pace and on your own schedule, with 24/7 online access to an eBook, practice quizzes, video cases, interactive exercises, study tools, and more.

Managing Leadership

LO1 Explain what leadership is and on what bases of power leaders influence others.

LO2 Describe the early trait and behavioural theories of leadership and their limitations.

LO3 Explain how contingency models of leadership enhance our understanding of effective leadership and management in organizations.

LO4 Compare and contrast transactional and transformational leadership.

LO5 Explain how gender, culture, and emotional intelligence affect leadership effectiveness.

Opening Case

Telecommunications Visionary Receives Canadian Business Leader Award

HOW CAN A MANAGER TRANSFORM A COMPANY IN A RAPIDLY CHANGING ENVIRONMENT?

Dean Mike Percy announced that Darren Entwistle—leader of TELUS Corporation and the longest-serving CEO amongst incumbent telecom companies globally—received the Alberta School of Business's 30th Canadian Business Leader Award (CBLA) on March 2, 2011, in front of a record crowd of over 900.[1]

"Being a recipient of the Canadian Business Leader Award is a genuine honour," Darren said. "I extend my heartfelt thanks to the entire TELUS team for their extraordinary commitment to our company's strategy, our customers, and the communities in which we live, work, and serve. I look forward to connecting with the students on March 2, as I believe this generation of Canadians has the courage to innovate by leveraging technology to answer our foremost challenges from healthcare delivery to Canada's global competitiveness."

Darren Entwistle has been President and CEO of TELUS Corporation since July 10, 2000. Over the last 12 years, during one of the most turbulent periods in Canadian telecommunications history, he has transformed TELUS from a regional telephone company into a leading national communications provider through a growth strategy focused on data and wireless. In 2000, TELUS became a national wireless provider with the $6.6 billion purchase of Clearnet. TELUS expanded its capabilities and reach through other acquisitions such as QuebecTel, Williams Communications Canada Inc., Emergis, and Black's Photography.

Today, TELUS is recognized worldwide for its innovation and strong financial performance with $10.4 billion of annual revenue. Notably,

from the beginning of 2000 through August 2012, TELUS has delivered the highest total shareholder returns among incumbent telecommunication companies on a global basis at 190 percent. Entwistle reversed TELUS's fortunes and robbed Bell Canada of big contracts, outpacing his rival in multiple verticals, particularly on the wireless front where TELUS's growth and profits have been nothing short of phenomenal.

Complementing TELUS's corporate performance is the company's commitment to being Canada's premier corporate citizen. In 2010, TELUS was recognized as the most outstanding philanthropic corporation globally by the United States–based Association of Fundraising Professionals. It was the first time a Canadian company had been recognized.[2] TELUS's philosophy is to "give where we live," and since 2000, TELUS and its team members have contributed $260 million to charitable and not-for-profit organizations and volunteered more than 4.2 million hours of service to local communities. Fourteen TELUS Community Boards, led by local community leaders, continue to

guide the company's local philanthropic initiatives from coast to coast across Canada.

TELUS is also committed to helping to transform the healthcare system in Canada, investing more than $1 billion and using innovative technology to improve efficiency and patient outcomes. Branham Group, a leading technology consultancy, has named TELUS the number-one healthcare IT company in Canada for five consecutive years.[3]

Guided by his belief in the TELUS team's ability to create sustainable value, Darren has taken the entirety of his annual cash salary compensation net of taxes in TELUS shares for two years, and will do so again in 2012. On the value of creating a quality corporate culture, Darren Entwistle said, "Competitors can copy your marketing or your products, but they can't re-create your corporate culture."[4]

He believes that his company's culture is its biggest sustainable single point of competitive advantage, and he encourages all TELUS leaders to develop diverse talent pools that foster continuous creativity and innovation. In this respect, Darren also believes training and development must be available for all employees and is an essential component of career development. Entwistle promotes this culture through four enduring corporate values created collaboratively by employees more than a decade ago: We embrace change and initiate opportunity, we have a passion for growth, we believe in spirited teamwork, and we have the courage to innovate.

Entwistle also strives for accountability through business performance. He is often quoted as saying, "What gets measured, gets done," and requires his leaders to set SMART (Specific, Measureable, Achievable and Accountable, Relevant, and Timebound) objectives that align with the company's strategic imperatives and corporate priorities.

On his communication style, a reporter for *The Globe and Mail* said he looked like a freshman but talked like an elder statesman giving a speech at the United Nations.[5] When Entwistle took on the role of CEO, he knew immediately that he had to transform the company in order to remain competitive

and thrive in a global economy. To Entwistle, TELUS was another landline dinosaur that wouldn't survive unless it crunched costs and learned how to make money in the new digital age. This is exactly what he did by inspiring the TELUS team through his drive and passion in establishing the company's strategic intent, "To unleash the power of the Internet to deliver the best solutions for Canadians at home, in the workplace, and on the move." To this day, TELUS is one of the only telcos globally that has had the discipline to stick with its strategy for more than 10 years.

Born in Montreal in 1962, Darren earned a Bachelor of Economics (Honours) degree from Concordia University, an MBA in Finance from McGill University, and a diploma in Network Engineering from the University of Toronto. Prior to joining TELUS, Darren, a 30-year veteran of the communications industry, spent seven years on the senior leadership team at Cable & Wireless in the United Kingdom, culminating with his appointment as President for the United Kingdom and Ireland operations in 1999.

After reading and understanding the concepts in this chapter, you should be able to answer the following questions:

1. *What traits and characteristics make Darren Entwistle an effective leader?*

2. *Is Entwistle a transformational leader? Why or why not?*

Overview

In the opening scenario, we see perhaps a new vision of leadership, one that goes beyond simply the traditional model of leader–follower and looks at the vision a manager or person in authority brings to the organization. In Chapter 1, we explained that one of the four principal tasks of managers is leading. Thus, it should come as no surprise that leadership is a key ingredient in effective management. When leaders are effective, their subordinates or followers are highly motivated, committed, and high-performing. When leaders are ineffective, chances are good that their subordinates do

not perform up to their capabilities, are de-motivated, and may be dissatisfied as well. Leadership is an important ingredient for managerial success at all levels of an organization: top management, middle management, and first-line management. Moreover, leadership is a key ingredient for managerial success for organizations large and small.

In this chapter, we describe what leadership is and examine the major leadership models that shed light on the factors that help make a manager an effective leader. *Trait and behaviour models* focus on what leaders are like and what they do. *Contingency models*—Fiedler's contingency model, Hersey-Blanchard's situational leadership theory, path-goal theory, and the leader substitutes model—take into account the complexity surrounding leadership and the role of the situation in leader effectiveness. We describe how managers can have dramatic effects in their organizations by means of transformational leadership. We also examine the relationship between gender and leadership, culture and leadership, and social intelligence and leadership. By the end of this chapter, you will have a good appreciation of the many factors and issues that managers face in their quest to be effective leaders.

LO1 Explain what leadership is and on what bases of power leaders influence others.

The Nature of Leadership

Leadership is the process by which a person exerts influence over other people and inspires, motivates, and directs their activities to help achieve group or organizational goals.[6] The person who exerts such influence is a **leader.** When leaders are effective, the influence they exert over others helps a group or organization achieve its performance goals. When leaders are ineffective, their influence does not contribute to, and often detracts from, goal attainment. As the opening case suggests, Darren Entwistle is taking multiple steps to inspire and motivate TELUS employees to help achieve organizational goals.

Beyond facilitating the attainment of performance goals, effective leadership increases an organization's ability to meet all the contemporary challenges discussed throughout this book, including the need to obtain a competitive advantage, the need to foster ethical behaviour, and the need to manage a diverse workforce fairly and equitably. Leaders who exert influence to help meet these goals increase their organization's chances of success.

In considering the nature of leadership, we first look at leadership styles and how they affect managerial tasks and at the influence of culture on leadership styles. We then focus on the key to leadership, *power*, which can come from a variety of sources. Finally, we consider the contemporary dynamic of empowerment and how it relates to effective leadership.

Personal Leadership Style and Managerial Tasks

A manager's **personal leadership style**— that is, the specific ways in which a manager

chooses to influence other people—shapes the way that the manager approaches planning, organizing, and controlling (the other principal tasks of managing). Consider Darren Entwistle's personal leadership style in the opening case. He has so much confidence in the long-term performance of his team at TELUS he is willing to take only stock options as salary.

Managers at all levels and in all kinds of organizations have their own personal leadership styles. Michael Tibeau, owner and manager of a dry-cleaning store in northeastern New Brunswick, for example, takes a hands-on approach to leadership. He has the sole authority for determining work schedules and job assignments for the 15 employees in his store (an organizing task), makes all important decisions by himself (a planning task), and closely monitors his employees' performance and rewards top performers with pay increases (a control task). His personal leadership style is effective in his organization. His employees are generally motivated, perform highly, and are satisfied, and his store is highly profitable.

In considering the nature of leadership, the age-old question for management thought arises: How do you get other people to follow and carry out tasks and orders effectively? Henri Fayol, writing early in the twentieth century, was very clear about the chain of command and believed in centralized control and decision making.[7] Max Weber and his three main historical paradigms of authority written in the mid twentieth century was one of the first social scientists to deal with this issue.[8] Mary Parker Follett addressed the issue of "giving orders" and obedience in a series of lectures published around the same time.[9] In fact, the entire Classical era of managerial thought, and most notably Frederick W. Taylor's scientific management theory, was consumed by this central question.[10] See Table 9.1.

Henry Mintzberg and other contemporary leadership theorists agree that no matter what one's leadership style, a key component of effective leadership is found in the *power* the leader has to affect other people's behaviour and to get them to act in certain ways.[11]

Power: The Key to Leadership

French and Raven depict five types of social power: *legitimate, reward, coercive, expert,* and *referent* (see Figure 9.1).[12]

Legitimate Power

Legitimate power is the authority a manager has by virtue of his or her position in

leadership The process by which an individual exerts influence over other people and inspires, motivates, and directs their activities to help achieve group or organizational goals.

leader An individual who is able to exert influence over other people to help achieve group or organizational goals.

personal leadership style The ways a manager chooses to influence others and how they approach planning, organizing, and controlling.

legitimate power The authority that a manager has by virtue of his or her position in an organization's hierarchy.

> **FIGURE 9.1** Sources of Managerial Power

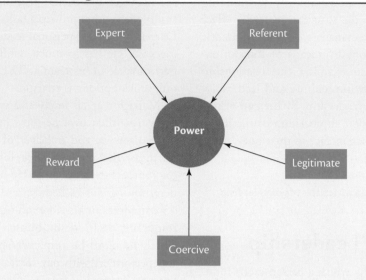

an organization's hierarchy. Personal leadership style often influences how a manager exercises legitimate power. Take the case of Carol Loray, who is a first-line manager in a greeting card company and leads a group of 15 artists and designers. Loray has the legitimate power to hire new employees, assign projects to the artists and designers, monitor their work, and appraise their performance. She uses this power effectively. She always makes sure that her project assignments match the interests of her subordinates as much as possible so that they will enjoy their work. She monitors their work to make sure they are on track but does not engage in close supervision, which can hamper creativity. She makes sure her performance appraisals are developmental, providing concrete advice for areas where improvements could be made. Recently, Loray negotiated with her manager to increase her legitimate power so that now she can initiate and develop proposals for new card lines.

Reward Power

Reward power is the ability of a manager to give or withhold tangible rewards (pay raises, bonuses, choice job assignments) and intangible rewards (verbal praise, a pat on the back, respect). As you learned in Chapter 8, members of an organization are motivated to perform at a high level by a variety of rewards. Being able to give or withhold rewards based on performance is a major source of power that allows managers to have a highly motivated workforce. Managers of salespeople in retail organizations like Harry Rosen and Future Shop, in car dealerships like General Motors and Ford, and in travel agencies like Marlin Travel and Sears Travel Company often use their reward power to motivate their subordinates. Subordinates in organizations such as these often receive commissions on whatever they sell and rewards for the quality of their customer service, which motivate them to do the best they can.

Effective managers use their reward power in such a way that subordinates feel that they are doing a good job and their efforts are appreciated. Ineffective managers use rewards in a more controlling manner (wielding the stick instead of offering the carrot), which signals to subordinates that the manager has

> **reward power** The ability of a manager to give or withhold tangible and intangible rewards.

> **TABLE 9.1** Management Gurus on Power and Authority

Henri Fayol (1841–1925)	Frederick W. Taylor (1856–1915)	Max Weber (1864–1920)	Mary Parker Follett (1868–1933)
Centralized, top-down decision making Unity in the chain of command	Scientific management Removes discretion/decision making from workers Managers plan tasks	Traditional authority Legal/Rational authority Charismatic authority	Law of the situation Integrative decision making

the upper hand. Managers also can take steps to increase their reward power.

One example of effective use of reward power occurred with Craig Johnston of Canada Post, who was rewarded for his bright idea with a $10 000 cheque, the respect of his bosses, and the admiration of his peers. He developed a time-saving device so that Canada Post could revamp its sorting line by jury-rigging its existing machinery to generate mail barcodes on the fly. Before his suggestion, packages without barcodes had to be manually sorted by clerks; this labour-intensive activity contributed to clogging up of the machines. The $10 000 was part of Canada Post's employee involvement award program—an initiative designed to encourage and reward innovation on the job.[13]

Coercive Power

Coercive power is the ability of a manager to persuade someone to do something that he or she otherwise would not. It includes the use of psychological and physical threats and actually perpetrating physical and mental harm. Sexual harassment is a form of coercive power. Other forms of power can be used in a coercive way. For example, reward power can be used to punish employees by withholding valuable outcomes like pay when the employee demonstrates undesirable behaviour such as frequent absenteeism. Referent power can become coercive if it is used to deceive people as is found in some religious cults. Managers who rely heavily on coercive power tend to be ineffective as leaders and sometimes even get fired themselves.

Excessive use of coercive power seldom produces high performance and is ethically questionable. Sometimes it amounts to a form of mental abuse, robbing workers of their dignity and causing excessive levels of stress. Overuse of coercive power can even result in dangerous working conditions. Better results and, importantly, an ethical workplace that respects employee dignity can be obtained by using reward power.

Expert Power

Expert power is based in the special knowledge, skills, and expertise that a leader possesses. The nature of expert power varies depending on the leader's level in the hierarchy. First-line and middle managers often have technical expertise relevant to the tasks that their subordinates perform. Their expert power gives them considerable influence over subordinates. Carol Loray has expert power: she is an artist herself and has drawn and designed some of her company's top-selling

greeting cards. Darren Entwistle, from this chapter's opening case, has expert power from more than 20 years' experience in telecommunications.

Some top managers derive expert power from their technical expertise. As a former Microsoft Chief Software Architect, inventor of Lotus Notes, and founder of Cocomo in 2012, Ray Ozzie has expertise in software design. Many top-level managers lack technical expertise, however, and derive their expert power from their abilities as decision makers, planners, and strategists. Jack Welch, the former, well-known leader and CEO of General Electric, summed it up this way: "The basic thing that we at the top of the company know is that we don't know the business. What we have, I hope, is the ability to allocate resources, people, and dollars."[14]

Effective leaders take steps to ensure that they have an adequate amount of expert power to perform their leadership roles. They may obtain additional training or education in their fields, make sure they keep up to date with the latest developments and changes in technology, stay abreast of changes in their fields through involvement in professional associations, and read widely to be aware of momentous changes in the organization's task and general environments. Expert power tends to be best used in a guiding or coaching manner rather than in an arrogant, high-handed manner.

Referent Power

Referent power is more informal than the other kinds of power. **Referent power** is a function of the personal characteristics of a leader. It is the power that comes from subordinates' and coworkers' respect, admiration, and loyalty. Leaders who are likeable and whom subordinates wish to use as a role model are especially likely to possess referent power.

In addition to being a valuable asset for top managers, referent power can help first-line and middle managers be effective leaders. Sally Carruthers, for example, is the first-level manager of a group of office workers in the finance department of a large university. Carruthers's secretaries are known to be among the best in the university. Much of their willingness to go above and beyond the call of duty has been attributed to Carruthers's warm and caring nature, which makes each of them feel important and valued. Managers can take steps to increase their referent power, such as taking time to get to know their subordinates and showing interest in and concern for them. Referent power is the power that managers

coercive power The ability to persuade someone to do something that he or she otherwise would not.

expert power Power that is based in the special knowledge, skills, and expertise that a leader possesses.

referent power Power that comes from subordinates' and coworkers' respect, admiration, and loyalty.

derive from the trust and commitment given to them by their colleagues because of who they are and how they are perceived. This is a precarious power source because if the respect and trust afforded to you falters, you can easily lose it.[15]

Empowerment: An Ingredient in Modern Management

More and more managers today are incorporating in their personal leadership styles an aspect that at first glance seems to be the opposite of being a leader. In Chapter 1, we described how **empowerment**—the process of giving employees at all levels in the organization the authority to make decisions, be responsible for their outcomes, improve quality, and cut costs—is becoming increasingly popular in organizations. When leaders empower their subordinates, the subordinates typically take over some of the responsibilities and authority that used to reside with the leader or manager, such as the right to reject parts that do not meet quality standards, the right to check one's own work, and the right to schedule work activities. Empowered subordinates are given the power to make some of the decisions that their leaders or supervisors used to make.

At first glance, empowerment might seem to be the opposite of effective leadership because managers allow subordinates to take a more active role in leading themselves. In actuality, however, empowerment can contribute to effective leadership for several reasons:

- Empowerment increases a manager's ability to get things done because the manager has the support and help of subordinates who may have special knowledge of work tasks.

- Empowerment often increases workers' involvement, motivation, and commitment, which helps ensure that they will be working toward organizational goals.

- Empowerment gives managers more time to concentrate on their pressing concerns because they spend less time on day-to-day supervisory activities.

Effective managers like Darren Entwistle realize the benefits of empowerment. Ineffective managers try to keep control over all decision making and force agreement from subordinates. The personal leadership style of managers who empower subordinates often includes developing subordinates so that they can make good decisions and being subordinates' guide, coach, and source of inspiration. Empowerment is a popular trend in Canada and the United States at companies as diverse as United Parcel Service of America Inc. (a package

empowerment The expansion of employees' knowledge, tasks, and decision-making responsibilities.

Empowered employees are more involved, motivated, and committed.

delivery company), Dominion Information Services Inc. (of Burnaby, B.C., which publishes *Super Pages* in B.C., Alberta, Ontario, and Quebec), and Redwood Plastics Corp. (a manufacturing company based in Langley, B.C.), and it is also taking off around the world.[16] Even companies in South Korea (such as Samsung, Hyundai, and Daewoo), in which decision making typically was centralized with the founding families, are empowering managers at lower levels to make decisions.[17]

Not every employee is a good candidate for empowerment, however. A study conducted by Professor Jia Lin Xie and colleagues at the University of Toronto's Joseph L. Rotman School of Management found that people who lack confidence can get ill from being put in charge of their own work. The researchers found that "workers who had high levels of control at work but lacked confidence in their abilities or blamed themselves for workplace problems were more likely to have lower antibody levels and experienced more colds and flus."[18]

Some of the difficulty with empowerment is that not all companies introduce it properly. Professor Dan Ondrack at the Rotman School of Management notes that for employees to be empowered, four conditions need to be met: (1) there must be a clear definition of the values and mission of the company; (2) the company must help employees acquire the relevant skills; (3) employees need to be supported in their decision making and not criticized when they try to do something out of the ordinary; and (4) workers need to be recognized for their efforts.[19] Thus, according to Gail Rieschi, president of Toronto-based VPI, a firm specializing in career and employment management, autonomy and empowerment "are two elements essential to job satisfaction—which, in turn, engenders greater commitment to the organization. It becomes, if managed correctly, a real win-win situation."[20]

Early Models of Leadership

Is there a difference between leadership and management? Harvard Business School Professor John Kotter suggests that "managers promote stability, while leaders press for change and only organizations that embrace both sides of the contradiction can survive in turbulent times."[21] Professor Rabindra Kanungo of McGill University reports growing agreement "among management scholars that the concept of 'leadership' must be distinguished from the concept of 'supervision/management.'"[22] Leaders look to the big picture, providing vision and strategy. Managers are charged with implementing vision and strategy; they coordinate and staff the organization, and handle day-to-day-problems.

Leading is such an important process in all organizations—nonprofit organizations, government agencies, and schools, as well as for-profit corporations—that it has been researched for decades. Early approaches to leadership, called the *trait model* and the *behaviour model*, sought to determine what effective leaders are like as people and what they do that makes them so effective.

Leadership theories developed before 1980 focused on the supervisory nature of leadership. Thus they were concerned with managing the day-to-day functions of employees. These theories took three different approaches to how supervision could be viewed: (1) do leaders have traits different from non-leaders? (2) should leaders engage in particular behaviours? (3) does the situation a leader faces matter? We briefly examine these approaches below.

The Trait Model

The trait model of leadership focused on identifying the personal characteristics that are responsible for effective leadership. Researchers thought effective leaders must have certain personal qualities that set them apart from ineffective leaders and from people who never become leaders. Decades of research (beginning in the 1930s) and hundreds of studies indicate that certain personal characteristics do appear to be associated with effective leadership (see Table 9.2 for a list of these).[23] Notice that although this model is called the "trait" model, some of the personal characteristics that it identifies are not personality traits per se; rather, they are concerned with a leader's skills, abilities, knowledge, and expertise. Leaders who do not possess these traits may be ineffective.

Traits alone, however, are not the key to understanding leader effectiveness. Some effective leaders do not possess all of these traits, and some leaders who do possess them are not effective in their leadership roles. This lack of a consistent relationship between leader traits and leader effectiveness led researchers to search for new explanations for effective leadership. Rather than focusing on what leaders are like (the traits they possess), researchers began to turn their attention to what effective leaders actually do—in other words, to the behaviours that allow effective leaders to influence their subordinates to achieve group and organizational goals.

The Behavioural Models

A variety of behavioural models of leadership exist, including the Ohio Studies,[24] the Michigan Studies,[25] and Blake and Mouton's managerial grid.[26] These models identify two basic kinds of leader behaviours that

> **TABLE 9.2** Traits and Personal Characteristics Related to Effective Leadership

Trait	Description
Intelligence	Helps managers understand complex issues and solve problems
Knowledge and expertise	Help managers make good decisions and discover ways to increase efficiency and effectiveness
Dominance	Helps managers influence their subordinates to achieve organizational goals
Self-confidence	Contributes to managers' effectively influencing subordinates and persisting when faced with obstacles or difficulties
High energy	Helps managers deal with the many demands they face
Tolerance for stress	Helps managers deal with uncertainty and make difficult decisions
Integrity and honesty	Help managers behave ethically and earn their subordinates' trust and confidence
Maturity	Helps managers avoid acting selfishly, control their feelings, and admit when they have made a mistake

many leaders in the United States, Germany, and other countries use to influence their subordinates: *consideration behaviours,* also known as concern for people and employee-centred behaviours; and *initiating structure,* also known as concern for production or task-oriented behaviours.

All of the behavioural theories suggest that leaders need to consider the nature of their subordinates when trying to determine the extent to which they should perform these two types of behaviours. At the root of leadership training courses is the notion that people can be taught the behaviours that allow them to be effective. As the Focus on the Social Economy feature illustrates, the Me to We Leadership training program helps youth learn how to make a difference in the lives of thousands worldwide.

Consideration

Leaders engage in **consideration or employee-centred behaviour** when they show subordinates that they trust, respect, and care about them. This behavioural leadership modelling is borne out with enthusiastic employees.[27] According to the company Sirota, survey intelligence specialists in attitude

research, employees start out with a company by being enthusiastic. What eventually gets in the way is management!

Managers, therefore, who truly look out for the well-being of their subordinates and who do what they can to help subordinates feel good and enjoy their work are performing consideration behaviours. With the increasing focus on the importance of high-quality customer service, many managers are realizing that when they are considerate to subordinates, subordinates are more likely to be considerate to customers and vice versa. In the opening case, Darren Entwistle engages in consideration when he fosters an inclusive, nurturing culture at TELUS.

> "Competitors can copy your marketing or your products, but they can't re-create your corporate culture!"
> *Darren Entwistle, CEO, TELUS*

consideration or employee-centred behaviour Behaviour indicating that a manager trusts, respects, and cares about subordinates.

initiating structure or task-oriented behaviours Behaviours that managers engage in to ensure that work gets done, subordinates perform their jobs acceptably, and the organization is efficient and effective.

Initiating Structure

Leaders engage in **initiating structure or task-oriented behaviours** when they focus on the goal rather than the process by taking steps to make sure that work gets done, subordinates perform their jobs acceptably, and the organization is efficient and

---

FOCUS ON > The Social Economy

From Me to We Leadership

Craig Kielburger was moved to do something about child slave labour in 1995 when he was just 12 years old. After reading an article about a child his same age who was sold into slavery and spent six years chained to a carpet weaving loom, he and a few school friends started a charity in Canada called Free the Children. Free the Children's mission is to end child poverty and exploitation through education and training for social change. Today, Free the Children is the largest network of children helping children in the world with over one million youth in 45 countries participating in the movement.[28]

One of the social enterprises used to fund the charitable work of Free the Children is called Me to We. Me to We Leadership courses and camps provide youth with

hands-on training in leading for social change. Youth facilitators teach young people about making environmentally sustainable decisions at home and abroad. Volunteer travel excursions to communities in which Free the Children are building schools and so on give youth the chance to use leadership skills to help change the world. The leadership programs at Me to We create life-altering experiences for youth who want to make a difference.

1. Go to the Me to We website. Does the leadership training offered at Me to We support or refute the behavioural models of leadership? Why?

2. In what ways does the leadership training at Me to We provide youth with transformational versus transactional skills?

effective. Assigning tasks to individuals or work groups, letting subordinates know what is expected of them, deciding how work should be done, making schedules, encouraging adherence to rules and regulations, and motivating subordinates to do a good job are all examples of initiating structure.[29] Michael Teckel, the manager of an upscale store selling imported men's and women's shoes in Winnipeg, engages in initiating structure when he establishes weekly work, lunch, and break schedules to ensure that the store has enough salespeople on the floor. Teckel also initiates structure when he discusses the latest shoe designs with his subordinates so that they are knowledgeable with customers, when he encourages adherence to the store's refund and exchange policies, and when he encourages his staff to provide high-quality customer service and to avoid a hard-sell approach.

The Managerial Grid

The managerial grid developed by Blake and Mouton provides a useful framework for managers to assess which set of behaviours have a propensity to dominate in their leadership style. See Figure 9.2. Five different leadership styles emerge from plotting behavioural dimensions on a simple grid. *Concern for people* is the degree to which the leader shows consideration, while concern for production is the degree to which the leader initiates structure. If a leader's behaviour is high in showing concern for people and low in showing *concern for production,* they fall into the *Country Club* style. While this type of leadership style may provide a fun and supportive environment for employees, the accomplishment of tasks and goals suffers. The *Impoverished* style shows a low concern for consideration behaviours on the part of the leader and a low concern for production. Needless to say, this type of leadership style tends to be ineffective. When leaders show a high concern for people and a high concern for production, they have the *Team Leader* management style. This creates an atmosphere of trust and respect that leads to high motivation and satisfaction and as a result high performance levels. According to Blake and Mouton, this combination exhibits the optimal leadership behaviours for effectiveness and efficiency. *Produce or Perish* leadership is the style that shows a strong emphasis on goal attainment at the expense of showing concern for the well-being of the employees. Formal rules and regulations as well as the fear of punishment tend to be used by these autocratic leaders. And finally, the *Middle of the Road* leadership style appears to show medium concern for people and production. This style, however, is not optimal, according to the model, because it requires compromise

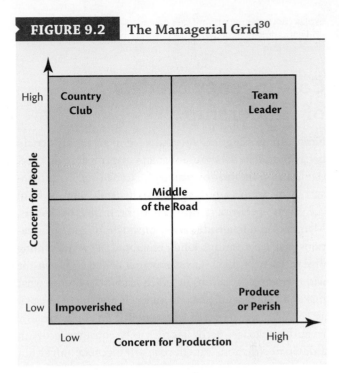

FIGURE 9.2 The Managerial Grid[30]

on both sets of concerns so as to leave them both unfulfilled resulting in average levels of performance.

You might expect that effective leaders and managers would perform both kinds of behaviours, but research has found that this is not necessarily the case. The relationship between performance of consideration and initiating-structure behaviours and leader effectiveness is not clear-cut. Some leaders are effective even when they do not perform consideration or initiating-structure behaviours, and some leaders are ineffective even when they do perform both kinds of behaviours. Like the trait model of leadership, the behaviour model alone cannot explain leader effectiveness.

Behavioural theories of leadership which assert that the most effective managers are high on both dimensions have been criticized for ignoring the particular circumstances in which the leader is operating. Just as the behavioural theories emerged as a critique of trait theory—by saying it is not the characteristics of the leader that matter but what they do—so too were the behavioural models criticized for assuming one style of leadership behaviours were appropriate in all situations. Realizing this, researchers began building more complicated models of leadership that focused not only on the leader's traits and behaviours but also on the situation or context in which leadership occurs. In the evolution of leadership theory, this led to the development of **contingency models of leadership.**

contingency models of leadership Models of leadership that take into account the variables in the situation or context in which leadership occurs.

Contingency Models of Leadership

Simply possessing certain traits or performing certain behaviours does not ensure that a manager will be an effective leader in all situations calling for leadership. Some managers who seem to possess the "right" traits and perform the "right" behaviours turn out to be ineffective leaders. Managers lead in a wide variety of situations and organizations and have various kinds of subordinates performing diverse tasks in many environmental contexts. Given the wide variety of situations in which leadership occurs, what makes a manager an effective leader in one situation (such as certain traits or certain behaviours) is not necessarily what that manager needs in order to be equally effective in a different situation. An effective army general might not be an effective university president, an effective manager of a restaurant might not be an effective manager of a clothing store, an effective coach of a hockey team might not be an effective manager of a fitness centre, and an effective first-line manager in a manufacturing company might not be an effective middle manager. The traits or behaviours that may contribute to a manager being an effective leader in one situation might actually result in the same manager being an ineffective leader in another situation.

Contingency models of leadership take into account the situation or context within which leadership occurs. So, for instance, while behavioural theories explored whether managers should be more employee-centred or more task-centred,

leader–member relations The extent to which followers like, trust, and are loyal to their leader; can be good or poor.

Leaders need to adapt to situational factors.

contingency theories answer: it depends (or is contingent) on the situation. According to contingency models, whether or not a manager is an effective leader is the result of the interplay between what the manager is like, what he or she does, and the situation in which leadership takes place. In this section, we discuss four prominent contingency models that shed light on what makes managers effective leaders: Fiedler's contingency model, Hersey-Blanchard's situational leadership theory, House's path-goal theory, and the leader substitutes model. As you will see, these leadership models are complementary. Each focuses on a somewhat different aspect of effective leadership in organizations.

Fiedler's Contingency Model

Fred E. Fiedler was among the first leadership researchers to acknowledge that effective leadership is contingent on, or depends on, the characteristics of the leader and of the situation. Fiedler's contingency model helps explain why a manager may be an effective leader in one situation and ineffective in another; it also suggests which kinds of managers are likely to be most effective in which situations.[31]

As with the trait approach, Fiedler hypothesized that personal characteristics can influence leader effectiveness. He used the term *leader style* to refer to a manager's characteristic approach to leadership and identified two basic leader styles: relationship-oriented and task-oriented. All managers can be described as having one style or the other.

Relationship-oriented leaders are mainly concerned with developing good relationships with their subordinates and being liked by them. Relationship-oriented managers focus on having high-quality interpersonal relationships with subordinates. This does not mean, however, that the job does not get done when such leaders are at the helm. It does mean that the quality of interpersonal relationships with subordinates is a prime concern for relationship-oriented leaders. *Task-oriented leaders* are mainly concerned with ensuring that subordinates perform at a high level. Task-oriented managers focus on task accomplishment and making sure the job gets done.

According to Fiedler, leadership style is an enduring characteristic; managers cannot change their style, nor can they adopt different styles in different kinds of situations. With this in mind, Fiedler identified three *situational characteristics* that are important determinants of how favourable a situation is for leading. He further determined in which situations a relationship-oriented leader and a task-oriented leader were most effective:

- **Leader–member relations:** The extent to which followers like, trust, and are loyal to their leader.

Situations are more favourable for leading when leader–member relations are good.

- **Task structure:** The extent to which the work to be performed is clear-cut so that a leader's subordinates know what needs to be accomplished and how to go about doing it. When task structure is high, situations are favourable for leading. When task structure is low, goals may be vague, subordinates may be unsure of what they should be doing or how they should do it, and the situation is unfavourable for leading.

- **Position power:** The amount of legitimate, reward, and coercive powers a leader has by virtue of his or her position in an organization. Leadership situations are more favourable for leading when position power is strong.

When a situation is favourable for leading, it is relatively easy for a manager to influence subordinates so that they perform at a high level and contribute to organizational efficiency and effectiveness. Therefore, it makes the most sense to be task-oriented because the relationship is already going well. In a situation unfavourable for leading, it is much more difficult for a manager to exert influence. This makes being task-oriented the most desirable behaviour for the leader. By taking all possible combinations of good and poor leader–member relations, high and low task structure, and strong and weak position power, Fiedler identified eight leadership situations, which vary in their favourability for leading. See Figure 9.3. After extensive research, Fiedler determined that relationship-oriented leaders are most effective in moderately favourable situations (IV, V, VI, and VII in Figure 9.3), and task-oriented leaders are most effective in very favourable situations (I, II, and III) or very unfavourable situations (VIII).

According to Fiedler, individuals cannot change their leadership style. Therefore, managers need to be placed in leadership situations that fit their style, or situations need to be changed to suit the manager. Situations can be changed—for example, by giving a manager more position power or by taking steps to increase task structure such as by clarifying goals. Take the case of Mark Compton, a relationship-oriented leader employed by a small construction company who was in a very unfavourable situation and having a rough time leading his construction crew. His subordinates did not trust him to look out for their well-being (poor leader–member relations); the construction jobs he supervised tended to be novel and complex (low task structure); and he had no control over the rewards and disciplinary actions his subordinates received (weak position power). Recognizing the need to improve matters, Compton's supervisor gave him the power to reward crew members with bonuses and overtime work as he saw fit and to discipline crew members for poor-quality work and unsafe on-the-job behaviour. As his leadership situation improved to moderately favourable, so too did Compton's effectiveness as a leader and the performance of his crew.

Research studies tend to support some aspects of Fiedler's model but also suggest that, like most theories, it needs some modifications.[32] Some researchers also find fault with the model's premise that leaders cannot alter their styles. That is, it is likely that at least some leaders

task structure The extent to which the work to be performed is clear-cut so that a leader's subordinates know what needs to be accomplished and how to go about doing it; can be high or low.

position power The amount of legitimate, reward, and coercive power that a leader has by virtue of his or her position in an organization; can be strong or weak.

> **FIGURE 9.3** Fiedler's Contingency Theory of Leadership

Relationship-oriented leaders are most effective in moderately favourable situations for leading (IV, V, VI, VII).
Task-oriented leaders are most effective in very favourable situations (I, II, III) or very unfavourable situations (VIII) for leading.

can diagnose the situation they are in and, when their style is inappropriate for the situation, modify their style so that it is more in line with what the leadership situation calls for.

Hersey-Blanchard's Situational Leadership Theory

Paul Hersey and Ken Blanchard's **situational leadership theory (SLT)**[33] has been incorporated into leadership training programs at numerous Fortune 500 companies. More than one million managers a year are taught its basic elements.[34]

SLT compares the leader–follower relationship to that between a parent and a child. Just as parents need to give more control to a child as the child becomes more mature and responsible, so too should leaders do this with employees. Hersey and Blanchard identify four specific leadership behaviours that managers can use to lead their employees: telling, selling, participating, and delegating. The styles vary in their degree of task-oriented behaviour and relationship-oriented behaviour. The appropriate style depends on the follower's ability and motivation:

- *Telling.* If a follower is *unable* and *unwilling* to do a task, the leader needs to give clear and specific directions (in other words, the leader needs to be highly directive).
- *Selling.* If a follower is *unable* but *willing,* the leader needs to display both high task orientation and high relationship orientation. The high task orientation will compensate for the follower's lack of ability. The high relationship orientation will encourage the follower to "buy into" the leader's desires (in other words, the leader needs to "sell" the task).
- *Participating.* If the follower is *able* but *unwilling,* the leader needs to use a supportive and participative style.
- *Delegating.* If the employee is both *able* and *willing,* the leader does not need to do much (in other words, a laissez-faire approach will work).

Figure 9.4 illustrates the relationship of leader behaviours to follower readiness.

Path-Goal Theory

Developed by Rotman School of Management professor Martin Evans in the late 1960s, and then expanded on by Robert House, **path-goal theory** focuses on what leaders can do to motivate their subordinates to reach group

and organizational goals.[35] The premise of path-goal theory is that effective leaders motivate subordinates to achieve goals by (1) clearly identifying the outcomes that subordinates are trying to obtain from the workplace, (2) rewarding subordinates with these outcomes for high performance and the attainment of work goals, and (3) clarifying for subordinates the *paths* leading to the attainment of work *goals.* Path-goal theory is a contingency model because it proposes that the steps that managers should take to motivate subordinates depend on both the nature of the subordinates and the type of work they do.

Based on the expectancy theory of motivation (see Chapter 8), path-goal theory provides managers with three guidelines to follow to be effective leaders:

1. *Find out what outcomes your subordinates are trying to obtain from their jobs and the organization.* These outcomes can range from satisfactory pay and job security to reasonable working hours and interesting and challenging job assignments. After identifying what these outcomes are, the manager should make sure that he or she has the reward power needed to distribute or withhold them.

2. *Reward subordinates for high performance and goal attainment with the outcomes they desire.*

3. *Clarify the paths to goal attainment for subordinates, remove any obstacles to high performance, and express confidence in subordinates' capabilities.* This does not mean that a manager needs to tell his or her subordinates what to do. Rather, it means that a manager needs to make sure that subordinates are clear about what they should be trying to accomplish and have the capabilities, resources, and confidence levels they need to be successful.

Path-goal theory identifies four kinds of behaviours that leaders can use to motivate subordinates:

- *Directive behaviours* include setting goals, assigning tasks, showing subordinates how to complete tasks, and taking concrete steps to improve performance.
- *Supportive behaviours* include expressing concern for subordinates and looking out for their best interests.
- *Participative behaviours* give subordinates a say in matters and decisions that affect them.

situational leadership theory (SLT) A contingency model of leadership that focuses on the followers' readiness.

path-goal theory A contingency model of leadership proposing that leaders can motivate subordinates by identifying their desired outcomes, rewarding them for high performance and the attainment of work goals with these desired outcomes, and clarifying for them the paths leading to the attainment of work goals.

> **FIGURE 9.4**   Hersey-Blanchard's Situational Leadership Styles

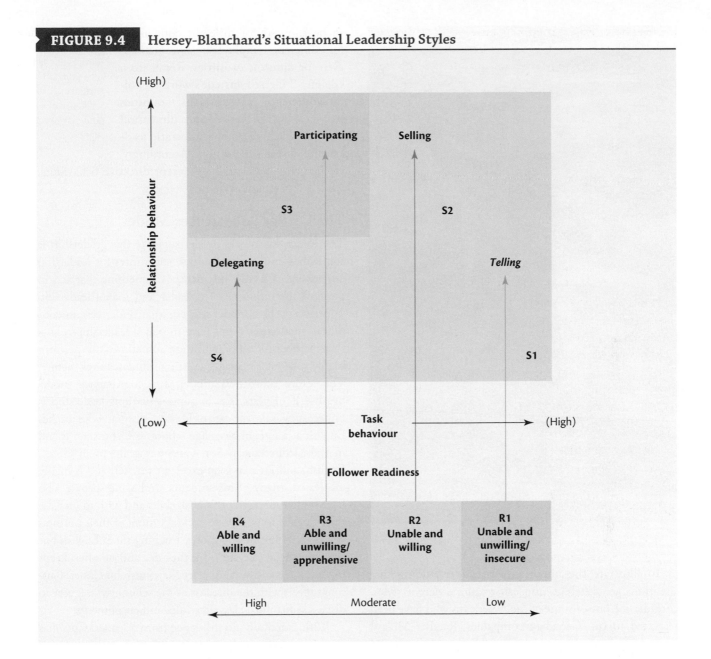

- *Achievement-oriented behaviours* motivate subordinates to perform at the highest level possible by, for example, setting very challenging goals, expecting that they be met, and believing in subordinates' capabilities.

Which of these behaviours should managers use to lead effectively? The answer to this question depends, or is contingent, on the nature of the subordinates and the kind of work they do.

Directive behaviours may be beneficial when subordinates are having difficulty completing assigned tasks, but they might be detrimental when subordinates are independent thinkers who work best when left alone. *Supportive* behaviours are often advisable when subordinates are experiencing high levels of stress. *Participative* behaviours can be particularly effective when subordinates' support of a decision is required. *Achievement-oriented* behaviours may increase motivation levels of highly capable subordinates who are bored from having too few challenges, but they might backfire if used with subordinates who are already pushed to their limits. Effective managers seem to have a knack for determining the kinds of leader behaviours that are likely to work in different situations and result in increased efficiency and effectiveness.

Direct supervision may be helpful when subordinates have trouble completing tasks.

to be adjusted for different companies, for different employees, and perhaps even for different countries. Recall from Chapter 2 Geert Hofstede's work on cultural differences across nations. Countries that have high power-distance dimension are more likely to accept autocratic leaders and direct supervision. Accordingly, Chinese employees tend to accept directive behaviours, while U.S. employees do not.

> **leader substitute**
> Characteristics of subordinates or characteristics of a situation or context that act in place of the influence of a leader and make leadership unnecessary.

The Leader Substitutes Model

The leader substitutes model suggests that leadership is sometimes unnecessary because substitutes for leadership are present. A **leader substitute** is something that acts in place of the influence of a leader and makes leadership unnecessary. This model suggests that under certain conditions managers do not have to play a leadership role—that members of an organization sometimes can perform highly without a manager exerting influence over them.[37] The leader substitutes model is a contingency model because it suggests that in some situations leadership is unnecessary. Take the case of David Cotsonas, who teaches English at a foreign-language school in Cyprus, an island in the Mediterranean Sea. Cotsonas is fluent in Greek, English, and French; is an excellent teacher; and is highly motivated. Many of his students are businesspeople who have some rudimentary English skills and wish to increase their fluency to be able to conduct more of their business in English. He enjoys not only teaching them English but also learning about the work they do, and he often keeps in touch with his students after they finish his classes. Cotsonas meets with the director of the school twice a year to discuss semiannual class schedules and enrollments.

With practically no influence from a leader, Cotsonas is a highly motivated top performer at the school. In his situation, leadership is unnecessary because substitutes for leadership are present. Cotsonas's teaching expertise, his motivation, and his enjoyment of his work all are substitutes for the influence of a leader—in this case, the school's director. If the school's director were to try to exert influence over the way Cotsonas goes about performing his job, Cotsonas would probably resent this infringement on his autonomy, and it is unlikely that his performance would improve because he is already one of the school's best teachers.

As in Cotsonas's case, both the *characteristics of subordinates*—such as their skills, abilities, experience, knowledge, and motivation—and the *characteristics of the situation or context*—such as the extent to which the work is interesting and enjoyable—can be substitutes for

To illustrate the importance of understanding that situations are different, and can require different styles, consider the fate of some of the Americans who have been recruited to run Canadian companies. Retailer Millard Barron was brought north to turn Zellers around, and American Bill Fields was supposed to save Hudson's Bay Co. Neither could replicate their American successes in Canada. Texas oilman J.P. Bryan was given the chance to restore profitability at two Canadian companies—Gulf Canada Resources Ltd. (now ConocoPhillips Company) and Canadian 88 Energy Corp. (now Esprit Exploration Limited)—and failed at both attempts.[36] Chief operating officer Gary Daichendt and chief technology officer Gary Kunis walked away from Nortel Corp. over management differences or "divergent management styles and different views of the future of the business" with the then CEO Bill Owens, who is facing little scrutiny in the criminal fraud trials that began in 2012 against three previous Nortel executives. These examples show the importance of understanding that one's leadership style may need leadership.[38] When work is interesting and enjoyable, as it is for Cotsonas, job holders do not need to be coaxed into performing because performing is rewarding in its own right. Similarly, when managers empower their subordinates or use *self-managed work teams* (discussed in detail in Chapter 10), the need for leadership influence from a manager is decreased because team members manage themselves.

Substitutes for leadership can increase organizational efficiency and effectiveness because they free up some of managers' valuable time and allow managers to focus their efforts on discovering new ways to improve organizational effectiveness. The director of the language school, for example, was able to spend much of his time making arrangements to open a second school in Rhodes, an island in the Aegean Sea, because of the presence of leadership substitutes, not only in the case of Cotsonas but in that of most of the other teachers at the school as well.

Bringing It All Together

Effective leadership in organizations occurs when managers take steps to lead in a way that is appropriate for the situation or context in which leadership occurs and the subordinates who are being led. The four contingency models of leadership just discussed help managers identify the necessary ingredients for effective leadership. They are complementary in that each one looks at the leadership question from a different angle. Fiedler's contingency model explores how a manager's leadership style needs to be matched to the leadership situation that the manager is in for maximum effectiveness. Hersey-Blanchard's situational leadership theory examines the need for leaders to adjust their style to match their followers' ability and motivation.

Tips **FOR MANAGERS**

Applying Contingency Models of Leadership

1. When two individuals are engaged in conflict and take a competing stance (Chapter 12), they tend to be highly assertive and unmotivated to find a solution to the problem. In this case, apply the Hersey-Blanchard SLT's *participating* style of leadership to encourage the parties to find a solution they can live with.

2. Increases in absenteeism and being late for work may be indications that the employee is burning out. Use positive reinforcement (Chapter 8) and *supportive* leader behaviours to reduce the lower level of performance.

3. Cultivate an inclusive culture with a highly skilled and highly motivated workforce so that employees can work in self-managed teams effectively. This will free up your time to develop and communicate a vision that inspires others to achieve the organization's goals.

House's path-goal theory focuses on how managers should motivate subordinates and describes the specific kinds of behaviours that managers can engage in to have a highly motivated workforce. The leadership substitutes model alerts managers to the fact that sometimes they do not need to exert influence over subordinates and thus can free up their time for other important activities. Table 9.3 recaps these four contingency models of leadership.

TABLE 9.3 Contingency Models of Leadership		
Model	**Focus**	**Key Contingencies**
Fiedler's contingency model	Describes two leader styles, relationship-oriented and task-oriented, and the kinds of situations in which each kind of leader will be most effective	The favourableness for leading depends on three contingency factors: leader–member relations, task-structure, and position power.
Hersey-Blanchard's-situational leadership theory	Describes how leaders adjust their styles to match their followers' ability and motivation	The styles that managers should use are contingent on the ability and motivation of subordinates
House's path-goal theory	Describes how effective leaders motivate their followers	The behaviours that managers should engage in to be effective leaders are contingent on the nature of the subordinates and the work they do
Leader substitutes model	Describes when leadership is unnecessary	Whether or not leadership is necessary for subordinates to perform highly is contingent on characteristics of the subordinates and the situation

Transactional and Transformational Models of Leadership

Transformational leadership is often contrasted with transactional leadership. In transactional leadership, managers use their reward and coercive powers to encourage high performance. **Transactional leadership** occurs when managers guide or motivate their subordinates in the direction of established goals. Transactional leaders use rewards to recognize appropriate behaviour. Under this kind of leadership, employees will generally meet performance expectations, though rarely will they exceed expectations.[39] When managers reward high performers, reprimand or otherwise punish low performers, and motivate subordinates by reinforcing desired behaviours and extinguishing or punishing undesired ones, they are engaging in transactional leadership. This style "results in performance below expectations, and discourages innovation and initiative in the workplace."[40] While leaders should not ignore poor performance, effective leaders emphasize how to achieve expectations, rather than dwelling on mistakes.

Hierarchical organizations still dominate Canada's "Most Respected Corporations,"[41] but some organizations are trying to be more innovative, faster moving, and more responsive to employees. These organizations have turned to a different style of leadership where leaders and managers not only are expected to perform supervisory tasks but also need to focus on vision-setting activities. These theories try to explain how certain leaders can achieve extraordinary performance from their followers, and they emphasize symbolic and emotionally appealing leadership behaviours.[42]

When managers have such dramatic effects on their subordinates and on an organization as a whole, they are engaging in transformational leadership. **Transformational leadership** occurs when managers change (or transform) their subordinates in three important ways[43]:

1. *Transformational managers make subordinates aware of how important their jobs are for the organization and how necessary it is for them to perform those jobs as best they can so that the organization can attain its goals.* At TELUS, Darren Entwistle took his entire 2010 cash salary in company shares. This demonstrated his strong belief in his team's ability to create sustainable value for the company.

2. *Transformational managers make their subordinates aware of the subordinates' own needs for personal growth, development, and accomplishment.* One of Entwistle's important steps at TELUS was to create an innovation-based organizational culture that encourages employees to reach their full potential so they will feel free to consider new ways of doing things at the company.

3. *Transformational managers motivate their subordinates to work for the good of the organization as a whole, not just for their own personal gain or benefit.* In transforming TELUS, Entwistle explained to employees the need for change at the company and that growth and improvement in productivity would make the company much stronger, thus benefiting everyone. All employees were encouraged to feel responsible for giving back to the community by engaging in philanthropic activities, for which the company won an award.

Many transformational leaders engage in transactional leadership. They reward subordinates for a job well done and notice and respond to substandard performance. But they also have their eyes on the bigger picture of how much better things could be in their organizations, how much more their subordinates are capable of achieving, and how important it is to treat their subordinates with respect and to help them reach their full potential.

Influencing Others

How do managers like Entwistle transform subordinates and produce dramatic effects in their organizations? There are at least three ways in which managers and other transformational leaders can influence their followers: by *being a charismatic leader,* by *stimulating subordinates intellectually,* and by *engaging in developmental consideration* (see Table 9.4).

Being a Charismatic Leader

Transformational managers such as Entwistle are **charismatic leaders.** They have a vision of how good things could be in their work groups and organizations,

transactional leadership Leaders who guide their subordinates toward expected goals by rewarding them for high performance and reprimanding them for low performance, with no expectation of exceeding expected behaviour.

transformational leadership Leadership that makes subordinates aware of the importance of their jobs and performance to the organization and aware of their own needs for personal growth, and that motivates subordinates to work for the good of the organization.

charismatic leaders Enthusiastic, self-confident leaders who are able to communicate clearly their vision of how good things could be.

TABLE 9.4	Transformational Leadership
Transformational Managers	
• Tend to be charismatic	
• Intellectually stimulate subordinates	
• Engage in developmental consideration	
Subordinates of Transformational Managers	
• Have increased awareness of the importance of their jobs and high performance	
• Are aware of their own needs for growth, development, and accomplishment	
• Work for the good of the organization and not just their own personal benefit	

and it is in contrast with the status quo. Their vision usually entails dramatic improvements in group and organizational performance as a result of changes in the organization's structure, culture, strategy, decision making, and other critical processes and factors. This vision paves the way for gaining a competitive advantage. From the opening case, it is clear that Darren Entwistle's vision for TELUS is to be a world leader not only in wireless data, but also in corporate citizenship by adopting a "give where we live" philosophy.

Charismatic leaders are excited and enthusiastic about their vision and clearly communicate it to their subordinates. The excitement, enthusiasm, and self-confidence of a charismatic leader contribute to the leader's being able to inspire followers to enthusiastically support his or her vision.[44] Darren Entwistle may look young for his age, but he speaks like a statesman giving a speech at the UN. People often think of charismatic leaders or managers as being "larger than life." The essence of charisma, however, is having a vision and enthusiastically communicating it to others. Thus, managers who appear to be quiet and earnest can also be charismatic.

The most comprehensive analysis of charismatic leadership was conducted by Professor Rabindra Kanungo at McGill University, together with Jay Conger.[45] Based on studies of managers from Canada, the United States, and India, they identified five dimensions that characterize charismatic leadership. These are shown in Table 9.5.

Does charismatic leadership really make a difference? An unpublished study by Robert House and some colleagues studying 63 American and 49 Canadian companies (including Nortel Networks, Molson [now Molson-Coors], Gulf Canada [now ConocoPhillips], and Manulife Financial) found that "between 15 and 25 percent of the variation in profitability among the companies was accounted for by the leadership qualities of their

CEO."[46] Charismatic leaders led the more profitable companies. During Entwistle's 10 years as CEO at TELUS, the company has delivered the highest shareholder returns among incumbent telecommunications companies on a global basis.

An increasing body of research shows that people who work for charismatic leaders are motivated to exert extra work effort and, because they like their leaders, they express greater satisfaction.[47] One of the most cited studies of the effects of charismatic leadership was done at the University of British Columbia in the early 1980s by Jane Howell (now at the Richard Ivey School of Business, University of Western Ontario) and Peter Frost.[48] The two found that those who worked under a charismatic leader generated more ideas, produced better results, reported higher job satisfaction, and showed stronger bonds of loyalty. Howell, in summarizing these results, says, "Charismatic leaders know how to inspire people to think in new directions."[49]

The accounting scandals and high-profile bankruptcies of North American companies, including Enron and WorldCom, suggest some of the dangers of charismatic leadership. WorldCom Inc.'s Bernard Ebbers and Enron Corp.'s Kenneth Lay "seemed almost a breed apart, blessed with unique visionary powers" when their companies were increasing stock prices at phenomenal rates in the 1990s.[50] After the scandals, however, there was some desire for CEOs with less vision and more ethical and corporate responsibility.

Stimulating Subordinates Intellectually

Transformational managers openly share information with their subordinates so that subordinates are aware of

TABLE 9.5	Key Characteristics of a Charismatic Leader

1. *Vision and articulation.* Has a vision—expressed as an idealized goal—that proposes a future better than the status quo; is able to clarify the importance of the vision in terms that are understandable to others.
2. *Personal risk.* Willing to take on high personal risk, incur high costs, and engage in self-sacrifice to achieve the vision.
3. *Environmental sensitivity.* Able to make realistic assessments of the environmental constraints and resources needed to bring about change.
4. *Sensitivity to follower needs.* Perceptive of others' abilities and responsive to their needs and feelings.
5. *Unconventional behaviour.* Engages in behaviours that are perceived as novel and counter to norms.

Source: Based on J.A. Conger and R.N. Kanungo, *Charismatic Leadership in Organizations* (Thousand Oaks, CA: Sage, 1998), p. 94.

intellectual stimulation Behaviour a leader engages in to make followers aware of problems and view these problems in new ways, consistent with the leader's vision.

developmental consideration Behaviour a leader engages in to support and encourage followers and help them develop and grow in the job.

problems and the need for change. The manager causes subordinates to view problems in their groups and throughout the organization from a different perspective, consistent with the manager's vision. Whereas in the past subordinates may not have been aware of some problems, may have viewed problems as a "management issue" beyond their concern, or may have viewed problems as insurmountable, the transformational manager's **intellectual stimulation** leads subordinates to view problems as challenges that they can and will meet and conquer. The manager engages and empowers subordinates to take personal responsibility for helping to solve problems.[51] For example, unlike other companies that often ask a team for an idea or to solve a problem and then tell them how much money they have to do it, Cirque du Soleil's leader Guy Laliberté instead would decide how much could be spent on a new show and then "expect the creative team to come up with their vision within its financial boundaries."[52]

Engaging in Developmental Consideration

When a manager engages in **developmental consideration,** he or she not only performs the consideration behaviours described earlier, such as demonstrating true concern for the well-being of subordinates, but also goes one step further. The manager goes out of his or her way to support and encourage subordinates, giving them opportunities to enhance their skills and capabilities and to grow and excel in their jobs.[53]

Research Support

The evidence supporting the superiority of transformational leadership is overwhelmingly impressive. For example, studies of Canadian, American, and German military officers found, at every level, that transformational leaders were considered more effective than their transactional counterparts (see Table 9.6).[54] Professor Jane Howell (at the University of Western Ontario) and her colleagues studied 250 executives and managers at a major financial services company and found that "transformational leaders had 34 percent higher business unit performance results than other types of leaders."[55] Under Entwistle, TELUS's growth and shareholder returns have been phenomenal. Studies also find that when leaders engage in transformational leadership, their subordinates tend to have higher levels of job satisfaction and performance.[56] Additionally, subordinates of transformational leaders may be more likely to trust their leaders and their organizations and feel that they are being fairly treated, which, in turn, may positively influence their work motivation (see Chapter 8).[57]

All organizations, no matter how large or small, successful or unsuccessful, can benefit when their managers engage in transformational leadership. Moreover, while the benefits of transformational leadership are often most

---

> **TABLE 9.6**   Transactional versus Transformational Leadership

Transactional Leadership	Transformational Leadership
Managers guide and motivate subordinates to achieve organizational goals through conventional methods such as direct supervision.	Produce dramatic effects for the organization's performance by inspiring subordinates to go above and beyond stated goals by modelling desired behaviours.
The status quo daily activities of planning, leading, organizing, and controlling are carried out effectively and efficiently.	Have vision that goes beyond the status quo entailing changes in the organization's structure, culture, strategy, decision making, and other critical variables for gaining a competitive advantage.
Subordinates meet performance expectations but rarely exceed them.	Subordinates perform at levels exceeding expectations.
Formal rules, regulations, and the fear of punishment discourage risk taking and innovation.	Show excitement and enthusiasm, trust and respect, and concern for subordinates' growth and development, encourage risk taking and initiative.
Managers rely on legitimate and reward power to exercise authority and recognize high and low levels of performance.	Are charismatic, possess referent power, intellectually stimulate subordinates and engage in developmental consideration to foster high performance.
The model is effective and efficient in a stable organizational environment.	Is an effective model in an unstable, dynamic environment where a change in the organization's course is desired or necessary to gain a competitive advantage.

apparent when an organization is in trouble, transformational leadership can be an enduring approach to leadership, leading to long-run organizational effectiveness.

LO5 Explain how gender, culture, and emotional intelligence affect leadership effectiveness.

Gender, Culture, Emotional Intelligence, and Leadership

There are many questions about whether men and women have different leadership styles and whether observed differences have more to do with personality differences across people rather than with explicit gender differences. Others consider whether leadership styles are the same cross-culturally and whether our North American leadership theories apply in other countries. More recently, the effects of *moods and emotions* of leaders on their effectiveness have gained notable attention. We consider these issues in the following sections.

Gender and Leadership

The increasing number of women entering the ranks of management as well as the problems some women face in their efforts to be hired as managers or promoted into management positions have prompted researchers to explore the relationship between gender and leadership. Although relatively more women are in management positions today than 10 years ago, relatively few women are in top management in larger organizations, and, in some organizations, even in middle management.

Although women make up 45 percent of the labour force in Canada, they fill only 32 percent of managerial roles, and only 12 percent of the senior management roles. In 2008, only 12 Fortune 500 companies had women CEOs.[58] In Canada, the growth of women-owned businesses is skyrocketing. In 2010, these businesses exceeded 1 million. Although female entrepreneurship is growing 60 percent faster than men's in Canada, just 4.3 percent of women's companies enjoy revenue of $1 million or more, while 10.7 percent of men's companies do.[59]

When women do advance to top-management positions, special attention is often focused on the fact that they are women. For example women CEOs of large companies are still rare; those who make it to the very top spot—such as Dianne Craig, CEO Ford Motor Co. of Canada in 2011; Canadian-born Andrea Jung, former CEO of Avon; and Virginia Rometty, CEO IBM in 2012—are very salient. While women have certainly made inroads into leadership positions in organizations, they continue to be very underrepresented in top leadership posts. For example, women

Andrea Jung—ex-CEO of Avon, the famous cosmetics producer—advanced to that rank after first serving as the company's president and chief operating officer.

held 3.2 percent of *Fortune* 500 CEO roles in 2011,[60] and 5.6 percent of *Financial Post* 500 CEO/Head roles.[61] The latter represents 27 of 500 companies. According to the Conference Board of Canada, rates of women in executive positions have virtually remained unchanged since 1987.[62] Nine best practices that help companies achieve greater gender equality are outlined in Table 9.7.[63]

Three companies worth noting that have supported women in leadership roles are:

- Canadian Pacific Railway—which has instituted a range of female-friendly workplace policies, supported by a strong communications program.

TABLE 9.7	Best Practices for Achieving Gender Diversity
• Using accountable search techniques	
• Identifying talent and providing succession planning initiatives	
• Setting up mentoring and coaching programs	
• Offering job rotation opportunities	
• Ensuring ongoing measurement	
• Creating an inclusive work environment through awareness training	
• Avoiding the glass cliff and token females	
• Highlighting role models and communicating success	
• Ensuring senior management support	

- Manitoba Lotteries Corporation—which has developed a comprehensive competency model and leveraged it to drive key changes to their talent systems.
- TD Bank Financial Group—which has a Women in Leadership committee and helps women network with and mentor each other.

Nevertheless, the challenges remain. All executives encounter difficulty with balancing work and life. With the demands of the job, which can easily add up to 60 to 80 hours of work per week, it is hard for executives to find time for life outside of work. Organizations must recognize that female and male executives in general face different work–life issues, and that the organization's culture regarding flexibility, control, capacity, and practical solutions must be tailored to the individual executive's needs if they want to support and encourage greater gender diversity in leadership roles.

A widespread stereotype of women is that they are nurturing, supportive, and concerned with interpersonal relations. Men are stereotypically viewed as being directive and focused on task accomplishment. Such stereotypes suggest that women tend to be more relationship-oriented as managers and engage in more consideration behaviours, whereas men are more task-oriented and engage in more initiating structure behaviours. Does the behaviour of actual male and female managers bear out these stereotypes? Do female managers lead in different ways than males? Are male or female managers more effective as leaders?

Research suggests that male managers and female managers who have leadership positions in organizations behave in similar ways.[64] Women do not engage in more consideration than do men, and men do not engage in more initiating structure than do women. Research does suggest, however, that leadership style may vary between women and men. Women tend to be somewhat more participative as leaders than men, involving subordinates in decision making and seeking their input.[65] Male managers tend to be less participative than female managers, making more decisions on their own and wanting to do things their own way. Moreover, research suggests that men tend to be harsher when they punish their subordinates than do women.[66]

There are at least two reasons why female managers may be more participative as leaders than are male managers.[67] First, subordinates may try to resist the influence of female managers more than they do the influence of male managers. Some subordinates may never have reported to a woman before, some may inappropriately see management roles as being more appropriate for men

than for women, and some may just resist being led by a woman. To overcome this resistance and encourage subordinates' trust and respect, female managers may adopt a participative approach.

A second reason why female managers may be more participative is that they sometimes have better interpersonal skills than do male managers.[68] A participative approach to leadership requires high levels of interaction and involvement between a manager and his or her subordinates, sensitivity to subordinates' feelings, and the ability to make decisions that may be unpopular with subordinates but necessary for reaching goals. Good interpersonal skills may help female managers have the effective interactions with their subordinates that are crucial to a participative approach.[69] To the extent that male managers have more difficulty managing interpersonal relationships, they may shy away from the high levels of interaction with subordinates that are necessary for true participation.

The key finding from research on leader behaviours, however, is that male and female managers do *not* differ significantly in their propensities to perform different leader behaviours. Even though they may be more participative, female managers do not engage in more consideration or less initiating structure than male managers.

Perhaps a question even more important than whether male and female managers differ in the leadership behaviours they perform is whether they differ in effectiveness. Consistent with the findings about leadership behaviours, research suggests that across different kinds of organizational settings, male and female managers tend to be equally *effective* as leaders.[70] Thus, there is no logical basis for stereotypes favouring male managers and leaders

Premiers Christy Clark of British Columbia and Alison Redford of Alberta.

or for the existence of the glass ceiling (an invisible barrier that seems to prevent women from advancing as far as they should in some organizations). Because women and men are equally effective as leaders, the increasing number of women in the workforce should result in a larger pool of highly qualified candidates for management positions in organizations, ultimately enhancing organizational effectiveness.[71]

Leadership Styles across Cultures

Some evidence suggests that leadership styles vary not only among individuals but also among countries or cultures. Some research suggests that European managers tend to be more humanistic or people-oriented than Japanese and American managers. The collectivistic culture in Japan places prime emphasis on the group rather than the individual, so the importance of individuals' own personalities, needs, and desires is minimized. Organizations in North America tend to be very profit-oriented and thus tend to downplay the importance of individual employees' needs and desires. Many countries in Europe have a more individualistic outlook than does Japan and a more humanistic outlook than does the United States, which may result in some European managers being more people-oriented than their Japanese or American counterparts. European managers, for example, tend to be reluctant to lay off employees, and when a layoff is absolutely necessary, they take careful steps to make it as painless as possible.[72]

Another cross-cultural difference that has been noted is in time horizons. Managers in any two countries often differ in their time horizons, but there also may be cultural differences. Canadian and American organizations tend to have a short-run profit orientation, which results in a leadership style emphasizing short-run performance. By contrast, Japanese organizations tend to have a long-run growth orientation, which results in Japanese managers' personal leadership styles emphasizing long-run performance. Justus Mische, now chair at the European organization Aventis (formerly Hoechst), has suggested that "Europe, at least the big international firms in Europe, have a philosophy between the Japanese long term and the United States short term."[73] Research on these and other global aspects of leadership is in its infancy, but as it continues, more cultural differences in managers' personal leadership styles may be discovered.

> **"Europe, at least the big international firms in Europe, have a philosophy between the Japanese long term and the United States short term."**
>
> *Justus Mische, Aventis*

Emotional Intelligence and Leadership

Do the moods and emotions leaders experience on the job influence their behaviour and effectiveness as leaders? Research suggests that this is likely to be the case. For example, one study found that when store managers experienced positive moods at work, salespeople in the stores they led provided high-quality customer-service and were less likely to quit.[74] Another study found that groups whose leaders experienced positive moods had better coordination, while groups whose leaders experienced negative moods exerted more effort; members of groups with leaders in positive moods also tended to experience more positive moods themselves; and members of groups with leaders in negative moods tended to experience more negative moods.[75]

Emotional intelligence is the ability to understand and manage one's own moods and emotions and the moods and emotions of other people. A leader's level of emotional intelligence may play a particularly important role in leadership effectiveness.[76] For example, emotional intelligence may help leaders develop a vision for their organizations, motivate their subordinates to commit to this vision, and energize them to enthusiastically work to achieve this vision. Moreover, emotional intelligence may enable leaders to develop a significant identity for their organization and instill high levels of trust and cooperation throughout the organization while maintaining the flexibility needed to respond to changing conditions.[77]

There are ways to cultivate the set of human skills that make up emotional intelligence.[78] See Table 9.8.

Emotional intelligence also plays a crucial role in how leaders relate to and deal with their followers, particularly when it comes to encouraging followers to be creative.[79] Creativity in organizations is an emotion-laden process, as it often entails challenging the status quo, being willing to take risks and accept and learn from failures, and doing much hard work to bring creative ideas to fruition in terms of new products, services, or procedures and processes when uncertainty is bound to be high.[80] Leaders who are high on emotional intelligence are more likely to understand all the emotions surrounding creative endeavours, to be able to awaken and support the creative pursuits

emotional intelligence
The ability to understand and manage one's moods and emotions and the moods and emotions of other people.

TABLE 9.8	Ways to Cultivate Emotional Intelligence

- Develop self-awareness, including managing your emotions (or self-regulation); this doesn't mean suppressing emotions, but not letting your disturbing emotions get in the way of life;

- Marshall your positive emotions and passions for a full life;

- Develop empathy, sensing how other people are feeling and a general social awareness;

- And, put that all together during social interactions.

of their followers, and to provide the kind of support that enables creativity to flourish in organizations.[81]

Leaders, like people everywhere, sometimes make mistakes. Emotional intelligence may also help leaders respond appropriately when they realize that they have made a mistake.

connect

Learn more on what it takes to become an emotionally intelligent leader in Connect.

Summary and Review

LO1 The Nature of Leadership Leadership is the process by which a person exerts influence over other people and inspires, motivates, and directs their activities to help achieve group or organizational goals. Leaders are able to influence others because they possess power. The five types of power available to managers are *legitimate power, reward power, coercive power, expert power,* and *referent power.* Many managers are using empowerment as a tool to increase their effectiveness as leaders.

LO2 Early Models of Leadership The *trait model* of leadership describes personal characteristics or traits that contribute to effective leadership. However, some managers who possess these traits are not effective leaders, and some managers who do not possess all the traits are nevertheless effective leaders. The *behaviour model* of leadership describes two kinds of behaviour that most leaders engage in: consideration and initiating structure. The managerial grid represents five styles of leadership based on the degree of behaviour along these two dimensions.

LO3 Contingency Models of Leadership Contingency models take into account the complexity surrounding leadership and the role of the situation in determining whether a manager is an effective or ineffective leader. *Fiedler's contingency model* explains why managers may be effective leaders in one situation and ineffective in another. *Hersey-Blanchard's situational leadership theory* examines the need for leaders to adjust their style to match their followers' level of ability and motivation. *House's path-goal theory* describes how effective managers motivate their subordinates by determining what outcomes their subordinates want, rewarding subordinates with these outcomes when they achieve their goals and perform at a high level, and clarifying the paths to goal attainment. The *leader substitutes model* suggests that sometimes managers do not have to play a leadership role because their subordinates perform highly without the manager having to exert influence over them.

LO4 Transactional and Transformational Models of Leadership Transactional leaders generally motivate their subordinates to meet expectations by rewarding high performance and extinguishing undesirable behaviours. Transformational leadership occurs when managers have dramatic effects on their subordinates and on the organization as a whole and inspire and energize subordinates to solve problems and improve performance. These effects include making subordinates aware of the importance of their own jobs and high performance; making subordinates aware of their own needs for personal growth, development, and accomplishment; and motivating subordinates to work for the good of the organization and not just their own personal gain. Managers can engage in transformational leadership by being charismatic leaders, by stimulating subordinates intellectually, and by engaging in developmental consideration. Transformational managers also often engage in transactional leadership by using their reward and coercive powers to encourage high performance.

LO5 Gender, Culture, Emotional Intelligence, and Leadership The number of female top executives has remained fairly constant over the last two decades; women continue to be underrepresented due to the unique challenges they face in balancing work–life issues. Female and male managers do not differ in the leadership behaviours that they perform, contrary to stereotypes suggesting that women are more relationship-oriented and men more task-oriented. Female managers sometimes are more participative than are male managers, however. Research has found that women and men are equally effective as managers and leaders. Studies have found differences in leadership styles across cultures. European leaders tend to be more people-oriented than either American or Japanese leaders. Leaders also differ in their time orientations, with American and Canadian leaders being more oriented toward the short term, while Japanese are oriented toward the longer term in their approach to leading. The moods and emotions leaders experience on the job, and their ability to effectively manage these feelings, can influence their effectiveness as leaders. Moreover, emotional intelligence has the potential to contribute to leadership effectiveness in multiple ways, including encouraging and supporting creativity among followers.

KEY TERMS

charismatic leader	initiating structure or task-oriented behaviours	position power
coercive power		referent power
consideration or employee-centred-behaviour	intellectual stimulation	reward power
	leader	situational leadership theory (SLT)
contingency models of leadership	leader–member relations	
	leader substitute	task structure
developmental consideration	leadership	transactional leadership
emotional intelligence	legitimate power	transformational leadership
empowerment	path-goal theory	
expert power	personal leadership style	

WRAP-UP TO ⟩⟩⟩ OPENING CASE

Telecommunications Visionary Receives Canadian Business Leader Award

HOW CAN A MANAGER TRANSFORM A COMPANY IN A RAPIDLY CHANGING ENVIRONMENT?

In March 2011, in front of a record crowd of over 900 at the Alberta School of Business, Dean Mike Percy announced that Darren Entwistle—leader of the TELUS Corporation and the longest-serving CEO amongst incumbent telecom companies globally—had received the school's 30th Canadian Business Leader Award (CBLA). After having read and understood the concepts in this chapter, you should be able to answer the following questions:

1. *What traits and characteristics make Darren Entwistle an effective leader?*

   ANSWER: Hundreds of studies since the 1930s have indicated that certain personal characteristics as well as skills and abilities are found in effective leaders like

Darren Entwistle. Traits such as intelligence, knowledge and expertise, dominance, self-confidence, high energy, tolerance for stress, integrity, honesty, and maturity are on the list. It is important to remember that some effective leaders may possess some or all of these traits, while some leaders who do possess them are not effective in their leadership roles. Darren Entwistle, however, is an effective leader who demonstrates several leader traits as CEO of TELUS Corp. His intelligence, knowledge, and expertise is shown in his education and in the previous management positions he has held in the United Kingdom. He has positioned TELUS as the dominant player in the wireless telecom space in Canada. He had the self confidence, energy, integrity, and maturity to turn the company's fortunes around after becoming CEO in 2000.

2. *Is Entwistle a transformational leader? Why or why not?*

ANSWER: Transformational leadership occurs when managers change (or transform) their subordinates in three important ways:

1. Transformational managers make subordinates aware of how important their jobs are for the organization and how necessary it is for them to perform those jobs as best they can so that the organization can attain its goals. At TELUS, Darren Entwistle took his entire 2010 cash salary in company shares. This demonstrated his strong belief in his team's ability to create sustainable value for the company.

2. Transformational managers make their subordinates aware of the subordinates' own needs for personal growth, development, and accomplishment. One of Entwistle's important steps at TELUS was to create an innovation-based organizational culture that encourages employees to reach their full potential so they will feel free to consider new ways of doing things at the company.

3. Transformational managers motivate their subordinates to work for the good of the organization as a whole, not just for their own personal gain or benefit. In transforming TELUS, Entwistle explained to employees the need for change at the company and that growth and improvement in productivity would make the company much stronger, thus benefiting everyone. All employees were encouraged to feel responsible for giving back to the community by engaging in philanthropic activities, for which the company won an award.

Management in Action

TOPICS FOR DISCUSSION AND ACTION

LEVEL 1 Knowledge & Comprehension

1. What is meant by "leadership," and on what bases of power do leaders influence others to take action that achieves organizational goals?
2. Describe trait and behavioural theories of leadership and their limitations.
3. Describe the leadership styles that evolve from the managerial grid. Which one is deemed to be optimal, and why? Is this style suitable in every situation?

LEVEL 2 Application & Analysis

4. Think of specific situations in which it might be especially important for a manager to engage in consideration and in initiating structure.

5. Interview a manager to find out how the three situational characteristics that Fiedler identified are affecting the manager's ability to provide leadership.

6. Discuss why substitutes for leadership can contribute to organizational effectiveness.

LEVEL 3 Synthesis & Evaluation

7. Listen to the following podcast by Jack Welch, former CEO of General Electric, "What Are 'Agents of Change' in Organizations?" (www.businessweek.com/mediacenter/qt/podcasts/welchway/welchway_10_10_08.mp3). Discuss the three characteristics of a "change agent" in organizations.

8. Compare and contrast transactional and transformational leadership styles.

9. Discuss why some people still think that men make better managers than do women, even though research indicates that men and women are equally effective as managers and leaders.

SELF-REFLECTION EXERCISE

Your school is developing a one-day orientation program for new students majoring in business. You have been asked to consider leading the group of students who will design and implement the orientation program. Develop a two- or three-page "handout" that shows whether the position is a natural fit for you. To do this, (1) identify your strengths and weaknesses in the sources of power you can bring to the project, and (2) discuss whether you would be a transactional leader or a transformation leader and why. Provide a strong concluding statement about whether or not you would be the best leader for this task.

SMALL GROUP BREAKOUT EXERCISE

Improving Leadership Effectiveness

Form groups of three to five, and appoint one member as the spokesperson who will communicate your findings and conclusions to the whole class when called on by the instructor. Then discuss the following scenario:

You are a team of human resource consultants who have been hired by Carla Caruso, an entrepreneur who started her own interior decorating business. At first, she worked on her own as an independent contractor. Then, because of a dramatic increase in the number of new homes being built, she decided to form her own company.

She hired a secretary/bookkeeper and four interior decorators. Caruso still does decorating jobs herself and has adopted a hands-off approach to leading the four decorators because she feels that interior design is a very personal, creative endeavour. Rather than paying the decorators on some kind of commission basis, she pays them a higher-than-average salary so that they are motivated to do what is best for their customers, not what will result in higher billings and commissions.

Caruso thought everything was going smoothly until customer complaints started coming in. These complaints were about the decorators being hard to reach, promising unrealistic delivery times, being late for or failing to keep appointments, and being impatient and rude when customers had trouble making up their minds. Caruso knows that her decorators are competent people and is concerned that she is not effectively leading and managing them. She has asked for your advice.

1. What advice can you give Caruso to either increase her power or use her existing power more effectively?

2. Does Caruso seem to be performing appropriate leadership behaviours in this situation? What advice can you give her about the kinds of behaviours she should perform?

3. How can Caruso increase the decorators' motivation to deliver high-quality customer service?

4. Would you advise Caruso to try engaging in transformational leadership in this situation? If not, why not? If so, what steps would you advise her to take?

BUSINESS PLANNING EXERCISE

Your professor may ask you to write a business plan for a new venture or a strategic plan for an existing venture. At the end of every chapter, you will have an opportunity to apply managerial and organizational concepts to the exercise of writing a business plan. Refer to Appendix A.

Your group is thinking about the management team for your new venture. You have to include a section in the business plan on what roles and responsibilities the management will undertake and what qualifies them to lead the organization.

1. Identify the traits you think the managers should possess for your venture.

2. Choose a functional area. Do you think a people-oriented leader or a production-oriented leader would best suit the situation? Why?

3. Would a transactional or transformational leader be more appropriate as the head of your organization?

MANAGING ETHICALLY EXERCISE

One of your subordinates has noticed that your expense account reports have repeatedly overstated your expenses because you always bill for an extra day, at the "daily rate," when you go out of town on company business. Your assistant knows that you have always been in town and working from home on that extra day. He has questioned your reports, as you have now submitted 15 of these for the year. How would you use your knowledge of power to resolve this dilemma? Which use of power would be most ethical, and why?

MANAGEMENT CHALLENGE EXERCISE

Napoleon on Leadership[82]

Jim Warthin is a friend of yours; he is also CEO of a small plastics firm and has invited you in to discuss a new book he has recently read on leadership and Napoleon Bonaparte.[83] He tells you in an email that the author of this text has identified Napoleon's six winning leadership principles. Jim wants to discuss these principles in the context of the leadership course that you both took when in business school together. He wants your trusted feedback.

1. Exactitude: He sought pinpoint precision through extensive research, continuous planning, and constant awareness of the situation he faced, which included meditating on what might occur—in other words, awareness, research, and continuous planning.

2. Speed: He recognized that momentum—mass times velocity—applied to achieving goals with people as well. "He knew that resistance causes momentum to fade. Increasing speed is about reducing resistance, increasing urgency, and providing focus by employing concentration of force and economy of force," the author says—in other words, reducing resistance, increasing urgency, and providing focus.

3. Flexibility: Napoleon ensured that his armies could react quickly to situations, yet operate according to a strategic plan. He organized his troops into mobile units and empowered them by providing knowledge of the mission and structuring them to operate independently; yet he also made sure they were operating under a unified doctrine and serving one ultimate leader—in other words, building teams that are adaptable, empowered, and unified.

4. Simplicity: He ensured his objectives were simple, his messages were simple, and his processes were simple, reducing confusion. "The art of war does not require complicated manoeuvre. The simplest are the best," Napoleon declared—in other words, clear simple objectives, messages, and processes.

5. Character: While driven by his ambition, Napoleon always maintained honour and integrity, calmness and responsibility, and encouraging respect of other cultures.

6. Moral force: "In war, everything depends upon morale," Napoleon said. People do their best work when they have self-confidence, feel what they are doing is worthwhile, and are recognized for their effort—in other words, providing order, purpose recognition, and rewards.

1. Are Napoleon's six principles more suited to a transformational leader or a transactional leader? Why?

MANAGEMENT PORTFOLIO PROJECT

Answer the following questions about the organization you have chosen to follow:

1. How would you characterize the leadership style of the CEO?

2. Do you consider the CEO to be a transactional or transformative leader, and why? Is the style appropriate for the environmental context in which the organization is situated?

3. What sources of power does he or she rely on most heavily?

VIDEO MANAGEMENT CASE   connect

Assessing Leadership Judgement[84]

Richard Davis, partner at RHR International, talks about what HR should do to assess whether a potential leader has good judgment.

1. How should we assess leadership judgment?

2. What are some practical methods we can use to judge leadership?

3. What is HR's role in judging leadership?

Management Case

Taking the Ted Out of Turner Broadcasting[85]

You may not have heard of Phil Kent. After all, the CEO of Turner Broadcasting is a whole lot quieter than Ted Turner, the so-called Mouth of the South who remained front and center long after selling his cable empire to Time Warner in the 1990s. But Kent has emerged from Turner's shadow and is fast becoming one of Time Warner's most important executives. If the media giant spins off its long-troubled AOL division as expected, the collection of channels that Kent oversees—including TNT, TBS, TCM, and CNN—will contribute nearly half of Time Warner's earnings.

In the past six years, Kent has taken on the broadcast networks with a smorgasbord of programming matched by few other cable outfits. As more ad dollars flow from broadcast to cable networks, he is on a mission to get advertisers to pay as much for time on Turner as they do the Big Four broadcasters. It's a campaign Kent plans to press in the coming weeks as advertisers gather in New York for the annual ad-buying ritual known as the upfronts.

Kent, 54, is the first person to run Turner without the looming presence of its mercurial founder, who stepped away from Time Warner in 2006. As such, Turner is a much changed place. "Under Ted," says Time Warner CEO Jeffrey L. Bewkes, "the top management was always Ted." Whereas Turner reveled in making his own news, Kent is the antithesis of the media executive. Although he learned the business working for legendary Hollywood power broker Michael Ovitz at Creative Artists Agency in the late 1980s, he finds Tinseltown self-promotion repellent and abhors the cult of the CEO. "He's definitely not a rock star chief executive," says Steven R. Koonin, one of Kent's top lieutenants.

At two key junctures of his career, Kent took himself out of the fray—both times when he wasn't having fun anymore. After working for Ovitz for six years, he bailed and embarked on an around-the-world trip, ignoring the blandishments of headhunters, who tracked him to a rooftop café in Marrakesh. In the 1990s, Kent worked at Turner, but he quit in 2001 after the AOL Time Warner merger. "Not until you leave a job do you appreciate that the sun really will rise and fall without you," he explains. "This does make you more fearless in making tough decisions. After all, if you've fired yourself, you're much less afraid of being fired."

Pump Up the Brands

Bewkes was looking for someone to make tough decisions when he lured Kent back to run Turner in 2003. At the time, the cable network was in a lull, and Bewkes, who turned HBO into a pop culture sensation, wanted Kent to pump up Turner's brands and create buzz around its channels.

Kent has invested heavily to broaden Turner's offerings in news, scripted shows, cartoons, and sports. To lure young, professional viewers, a coveted cohort, Kent pushed TNT and TBS into original programming with marquee names. TNT's *The Closer,* starring Kyra Sedgwick as a sugar-addicted police chief, has become one of cable's top-rated shows. Ditto for *Saving Grace,* which features Holly Hunter as an Oklahoma cop with a dark past and a guardian angel.

Kent backed Adult Swim, a comedy channel that appears on Turner's Cartoon Network in the evenings. This network-within-a-network has allowed Turner to reel in two key demographics: teenage and early-twentysomething males, who watch the racy fare on Adult Swim at night, and kids and their parents, who watch the cartoons during the rest of the day. This year, TNT and TBS will air 13 original shows, versus none in 2003.

Kent's strategy is attracting a range of blue-chip advertisers, among them T-Mobile, DirecTV, Hewlett-Packard, and Procter & Gamble. Under Kent, Turner revenues, a mix of ad dollars and distribution fees, have nearly doubled, to $7 billion, according to people familiar with the numbers. So has cash flow, to $2.3 billion. (Time Warner does not break them out.)

By many accounts, Turner has become a far more inclusive place since Kent took the reins. Kent says his sabbaticals taught him that the CEO mania for scheduling every moment of the day is counterproductive. Splitting his weeks between Turner's headquarters in Atlanta and New York, he leaves time for colleagues, walking the halls and popping into people's offices. Koonin says it was during one of those office visits that he and Kent talked about focusing more on underserved audiences. That chat led eventually to offering comedian George Lopez his own late-night talk show on TBS to compete with Conan and Dave and bring in Hispanic viewers.

Kent's tenure hasn't been seamless. In 2007 he was forced to apologize for an Adult Swim guerrilla marketing stunt in Boston involving cartoonish devices that passersby mistook for bombs. This month, TNT canceled the advertising comedy *Trust Me* after just one season. Now, as Turner emerges as a more important part of a leaner Time Warner, Kent will have to morph into a role that makes him uneasy: the high-profile CEO.

Investors will be watching closely to see if he can, in fact, get advertisers to pay more for commercial airtime on Turner channels. Cable networks typically get a third or so less in advertising rates versus the broadcast networks. Kent acknowledges changing that dynamic won't be easy but says, "We can do a much better job of selling [the Turner] story."

1. How would you describe Phil Kent's personal leadership style?
2. What traits do you think he is high on?
3. What behaviours do you think he is likely to engage in?
4. Do you think Phil Kent is a transformational leader? Why or why not?

Source: Tom Lowry, "Taking the Ted Out of Turner Broadcasting." Reprinted from the May 4, 2009 issue of *BusinessWeek* by special permission. Copyright © 2009 by The McGraw-Hill Companies, Inc.

McGraw-Hill **connect**

Connect allows you to practise important concepts at your own pace and on your own schedule, with 24/7 online access to an eBook, practice quizzes, video cases, interactive exercises, study tools, and more.

10

Managing Teams

LEARNING OUTCOMES

LO1 Explain why groups and teams are key contributors to organizational effectiveness.

LO2 Identify the different types of groups and teams that help managers and organizations achieve their goals.

LO3 Explain how different elements of group dynamics influence the functioning and effectiveness of groups and teams.

LO4 Explain how group decision making can be improved by minimizing groupthink and fostering creativity and innovation.

LO5 Describe how managers can create high-performing teams by motivating group members to achieve organizational goals, reducing social loafing, and managing conflict effectively.

Opening Case

Virgin Group's Richard Branson: People Are Your Biggest Asset—Treat Them Like It[1]

HOW CAN MANAGERS USE TEAMS TO GAIN A COMPETITIVE ADVANTAGE?

How a new company treats its customers often decides whether it will be successful. Great businesses are good at turning customers into advocates for their companies. This means that their marketing efforts are supported by customer word-of-mouth and positive comments on review sites and social media channels.

The retention of customers is important to any company; after all, it makes more sense to keep the good customers you have than to continually chase new ones. In the travel sector, companies have to take customer service seriously if they hope to succeed, because a wonderful flight, train journey—or soon, we hope, a space trip—begins and ends with great service. While a company may be able to find ways to improve the interiors of their planes or trains, perhaps installing more comfortable seats and serving better meals, that expensive technology and luxurious design will count for nothing if customer service is shoddy.

I was recently reminded of how important customer service is for all businesses, both new and established, when I reconnected with the team at Virgin America and saw how they train their new employees. I came away with three key lessons that can be applied at any company.

First, an investment in your employees is an investment in your company. All airlines must ensure that everyone on staff, from pilots to ground workers, has rigorous operational, safety, security and even medical training; but at Virgin America, that's just the beginning. Our staff must also complete a broader immersion in brand values through

a two-day annual "brand bath," which the company calls Refresh. At those retreats, they focus on improving customer experience across the airline.

The flight crews are brought together with colleagues from different departments and trained in conflict resolution, hospitality and emotional intelligence, to help employees truly understand the customer's perspective; to resolve issues and not push them up the chain.

As an entrepreneur, how can you bring your team together to solve problems and build their trust in each other? At a small business, this might be as simple as starting a tradition of eating lunch together and talking about how work is progressing.

Second, always lead from the front. At Refresh, Virgin America CEO David Cush often holds question-and-answer sessions with employees to ensure that he personally addresses their concerns. This is the first step in building bonds between front-line staff and senior managers, which helps to create easy and open communications.

I've argued on a few recent occasions in these pages that executives and managers must step away from their desks and get to know their staff. If your company is too big for regular meetings, spending a few hours handling customer complaints yourself or working on the factory floor will help you understand what's really going on—and to break down any silos in your business.

Finally, make sure employees have the tools they need to succeed. Refresh teaches Virgin America employees how to solve problems on their own—a key to great customer service. This is an unusual approach; most businesses impose restrictions on their staff in terms of the types of problems employees can solve and the authority they have to do so. But our experience shows that the best solution is to provide people with the skills and confidence they need to deal with problems on their own, without sticking to a script or following a flow chart.

Most often, what's missing is information. If, in your meetings with your staff or during your time on the floor, you notice that employees are groping for answers, it's time to take action. Remove limits on access to databases; invest in new information technology; do whatever it takes to make sure that they can take initiative on their own. Celebrate successes in internal communications, to encourage others.

In tough times, when your competitors are cutting costs, it might be tempting to follow their lead and cut back on customer service. But slashing prices is not the only solution. Every customer is valuable; a thriving company is built on relationships, not just the bottom line.

After reading and understanding the concepts in this chapter, you should be able to answer the following questions:

1. *How do teams at Virgin America contribute to organizational effectiveness?*

2. *What types of teams are encouraged in this case?*

3. *How do the managers in this case create group cohesiveness and why is this important for high performance?*

Overview

Virgin Group companies are not alone in using groups and teams to improve organizational effectiveness. Managers in companies large and small are using groups and teams to enhance performance, increase responsiveness to customers, spur innovation, and motivate employees. In this chapter, we look in detail at how groups and teams can contribute to organizational effectiveness and at the

types of groups and teams used in organizations. We discuss how different elements of group dynamics influence the functioning and effectiveness of groups, and we describe how managers can motivate group members to achieve organizational goals and reduce social loafing in groups and teams. By the end of this chapter, you will appreciate why the effective management of groups and teams is a key ingredient for organizational performance and effectiveness. See Figure 10.1.

FIGURE 10.1 Groups' and Teams' Contributions to Organizational Effectiveness

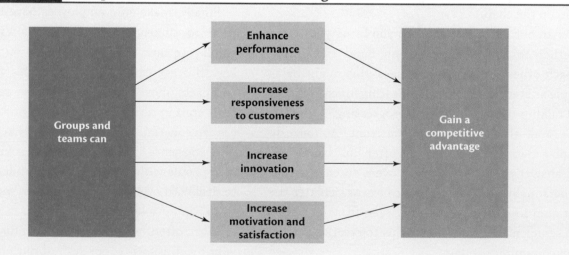

LO1 Explain why groups and teams are key contributors to organizational effectiveness.

Groups, Teams, and Organizational Effectiveness

It is difficult to escape reading about teams if you pick up almost any business magazine. Teams are widely used these days. A Conference Board of Canada report found that more than 80 percent of its 109 respondents used teams in the workplace.[2] In the United States, at least half of the employees at 80 percent of Fortune 500 companies work in teams, while 68 percent of small manufacturers use teams in their production areas.[3]

A **group** may be defined as two or more people who interact with each other to reach certain goals or meet certain needs.[4] A **team** is a group whose members work *intensely* with each other and have regular interaction to achieve a specific common goal or vision. As these definitions imply, all teams are groups, but not all groups are teams. The two characteristics that distinguish teams from groups are the *intensity* with which team members work together, the frequency of interaction and the presence of a *specific, overriding team goal or objective*. See Figure 10.2. At Virgin America, managers formed a team that worked intensively to achieve the goal of improving customer service. In contrast, the accountants who work in a small chartered accounting firm are a group: they may interact infrequently with one another to achieve goals such as keeping up to date on the latest changes in accounting rules and regulations, maintaining a smoothly functioning office, satisfying clients, and attracting new clients. But they are not a team because they do not work intensely and regularly with one another toward a common goal. Each accountant concentrates on serving the needs of his or her own clients.

Throughout this chapter, when we use the term *group* we are referring to both groups *and* teams. As you might imagine, because members of teams work intensely together, teams can sometimes be difficult to form and it may take time for members to learn how to effectively work together. In this section, we look at each of these contributions in turn.

Groups and Teams as Performance Enhancers

One of the main advantages of using groups is the opportunity to obtain a type of synergy: People working in teams are able to produce more or higher quality outputs than would have been produced if each person had worked separately and all their individual efforts had been combined. The essence of synergy is captured in the saying "The whole is more than the sum of its parts." Factors that can contribute to synergy in groups include the ability of group members to bounce ideas off one another, to correct one another's mistakes, to solve problems immediately as they arise, to bring a diverse knowledge base to bear on a problem or goal, and to accomplish work that is too vast or all-encompassing for any one individual to achieve on his or her own.

To take advantage of the potential for synergy in groups, managers need to make sure that groups are composed of members who have complementary skills and

group Two or more people who interact with each other to reach certain goals or meet certain needs.

team A group whose members work intensely with each other to achieve a specific common goal or objective.

FIGURE 10.2 | **Differences between Groups and Teams**

Groups	Teams
• Two or more people	• Two or more people
• Interact loosely	• Intense, regular, and frequent interaction
• Purpose to achieve organizational goals	• Specific team vision or purpose that supports organizational goals

knowledge relevant to the group's work. For example, at Hallmark Cards, synergies are created by bringing together all the different functions needed to create and produce a greeting card in a cross-functional team (a team composed of members from different departments or functions). For instance, artists, writers, designers, and marketing experts work together as members of a team to develop new cards.[5]

At Hallmark, the skills and expertise of the artists complement the contributions of the writers and vice versa. Managers also need to give groups enough autonomy so that the groups, rather than the manager, are solving problems and determining how to achieve goals and objectives, as is true in the cross-functional teams at Hallmark and the teams formed at Virgin America in the opening case. To promote synergy, managers need to empower their subordinates and be coaches, guides, and resources for groups while refraining from playing a more directive or supervisory role. The potential for synergy in groups may be the reason why more and more managers are incorporating empowerment into their personal leadership styles (see Chapter 9).

Groups, Teams, and Responsiveness to Customers

Being responsive to customers is not always easy. In manufacturing organizations, for example, customers' needs and desires for new and improved products have to be balanced against engineering constraints, production costs and feasibilities, government safety regulations, and marketing challenges. Being responsive to customers often requires the wide variety of skills and expertise found in different departments and at different levels in an organization's hierarchy. Sometimes, for example, employees at lower levels in an organization's hierarchy, such as sales representatives for a computer company, are closest to its customers and the most attuned to their needs. However, lower-level employees like salespeople often lack the technical expertise needed to come up with new product ideas; such expertise is found in the research and development department. Bringing salespeople, research and development experts, and members of other departments together in a group or cross-functional team can enhance responsiveness to customers by increasing the skills and expertise available. Consequently, when managers form a team, they need to make sure that the diversity of expertise and knowledge needed to be responsive to customers exists within the team; this is why cross-functional teams are so popular. At Virgin America, everyone on staff, from pilots and flight crews to ground workers, come together to solve problems in enhancing the customer's experience.

Two people are often better than one in creating a high performing organization.

In a cross-functional team, the expertise and knowledge in different organizational departments are brought together in the skills and knowledge of the team members. Managers of high-performing organizations are careful to determine which types of expertise and knowledge are required for teams to be responsive to customers, and they use this information in forming teams.

Teams and Innovation

Innovation—the implementation of creative ideas for new products, new technologies, new services, or even new organizational structures—is essential for organizational effectiveness. Often, an individual working alone does not possess the extensive and diverse set of skills, knowledge, and expertise required for successful innovation. Managers can better encourage innovation by creating teams of diverse individuals who together have the knowledge relevant to a particular type of innovation, rather than by relying on individuals working alone. Using teams to innovate has other advantages as well. First, team members can often uncover one another's errors or false assumptions; an individual acting alone would not be able to do this. Second, team members can critique one another's approaches when need be and build off one another's strengths while compensating for weaknesses (one of the advantages of devil's advocacy, discussed later in this chapter).

To further promote innovation, managers are well advised to empower teams and make their members fully responsible and accountable for the innovation process. The manager's role is to provide guidance, assistance, coaching, and the resources team members need and *not* to closely direct or supervise their activities. At Virgin, rather than follow orders or scripts developed by management, managers provide people with the skills and confidence they need to deal with problems on their own. To speed innovation, managers also need to form teams in which each member brings some unique resource to the team, such as engineering prowess, knowledge of production, marketing expertise, or financial savvy. Successful innovation sometimes requires that managers form teams with members from different countries and cultures. Amazon uses teams to spur innovation, and many of the unique features on its website that enable it to be responsive to customers and meet their needs have been developed by teams. For example, it was a team that developed "Search inside the Book," which allows customers to search and read content from over 100 000 books.[6]

Groups and Teams as Motivators

Managers often decide to form groups and teams to accomplish organizational goals and then find that using groups and teams brings additional benefits. Members of groups, and especially members of teams (because of the higher intensity of interaction in teams), are likely to be more highly motivated and satisfied than they would have been while working on their own. The experience of working alongside other highly charged and motivated people can be very stimulating. Team members more readily see how their efforts and expertise directly contribute to the achievement of team and organizational goals, and they feel personally responsible for the outcomes or results of their work. This has been the case at Hallmark Cards.

The increased motivation and satisfaction that can accompany the use of teams can also lead to other outcomes, such as low absenteeism and turnover. Working in a group or team can also satisfy organizational members' needs for engaging in social interaction and feeling connected to other people. For workers who perform highly stressful jobs, such as hospital emergency and operating room staff, group membership can be an important source of social support and motivation. Family members or friends may not be able to fully understand or appreciate some sources of work stress that these group members experience firsthand. Moreover, group members may cope better with work stressors when they are able to share them with other members of their group. In addition, groups often devise techniques to relieve stress, such as the telling of jokes among hospital operating room staff.

Why do managers in all kinds of organizations rely so heavily on groups and teams? Effectively managed groups and teams can help managers in their quest for high performance, responsiveness to customers, and employee motivation. Before explaining how managers can effectively manage groups, however, we will describe the types of groups that are formed in organizations.

> **formal groups** Groups that managers establish to achieve organizational goals.

Identify the different types of groups and teams that help managers and organizations achieve their goals.

LO2

Types of Groups and Teams

To achieve their goals of high performance, responsiveness to customers, innovation, and employee motivation, managers can form various types of groups and teams (see Figure 10.3). **Formal groups** are those managers establish to achieve organizational goals. The formal work groups are *cross-functional* teams composed of members from

> ### FIGURE 10.3 Types of Groups and Teams in Organizations

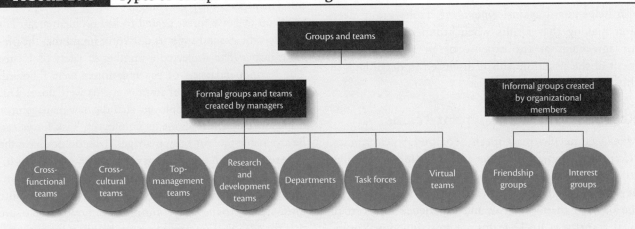

different departments, such as those at Hall-mark Cards, and *cross-cultural* teams composed of members from different cultures or countries, such as the teams at global car-makers. As you will see, some of the groups discussed in this section also can be considered to be cross-functional (if they are composed of members from different departments) or cross-cultural (if they are composed of members from different countries or cultures).

Sometimes organizational members, managers or nonmanagers, form groups because they feel that groups will help them achieve their own goals or meet their own needs (for example, the need for social interaction). Groups formed in this way are **informal groups.** Four nurses who work in a hospital and have lunch together twice a week constitute an informal group.

The Top-Management Team

A central concern of the CEO and president of a company is to form a top-management team to help the organization achieve its mission and goals. Top-management teams are responsible for developing the strategies that produce an organization's competitive advantage; most have between five and seven members. In forming their top-management teams, CEOs are well advised to stress diversity—in expertise, skills, knowledge, and experience. Thus, many top-management teams are **cross-functional teams:** they include members of different departments, such as finance, marketing, production, and engineering. Diversity helps ensure that the top-management team will have all the background and resources it needs to make good decisions. Diversity also helps guard against *groupthink,* faulty group decision making that results when group members strive for agreement at the expense of an accurate assessment of the situation; this is discussed in detail later in this chapter.

Research and Development Teams

Managers in pharmaceuticals, computers, electronics, electronic imaging, and other high-tech industries often create **research and development teams** to develop new products. Managers select R&D team members on the basis of their expertise and experience in a certain area. Sometimes R&D teams are cross-functional teams

informal groups Groups that managers or nonmanagerial employees form to help achieve their own goals or meet their own needs.

cross-functional teams Groups of individuals from different departments brought together to perform organizational tasks.

research and development teams Teams whose members have the expertise and experience needed to develop new products.

department A group composed of subordinates who report to the same supervisor; also called a unit.

task force A cross-functional team charged with solving a specific problem or addressing a specific issue within a fixed timeframe.

with members from departments such as engineering, marketing, and production in addition to members from the research and development department.

Departments

Subordinates who report to the same supervisor form a **department.** When top managers design an organization's structure and establish reporting relationships and a chain of command, they are essentially creating units or departmental groups. *Departments* or *units* perform a significant amount of the work in many organizations. In order to have these types of groups help an organization gain a competitive advantage, managers need to motivate group members to perform at a high level, and managers need to be effective leaders. Examples of departmental groups include the salespeople at The Bay who report to the same supervisor, the employees of a small swimming pool sales and maintenance company who report to a general manager, the telephone operators at Manulife Financial insurance company who report to the same supervisor, and workers on an automobile assembly line at Ford Canada who report to the same first-line manager.

Task Forces

Managers form **task forces** to accomplish specific goals or solve problems in a certain period; task forces are sometimes called *ad hoc committees.* When Vancouver Island–based Myra Falls copper and zinc mine was purchased in 1998 by Swedish-controlled Boliden AB, the mine had been facing labour strife for years.[7] Boliden sent over a new mine manager to help get things in order. His first job was to set up five task forces geared to key problem areas. For instance, the ground support task force found that the previous owners had neglected a number of safety problems. The recommendations of the task forces were followed, and $15 million worth of improvements were done. This sent a strong signal to employees that the new management team was concerned about its employees. Task forces can be a valuable tool for busy managers who do not have the time to explore an important issue in depth on their own.

Sometimes organizations need to address a long-term or enduring problem or issue, such as how to contribute most usefully to the local community or how to make sure that the organization provides opportunities for potential employees with disabilities. Task forces that are relatively permanent are often referred to as **standing committees.** Membership in standing committees changes over time. Members may have, for example, a two or three-year term on the committee and then rotate off. Memberships expire at varying times so that there are always some members with experience on the committee. Managers form and maintain standing committees to make sure that important issues continue to be addressed.

After the South Asia Boxing Day 2004 tsunami devastation, then UN Secretary-General Kofi Annan launched the Millennium Project. He set up 10 international task forces to come up with concrete, innovative proposals to achieve the agreed-on goals originally envisioned in the 2002 *Investing in Development* report.[8] Eight goals were set to be achieved by 2015. While some saw all of this as visionary, others, of course, saw the effort more cynically. As you read the list below, reflect back to the discussion on emotional and social intelligence from Chapter 9. While goals and targets may be envisioned and articulated, it takes courage, emotional and social intelligence, an ability to deal with conflict and political forces, and a leadership vision to make such efforts fruitful.

The eight goals set up to be achieved by 2015 were:

1. To halve the number of people living on less than $1 a day.

2. To make primary education available to every child.

3. To reduce child mortality by two-thirds.

4. To cut maternal mortality by three-quarters.

5. To promote gender equality.

6. To reverse the spread of HIV/AIDS and malaria.

7. To halt the loss of environmental resources.

8. To create a global partnership for development.

Self-Managed Work Teams[9]

Self-managed (or self-directed) work teams are teams whose members are empowered and have the responsibility and autonomy to complete identifiable pieces of work. On a day-to-day basis, team members decide what the team will do, how it will do it, and which team members will perform specific tasks.[10] Managers provide self-managed work teams with their overall goals (such as assembling defect-free computer keyboards) but let team members decide how to meet those goals. Managers usually form self-managed work teams to improve quality, increase motivation and satisfaction, and lower costs.

Managers can take a number of steps to ensure the effectiveness of self-managed teams.

Often, by creating self-managed work teams, they combine tasks that individuals used to perform on their own, so the team is responsible for the whole set of tasks that yield an identifiable output or end product. The Conference Board of Canada found that self-directed work teams are used in a variety of manufacturing environments (e.g., the auto and chemicals industries) and service environments (e.g., hotels, banks, and airlines).[11]

Managers can take a number of steps to ensure that self-managed work teams are effective and help an organization achieve its goals[12]:

- Give teams enough responsibility and autonomy to be truly self-managing. Refrain from telling team members what to do or solving problems for them even if you (as a manager) know what should be done.

- Make sure that a team's work is sufficiently complex so that it entails a number of different steps or procedures that must be performed and results in some kind of finished end product.

- Carefully select members of self-managed work teams. Team members should have the diversity of skills needed to complete the team's work, have the ability to work with others, and want to be part of a team.

- Recognize that self-managed work teams need guidance, coaching, and support, not direct supervision. Managers should be a resource for teams to turn to when needed.

standing committee A relatively permanent task force charged with addressing long-term, enduring problems or issues facing an organization.

self-managed (or self-directed) work teams Groups of employees who supervise their own activities and monitor the quality of the goods and services they provide.

- Analyze what type of training team members need, and provide it. Working in a self-managed work team often requires that employees have more extensive technical and interpersonal skills.

Managers in a wide variety of organizations have found that self-managed work teams help the organization achieve its goals.[13] However, self-managed work teams can run into trouble. Case studies of Canadian plastics companies made it absolutely clear that teamwork is appropriate to certain types of workplaces and not to others.[14] Canadian General Tower Limited had mixed results with using self-directed teams. At the plant's dry laminating facility such teams were abandoned after no significantly positive results could be observed. The company does, however, operate a small distribution centre in Brantford, Ontario, where the employees work in a self-directed team environment and no grievances or turnover have resulted. Problems with self-managed teams include members' reluctance to discipline one another by, for example, withholding bonuses from members who are not performing up to par or by firing members.[15]

They are also reluctant to evaluate each other's performance and determine pay levels. One reason for team members' discomfort may be the close personal relationships they sometimes develop with each other. In addition, sometimes members of self-managed work teams actually take longer to accomplish tasks, such as when team members have difficulties coordinating their efforts.

Virtual Teams

Virtual teams are teams whose members rarely or never meet face to face and instead interact by using various forms of information technology such as email, computer networks, telephones, faxes, and video conferences. As organizations become increasingly global and have operations in far-flung regions of the world, and as the need for specialized knowledge increases due to advances in technology, virtual teams allow managers to create teams to solve problems or explore opportunities without being limited by the need for team members to be working in the same geographic location.[16]

virtual team A team whose members rarely or never meet face to face and interact by using various forms of information technology such as email, computer networks, telephones, faxes, and video conferences.

Take the case of an organization that has manufacturing facilities in Australia, Canada, the United States, and Mexico, and is encountering a quality problem in a complex manufacturing process. Each of its manufacturing facilities has a quality control team that is headed by a quality control manager. The vice-president for production does not try to solve the problem by forming and leading a team at one of the four manufacturing facilities; instead, she forms and leads a virtual team composed of the quality control managers of the four plants and the plants' general managers. Team members communicate via email and video conferencing, and a wide array of knowledge and experience is utilized to solve the problem.

The principal advantage of virtual teams is that they enable managers to disregard geographic distances and form teams whose members have the knowledge, expertise, and experience to tackle a particular problem or take advantage of a specific opportunity.[17] Virtual teams can include members who are not employees of the organization itself. For example, a virtual team might include members of an organization that is used for outsourcing. More and more companies—including Hewlett-Packard, PricewaterhouseCoopers, and Kodak—are either using or exploring the use of virtual teams.[18]

Increasing globalization is likely to result in more organizations relying on virtual teams to a greater extent.[19] One of the major challenges members of virtual teams face is building a sense of camaraderie and trust among team members who rarely, if ever, meet face-to-face. To address this challenge, some organizations schedule recreational activities, such as ski trips, so that virtual team members can get together. Other organizations make sure that virtual team members have a chance to meet in person soon after the team is formed and then schedule periodic face-to-face meetings to promote trust, understanding, and cooperation in the teams.[20] The need for such meetings is underscored by research that suggests that while some virtual teams can be as effective as teams that meet face-to-face, virtual team members might be less satisfied with teamwork efforts and have fewer feelings of camaraderie or cohesion. (Group cohesiveness is discussed in more detail later in the chapter.)[21]

Research also suggests that it is important for managers to keep track of virtual teams and intervene when necessary by, for example, encouraging members of teams who do not communicate often enough to monitor their team's progress and make sure that team members actually have the time and are recognized for their virtual teamwork.[22] Additionally, when virtual teams are experiencing downtime or rough spots, managers might try to schedule face-to-face team time to bring team members together and help them focus on their goals.[23] Some virtual teams periodically meet face-to-face to promote trust, understanding, and cooperation in the team.

Researchers at the London Business School, including Professor Lynda Gratton, recently studied global virtual teams to try to identify factors that might help such teams be effective.[24] Based on their research, Gratton suggests that when forming virtual teams it is helpful to include a few members who already know each other, other members who are very well connected to people outside of the team, and, when possible, members who have volunteered to be a part of the team.[25] It is also advantageous for companies to have some kind of online site where team members can learn more about each other and the kinds of work they are engaged in, and in particular, a shared online workspace that team members can access around the clock.[26] Frequent communication is beneficial. Additionally, virtual team projects should be perceived as meaningful, interesting, and important by their members to promote and sustain their motivation.[27]

Friendship Groups

The groups described so far are formal groups created by managers. **Friendship groups** are informal groups composed of employees who enjoy one another's company and socialize with one another. Members of friendship groups may have lunch together, take breaks together, or meet after work for meals, sports, or other activities.

Founders Art Cooley, Charlie Wurster, and Dennis Puleston started EDF in 1967 to protect humans and wildlife from DDT.

Friendship groups help satisfy employees' needs for interpersonal interaction, can provide needed social support in times of stress, and can contribute to people's feeling good at work and being satisfied with their jobs. Managers themselves often form friendship groups. The informal relationships that managers build in friendship groups can often help them solve work-related problems because members of these groups typically discuss work-related matters and offer advice.

Interest Groups

Employees form informal **interest groups** when they seek to achieve a common goal related to their membership in an organization. Employees may form interest groups, for example, to encourage managers to consider instituting flexible working hours, providing on-site child care, improving working conditions, or more proactively supporting environmental protection, as was the case with the Environmental Defense Fund showcased in the Focus on the Social Economy feature. Interest groups can provide managers with valuable insights into the issues and concerns that are foremost in employees' minds. They also can signal the need for change.

Explain how different elements of group dynamics influence the functioning and effectiveness of groups and teams. **LO3**

Group Dynamics

How groups and teams function and how effective they will ultimately be depends on a number of characteristics and processes known collectively as **group dynamics**. In this section, we discuss five key elements of group dynamics: group size and roles; group leadership; group development; group norms; and group cohesiveness. As we mentioned earlier in the chapter, teams and groups are not the same thing, though some of their processes are similar. Thus, much of what we call group dynamics here also applies to teams.

Group Size and Roles

Managers need to take group size and group roles into account as they create and maintain high-performing groups and teams.

Group Size

The number of members in a group can be an important determinant of members' motivation and commitment

friendship groups Informal groups composed of employees who enjoy one another's company and socialize with one another.

interest groups Informal groups composed of employees seeking to achieve a common goal related to their membership in an organization.

group dynamics The ways in which group members interact determines their effectiveness.

FOCUS ON ❯ *The Social Economy*

The Environmental Defense Fund

In the 1960s, the pesticide DDT was used widely. It caused eggshells to thin and break, threatening the survival of magnificent birds like the osprey, bald eagle and peregrine falcon. It is a persistent poison that works its way up the food chain, endangering people, too.

In Long Island, New York, a small conservation group included a researcher who had been documenting the decline of the osprey for more than a decade. He found that unhatched osprey eggs contained significant concentrations of DDT. The group appealed to the county to stop using DDT. The mosquito control commission replied that DDT killed mosquitos cheaply and easily, so they would continue to use it.

So the group tried a novel approach, common today but unheard of in the late 1960s: The scientists teamed up with a lawyer and went to court on behalf of the environment.

After many months of preparation, the case was strong. Not only was DDT poisoning birds and crustaceans, but it was also of declining value in mosquito control, as the insects became resistant to it. In 1966, the court imposed a ban on DDT. In 1970, the governor enacted a statewide ban, based largely on the testimony from that Long Island case. And in 1972, the lawyers and scientists played a major role in securing a nationwide ban. The osprey has since made a dramatic recovery, and the bald eagle and peregrine falcon have been removed from the endangered species list.

That first court victory presented the local group with a choice. Because this was the first case of its kind, it roused national interest, "out of all proportion to the actual results achieved." Appeals for help came pouring in from across the country, many more than a small group of volunteers could address. They decided to organize more formally and attempt to raise funds to expand their work. In 1967, they incorporated as Environmental Defense Fund.[28]

1. Are the founders of the EDF a group or a team? Why?

2. What type of group did the founders of the EDF create?

---

and of group performance. There are several advantages to keeping a group relatively small—between two and nine members. Compared with members of large groups, members of small groups tend to

- interact more with each other and find it easier to coordinate their efforts;
- be more motivated, satisfied, and committed;
- find it easier to share information; and
- be better able to see the importance of their personal contributions for group success.

Recognizing these advantages, Nathan Myhrvold, former chief technology officer at Microsoft Corporation, found that eight is the ideal size for the types of R&D teams he would form to develop new software.[29] A disadvantage of small groups is that members have fewer resources available to accomplish their goals.

Large groups—with 10 or more members—also offer some advantages. They have at their disposal more resources to achieve group goals than do small groups. These resources include the knowledge, experience, skills, and abilities of group members as well as their actual time and effort. Large groups also have advantages stemming from the **division of labour**—splitting the work to be performed into particular tasks and assigning tasks to individuals. Individuals who specialize in particular tasks are likely to become skilled at performing those tasks and contribute significantly to high group performance.

Large groups suffer a number of problems, including greater communication and coordination difficulties and lower levels of motivation, satisfaction, and commitment. It is clearly more difficult to share information and coordinate activities when you are dealing with 16 people rather than 8. Moreover, members of large groups might not feel that their efforts are really needed and sometimes might not even feel a part of the group.

In deciding on the appropriate size for any group, managers attempt to gain the advantages of small-group size and, at the same time, form groups with sufficient resources to accomplish their goals and have a well-developed division of labour. As a general rule of thumb, groups should have

division of labour
Splitting the work to be performed into particular tasks and assigning tasks to individual workers.

no more members than necessary to achieve a division of labour and provide the resources needed to achieve group goals. In R&D teams, for example, group size is too large when

- members spend more time communicating what they know to others rather than applying what they know to solve problems and create new products;
- individual productivity decreases; and
- group performance suffers.[30]

Group Roles

A **group role** is a set of behaviours and tasks that a member of a group is expected to perform because of his or her position in the group. Members of cross-functional teams, for example, are expected to perform roles relevant to their special areas of expertise. In our earlier example of cross-functional teams at Hallmark Cards, it is the role of writers on the teams to create verses for new cards, the role of artists to draw illustrations, and the role of designers to put verse and artwork together in an attractive and appealing card design. The roles of members of top-management teams are shaped primarily by their areas of expertise—production, marketing, finance, research and development—but members of top-management teams also typically draw on their broad-based expertise as planners and strategists.

In forming groups and teams, managers need to communicate clearly the expectations for each group role, what is required of each member, and how the different roles in the group fit together to accomplish group goals. Managers also need to realize that group roles change and evolve as a group's tasks and goals change and as group members gain experience and knowledge. Thus, to get the performance gains that come from experience or "learning by doing," managers should encourage group members to take the initiative to modify their assigned roles by taking on extra responsibilities as they see fit. This process, called **role making,** can enhance individual and group performance.

Beyond the simple roles that each person fulfills in order to complete the task at hand, two major kinds of roles need to be discussed: task-oriented roles and maintenance roles. **Task-oriented roles** are performed by group members to make sure that the group accomplishes its tasks. **Maintenance roles** are carried out to make sure that team members have good relationships. For teams to

Managers communicate the expectations for each group role and what is required of each member.

be effective there needs to be some balance between task orientation and relationship maintenance. Table 10.1 identifies a number of task-oriented and maintenance roles that you might find in a team.

In self-managed work teams and some other groups, group members themselves are responsible for creating and assigning roles. Many self-managed work teams also pick their own team leaders. When group members create their own roles, managers should be available in an advisory capacity, helping group members effectively settle conflicts and disagreements. At Johnsonville Foods, for example, the position titles of first-line managers were changed to "advisory coach" to reflect the managers' new role vis-à-vis the self-managed work teams they oversee.[31]

Group Leadership

All groups and teams need leadership, as Richard Branson learned in the opening case. Indeed, as we discussed in detail in Chapter 9, effective leadership is a key ingredient for high-performing groups, teams, and organizations. Sometimes managers assume the leadership role, as is the case in many department-type groups and top-management teams. Or a manager may appoint a member of a group who is not a manager to be group leader or chairperson, as is the case in a task force or standing committee. In other cases, group or team members may choose their own leaders, or a leader may emerge naturally as group members work together to achieve group goals. When managers empower members of

group role A set of behaviours and tasks that a member of a group is expected to perform because of his or her position in the group.

role making Taking the initiative to modify an assigned role by taking on extra responsibilities.

task-oriented roles A role performed by group members to make sure the task gets done.

maintenance roles Roles performed by group members to make sure there are good relationships among group members.

TABLE 10.1 Roles Required for Effective Group Functioning

	Function	Description	Example
Roles that build task accomplishment	Initiating	Stating the goal or problem, making proposals about how to work on it, and setting time limits.	"Let's set up an agenda for discussing each of the problems we have to consider."
	Seeking information and opinions	Asking group members for specific factual information related to the task or problem, or for their opinions about it.	"What do you think would be the best approach to this, Jack?"
	Providing information and opinions	Sharing information or opinions related to the task or problems.	"I worked on a similar problem last year and found . . ."
	Clarifying	Helping one another understand ideas and suggestions that come up in the group.	"What you mean, Sue, is that we could . . .?"
	Elaborating	Building on one another's ideas and suggestions.	"Building on Don's idea, I think we could . . ."
	Summarizing	Reviewing the points covered by the group and the different ideas stated so that decisions can be based on full information.	Appointing a recorder to write notes on a blackboard.
	Consensus testing	Periodic testing about whether the group is nearing a decision or needs to continue discussion.	"Is the group ready to decide about this?"
Roles that build and maintain a group	Harmonizing	Mediating conflict among other members, reconciling disagreements, and relieving tensions.	"Don, I don't think you and Sue really see the question that differently."
	Compromising	Admitting error at times of group conflict.	"Well, I'd be willing to change if you provided some help on . . ."
	Gatekeeping	Making sure all members have a chance to express their ideas and feelings and preventing members from being interrupted.	"Sue, we haven't heard from you on this issue."
	Encouraging	Helping a group member make his or her point and establishing a climate of acceptance in the group.	"I think what you started to say is important, Jack. Please continue."

Source: D. Ancona, T. Kochan, M. Scully, J. Van Maanen, D.E. Westney. "Team Processes," in *Managing for the Future* (Cincinnati, OH: South-Western College. Publishing 1996).

self-managed work teams, they often let group members choose their own leaders. Some self-managed work teams find it effective to rotate the leadership role among their members. Whether leaders of groups and teams are managers or not and whether they are appointed by managers (often referred to as *formal leaders*) or emerge naturally in a group (often referred to as *informal leaders*), they play an important role in ensuring that groups and teams perform up to their potential.

Group Development Over Time

As many managers overseeing self-managed teams have learned, it sometimes takes a self-managed work team two or three years to perform up to its true capabilities.[32] As their experience suggests, what a group is capable of achieving depends in part on its stage of development. Knowing that it takes considerable time for self-managed work teams to get up and running has helped managers have realistic expectations for new teams and know that they need to provide new team members with considerable training and guidance.

Every group's development over time is somewhat unique. However, researchers have identified five stages of group development that many groups seem to pass through (see Figure 10.4)[33]:

- *Forming.* Members try to get to know each other and reach a common understanding of what the group is trying to accomplish and how group members should behave. During this stage, managers should strive to make each member feel like a valued part of the group.

- *Storming.* Group members experience conflict and disagreements because some members do not wish to submit to the demands of other group members. Disputes may arise over who should lead the group. Self-managed work teams can be particularly vulnerable during the storming stage. Managers need to keep an eye on groups at this stage to make sure that the conflict does not get out of hand.

- *Norming.* Close ties between group members develop, and feelings of friendship and camaraderie emerge. Group members arrive at a consensus about what goals they should be aiming to achieve and how group members should behave toward one another.

- *Performing.* The real work of the group gets accomplished during this stage. Depending on the type of group in question, managers need to take different steps at this stage to help ensure that groups are effective. Managers of departments need to make sure that group members are motivated and that they are effectively leading group members. Managers overseeing self-managed work teams have to empower team members and make sure that teams are given enough responsibility and autonomy at the performing stage.

- *Adjourning.* This stage applies only to groups that eventually are disbanded, such as task forces. During adjourning, a group is dispersed. Sometimes, adjourning takes place when a group completes a finished product, such as when a task force evaluating the pros and cons of providing on-site child care produces a report supporting its recommendation.

Managers need a flexible approach to group development and need to keep attuned to the different needs and requirements of groups at the various stages.[34] Above all else, and regardless of the stage of development, managers need to think of themselves as *resources* for groups and

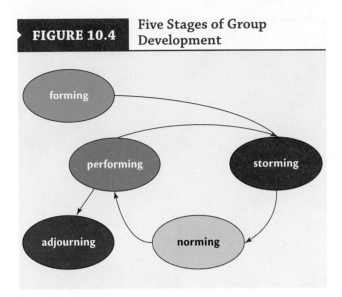

FIGURE 10.4 Five Stages of Group Development

recognize that the stages of development are not linear. Groups can move between the different stages as different events affect its development. Thus, managers always should be trying to find ways to help groups and teams function more effectively.

Group Norms

All groups, whether top-management teams, self-managed work teams, or departments, need to control their members' behaviour to ensure that the group performs well and meets its goals. Roles as well as group norms control behaviour in groups.[35] **Group norms** are shared guidelines or rules for behaviour that most group members follow. Groups develop norms for a wide variety of behaviours, including working hours, the sharing of information among group members, how certain group tasks should be performed, and even how members of a group should dress.

Managers should encourage members of a group to develop norms that contribute to group performance and the attainment of group goals. These could include group norms that dictate that each member of a cross-functional team should always be available for the rest of the team when his or her input is needed, return phone calls as soon as possible, inform other team members of travel plans, and give team members a phone number at which he or she can be reached when travelling on business. Virtual teams such as those at Ryder System Inc. in Mississauga, Ontario, establish such norms as how often to have conference calls and how often they should meet face to face in order to increase their ability to communicate effectively.

group norms Shared guidelines or rules for behaviour that most group members follow.

Deviance from group norms can increase the performance of an organization.

Conformity and Deviance

Group members conform to norms for three reasons:

1. They want to obtain rewards and avoid punishments.

2. They want to imitate group members whom they like and admire.

3. They have internalized the norm and believe it is the right and proper way to behave.[36]

Consider the case of Robert King, who conformed to his department's norm of attending a fund-raiser for a community food bank. King's conformity could be due to (1) his desire to be a member of the group in good standing and to have friendly relationships with other group members (rewards), (2) his copying the behaviour of other members of the department whom he respects and who always attend the fundraiser (imitating other group members), or (3) his belief in the merits of supporting the activities of the food bank (believing that is the right and proper way to behave).

Failure to conform, or deviance, occurs when a member of a group violates a group norm. Deviance signals that a group is not controlling one of its members' behaviours. Groups generally respond to members who behave defiantly in one of three ways[37]:

1. The group might try to get the member to change his or her deviant ways and conform to the norm. Group members might try to convince the member of the need to conform, or they might ignore or even punish the deviant. For example, in a Jacksonville Foods plant, Liz Senkbiel, a member of a self-managed work team responsible for weighing sausages, failed to conform to a group norm dictating that group members should periodically clean up an untidy interview room. Because Senkbiel refused to take part in the team's cleanup efforts, team members reduced her monthly bonus by about $225 for a two-month period.[38] Senkbiel clearly learned the costs of deviant behaviour in her team.

2. The group might expel the member.

3. The group might change the norm to be consistent with the member's behaviour.

That last alternative suggests some deviant behaviour can be functional for groups when performance norms are low. Deviance is functional for a group when it causes group members to stop and evaluate norms that may be dysfunctional but that are taken for granted by the group. Often, group members do not think about why they behave in a certain way or why they follow certain norms. Deviance can cause group members to reflect on their norms and change them when appropriate, such as when a new employee comes up with a new procedure because she was not aware of "the right way" to do something, and everyone realizes her suggestion is a better way.

Take the case of a group of receptionists in a beauty salon who followed the norm that all appointments would be handwritten in an appointment book and, at the end of each day, the receptionist on duty would enter the appointments into the salon's computer system, which printed out the hairdressers' daily schedules. One day, a receptionist decided to enter appointments directly into the computer system at the time they were being made, bypassing the appointment book. This deviant behaviour caused the other receptionists to think about why they were using the appointment book in the first place, since all appointments could be entered into the computer directly. After consulting with the owner of the salon, the group changed its norm. Now appointments are entered directly into the computer, which saves time and cuts down on scheduling errors.

Encouraging a Balance of Conformity and Deviance

In order for groups and teams to be effective and help an organization gain a competitive advantage, they need to have the right balance of conformity and deviance (see Figure 10.5). A group needs a certain level of conformity to ensure that it can control members' behaviour and channel it in the direction of high performance and group goal accomplishment. A group also needs a certain level of deviance to ensure that dysfunctional norms are discarded and replaced with functional ones. Balancing conformity and deviance is a pressing concern for all groups, whether they are top-management teams, R&D teams, departments, or self-managed work teams.

The extent of conformity and reactions to deviance within groups are determined by group members themselves. The three bases for conformity just described are powerful forces that more often than not result in group members' conforming to norms. Sometimes these forces are so strong that deviance rarely occurs in groups, and when it does, it is stamped out.

Managers can take several steps to ensure that there is enough tolerance of deviance in groups so that group members are willing to deviate from dysfunctional norms and, when deviance occurs in their group, reflect on the appropriateness of the violated norm and change the norm if necessary.

First, managers can be role models for the groups and teams they oversee. When managers encourage and accept employees' suggestions for changes in procedures, do not rigidly insist that tasks be accomplished in a certain way, and admit when a norm that they once supported is no longer functional, they signal to group members that conformity should not come at the expense of needed changes and improvements. Second, managers should let employees know that there are always ways to improve group processes and performance levels and thus opportunities to replace existing norms with norms that will better enable a group to achieve its goals and perform at a high level. Third, managers should encourage members of groups and teams to periodically assess the appropriateness of their existing norms.

> **FIGURE 10.5** Balancing Conformity and Deviance in Groups

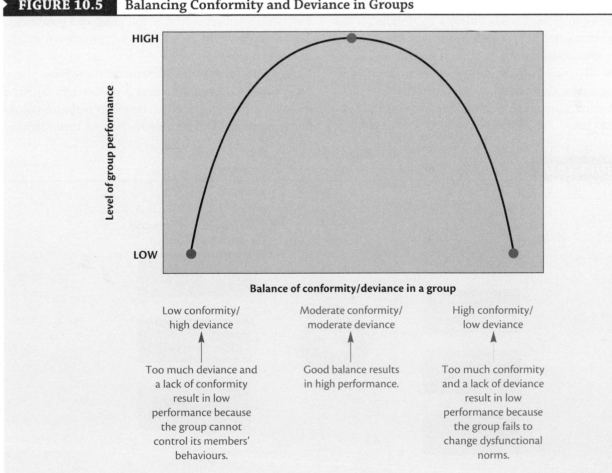

Group Cohesiveness

Another important element of group dynamics that affects group performance and effectiveness is **group cohesiveness,** the degree to which members are attracted or loyal to their group or team.[39] When group cohesiveness is high, individuals strongly value their group membership, find the group very appealing, and have strong desires to remain part of the group. When group cohesiveness is low, group members do not find their group particularly appealing and have little desire to retain their group membership. Research suggests that managers should aim to have a moderate level of cohesiveness in the groups and teams they manage because that is most likely to contribute to an organization's competitive advantage.

Consequences of Group Cohesiveness

There are three major consequences of increasing group cohesiveness: level of participation within a group, level of conformity to group norms, and emphasis on group goal accomplishment (see Figure 10.6).[40]

As group cohesiveness grows, the extent of group members' participation within the group increases. Increasing levels of group cohesiveness result in increasing levels of conformity to group norms. This is a good thing for the organization when the performance norms are high. But when performance norms are low, groups need a good dose of deviance to shake things up and adopt better working habits. And finally, as group cohesiveness grows, emphasis on group goal accomplishment also increases within a group.

A moderate level of cohesiveness motivates group members to accomplish both group and organizational goals. A moderate level of group cohesiveness helps ensure that group members take an active

part in the group and communicate effectively with each other. The reason managers may not want to encourage high levels of cohesiveness is illustrated by the example of two cross-functional teams responsible for developing new toys. Members of the highly cohesive Team Alpha often have lengthy meetings that usually start with non-work-related conversations and jokes, meet more often than most of the other cross-functional teams in the company, and spend a good portion of their time communicating the ins and outs of their department's contribution to toy development to other team members. Members of the moderately cohesive Team Beta generally have efficient meetings in which ideas are communicated and discussed as needed, do not meet more often than necessary, and share the ins and outs of their expertise with one another to the extent needed for the development process. Teams Alpha and Beta have both developed some top-selling toys. However, it generally takes Team Alpha 30 percent longer to do so than Team Beta. This is why too much cohesiveness can be too much of a good thing. Thus a moderate degree of cohesiveness often yields the best outcome.

As group cohesiveness increases, the emphasis placed on group goal accomplishment also increases within a group. A very strong emphasis on group goal accomplishment, however, does not always lead to organizational

FIGURE 10.6 **Sources and Consequences of Group Cohesiveness**

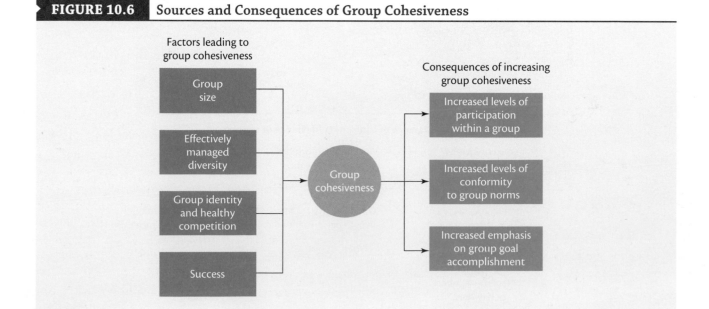

effectiveness. For an organization to be effective and gain a competitive advantage, the different groups and teams in the organization must cooperate with one another and be motivated to achieve *organizational goals,* even if doing so sometimes comes at the expense of the achievement of group goals. A moderate level of cohesiveness motivates group members to accomplish both group and organizational goals. High levels of cohesiveness can cause group members to be so focused on group goal accomplishment that they may strive to achieve group goals no matter what—even when doing so jeopardizes organizational performance.

At the toy company, the major goal of the cross-functional teams was to develop new toy lines that were truly innovative, utilized the latest in technology, and were in some way fundamentally distinct from other toys on the market. When it came to the rabbit project, Team Alpha's high level of cohesiveness contributed to its continued emphasis on its group goal of developing an innovative line of toys; thus, the team stuck with its usual design process. Team Beta, in contrast, realized that developing the new line of toys quickly was an important organizational goal that should take precedence over the group's goal of developing groundbreaking new toys, at least in the short run. Team Beta's moderate level of cohesiveness contributed to team members' doing what was best for the toy company in this case.

Four factors contribute to the level of group cohesiveness (see Figure 10.6).[41] By influencing these *determinants of group cohesiveness,* managers can raise or lower the level of cohesiveness to promote moderate levels of cohesiveness in groups and teams.

- *Group size*—To promote cohesiveness in groups, when feasible, managers should form groups that are small to medium in size (about 2 to 15 members). If a group is low in cohesiveness and large in size, managers might want to consider the feasibility of dividing the group in two and assigning different tasks and goals to the two newly formed groups.
- *Effectively managed diversity*—Diverse groups often come up with more innovative and creative ideas. One reason cross-functional teams are so popular in organizations like Hallmark Cards is that the diversity in expertise represented in the teams results in higher levels of team performance. In forming groups and teams, managers need to make sure that the diversity in knowledge, experience, expertise, and other characteristics necessary for group goal accomplishment is represented in the new groups.

Managers then have to make sure that this diversity in group membership is effectively managed so that groups will be cohesive (see Chapter 3).
- *Group identity and healthy competition*—When group cohesiveness is low, managers can often increase it by encouraging groups to develop their own identities or personalities and to engage in healthy competition. If groups are too cohesive, managers can try to decrease cohesiveness by promoting organizational (rather than group) identity and making the organization as a whole the focus of the group's efforts. Excessive levels of cohesiveness also can be reduced by reducing or eliminating competition among groups and rewarding cooperation.
- *Success*—When it comes to promoting group cohesiveness, there is more than a grain of truth to the saying "Nothing succeeds like success." As groups become more successful, they become increasingly attractive to their members, and their cohesiveness tends to increase. When cohesiveness is low, managers can increase cohesiveness by making sure that a group can achieve some noticeable and visible successes.

A note of caution: In 1972 psychologist Janis Irving named a phenomenon called "groupthink."[42] The group cohesiveness in groupthink becomes dysfunctional. In other words, the group's decision-making processes become faulty because members do not consider all the alternatives and seek unanimity at the expense of quality decisions. To challenge such groupthink, a critical analysis of how the group makes decisions needs to occur. We now turn to this topic.

Explain how group decision making can be improved by minimizing groupthink and fostering creativity and innovation. **LO4**

Group Decision Making

Many, perhaps most, important organizational decisions are made by groups of managers rather than by individuals. Group decision making is superior to individual decision making in several respects. When managers work as a team to make decisions and solve problems, their choices of alternatives are less likely to fall victim to the biases and errors discussed previously. They are able to draw on the combined skills, competencies, and accumulated knowledge of group members, and thereby improve their ability to generate feasible alternatives and make good decisions. Group decision making also allows managers to process

groupthink A pattern of faulty and biased decision making that occurs in groups whose members strive for agreement among themselves at the expense of accurately assessing information relevant to a decision.

more information and to correct each other's errors. In the implementation phase, all managers affected by the decisions agree to cooperate. When a group of managers makes a decision, as opposed to one top manager making a decision and imposing it on subordinate managers, it is more probable that the decision will be implemented successfully.

Nevertheless, some disadvantages are associated with group decision making. Groups often take much longer than individuals to make decisions. Getting two or more managers to agree to the same solution can be difficult because managers' interests and preferences are often different. In addition, just like decision making by individual managers, group decision making can be undermined by biases. A major source of group bias is groupthink.

The Perils of Groupthink

Groupthink is a pattern of faulty and biased decision making that occurs in groups whose members strive for agreement among themselves at the expense of accurately assessing information relevant to a decision.[43] When individuals are subject to groupthink, they collectively embark on a course of action without developing appropriate criteria to evaluate alternatives. Typically, a group rallies around a strong individual and the course of action that the individual supports. Group members become blindly committed to that course of action without evaluating its merits. Commitment is often based on an emotional—rather than objective—assessment of the best course of action.

We have all seen the symptoms of the groupthink phenomenon[44]:

- *Illusion of invulnerability.* Group members become overconfident, and this causes them to take extraordinary risks.

- *Assumption of morality.* Group members believe that the group's objectives are morally right, and so they do not debate the ethics of their actions.

- *Rationalized resistance.* No matter how strongly the evidence may contradict their basic assumptions, group members rationalize that

their assumptions are correct and that the negative evidence is faulty.

- *Peer pressure.* Members who express doubts about any of the group's shared views are pressured to ignore their concerns and to support the group.

- *Minimized doubts.* Members who have doubts or hold differing points of view may keep silent about their misgivings and even minimize to themselves the importance of their doubts.

- *Illusion of unanimity.* If someone does not speak, it is assumed that he or she agrees with the group. In other words, silence becomes viewed as a "yes" vote.

Pressures for agreement and harmony within a group have the unintended effect of discouraging individuals from raising issues that run counter to majority opinion. For example, a colourful character named Sherman Kent, a onetime history professor at Yale, known as "Buffalo Bill, the Cultured Cowboy" because he wore red suspenders, could tell bawdy jokes, and use barnyard language, had also previously taught CIA personnel for 17 years how important it was for intelligence analysts to challenge their assumptions, to acknowledge uncertainty and ambiguity, to watch for their own biases, and to meet the needs of policymakers without being seduced by them. When the U.S. Senate Select Committee on Intelligence brought out its paper in July 2004, it cited Professor Kent as the person whose admonitions had been ignored, so much so that "intelligence officials did not explain the uncertainties behind their judgment that Iraq was pursuing biological, chemical, and nuclear weapons." Instead, intelligence analysts fell into "groupthink."[45]

Considerable anecdotal evidence exists to suggest the negative implications of groupthink in organizational settings, but very little empirical work has been conducted in organizations on the subject of groupthink.[46] In fact, more recently, groupthink has been criticized for overestimating the link between the decision-making process and its outcome[47] and for suggesting that its effect is uniformly negative.[48] A study of groupthink in five large corporations reported that elements of groupthink may affect decision making differently. For instance, the illusion of vulnerability, the belief in inherent group morality, and the illusion of unanimity often led to greater team performance, counter to what the original groupthink proposals suggest.[49]

> **"[I]ntelligence officials did not explain the uncertainties behind their judgment that Iraq was pursuing biological, chemical, and nuclear weapons."**
>
> **U.S. Senate Committee on Intelligence**

Improving Group Decision Making

A variety of steps can be taken to improve group decision making.[50] Managers should encourage group leaders to be impartial in their leadership, and actively seek input from all group members. Leaders should avoid expressing their own opinions in the early stages of discussion.

Another strategy to improve group decision making is to encourage one group member to play the role of the devil's advocate. **Devil's advocacy** is a critical analysis of a preferred alternative to pinpoint its strengths and weaknesses before it is implemented (see Figure 10.7).[51] Typically, one member of the decision-making group plays the role of the devil's advocate. The devil's advocate critiques and challenges the way the group evaluated alternatives and chose one over the others. The purpose of devil's advocacy is to identify all the reasons that might make the preferred alternative unacceptable after all. In this way, decision makers can be made aware of the possible perils of recommended courses of action.

Another way to improve group decision making is to promote diversity in decision-making groups.[52] Bringing together male *and* female managers from various ethnic, national, and functional backgrounds broadens the range of life experiences and opinions that group members can draw from as they generate, assess, and choose among alternatives. Moreover, diverse groups are sometimes less prone to groupthink because group members already differ from each other and thus are less subject to pressures for uniformity. The Swiss firm The BrainStore takes advantage of diversity to improve decision making by mixing children and managers together.

Promoting Group Creativity

To encourage creativity at the group level, organizations can make use of group problem-solving techniques that promote creative ideas and innovative solutions. These techniques can also be used to prevent groupthink and to help managers and employees uncover biases. Here, we look at three group decision-making techniques: *brainstorming,* the *nominal group technique,* and the *Delphi technique.*

Brainstorming

Brainstorming is a group problem-solving technique in which individuals meet face to face to generate and debate a wide variety of alternatives from which to make a decision.[53] Generally, from 5 to 15 individuals meet in a closed-door session and proceed like this:

- One person describes in broad outline the problem the group is to address.

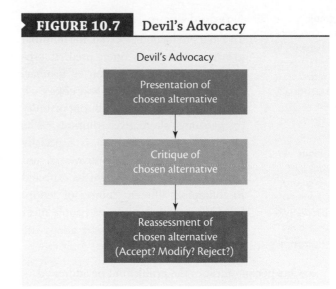

FIGURE 10.7 Devil's Advocacy

Devil's Advocacy

Presentation of chosen alternative

↓

Critique of chosen alternative

↓

Reassessment of chosen alternative (Accept? Modify? Reject?)

- Group members then share their ideas and generate alternative courses of action.

- As each alternative is described, group members are not allowed to criticize it, and everyone withholds judgment until all alternatives have been heard. One member of the group records the alternatives on a flip chart.

- Group members are encouraged to be as innovative and radical as possible. Anything goes; and the greater the number of ideas put forth, the better. Moreover, group members are encouraged to "piggyback"—that is, to build on each other's suggestions.

- When all alternatives have been generated, group members debate the pros and cons of each and develop a short list of the best alternatives.

Brainstorming is very useful in some problem-solving situations—for example, when trying to find a new name for a perfume or for a model of car. But sometimes individuals working alone can generate more alternatives. The main reason, it seems, is the **production blocking** that occurs in groups because members cannot always simultaneously make sense of all the alternatives being generated, think up additional alternatives, and remember what they were thinking.[54]

devil's advocacy
Critical analysis of a preferred alternative, made by a group member who plays the role of devil's advocate to defend unpopular or opposing alternatives for the sake of argument.

brainstorming A group problem-solving technique in which individuals meet face to face to generate and debate a wide variety of alternatives from which to make a decision.

production blocking A loss of productivity in brainstorming sessions due to the unstructured nature of brainstorming.

Nominal Group Technique

To avoid production blocking, the **nominal group technique** is often used. It provides a more structured way of generating alternatives in writing and gives each individual more time and opportunity to generate alternative solutions. The nominal group technique is especially useful when an issue is controversial and when different people might be expected to champion different courses of action. Generally, a small group of people meet in a closed-door session and adopt the following procedures:

- One person outlines the problem to be addressed, and 30 or 40 minutes are allocated for each group member to write down ideas and solutions. Group members are encouraged to be innovative.

- Individuals take turns reading their suggestions to the group. One person writes the alternatives on a flip chart. No criticism or evaluation of alternatives is allowed until all alternatives have been read.

- The alternatives are then discussed, one by one, in the sequence in which they were first proposed. Group members can ask for clarifying information and critique each alternative to identify its pros and cons.

- When all alternatives have been discussed, each group member ranks all the alternatives from most preferred to least preferred, and the alternative that receives the highest ranking is chosen.[55]

Delphi Technique

Both nominal group technique and brainstorming require people to meet together to generate creative ideas and engage in joint problem solving. What happens if people are in different cities or in different parts of the world and cannot meet face to face? Videoconferencing is one way to bring distant people together to brainstorm. Another way is to use the **Delphi technique,** a written approach to creative problem solving.[56] The Delphi technique works like this:

- The group leader writes a statement of the problem and a series of questions to which participating individuals are to respond.

- The questions are sent to the managers and departmental experts who are most knowledgeable about the problem; they are asked to generate solutions and mail the questionnaire back to the group leader.

- The group leader records and summarizes the responses. The results are then sent back to the participants, with additional questions to be answered before a decision can be made.

- The process is repeated until a consensus is reached and the most suitable course of action is clear.

Describe how managers can create high-performing teams by motivating group members to achieve organizational goals, reducing social loafing, and managing conflict effectively. **LO5**

Managing Groups and Teams for High Performance

Now that you have a good understanding of the reasons why groups and teams are so important for organizations, the types of groups that managers create, and group dynamics, group decision making, and the perils of groupthink, we consider additional steps that managers can take to make sure groups and teams perform highly and contribute to organizational effectiveness. Managers who want top-performing groups and teams need to (1) motivate group members to achieve organizational goals, (2) reduce social loafing, and (3) help groups manage conflict effectively.

Motivating Group Members to Achieve Organizational Goals

When work is difficult, tedious, or requires a high level of commitment and energy, managers cannot assume that group members will always be motivated to work toward the achievement of organizational goals. Consider the case of a group of house painters who paint the interiors and exteriors of new homes for a construction company and are paid on an hourly basis. Why should they strive to complete painting jobs quickly and efficiently if doing so will just make them feel more tired at the end of the day and they will not receive any tangible benefits? It makes more sense for the painters to adopt a more relaxed approach, to take frequent breaks, and to work at a leisurely pace.

> **"Every customer is valuable; a thriving company is built on relationships, not just the bottom line."**
>
> *Richard Branson, CEO, Virgin Group*

This relaxed approach, however, impairs the construction company's ability to gain a competitive advantage because it raises costs and increases the time needed to complete a new home.

Managers can motivate members of groups and teams to reach organizational goals and create a competitive advantage by making sure that the members themselves benefit when the group or team performs highly. If members of a self-managed work team know that they will receive a percentage of any cost savings that the team discovers and implements, they probably will try to cut costs. For example, Canadian Tire offers team incentives to employees of its gas bars. "Secret" retail shoppers visit the outlets on a regular basis and score them on such factors as cleanliness, manner in which the transaction was processed, and the types of products offered, using a 100-point scoring system. Scores above a particular threshold provide extra compensation that is shared by the team. Xerox Canada, through its XTRA program, rewards districts for achieving profit and customer satisfaction targets. Everyone in the district shares equally in the bonuses.

Managers often rely on some combination of individual and group-based incentives to motivate members of groups and teams to work toward reaching organizational goals and a competitive advantage. When individual performance within a group can be assessed, pay is often determined by individual performance or by both individual and group performance. When individual performance within a group cannot be assessed accurately, then group performance should be the key determinant of pay levels. Many companies that use self-managed work teams base team members' pay in part on team performance.[57] A major challenge for managers is to develop a fair pay system that will lead to both high individual motivation and high group or team performance.

In addition to monetary rewards, benefits that managers can make available to group members when a group performs highly could also include equipment and computer software, awards and other forms of recognition, and choice future work assignments. For example, members of self-managed work teams that develop new software at companies such as Microsoft often value working on interesting and important projects, and so members of teams that perform highly are rewarded with interesting and important new projects.

Reducing Social Loafing in Groups

We have been focusing on the steps that managers can take to encourage high levels of performance in groups.

Managers, however, need to be aware of an important downside to group and teamwork: the potential for social loafing, which reduces group performance. **Social loafing** is the tendency of individuals to put forth less effort when they work in groups than when they work alone.[58] Have you ever watched one or two group members who never seemed to be pulling their weight? Have you ever worked in a student club or committee in which some members always seemed to be missing meetings and never volunteered for activities? Have you ever had a job in which one or two of your coworkers seemed to be slacking off because they knew that you or other members of your work group would make up for their low levels of effort? If you have, you have witnessed social loafing in action.

Social loafing can occur in all kinds of groups and teams and in all kinds of organizations. It can result in lower group performance and may even prevent a group from reaching its goals. Fortunately, managers can take

> **social loafing** The tendency of individuals to put forth less effort when they work in groups than when they work alone.

Managers must tie rewards and benefits to high levels of performance.

steps to reduce social loafing and sometimes completely eliminate it. Here, we look at three:

1. *Making sure that individual contributions to a group are identifiable.* Some people may engage in social loafing when they work in groups because they think that they can hide in the crowd—that no one will notice if they put forth less effort than they should. Other people may think that if they put forth high levels of effort and make substantial contributions to the group, their contributions will not be noticed and they will receive no rewards for their work—so why bother?[59]

   One way in which managers can effectively eliminate social loafing is by making individual contributions to a group identifiable so that group members perceive that low and high levels of effort will be noticed and individual contributions evaluated.[60] Managers can accomplish this by assigning specific tasks to group members and holding them accountable for their completion. Take the case of a group of eight employees responsible for reshelving returned books in a large public library in Vancouver. The head librarian was concerned that there was always a backlog of seven or eight carts of books to be reshelved, even though the employees never seemed to be particularly busy and some even found time to sit down and read newspapers and magazines. The librarian decided to try to eliminate the apparent social loafing by assigning each employee sole responsibility for reshelving a particular section of the library. Because the library's front-desk employees sorted the books by section on the carts as they were returned, holding the shelvers responsible for particular sections was easily accomplished. Once the shelvers knew that the librarian could identify their effort or lack of effort, there were rarely any backlogs of books to be reshelved.

   Sometimes the members of a group can cooperate to eliminate social loafing by making individual contributions identifiable. For example, in a small security company, members of a self-managed work team who assemble control boxes for home alarm systems start each day by deciding who will perform which tasks that day and how much work each member and the group as a whole should strive to accomplish. Each team member knows that, at the end of the day, the other team members will know exactly how much he or she has accomplished. With this system in place, social

It's the manager's job to reduce social loafing.

loafing never occurs in the team. Remember, however, that in some teams, individual contributions cannot be made identifiable.

2. *Emphasizing the valuable contributions of each individual group member.* Another reason why social loafing may occur is that people sometimes think that their efforts are unnecessary or unimportant when they work in a group. They feel the group will accomplish its goals and perform at an acceptable level whether or not they personally perform at a high level. To counteract this belief, when managers form groups they should assign individuals to a group on the basis of the valuable contributions that *each* person can make to the group as a whole. Individuals who feel their contributions matter will be less likely to engage in social loafing.

3. *Making sure that the group size is not too large* (see Figure 10.8). As size increases, identifying individual contributions becomes increasingly difficult and members are increasingly likely to think that their individual contributions are not very important. To overcome this, managers should form groups with no more members than are needed to accomplish group goals and perform at a high level.[61]

Helping Groups to Manage Conflict Effectively

At some point or other, practically all groups experience conflict either within the group (*intragroup conflict*) or with other groups (*intergroup conflict*). In Chapter 12, we discuss the sources of conflict and explore ways to

| FIGURE 10.8 | Three Ways to Reduce Social Loafing |

Making individual contributions to a group identifiable when possible

Emphasizing the valuable contributions of individual members

Keeping group size at an appropriate level

Reduce → Social loafing

task-related conflict
Members of the group perceive a problem or have a disagreement about the nature of the task or project.

relationship conflict
Members of the group perceive each other's attitudes as a problem.

manage it effectively. As you will learn there, individuals often have turbulent working relationships that call for managers to take steps to help individuals manage conflict and disagreements. Here, we focus on the types of conflict that emerge within groups and what managers can do to handle it effectively.

Task-related conflict (or *constructive conflict*) occurs when the members of the group perceive a problem or have a disagreement about the nature of the task or project, not in the way the members are relating to one another. This type of conflict is relatively easy to resolve by seeking clarification about the nature of the task or problem to be solved. **Relationship conflict,** on the other hand, occurs when members of the group perceive each other's attitudes as the problem. Differences in opinions are viewed as personal attacks that

threaten to derail the project. Managers should practise the following four strategies to diminish and discourage relationship conflict:

1. *Reduce interpersonal hostility by developing high levels of emotional intelligence:* Team members with high levels of emotional intelligence are less likely to fly off the handle when disagreements arise (see Chapter 9).

2. *Promote cohesiveness:* Teams with high levels of loyalty and commitment are more tolerant of emotional outbreaks and tend not to become personally offended when the conversation gets heated.

3. *Promote positive group norms:* Supportive group norms such as encouraging open and honest discussion and practising maintenance roles such as "gatekeeping" that promotes participation can diminish relationship conflict.

4. *Collaborating conflict-handling behaviour:* When conflicting members of the group can collaborate by asserting their interests and point of view clearly, without being aggressive, and genuinely desire to have a positive outcome to the disagreement, a win–win situation can result. On the other hand, if group members' conflict-handling behaviours focus on competing or forcing their own take on the situation, relationship conflict will likely escalate.

Managers rely on strategies to reduce dysfunctional conflict.

Tips **FOR MANAGERS**

Building Teams for High Performance[62]

1. Clarify roles and responsibilities for team members so they work together effectively.

2. Manage interpersonal conflicts among team members.

3. Maximize team productivity by encouraging group discussion and problem solving.

4. Overcome organizational, management, and employee barriers to teamwork through the focus on enhancing the emotional intelligence of team members.

5. Identify and manage team rewards effectively.

Summary and Review

LO1 Groups, Teams, and Organizational Effectiveness A group is two or more people who interact with each other to reach certain goals or meet certain needs. A team is a group whose members work intensely with each other to achieve a specific common goal or objective. Groups and teams can contribute to organizational effectiveness by enhancing performance, increasing responsiveness to customers, increasing innovation, and being a source of motivation for their members.

LO2 Types of Groups and Teams Formal groups are groups that managers establish to achieve organizational goals; they include cross-functional teams, cross-cultural teams, top-management teams, research and development teams, departments, task forces, self-managed work teams, and virtual teams. Informal groups are groups that employees form because they believe that the groups will help them achieve their own goals or meet their needs; they include friendship groups and interest groups.

LO3 Group Dynamics Key elements of group dynamics are group size and roles, group leadership, group development, group norms, and group cohesiveness. The advantages and disadvantages of large and small groups suggest that managers should form groups with no more members than are needed to provide the human resources the group needs to reach its goals and use a division of labour. A group role is a set of behaviours and tasks that a member of a group is expected to perform because of his or her position in the group. All groups and teams need leadership. Five stages of development that many groups pass through are *forming, storming, norming, performing,* and *adjourning.* Group norms are shared rules of behaviour that most group members follow. To be effective, groups need a balance of conformity and deviance. Conformity allows a group to control its members' behaviours in order to achieve group goals; deviance provides the impetus for needed change. Group cohesiveness is the attractiveness of a group or team to its members. As group cohesiveness increases, so, too, do the level of participation and communication within a group, the level of conformity to group norms, and the emphasis on group goal accomplishment. Managers should strive to achieve a moderate level of group cohesiveness in the groups and teams they manage.

LO4 Group Decision Making Managers must be aware of the perils of groupthink, where members strive to reach a decision without considering all the alternatives sufficiently. Managers can minimize *groupthink* by playing the *devil's advocate* and foster creativity and innovation to improve decision making by using three techniques. (1) *Brainstorming* involves generating lots of innovative alternatives, without judgment, in a face-to-face environment. The assessment of the alternatives comes after the brainstorm. (2) The *nominal group technique* allows group members to generate alternatives individually and write them down for later consideration by the whole group. (3) The *Delphi technique* is used to solve problems by allowing experts to generate and debate appropriate solutions and courses of action.

LO5 Managing Groups and Teams for High Performance To make sure that groups and teams perform at a high level, managers need to motivate group members to work toward the achievement of organizational goals and reduce social loafing and conflict. Managers can motivate members of groups and teams to work toward the achievement of organizational goals by making sure that members personally benefit when the group or team performs at a high level.

KEY TERMS

brainstorming	group norms	role making
cross-functional teams	group role	self-managed (or self-
Delphi technique	groupthink	directed) work teams
department	informal groups	social loafing
devil's advocacy	interest groups	standing committee
division of labour	maintenance roles	task forces
formal groups	nominal group technique	task-oriented roles
friendship groups	production blocking	task-related conflict
group	relationship conflict	team
group cohesiveness	research and development	virtual team
group dynamics	teams	

>>>> WRAP-UP TO >>>> (OPENING CASE)

Virgin Group's Richard Branson: People Are Your Biggest Asset—Treat Them Like It

HOW CAN MANAGERS USE TEAMS TO GAIN A COMPETITIVE ADVANTAGE?

"In the travel sector, companies have to take customer service seriously if they hope to succeed, because a wonderful flight, train journey—or soon, we hope, a space trip—begins and ends with great service. While a company may be able to find ways to improve the interiors of their planes or trains, perhaps installing more comfortable seats and serving better meals, that expensive technology and luxurious design will count for nothing if customer service is shoddy." After having read and understood the concepts in this chapter, you should be able to answer the following questions:

1. *How do teams at Virgin America contribute to organizational effectiveness?*

ANSWER: Groups and teams can help an organization gain a competitive advantage because they can (1) enhance its performance, (2) increase its responsiveness to customers, (3) increase innovation, and (4) increase employees' motivation and satisfaction. The Refresh teams at Virgin America are a diverse group of employees including pilots, flight crew, ground crew, and members from all departments who come together to get trained in conflict resolution, hospitality, and emotional intelligence to help employees truly understand the customer's perspective by creating synergy from coordinating perspectives and experience across departments. The cross-functional teams draw on the expertise and knowledge from different departments to determine what is required to be responsive to customers. To promote innovation, the Refresh teams at Virgin America are left alone to solve problems that arise, rather than relying on scripts or flow charts provided by management. Working in teams at Virgin America can be motivating for the members by stimulating creative problem solving, engaging in social interaction, feeling connected to others, and sharing techniques for relieving stress and dealing effectively with conflict: all key ingredients of increasing responsiveness to customers.

2. *What types of teams are encouraged in this case?*

ANSWER: Many types of teams and groups are found in organizations that help managers achieve organizational goals. A team is a group whose members work intensely with each other to achieve a specific common goal or objective. At Virgin America, formal, cross-functional teams are formed by managers, where members from different departments are brought together to work toward a common goal. In this case the common goal is to enhance the customer's experience. The teams formed at Refresh are also task forces, set up as temporary teams assigned a specific task, as opposed to standing committees that are permanent. They are also self-managed teams, given the responsibility and autonomy to solve problems without managerial supervision.

3. *How do the managers in this case create group cohesiveness and why is this important for high performance?*

ANSWER: Group cohesiveness is the degree to which members are attracted and loyal to their group or team. As group cohesiveness increases, members' participation, conformity to group norms, and motivation to achieve group goals increases. Managers at Virgin America encourage two-way question-and-answer sessions with employees to help build bonds among members and senior management, thus strengthening loyalty and conformity to norms and motivation to accomplish organizational goals. Too much cohesiveness may lead to dysfunctional outcomes for the organization because highly cohesive teams often focus on group goals at the expense of goals that are effective for the organization as a whole. Too much cohesiveness may also result in groupthink, where faulty and biased decision making occurs in groups whose members strive for agreement among themselves at the expense of accurately assessing information relevant to a decision. Managers at Virgin America, and managers in general, strive to create moderately cohesive groups and teams to enhance organizational effectiveness and promote high performance.

Management in Action

TOPICS FOR DISCUSSION AND ACTION

LEVEL 1 Knowledge & Comprehension

1. Describe how teams can increase an organization's competitive advantage.

2. Describe the different types of groups and teams found in organizations.

3. Describe three techniques managers can use to improve group decision making and promote creativity.

LEVEL 2 Application & Analysis

4. Explain why and how managers would use self-managed teams to achieve organizational goals. What are some of the disadvantages to using self-managed teams?

5. Listen to the *BusinessWeek* podcast (or similar) at www.businessweek.com/mediacenter/ qt/podcasts/climbing/climbing_01_29_08.mp3 called "Climbing the Ladder." Describe the four archetypal personalities found in organizations and what roles they play in a high-performing team.

6. Describe the task and maintenance roles for effective group functioning. Which do you think are the most important, and why?

LEVEL 3 Synthesis & Evaluation

7. Teams should have a moderate level of cohesiveness and a balance of conformity and deviance from group norms. Why are these levels important to the performance of the team?

8. Imagine that you are the manager of a hotel. What steps will you take to reduce social loafing by members of the cleaning staff who are responsible for keeping all common areas and guest rooms spotless?

9. Analyze the pitfalls of groupthink. How can group conflict be resolved?

SELF-REFLECTION EXERCISE

Diagnosing Group Failures

Think about the last dissatisfying or discouraging experience you had as a member of a group or team. Perhaps the group did not accomplish its goals, perhaps group members could agree about nothing, or perhaps there was too much social loafing. Now answer the following questions.

1. What type of group was this?

2. Were group members motivated to achieve group goals? Why, or why not?

3. What were the group's norms? How much conformity and deviance existed in the group?

4. How cohesive was the group? Why do you think the group's cohesiveness was at this level? What consequences did this level of group cohesiveness have for the group and its members?

5. Was social loafing a problem in this group? Why, or why not?

6. What could the group's leader or manager have done differently to increase group effectiveness?

7. What could group members have done differently to increase group effectiveness?

SMALL GROUP BREAKOUT EXERCISE

Creating a Cross-Functional Team

Form groups of three or four, and appoint one member as the spokesperson who will communicate your findings to the whole class when called on by the instructor. Then discuss the following scenario:

You are a group of managers in charge of food services for a large university. Recently, a survey of students, faculty, and staff was conducted to evaluate customer satisfaction with the food services provided by the university's eight cafeterias. The results were disappointing, to put it mildly. Complaints ranged from dissatisfaction with the type and range of meals and snacks provided, operating hours, and food temperature, to unresponsiveness to current concerns about the importance of low-carb/high-protein diets and the preferences of vegetarians. You have decided to form a cross-functional team to further evaluate reactions to the food services and to develop a proposal for changes that can be made to increase customer satisfaction.

1. Indicate who should be on this important cross-functional team and why.
2. Describe the goals the team should be trying to achieve.
3. Describe the different roles team members will need to perform.
4. Describe the steps you will take to help ensure that the team has a good balance between conformity and deviance and a moderate level of cohesiveness.

BUSINESS PLANNING EXERCISE

Your professor may ask you to write a business plan for a new venture or a strategic plan for an existing venture. At the end of every chapter, you will have an opportunity to apply managerial and organizational concepts to the exercise of writing a business plan. Refer to Appendix A.

You and your business planning team realize that you might have to operate as a virtual team because it turns out that each of you has a different work and class schedule, so there is almost no time when more than three people could meet face to face. As you know, virtual teams have benefits, but they also face problems.

1. How will you build group cohesiveness in this team?
2. Write out a "team effectiveness contract" that includes how the group will divide the labour of writing the business plan (what roles and responsibilities will each member take on), what norms might help the group function, how the team will prevent social loafing and what will be the consequences for not meeting commitments.

MANAGING ETHICALLY EXERCISE

Moon Fuel uses self-managed teams to develop and produce new websites. Some of the members of the team are engaged in social loafing, and other members of the team are reluctant to say anything. Team members are supposed to provide performance evaluations of each other at the end of each project, but some rate everyone equally to avoid conflict. This practice has caused low morale on the team because hard work results in the same pay as does loafing. Some team members are complaining that it is unethical to rate everyone the same way when individual performances differ so much. One team member has come to you for advice because you are an expert in team performance and ethics. What would you advise this team member to do? How could the team's performance be improved?

MANAGEMENT CHALLENGE EXERCISE

Building Team Spirit[63]

Jim Clemmer, based in Kitchener, Ontario, is a professional speaker, workshop/retreat leader, and author of *Growing the Distance* and *The Leader's Digest.* He says that "team spirit is the catalyst every organization needs to achieve outstanding performance." Indeed, he goes on to say that the "emotional commitment of the people using the tools and executing the plans is what determines whether companies sink or soar." He further explains how companies can kill or build spirit.

Because of your knowledge and skill in team-based performance, you have been called into discussions with the two founding partners and 10 employees of a new specialty tire company about to open its doors in Winnipeg, Manitoba. Many of these people have been friends to this point, but the owners want to get the company going on the right footing, especially because during the planning stage owners had tolerated the use of wireless devices in meetings. They notice now that some members are beginning to resent this "extra presence" while the team is doing its best to communicate. The owners have discovered that bored staff are simply emailing one another—literally "under the table."

1. What do you think is the problem here?
2. What is your best advice regarding team-building for this group?

MANAGEMENT PORTFOLIO PROJECT

Answer the following questions about the organization you have chosen to follow:

1. What types of groups and teams can you identify in this organization?
2. Does this organization use self-managed teams? How are they organized?
3. Does this organization use virtual teams? If so, in what areas of the operation do they function?
4. Can you identify any conflicts in this organization? What caused them, and how would you resolve them?

VIDEO MANAGEMENT CASE

"It's About the Team": How Canadian Tire Changed Its Staffing Processes[64]

Liza Provenzano, associate vice-president of employee relations, safety, and HR policy at Canadian Tire, talks about how her team centralized its staffing function and examined current processes in order to identify waste in hiring practices.

1. How did Canadian Tire use a team approach to centralizing its staffing function?

Management Case

"Nobody Has a Good Day in Space If the Team Has a Bad Day"[65]

Although a small firm, Neptec Design Group has learned how to work with big space agencies by thinking like them.

Pound for pound, Neptec Design Group Ltd. of Ottawa punches way above its weight in the aerospace industry: a 100-person firm that in its 20 years has loaded its technology onto six space flights for NASA. The key to its success as a mid-size company is in being a team player, which means solving problems the way its customers want them solved, says Iain Christie, Neptec's chief executive. "Nobody has a good day in space if the team has a bad day," he says.

Neptec designs and builds advanced sensors and robotics for space, defence and industry, specializing in the development and operation of 3D vision systems for equipment inspection and positioning. This year, it became the first company outside the United States to win NASA's George M. Low Award for quality and performance.

Beyond Canada and the United States, Neptec has contracts with the Japanese Space Agency and the European Space Agency, and is in talks to do work in Russia. It is also seeking partners abroad for Neptec Technologies Corp., a start-up that hopes to put the company's technological expertise to work for industries such as defence and energy.

Christie, 46, received his PhD in physics from the University of Ottawa. Most of the company's staff have been trained at Canadian universities, including the University of Waterloo, Carleton University and Laval University.

Why did you win NASA's George M. Low Award?

We do things the NASA way. We understand not just explicitly what they want, but implicitly the way they need to see this thing done. They understand that when we're on the team, we're on the team. Nobody has a good day in space if the team has a bad day.

Can you explain what you mean by doing things the way NASA needs to see them done?

When I first went down to the Johnson Space Centre in Houston very early in my career, I spent time working on the space vision system, which we eventually used to put together the space station. It used a camera to look at targets. We thought it would be better to use two cameras. I had worked for a year figuring out how to generate, as we call it, the two-camera algorithm. So I went down to NASA to work as our liaison down there, and the very first day we had a meeting and I said, "We have this two-camera algorithm and it will make things a lot better; it's a lot more accurate and it'll solve your problems." The first guy to speak up said, "That's very interesting, but we have to be single-fault tolerant, meaning if we lose one camera, we can still do it. So in order to do what you're asking, we'd need at least three, maybe four cameras. So we can't do it. I'm sorry, you can't use your two-camera algorithm. What else do you have?" So that was my first lesson. Solving the problem the way you want to might be great, but if you can't really understand what the customer wants and do it their way, you haven't really solved the problem.

What did you learn from that?

The most important feature in solving problems is not only understanding the constraints the customer is willing to write down for you, but to understand their implicit constraints as well. The ones that come from their culture—the single-fault tolerance is written into the NASA documentation, but it's also very much a part of their culture. They don't consider doing anything any other way. When you can get to the point where they say, "but did you do this, did you do that, does it do this," and you have the right answer, they begin to relax and believe that "when these guys bring us the solution, it's going to be the NASA solution. It's not going to be the Neptec solution."

Is that the key to your company's success?

Our ability to make ourselves part of our customers' teams and adopt their constraints, attitudes and goals is what keeps our customers coming back, and staying very loyal to us. A lot of large companies like the innovation they get from the small companies, but they distrust it because they don't know how to control it. They don't know if they can trust the product they get. They don't know if it's going to be reliable or consistent.

What's the biggest limitation of being small?

Any business that is focused on cash flow instead of balance sheets is a small business. And we're a small business. The biggest constraint of being small is you can make long-term plans and long-term strategies, but you're always at the mercy of short-term issues, and one way or other those issues always end up coming back to cash. The wolf is never far enough from the door to let you truly put aside short-term considerations for the long-term one.

It's great to know you can find talented staff in Canada.
We really do have a first-rate post-secondary education system. And we have a society that allows people to focus on their employment. Because we live in a very stable society with very little social unrest or problems, people are able to put their energies and their creativity into their employment, which is a great benefit to the people that employ them.

1. How does Neptec's team contribute to the organizational effectiveness of NASA?
2. What is the key to success of Neptec's team approach?
3. How does groupthink play a role in this case?

Mc Graw Hill **connect**™

Connect allows you to practise important concepts at your own pace and on your own schedule, with 24/7 online access to an eBook, practice quizzes, video cases, interactive exercises, study tools, and more.

Managing Human Resources

Opening Case

Effectively Managing Human Resources at the Four Seasons

HOW CAN MANAGERS PROMOTE HIGH LEVELS OF PERSONALIZED CUSTOMER SERVICE IN AN INDUSTRY KNOWN FOR HIGH EMPLOYEE TURNOVER?

Four Seasons Hotels and Resorts is one of only about 14 companies to be ranked one of the "100 Best Companies to Work For" every year since *Fortune* magazine started this annual ranking of companies over 12 years ago.[1] And the Four Seasons often receives other awards and recognition based on customers' responses.[2] In an industry in which annual turnover rates are over 35 percent, turnover for the Four Seasons is around 18 percent.[3] Evidently, employees and customers alike are very satisfied with the way they are treated at the Four Seasons. Understanding that the two are causally linked is perhaps the key to the Four Seasons' success. As the Four Seasons' founder, chairman of the board, and CEO Isadore Sharp suggests, "How you treat your employees is how you expect them to treat the customer."[4]

The Four Seasons was founded by Canadian-born Sharp in 1961. After opening and running both small and large hotels, Sharp decided that he could provide customers with a very different kind of hotel experience by trying to combine the best features of both kinds of hotel experiences—the sense of closeness and personal attention that a small hotel brings with the amenities of a big hotel to suit the needs of business travellers.[5]

Sharp sought to provide the kind of personal service that would really help business travellers on the road—providing them with the amenities they have at home and in the office and miss when travelling on

business. Thus, the Four Seasons was the first hotel chain to provide many amenities such as bathrobes and shampoo.[6] While these are relatively concrete ways of personalizing the hotel experience, Sharp realized that the ways in which employees treat customers are just as, or perhaps even more, important. When employees view each customer as an individual with his or her own needs and desires, and empathetically try to meet these needs and desires and help customers both overcome any problems or challenges they face and truly enjoy their hotel experience, customers are likely to be both loyal and highly satisfied.[7]

Sharp has always realized that in order for employees to treat customers well, the Four Seasons needs to treat its employees well. Salaries are relatively high at the Four Seasons, by industry standards (i.e., between the 75th and 90th percentiles), employees participate in a profit-sharing plan, and the company contributes to their pension plans. All employees are provided with free meals in the hotel cafeteria, have access to staff showers and a locker room, and are provided with an additional, highly attractive benefit: once a new employee has worked for the Four Seasons for six months, he or she can stay for three nights free at any Four Seasons hotel or resort in the world. After a year of employment, this benefit increases to six free nights and it continues to increase as tenure with the company increases.[8]

All aspects of human resource management at the Four Seasons are oriented around ensuring that the guiding principle behind all Four Seasons operations is upheld. As Sharp indicates, all employees and managers should "deal with others—partners, customers, coworkers, everyone—as we would want them to deal with us."[9]

All job applicants to the Four Seasons, regardless of level or area, have a minimum of four interviews, one of which is with the general manager of the property.[10] The Four Seasons devotes so much attention to hiring the right people because of the importance of each and every employee providing a consistently high level of empathetic and responsive customer service.[11]

New hires participate in a three-month training program that includes improvisation activities to help them learn how to anticipate guests' needs, requirements, and actions and appropriately respond to them.[12] The aim of training is to help ensure that all employees, regardless of area or function, provide consistently high-quality and highly responsive customer service. Since customer service is everyone's responsibility, the Four Seasons has no separate customer service department per se. Training is an ongoing activity at the Four Seasons and never really stops.[13]

The Four Seasons also tends to promote from within.[14] For example, while recent college graduates may start out as assistant managers, those who do well and have high aspirations could potentially become general managers in less than 15 years. This helps to ensure that managers have empathy and respect for those in lower-level positions as well as the ingrained ethos of treating others (employees, subordinates, coworkers, and customers) the way they would like to be treated themselves. All in all, the way in which the Four Seasons manages its human resources helps to ensure that customers are treated very well indeed.[15]

After reading and understanding the concepts in this chapter, you should be able to answer the following questions:

1. *How does Isadore Sharp employ a human resource system that creates an outstanding experience for customers at the Four Seasons?*

2. *How does the Four Seasons manage the components of its HR system?*

Overview

Managers are responsible for acquiring, developing, protecting, and using the resources that an organization needs to be efficient and effective. One of the most important resources in all organizations is human resources—the people involved in the production and distribution of goods and services. Human resources include all members of an organization, ranging from top managers to entry-level employees. In previous chapters, we saw how the aging of the workforce is "unprecedented." At the same time, younger workers may experience the upside of an aging workforce. Effective human resource managers—like Isadore Sharp in the opening case—realize how valuable human resources are and take active steps to make sure that their organizations build and fully utilize their human resources to gain a competitive advantage.

This chapter examines how managers can tailor their human resource management system to their organization's strategy and structure. We discuss in particular the major components of human resource management: recruitment and selection, training and development, performance appraisal, pay and benefits, and labour relations in the context of the Canadian legal framework. By the end of this chapter, you will understand the central role that human resource management plays in creating a high-performing organization.

Describe the legal framework of human resource management in Canada. **LO1**

The Legal Framework of Human Resource Management in Canada

Several key pieces of legislation govern the management of human resources (HR) in Canada. The laws have been developed to protect the rights of employers and employees. HR managers must be aware of the legal and political environment in which they do their work. Failure to adhere to the legislation governing employment standards, labour relations, health and safety, employment equity, and other employment-related regulations, such as the *Charter of Rights and Freedoms,* knowingly or unknowingly, can result in severe penalties to managers and employers. The HR manager has the responsibility to avoid **intentional discrimination** (deliberately using prohibited grounds, such as race, religion, and sex, when making employment decisions) and **unintentional discrimination** (unfair practices and policies that have an

intentional discrimination The illegal practice of deliberately using prohibited grounds, such as race, religion and sex, when making employment decisions.

unintentional discrimination Unfair practices and policies that have an adverse impact on specific groups for reasons unrelated to the job.

adverse impact on specific groups for reasons that are unrelated to the job). In this chapter, we look at two pieces of legislation that make up the legal environment of HR management in Canada: the *Employment Standards Act* and the *Canadian Human Rights Act*.

The *Employment Standards Act* sets out minimum standards for the private sector in federal, provincial, and territorial legislation. It deals with the minimum age for employment, hours of work and overtime pay, minimum wages, equal pay, the weekly rest-day, general holidays with pay, annual vacations with pay, parental leave, and individual and group terminations of employment. It also deals with mandatory retirement and whistleblower protection rights. Minimum employee entitlements are established for each element covered by the Act.

The *Canadian Human Rights Act* covers all businesses under federal jurisdiction. Each province and territory has its own human rights legislation that prohibits discrimination based on specific grounds. There are differences across the nation. For example, in British Columbia, Prince Edward Island, Quebec, and Yukon, it is considered discriminatory to reject an applicant for employment based on a record of criminal conviction. This is not a prohibited ground of discrimination in any other of the 14 jurisdictions in Canada. All jurisdictions prohibit discrimination on the grounds of race, colour, religion or creed, physical and mental disability, sex (including pregnancy and childbirth), and marital status. All areas have policies related to discrimination on the basis of age; however, the protected age groups differ. Human resource managers must act according to the legislation that governs their jurisdiction in hiring and firing employees. Failure to do so may result in charges of discrimination and may lead to increasingly large fines and settlements.

It is important to note that the *Employment Standards Act* and the *Human Rights Act* do not restrict employers' right and ability to reward high-performing employees and discipline employees for not meeting productivity standards or following company rules, as long as such rewards and punishments are based on *job-related criteria* and not on prohibited grounds.

A note on health and safety: Every human resource manager must pay attention to maintaining a healthy and safe working environment. It is estimated that indirect costs can be as much as two to 10 times more than the direct costs of an accident. The Canadian government

> "How you treat your employees is how you expect them to treat the customer."
> *Isadore Sharp, CEO, Four Seasons*

has recognized this importance of health and safety as well. However, in Canada, unlike in the United States, there is no federal body to which organizations report. Rather, Canada has health and safety regulations and enforcement agencies by province and territory. What can be called Canadian health and safety net legislation would include the following: the Canada Labour Code,[16] WHMIS (Workplace Hazardous Materials Information System),[17] Workers' Compensation,[18] Canadian Centre for Occupational Health and Safety,[19] and the *Occupational Health and Safety Act*.[20]

We now turn to the activities that managers engage in to attract, develop, and retain high-performing employees.

Explain why strategic human resource management and human resources planning can help an organization gain a competitive advantage. **LO2**

Strategic Human Resource Management

Human resource management (HRM) includes all the activities that managers engage in to attract and retain employees and to ensure that they perform at a high level and contribute to the accomplishment of organizational goals. These activities make up an organization's human resource management system, which has five major components: recruitment and selection, training and development, performance appraisal and feedback, pay and benefits, and labour relations. See Figure 11.1. **Strategic human resource management** is the process by which managers design the components of an HRM system to be consistent with each other, with other elements of organizational architecture, and with the organization's strategy and goals.[21] The objective of strategic HRM is the development of an HRM system that enhances an organization's efficiency, quality, innovation, and responsiveness to customers—the four building blocks of competitive advantage, which we discussed in Chapter 2. At the Four Seasons in the opening case, HRM practices ensure that all employees provide excellent customer service.

human resource management (HRM) Activities that managers engage in to attract and retain employees and to ensure that they perform at a high level and contribute to the accomplishment of organizational goals.

strategic human resource management The process by which managers design the components of a human resource management system to be consistent with each other, with other elements of organizational architecture, and with the organization's strategy and goals.

| FIGURE 11.1 | Components of a Human Resource Management System |

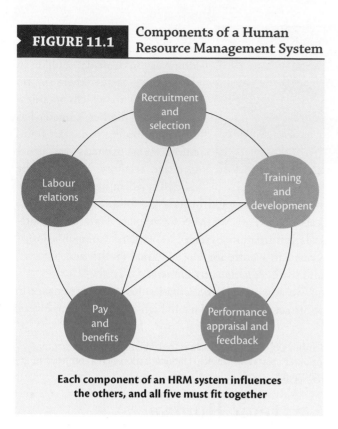

Each component of an HRM system influences the others, and all five must fit together

Human Resource Planning

Human resource planning includes all the activities that managers use to forecast their current and future needs for human resources. Current human resources are the employees an organization needs today to provide high-quality goods and services to customers. Future human resources are the employees the organization will need at some later date to achieve its longer-term goals. As part of human resource planning, managers must make both demand forecasts and supply forecasts. *Demand forecasts* estimate the qualifications and numbers of employees an organization will need given its goals and strategies. *Supply forecasts* estimate the availability and qualifications of current employees now and in the future and the supply of qualified workers in the external labour market. One of the factors facing some amusement parks is that not enough teenagers are available or willing to work at them. With low supply, they have had to look to senior citizens as an alternative supply of labour.

As a result of their human resource planning, managers sometimes decide to **outsource** to fill some of their human resource needs. Instead of recruiting and selecting employees to produce goods and services, managers contract with people who are not members of their organization to produce goods and services. Managers in publishing companies, for example, frequently contract with freelance editors to copyedit books that they intend to publish. The People Bank is an organization that provides temporary typing, clerical, and secretarial workers to managers who want to use outsourcing to fill some of their human resource requirements in these areas. EMBERS Staffing Solutions provides construction and warehouse staff.

Two reasons why human resource planning sometimes leads managers to outsource are flexibility and cost. First, outsourcing can give managers increased *flexibility,* especially when accurately forecasting human resource needs is difficult, human resource needs fluctuate over time, or finding skilled workers in a particular area is difficult. Second, outsourcing can sometimes allow managers to make use of human resources at a lower *cost.* When work is outsourced, costs can be lower for a number of reasons: the organization does not have to provide benefits to workers; managers are able to contract for work only when the work is needed; and managers do not have to invest in training. Outsourcing can be used for functional activities such as after-sales service on appliances and equipment, legal work, and the management of information systems.

Outsourcing does have its disadvantages, however.[22] When work is outsourced, managers may lose some control over the quality of goods and services. Also, individuals performing outsourced work may have less knowledge of organizational practices, procedures, and goals and less commitment to an organization than regular employees. In addition, unions resist outsourcing because it has the potential to eliminate some of their members. To gain some of the flexibility and cost savings of outsourcing and avoid some of its disadvantages, a number of organizations, such as Microsoft and IBM, rely on a pool of temporary employees to, for example, debug programs.

A major trend reflecting the increasing globalization of business is the outsourcing of office work, computer programming, and technical jobs from the United States and countries in Western Europe, with high labour costs, to countries like India and China, with low labour costs.[23] For example, computer programmers in India and China earn a fraction of what their U.S. counterparts earn. According to estimates by Gartner Inc., outsourcing (or *offshoring,* as it is also called when work is outsourced to other countries) of information technology and business process work is valued at over $34 billion per year.

As companies gain experience in outsourcing software and technological services, managers are learning what kinds

human resource planning Activities that managers use to forecast their current and future needs for human resources.

outsource To use outside suppliers and manufacturers to produce goods and services.

of work can be effectively outsourced and what work should probably not be outsourced. In India, for example, the workforce is highly trained and motivated, and cities like Bangalore are bustling with high-tech jobs and companies like Infosys Technologies, providing software services to companies abroad. Managers who have outsourcing experience have found that outsourcing works best for tasks that can be rule-based, do not require closeness/familiarity with customers and/or the customs and culture of the country in which the company is based, and do not require creativity.[24] When the work requires the recognition and solution of problems rather than the application of pre-existing algorithms, creativity in developing solutions, and independent thinking and judgment without the guidance of standard operating procedures, performance might suffer from outsourcing. Essentially, the more complex and uncertain the work and the more it depends on being close to customers and the company itself, the less advantageous outsourcing tends to be.[25]

Nonetheless, there are many kinds of tasks that can be effectively outsourced, and the cost savings for these tasks can be considerable.[26] And some managers believe that many tasks can be effectively outsourced, even those requiring creativity. Some of the advantages and disadvantages are shown in Table 11.1.

The assessment of both current and future human resource needs helps managers determine whom they should be trying to recruit and select to achieve organizational goals *now* and in the *future*. See Figure 11.2. As workers age, and retire, they take valuable knowledge about the ins and outs of getting a job done with them. This is why succession planning is becoming a critical need. In recent years, Montreal-based BCE has created a new position, "chief talent officer," who is responsible for executive recruitment, compensation, and succession planning to make sure that BCE's companies have the right leadership and talent as BCE looks toward the future.[27]

Succession planning helps ensure that valuable knowledge is not lost to the organization when workers leave or retire. It must be well thought out. Human resources managers often use **personnel replacement charts** as tools in this process. A personnel replacement chart is an examination of all current positions, along with who holds them, what their skills and qualifications are, and whether or not their performance levels make them suitable for promotion as positions become available. In order to create a replacement chart, a thorough analysis of each position is required. See Figure 11.3 for an example of a typical personnel replacement chart.

> **personnel replacement charts** A graphic illustration of current positions, who holds them, and whether they have the skills and qualifications necessary for succession planning.

> **TABLE 11.1** Advantages and Disadvantages of Outsourcing Human Resources

Examples	Advantages	Disadvantages
Computer software companies outsourcing programming work to India Contracting out activities to companies that specialize in HRM	Takes advantage of lower labour costs Provides flexibility by allowing the company to focus on core competencies Reduces costs: when a company outsources, it does not have to provide benefits to full-time workers or invest in training	Lose control over the quality of goods and services. Companies hired to do the work have less knowledge of organizational practices, procedures, and goals. Outsourced employees have less commitment to an organization than do regular, full-time employees. The potential to eliminate members' jobs creates resistance to outsourcing by labour unions.

> **FIGURE 11.2** HRM Planning and Job Analysis

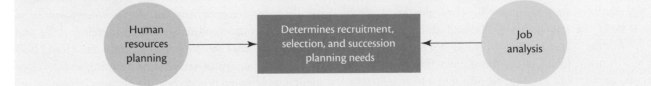

FIGURE 11.3 **A Typical Personnel Replacement Chart**

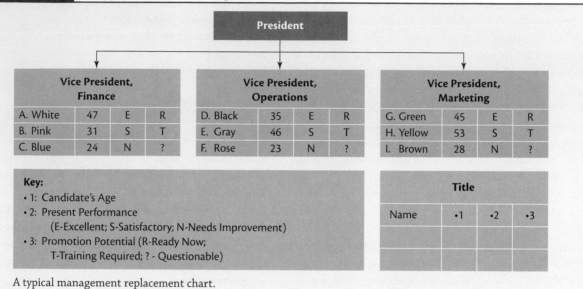

A typical management replacement chart.

Job Analysis

Job analysis is the process of identifying (1) the tasks, duties, and responsibilities that make up a job (the *job description*), and (2) the knowledge, skills, and abilities needed to perform the job (the *job specifications*).[28] For each job in an organization, a job analysis needs to be done.

A job analysis can be done in a number of ways, including by observing current employees as they perform the job or by interviewing them. Often, managers rely on questionnaires completed by job holders and their managers. The questionnaires ask about the skills and abilities needed to perform the job, job tasks and the amount of time spent on them, responsibilities, supervisory activities, equipment used, reports prepared, and decisions made.[29]

A trend, in some organizations, is toward more flexible jobs in which tasks and responsibilities change and cannot be clearly specified in advance. For these kinds of jobs, job analysis focuses more on determining the skills and knowledge workers need to be effective and less on specific duties.

When managers complete human resource planning and job analyses for all jobs in an organization, they know their human resource needs and the jobs they need to fill. They also know what knowledge, skills, and abilities potential employees will need to perform those jobs. At this point, the first component of HRM, recruitment and selection, can begin. Before looking in depth at recruitment and selection processes, we give a brief overview of each component and how they fit together with the strategy and structure of the organization.

Describe the five components of human resources management and explain how they fit together with the strategy and structure of the organization. **LO3**

Overview of the Components of HRM

An organization's human resource management system has five major components: (1) recruitment and selection, (2) training and development, (3) performance appraisal and feedback, (4) pay and benefits, and (5) labour relations (refer to Figure 11.1). Managers use *recruitment and selection,* the first component of an HRM system, to attract and hire new employees who have the abilities, skills, and experiences that will help an organization achieve its goals. For example, Cirque du Soleil recruits its members from all over the world. About 70 percent of recruits come from a sports background, which is well suited for training in acrobatics, a core part of their entertainment experience.

After recruiting and selecting employees, managers use the second component, *training and development,* to ensure that organizational members develop skills and abilities that will enable them to perform their jobs effectively in the present and the future. Training and development is an ongoing process because changes in technology and the environment, as well as in an organization's goals

job analysis Identifying the tasks, duties, and responsibilities that make up a job and the knowledge, skills, and abilities needed to perform the job.

and strategies, often require organizational members to learn new techniques and ways of working.

At Cirque, new recruits have the discipline and technical skills but usually lack the acrobatic and artistic skills. Extensive training removes this gap and positions the company to gain a competitive advantage.

The third component, *performance appraisal and feedback,* serves two purposes in HRM. First, performance appraisal can provide managers with the information they need to make good human resources decisions—decisions about how to train, motivate, and reward organizational members.[30] Thus, the performance appraisal and feedback component is a kind of control system that can be used with management by objectives (discussed in Chapters 5 and 13). Second, performance feedback from performance appraisal serves a developmental purpose for the members of an organization. When managers regularly evaluate their subordinates' performance, they can provide subordinates with valuable information about their strengths and weaknesses and the areas in which they need to concentrate. On the basis of performance appraisals, managers distribute pay to employees.

In the fourth component of HRM, *pay and benefits,* managers distribute pay to employees, first by determining their starting salaries, and later by determining whether raises or bonuses should be given. By rewarding high-performing organizational members with pay raises, bonuses, and the like, managers increase the likelihood that an organization's most valued human resources are motivated to continue their high levels of contribution to the organization. Moreover, when pay is linked to performance, high-performing employees are more likely to stay with the organization, and managers are more likely to be able to fill open positions with highly talented individuals. Benefits such as health insurance are important outcomes that employees receive by virtue of their membership in an organization.

Last but not least, *labour relations* includes the steps that managers take to develop and maintain good working relationships with the labour unions that may represent their employees' interests. For example, an organization's labour relations component can help managers establish safe working conditions and fair labour practices in their offices and plants.

Managers must ensure that all five of these components fit together and complement their companies' structure, strategy, and control systems.[31] For example, if managers decide to decentralize authority and empower employees, they need to invest in training and development to ensure that lower-level employees have the knowledge and expertise they need to make the decisions that top

managers would make in a more centralized structure. If the organization is following a differentiation strategy, they may require more highly skilled employees to create a competitive advantage, whereas a cost-leadership strategy may rely on cheaper, unskilled labour. Hierarchical organizations that rely on bureaucratic rules and regulations often rely on fear of punishment to control employee behaviour. Flatter, more flexible organizational structures rely less on formal rules and more on shared values to guide appropriate employee behaviour. Forms of control are discussed in more depth in Chapter 13.

Each of the five components of HRM influences the others.[32] The kinds of people that the organization attracts and hires through recruitment and selection, for example, determine (1) the training and development that are necessary, (2) the way performance is appraised, and (3) the appropriate levels of pay and benefits. We turn now to an examination of each component.

Recruitment and Selection

After managers engage in human resource planning and job analysis, they can start to recruit and select employees. **Recruitment** includes all the activities that managers use to develop a pool of qualified candidates for open positions.[33] **Selection** is the process by which managers determine the relative qualifications of job applicants and their potential for performing well in a particular job.

> **recruitment** Activities that managers use to develop a pool of qualified candidates for open positions.
>
> **selection** The process that managers use to determine the relative qualifications of job applicants and the individuals' potential for performing well in a particular job.

Managers seek to develop a pool of qualified candidates when recruiting.

External and Internal Recruitment

Recently, *The Economist* devoted a 15-page special report to what it called "The Search for Talent: Why It's Getting Harder to Find."[34] They speak about the world's most valuable commodity—talent—getting more and more difficult to find. Brainpower is the *intangible asset* that now describes the word "talent." What is making things difficult in finding "talent" is the collapse of loyalty and the shortage of "trained brains." While in times past business discussions on the global economy were on the "balance of power," today the emphasis is on the "balance of brains."[35] Who will be the winner in the competition for global brainpower? *The Economist* refers to Clyde Prestowitz's book *Three Billion New Capitalists: The Great Shift of Wealth and Power to the East,* where he quotes a Chinese friend: "We've had a couple of hundred bad years, but now we're back."[36] Welcome to the challenge and race for talent! HR managers generally use two types of recruiting talent: external and internal, which are now supplemented by recruiting over the Internet. See Figure 11.4.

External Recruiting

When managers do external recruiting to fill open positions, they look outside the organization for people who have not worked for the organization before. There are many ways in which managers can recruit externally—advertisements in newspapers and magazines, open houses for students, career counsellors at high schools and colleges, career fairs at colleges, recruitment meetings with groups in the local community, and notices on the Web.

Many large organizations send teams of interviewers to college campuses to recruit new employees. External recruitment can also take place through informal networks, such as when current employees inform friends about open positions in their companies or recommend people they know to fill vacant spots. Some organizations use employment agencies for external recruitment, and some external recruitment takes place simply through walk-ins, where job hunters come to an organization and inquire about employment possibilities. An example of an employment agency that provides a source of labour in the construction and maintenance sectors is featured in our Focus on the Social Economy.

With all the downsizings and corporate layoffs that have taken place in recent years, you might think that external recruiting would be a relatively easy task for managers. However, it often is not, because even though many people may be looking for jobs, many of the jobs that are opening up require skills and abilities that these job hunters do not have. Managers needing to fill vacant positions and job hunters seeking employment opportunities are increasingly relying on the Internet to make connections with each other through employment websites such as Monster.com[37] and Jobline International. Jobline is Europe's largest electronic recruiting site, with operations in 12 countries.[38] Major corporations such as Coca-Cola, Cisco, Ernst & Young, Canon, and Telia have relied on Jobline to fill global positions.[39] Job postings for international recruitment are often placed online in trade journals and news magazines like *The Times* and *The Economist.*

> **FIGURE 11.4** Sources of Internal and External Recruitment[40]

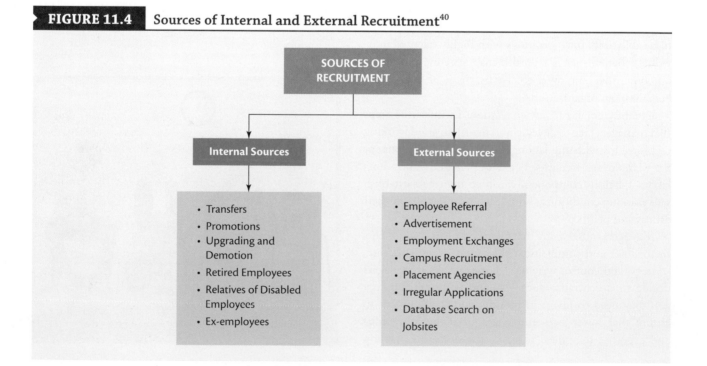

Selecting the right people for the job leads to high performing organizations.

Marilyn Mackes, the executive director for the U.S. National Association of Colleges and Employers, published that whereas in the past employers used social networking sites "to check profiles of potential hires," today "more than half will use the sites to network with potential candidates."[41]

External recruiting has both advantages and disadvantages for managers. Advantages include having access to a potentially large applicant pool; being able to hire people who have the skills, knowledge, and abilities the organization needs to achieve its goals; and being able to bring in newcomers who may have a fresh approach to problems and be up to date on the latest technology. These advantages have to be weighed against the disadvantages, however, including lower morale if current employees feel that there are individuals within the company who should be promoted. External recruitment also has high costs. Employees recruited externally lack knowledge about the inner workings of the organization and may need to receive more training than those recruited internally. Finally, with external recruitment, there is always uncertainty about whether the new employees actually will be good performers. Nonetheless, there are steps managers can take to reduce some of the uncertainty surrounding external recruitment. For example, Vancouver-based Angiotech Pharmaceuticals Inc. solves this problem by working with potential employees years before they are ready to be hired. The company provides research money to graduate students at the University of British Columbia who are working on projects closely related to Angiotech's needs.

FOCUS ON ❯ *The Social Economy*

EMBERS (Eastside Movement for Business & Economic Renewal Society)

EMBERS (Eastside Movement for Business & Economic Renewal Society) is a non-profit agency that works to combat poverty and assists in the revitalization of Vancouver's inner city by facilitating community-based business development. They do this by helping individuals and groups start small businesses and social enterprises. They offer self-employment training, one-on-one business coaching, and work with residents, community groups, and other stakeholders to develop plans, strategies, and specific ventures to improve the lives of residents and build a healthy community.

In 2008, EMBERS launched EMBERS Staffing Solutions as a way to reach more people and have a greater impact in the community. The only socially responsible,

non-profit staffing agency in Canada, they provide companies with high quality blue-collar workers on a monthly, weekly, or daily basis. Their candidates are talented, reliable, and proven workers in the construction, warehouse, and other sectors. All profits from EMBERS Staffing Solutions are reinvested back into EMBERS Staffing Solutions employment programs to help to improve the lives and skills of workers.

Paying out over $900 000 in wages and benefits to date, EMBERS Staffing Solutions has hired over 550 individuals of which more than 200 have transitioned into working full time.[42]

1. With which component of an HR system does EMBERS Staffing Solutions help organizations?

Internal Recruiting

When recruiting is internal, managers turn to existing employees to fill open positions. Employees recruited internally want either **lateral moves** (job changes that entail no major changes in responsibility or authority levels) or promotions. Internal recruiting has several advantages. First, internal applicants are already familiar with the organization (including its goals, structure, culture, rules, and norms). Second, managers already know internal candidates; they have considerable information about their skills and abilities and actual behaviour on the job. Third, internal recruiting can help boost levels of employee motivation and morale, both for the employee who gets the job and for other workers. Those who are not seeking a promotion or who may not be ready for a promotion can see that it is a possibility for the future, or a lateral move can alleviate boredom once a job has been fully mastered and also provide a useful way to learn new skills. Finally, internal recruiting is normally less time-consuming and expensive than external recruiting. As we say in the opening case, the Four Seasons hotel chain often promotes from within. A new college graduate can start as an assistant manager and, if they have the right stuff, within 15 years advance to a general hotel manager.

Given the advantages of internal recruiting, why do managers rely on external recruiting as much as they do? The answer lies in the disadvantages to internal recruiting—among them, a limited pool of candidates and a tendency among those candidates to be set in the organization's ways. Often, the organization simply does not have suitable internal candidates. Sometimes, even when suitable internal applicants are available, managers may rely on external recruiting to find the very best candidate or to help bring new ideas and approaches into the organization. When organizations are in trouble and performing poorly, external recruiting is often relied on to bring in managerial talent with a fresh approach.

The Selection Process

Once managers develop a pool of applicants for open positions through the recruitment process, they need to find out whether each applicant is qualified for the position and whether he or she is likely to be a good performer. If more than one applicant meets these two conditions, managers must further determine which applicants are likely to be better performers than others. They have several selection tools to help them sort out the relative qualifications of job applicants and to appraise applicants' potential for being good performers in a particular job. Those tools include background information, interviews, tests, and references.[43]

Selection techniques must be valid and reliable.

All selection techniques must be valid *and* reliable. To be a **valid selection technique,** it must determine the candidates' likely performance (success or failure) on the job. Validity is the degree to which the test predicts performance on the tasks or job in question. Does a physical ability test used to select firefighters, for example, actually predict on-the-job performance? Do assessment centre ratings actually predict managerial performance? Do keyboarding tests predict secretarial performance? These are all questions of validity. Honesty tests, for example, are controversial because it is not clear that they validly predict honesty in such jobs as retailing and banking.

If the test is unrelated to performing the job, it is invalid and managers can be subject to charges of discrimination if the candidate is not chosen. For example, it would be invalid for a manager to use a test of strength to select a candidate for a word processing job. The test of strength has no relation to how the candidate will perform the tasks of a word processor. Women have long been unable to access many of the jobs traditionally held by men because of invalid selection techniques. To be a **reliable selection technique,** it must yield consistent results

lateral moves Job changes that entail no major changes in responsibility or authority levels.

valid selection technique A test or tool that measures the candidates' likely success or failure of performing the job.

reliable selection technique A test or tool that yields consistent results when repeated.

when repeated over time. Reliability is the degree to which the test or tool measures the same thing each time it is administered. In the previous example, if the word-processing candidate is given a typing test, if it is reliable it should yield similar performance results, without a significant deviation, when repeated some time later.

Background Information

To aid in the selection process, managers obtain background information from job applications and from résumés. Such information might include highest levels of education obtained, university or college majors and minors, type of college or university attended, years and type of work experience, and mastery of foreign languages. Background information can be helpful both to screen out applicants who are lacking key qualifications (such as a post-secondary degree) and to determine which qualified applicants are more promising than others (e.g., applicants with a BSc may be acceptable, but those who also have an MBA are preferable).

Increasing numbers of organizations are performing background checks to verify that the background information prospective employees provide is accurate (and also to uncover any negative information such as crime convictions).[44] According to ADP Employer Services, an outsourcing company that performs payroll and human resource functions for organizations, more and more companies are performing background checks on prospective employees and are uncovering inaccuracies, inconsistencies, and negative information such as prior convictions or driving violations.[45]

Interviews

Virtually all organizations use interviews during the selection process. The interview process is intended to create a perception of the candidate to try to determine if they are a good match for the job and fit well with the culture of the organization. Interviews should also be used to give potential candidates a *realistic job preview*. A **realistic job preview (RJP)** involves communicating the good and bad aspects of a job to a candidate to prevent mismatched expectations and high turnover. Four Seasons has a substantially lower turnover rate than the rest of the industry, because potential employees understand from the beginning the difficulties and rewards of creating a first class hotel experience for customers.

Two general types of interviews are *structured* and *unstructured*. In a structured interview, managers ask each applicant the same standard questions (such as "What are your unique qualifications for this position?" and "What characteristics of a job are most important for you?").

Interviews provide the employer and candidate with valuable information.

Particularly informative questions may be those where the actual answering allows an interviewee to demonstrate skills and abilities needed for the job. Sometimes called **situational interview questions,** these questions present interviewees with a scenario that they would likely encounter on the job and ask them to indicate how they would handle it.[46] For example, applicants for a sales job may be asked to indicate how they would respond to a customer who complains about waiting too long for service, a customer who is indecisive, and a customer whose order is lost.

Practically all organizations use some kind of interview during the selection process. At Four Seasons, a minimum of four interviews are conducted, no matter what level of position is applied for, to ensure the candidates have the empathy required to be responsive to customers' needs.

Behavioural interview questions focus on relevant past job-related behaviours. They involve describing a situation and asking the candidate how they handled it. While situational interview questions ask candidates how they would deal with a specific situation *in the future,* behavioural interview questions ask them to describe how they reacted to a specific situation *in the past.* See Figure 11.5.

An **unstructured interview** proceeds more like an ordinary conversation. The interviewer feels free to ask probing questions to discover what the applicant is like and does not ask a fixed set of questions prepared in advance. In general, a **structured interview,** where questions

realistic job preview (RJP) Communicating the good and bad aspects of a job to a candidate to prevent mismatched expectations and high turnover.

situational interview questions Ask candidates how they would deal with a situation they might encounter on the job.

behavioural interview questions Ask candidates how they dealt with a situation they encountered on the job.

unstructured interview Unplanned questions asked as points of interest arise in the conversation.

structured interview Formal questions asked in a set sequence.

> **FIGURE 11.5** **Examples of Interview Question Types**

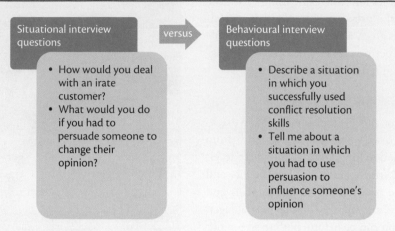

are asked in set sequence, is superior to the unstructured interview because it is more likely to yield information that will help identify qualified candidates and is less subjective. Also, evaluations based on structured interviews may be less likely to be influenced by the biases of the interviewer than evaluations based on unstructured interviews.

Even when structured interviews are used, however, there is always the potential for the biases of the interviewer to influence his or her judgment. The similar-to-me effect can cause people to perceive others who are similar to themselves more positively than they perceive those who are different and illustrates how stereotypes can result in inaccurate perceptions. It is important for interviewers to be trained to avoid these biases and sources of inaccurate perceptions as much as possible. Many of the approaches to increasing diversity awareness and diversity skills described in Chapter 3 can be used to train interviewers to avoid the effects of biases and stereotypes. In addition, using multiple interviewers can be advantageous, for their individual biases and idiosyncrasies may cancel one another out.[47]

When conducting interviews, managers have to be careful not to ask questions that are irrelevant to the job in question, or their organizations run the risk of costly lawsuits. It is inappropriate and illegal, for example, to inquire about an interviewee's spouse or to ask questions about whether an interviewee plans to have children. Questions such as these, which are irrelevant to job performance, are *invalid* and may be viewed as discriminatory and violate human rights legislation. Thus, interviewers also need to be instructed in what is required under the legislation and informed about questions that may be seen as violating those laws.

Pencil and Paper Tests

Potential employees may be asked to take paper-and-pencil tests. The two main kinds of paper-and-pencil tests used for selection purposes are ability tests and personality tests. **Ability tests** assess the extent to which applicants possess the skills necessary for job performance, such as verbal comprehension or numerical skills. Autoworkers hired by General Motors, Chrysler, and Ford, for example, are typically tested for their ability to read and to do mathematics.[48]

Personality tests measure personality traits and characteristics relevant to job performance. Employers keen to find and retain the right workers are turning to personality testing to help everything from recruiting to promoting to team building. Proponents call them essential, but critics worry that they sometimes can be invasive, ineffective, even borderline illegal.[49] Some retail organizations, for example, give job applicants honesty tests to determine how trustworthy they are. The use of personality tests (including honesty tests) for hiring purposes is controversial. Some critics maintain that honesty tests do not really measure honesty (i.e., they are not valid) and can be subject to faking by job applicants. Before using any paper-and-pencil tests for selection purposes, managers must have sound evidence that the tests are actually good predictors of performance on the job in question. Managers who use tests without such evidence may be subject to costly discrimination lawsuits.

For jobs that require physical abilities—such as firefighting, garbage collecting, and package delivery—managers' selection tools include **physical ability tests**

ability tests Assess the skills necessary to perform the job well.

personality tests Measure personality traits and characteristics relevant to job performance.

physical ability tests Measure physical strength and stamina.

that measure physical strength and stamina. Autoworkers are typically tested for mechanical dexterity because this physical ability is an important skill for high job performance in many auto plants.[50]

Performance Tests

Performance tests measure job applicants' performance on actual job tasks. Applicants for secretarial positions, for example, are typically required to complete a typing test that measures how quickly and accurately they are able to type. Applicants for middle and top-management positions are sometimes given short-term projects to complete—projects that mirror the kinds of situations that arise in the job being filled—to assess their knowledge and problem-solving capabilities.[51]

Assessment centres, first used by AT&T, take performance tests one step further. In a typical assessment centre, about 10 to 15 candidates for managerial positions participate in a variety of activities over a few days. During this time they are assessed for the skills an effective manager needs—problem-solving, organizational, communication, and conflict-resolution skills. Some of the activities are performed individually; others are performed in groups. Throughout the process, current managers observe the candidates' behaviour and measure performance. Summary evaluations are then used as a selection tool.

performance tests
Measure the candidate's ability to perform actual job tasks.

References

Applicants for many jobs are required to provide references from former employers or other knowledgeable sources (such as a college instructor or adviser) who know the applicant's skills, abilities, and other personal characteristics. These individuals are asked to provide candid information about the applicants. References are often used at the end of the selection process to confirm a decision to hire. Yet, the fact that many former employers are reluctant to provide negative information in references sometimes makes it difficult to interpret what a reference is really saying about an applicant.

In fact, several recent lawsuits filed by applicants who felt that they were unfairly denigrated or had their privacy invaded by unfavourable references from former employers have caused managers to be increasingly wary of providing any kind of negative information in a reference, even if it is accurate. For jobs in which the job holder is responsible for the safety and lives of other people, however, failing to provide accurate negative information in a reference does not just mean that the wrong person might get hired but may also mean that other people's lives will be at stake. See Figure 11.6 for a summary of the typical steps in the hiring process.

In summary, managers have an ethical and legal obligation to use reliable and valid selection tools. Yet reliability and validity are matters of degree rather than all-or-nothing characteristics. Thus, managers should

FIGURE 11.6   **Typical Steps in the Hiring Process**

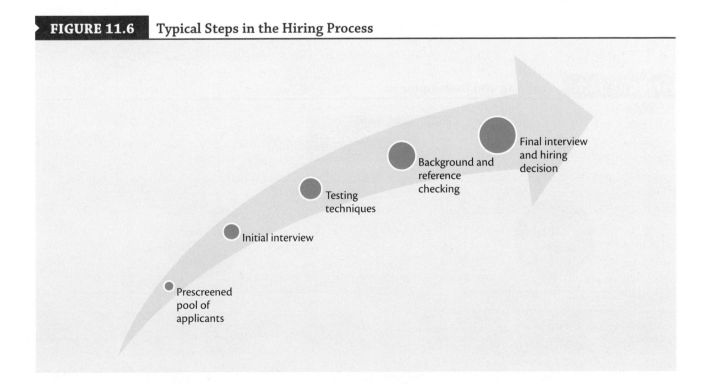

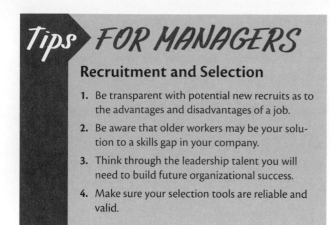

strive to use selection tools in such a way that they can achieve the greatest degree of reliability and validity. For ability tests of a particular skill, managers should keep up to date on the latest advances in the development of valid paper-and-pencil tests and use the test with the highest reliability and validity ratings for their purposes. Regarding interviews, managers can improve reliability by having more than one person interview job candidates.

Training and Development

Training and development help ensure that organizational members have the knowledge and skills they need to perform their jobs effectively, take on new responsibilities, and adapt to changing conditions. **Training** focuses mainly on teaching organizational members how to perform their current jobs and on helping them acquire the knowledge and skills they need to be effective performers. New hires at the Four Seasons participate in a three-month training program that includes improvisation activities to help them learn how to anticipate guests' needs, requirements, and actions and appropriately respond to them.

Development focuses on building the knowledge and skills of organizational members so that they will be prepared to take on new responsibilities and challenges. Training tends to be used more often at lower levels of an organization; development tends to be used more often with professionals and managers.

Before creating training and development programs, managers should perform a **needs assessment** in which they determine which employees need training or development and what type of skills or knowledge they need to acquire (see Figure 11.7).[52]

Types of Training

There are two types of training: classroom instruction and on-the-job training. Apprenticeships include both types.

Classroom Instruction

Through classroom instruction, employees acquire knowledge and skills in a classroom setting. This instruction

training Teaching organizational members how to perform their current jobs and helping them acquire the knowledge and skills they need to be effective performers.

development Building the knowledge and skills of organizational members so that they will be prepared to take on new responsibilities and challenges.

needs assessment An assessment to determine which employees need training or development and what type of skills or knowledge they need to acquire.

> **FIGURE 11.7** Training and Development

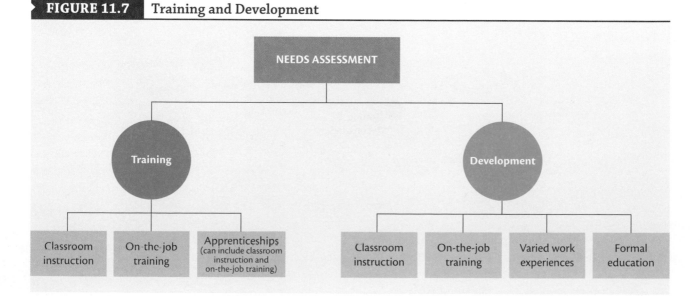

may take place within the organization or outside it, such as courses at local colleges and universities. Many organizations actually establish their own formal instructional divisions—some are even called "colleges"—to provide needed classroom instruction.

Classroom instruction frequently includes the use of videos and role playing in addition to traditional written materials, lectures, and group discussions. *Videos* can be used to demonstrate appropriate and inappropriate job behaviours. For example, by watching an experienced salesperson effectively deal with a loud and angry customer in a video clip, inexperienced salespeople can develop skills in handling similar situations. During *role playing*, trainees either directly participate in or watch others perform actual job activities in a simulated setting. At McDonald's Hamburger University, for example, role playing helps franchisees acquire the knowledge and skills they need to manage their restaurants.

Simulations also can be part of classroom instruction, particularly for complicated jobs that require an extensive amount of learning and in which errors carry a high cost. In a simulation, key aspects of the work situation and job tasks are duplicated as closely as possible in an artificial setting. For example, air traffic controllers are trained by simulations because of the complicated nature of the work, the extensive amount of learning involved, and the very high costs of air traffic control errors.

On-the-Job Training

In **on-the-job training,** learning occurs in the work setting as employees perform their job tasks. On-the-job training can be provided by coworkers or supervisors or can occur simply as jobholders gain experience and knowledge from doing the work. Newly hired waiters and waitresses in chains such as Red Lobster or the Olive Garden often receive on-the-job training from experienced employees. The supervisor of a new bus driver for a campus bus system may ride the bus for a week to ensure that the driver has learned the routes and follows safety procedures. For all on-the-job training, employees learn by doing.

Managers often use on-the-job training on a continuing basis to ensure that their subordinates keep up to date with changes in goals, technology, products, or customer needs and desires. For example, sales representatives at Mary Kay Cosmetics Inc. receive ongoing training so that they not only are knowledgeable about new cosmetic products and currently popular colours but also are reminded of Mary Kay's guiding principles. Mary Kay's expansion into Russia has been very successful, in part because of the ongoing training that Mary

Kay's Russian salespeople receive.[53] At many restaurants, new employees receive on-the-job training by shadowing more experienced waiters and waitresses as they go about their work.

Types of Development

Although both classroom instruction and on-the-job training can be used for development purposes as well as training, development often includes additional activities such as varied work experiences and formal education.

Varied Work Experiences

Top managers need to develop an understanding of, and expertise in, a variety of functions, products and services, and markets. To develop executives who will have this expertise, managers frequently make sure that employees with high potential have a wide variety of different job experiences, some in line positions and some in staff positions. Varied work experiences broaden employees' horizons and help them think more about the big picture. For example, one- to three-year stints overseas are being used increasingly to provide managers with international work experiences. With organizations becoming more global, managers need to develop an understanding of the different values, beliefs, cultures, regions, and ways of doing business in different countries.

Another development approach is mentoring. A *mentor* is an experienced member of an organization who provides advice and guidance to a less experienced member, called a *protégé*. Having a mentor can help managers seek out work experiences and assignments that will contribute to their development and can enable them to gain the most possible from varied work experiences.[54] While some mentors and protégés hook up informally, organizations have found that formal mentorship programs can be valuable ways to contribute to the development of managers and all employees.

Formal mentoring programs ensure that mentoring takes place in an organization, structure the process, and make sure that diverse organizational members have equal access to mentors. Participants receive training, efforts are focused on matching up mentors and protégés so that meaningful developmental relationships ensue, and organizations can track reactions and assess the potential benefits of mentoring. Formal mentoring programs can also ensure that diverse members of an organization receive the benefits of mentoring. A study conducted by David A. Thomas, a professor at the Harvard Business School, found that members of racial minority

on-the-job training
Training that takes place in the work setting as employees perform their job tasks.

groups at three large corporations who were very successful in their careers had the benefit of mentors. Formal mentorship programs help organizations make this valuable development tool available to all employees.[55]

When diverse members of an organization lack mentors, their progress in the organization and advancement to high-level positions can be hampered. Ida Abbott, a lawyer and consultant on work-related issues, recently presented a paper to the Minority Corporate Counsel Association in which she concluded, "The lack of adequate mentoring has held women and minority lawyers back from achieving professional success and has led to high rates of career dissatisfaction and attrition."[56]

Mentoring can benefit all kinds of employees in all kinds of work.[57] John Washko, a manager at the Four Seasons hotel chain, benefited from the mentoring he received from Stan Bromley on interpersonal relations and how to deal with employees; mentor Bromley, in turn, found that participating in the Four Seasons' mentoring program helped him develop his own management style.[58] More generally, development is an ongoing process for all managers, and mentors often find that mentoring contributes to their own personal development.

Formal Education

Many large corporations reimburse employees for tuition expenses they incur while taking college courses and obtaining advanced degrees. This is not just benevolence on the part of the employer or even a simple reward given to the employee; it is an effective way to develop employees who are able to take on new responsibilities and more challenging positions. For similar reasons, corporations spend thousands of dollars sending managers to executive development programs such as executive MBA programs. In these programs, experts teach managers the latest in business and management techniques and practices.

To save time and travel costs, managers are increasingly relying on *long-distance learning* to formally educate and develop employees. Using videoconferencing technologies, business schools such as Athabasca University and the University of Toronto, Rotman School of Management are teaching courses on video screens in corporate conference rooms. Business schools are also customizing

> ❝ **"The lack of adequate mentoring has held women and minority lawyers back from achieving professional success and has led to high rates of career dissatisfaction and attrition."** ❞
>
> *Ida Abbott*

courses and degrees to fit the development needs of employees in a particular company.

Transfer of Training and Development

Whenever training and development take place off the job or in a classroom setting, it is vital for managers to promote the transfer of the knowledge and skills acquired *to the actual work situation*. Trainees should be encouraged and expected to use their newfound expertise on the job.

Performance Appraisal and Feedback

The recruitment/selection and the training/development components of a human resource management system ensure that employees have the knowledge and skills they need to be effective now and in the future. Performance appraisal and feedback complement recruitment, selection, training, and development. **Performance appraisal** is the evaluation of employees' job performance and contributions to their organization. **Performance feedback** is the process through which managers share performance appraisal information with their subordinates, give subordinates an opportunity to reflect on their own performance, and develop, with subordinates, plans for the future. In order for performance feedback to occur, performance appraisal must take place. Performance appraisal could take place without providing performance feedback, but wise managers are careful to provide feedback because it can contribute to employee motivation and performance.

Performance appraisal and feedback contribute to the effective management of human resources in two ways. Performance appraisal gives managers important information on which to base human resource decisions.[59] Decisions about pay raises, bonuses, promotions, and job moves all hinge on the accurate appraisal of performance. Performance appraisal also can help managers determine which workers are candidates for training and development and in what areas. Performance feedback encourages

performance appraisal The evaluation of employees' job performance and contributions to their organization.

performance feedback The process through which managers share performance appraisal information with subordinates, give subordinates an opportunity to reflect on their own performance, and develop, with subordinates, plans for the future.

high levels of employee motivation and performance. It alerts good performers that their efforts are valued and appreciated and alerts poor performers that their lacklustre performance needs improvement. Performance feedback can provide both good and poor performers with insight into their strengths and weaknesses and ways in which they can improve their performance in the future.

Types of Performance Appraisal

Performance appraisal focuses on the evaluation of traits, behaviours, and results.[60]

Trait Appraisals

When trait appraisals are used, managers assess subordinates on personal characteristics that are relevant to job performance, such as skills, abilities, or personality. A factory worker, for example, may be evaluated based on her ability to use computerized equipment and perform numerical calculations. A social worker may be appraised based on his empathy and communication skills.

Three disadvantages of trait appraisals often lead managers to rely on other appraisal methods. First, possessing a certain personal characteristic does not ensure that the personal characteristic will actually be used on the job and result in high performance. For example, a factory worker may possess superior computer and numerical skills but be a poor performer due to low motivation. The second disadvantage of trait appraisals is linked to the first. Because traits do not always show a direct association with performance, workers and courts of law may view them as unfair and potentially discriminatory. The third disadvantage of trait appraisals is that they often do not enable managers to provide employees with feedback that they can use to improve performance. Because trait appraisals focus on relatively enduring human characteristics that change only over the long term, employees can do little to change their behaviour in response to performance feedback from a trait appraisal. Telling a social worker that he lacks empathy provides him with little guidance about how to improve his interactions with clients, for example. These disadvantages suggest that managers should use trait appraisals only when they can demonstrate that the assessed traits are accurate and important indicators of job performance.

Behaviour Appraisals

Through behaviour appraisals, managers assess how workers perform their jobs—the actual actions and behaviours that workers exhibit on the job. Whereas trait appraisals assess what workers are *like,* behaviour appraisals assess what workers *do.* For example, with a behaviour appraisal, a manager might evaluate a social worker on the extent to which he looks clients in the eye when talking with them, expresses sympathy when they are upset, and refers them to community counselling and support groups geared toward the specific problem they are encountering. Behaviour appraisals are especially useful when *how* workers perform their jobs is important. In educational organizations such as high schools, for example, the number of classes and students taught is important, but also important are how they are taught and the methods teachers use to ensure that learning takes place.

Behaviour appraisals have the advantage of providing employees with clear information about what they are doing right and wrong and how they can improve their performance. And because behaviours are much easier for employees to change than traits, performance feedback from behaviour appraisals is more likely to lead to performance improvements.

Graphic Rating Scale Method

The most popular method of employee performance appraisal is called the graphic rating scale method. In this method, the appraiser scores the employee on a number of characteristics that reflect performance levels in such areas as quality, productivity, job knowledge, reliability, availability, and ability to work independently or in a team. Specific behavioural descriptions are used for each area that relate to the current job requirements. Points are assigned for each rating and are totalled and averaged for an overall performance score. See Figure 11.8.

Result Appraisals

For some jobs, *how* people perform the job is not as important as *what* they accomplish or the results they obtain. With result appraisals, managers appraise performance by the results or the actual outcomes of work behaviours. Take the case of two new-car salespersons. One salesperson strives to develop personal relationships with her customers. She spends hours talking to them and frequently calls them up to see how their decision-making process is going. The other salesperson has a much more hands-off approach. He is very knowledgeable, answers customers' questions, and then waits for them to come to him. Both salespersons sell, on average, the same number of cars, and the customers of both are satisfied with the service they receive, according to postcards that the dealership mails to customers asking for an assessment of their satisfaction. The manager of the dealership appropriately uses result appraisals (sales and customer satisfaction) to evaluate the salespeople's performance because it does not matter which behaviour salespeople use to sell

FIGURE 11.8 Elements Included in a Graphic Rating Scale Performance Appraisal

Factors	Rating	Scale	Points and comments
Quality—The degree of excellence and thoroughness of the work performed	**Outstanding**—Performance is exceptional and superior to others	100–90	☐
Productivity—The amount of work done in a specific period	**Very good**—High levels of performance that consistently exceed requirements	90–80	☐
Job knowledge—The specialized skills and information used on the job	**Good**—Competent and reliable level of performance	80–70	☐
Reliability—The degree of trustworthiness to complete the task and follow up	**Improvement needed**—Performance falls below requirements in some areas	70–60	☐
Availability—The rate of absenteeism and punctuality of the employee	**Unsatisfactory**—Performance levels are unacceptable	Below 60	☐
Independence—The degree to which the employee must be supervised			☐
Team work—The ability to work well as a member of a group			☐

cars as long as they sell the desired number and satisfy customers. If one salesperson sells too few cars, however, the manager can give that person performance feedback about his or her low sales.

Objective and Subjective Appraisals

Whether managers appraise performance in terms of traits, behaviours, or results, the information they assess is either *objective* or *subjective*. **Objective appraisals** are based on facts and are likely to be numerical—the number of cars sold, the number of meals prepared, the number of times late, the number of audits completed. Managers often use objective appraisals when results are being appraised because results tend to be easier to quantify than traits or behaviours. When *how* workers perform their jobs is important, however, subjective behaviour appraisals are more appropriate than result appraisals.

Subjective appraisals are based on managers' perceptions of traits, behaviours, or results. Because subjective appraisals rest on managers' perceptions, there is always the chance that they are inaccurate. This is why both researchers and managers have spent considerable time and effort on determining the best way to develop reliable and valid subjective measures of performance.

objective appraisal An appraisal that is based on facts and is likely to be numerical.

subjective appraisal An appraisal that is based on perceptions of traits, behaviours, or results.

Who Appraises Performance?

We have been assuming that managers or the supervisors of employees evaluate performance. This is a pretty fair assumption, as supervisors are the most common appraisers of performance. Performance appraisal is an important part of most managers' job duties. It is managers' responsibility to motivate their subordinates to perform at a high level, and managers make many of the decisions that hinge on performance appraisals, such as decisions about pay raises or promotions. Appraisals by managers can, however, be usefully supplemented by appraisals from other sources (see Figure 11.9).

FIGURE 11.9 Who Appraises Performance?

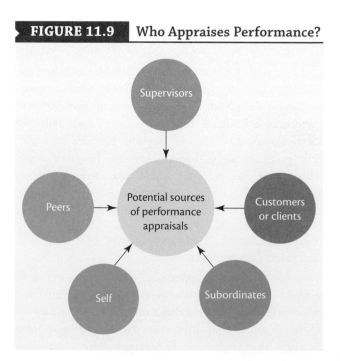

Self, Peers, Subordinates, and Clients

When self-appraisals are used, managers supplement their evaluations with an employee's assessment of his or her own performance. Peer appraisals are provided by an employee's coworkers. Especially when subordinates work in groups or teams, feedback from peer appraisals can motivate team members while providing managers with important information for decision making. A growing number of companies are having subordinates appraise their managers' performance and leadership as well. And sometimes customers or clients provide assessments of employee performance in terms of responsiveness to customers and quality of service.

Although appraisals from each of these sources can be useful, managers need to be aware of potential issues that may arise when they are used. Subordinates sometimes may be inclined to inflate self-appraisals, especially if organizations are downsizing and they are worried about their job security. Managers who are appraised by their subordinates may fail to take needed but unpopular actions for fear that their subordinates will appraise them negatively. Some of these potential issues can be mitigated to the extent that there are high levels of trust in an organization. Online surveys that ensure anonymity are increasingly being used by large companies to solicit performance appraisals.

360-Degree Performance Appraisals

To improve motivation and performance, some organizations include **360-degree appraisals** and feedback in their performance appraisal systems, especially for managers. In a 360-degree appraisal, an individual's performance is appraised by a variety of people, such as self, peers or coworkers, subordinates, superiors, and sometimes even customers or clients. The individual receives feedback based on evaluations from these multiple sources.

The growing number of companies using 360-degree appraisals and feedback includes Celestica (Toronto); InSystems (Markham, Ontario); Dominion Information Services (Burnaby, B.C.); and Hudson's Bay (Toronto). A 360-degree appraisal and feedback is not always as clear-cut as it might seem. On the one hand, some subordinates may try to get back at their managers by giving them negative evaluations, especially when evaluations are anonymous (to encourage honesty and openness). On the other hand, some managers may coach subordinates to give—or even threaten punishment if they fail to give—positive evaluations.

Peers often are very knowledgeable about performance but may be reluctant to provide an accurate and negative appraisal of someone they like or a positive appraisal of someone they dislike. In addition, whenever peers, subordinates, or anyone else evaluates an employee's performance, managers must be sure that the evaluators are actually knowledgeable about the performance dimensions being assessed. For example, subordinates should not evaluate their supervisor's decision making if they have little opportunity to observe this dimension of his or her performance.

These potential problems with 360-degree appraisals and feedback do not mean that they are not useful. Rather, they suggest that in order for 360-degree appraisals and feedback to be effective, trust is needed throughout the organization. More generally, trust is a critical ingredient in any performance appraisal and feedback procedure. Managers using 360-degree appraisals and feedback also have to consider carefully the pros and cons of using anonymous evaluations and of using the results of the appraisals for decision-making about important issues such as pay raises.[61]

Even when 360-degree appraisals are used, it is sometimes difficult to design an effective process by which subordinates' feedback can be communicated to their managers. Advances in information technology provide organizations with a potential solution to this problem. For example, ImproveNow.com has online questionnaires that subordinates fill out to evaluate the performance of their managers and provide the managers with feedback. Each subordinate of a particular manager completes the questionnaire independently, all responses are tabulated, and the manager is given specific feedback on behaviours in a variety of areas, such as rewarding good performance, looking out for subordinates' best interest and being supportive, and having a vision for the future.[62]

Effective Performance Feedback

In order for the performance appraisal and feedback component of a human resource management system to encourage and motivate high performance, managers must provide their subordinates with performance feedback. To generate useful information to pass on to subordinates, managers can use both formal and informal appraisals. **Formal appraisals** are conducted at set times during the year and are based on performance dimensions and measures that have been specified in advance. A salesperson, for example, may be evaluated by his or her manager twice a year on the performance dimensions of sales and customer service, sales being measured from sales reports

360-degree appraisal
A performance appraisal by peers, subordinates, superiors, and sometimes clients who are in a position to evaluate a manager's performance.

formal appraisals
Appraisals conducted at a set time during the year and based on performance dimensions and measures that were specified in advance.

and customer service being measured by the number of complaints received. **Informal appraisals**—unscheduled appraisals of ongoing progress and areas for improvement—may occur at the request of the employee. Moreover, when job duties, assignments, or goals change, informal appraisals can provide workers with timely feedback concerning how they are handling their new responsibilities.

An integral part of a formal appraisal is a meeting between the manager and the subordinate in which the subordinate is given feedback on his or her performance.

Managers often dislike providing performance feedback, especially when the feedback is negative, but doing so is an important managerial activity. Here are some guidelines for effectively giving performance feedback that will contribute to employee motivation and performance:

- *Be specific and focus on behaviours or outcomes that are correctable and within a worker's ability to improve.* Example: Telling a salesperson that he or she is too shy when interacting with customers is likely to do nothing more than lower the person's self-confidence and prompt him or her to become defensive. A more effective approach is to give the salesperson feedback about specific behaviours to engage in—greeting customers as soon as they enter the department, asking customers whether they need help, and volunteering to help customers find items if they seem to be having trouble.

- *Approach performance appraisal as an exercise in problem-solving and solution-finding, not criticizing.* Example*:* Rather than criticizing a financial analyst for turning reports in late, the manager helps the analyst determine why the reports are late and identify ways to better manage time.

- *Express confidence in a subordinate's ability to improve.* Example: Instead of being skeptical, a first-level manager tells a subordinate in confidence that the subordinate can increase quality levels.

- *Provide performance feedback both formally and informally.* Example: The staff of a preschool receives feedback from formal performance appraisals twice a year. The director of the school also provides frequent informal feedback such as complimenting staff members on creative ideas for special projects, noticing when they do a particularly good job of handling a difficult child, and pointing out when they provide inadequate supervision.

- *Praise instances of high performance and areas of a job in which an employee excels.* Example: Rather than focusing on just the negative, a manager discusses the areas the subordinate excels in as well as areas in need of improvement.

- *Avoid personal criticisms, and treat subordinates with respect.* Example: An engineering manager acknowledges subordinates' expertise and treats them as professionals. Even when the manager points out performance problems to subordinates, it is important to refrain from criticizing them personally.

- *Agree to a timetable for performance improvements.* Example: A first-level manager and subordinate decide to meet again in one month to determine whether quality has improved.

In following these guidelines, managers need to keep in mind *why* they are giving performance feedback: to encourage high levels of motivation and performance. Moreover, the information that managers gather through performance appraisal and feedback helps them determine how to distribute pay raises and bonuses.

Pay and Benefits

Pay includes employees' base salaries, pay raises, and bonuses and is determined by a number of factors such as characteristics of the organization and the job and levels of performance. Employee *benefits* are based on membership in an organization (and not necessarily on the particular job held) and include sick days, vacation days, and medical and life insurance. In Chapter 8, we discussed the ways in which pay can be used to motivate organizational members to perform at a high level, as well as the different kinds of pay plans managers can use to help an organization achieve its goals and gain a competitive advantage. It is important for pay to be linked to behaviours or results that contribute to organizational effectiveness. Here we focus on how organizations determine their pay levels and pay structures.

Pay Level

Pay level is a broad comparative concept that refers to how an organization's pay incentives compare, in general, to those of other organizations in the same industry employing similar kinds of workers. Managers must decide whether they want to offer relatively high wages, average wages, or relatively low wages. At Four Seasons, as we saw in the opening case, pay levels are set at the high end of

informal appraisals
Unscheduled appraisals of ongoing progress and areas for improveent.

pay level The relative position of an organization's pay incentives in comparison with those of other organizations in the same industry employing similar kinds of workers.

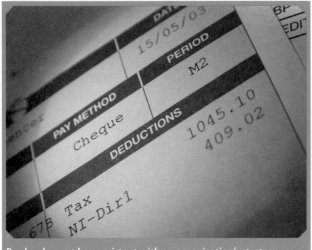

Pay levels must be consistent with an organization's strategy.

the industry, between the 75th and 90th percentile. High wages help ensure that an organization is going to be able to recruit, select, and retain high performers, but high wages also raise costs. Low wages give an organization a cost advantage but may undermine the organization's ability to select and recruit high performers and motivate current employees to perform at a high level. Either of these situations may lead to inferior quality or inferior customer service.

In determining pay levels, managers should take their organization's strategy into account. A high pay level may prohibit managers from effectively pursuing a low-cost strategy. But a high pay level may be well worth the added costs in an organization whose competitive advantage lies in superior quality and excellent customer service, as is the case with the Four Seasons. As one might expect, hotel and motel chains with a low-cost strategy, such as Days Inn and Holiday Inns, have lower pay levels than do chains striving to provide high-quality rooms and services, such as Four Seasons and Hyatt Regency.

Pay Structure

After deciding on a pay level, managers have to establish a pay structure for the different jobs in the organization. A **pay structure** clusters jobs into categories that reflect their relative importance to the organization and its goals, levels of skills required, and other characteristics that managers consider important. Pay ranges are established for each job category. Individual job holders' pay within job categories is then determined by such factors as performance, seniority, and skill levels.

There are some interesting global differences in pay structures. Large corporations based in the United States tend to pay their CEOs and top managers higher salaries than do their Canadian, European, or Japanese counterparts. Also, the pay differential between employees at the bottom of the corporate hierarchy and those higher up is much greater in U.S. companies than in other companies.[63]

Concerns have been raised over whether it is equitable or fair for CEOs of large companies to be making millions of dollars in years when their companies are restructuring and laying off a large portion of their workforces.[64] Additionally, the average CEO in the United States typically earns over 430 times what the average hourly worker earns.[65] In Canada, the top CEOs earn about 190 times the average worker.[66] Is a pay structure with such a huge pay differential ethical? Shareholders and the public are increasingly asking this very question and asking large corporations to rethink their pay structures.[67] Also troubling are the millions of dollars in severance packages that some CEOs receive when they leave their organizations. In an era in which many workers are struggling to find and keep jobs and make ends meet, more and more people are questioning whether it is ethical for some top managers to be making so much money.[68] Income inequality was at the root of the Occupy Wall Street and subsequent "Occupy" protests in cities around Canada and the world in 2011.

pay structure The arrangement of jobs into categories that reflect their relative importance to the organization and its goals, levels of skill required, and other characteristics.

Benefits

Employee benefits are based on membership in an organization (and not necessarily on the particular job held) and include sick days, vacation days, and medical and life insurances. Mandatory employee benefits

Frank Stronach, founder and CEO of Magna International Inc., earned $61.8 million in 2010.

vary across provinces; however, organizations are legally required to pay into workers' compensation, social insurance, and employment insurance for their employees. Workers' compensation provides employees with financial assistance if they become unable to work because of a work-related injury or illness. Social insurance provides financial assistance to retirees and disabled former employees. Employment insurance provides financial assistance to employees who lose their jobs through no fault of their own.

Other benefits—such as extended health insurance, dental insurance, vacation time, pension plans, life insurance, flexible working hours, company-provided daycare, and employee assistance and wellness programs—are provided at the option of employers. Recall how a very attractive benefit at the Four Seasons in the opening case is being able to stay for free in any of the company's hotels and resorts. Benefits enabling workers to simultaneously balance the demands of their jobs and of their lives away from the office or factory are of growing importance for many workers who have competing demands on their all-too-scarce time and energy. Benefits mandated by public policy and benefits provided at the option of employers cost organizations a substantial amount of money.

In some organizations, top managers decide which benefits might best suit the organization and employees and offer the same benefit package to all employees. Other organizations, realizing that employees' needs and desires for benefits might differ, offer **cafeteria-style benefit plans** that let employees themselves choose the benefits they want, from among such options as day care, flextime, tuition credits, on-site fitness centres, and extended medical and dental plans. Cafeteria-style benefit plans sometimes assist managers in dealing with employees who feel unfairly treated because they are unable to take advantage of certain benefits available to other employees who, for example, have children. Some organizations have success with cafeteria-style benefit plans; others find them difficult to manage.

cafeteria-style benefit plans Plans from which employees can choose the benefits that they want.

labour relations The activities that managers engage in to ensure that they have effective working relationships with the labour unions that represent their employees' interests.

Labour Relations

Labour relations are the activities that managers engage in to ensure that they have effective working relationships with the labour unions that represent their employees' interests. As a way to deal with the unethical and unfair treatment of workers, the federal and provincial governments created the Canada Labour Code, the *Canadian Human Rights Act*,

and provincial Employment Standards laws. However, some employees believe that unions will be more effective than codes and laws in protecting their rights.

Unions exist to represent workers' interests in organizations. Given that managers have more power than rank-and-file workers and that organizations have multiple stakeholders, there is always the potential that managers might take steps that benefit one set of stakeholders such as shareholders while hurting another such as employees. For example, managers may decide to speed up a production line to lower costs and increase production in the hopes of increasing returns to shareholders. Speeding up the line, however, could hurt employees forced to work at a rapid pace and may increase the risk of injuries. Also, employees receive no additional pay for the extra work they are performing. Unions would represent workers' interests in a scenario such as this one.

The first step in the labour relations process is for workers to seek collective representation to further their interests in the organization. The reasons they might desire to unionize are many:

- Shareholder interests overshadow those of the workers
- Dissatisfaction with wages, benefits, and working conditions
- Lack of a safe work environment
- Lack of job security
- Lack of proper training
- Perceived inequities in pay
- Unfair policies and practices
- Dissatisfaction with management
- Inability to communicate concerns and effect change

Caterpillar closed its London, Ontario Electro-Motive plant after locking out employees in 2012.

- Lack of opportunities for advancement, growth, and role in decision making
- The belief that unionization may improve working conditions
- The belief that a united group wields more power than an individual

Although these would seem to be potent forces for unionization, some workers are reluctant to join unions. Individual workers may reject unionization for a number of reasons, including the perception that the leaders are corrupt, or they simply do not want to pay union dues. Employees also might not want to be forced into doing something they do not want to, such as striking because the union thinks it is in their best interest. Moreover, although unions can be a positive force in organizations, sometimes they also can be a negative force, impairing organizational effectiveness. For example, when union leaders resist needed changes in an organization or are corrupt, organizational performance can suffer.

In order for a union to become the bargaining unit for a group of employees, it must attain acceptance by the majority of eligible employees and be certified by the Labour Relations Board (LRB). See Figure 11.10. During an organizing campaign, employers must make sure they do not question employees about their union activities or use "undue influence" by promising to increase wages and benefits in a way that could be perceived as a bribe for remaining nonunionized or, for that matter, by threatening employees' jobs if they support unionization.

Once a union is recognized by the employer and the LRB as the bargaining unit for a group of employees, **collective bargaining**—negotiations between the labour union and the employer—take place to arrive at a mutually acceptable **collective agreement** pertaining to the terms and conditions of employment for a specified period of time. Once a collective agreement is signed, both the union members and the management are required to abide by the provisions. When disagreements over the administration of the agreement or violations of the terms arise, they are handled and settled by the *grievance procedure*. When the timeframe of the agreement has ended and a new collective agreement has not been reached, neither party is bound by its terms and conditions. In such a case, the union is in a legal strike position, and the employer has the potential to lock out the workers. Both *strikes* and *lockouts* involve work stoppages. In the first month of 2012, there were two strikes and two lockouts in companies with more than 500 employees in Canada. The lockouts were at Rio Tinto Alcan and Electro-Motive Canada Co. In 2011, there were 14 work stoppages involving 500 or more employees in Canada.[69]

> **collective bargaining**
> Negotiations between labour unions and managers to resolve conflicts and disputes about issues such as working hours, wages, working conditions, and job security.
>
> **collective agreement**
> A mutually agreed upon set of provisions that govern working conditions between a union and an employer for a set period of time.

Trends in Labour Relations

Canada and the United States have differential rates of unionization. Statistics Canada shows that in 2010, 31.5 percent of the Canadian workforce was unionized, down from the 38 percent in 1981. In the United States, only 14.8 percent of the workers are unionized. Declines in the industrial sectors of the economy, such as manufacturing, where unions have traditionally been strong are often viewed as the reasons for declining unionization in the United States. The growth in service sector employment, which is often viewed as more difficult to organize, is also seen as a reason. In Canada, however, almost 40 percent of service workers are unionized, while approximately 7 percent belong to unions in the United States. On the macro level, the main argument for differences between the countries is labour law and the structure of the political system in each country.[70]

Several provincial governments have passed legislation in the last decade that hinders the impact of unions. In 2012, the legislature of British Columbia passed Bill 22, which prohibits teachers to strike. The legislation was announced the same day as the B.C. LRB granted teachers the right to conduct a three-day general strike. In late 2001, Ontario changed its *Labour Relations Act* to require employers to post information in the workplace about how a union can be decertified. In the 2000–2001 fiscal year in Ontario, there were 521 certifications and 59 decertifications. In the next year,

FIGURE 11.10   **The Process of Labour Relations**

Desire to unionize → Campaign for certification → Recognition by the employer and Labour Relations Board → Collective bargaining → Collective agreement → Administration of the collective agreement there were 307 certifications and 85 decertifications. In Quebec, the government managed to push through legislation to force the reduction of the number of unions bargaining in such institutions as hospitals. In one case, the number of unions dropped from 88 to 4. Other legislation, despite strong union objections, made it easier for public institutions such as hospitals to outsource some services, for example, food and laundry services.[71] In Saskatchewan, Bill 6, *Trade Union Amendment Act, 2008,* came into force on May 14, 2008, and made significant amendments to the *Trade Union Act* (TUA). Any application for certification or decertification of a union must now be determined by a mandatory secret ballot vote. Furthermore, the level of employee support necessary for an application for certification or decertification, previously unspecified in the TUA (except in the case of an application to displace a certified union, which was set at 25 percent), is now fixed at 45 percent. Finally, the timeframe within which evidence of employee support must be obtained has been reduced to 90 days and employers have been given more leeway to communicate facts and opinions to their employees during union drives.[72]

The impact of labour relations on human resource management is considerable. Once a collective agreement is signed, the HR department typically expands to include a labour relations specialist and thus affects the organizational structure of the company. Managers may have their power to make decisions diminished as union leaders typically increase their participation in issues that affect their members. Reward power is lessened, as pay levels and pay structures are set out in the terms of the collective agreement. Some managers resent the loss of authority that having to abide by the collective agreement sometimes entails. HR managers tend to keep more paper records of employee assignments and behaviours, as this is crucial at grievance and arbitration hearings. Overall, union leaders and managers must recognize the need to build effective cooperative working relationships in order to remain competitive long before they get to the bargaining table to negotiate a collective agreement. It is in their mutual interests to ensure that labour strife is avoided.

Summary and Review

LO1 The Legal Framework of Human Resource Management in Canada   Several key pieces of legislation govern the management of human resources in Canada. The Canadian *Human Rights Act* and the *Employment Standards Act* ensure minimum employee entitlements are standardized across the country and that *intentional and unintentional discrimination* is prohibited based on specific grounds.

LO2 Strategic Human Resource Management   *Human resource management* (HRM) includes all the activities that managers use to ensure that their organizations are able to attract, retain, and utilize human resources effectively. *Strategic HRM* is the process by which managers design the components of an HRM system to be consistent with each other, and with the organization's strategies, structure, and goals. *Human resource planning* includes all the activities managers engage in to forecast their current and future needs for human resources. *Job analysis* is the process of identifying (1) the tasks, duties, and responsibilities that make up a job and (2) the knowledge, skills, and abilities needed to perform the job.

LO3 Overview of the Components of HRM   The five major components of human resource management are: (i) recruitment and selection, (ii) training and development, (iii) performance appraisal and feedback, (iv) pay and benefits, and (v) labour relations. *Recruitment* includes all the activities that managers engage in to develop a pool of qualified applicants for open positions. *Selection* is the process by which managers determine the relative qualifications of job applicants and their potential for performing well in a particular job. *Training* focuses on teaching organizational members how to perform effectively in their current jobs. Development focuses on broadening organizational members' knowledge and skills so that employees will be prepared to take on new responsibilities and challenges. *Performance appraisal* is the evaluation of employees' job performance and contributions to their organization. *Performance feedback* is the process through which managers share performance appraisal information with their subordinates; give subordinates an opportunity to reflect on their own performance; and help subordinates develop plans for the future. Performance appraisal provides managers with useful information for decision making about pay and promotions. Performance feedback can encourage high levels of motivation and performance. *Pay level* is the relative position of an organization's pay incentives in comparison with those of other organizations in the same industry employing similar kinds of employees. A *pay structure* clusters jobs into categories that reflect their relative importance to the organization and its goals, levels of skill required, and other characteristics. Pay ranges are established for each job category. Organizations are legally required to provide certain *benefits* to their employees; other benefits are provided at the discretion of employers. *Labour relations* are the activities that managers engage in to ensure that they have effective working relationships with the labour unions that represent their employees' interests.

KEY TERMS

ability tests	collective agreement	human resource
behavioural interview	collective bargaining	management (HRM)
questions	development	human resource planning
cafeteria-style benefit plans	formal appraisals	informal appraisals

intentional discrimination	performance feedback	situational interview
job analysis	performance tests	questions
labour relations	personality tests	strategic human resource
lateral moves	personnel replacement	management
needs assessment	chart	structured interview
objective appraisals	physical ability tests	subjective appraisal
on-the-job training	realistic job preview (RJP)	360-degree appraisal
outsource	recruitment	training
pay level	reliable selection	unintentional discrimination
pay structure	technique	unstructured interview
performance appraisal	selection	valid selection technique

WRAP-UP TO >>> OPENING CASE

Effectively Managing Human Resources at the Four Seasons

HOW CAN MANAGERS PROMOTE HIGH LEVELS OF PERSONALIZED CUSTOMER SERVICE IN AN INDUSTRY KNOWN FOR HIGH EMPLOYEE TURNOVER?

Four Seasons Hotels and Resorts is one of only about 14 companies to be ranked one of the "100 Best Companies to Work For" every year since *Fortune* magazine started this annual ranking of companies over 12 years ago.[73] And the Four Seasons often receives other awards and recognition based on customers' responses.[74] In an industry in which annual turnover rates are over 35 percent, turnover at the Four Seasons is around 18 percent.[75] Evidently, employees and customers alike are very satisfied with the way they are treated at the Four Seasons. Understanding that the two are causally linked is perhaps the key to the Four Seasons' success. As the Four Seasons' founder, chairman of the board, and CEO Isadore Sharp suggests, "How you treat your employees is how you expect them to treat the customer."[76] After having read and understood the concepts in this chapter, you should be able to answer the following questions:

1. *How does Isadore Sharp employ a human resource system that creates an outstanding experience for customers at the Four Seasons?*

    ANSWER: Isadore Sharp creates a competitive advantage in an industry with extremely high turnover rates by building outstanding customer responsiveness. Sharp has always realized that in order for employees to treat customers well, the Four Seasons needs to treat its employees well. When employees view each customer as an individual with his or her own needs and desires, and empathetically try to meet these needs and desires and help customers both overcome any problems or challenges they face and truly enjoy their hotel experience, customers are likely to be both loyal and highly satisfied.

2. *How does the Four Seasons manage the components of its HR system?*

    ANSWER: The five components of a human resource system are: (1) recruitment and selection, (2) training and development, (3) performance appraisal, (4) pay and benefits, and (5) labour relations. In this case, we find that the Four Seasons focuses a lot of attention on the selection of employees. Applicants are interviewed a minimum of four times to make sure they can provide a high level of empathy to the customer. Internal recruiting through promotion is evident. Recent college graduates may start out as assistant managers; those who do well and have high aspirations could potentially become general managers in less than 15 years. This helps to ensure that managers have empathy and respect for those in lower-level positions as well as the ingrained ethos of treating others (employees, subordinates, coworkers, and customers) the way they would like to be treated themselves. Training of employees and development of potential managers is ongoing at Four Seasons. New hires participate in a three-month training program that includes improvisation activities to help new hires learn how to anticipate guests' needs, requirements, and actions and appropriately respond to them. Varied work experiences such as mentoring of managers is used at the Four Seasons. A mentor is an experienced member of an organization who provides advice and guidance to a less experienced member. No mention of how employee performance is appraised is made in this case, nor how employees and management negotiated working conditions. Pay and benefits, however, are discussed. Salaries are relatively high at the Four Seasons, by industry standards (i.e., between the 75th and 90th percentiles), employees participate in a profit-sharing plan, and the company contributes to their pension plans. All employees are provided with free meals in the hotel cafeteria, have access to staff showers and a locker room, and are provided with an additional, highly attractive benefit. Once a new employee has worked for the Four Seasons for six months, he or she can stay for three nights free at any Four Seasons hotel or resort in the world. After a year of employment, this benefit increases to six free nights and it continues to increase as tenure with the company increases. The Four Seasons' human resource management philosophy and practice translate into happy employees—which means happy customers.

Management in Action

TOPICS FOR DISCUSSION AND ACTION

LEVEL 1 Knowledge & Comprehension

1. Describe the five components of an HRM system.

2. Discuss the reasons why an organization might outsource its human resources. What problems can arise?

3. Describe the best way for managers to give performance feedback to subordinates.

LEVEL 2 Application & Analysis

4. Discuss why it is important for the components of the HRM system to be in sync with an organization's strategy and structure and with each other.

5. Interview a manager in a local organization to determine how that organization recruits and selects employees.

6. How can managers avoid charges of discrimination in their hiring practices? Describe the legal framework of HRM in Canada.

LEVEL 3 Synthesis & Evaluation

7. Evaluate the pros and cons of 360-degree performance appraisals and feedback. Would you like your performance to be appraised in this manner? Why, or why not?

8. Discuss why two restaurants in the same community might have different pay levels.

9. Listen to Jack and Suzy Welch's podcast called "Team Building: Wrong and Right" at www.businessweek.com/mediacenter/qt/podcasts/welchway/welchway_11_14_08%201.mp3. What three things do they argue a leader should not do when hiring and putting together a high-performing team?

SELF-REFLECTION EXERCISE

Analyzing Human Resource Management Systems

Think about your current job or a job that you had in the past. If you have never had a job, then interview a friend or family member who is currently working. Answer the following questions about the job you have chosen:

1. How are people recruited and selected for this job? Are the recruitment and selection procedures that the organization uses effective or ineffective? Why?

2. What training and development do people who hold this job receive? Is it appropriate? Why, or why not?

3. How is performance of this job appraised? Does performance feedback contribute to motivation and high performance on this job?

4. What levels of pay and benefits are provided for this job? Are these levels of pay and benefits appropriate? Why, or why not?

SMALL GROUP BREAKOUT EXERCISE

Building a Human Resource Management System

Form groups of three or four, and appoint one group member as the spokesperson who will communicate your findings to the whole class when called upon by the instructor. Then discuss the following scenario:

You and your two or three partners are engineers with a business minor who have decided to start a consulting business. Your goal is to provide manufacturing-process engineering and other engineering services to large and small organizations. You forecast that there will be an increased use of outsourcing for these activities. You have discussed with managers in several large organizations the services you plan to offer, and they have expressed considerable interest. You have secured funding to start the business and are now building the HRM system. Your human resources planning suggests that you need to hire between five and eight experienced engineers with good communication skills, two clerical/secretarial workers, and two MBAs who between them will have financial, accounting, and human resources skills. You are striving to develop an in-house approach to building your human resources that will enable your new business to prosper.

1. Describe the steps you will take to recruit and select (a) the engineers, (b) the clerical/secretarial workers, and (c) the MBAs.

2. Describe the training and development the engineers, the clerical/secretarial workers, and the MBAs will receive.

3. Describe how you will appraise the performance of each group of employees and how you will provide feedback.

4. Describe the pay level and pay structure of your consulting firm.

BUSINESS PLANNING EXERCISE

Your professor may ask you to write a business plan for a new venture or a strategic plan for an existing venture. At the end of every chapter, you will have an opportunity to apply managerial and organizational concepts to the exercise of writing a business plan. Refer to Appendix A.

After reading this chapter, you and your business planning team realize that you must develop a human resources plan for your venture and include this in your business plan. Using the HRM tools in this chapter, answer the following:

1. How will you
   a. recruit,
   b. select, and
   c. train and develop your employees?
2. Write a job description and specification for a bartender (if appropriate) and other personnel you will need to hire in your first year of operation.
3. How you will appraise your employees' performances?
   - Refer to the material in the chapter to determine the methods of appraising employee performance that would be appropriate for your organization.
4. How much should you pay each category of employees for their inputs?
   - Will you offer wages at, above, or below the industry standards? Justify your answer in terms of the strategy of the venture.
5. What, if any, benefits will you offer aside from the mandatory benefits?

   - Determine the mandatory benefits you must provide as an employer in your province. Describe these and others you intend to provide. What are the costs of these benefits, and why would you offer them to your employees?

MANAGING ETHICALLY EXERCISE

Nadia Burowsky has recently been promoted to a managerial position in a large downtown bank. Before her promotion, she was one of a group of bank tellers who got together weekly and complained about their jobs. Burowsky enjoyed these get-togethers because she is recently divorced, and they provided a bit of a social life for her. In Burowsky's new role, she will be conducting performance appraisals and making decisions about pay raises and promotions for these same tellers. Burowsky reports to you, and you are aware of her former weekly get-togethers with the tellers. Is it ethical for her to continue attending these social functions? How might she effectively manage having relationships with co-workers and evaluating them?

MANAGEMENT CHALLENGE EXERCISE

As Canada's economy grew stronger after the recession of 2008–2009, a new power emerged in the executive suite. Many companies began shifting from cutback-survival mode to embracing such enlightened concepts as growth, expansion, and a healthy corporate culture. Canada's human resource specialists finally began getting away from planning layoffs and calculating severance packages to building productive teams, enhancing employee motivation, and creating a winning corporate culture. In some companies, HR's new role is not just evolutionary but revolutionary. A prominent medical products company, for instance, recently appointed its HR vice-president as VP of marketing. One large retailer promoted its former head of HR to country manager. In a recovering economy, it figured its biggest challenge is not merchandising, but improving the quality of customer service and building staff morale. Similarly, a high-tech firm created a senior HR position to forge a new corporate culture. The company knew it had more than enough software engineers on staff (most of them recruited right out of college) but realized it now needed more people who could challenge the culture—develop new markets, build relationships, and foster risk-taking in a company that had always talked things to death. The HR executive's mandate: Find tech-savvy business leaders and hire them now, even if their job does not exist yet. Because of your expertise, your advice is now being sought by a well-known mid-sized company in your area.

1. What course of action would you recommend to the executives to fulfill their mandate?

MANAGEMENT PORTFOLIO PROJECT

Answer the following questions about the organization you have chosen to follow:

1. Find out and report on how your organization plans for its human resources. What are the forces operating on this firm that make it easy or difficult to forecast its future supply of and demand for employees?

2. Describe the training and development programs for employees and managers in this organization.

3. What methods of employee performance appraisals are used in this company? How are they different for different categories of employees?

4. Describe the company's compensation and benefits system. Would this system motivate you to work for this company? Why, or why not?

5. Discuss whether or not the company's HRM system is compatible with its strategy and organizational structure. If not, make recommendations as to how to reach a better fit.

6. If the organization is unionized, describe the state of its labour relations.

VIDEO MANAGEMENT CASE

Talent Management at the City of Brampton

Lisa Murray, skills development and education specialist at the Ontario municipality of Brampton, talks about how her organization handles talent management.

1. How does the City of Brampton strive to gain a competitive advantage when it comes to developing talented employees from recruitment to retirement?

Management Case

Chain of Knowledge: Boomers Filling the Gaps[77]

"It's a bit of a paradigm shift," says David Lathrop, president of Grey Fox Associates Inc.[78] "The world is slowly coming to realize there is a real need (for senior management expertise) that isn't a full-time need." And so a growing number of baby boomers with senior-level business experience will be recruited to fill a niche created by their retiring colleagues, who are leaving a skills gap in their wake.

David Lathrop and Bob Eccleston, 57-year-old information technology executives, felt the sting of downsizing. They wanted to capitalize on their expertise in a way that gave them the work flexibility they wanted—and could afford—at this stage in life. So they set up a consulting business that allows them to work 40 or 50 hours a month on a contract basis to client companies that need to develop the skills of current, and often much more inexperienced, leaders. "It's about providing very senior-level help, but in very small and manageable quantities in a way that a customer can see great value," says Eccleston, who was "downsized" three times before deciding to venture in a different direction.

Most human resource experts agree there will be a relatively sudden lack of senior experience in the market once the majority of baby boomers retire, leaving unprepared companies scrambling to find the qualified talent to replace them. Increasingly, firms such as Grey Fox are offering their services by coaching and mentoring up-and-coming leaders while keeping their own hands in the business world, Eccleston says. "You get so much satisfaction out of taking what you've learned over 35 years and helping these people get through those bumps in their careers." Lathrop says the goal is to recruit more partners with the same amount of experience and wisdom so the chain of knowledge continues moving along to the next generation of business leaders. The trend has also given rise to the increased use of interim managers, or contract executives who take over the helm of a department or company until a replacement can be groomed or recruited. "What [more junior executives] really need is just a few hours a week of someone with 30-plus years behind them who has kind of seen it all to hold them by the hand and get them through those difficult moments," Eccleston says.

1. Why is the recruitment of older employees important in managing the skills gap?
2. What is the paradigm shift that David Lathrop refers to?

Mc Graw Hill connect™

Connect allows you to practise important concepts at your own pace and on your own schedule, with 24/7 online access to an eBook, practice quizzes, video cases, interactive exercises, study tools, and more.

Managing Communication and Conflict

Opening Case

Canadian Drug Maker Goes Social to Help Supply Chain Crisis[1]

HOW CAN MANAGERS CREATE A COMPETITIVE ADVANTAGE BY USING TECHNOLOGY TO HELP IMPROVE COMMUNICATIONS?

A few years ago, a Canadian pharmaceutical company found that it was in constant crisis mode, and its way out of the chaos lay in getting everyone to communicate.

The company, Ratiopharm Canada, was having a hard time being flexible enough to meet changes in demand. For example, the supply chain unit might not know for as long as four months that there had been a slowdown in production because of a manufacturing snafu or a quality control issue.

Ratiopharm found the answer was to get everyone to communicate. The generic drug manufacturer made that happen by using social collaboration tools. "When the entire operation is stressed, it reverts to crisis mode," said Antonio Martins, who was vice-president of supply chain in 2005 when he first introduced social collaboration tools at Ratiopharm. "We were in constant crisis mode. When the stress is lifted, suddenly things can be more orderly. . . . The entire operation becomes much more efficient."

Martins, who is the former vice-president of supply chain at Teva Canada, which bought Ratiopharm in 2010, said the problem stemmed from a lack of communication in the supply chain. If something went wrong anywhere in the supply chain process, it might be two to four months before the people who needed to know found out about it.

So how do you bridge such a chasm of communication? Martins turned to Web 2.0 technology and social collaboration tools, starting with Microsoft's SharePoint, then switching to tools from Strategy-Nets

and later Moxie Software, which is what the company uses today.

Martins said collaboration tools fixed the communication problems employees were having, and the improvement in communication fixed Ratiopharm's supply chain problem. Addressing those issues ultimately fixed the company's service problems and eventually saved jobs and enabled the company to survive during rocky times in the pharmaceutical industry.

Martins explained that back around 2005, Ratiopharm was having trouble because it took so long to find out that there had been a snafu somewhere along the supply chain. For instance, if unsightly black specks from a foreign substance suddenly appeared in the ingredients used to make a batch of tablets, the manufacturing process would have to be stopped and the tainted tablets would have to be removed.

"That batch that's sitting in barrels—we're waiting for them and we don't know something is wrong," he said. "We have to detect what's going on as soon

as possible. . . . We didn't want the situation to go through a hierarchy because that takes too long for bosses to talk to bosses."

Martins noted that at that point the company had started using SharePoint, so he got his employees to use the software's message board. "Individuals would post the problem and other individuals would solve the problem," he explained. "We went from it taking two to four months to find out there was a problem, to two to four weeks, and then to a few hours or a couple of days."

SharePoint had worked well, but Ratiopharm wanted more social tools, so in 2007 Martins moved to Strategy-Nets software and extended the collaboration program beyond the supply chain to include customer service, sales, and marketing.

From Strategy-Nets, Ratiopharm moved to Moxie Software, which includes tools for real-time conversations, blogs, wikis, and document sharing. Martins said he also liked Moxie's offering because it has a sound architecture and is based on an open-source platform. Once people in different departments were connected, they could make better market predictions and "react before business flash-floods hit," Martins said.

The expanded use of collaboration software, and the move to richer and more varied tools, helped the company achieve a service level of 98 percent for three years in a row. Moreover, Ratiopharm was able to manufacture its products three times faster, improving its ability to meet demand—even surprise spikes in demand.

"You establish environments in which employees can declare there's a problem," Martins said. "Collaboration allows us to see what's going on in-house. . . . If you're talking about how your company produces, you have a core that makes everything faster."

After reading and understanding the concepts in this chapter, you should be able to answer the following questions:

1. *In what ways was communication at Ratiopharm Canada ineffective?*

2. *How did going "social" help Ratiopharm Canada solve its communication problems?*

3. *What degree of information richness is achieved through social media channels?*

Overview

As Ratiopharm's initiatives suggest, developing new IT to improve communication and decision making is a vital managerial task. Communication is an essential component in the fabric of a healthy workplace. In addition to warding off toxic work environments, effective communication can be the lifeblood of work each day. Ineffective communication is detrimental for managers, employees, and organizations; it can lead to conflict, poor performance, strained interpersonal relations, poor service, and dissatisfied customers. Managers at all levels need to be good communicators in order for an organization to be effective and gain a competitive advantage.

In this chapter, we describe the nature of communication and the communication process and explain why it is so important for all managers and their subordinates to be effective communicators. We describe the communication media available to managers, and the factors that managers need to consider in selecting a communication medium for each message they send. We describe the communication skills that help individuals be effective senders and receivers of messages. We describe conflict, and the strategies that managers can use to resolve it effectively. One major conflict-resolution technique—negotiation—is dealt with in detail, outlining the steps managers can take to be good negotiators. By the end of this chapter, you will have a good appreciation of the nature of communication and the steps that all organizational members can take to ensure that they are effective communicators. You will also become aware of the skills necessary to manage organizational conflict.

Explain why effective communication—the sharing of information—helps an organization gain a competitive advantage, and describe the communication process. **LO1**

The Importance of Communication in Organizations

Communication is the sharing of information between two or more individuals or groups to reach a common understanding.[2] Some organizations are more effective at doing this than are others, as we saw in the opening case. First and

communication The sharing of information between two or more individuals or groups to reach a common understanding.

foremost, communication, no matter how electronically based, is a human endeavour and involves individuals and groups. Second, communication does not take place unless a common understanding is reached. Thus, if you try to call a business to speak to a person in customer service or billing and you are bounced back and forth between endless automated messages and menu options and eventually hang up in frustration, communication has not taken place.

In Chapter 1, we explained that in order for an organization to gain a competitive advantage managers must strive to increase efficiency, quality, responsiveness to customers, and innovation. Good communication is essential for attaining each of these four goals and thus is a necessity for gaining a competitive advantage.

Managers can *increase efficiency* by updating the production process to take advantage of new and more efficient technologies and by training workers to operate the new technologies and expand their skills. Good communication is necessary for managers to learn about new technologies, implement them in their organizations, and train workers in how to use them. Similarly, *improving quality* hinges on effective communication. Managers need to communicate to all members of an organization the meaning and importance of high quality and the routes to attaining it. Subordinates need to communicate quality problems and suggestions for increasing quality to their superiors, and members of self-managed work teams need to share their ideas for improving quality with each other.

Good communication can also help to increase *responsiveness to customers*. When the organizational members who are closest to customers, such as salespeople in department stores and tellers in banks, are empowered to communicate customers' needs and desires to managers, managers are better able to respond to these needs. Managers, in turn, must communicate with other organizational members to determine how best to respond to changing customer preferences. As discussed in Chapter 5, effective communication is particularly important when managing crises. Maple Leaf Foods is widely considered a textbook example of successfully communicating with customers for the way it handled Canada's largest food recall ever due to a deadly outbreak of listeria at one of its meat plants in August 2008. CEO Michael McCain quickly responded to the recall by holding a press conference, as well as recording a YouTube video detailing the steps Maple Leaf was taking to resolve the problems. The company also bought advertisements in newspapers and on television to inform customers further. The CEOs of Research In Motion (RIM), on the other hand, waited until the problem of the worldwide BlackBerry outage

Effective communication skills are important for managers.

in 2011 was essentially resolved before co-CEO Mike Lazaridis went on YouTube to give an update.

Innovation, which often takes place in cross-functional teams, also requires effective communication. Members of a cross-functional team developing a new kind of compact disc player, for example, must communicate effectively with each other to develop a disc player that customers will want, that will be of high quality, and that can be produced efficiently. Members of the team also must communicate with managers to secure the resources they need to develop the disc player and keep the managers informed of progress on the project.

Effective communication is necessary for managers and all members of an organization to increase efficiency, quality, responsiveness to customers, and innovation and thus gain a competitive advantage for their organization. Managers therefore must have a good understanding of the communication process if they are to perform effectively. Work that is truly team-based entails a number of highly interdependent yet distinct components, and involves team members with distinct areas of expertise who need to closely coordinate their efforts. Collaboration software can be a powerful communication tool, as profiled in the opening case.

The Communication Process

The communication process consists of two phases. In the *transmission phase,* information is shared between two or more individuals or groups. In the *feedback phase,* a common understanding is reached. In both phases, a number of distinct stages must occur for communication to take place (see Figure 12.1).[3]

The **sender** (the person or group wishing to share information with some other person or group) starts the transmission phase by deciding on the **message** (the information to communicate). Then the

sender The person or group wishing to share information.

message The information that a sender wants to share.

FIGURE 12.1 The Communication Process

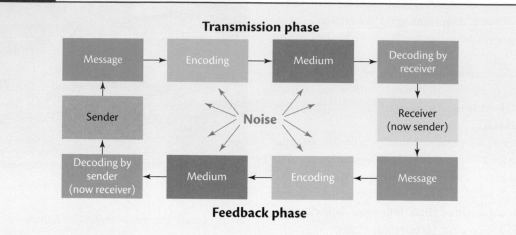

sender translates the message into symbols or language, a process called **encoding.** Often, messages are encoded into words but they could also be symbols, such as :-) or a stop sign. **Noise** is a general term that refers to anything that hampers any stage of the communication process.

Once encoded, a message is transmitted through a medium to the **receiver,** the person or group for which the message is intended. A **medium** is simply the pathway—such as a phone call, a letter, a memo, or face-to-face communication in a meeting—through which an encoded message is transmitted to a receiver. At the next stage, the receiver interprets and tries to make sense of the message, a process called **decoding.** This is a critical point in communication.

The feedback phase is begun by the receiver (who becomes a sender). The receiver decides what message to send to the original sender (who becomes a receiver), encodes it, and transmits it through a chosen medium (see Figure 12.1). The message might contain a confirmation that the original message was received and understood, a restatement of the original message to make sure that it was correctly interpreted, or a request for more information. The original sender decodes the message and makes sure that a common understanding has been reached. If the original sender determines that a common understanding has not been reached, the sender and receiver go through the whole process as many times as needed to reach

a common understanding. Failure to listen to employees prevents many managers from receiving feedback and reaching a common understanding with their employees. Feedback eliminates misunderstandings, ensures that messages are correctly interpreted, and enables senders and receivers to reach a common understanding.

The encoding of messages into words, written or spoken, is **verbal communication.** We also encode messages without using written or spoken language; **nonverbal communication** shares information by means of facial expressions (smiling, raising an eyebrow, frowning, dropping one's jaw), body language (posture, gestures, nods, shrugs), and even style of dressing (casual, formal, conservative, trendy). "People make judgments about you based on how you look. If you're sloppily dressed or look like you're going to the beach, you'll leave a negative impression on clients and other employees," warns Natasha vandenHoven, senior vice-president of human resources at Aon Consulting in Toronto.[4]

encoding Translating a message into understandable symbols or language.

noise Anything that hampers any stage of the communication process.

receiver The person or group for which a message is intended.

medium The pathway through which an encoded message is transmitted to a receiver.

decoding Interpreting and trying to make sense of a message.

verbal communication The encoding of messages into words, either written or spoken.

nonverbal communication The encoding of messages by means of facial expressions, body language, and styles of dressing.

Feedback eliminates misunderstandings.

Nonverbal communication can reinforce verbal communication. Just as a warm and genuine smile can support words of appreciation for a job well done, a concerned facial expression can support words of sympathy for a personal problem. In such cases, similarity between verbal and nonverbal communication helps ensure that a common understanding is reached. This is not always as straightforward as it appears. Nonverbal gestures are culturally constructed; that is, different cultures perceive and interpret the symbols differently. For example, the thumbs-up sign in Western cultures indicates "all is good," but in the Middle East it is a gesture of insult. Similarly, maintaining eye contact is viewed as a sign of engagement and attentiveness in Canada, but in Japan it is viewed as rude behaviour and an invasion of privacy.[5]

Nonverbal cues, such as an intense look exchanged by two people, can provide managers and employees with vital information that helps them make better decisions. Sometimes when members of an organization decide not to express a message verbally, they inadvertently do so nonverbally. People tend to have less control over nonverbal communication, and often a verbal message that is withheld gets expressed through body language or facial expressions. For instance, a manager who agrees to a proposal that she or he actually is not in favour of may unintentionally communicate disfavour by grimacing.

Sometimes nonverbal communication is used to send messages that cannot be sent through verbal channels.

> "People make judgments about you based on how you look. If you're sloppily dressed or look like you're going to the beach, you'll leave a negative impression on clients and other employees."
>
> *Natasha VandenHoven,*
> *Aon Consulting*

Many lawyers are well aware of this communication tactic. Lawyers are often schooled in techniques of nonverbal communication, such as choosing where to stand in the courtroom for maximum effect and using eye contact during different stages of a trial. Lawyers sometimes get into trouble for using inappropriate nonverbal communication in an attempt to influence juries.

It is important to be aware of nonverbal aspects of communication, as well as the literal meaning of the words. You should particularly be aware of contradictions between the messages. A manager may say it is a good time to discuss a raise but then keep looking at the clock. This nonverbal signal may indicate that this is really *not* a good time to talk. Thus actions can speak louder (and more accurately) than words. A variety of popular books help one interpret body language. However, do use some care. For instance, while it is often thought that crossing your arms in front of your chest conveys resistance to a message, you might do this simply because you feel cold.

When managers and other members of an organization are ineffective communicators, organizational performance suffers, and any competitive advantage the organization might have is likely to be lost. Moreover, poor communication sometimes can be downright dangerous and even lead to tragic and unnecessary loss of human life. For example, researchers from Harvard University studied the causes of mistakes, such as a patient receiving the wrong medication, in two large hospitals in the Boston area. They discovered that some mistakes in hospitals occur because of communication problems—physicians not having the information they need to correctly order medications for their patients, or nurses not having the information they need to correctly administer medications. The researchers concluded that some of the responsibility for these mistakes lies with hospital management, which has not taken active steps to improve communication.[6]

Nonverbal messages are just as important as verbal and written ones.

The Role of Perception in Communication

Perception plays a central role in communication and affects both transmission and feedback. **Perception** is the process through which people select, organize,

> **perception** The process through which people select, organize, and interpret sensory input to give meaning and order to the world around them.

and interpret sensory input to give meaning and order to the world around them. But it is inherently subjective and influenced by people's personalities, values, attitudes, and moods, as well as by their culture, experience, and knowledge. Thus, when senders and receivers communicate with each other, they are doing so based on their own subjective perceptions. The encoding and decoding of messages and even the choice of a medium hinge on the perceptions of senders and receivers.

In addition, perceptual biases can hamper effective communication. Recall from Chapter 3 that *biases* are systematic tendencies to use information about others in ways that result in inaccurate perceptions. In Chapter 3, we described a number of biases that can result in diverse members of an organization being treated unfairly. These same biases also can lead to ineffective communication. For example, stereotypes—simplified and often inaccurate beliefs about the characteristics of particular groups of people—can interfere with the encoding and decoding of messages.

One group that has suffered extensively over the years from unwarranted stereotyping has been Canada's Aboriginal population. Today, however, Aboriginal entrepreneurs are growing in number and moving beyond their roots.[7] Orrin Benn, president of the Canadian Aboriginal and Minority Supplier Council (CAMSC), is working hard to make sure Aboriginal entrepreneurs succeed in growing their businesses. Otherwise, as he points out, given the stereotypical perceptions, "Canada loses." John Bernard, president and founder of Donna Cona Inc., Canada's largest Aboriginal-owned technology firm, has experienced first-hand the unique challenges facing Aboriginal and minority entrepreneurs. He readily admits that being Aboriginal makes it that much harder to gain access to the supply chains of major corporations. For example,

Six months after beating out IBM and CGI to design the infrastructure for Nunavut residents to communicate across the two million-square-kilometre expanse of Canada's largest territory, Mr. Bernard learned that the fact he was aboriginal could have cost him the contract. "I was at an event with the CIO of the Nunavut project and he asked if I was aboriginal. I said, 'Yes, isn't that one of the reasons we won?' And he said, 'Oh God, no. You won because you had the best proposal. In fact,' he said, 'if we had known you were aboriginal that would have gone against you.' Why? Because of the stereotype that aboriginal firms do not deliver. If an aboriginal company makes a mistake, it reflects on the entire community. That is a huge obstacle to overcome."[8]

Instead of relying on stereotypes, effective communicators strive to perceive other people accurately by focusing on their actual behaviours, knowledge, skills, and abilities. Accurate perceptions, in turn, contribute to effective communication.

Good communication is essential for organizations to function effectively. Managers spend about 85 percent of their time engaged in some form of communication, whether in meetings, in telephone conversations, through email, or in face-to-face interactions. Employees also need to be effective communicators.[9] When all members of an organization are able to communicate effectively with each other and with people outside the organization, the organization is much more likely to perform highly and gain a competitive advantage.

Define information richness, and describe the information richness of communication media available to managers. **LO2**

Information Richness and Communication Media

To be effective communicators, individuals need to select an appropriate communication medium for *each* message they send. Should a change in procedures be communicated to subordinates in a memo or sent as email? Should a congratulatory message about a major accomplishment be communicated in a letter, in a phone call, or over lunch? Should a layoff announcement be made in a memo or at a plant meeting? Should the members of a purchasing team travel to Europe to finalize a major agreement with a new supplier, or should they do this through electronic files and faxes? Managers deal with these questions day in and day out.

There is no one best communication medium. In choosing a communication medium for any message, individuals need to consider three factors:

- *The level of information richness that is needed.* **Information richness** is the amount of information a communication medium can carry and the extent to which the medium enables sender and receiver to reach a common understanding.[10] The communication media that managers use vary in their information richness (see Figure 12.2).[11] Media high in information richness are able to carry a lot of information and generally enable receivers and senders to come to a common understanding.

- *The time needed for communication.* Managers' and other organizational

information richness
The amount of information that a communication medium can carry and the extent to which the medium enables sender and receiver to reach a common understanding.

FIGURE 12.2   The Information Richness of Communication Media

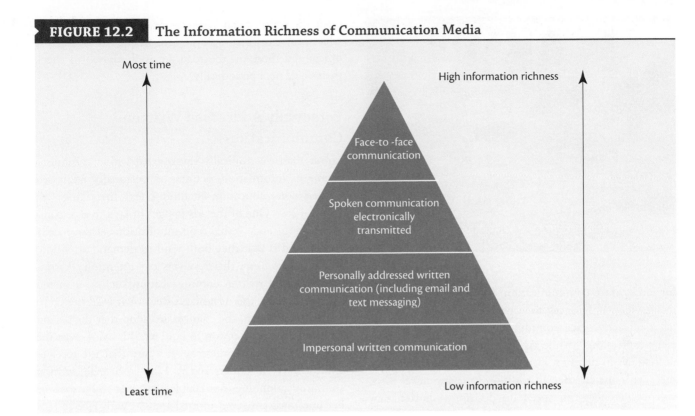

members' time is valuable, and this affects the way messages should be sent.

- *The need for a paper or electronic trail.* An individual may want written documentation that a message was sent and received.

In the remainder of this section, we examine four types of communication media that vary along these three dimensions: information richness, time, and need for a paper or electronic trail.[12]

Face-to-Face Communication

Face-to-face communication has the highest information richness. When individuals communicate face to face, they not only can take advantage of verbal communication but also can interpret each other's nonverbal signals, such as facial expressions and body language. A look of concern or puzzlement can sometimes tell more than a thousand words, and individuals can respond to these nonverbal signals on the spot. Face-to-face communication also enables instant feedback. Points of confusion, ambiguity, or misunderstanding can be resolved, and individuals can cycle through the communication process as many times as they need to in order to reach a common understanding.

Management by wandering around (MBWA) is a face-to-face communication technique that is effective for many managers at all levels in an organization.[13] Rather than scheduling formal meetings with subordinates, managers walk around work areas and talk informally with employees about issues and concerns that both employees and managers may have. These informal conversations provide managers and subordinates with important information and at the same time foster the development of positive relationships. William Hewlett and David Packard, founders and former top managers of Hewlett-Packard, found management by wandering around to be a highly effective way to communicate with their employees.

Because face-to-face communication is highest in information richness, you might think that it should always be the medium of choice. This is not the case, however, because of the amount of time it takes and the lack of a paper or electronic trail resulting from it. For messages that are important, personal, or likely to be misunderstood, it is often well worth the time to use face-to-face communication and, if need be, supplement it with some form of written communication documenting the message.

Advances in information technology are providing managers with new and close alternative communication media

management by wandering around (MBWA) A face-to-face communication technique in which a manager walks around a work area and talks informally with employees about issues and concerns.

Videoconferencing can effectively facilitate meetings by retaining a personal feeling.

for face-to-face communication. Many organizations are using videoconferences to capture some of the advantages of face-to-face communication (such as access to facial expressions), while saving time and money because individuals in different locations do not have to travel to meet with one another. In addition to saving travel costs, videoconferences can speed up decisions, shorten new product development time, and lead to more efficient meetings. Some managers have found that meetings are 20 to 30 percent shorter when they use videoconferences instead of face-to-face meetings.[14]

Spoken Communication Electronically Transmitted

After face-to-face communication, spoken communication electronically transmitted over the phone is second-highest in information richness (see Figure 12.2). Although individuals communicating over the phone do not have access to body language and facial expressions, they do have access to the tone of voice in which a message is delivered, the parts of the message the sender emphasizes, and the general manner in which the message is spoken, in addition to the actual words themselves. Thus, phone conversations have the capacity to convey extensive amounts of information. Individuals also can ensure that mutual understanding is reached because they can get quick feedback over the phone and can answer questions.

Voice mail systems and answering machines also allow people to send and receive verbal electronic messages. Voice mail systems are companywide systems that enable senders to record messages for members of an organization who are away from their desks and allow receivers to access their messages when hundreds of kilometres away

from the office. Such systems are obviously a necessity when managers or employees are frequently out of the office, and those on the road are well advised to check their voice mail periodically.

Personally Addressed Written Communication

Lower than electronically transmitted verbal communication in information richness is personally addressed written communication including text messaging (see Figure 12.2). One of the advantages of face-to-face communication and verbal communication electronically transmitted is that they both tend to demand attention, which helps ensure that receivers pay attention. Personally addressed written communication such as a memo or letter also has this advantage. Because it is addressed to a particular person, the chances are good that the person will actually pay attention to (and read) it. Moreover, the sender can write the message in a way that the receiver is most likely to understand it. Like voice mail, written communication does not enable a receiver to have his or her questions answered immediately as with face-to-face communication, but when messages are clearly written and feedback is provided, common understanding can still be reached.

Even if managers use face-to-face communication, a follow-up in writing is often needed for messages that are important or complicated and need to be referred to later on. This is precisely what Karen Binder, a disability claims administrator at Manulife Financial, did when she needed to tell one of her subordinates about an important change in the way the company would be handling denials of insurance benefits. Binder met with the subordinate and described the changes face-to-face. Once she was sure that the subordinate understood them, she handed her a sheet of instructions to follow, which essentially summarized the information they had discussed.

Email, Twitter, Facebook, and Blogs

Email, Twitter, Facebook, and blogs also fit into this category of communication media because senders and receivers are communicating through personally addressed written words. However, the words are appearing on their personal computer screens rather than on pieces of paper. Short forms of written words and symbols are often used when space is limited, as it is on Twitter. Email and text messaging is becoming so widespread in the business world that managers are even developing their own etiquette. For instance, messages in capital letters are often perceived as being shouted or screamed.

While the growing use of email and texting has enabled better communication within organizations, not all benefits have been positive. Many individuals complain of "email overload," and being unable to keep up with all the emails and texts that arrive. In addition, employees often find their electronic mailboxes clogged with junk mail. In a recent survey, more than half of the organizations surveyed acknowledged some problems with their email systems.[15]

To avoid these and other costly forms of email abuse, managers need to develop a clear policy specifying what company email can and should be used for and what is out of bounds. Managers also should clearly communicate this policy to all members of an organization as well as describe both the procedures that will be used when email abuse is suspected and the consequences that will result when email abuse is confirmed.

The increasing use of voice mail and email in companies large and small has led to some ethical concerns. These forms of communication are not necessarily private. The federal *Privacy Act* and the *Access to Information Act* apply to all federal government departments, most federal agencies, and some federal Crown corporations, but many private-sector employees are not covered by privacy legislation. Only Quebec's privacy act applies to the entire private sector.

The ethics of listening to other people's voice mail or reading their email are likely to be a growing concern for many managers. A recent survey of more than 2000 large American firms found that 38 percent reported that they "store and review" employee email messages.[16] The Ontario, Manitoba, and British Columbia governments have told their employees that email will be monitored if abuse is suspected. The governments' positions are that the Internet and email should be used only for business purposes.

Impersonal Written Communication

Impersonal written communication is lowest in information richness and is well suited for messages that need to reach a large number of receivers. Because such messages are not addressed to particular receivers, feedback is unlikely, so managers must make sure that messages sent by this medium are written clearly in language that all receivers will understand.

Managers can use impersonal written communication, including company newsletters, for various types of messages, including rules, regulations, policies, newsworthy information, and announcements of changes in procedures or the arrival of new organizational members.

Impersonal written communication also can be used to communicate instructions about how to use machinery or how to process work orders or customer requests. For these kinds of messages, the paper trail left by this communication medium can be invaluable for employees. Much of this information is also being posted to company intranets. The danger with impersonal communication, however, is that some individuals will not read it, so it is important that employees are made aware of important messages.

Like personal written communication, impersonal written communication can be delivered and retrieved electronically, and this is increasingly being done in companies large and small. Unfortunately, the ease with which electronic messages can be spread has led to their proliferation. The electronic inboxes of many managers and workers are backlogged, and they rarely have time to read all the electronic work-related information available to them. The problem with such **information overload**—a superabundance of information—is the potential for important information to be ignored or overlooked while tangential information receives attention. Moreover, information overload can result in thousands of hours and millions in dollars in lost productivity.

Advances in Information Technology

Computer-based information technology can greatly facilitate and improve the communication process. It has allowed managers to develop computer-based

> **information overload**
> A superabundance of information that increases the likelihood that important information is ignored or overlooked and tangential information receives attention.

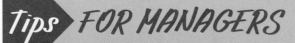

FOR MANAGERS

Information Richness and Communication Media

1. When you have something to communicate that is important, emotion-based, and personal, use face-to-face communication.

2. Use videoconferencing when distance, weather, or cost hinders face-to-face communication.

3. Consider introducing "Email-Free Friday," recommended by Sport England.

4. Whether or not privacy is protected by law or contract, foster a workplace culture where privacy is valued and respected.

management information systems that provide timely, complete, relevant, and high-quality information. As we discussed in Chapter 4, technology allows companies to improve their responsiveness to customers, minimize costs, and thus improve their competitive position. The link between information systems, communication, and competitive position is an important one that may determine the success or failure of organizations in an increasingly competitive global environment.

Wireless Communications

A trend of considerable significance for information systems has been the rapid growth of wireless communication technologies, particularly digital communications. Wireless communication is significant for the information technology revolution because it facilitates linking together people and computers, which greatly increases their decision-making ability. An engineer or salesperson working in the field can send information to, and receive information from, the home office by using the wireless capability built into smartphones, laptops, and tablets.

Computer Networks

The tumbling price of computing power and information and the use of wireless communication channels have facilitated **networking,** the exchange of information through a group or network of interlinked computers. The most common arrangement now emerging is a three-tier network consisting of clients, servers, and a mainframe (see Figure 12.3). At the outer nodes of a typical three-tier network are the personal computers (PCs) that sit on the desks of individual users. These personal computers, referred to as *clients,* are linked to a local *server,* a high-powered midrange computer that "serves" the client personal computers. Servers often store power-hungry software programs that can be run more effectively on a server than on individuals' personal computers. Servers may also manage several printers that can be used by hundreds of clients; servers also store data files and handle email communications between clients. The client computers linked directly to a server constitute a *local area network (LAN).* Within any organization there may be several LANs—for example, one in every division and function.

At the hub of a three-tier system are *mainframe computers,* large and powerful computers that can be used to store and process vast amounts of information. The mainframe can also be used to handle electronic

networking The exchange of information through a group or network of interlinked computers.

FIGURE 12.3 A Typical Three-Tier Information System

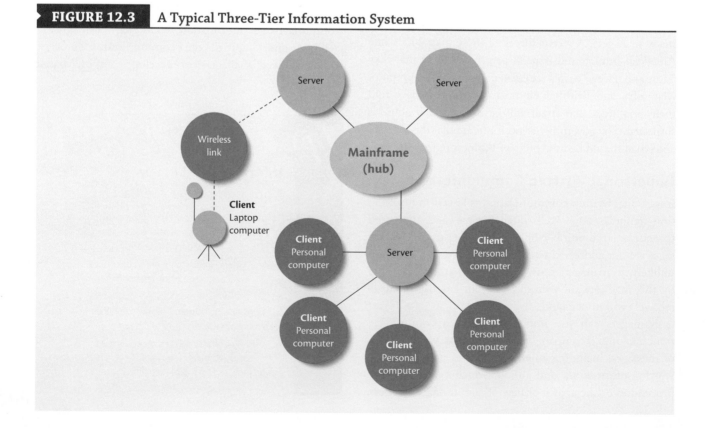

communications between personal computers situated in different LANs. In addition, the mainframe may be connected to mainframes in other organizations and, through them, to LANs in other organizations. Increasingly, the Internet, a worldwide network of interlinked computers, is used as the conduit for connecting the computer systems of different organizations.

A manager with a personal computer hooked into a three-tier system can access data and software stored in the local server, in the mainframe, or through the Internet in computers based in another organization. A manager can therefore communicate electronically with other individuals hooked into the system, whether they are in the manager's LAN, in another LAN within the manager's

organization, or in another organization altogether. Moreover, because of the growth of wireless communications, an individual with the proper equipment can hook into the system from any location—at home, on a boat, on the beach, in the air—anywhere a wireless communications link can be established.

Software Developments

If computer hardware has been developing rapidly, so has computer software. **Operating system software** tells the computer hardware how to run. **Applications software,** such as programs for word processing, spreadsheets,

> **operating system software** Software that tells computer hardware how to run.
>
> **applications software** Software designed for a specific task or use.

FOCUS ON ❯ *The Social Economy*

Framework

Framework is a non-profit organization that has two core programs: Timeraiser and Civic Footprint.[17]

Timeraiser is a silent art auction with a difference. People bid time, not money, on works of art by local emerging artists. Timeraiser artists are paid fair market value for their work.

During the event, people match their skills to the needs of the agencies and groups seeking volunteers. After finding a match, the volunteers bid their time on the artwork.

"The Timeraiser connects people to causes and causes to people. We reach out to young professionals who are looking for ways to get involved, but aren't quite sure how. The Timeraiser brings together local agencies who are looking for skilled volunteers, while celebrating the work of artists in the community."[18]

Civic Footprint is a program that helps people participate in community and civic activities by volunteering for causes and participating at events that interest them. The program allows people to plan and track their Civic Footprint, which helps to build a lifetime of civic engagement.

"In the same way that you want to make your carbon footprint as small as possible, we want you to grow your Civic Footprint to be as large as possible. We aim to generate volunteer hours in the community while encouraging skilled volunteerism."[19]

Framework uses online applications (website and blog) to showcase interesting non-profit initiatives across Canada and shows ways volunteers can get involved.

On communication, Framework has this to say:

"As a non-profit operating in several timezones, we quickly recognized the need to have accessible,

collaborative documents available to our staff and volunteers regardless of their location. In order to be agile, expand the Timeraiser program, and further develop Civic Footprint, we need the ability to share and edit documents from anywhere. Like many non-profit organizations, we operate within a limit budget, changing staff models and shifting technologies. How do you build a strong organizational core when some or all of your organization's knowledge can leave with a staff member? It can also be extremely challenging to invest in new technologies, software languages and social media tools without full-time support and maintenance of these technologies.

"Using Google Applications and Salesforce.com, we can keep up to date records of our contacts, plan and execute projects, and collaborate on documents and website development. We connect the work built in Google Applications with our external Social Media tools, primarily Facebook, Twitter, and our blog. We also produce unique information and e-learning videos that are posted to YouTube and promoted through Twitter. Although the ratio of Software as a Service to Desktop Software applications is 33:4, we do utilize and appreciate Desktop Software applications on occasion.

"We have looked closely at the possibilities and flexibility that a cloud computing model offers over a traditional server-based model, and have concluded that cloud computing suits the needs of our organization best."[20]

1. What are the communication challenges for Framework's programs?

artificial intelligence
Behaviour performed by a machine that would be called intelligent if performed by a human being.

graphics, and database management, is software developed for a specific task or use. The increase in the power of computer hardware has allowed software developers to write increasingly powerful programs that are, at the same time, increasingly user-friendly. By harnessing the rapidly growing power of microprocessors, applications software has vastly increased the ability of managers to acquire, organize, manipulate, and transmit information. In doing so, it also has increased the ability of managers to coordinate and control the activities of their organization and to make decisions, as discussed earlier in Chapter 4.

As illustrated by the non-profit organization Framework, featured in our Focus on the Social Economy, the need for real-time information can be crucial to the success of a venture.

Artificial intelligence is another interesting and potentially fruitful software development. **Artificial intelligence** has been defined as behaviour by a machine that would be called intelligent if performed by a human being.[21] Artificial intelligence has already made it possible to write programs that can solve problems and perform simple tasks. For example, software programs variously called "software agents," "softbots," or "knowbots" can be used to perform simple managerial tasks such as sorting through reams of data or incoming e-mail messages to look for important data and messages. The interesting feature of these programs is that from "watching" a manager sort through such data they can "learn" what his or her preferences are. Having done this, they then can take over some of this work from the manager, freeing up more time for work on other tasks. Most of these programs are in the development stage, but they may be commonplace within a decade.[22]

Another software development that is starting to have an impact on the manager's job is speech recognition software. Currently, speech recognition software must be "trained" to recognize and understand each individual's voice, and it requires the speaker to pause after each word. The increasing power of microprocessors, however, has enabled the development of faster speech recognition programs that can handle more variables and much greater complexity. Now a manager driving down the road may be able to communicate with a computer through a wireless link and give that computer complex voice instructions.[23]

Limitations of Information Systems

Despite their usefulness, information systems have some limitations. A serious potential problem is the one noted at the beginning of this chapter. In all of the enthusiasm for management information systems, electronic communication by means of a computer network, and the like, a vital human element of communication may be lost. Some kinds of information cannot be aggregated and summarized on an MIS report because of issues surrounding information richness. Very rich information is often required to coordinate and control an enterprise and to make informed decisions, far beyond that which can be quantified and aggregated.

The importance of information richness is a strong argument in favour of using electronic communication to *support* face-to-face communication, not to replace it. For example, it would be wrong to make a judgment about an individual's performance merely by "reading the numbers" provided by a management information system. Instead, the numbers should be used to alert managers to individuals who may have a performance problem. The nature of this performance problem should then be explored in a face-to-face meeting, during which rich information can be gathered. As a top Boeing manager noted, "In our company, the use of e-mail and video-conferencing has not reduced the need to visit people at other sites; it has increased it. E-mail has facilitated the establishment of communications channels between people who previously would not communicate, which is good, but direct visits are still required to cement any working relationships that evolve out of these electronic meetings."[24]

Developing Communication Skills

There are various kinds of barriers to effective communication in organizations. Some barriers have their origins in senders. When messages are unclear, incomplete, or difficult to understand, when they are sent over an inappropriate medium, or when no provision for feedback is made, communication suffers. Other communication barriers have their origins in receivers. When receivers pay no attention to, do not listen to, or make no effort to understand the meaning of a message, communication is likely to be ineffective.

To overcome these barriers and effectively communicate with others, managers (as well as other organizational members) must possess or develop certain communication skills. Some of these skills are particularly important when individuals send messages, and others are critical when individuals receive messages. These skills help ensure not only that individuals will be able to share information but also that they will have the information they need to make good decisions and take action and be able to reach a common understanding with others.

Communication Skills for Senders

Individuals can make sure that they consider all of the steps of the communication process when they are engaging in communication. They can also develop their skills in giving feedback. We discuss each of these issues in turn.

Improving the Communication Process

Table 12.1 summarizes seven communication skills that help ensure that when individuals send messages, they are properly understood and the transmission phase of the communication process is effective. Let us see what each skill entails.

1. *Send Clear and Complete Messages* Individuals need to learn how to send a message that is clear and complete. A message is clear when it is easy for the receiver to understand and interpret, and it is complete when it contains all the information that the sender and receiver need to reach a common understanding. In trying to send messages that are both clear and complete, managers must learn to anticipate how receivers will interpret messages and adjust messages to eliminate sources of misunderstanding or confusion.

2. *Encode Messages in Symbols the Receiver Understands* Individuals need to appreciate that when they encode messages, they should use symbols or language that the receiver understands. When sending messages in English to receivers whose native language is not English, for example, it is important to use commonplace vocabulary and to avoid clichés that, when translated, may make little sense and in some cases are unintentionally comical or insulting.

   Jargon, specialized language that members of an occupation, group, or organization develop to facilitate communication among themselves, should

never be used to communicate with people outside the occupation, group, or organization. For example, truck drivers refer to compact cars as "roller skates," highway dividing lines as "paints," and orange barrels around road construction areas as "Schneider eggs." Using this jargon among themselves results in effective communication because they know precisely what is being referred to. But if a truck driver used this language to send a message (such as "That roller skate can't stay off the paint") to a receiver who did not drive trucks, the receiver would not know what the message meant.[25]

3. *Select a Medium Appropriate for the Message* When choosing among communication media, individuals need to take into account the level of information richness required, time constraints, and the need for a paper or electronic trail. A primary concern in choosing an appropriate medium is the nature of the message. Is it personal, important, nonroutine, and likely to be misunderstood and in need of further clarification? If it is, face-to-face communication is likely to be in order.

4. *Select a Medium That the Receiver Monitors* Another factor that individuals need to take into account when selecting a communication medium is whether it is one that the receiver uses. Not everyone checks voice mail and email routinely. Many people simply select the medium that they themselves use the most and are most comfortable with, but doing this can often lead to ineffective communication. No matter how much an individual likes email, sending an email message to someone else who never checks his or her email is useless. Learning which individuals like things in writing and which prefer face-to-face interactions and then using the appropriate medium enhances the chance that receivers will actually receive and pay attention to messages.

   A related consideration is whether receivers have disabilities that limit their ability to decode certain kinds of messages. A visually impaired receiver, for example, cannot read a written message. Managers should ensure that their employees with disabilities have resources available to communicate effectively with others.

5. *Avoid Filtering and Information Distortion* **Filtering** occurs when senders withhold part of a message

---

TABLE 12.1	Seven Communication Skills for Managers as Senders of Messages

1. Send messages that are clear and complete.
2. Encode messages in symbols that the receiver understands.
3. Select a medium that is appropriate for the message.
4. Select a medium that the receiver monitors.
5. Avoid filtering and information distortion.
6. Ensure that a feedback mechanism is built into messages.
7. Provide accurate information to ensure that misleading rumours are not spread.

jargon Specialized language that members of an occupation, group, or organization develop to facilitate communication among themselves.

filtering Withholding part of a message out of the mistaken belief that the receiver does not need or will not want the information.

because they (mistakenly) think that the receiver does not need the information or will not want to receive it. Filtering can occur at all levels in an organization and in both vertical and horizontal communication. Rank-and-file employees may filter messages they send to first-line managers, first-line managers may filter messages to middle managers, and middle managers may filter messages to top managers. Such filtering is most likely to take place when messages contain bad news or problems that subordinates are afraid they will be blamed for.

Information distortion occurs when the meaning of a message changes as the message passes through a series of senders and receivers. Some information distortion is accidental—due to faulty encoding and decoding or to a lack of feedback. Other information distortion is deliberate. Senders may alter a message to make themselves or their groups look good and to receive special treatment. The **grapevine** is the informal way of communicating information throughout an organization that is based on a gossip network. Surprisingly, much of the information that is sent and received through the grapevine is seldom distorted. Managers can use the grapevine to their advantage by floating new ideas and gauging the reaction of employees before actually implementing change.

Managers themselves should avoid filtering and distorting information. But how can they eliminate these barriers to effective communication throughout their organization? They need to establish trust throughout the organization. Subordinates who trust their managers believe that they will not be blamed for things beyond their control and will be treated fairly. Managers who trust their subordinates provide them with clear and complete information and do not hold things back.

6. *Include a Feedback Mechanism in Messages* Because feedback is essential for effective communication, individuals should build a feedback mechanism into the messages they send. They either should include a request for feedback or indicate when and how they will follow up on the message to make sure that it was received and understood. When writing letters and memos or sending faxes, one can request that the receiver respond with comments and suggestions in a letter, memo, or fax; schedule a meeting to discuss the issue; or follow up with a phone call. Building feedback mechanisms such as these into messages ensures that messages are received and understood.

7. *Provide Accurate Information* **Rumours** are unofficial pieces of information of interest to organizational members but with no identifiable source. Rumours spread quickly once they are started, and usually they concern topics that organizational members think are important, interesting, or amusing. Rumours, however, can be misleading and can cause harm to individual employees and to an organization when they are false, malicious, or unfounded. Managers can halt the spread of misleading rumours by providing organizational members with accurate information on matters that concern them.

information distortion Changes in the meaning of a message as the message passes through a series of senders and receivers.

grapevine An informal communication network among people in organizations.

rumours Unofficial pieces of information of interest to organizational members but with no identifiable source.

Giving Feedback

We have discussed the importance of feedback in making sure that communication is understood. We can also talk about providing feedback more generally, because communicating feedback is an important task for managers. While positive feedback is easier to give, many individuals do not provide such feedback. Most people find giving negative feedback more difficult. Individuals can learn from feedback, whether it is positive or negative, so providing it in a timely fashion is important. The following suggestions can lead to more effective feedback:

- *Focus on specific behaviours.* Individuals should be told what it was that they did well or poorly, rather than simply being told that they did a good job. They can learn more from comments such as "You were very organized in your presentation," or "You managed your time effectively on this project," than when told simply, "Great job."

- *Keep feedback impersonal.* When giving feedback, you should describe the behaviour rather than judge or evaluate the person.[26] Particularly, when giving negative feedback it is easy to focus on personal characteristics (rudeness, laziness, incompetence, etc.), but this rarely helps the person learn from mistakes. It is better to explain that the report was late, contained a number of errors, and was missing an important section.

- *Keep feedback goal-oriented.* Feedback should not be given just because it will make you feel better. Rather, it should have a goal, such as improving performance the next time.

- *Make feedback well-timed.* Feedback should be given shortly after the behaviour occurs. This ensures that the individual remembers the event and also is more likely to result in change if change is needed. Giving feedback to someone six months later, during a performance review, is usually not helpful. If a situation has provoked an emotional response in you, however, delaying feedback until you have had time to lessen the emotional impact is wise.

- *Direct negative feedback toward behaviour that the receiver can control.* When giving negative feedback, consider which things the individual can fix and which are out of his or her control. Criticizing someone's writing skills and then suggesting that the person take a writing course focuses on behaviour that can be controlled. Criticizing someone for not sending an important email when the company's network was down is not likely a situation the individual can fix or control.

Communication Skills for Receivers

Senders also receive messages, and thus they must possess or develop communication skills that allow them to be effective receivers of messages. Table 12.2 summarizes three of these important skills, which we examine in greater detail.

1. Pay Attention

When individuals are overloaded and forced to think about several things at once, they sometimes do not pay sufficient attention to the messages they receive. To be effective, however, individuals should always pay attention to messages they receive, no matter how busy they are. For example, when discussing a project with a subordinate, an effective manager focuses on the project and not on an upcoming meeting with his or her own boss. Similarly, when individuals are reading written forms of communication, they should focus their attention on understanding what they are reading and not be sidetracked into thinking about other issues.

TABLE 12.2	**Three Communication Skills for Managers as Receivers of Messages**

1. Pay attention.

2. Be a good listener.

3. Be empathetic.

2. Be a Good Listener

Part of being a good communicator is being a good listener. This is an essential communication skill for all organizational members. Being a good listener is surprisingly more difficult than you might realize, however. The average person speaks at a rate of 125 to 200 words per minute, but the average listener can effectively process up to 400 words per minute. Therefore listeners are often thinking about other things when someone is speaking to them.

It is important to engage in active listening, which requires paying attention, interpreting, and remembering what was said. Active listening requires making a conscious effort to hear what a person is saying and interpreting it to see that it makes sense. Being a good listener is an essential communication skill in many different kinds of organizations, from small businesses to large corporations.

Organizational members can practise the following behaviours to become active listeners[27]:

1. *Make eye contact if it is culturally appropriate.* Eye contact lets the speaker know that you are paying attention, and it also lets you pick up nonverbal cues. Making eye contact in Japan is considered rude behaviour, and so being a good listener requires being culturally sensitive.

2. *Exhibit affirmative nods and appropriate facial expressions.* By nodding your head and exhibiting appropriate facial expressions, you further show the speaker that you are listening.

3. *Avoid distracting actions or gestures.* Do not look at your watch, shuffle papers, play with your pencil, or engage in similar distractions when you are listening to someone. These actions suggest to the speaker that you are bored or uninterested. The actions also mean that you probably are not paying full attention to what is being said.

4. *Ask questions.* The critical listener analyzes what he or she hears and asks questions. Asking questions provides clarification and reduces ambiguity, leading to greater understanding. It also assures the speaker that you are listening.

5. *Paraphrase.* Paraphrasing means restating in your own words what the speaker has said. The effective listener uses such phrases as "What I hear you saying is . . ." or "Do you mean . . . ?" Paraphrasing is a check on whether you are listening carefully and accurately.

6. *Avoid interrupting the speaker.* Interruptions can cause the speaker to lose his or her train of thought

and cause the listener to jump to wrong conclusions based on incomplete information.

7. *Do not overtalk.* Most of us prefer talking to listening. However, a good listener knows the importance of taking turns in a conversation.

8. *Make smooth transitions between the roles of speaker and listener.* The effective listener knows how to make the transition from listener role to speaker role, and then back to being a listener. It is important to listen rather than plan what you are going to say next.

3. Be Empathetic

Receivers are empathetic when they try to understand how the sender feels and try to interpret a message from the sender's perspective, rather than viewing a message from only their own point of view.

LO3 Identify the sources of organizational conflict and understand how conflict is handled by individuals.

Organizational Conflict

Organizational conflict often arises as the result of communication breakdowns among individuals or units. **Organizational conflict** is the discord that arises when the goals, interests, or values of different individuals or groups are incompatible and those individuals or groups block or thwart each other's attempts to achieve their objectives.[28] Recall from Chapter 10 how managers can resolve *relationship* and *task-related conflict* within and among groups.

Conflict is an inevitable part of organizational life because the goals of different stakeholders such as managers and workers are often incompatible. Organizational conflict also can exist between departments and divisions that compete for resources or even between managers who may be competing for promotion to the next level in the organizational hierarchy.

Though many people dislike conflict, it is not always dysfunctional. Too little conflict can be as bad as too much conflict, but a medium level of conflict can encourage a variety of perspectives that improve organizational functioning and effectiveness and help decision making. Conflict is a force that needs to be managed rather than eliminated.[29] Managers should never try to eliminate all conflict but rather should try to keep conflict at a moderate and functional level to promote change efforts

organizational conflict
The discord that arises when the goals, interests, or values of different individuals or groups are incompatible and those individuals or groups block or thwart each other's attempts to achieve their objectives.

Too much conflict can be dysfunctional for a high-performing organization.

that benefit the organization. To deal with conflict effectively, managers should understand the sources of conflict in organizations and understand how individuals behave when they are engaged in conflict.

Sources of Organizational Conflict

Organizational conflict can happen between individuals, within a group or department, between groups or departments, or even across organizations. Conflict can arise for a variety of reasons. Within organizations conflict occurs for such reasons as incompatible goals and time horizons, overlapping authority, task interdependencies, incompatible evaluation or reward systems, scarce resources, and status inconsistencies (see Figure 12.4).[30]

Overlapping Authority

Recall from Chapter 6 the organizational structure called a *matrix* structure. The matrix structure groups people and resources by function and product. Team members from different functional areas come together to develop new products. This kind of structure is very flexible and allows for creative innovation in product development. The drawback, as you recall, is that team members report to two bosses: the manager of the functional area, and the leader of the product team. As you can imagine, this dual reporting mechanism may cause conflicting demands on team members who do not know which manager to satisfy first. Also, functional and team managers may come into conflict over precisely who is in charge of which team members and for how long. Overlapping authority, as in the case with the matrix structure, can be a source of conflict.

Task Interdependencies

When people and work units depend on other people and work units for information, materials, or assistance,

► FIGURE 12.4   Sources of Conflict in Organizations

task interdependence exists. Highly interdependent work units require better coordination, communication, and mutual adjustment to maintain work performance. The higher the level of task interdependence, the greater the risk of conflict, because there is a greater chance that each side will disrupt or interfere with the other side's work. Take, for example, the production process of a soft drink manufacturer. The workers that fill, pack, and ship the full bottles depend on the workers who create the glass bottles to send them down the line in an orderly and timely fashion. If there is a problem with the production of the glass bottles, the work at the other end of the line is disrupted.

Incompatible Evaluation or Reward Systems

Often managers develop employee performance and reward systems that create conflict among groups because they contradict and run counter to each group's goals. Continuing with the soft drink manufacturing example, conflict may arise if the bottle producers and the fillers and packers are evaluated for producing different outcomes. Let's say the bottle fillers are evaluated on the quantity of bottles produced and forwarded down the line for filling. Those workers are rewarded for meeting or exceeding the goals set by their manager for the number of bottles produced per shift. At the other end of the production line, the fillers and packers are evaluated on product quality and receive bonuses for minimizing customer complaints and returns. The fillers and packers are therefore motivated to reject any bottles that don't

meet quality standards. But the fewer bottles rejected by employees at the filling end, the bigger the bonuses of employees at the bottle making end. The way that managers designed the evaluation and reward system of the two work groups creates conflict between them. Bottle makers complain the fillers are too picky about quality and the fillers don't like the bottle makers questioning their quality control decisions.

Scarce Resources

When resources are scarce, such as when cutbacks have to be made, people are motivated to compete with others who also need those resources to achieve their objectives. Division heads and plant managers may experience this conflict over allocation of budgets, because there is rarely enough money to meet everyone's needs.

Status Inconsistencies

Unclear job expectations increase the possibility that some people will be working at cross purposes. Often referred to as *role ambiguity,* unclear sets of expectations over responsibilities can lead to conflict and weaken the performance of an organization. Titles carry not only status—that is, formal authority within the hierarchy of an organization—but also expectations about responsibility and accountability. An employee may be asked to take on some managerial tasks without being given the title, status, and recognition of the formal managerial position. This can cause problems between employees who feel they don't have to do what they are asked because the person giving the direction has no status as a manager. Moreover, the person being asked to assume the responsibilities of managing while being denied the power and rewards of the position may come to resent the situation. Status inconsistencies in organizations create conflict.

Incompatible Goals and Time Horizons

One of the main sources of conflict is incompatible goals and time horizons among people or departments. Consider again the relationship between the bottle makers and the bottle fillers on the production line of the soft drink manufacturer. The fillers want to avoid complaints about product quality, whereas the bottle makers want to minimize the number of units rejected by the fillers. The fillers achieve their goal by being meticulous about the quality of bottles packaged and delivered to clients, but this conflicts with the bottle makers' goal of producing as many bottles as possible. These competing objectives cause conflict.

Sometimes different departments have different time constraints for completing their work which create tension between them. For example, the production department of a magazine sets a limit on when the last advertisement has to be booked for the next issue to ensure there is enough time for production and printing. This conflicts with the interests of the salespeople. The salespeople want to close as many sales as possible to maximize their commission. One more day of sales could make a significant difference to their take-home pay, so they constantly try to push back the closing date.

Similarly, the R&D departments are usually operating on a long-term time frame when they develop new products. Product deadlines are set so that marketing and sales departments can create campaigns to promote the new products within a particular budget year. If the research and development of a new product extends beyond the anticipated timeframe, the marketing and sales department might lose their allotted budget. The pressure to finalize the product so that the marketing can begin can create conflict.

Conflict-Handling Behaviours

Regardless of the source of the conflict, knowing how individuals handle conflict is an important skill for the manager who may have to intervene to resolve it. As 19th-century American philosopher and psychologist William James said, "Whenever you're in conflict with someone, there is one factor that can make the difference between damaging your relationship and deepening it.

That factor is attitude."[31] The behaviours for handling conflict fall along two dimensions: *cooperativeness* (the degree to which one party tries to satisfy the other party's concerns) and *assertiveness* (the degree to which one party tries to satisfy his or her own concerns).[32] This can be seen in Figure 12.5. From these two dimensions emerge five conflict-handling behaviours:

- *Avoiding.* Withdrawing from conflict.
- *Competing.* One person tries to satisfy his or her own interests, without regard to the interests of the other party.
- *Compromising.* Each party is concerned about its own goal accomplishment and the goal accomplishment of the other party and is willing to engage in a give-and-take exchange and to make concessions until a reasonable resolution of the conflict is reached.
- *Accommodating.* One person tries to please the other person by putting the other's interests ahead of his or her own.
- *Collaborating.* The parties to a conflict try to satisfy their goals without making any concessions and instead come up with a way to resolve their differences that leaves them both better off.

When the parties to a conflict are willing to cooperate with each other and devise a solution that each finds acceptable (through compromise or collaboration), an organization is more likely to achieve its goals.

Describe conflict management strategies that managers can use to resolve individual and organizational conflict effectively. **LO4**

Conflict Management Strategies

Conflict management strategies that ensure conflicts are resolved in a functional manner focus on individuals, groups, and on the organization as a whole. Below, we describe strategies that focus on individuals: increasing diversity awareness and skills, practising job rotation or temporary assignments, and using permanent transfers or dismissals when necessary. We also describe two strategies that focus on the organization as a whole: changing an organization's structure or culture and directly altering the source of conflict. Finally, distributive and integrative negotiation techniques are analyzed as methods to resolve intergroup conflict.

> **FIGURE 12.5** Dimensions of Conflict-Handling Behaviours

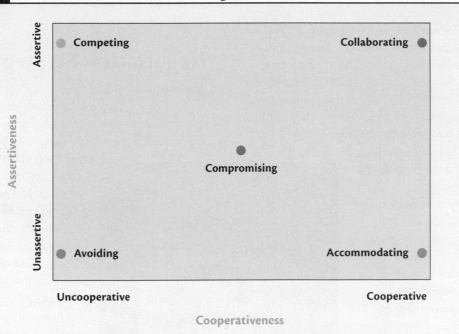

Source: Adapted from K.W. Thomas, "Toward Multi-Dimensional Values in Teaching: The Example of Conflict Behaviors," Table 2: Situations in Which to Use the Five Conflict-Handling Modes as Reported by 28 Chief Executives of Organizations, p. 487. *Academy of Management Review*, Vol. 2, No. 3, July 1977.

Strategies Focused on Individuals

1. *Increasing Awareness of Individual Differences* Much conflict arises because individuals are not aware of how differences in linguistic styles, personalities, backgrounds, and job requirements affect interactions. For example, differences in linguistic styles may lead some men in work teams to talk more and take more credit for ideas than would women in those teams. These communication differences can result in conflict when the men incorrectly assume that the women are uninterested or less capable because they participate less and the women incorrectly assume that the men are being bossy and are not interested in their ideas because they seem to do all the talking. Conflict can also arise when coworkers are unaware of the demands of each other's jobs and place unrealistic expectations on someone to complete a project. When individuals are aware of the source of conflict, they can take steps to interact with each other more effectively. Awareness can be increased through diversity training, open communication, and job rotation or temporary assignments that increase understanding of the work activities and demands that others in the organization face.

2. *Using Permanent Transfers or Dismissals* Sometimes when other conflict resolution strategies do not work, managers may need to take more drastic steps, starting with job rotation and temporary assignment then progressing to permanent transfers or dismissals.

Suppose two first-line managers who work in the same department are always at each other's throats; frequent bitter conflicts arise between them, even though they both seem to get along well with the other people they work with. No matter what their supervisor does to increase their understanding of each other, these conflicts keep occurring. In this case, the supervisor may want to transfer one or both managers so that they do not have to interact as frequently.

When dysfunctionally high levels of conflict occur among top managers who cannot resolve their differences and understand each other, it may be necessary for one of them to leave the company.

Strategies Focused on the Organization

1. *Changing Structure or Culture.* Conflict can signal the need for changes in an organization's structure or culture. Sometimes, managers can effectively resolve conflict by changing the organizational structure they use to group people and tasks.[33] As an organization grows, for example, the *functional structure* that was effective when the organization was small may no longer be effective, and a shift to a product structure might effectively resolve conflicts (see Chapter 6).

Managers also can effectively resolve conflicts by increasing levels of integration in an organization. When individuals from different departments are assigned to the same team, they can directly resolve issues on the spot, rather than going through departments.

Sometimes managers may need to take steps to change an organization's culture to resolve conflicts (see Chapter 7). Norms and values in an organizational culture might inadvertently promote dysfunctionally high levels of conflicts that are difficult to resolve. For instance, norms that stress respect for formal authority may create conflict that is difficult to resolve when an organization creates self-managed work teams. Values stressing individual competition may make it difficult to resolve conflicts when organizational members need to put others' interests ahead of their own. In circumstances such as these, taking steps to change norms and values can be an effective conflict-resolution strategy.

2. *Altering the Source of Conflict.* When conflict is due to overlapping authority, status inconsistencies, and incompatible evaluation or reward systems, managers can sometimes effectively resolve the conflict by directly altering the source of conflict. For example, managers can clarify the chain of command and reassign tasks and responsibilities to resolve conflicts due to overlapping authority.

> "Whenever you're in conflict with someone, there is one factor that can make the difference between damaging your relationship and deepening it. That factor is attitude."
>
> *William James*

negotiation A method of conflict resolution in which the parties in conflict consider various alternative ways to allocate resources to each other in order to come up with a solution acceptable to them all.

distributive negotiation Adversarial negotiation in which the parties in conflict compete to win the most resources while conceding as little as possible.

integrative bargaining Cooperative negotiation in which the parties in conflict work together to achieve a resolution that is good for them all.

Differentiate between distributive and integrative bargaining and demonstrate how negotiation can be used to resolve intergroup conflict. **LO5**

Negotiation Strategies

A particularly important conflict-resolution technique for managers and other organizational members to use in situations in which the parties to a conflict have approximately equal levels of power is negotiation. During **negotiation,** the parties to a conflict try to come up with a solution acceptable to themselves by considering various alternative ways to allocate resources to each other.[34]

There are two major types of negotiation—distributive negotiation and integrative bargaining.[35] In **distributive negotiation,** the parties perceive that they have a "fixed pie" of resources that they need to divide up.[36] They take a competitive, adversarial stance. Each party realizes that he or she must concede something but is out to get the lion's share of resources.[37] The parties see no need to interact with each other in a collaborative way and do not care if their interpersonal relationship is damaged or destroyed by their competitive negotiations.[38] Distributive negotiation tends to take on a win–lose orientation. The parties tend to rely on power and politics to gain an advantage. A win–lose situation may occasionally be appropriate when the conflict really is over a fixed resource, but few organizational conflicts are due to perfectly opposing interests and fixed resources. In most cases, creative solutions are possible.

In **integrative bargaining,** the parties adopt a win–win orientation by perceiving that they might be able to increase the resource pie by trying to come up with a creative solution to the conflict. They do not view the conflict competitively, as a win-or-lose situation; instead, they view it cooperatively, as a win–win situation in which all parties can gain. Integrative bargaining is characterized by trust, information sharing, and the desire of all parties to achieve a good resolution of the conflict.[39] For the conflicting parties to show a commitment to integrative bargaining, each side

Negotiating an agreement should be a win–win situation.

would need to figure out ways to address some of the needs of the other, rather than simply taking an adversarial position.

There are five strategies that individuals can rely on to increase the odds of a win–win solution[40]:

- *Emphasize the big-picture goals.* This reminds individuals that they are working together for a larger purpose or goal despite their disagreements.

- *Focus on the problem, not the people.* All parties to a conflict need to keep focused on the source of the conflict and avoid the temptation to discredit each other by personalizing the conflict.

- *Focus on interests, not demands.* Demands are what a person wants, and interests are why the person wants them. When two people are in conflict, it is unlikely that the demands of both can be met. Their underlying interests often can be met, creating a win–win solution.

- *Create new options for joint gain.* Rather than having a fixed set of alternatives from which to choose, the parties can come up with new alternatives that might even expand the resource pie.

- *Focus on what is fair.* Emphasizing fairness will help the parties come to a mutual agreement about what the best solution to the problem is.

Any and all of these strategies would help the conflicting parties negotiate with each other more effectively. When managers pursue these five strategies and encourage other organizational members to do so, they are more likely to resolve their conflicts effectively. In addition, throughout the negotiation process, managers and other organizational members need to be aware of, and on their guard against, the biases that can lead to faulty decision making (see Chapter 4).[41]

Collective Bargaining

Recall from Chapter 11 that *collective bargaining* is negotiation between labour unions and managers to resolve conflicts and disputes about important issues such as working hours, wages, benefits, working conditions, and job security. Once an agreement between management and union members has been reached (sometimes with the help of a neutral third party called a *mediator*), union leaders and managers sign a contract spelling out the terms of the collective bargaining. This is called a *collective agreement.*

Collective bargaining is an ongoing consideration in labour relations. After an agreement is signed it must be administered, and the rules governing working conditions must be followed by both parties. However, disagreement and conflicts can arise over the interpretation of the contract. In these cases, a neutral third party known as an *arbitrator* is usually called in to resolve the conflict. An important component of a collective agreement is a *grievance procedure* through which workers who feel they are not being fairly treated are allowed to voice their concerns and have their interests represented by the union. Employees who feel they were unjustly fired in violation of a union contract, for example, may file a grievance, have the union represent them, and get their jobs back if an arbitrator agrees with them. See Chapter 11 for more on labour relations.

Summary and Review

LO1 The Importance of Communication in Organizations Effective communication is the sharing of information between two or more individuals or groups to reach a common understanding. Good communication is necessary for an organization to gain a competitive advantage. Communication takes place in a cyclical process that has two phases: *transmission* and *feedback.*

LO2 Information Richness and Communication Media Information richness is the amount of information a communication medium can carry and the extent to which the medium enables the sender and receiver to reach a common understanding. Four categories of communication media in descending order of information richness are *face-to-face communication* (includes videoconferences), *spoken communication electronically transmitted* (includes voice mail), *personally addressed written communication* (includes email and texting), and *impersonal written communication.* Advances in technology have significantly affected managerial communication.

LO3 Organizational Conflict Organizational conflict is the discord that arises when the goals, interests, or values of different individuals or groups clash, and those individuals or groups block or thwart each other's attempts to achieve their objectives. Sources of organizational conflict include *incompatible goals* and *time horizons, overlapping authority, task interdependencies, incompatible evaluation and reward systems, scarce resources,* and *status inconsistencies.*

LO4 Conflict Management Strategies Individuals handle conflict along two dimensions, their level of cooperativeness and their level of assertiveness, which give rise to five types of conflict-handling behaviours: *competing, avoiding, compromising, accommodating,* and *collaborating.* The collaboration behaviour tends to yield a win–win resolution. Conflict management strategies focused on individuals include increasing awareness of the sources of conflict, increasing diversity awareness and skills, and using permanent transfers or dismissals when necessary. Strategies focused on the whole organization include changing an organization's structure or culture and altering the source of conflict.

LO5 Negotiation Strategies Negotiation is a conflict resolution technique used when parties have approximately equal levels of power and try to come up with an acceptable way to allocate resources to each other. In *distributive negotiation,* the parties perceive that there is a fixed level of resources for them to allocate, and each competes to receive as much as possible at the expense of the others. In *integrative bargaining,* the parties perceive that they may be able to increase the resource pie by coming up with a creative solution to the conflict, trusting each other, and cooperating with each other to achieve a win–win resolution. Five strategies that managers can use to facilitate integrative bargaining are to emphasize big-picture goals; focus on the problem, not the people; focus on interests, not demands; create new options for joint gain; and focus on what is fair. *Collective bargaining* is the process through which labour unions and managers negotiate collective agreements.

KEY TERMS

applications software	information richness	nonverbal communication
artificial intelligence	integrative bargaining	operating system
communication	jargon	software
decoding	management by wandering	organizational conflict
distributive negotiation	around (MBWA)	perception
encoding	medium	receiver
filtering	message	rumours
grapevine	negotiation	sender
information distortion	networking	verbal communication
information overload	noise	

WRAP-UP TO OPENING CASE

Canadian Drug Maker Goes Social to Help Supply Chain Crisis

A few years ago, a Canadian pharmaceutical company found that it was in constant crisis mode, and its way out of the chaos lay in getting everyone to communicate. After having read and understood the concepts in this chapter, you should be able to answer the following questions:

1. *In what ways was communication at Ratiopharm Canada ineffective?*

ANSWER: Effective communication occurs when both the sender and the receiver of the message have the same understanding in a timely manner. Barriers to effective communication may stem from messages being unclear, incomplete, or difficult to understand, when they are sent over an inappropriate medium, or when no provision for feedback is made. In this case, the problem stemmed from a lack of communication in the supply chain. If something went wrong anywhere in the supply chain process, it might be two to four months before the people who needed to know found out about it.

2. *How did going "social" help Ratiopharm Canada solve its communication problems?*

ANSWER: Using social collaboration tools such as Web 2.0, SharePoint, Strategy-Nets, and Moxie Software fixed Ratiopharm's communication problems. These social tools allowed employees to communicate and solve problems anywhere along the supply chain, and eventually in customer service, sales, and marketing. Using message board technology, employees would post the problem and others would solve it, cutting the detection and fixing time down from four months to a few hours. The expanded use of collaboration software, and the move to richer and more varied tools, helped the company achieve a service level of 98 percent for three years in a row. Ratiopharm was also able to manufacture its products three times faster, improving its ability to meet demand.

3. *What degree of information richness is achieved through social media channels?*

ANSWER: Information richness is the amount of information a communication medium can carry and the extent to which the medium enables sender and receiver to reach a common understanding. Using social media channels such as tools for real-time conversations, blogs, wikis, and document sharing allows employees at Ratiopharm to have a high level of richness. Media high in information richness are able to carry a lot of information and generally enable receivers and senders to come to a common understanding and solve problems quickly.

Management in Action

TOPICS FOR DISCUSSION AND ACTION

LEVEL 1 Knowledge & Comprehension

1. Describe the communication process. Why is perception important?

2. Describe the sources of organizational conflict. Which type of strategies—those that focus on the individual or those that focus on the structure and culture of the organization—are suitable to diminish each source?

3. Describe five types of conflict-handling behaviours.

LEVEL 2 Application & Analysis

4. Explain why ineffective communication occurs.

5. Interview a manager to determine the kinds of conflicts that occur in the organization and the strategies that are used to manage them.

6. Which medium (or media) do you think would be appropriate for a manager to use when sending the following messages to a subordinate?

   a. Getting a raise

   b. Not receiving a promotion

   c. Disciplining an employee for being consistently late

   d. Adding job responsibilities

   e. Creating the schedule for company holidays for the upcoming year. Explain your choices.

LEVEL 3 Synthesis & Evaluation

7. Why is integrative bargaining a more effective way of resolving conflicts than is distributive negotiation?

8. Evaluate the advances in information technology and discuss their limitations for the manager who wants to communicate effectively.

9. Listen to the podcast by Jack and Suzy Welch called "The Connected Leader: How Will the Internet Change Leadership?" at www.businessweek.com/mediacenter/qt/podcasts/welchway/welchway_06_13_08.mp3. How do they describe the changes to the manager's job in the way that information is communicated via the Internet?

SELF-REFLECTION EXERCISE

Consider a person with whom you have had difficulty communicating. Using the communication skills for senders as a start, analyze what has gone wrong with the communication process with that person. What can be done to improve communication? To what extent did sender and receiver problems contribute to communication breakdown?

SMALL GROUP BREAKOUT EXERCISE

Negotiating a Solution

Form groups of three or four. One member of your group will play the role of Jane Rister, one member will play the role of Michael Schwartz, and one or two members will be observer(s) and spokesperson(s) for your group.

Jane Rister and Michael Schwartz are assistant managers in a large department store. They report directly to the store manager. Today they are meeting to discuss important problems that they need to solve but on which they disagree.

The first problem hinges on the fact that either Rister or Schwartz needs to be on duty whenever the store is open. For the last six months, Rister has taken most of the least desirable hours (nights and weekends). They are planning their schedules for the next six months. Rister hopes Schwartz will take more of the undesirable times, but Schwartz has informed Rister that his wife has just started a nursing job that requires her to work weekends, so he needs to stay home on weekends to take care of their infant daughter.

The second problem concerns a department manager who has had a hard time retaining sales people in his department. The turnover rate in his department is twice that of the other departments in the store. Rister thinks the manager is ineffective and wants to fire him. Schwartz thinks the high turnover is a fluke and the manager is effective.

The last problem concerns Rister's and Schwartz's vacation schedules. Both managers want to take off the week of July 1, but, as mentioned above, one of them needs to be in the store whenever it is open.

1. The group members playing Rister and Schwartz assume their roles and negotiate a solution to these three problems.

2. Observers take notes on how Rister and Schwartz negotiate solutions to their problems.

3. Observers determine the extent to which Rister and Schwartz use distributive negotiation or integrative bargaining to resolve their conflicts.

4. When called on by the instructor, observers communicate to the rest of the class how Rister and Schwartz resolved their conflicts, whether they used distributive negotiation or integrative bargaining, and their actual solutions.

BUSINESS PLANNING EXERCISE

Your professor may ask you to write a business plan for a new venture or a strategic plan for an existing venture. At the end of every chapter, you will have an opportunity to apply managerial and organizational concepts to the exercise of writing a business plan. Refer to Appendix A.

After reading this chapter you and your team realize that you will have to negotiate with many different people when operating your venture.

1. Make a list of all the parties you will have to negotiate with in order to operate the venture.

2. Which negotiation strategy will you use with each of the parties, and why?

MANAGING ETHICALLY EXERCISE

About 75 percent of medium and large companies that were surveyed engaged in some kind of monitoring of employees' email and Internet activities. Critics say this is an invasion of privacy. Proponents say that Web surfing costs millions of dollars in lost productivity. What is your opinion of Web surfing? To what extent should it be allowed? When does Internet use at work become unethical? To what extent should it be monitored? When does monitoring become unethical?

MANAGEMENT CHALLENGE EXERCISE

Assume you are a middle-level manager at a data processing company. After monitoring the online user statistics, it is evident that several employees are using company time to send personal emails. You have been asked by your boss to create a company policy on personal emails at work and send a memo to the employees describing it. Share your thoughts with two other students, and consolidate everyone's thoughts on the policy into one memo.

MANAGEMENT PORTFOLIO PROJECT

Answer the following questions about the organization you have chosen to follow:

1. What kinds of communication media are commonly used in this organization for the various types of messages? Are the media appropriate for the messages?

2. Have there been any examples of organizational conflict? What was the nature of the conflict, and how was it resolved?

VIDEO MANAGEMENT CASE   connect

Could You Go Without Technology for a Week?

In this NBC feature, *Forbes* editor Dennis Neal tries to go a week without his cell phone, BlackBerry, and email and finds it nearly impossible to do his job, communicate with his family, and manage personal business.

1. How do cell phones and email rank on the information richness scale? When would making a phone call be more effective than sending an email, and vice versa?

2. What are the advantages and disadvantages of using email to communicate?

3. What are some indications—from Dennis Neal's experience and your observations—that people may be too dependent on communications technology?

Management Case

Anthony Lacavera—CEO Wind Mobile[42]

Wind Mobile CEO Tony Lacavera would like to see the government clamp down the regulations now in place regarding tower sharing. He says while it sounds good in theory to have the Big Three share infrastructure, having it actually transpire is often a slow, arduous process.

"We've been very vocal about the need for tower sharing and roaming policies to be overhauled and penalties to be put in place when it doesn't happen," Lacavera tells us.

"A very big part of our network rollout we're trying to make is a collaborative effort particularly in certain municipalities where new towers would not be an ideal thing for residents and businesses for a variety of reasons."

"We've been very clear to both industry officials and competitors that we're going to build our network regardless, and of course the big guys would like to slow us down as much as possible," he continued. "Unfortunately the government is not pushing these guys enough in cases where it makes sense to share and they know they can get away with not working cooperatively with competitors."

Lacavera says it doesn't amount to an actual barrier, but admits it does slow companies such as his down considerably. Tower sharing and roaming remain critical issues for Wind Mobile.

"Even more important for us is that the government has really cut off the lifeblood of new competitors and not in not permitting us to buy sufficient spectrum and not even acknowledging the grotesque inequity and imbalance there is in spectrum allocation in this country with three carriers that operate two networks owning over 85 per cent of all the spectrum."

While Lacavera doesn't squarely lay blame on the slowdown on the Ministry of Industry and Minister Christian Paradis, it's obvious he'd like to see more done at the federal level.

"I recognize there are a lot of competing agendas here in trying to generate cooperation and I don't want to diminish the complexity of the task in front of him (Paradis)," Lacavera notes. "However, I do think he's capitulating to the incumbent interests when he doesn't push them to share infrastructure towers where they're clearly not strategic assets for them."

There's a lot of sites where Wind Mobile has built stand-alone towers in eyesight of a Bell tower that they are sharing with Telus and a Rogers tower, which to Lacavera seems to make little, if any, sense at all.

"We're quite willing to pay a commercial level of rent to put our equipment on the towers, which would generate new revenue for them and lower costs."

"If I was in their shoes I'd probably be trying to put up the same obstacles," Lacavera admits. "But someone has to get them to stop playing these games."

Clearly that someone needs to be the federal government.

What baffles Lacavera and some of the other smaller telecom companies is that the obstacles are very transparent, leaving them wondering why it continues to be allowed. It makes them feel as if there is no refereeing system to make it stop—and clearly that referee needs to be the federal government. Lacavera also doesn't see why the Big Three are so worried about sharing.

"I've always made the point that, in the case with Rogers, instead of stopping us from sharing with you, why don't you just offer your customers a better product and service?"

Meanwhile, Minister of Industry Christian Paradis noted that there's no plan on the horizon to ease restrictions on foreign ownership for the larger telecoms—Bell, Telus and Rogers, but in any event, Lacavera says that's not a big concern to him or likely any of the other small telecoms.

"There's no meaningful difference to small competitors whether they open up to the big guys or not," he states. "Because they already have a significant and established market presence they have a very attractive cost of capital."

In order for some of the fledgling telecoms to remain viable, it's a distinct possibility that there will need to be some consolidation and convergence of assets as time goes on. It could be in the form of mergers or acquisitions, or the sharing of customer bases and networks. Whether they band together or go it alone, one thing is certain based on what the government has come up with—the players must cooperate in order to survive.

Over the long haul it's not unrealistic to believe companies such as Wind Mobile, Public Mobile and Mobilicity may try and combine forces in order to have a better chance at taking on the giants in the industry.

1. What is the root of the conflict experienced by Wind Mobile?

2. Put yourself in the position of management consultant to Wind Mobile. What recommendations to the CEO would you make to resolve the situation?

3. Is integrative or distributive bargaining more appropriate in this case? Why?

McGraw Hill connect™

Connect allows you to practise important concepts at your own pace and on your own schedule, with 24/7 online access to an eBook, practice quizzes, video cases, interactive exercises, study tools, and more.

End of Part V: Continuing Case

CARROT TOPS: MANAGING HIGH PERFORMANCE LEVELS

Janet's team of courteous and knowledgeable drivers know their way around the city. Sometimes, however, she gets complaints from the drivers that the schedules and routes she assigns them leads them to drop off early or late or unable to deliver at all. Some have suggested she overmanages the drivers; that she should empower them to set their own routes and schedules.

To make matters worse, another grocery store manager in the area announced in a press release that they have started home delivery. This is a relatively new store and fortunately, Janet thought, although they offer organic food, it is of inferior quality. Nevertheless, one of the five drivers Janet supervises has quit and gone to work for the competition. He voiced his dissatisfaction with Janet's management methods to anyone who would listen and was not interested in working out any differences they had. He soon had all the drivers complaining, but not offering any solutions. Janet admits that the organization of the delivery system is ad hoc, understaffed, and could be improved, but she believes that her employees should nevertheless follow her directions. She is, after all, their boss! Now she will have to go through the hassle of recruiting, hiring, and keeping a new driver.

Drawing on all segments of this case:

1. What type of team structure would you recommend Janet use with the drivers to encourage high performance?
2. Suggest a total rewards strategy for motivating the drivers.
3. Identify an example of groupthink.
4. Describe the conflict handling behaviour adopted (a) by the driver who quit, and (b) by Janet.
5. Using all of the components of human resources management, describe the process Janet should use to hire a new driver for Carrot Tops.
6. Is Janet a transformational or transactional leader? Explain your answer.

PART VI

CHAPTER 13

Managing Control and Operations

LEARNING OUTCOMES

LO1 Define organizational control and discuss how it contributes to gaining a competitive advantage and why it is important to overall performance.

LO2 Describe the steps in the process of control.

LO3 Describe three systems of control used in operations management.

LO4 Identify how output, behavioural, and clan controls coordinate and motivate employees to achieve organizational goals.

LO5 Explain how *innovative* and *conservative* cultures control managerial action.

Opening Case

A Husky Solution for Organizational Control[1]

One company that has become a poster child for innovative control measures and progressive employee management is Husky Injection Molding Systems of Bolton, Ontario. The company has constructed a culture of innovation and proactively addresses issues of control in the workplace.

Husky Injection Molding Systems is a global supplier of injection moulding equipment and services to the plastics industry. With one of the broadest product lines in the industry, customers use Husky equipment and services to manufacture a wide range of products, such as bottles and caps for beverages, containers for food, medical components, and consumer electronic parts. The company has more than 40 service and sales offices, supporting customers in more than 100 countries. Husky's manufacturing facilities are located in Canada, the United States, Luxembourg, Austria, and China.[2]

Husky offers a range of software tools that are designed for predictive, preventative, and proactive maintenance, as well as productivity and process monitoring. This provides customers with real-time solutions to maximize productivity, more accurately monitor factory processes, and resolve equipment problems to reduce downtime.[3]

In addition to manufacturing controls, Husky offers employees an on-site daycare centre, and in the onsite cafeterias, healthy options are served. Beef, chicken, fish, tofu, and herbal teas are available, along with a customized salad bar.

Husky also has a wellness centre that employs a naturopath and a full-time massage therapist and chiropractor. At the fitness centre,

yoga is among the daily classes on offer. Husky sees employee wellness as a priority and does realize the return on investment. The company's rate of absenteeism is below the national average. Spending on its drug plan, which also covers naturopathic remedies, comes in at half the national average. Workers' Compensation Board claims are 1.35 percent for every 200 000 hours of operation, compared with the industry average of 5.5 percent per 200 000 hours. The company also offers the usual employee assistance programs for those who are in distress—which takes a burden off managers.

After reading and understanding the concepts in this chapter, you should be able to answer the following question:

1. *What is Husky doing to create organizational control?*

Overview

As discussed in Chapter 6, one major task facing managers is organizing—that is, establishing the structure of task and reporting relationships that allows organizational members to use resources most efficiently and effectively. Structure alone, however, does not provide the incentive or motivation for people to behave in ways that help achieve organizational goals. The purpose of organizational control is to provide managers with a means of motivating subordinates to work toward achieving organizational goals, and to provide managers with specific feedback on how well an organization and its members are performing. Organizational structure provides an organization with a skeleton, to which organizational control and culture add the muscles, sinews, nerves, and sensations that allow managers to regulate and govern the organization's activities. The managerial functions of organizing and controlling are inseparable, and effective managers, such as those at Husky in the opening case, must learn to make them work together harmoniously.

In this chapter, we look in detail at the nature of organizational control and describe the steps in the control process. We discuss three systems of control used in operations and supply chain management. Next we address corporate governance issues. How is managerial behaviour held accountable? We then look at types of controls managers can use to motivate and control resources and people: *output, behavioural,* and *clan controls*. Finally, we discuss how *innovative* and *conservative* cultures shape managerial approaches to planning, organizing, leading, and controlling.[4] By the end of this chapter, you will appreciate the rich variety of control measures available to managers and understand why developing an appropriate control system is vital to increasing the performance of an organization and its members.

Controlling ensures the smooth operation of the organization.

hope will allow the organization to use resources most effectively to create value for customers. In *controlling,* managers monitor and evaluate whether their organization's strategy and structure are working as intended, how they could be improved, and how they might be changed if they are not working.

Control, however, does not mean just reacting to events after they have occurred. It also means keeping an organization on track, anticipating events that might occur, and then changing the organization to respond to whatever opportunities or threats have been identified. Control is concerned with keeping employees motivated, focused on the important productivity problems confronting the organization, and working together to make the changes that will help an organization perform better over time. As the opening case illustrates, Husky Injection Molding develops innovative approaches to controlling.

Organizational Control and Building a Competitive Advantage

To understand the importance of organizational control, consider how it helps managers obtain superior efficiency, quality, responsiveness to customers, and innovation—the four building blocks of competitive advantage.

To determine how efficiently they are using their resources, managers must be able to accurately measure how many units of inputs (raw materials, human resources, and so on) are being used to produce a unit of output. Managers also must be able to measure how many units of outputs (goods and services) are being produced. Increases in **productivity**, the output of goods and services relative to

LO1 Define organizational control and discuss how it contributes to gaining a competitive advantage and why it is important to overall performance.

What Is Organizational Control?

As noted in Chapter 1, **controlling** is the process that managers use to monitor and evaluate how efficiently and effectively an organization and its members are achieving organizational goals and taking action to maintain or improve performance. As discussed in previous chapters, in *planning* and *organizing* managers develop the organizational strategy and then create the structure that they

controlling The process of monitoring and evaluating how well an organization is achieving its goals and taking action to maintain or improve performance; one of the four principal functions of management.

productivity The output of goods and services relative to the inputs.

the inputs, is the measure of an organization's efficiency. A control system contains the measures or yardsticks that allow managers to assess how efficiently the organization is producing goods and services. Managers can use **benchmarking**, comparing their performance on specific dimensions with the performance of high-performing organizations to decide how to increase productivity. For example, when Xerox was doing poorly in the 1980s it benchmarked the efficiency of its distribution operations against those of L.L. Bean, the efficiency of its central computer operations against those of John Deere, and its marketing abilities against those of Procter & Gamble. Those companies are renowned for their skills in those different areas, and by studying how they performed, Xerox was able to dramatically increase its own performance.

Moreover, if managers experiment with changing the way the organization produces goods and services to find a more efficient way of producing them, managers can adopt **Six Sigma** principles. Adopting these principles ensures that an organization's products and services are as free of errors or defects as possible through a variety of human resources and customer service initiatives. Jack Welch, former CEO of General Electric Company, has indicated that these initiatives have saved his company millions of dollars, and other companies, such as Maple Leaf Foods, TD Financial Group, Whirlpool, and Canadian Pacific, also have implemented Six Sigma initiatives. In order for such initiatives to be effective, however, top managers have to be committed to qualifying as Six Sigma "black belts," employees must be motivated, and there must be demand for the products or services of the organization in the first place. For example, if top managers are not committed to the quality initiative, they may not devote the necessary time and resources to make it work and may lose interest in it prematurely.[5]

Controlling is the key to organizational success.

Today, much of the competition among organizations revolves around increasing the quality of goods and services. In the car industry, for example, cars within each price range compete against one another in features, design, and reliability. Thus, whether a customer will buy a Ford Taurus, GM Grand Prix, Chrysler Sebring, Toyota Camry, or Honda Accord depends significantly on the quality of each product. Organizational control is important in determining the quality of goods and services because it gives managers feedback on product quality. If the managers of carmakers consistently measure the number of customer complaints and the number of new cars returned for repairs, or if school principals measure how many students drop out of school or how achievement scores on nationally based tests vary over time, they have a good indication of how much quality they have built into their product—be it an educated student or a car that does not break down. **Total quality management (TQM)** is an approach to continuous improvement based on creating superior quality at every stage of production through teamwork or quality circles used to solve production problems. The teams who actually do the work and perform the tasks make decisions or recommendations on how to improve the process. Effective managers create a control system that consistently monitors the quality of goods and services so that they can make continuous improvements to quality—an approach to change that gives them a competitive advantage.

Managers can also help make their organizations more responsive to customers if they develop a control system that allows them to evaluate how well customer-contact employees are performing their jobs. Monitoring employee behaviour can help managers find ways to increase employees' performance levels, perhaps by revealing areas in which skill training can help employees or by finding new procedures that allow employees to perform their jobs better. When employees know that their behaviours are being monitored, they may also have more incentive to be helpful and consistent in how they act toward customers. To improve customer service, for example, Ford regularly surveys customers about their experiences with particular Ford dealers. If a dealership receives too many customer complaints, Ford's managers investigate the dealership to uncover the sources of the problems and suggest solutions; if necessary, they might

benchmarking Comparing performance on specific dimensions with the performance of high-performing organizations.

Six Sigma A technique for improving performance based on error-free production and service provision.

total quality management (TQM) An approach to continuous improvements in quality at every stage of production.

> **FIGURE 13.1** The Importance of Control

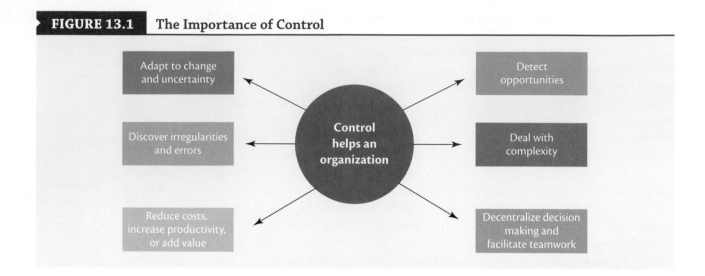

Adapt to change and uncertainty

Discover irregularities and errors

Reduce costs, increase productivity, or add value

Control helps an organization

Detect opportunities

Deal with complexity

Decentralize decision making and facilitate teamwork

even threaten to reduce the number of cars a dealership receives to force the dealer to improve the quality of its customer service.

Finally, controlling can raise the level of innovation in an organization. Successful innovation takes place when managers create an organizational setting in which employees feel empowered to be creative and in which authority is decentralized to employees so that they feel free to experiment and take risks. Deciding on the appropriate control systems to encourage risk taking is an important management challenge in developing an innovative organizational culture, as we discussed in Chapter 7.

The Importance of Control to Organizational Performance

Control systems are intended to make organizations more successful. As we see in Figure 13.1, they help managers adapt to change and uncertainty, discover irregularities and errors, reduce costs, increase productivity or add value, detect opportunities, deal with complexity, decentralize decision making, and facilitate teamwork. See Figure 13.1.[6]

1. *Adapt to change and uncertainty.* We described in Chapter 2 how managers face uncertain task and external environments. New suppliers and customers can appear, as well as new technologies and regulations. Control systems help managers anticipate these changes and be prepared for them.

2. *Discover irregularities and errors.* There may be problems with quality control, customer service, or even human resource management. Control systems help managers uncover these problems before they become too serious to overcome.

3. *Reduce costs, increase productivity, or add value.* Control systems can be used to reduce labour or production costs, to improve productivity, or to add value to a product, making it more attractive to a customer.

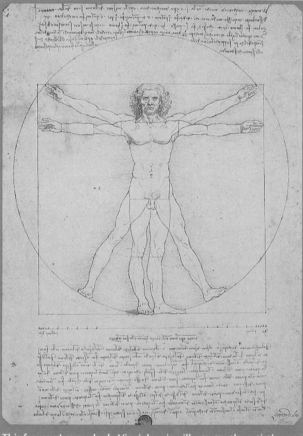

This famous Leonardo da Vinci drawing illustrates the artist's concern for understanding how the human body controls its own movements and how the different parts of the body work together to maintain the body's integrity. The interconnection of the body is similar to the way in which various departments operate in an organization.

4. *Detect opportunities.* Control systems can help managers identify new markets, demographic changes, new suppliers, and other opportunities.

5. *Deal with complexity.* When organizations become large, it sometimes becomes impossible to know what the different units are doing. This is particularly the case when two companies merge. There may be redundancies in product lines or employees. Control systems help managers deal with these complexities.

6. *Decentralize decision making and facilitate teamwork.* When control systems are in place, managers can allow employees to make more decisions, and work in teams.

LO2 Describe the steps in the process of control.

Steps in the Control Process

The control process can be broken down into four steps: *establishing standards of performance,* then *measuring, comparing,* and *evaluating actual performance* (see Figure 13.2).[7]

Step 1: Establish the Standards of Performance

At Step 1 in the control process, managers decide on the standards of performance, goals, or targets that they will use to evaluate the performance of either the entire organization or some part of it, such as a division, a function, or an individual. The standards of performance that managers select measure efficiency, quality, responsiveness to customers, and innovation.[8] If managers decide to pursue a low-cost strategy, for example, they need to measure efficiency at all levels in the organization.

At the corporate level, a standard of performance that measures efficiency is *operating costs*—the actual costs associated with producing goods and services, including all employee-related costs. Top managers might set a corporate goal of "reducing operating costs by 10 percent for the next three years" to increase efficiency. Corporate managers might then evaluate divisional managers for their ability to reduce operating costs within their respective divisions, and divisional managers might set cost-savings targets for functional managers. Thus, performance standards selected at one level affect those at the other levels, and ultimately individual managers are evaluated for their ability to reduce costs. For example,

> **FIGURE 13.2** **Steps in Organizational Control**

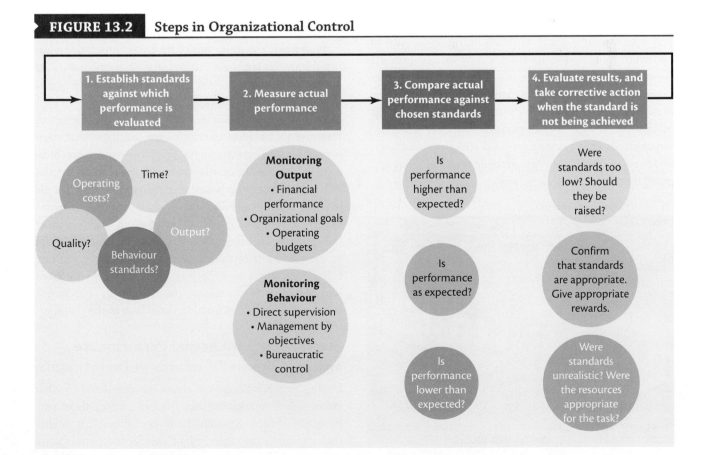

S.I. Newhouse, the owner of Condé Nast Publications Inc., which produces magazines such as *GQ, Vanity Fair, Vogue,* and *Wired,* started an across-the-board attempt to reduce costs so that he could reverse the company's losses and instructed all divisional managers to begin a cost-cutting program. When Newhouse decided to retire, he chose Steven T. Florio to replace him. Florio had been the division head who had been most successful in reducing costs and increasing efficiency at *The New Yorker* magazine.

Managers can set a variety of standards, including time, output, quality, and behaviour standards. *Time standards* refer to how long it is supposed to take to complete a task. Some companies, for instance, instruct staff that all emails must be answered within 24 hours. *Output standards* refer to the quantity of the service or product the employee is to produce. *Quality standards* refer to the level of quality expected in the delivery of goods or services. For instance, a company might set what it considers an acceptable level of defects. Or a retail store might set a standard of one complaint per thousand customers served. Finally, a company might set *behaviour standards,* which can govern such factors as hours worked, dress code, or how one interacts with others.

Managers must be careful to choose standards of performance that are not harmful in unintended ways. If managers focus on just one issue (such as efficiency) and ignore others (such as determining what customers really want and innovating a new line of products to satisfy them), managers may end up hurting their organization's performance. Being aware of this threat, managers at Husky take a proactive approach to organizational control and emphasize not only efficiency (what needs to get done), but also effectiveness (how it is done) by creating an organizational culture that supports their employees' well-being.

Husky takes a proactive approach to organizational control.

Step 2: Measure Actual Performance

Once managers have decided which standards or targets they will use to evaluate performance, the next step in the control process is to measure actual performance. In practice, managers can measure or evaluate two things: (1) the actual *outputs* that result from the behaviour of their members and (2) the *behaviours* themselves (hence the terms *output control* and *behaviour control*).[9]

Sometimes both outputs and behaviours can be easily measured. Measuring outputs and evaluating behaviour are relatively easy in a fast-food restaurant, for example, because employees are performing routine tasks. Managers of a fast-food restaurant can measure outputs quite easily by counting how many customers their employees serve and how much money customers spend. Managers can easily observe each employee's behaviour and quickly take action to solve any problems that may arise.

When an organization and its members perform complex, nonroutine activities that are difficult to measure, it is much more difficult for managers to measure outputs or behaviour.[10] It is very difficult, for example, for managers in charge of R&D departments at RIM or TELUS to measure performance or to evaluate the performance of individual members because it can take 5 or 10 years to determine whether the new products that scientists are developing are going to be profitable. Moreover, it is impossible for a manager to measure how creative a research scientist is by watching his or her actions.

In general, the more nonroutine or complex organizational activities are, the harder it is for managers to measure outputs or behaviours.[11] Outputs, however, are usually easier to measure than behaviours because they are more tangible and objective. Therefore, the first kinds of performance measures that managers tend to use are those that measure outputs. Then managers develop performance measures or standards that allow them to evaluate behaviours in order to determine whether employees at all levels are working toward organizational goals. Some simple behaviour measures are: Do employees come to work on time? Do employees consistently follow the established rules for greeting and serving customers? Each type of output and behaviour control and the way it is used at the different organizational levels—corporate, divisional, functional, and individual—is discussed in detail later in the chapter.

Step 3: Compare Actual Performance against Chosen Standards of Performance

During Step 3, managers evaluate whether—and to what extent—performance deviates from the standards of performance chosen in Step 1. If performance is higher than expected, managers might decide that performance

FIGURE 13.3 Variance Analysis

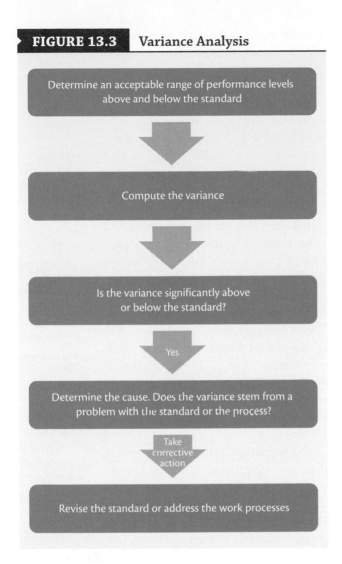

Determine an acceptable range of performance levels above and below the standard

Compute the variance

Is the variance significantly above or below the standard?

Yes

Determine the cause. Does the variance stem from a problem with the standard or the process?

Take corrective action

Revise the standard or address the work processes

standards are too low and may raise them for the next period to challenge subordinates.[12] Managers at Japanese companies are well known for the way they try to raise performance in manufacturing settings by constantly raising performance standards to motivate managers and employees to find new ways to reduce costs or increase quality.

However, if performance is too low and standards were not reached, or if standards were set so high that employees could not achieve them, managers must decide whether the deviation is substantial enough to warrant taking corrective action.[13] A variance analysis can be used to determine if corrective action is appropriate. See Figure 13.3. If managers are to take any form of corrective action, Step 4 is necessary.

Step 4: Evaluate the Result and Initiate Corrective Action if Necessary

The final step in the control process is to evaluate the results and take corrective action if necessary to meet performance standards. Whether performance standards have been met or not, managers can learn a great deal during this step: If managers decide that the level of performance is unacceptable, they must try to solve the problem. Sometimes, performance problems occur because the standard was too high—for example, a sales target was too optimistic and impossible to achieve. In this case, adopting more realistic standards can reduce the gap between actual performance and desired performance. However, if managers determine that something in the situation is causing the problem, then to raise performance they will need to change the way in which resources are being used.[14] Perhaps the latest technology is not being used, perhaps workers lack the advanced training they need to perform at a higher level, perhaps the organization needs to buy its inputs or assemble its products abroad to compete against low-cost rivals, or perhaps it needs to restructure itself or re-engineer its work processes to increase efficiency. If managers decide that the level has been achieved or exceeded, they can consider whether the standard set was too low. However, they might also consider rewarding employees for a job well done.

The simplest example of a control system is the thermostat in a home. By setting the thermostat, you establish the standard of performance with which actual temperature is to be compared. The thermostat contains a sensing or monitoring device, which measures the actual temperature against the desired temperature. Whenever there is a difference between them, the furnace or air-conditioning unit is activated to bring the temperature back to the standard. In other words, corrective action is initiated. This is a simple control system, for it is entirely self-contained and the target (temperature) is easy to measure. In the opening case,

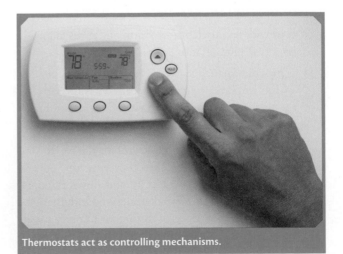

Thermostats act as controlling mechanisms.

we saw how Husky's predictive maintenance program software alerts customers when thresholds are breached so that they can take corrective action and reduce down time.

Establishing targets and designing measurement systems can be difficult for managers. Because of the high level of uncertainty in the organizational environment, managers rarely know what might happen. Thus it is vital for managers to design control systems to alert them to problems so that these can be dealt with before they become threatening. Another issue is that managers are not just concerned with bringing the organization's performance up to some predetermined standard; they want to push that standard forward, to encourage employees at all levels to find new ways to raise performance. Husky's attention to the well-being of its employees demonstrates the high return on investment from being proactive.

LO3 Describe three systems of control used in operations management.

Control Systems and Operations Management

As we see from the control process described above, managers need effective control systems to help them evaluate whether they are staying on target with their planned performance. **Control systems** are formal target-setting, monitoring, evaluation, and feedback systems that provide managers with information about whether the organization's strategy and structure are working efficiently and effectively.[15] Effective control systems alert managers when something is going wrong and give them time to respond to opportunities and threats. An effective control system has three characteristics:

- It is flexible enough to allow managers to respond, as necessary, to unexpected events.

- It provides accurate information and gives managers a true picture of organizational performance.

- It provides managers with the information in a timely manner because making decisions on the basis of outdated information is a recipe for failure.

New forms of information technology have revolutionized control systems because they ease the flow of accurate and timely information up and down the organizational hierarchy and between functions and divisions. Today, employees at all levels of the organization routinely feed information into a company's information system or

network and start the chain of events that affect decision making at some other part of the organization. This could be the department-store clerk whose scanning of purchased clothing tells merchandise managers what kinds of clothing need to be reordered; or the salesperson in the field who uses a wireless laptop to send information about customers' changing needs or problems.

Operations management is the process of managing the use of materials and other resources in producing an organization's goods and services. Operations managers include titles such as manufacturing managers, purchasing managers, and logistics (transportation) managers. These managers focus on the five "Ps" of the organization's operations: *people* (the labour force), *plants* (facilities), *parts* (inputs), *processes* (technology and work flow), and *planning and control systems* (standards and measures for quality control).

A **production system** is the system that an organization uses to acquire inputs, convert inputs into outputs, and dispose of the outputs (goods or services). **Operations managers** are managers who are responsible for managing an organization's production system. They do whatever it takes to transform inputs into outputs. Their job is to manage the three stages of production—acquisition of inputs, control of conversion processes, and disposal of goods and services—and to determine where operating improvements might be made in order to increase quality, efficiency, and responsiveness to customers and so give an organization a competitive advantage (see Figure 13.4).

In managing a production system, operations managers focus on the three stages of the process of taking the raw materials and transforming them into a useable finished product or service. Operations management techniques are developed to measure performance at each stage (see Figure 13.4).

Feedforward Control

Before the work begins, managers use **feedforward control** to anticipate possible problems that they can then avoid once the work is underway.[16] For example, by giving stringent product specifications to suppliers in advance (a form of performance target), an organization

control systems Formal target-setting, monitoring, evaluation, and feedback systems that provide managers with information about how well the organization's strategy and structure are working.

operations management The process of managing the use of materials and other resources in producing an organization's goods and services.

production system The system that an organization uses to acquire inputs, convert the inputs into outputs, and dispose of the outputs.

operations managers Managers who are responsible for managing an organization's production system.

feedforward control Control that allows managers to anticipate and deal with potential problems.

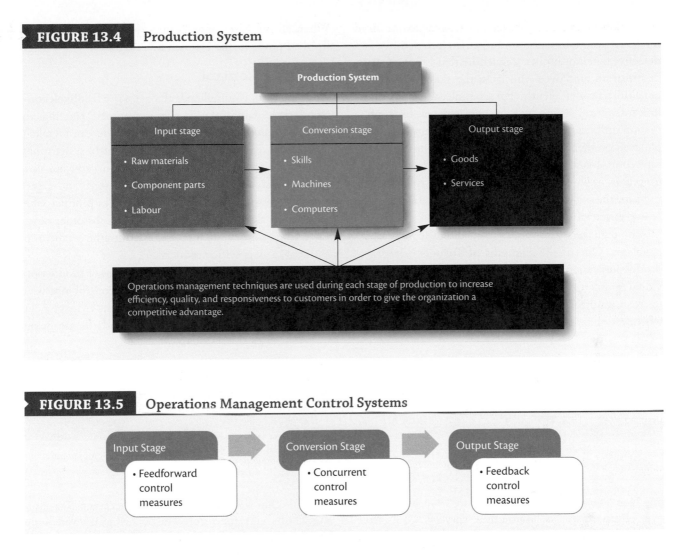

> **FIGURE 13.4** Production System

> **FIGURE 13.5** Operations Management Control Systems

can control the quality of the inputs it receives from its suppliers and thus avoid potential problems at the conversion stage (see Figure 13.5). Similarly, by screening job applicants and using several interviews to select the most highly skilled people, managers can lessen the chance that they will hire people who lack the skills or experience needed to perform effectively. Another form of feedforward control is the development of management information systems that provide managers with timely information about changes in the task and general environments that may impact their organization later on. Effective managers always monitor trends and changes in the external

environment to try to anticipate problems. Husky uses feedforward control measures by offering on-site child care, subsidized healthy food, fitness classes, and a subsidized drug plan. The return on investment is lower absenteeism and accident claims.

Concurrent Control

During the conversion phase, **concurrent control** gives managers immediate feedback on how efficiently inputs are being transformed into outputs so that managers can correct problems as they

> "**Components such as pumps, electric motors and seals all have finite lifespans, so to be able to predict the need for maintenance, before failure occurs, is a significant step forward in increasing customer asset utilization.**"
>
> *Keith Boss, Husky's ex-Vice President of Parts and Service*

concurrent control
Control that gives managers immediate feedback on how efficiently inputs are being transformed into outputs so that managers can correct problems as they arise.

arise. Concurrent control alerts managers to the need for quick reaction to the source of the problem, be it a defective batch of inputs, a machine that is out of alignment, or an employee who lacks the skills necessary to perform a task efficiently. For example, Husky's Smartlink software gives production managers real-time information on breaches of threshold levels in temperature or oil levels on their injection moulding machines. Concurrent control is at the heart of total quality management programs, in which employees are expected to constantly monitor the quality of the goods or services they provide at every step of the production process and inform managers as soon as they discover problems. One of the strengths of Toyota's production system, for example, is that individual employees are given the authority to push a button to stop the assembly line whenever they discover a quality problem.

> **feedback control** Control that gives managers information about customers' reactions to goods and services so that corrective action can be taken if necessary.

When all problems have been corrected, the result is a finished product that is much more reliable.

Feedback Control

Once the work is completed, managers use **feedback control** to provide information about customers' reactions to goods and services so that corrective action can be taken if necessary. For example, a feedback control system that monitors the number of customer returns alerts managers when defective products are being produced, and a system that measures increases or decreases in product sales alerts managers to changes in customer tastes so they can increase or reduce the production of specific products.

To summarize, all processes of production (and service provision) have control measures at each stage in the operations management process to determine if standards are being

---

FOCUS ON ❯ *The Social Economy*

Ten Thousand Villages

Ten Thousand Villages began in 1946 when Edna Ruth Byler, a Mennonite Central Committee (MCC) worker, visited volunteers in Puerto Rico who were teaching sewing classes in an effort to help improve the lives of women living in poverty.

From this trip, Edna brought several pieces of embroidery home to sell to friends and neighbours. The pieces became quite popular and she soon added cross-stitch needlework from Palestinian refugees and hand-carved Haitian woodenware to her inventory.

In the early 1970s, the flourishing project moved out of Byler's basement and became SELFHELP CRAFTS, an official MCC program. Thousands of loyal customers and volunteers have helped to build this program into the strong alternative trading organization that, in 1996, became known as Ten Thousand Villages.

Commerce with a Conscience

Men and women around the world have a simple dream—to earn an honest living, provide a home, food and education for their children, and to be gainfully employed in a job that brings dignity and joy. Ten Thousand Villages partners with thousands of talented artisans in a healthy business relationship.

Often referred to as "Fair Trade," the philosophy of helping to build a sustainable future is based on the principle that trade should have a conscience. Through Fair Trade, artisans receive respect, dignity and hope from working hard and earning fair value for their work.

Ten Thousand Villages is a nonprofit Fair Trade Organization (FTO). FTOs are non-governmental organizations designed to benefit artisans, not to maximize profits. They market products from handicraft and agricultural organizations based in low-income countries, providing consumers with products that have been fairly purchased from sustainable sources.

Ten Thousand Villages is a member of the World Fair Trade Organization (WFTO), a global network of Fair Trade Organizations. WFTO's mission is to improve the livelihood and well-being of disadvantaged producers by linking and promoting Fair Trade organizations and speaking out for greater justice in world trade. Over 270 FTOs in 60 countries form the basis of this network.[17]

1. Visit the World Fair Trade Organization website and research its role in improving the lives of producers in poor countries.

2. How can operations managers practise feedforward control measures that ensure ethical and fair trade principles in managing production systems?

met. If significant deviations between the actual performance and the objective are found, operations managers can take action to correct the situation anywhere along the supply chain.

In the global economy today, supply chains are complex and often not very transparent. Workers in developing nations who supply raw materials often do not get the rewards or benefits from their labour that are expected elsewhere. An ethical movement toward fair trade instead of free trade was the inspiration for Ten Thousand Villages, the organization featured in our Focus on the Social Economy. Increasingly, consumers are demanding fair trade principles in operations management.

LO4 Identify how output, behavioural, and clan controls coordinate and motivate employees to achieve organizational goals.

Types of Control to Coordinate and Motivate Employees

Managers need to determine internal control measures that will motivate employees and ensure that they perform effectively. In the following sections, we consider the three most important types of control that managers use to coordinate and motivate employees: *output control, behaviour control,* and *clan control.* Managers use all three to govern and regulate organizational activities, no matter what specific organizational structure is in place.

Output Control

All managers develop a system of output control for their organizations. First, they choose the goals or output performance standards or targets that they think will best measure factors such as efficiency, quality, innovation, and responsiveness to customers. Then they measure to see whether the performance goals and standards are being achieved at the corporate, divisional, or functional and individual levels of the organization. The three main mechanisms that managers use to assess output or performance are financial measures, organizational goals, and operating budgets.

Financial Measures of Performance

Top managers are most concerned with overall organizational performance and use various financial measures to evaluate performance. The most common are *profit ratios, liquidity ratios, leverage ratios,* and *activity ratios.* They are discussed below and summarized in Table 13.1.[18]

TABLE 13.1	Four Measures of Financial Performance	
Profit Ratios		Measures how well managers are using the organization's resources to generate profits. A simple ROI can be thought of as: gains minus investment costs divided by investment costs.
Return on investment	$= \dfrac{\text{Net profit after taxes}}{\text{Total assests}}$	
Gross profit margin	$= \dfrac{\text{Sales revenue} - \text{Cost of goods sold}}{\text{Sales revenue}}$	The difference between the amount of revenue generated from the product and the resources used to produce the product.
Liquidity Ratios		Do managers have resources available to meet claims of short-term creditors?
Current ratio	$= \dfrac{\text{Current assests}}{\text{Current liabilities}}$	
Quick ratio	$= \dfrac{\text{Current assests} - \text{Inventory}}{\text{Current liabilities}}$	Can managers pay off claims of short-term creditors without selling inventory?
Leverage Ratios		To what extent have managers used borrowed funds to finance investments?
Debt-to-assets ratio	$= \dfrac{\text{Total debt}}{\text{Total assets}}$	
Times-covered ratio	$= \dfrac{\text{Profit before interest and taxes}}{\text{Total interest charges}}$	Measures how far profits can decline before managers cannot meet interest charges. If ratio declines to less than 1, the organization is technically insolvent.
Activity Ratios		Measures how efficiently managers are turning inventory over so excess inventory is not carried.
Inventory turnover	$= \dfrac{\text{Cost of goods sold}}{\text{Inventory}}$	
Days sales outstanding	$= \dfrac{\text{Accounts receivable}}{\dfrac{\text{Total sales}}{360}}$	Measures how efficiently managers are collecting revenues from customers to pay expenses.

* *Profit ratios* measure how efficiently managers are using the organization's resources to generate profits. *Return on investment (ROI),* an organization's net profit after taxes divided by its total assets, is the most commonly used financial performance measure because it allows managers of one organization to compare performance with that of other organizations. ROI allows managers to assess an organization's competitive advantage. *Gross profit margin* is the difference between the amount of revenue generated by a product and the resources used to produce the product. This measure provides managers with information about how efficiently an organization is using its resources and about how attractive customers find the product. It also provides managers with a way to assess how well an organization is building a competitive advantage.

* *Liquidity ratios* measure how well managers have protected organizational resources so as to be able to meet short-term obligations. The *current ratio* (current assets divided by current liabilities) tells managers whether they have the resources available to meet the claims of short-term creditors. The *quick ratio* tells whether they can pay these claims without selling inventory.

* *Leverage ratios* such as the *debt-to-assets ratio* and the *times-covered ratio* measure the degree to which managers use debt (borrow money) or equity (issue new shares) to finance ongoing operations. An organization is highly leveraged if it uses more debt than equity. Debt can be very risky when profits fail to cover the interest on the debt.

* *Activity ratios* provide measures of how well managers are creating value from organizational assets. *Inventory turnover* measures how efficiently managers are turning inventory over so that excess inventory is not carried. *Days sales outstanding* provides information on how efficiently managers are collecting revenue from customers to pay expenses.

The objectivity of financial measures of performance is the reason why so many managers use them to assess the efficiency and effectiveness of their organizations. When an organization fails to meet performance standards such as ROI, revenue, or stock price targets, managers know that they must take corrective action. Thus, financial controls tell managers when a corporate reorganization might be necessary, when they should sell off divisions and exit from businesses, or when they should rethink their corporate-level strategies.[19] For example, Starbucks had to rethink its corporate strategy after profits declined by 53 percent in 2008.[20]

While financial information is an important output control, on its own it does not provide managers with all the information they need about whether the plans they have made are being met. Financial results inform managers about the results of decisions they have already made; they do not tell managers how to find new opportunities to build competitive advantage in the future. To encourage a future-oriented approach, top managers, in their planning function, establish organizational goals that provide direction to middle and first-line managers. As part of the control function, managers evaluate whether those goals are being met.

Organizational Goals

Once top managers, in consultation with lower-level managers, have set the organization's overall goals, they then establish performance standards for the divisions and functions. These standards specify for divisional and functional managers the level at which their units must perform if the organization is to reach its overall goals.[21] For instance, if the goals for the year include improved sales, quality, and innovation, sales managers might be evaluated for their ability to increase sales, materials managers for their ability to increase the quality of inputs or lower their costs, and R&D managers for the number of products they innovate or the number of patents they receive. By evaluating how well performance matches up to the goals set, managers at all levels can determine whether the plans they had made are being met, or whether adjustments need to be made in either the plans

Financial measures illustrate the level of efficiency in organizations.

Operating budgets are an output control measure.

or the behaviours of managers and employees. Thus goals can be a form of control by providing the framework for what is evaluated and assessed.

Output control is used at every level of the organization, and it is vital that the goals set at each level harmonize with the goals set at other levels so that managers and other employees throughout the organization work together to attain the corporate goals that top managers have set.[22] It is also important that goals be set appropriately so that managers are motivated to accomplish them. If goals are set at an impossibly high level, managers might work only half-heartedly to achieve them because they are certain they will fail. In contrast, if goals are set so low that they are too easy to achieve, managers will not be motivated to use all their resources as efficiently and effectively as possible. Research suggests that the best goals are *specific, difficult goals*—goals that challenge and stretch managers' ability but are not out of reach and do not require an impossibly high expenditure of managerial time and energy. Such goals are often called *stretch goals.*

Deciding what is a specific, difficult goal and what is a goal that is too difficult or too easy is a skill that managers must develop. Based on their own judgment and work experience, managers at all levels must assess how difficult a certain task is, and they must assess the ability of a particular subordinate manager to achieve the goal. If they do so successfully, challenging, interrelated goals—goals that reinforce one another and focus on achieving overall corporate objectives—will energize the organization.

Operating Budgets

Once managers at each level have been given a goal or target to achieve, the next step in developing an output control system is to establish operating budgets that regulate how managers and employees reach those goals.

An **operating budget** is a feedforward control measure that states how managers intend to use organizational resources to achieve organizational goals efficiently. Typically, managers at one level allocate to subordinate managers a specific amount of resources to produce goods and services. Once they have been given a budget, these lower-level managers must decide how to allocate resources for different organizational activities. They are then evaluated for their ability to stay within budget and to make the best use of available resources. For example, managers at Husky's European division might have a budget of $50 million to spend on developing and selling a new line of injection moulding machines. They must decide how much money to allocate to the various functions such as R&D, engineering, and sales so that the division generates the most customers and revenue.

Large organizations often treat each division as a singular or stand-alone responsibility centre. Corporate managers then evaluate each division's contribution to corporate performance. Managers of a division may be given a fixed budget for resources and evaluated for the amount of goods or services they can produce using those resources (this is a *cost* or *expense* budget approach). Or managers may be asked to maximize the revenues from the sales of goods and services produced (a *revenue* budget approach). Or managers may be evaluated on the difference between the revenues generated by the sales of goods and services and the budgeted cost of making those goods and services (a *profit* budget approach). Japanese companies' use of operating budgets and challenging goals to increase efficiency is instructive in this context.

In summary, three components—objective financial measures, performance standards derived from goals, and appropriate operating budgets—are the essence of effective output control. Most organizations develop sophisticated output control systems to allow managers at all levels to maintain an accurate picture of the organization so that they can move quickly to take corrective action as needed.[23] Output control is an essential part of management.

Problems with Output Control

Boards of directors have to adopt new organizational output accounting control systems with managers and executives in order to reduce potential ethical conflicts. When designing an output control system, managers must be careful to avoid some pitfalls, as shown in Figure 13.6. First, they must be sure that their output standards motivate managers

operating budget A budget that states how managers intend to use organizational resources to achieve organizational goals.

FIGURE 13.6 Pitfalls of Output Control

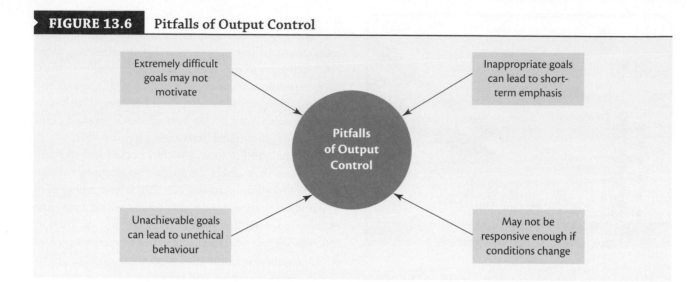

at all levels and do not cause managers to behave in inappropriate ways to achieve organizational goals. Scotia McLeod's system of rewarding for each individual trade ended up creating "churning." Brokers advised clients to trade too much, and this led to investigations by regulatory bodies, as well as fines and discipline against the brokerages and individual brokers.

Problems can also occur if the standards that are set turn out to be unrealistic. Suppose that top managers give divisional managers the goal of doubling profits over a three-year period. This goal seems challenging and reachable when it is jointly agreed upon, and in the first two years profits go up by 70 percent. In the third year, however, an economic recession hits and sales plummet. Divisional managers think it is increasingly unlikely that they will meet their profit goal. Failure will mean losing the substantial monetary bonus tied to achieving the goal. How might managers behave to try to preserve their bonuses?

One course of action they might take is to find ways to reduce costs, since profit can be increased either by raising revenues or by reducing costs. Thus, divisional managers might cut back on expensive research and development activities, delay maintenance on machinery, reduce marketing expenditures, and lay off middle managers and employees to reduce costs so that at the end of the year they will make their target of doubling profits and will receive their bonuses. This tactic might help them achieve a short-term goal—doubling profits—but such actions could hurt long-term profitability or ROI (because a cutback in R&D can reduce the rate of product innovation, a cutback in marketing will lead to the loss of customers, and so on).

The long term is what corporate managers should be most concerned about. Thus, top managers must

consider carefully how flexible they should be when using output control. If conditions change (as they will because of uncertainty in the task and general environments), it is probably better for top managers to communicate to managers lower in the hierarchy that they are aware of the changes taking place and are willing to revise and lower goals and standards. Indeed, most organizations schedule yearly revisions of their five-year plan and goals.

Second, the inappropriate use of output control measures can lead managers and employees to behave unethically. If goals are too challenging, employees may be motivated to behave unethically toward customers, as sometimes happens in brokerage firms. Scotia McLeod has moved to a fee-based system to change the way in which its brokers are rewarded in order to reduce potential ethical conflicts.

The message is clear: Although output control is a useful tool for keeping managers and employees at all levels motivated and the organization on track, it is only a guide to appropriate action. Output controls need to be flexible enough to accommodate changes in the organization's environment. Therefore, managers must be sensitive to how they use output control and constantly monitor its effects at all levels in the organization.

Behaviour Control

Organizational structure is often viewed as a way of achieving control by designating who reports to whom and what the responsibilities of each individual are. However, structure by itself does not provide any mechanism that motivates managers and nonmanagerial employees to behave in ways that make the structure work or even improve the way it works—hence the need for control. Output control is one way to motivate people; behaviour

> **FIGURE 13.7**   Types of Control Measures to Coordinate and Motivate Employees

Type of Control	Mechanisms of Control
Output control	Financial measures of performance Organizational goals Operating budgets
Behaviour control	Corporate governance Direct supervision Management by objectives Bureaucratic rules
Clan control	Values Norms Socialization

control is another. In this section, we begin by examining the ways that managerial behaviour can be held accountable through *corporate governance* principles. We end with a discussion of three mechanisms that managers can use to keep subordinates on track and make organizational structures work as they are designed to work: *direct supervision, management by objectives,* and *bureaucratic rules and operating procedures* (see Figure 13.7).

Corporate Governance and Control

After the Enron and WorldCom scandals arose in the early twenty-first century around corporate financial reporting, the ways that top managers account for and report their performance has been called into question. Canadian-born CEO of WorldCom Bernard Ebbers made dubious accounting judgments that misrepresented the actual performance level of the company in an effort to keep the share price high and investors happy. Instead, the fraudulent activity landed him in jail, and the company went bankrupt. In the case of Enron, the CFO Andrew Fastow set up accounting practices that allowed him to defraud investors as well as disguise the declining performance to shareholders. These and other more recent financial scandals around the world, such as Satyam in India, Nortel Networks, Goldman Sachs, Hollinger Inc., Bank of America, and Facebook, have resulted in reforms to the way that corporations approach corporate governance and accountability. **Corporate governance** practices are the processes companies use to be accountable to stakeholders, including investors, employees, the environment, and communities. The failure of the self-governing practices of corporations has led shareholders, particularly institutional investors, to become more active in

corporate governance
The processes companies use to be accountable to stakeholders, including investors, employees, the environment, and communities.

controlling the management of their assets and scrutinizing top managerial behaviour.

How do companies make managerial behaviour accountable? Take tech giant Research In Motion (RIM), for example. RIM's annual income grew by 45 000 percent in its first 10 years of operation. With such rapid growth, how did the company maintain control and compliance to regulatory standards in accounting?

In 2006, RIM undertook a voluntary internal review of its stock option granting practices after accounting errors were found in connection with the administration of certain stock options between February 2002 and August 2006. The internal review resulted in some significant changes to RIM's governance structure. First, the roles of chairman of the board and CEO were separated. The chair became a nonexecutive role after Jim Balsillie voluntarily stepped down but maintained the position of co-CEO with Mike Lazaridis, who also held the position of president of the company. Second, an oversight committee of the board of directors was formed to implement changes to the company's board, audit committee, compensation committee, and nominating committee and to change various management roles. Although no employees were asked to leave the company as a result of the uncovering of errors in governance, RIM did have to restate several years' financial statements and made significant changes to its organizational structure as a result.

"We are satisfied with the thoroughness of the review and we believe that the resulting enhancements to governance and controls will make RIM even stronger as it continues to grow and lead in the thriving market it pioneered," said Estill and Richardson, who sat on the special committee investigating the issue in a joint statement. "It must also be said that we have the utmost confidence in Jim Balsillie and the senior management team. Over the last 10 years, incredible results have been accomplished under their stewardship, including an increase in RIM's annual revenue by more than 45 000 percent and an increase in RIM's share price by more than 10 000 percent. These results speak loudly about the management team and the value of their leadership to RIM and its shareholders."[24] In 2012, after market share declined, RIM's co-CEOs stepped down and passed the reins to Thorsten Heins. Unexpectedly, Balsillie then resigned from the board of directors, while Lazaridis remained.

In light of these developments, the role of the board of directors has undergone substantial reform (see Figure 13.8). Nell Minow, editor of The Corporate Library, an independent U.S.–based research firm that rates boards of directors of public companies and compiles research on corporate governance issues, put the matter like this: "boards of directors are like subatomic particles—they behave differently when they are observed."[25] To encourage boards and top managers to do their jobs in a more transparent and effective way, government legislation and guidelines set out by stakeholder groups have been developed. In 2002, the *Sarbanes–Oxley Act* was passed in the United States, imposing considerable demands on board members of publicly

> "Boards of directors are like subatomic particles— they behave differently when they are observed."
>
> *Nell Minow*

traded companies with respect to accountability. Similar but far less tough rules were adopted by most Canadian provincial securities commissions. Principles and guidelines go beyond promoting accountability in financial matters.

Figure 13.9 illustrates the Ceres 14-point Climate Change Governance Checklist used by the largest pension fund in the United States, the California Public Employees Retirement System (calPERS), to decide in which companies to invest. Transparent corporate governance systems and adopting a sustainability strategy are increasingly important control measures for creating a competitive advantage as more vigilant shareholders are also more socially responsible in terms of demanding economic, environmental, and social impact returns (triple-bottom-line returns).

Direct Supervision

The most immediate and potent form of behaviour control is direct supervision by managers who actively monitor and observe the behaviour of their subordinates, educate subordinates about the behaviours that are appropriate or inappropriate, and intervene to take corrective action as needed. When managers personally supervise subordinates, they lead by example and in this

> **FIGURE 13.8** Reforms to the Role of the Board of Directors

Old versus New Corporate Governance Roles

CEO also holds Chair of the Board of Directors (BoD) position	Top Management is independent from the Board of Directors
• BoD self governs decisions and practices	• BoD monitors the CEO and control systems
• BoD members held close professional and/or personal ties to the corporation	• BoD members are independent of the corporation
• BoD relied on top management expertise	• BoD members possess relevant industry, company, governance and functional area expertise
• BoD met infrequently with little access to relevant information needed to perform their duties	• BoD meets frequently with all required resources
• Insider trading and other activities not publically disclosed	• Activities and transactions are communicated in a timely and transparent manner
	• Independent internal audit committee

> **FIGURE 13.9**   The Ceres 14-Point Climate Change Governance Checklist[26]

Board Oversight

- 1. Board is actively engaged in climate change policy and has assigned oversight responsibility to board member, board committee, or full board.

Management Execution

- 2. Chairman/CEO assumes leadership role in articulating and executing climate change policy.
- 3. Top executives and/or executive committees assigned to manage climate change response strategies.
- 4. Climate change initiatives are integrated into risk management and mainstream business activities.
- 5. Executive officers' compensation is linked to attainment of environmental goals and GHG targets.

Public Disclosure

- 6. Securities filings disclose material risks and opportunities posed by climate change.
- 7. Public communications offer comprehensive, transparent presentation of response measures.

Emissions Accounting

- 8. Company calculates and registers GHG emissions savings and offsets from operations.
- 9. Company conducts annual inventory of GHG emissions and publicly reports results.
- 10. Company has an emissions baseline by which to gauge future GHG emissions trends.
- 11. Company has third-party verification process for GHG emissions data.
- 12. Company sets absolute GHG emission reduction targets for facilities, energy use, business travel, and other operations (including direct emissions).

Strategic Planning

- 13. Company participates in GHG emissions trading programs—up to 30.
- 14. Company pursues business strategies to reduce GHG emissions, minimize exposure to regulatory and physical risks, and maximize opportunities from changing market forces and emerging controls.

way can help subordinates develop and increase their own skill levels (leadership is the subject of Chapter 9). Thus, control through personal supervision can be a very effective way of motivating employees and promoting behaviours that increase efficiency and effectiveness.[27]

Nevertheless, certain problems are associated with direct supervision.

- It is very expensive. A manager can personally manage only a small number of subordinates effectively. Therefore, direct supervision requires a lot of managers, and this will raise costs.

- It can demotivate subordinates if they feel that they are not free to make their own decisions. Subordinates may avoid responsibility if they feel that their manager is waiting to reprimand anyone who makes the slightest error.

- For many jobs, direct supervision is simply not feasible. The more complex a job is, the more difficult it is for a manager to evaluate how well a subordinate is performing.

For all of these reasons, output control is usually preferred to behaviour control. Indeed, output control tends to be the first type of control that managers at all levels use to evaluate performance.

Management by Objectives

To provide a framework within which to evaluate subordinates' behaviour and, in particular, to allow managers to monitor progress toward achieving goals, many organizations implement some version of *management by objectives (MBO)*.

Management by objectives is a system of evaluating subordinates for their ability to achieve specific organizational goals or performance standards.[28] Most organizations make some use of management by objectives because it is pointless to establish goals and then fail to communicate the goals and their measurement to employees. Management by objectives involves three specific steps:

management by objectives A system of evaluating subordinates for their ability to achieve specific organizational goals or performance standards.

- Step 1. *Specific goals and objectives are established at each level of the organization.*

  Management by objectives starts when top managers establish overall organizational objectives, such as specific financial performance targets. Objective setting then cascades down throughout the organization as managers at the divisional and functional levels set their own objectives to achieve the corporate objectives.[29] Finally, first-line managers and workers jointly set objectives that will contribute to achieving functional goals.

- Step 2. *Managers and their subordinates together determine the subordinates' goals.*

  An important characteristic of management by objectives is its participatory nature. Managers at every level sit down with the subordinate managers who report directly to them, and together they determine appropriate and feasible goals for the subordinate and bargain over the budget that the subordinate will need so as to achieve his or her goals. The participation of subordinates in the objective-setting process is a way of strengthening their commitment to achieve their goals.[30] Another reason why it is so important for subordinates (both individuals and teams) to participate in goal setting is to enable them to tell managers what they think they can realistically achieve.[31]

- Step 3. *Managers and their subordinates periodically review the subordinates' progress toward meeting goals.*

  Once specific objectives have been agreed upon for managers at each level, managers are accountable for meeting those objectives. Periodically, they sit down with their subordinates to evaluate their progress. Normally, salary raises and promotions are linked to the goal-setting process.

From a control perspective, the important element of MBO is step 3: that managers and their subordinates need to periodically review the subordinates' progress toward meeting goals. Managers and employees who achieve their goals receive greater rewards than those who fall short. (The issue of how to design reward systems to motivate managers and other organizational employees is discussed in Chapter 8.)

In companies that decentralize responsibility for the production of goods and services to empowered teams and cross-functional teams, management would review the accomplishments of the team, and then the rewards would be linked to team performance as well as the performance of any one team member. For either the individual or team situation, MBO creates the conditions for providing standards that are evaluated.

Cypress Semiconductor offers an interesting example of how IT can be used to manage the MBO process quickly and effectively. In the fast-moving semiconductor business a premium is placed on organizational adaptability. At Cypress, CEO T.J. Rodgers was facing a problem. How could he control his growing 1500-employee organization without developing a bureaucratic management hierarchy? Rodgers believed that a tall hierarchy hinders the ability of an organization to adapt to changing conditions. He was committed to maintaining a flat and decentralized organizational structure with a minimum of management layers. At the same time, he needed to control his employees to ensure that they perform in a manner consistent with the goals of the company.[32] How could he achieve this without resorting to direct supervision and the management hierarchy that it implies?

To solve this problem, Rodgers implemented an online information system through which he can manage what every employee and team is doing in his fast-moving and decentralized organization. Each employee maintains a list of 10 to 15 goals, such as "Meet with marketing for new product launch" or "Make sure to check with customer X." Noted next to each goal are when it was agreed upon, when it is due to be finished, and whether it has been finished. All of this information is stored on a central computer. Rodgers claims that he can review the goals of all employees in about four hours and that he does so each week.[33] How is this possible? He manages by exception and looks only for employees who are falling behind. He then calls them, not to scold but to ask whether there is anything he can do to help them get the job done. It takes only about half an hour each week for employees to review and update their lists. This system allows Rodgers to exercise control over his organization without resorting to the expensive layers of a management hierarchy and direct supervision.

Bureaucratic Control

When direct supervision is too expensive and management by objectives is inappropriate, managers might turn to another mechanism to shape and motivate employee behaviour: bureaucratic control. **Bureaucratic control** is control by means of a comprehensive system of rules and **standard operating procedures (SOPs)** that standardize the

bureaucratic control
Control of behaviour by means of a comprehensive system of rules and standard operating procedures.

standard operating procedures (SOPs)
Rules and policies that standardize behaviours.

behaviour of divisions, functions, and individuals. All organizations use bureaucratic rules and procedures, but some use them more than others.[34]

Rules and SOPs guide behaviour and specify what employees are to do when they confront a problem that needs a solution. It is the responsibility of a manager to develop rules that allow employees to perform their activities efficiently and effectively. When employees follow the rules that managers have developed, their behaviour is *standardized*—actions are performed in the same way time and time again—and the outcomes of their work are predictable. In addition, to the degree that managers can make employees' behaviour predictable, there is no need to monitor the outputs of behaviour because standardized behaviour leads to standardized outputs.

Suppose a worker at Toyota comes up with a way to attach exhaust pipes that reduces the number of steps in the assembly process and increases efficiency. Always on the lookout for ways to standardize procedures, managers make this idea the basis of a new rule: "From now on, the procedure for attaching the exhaust pipe to the car is as follows. . . ." If all workers followed the rule to the letter, every car would come off the assembly line with its exhaust pipe attached in the new way, and there would be no need to check exhaust pipes at the end of the line. In practice, mistakes and lapses of attention do happen, so output control is used at the end of the line, and each car's exhaust system is given a routine inspection. However, the number of quality problems with the exhaust system is minimized because the rule (bureaucratic control) is being followed.

> **discipline** Managerial control through administering punishment when undesired workplace behaviours, such as absenteeism, lack of punctuality, and low performance, are exhibited, in an attempt to decrease their frequency.

Service organizations such as retail stores and fast-food restaurants try to standardize the behaviour of employees by instructing them on the correct way to greet customers or the appropriate way to serve or bag food. Employees are trained to follow the rules that have proven to be most effective in a particular situation. The better trained the employees are, the more standardized is their behaviour and the more trust managers can have that outputs (such as food quality) will be consistent.

Inconsistent behaviour and undesired behaviour on the part of employees such as not showing up for work, coming late, and performing poorly should be formally addressed through discipline. **Discipline** is administering punishment when undesired behaviours are exhibited, in an attempt to decrease the frequency of those actions. It is based on learning theory (discussed in Chapter 8). Management introduces an unpleasant stimulus, such as a reprimand or withholding pay when, for example, an employee performs poorly executed work. If discipline is given in an objective, fair, and consistent way that makes clear to the employee what the undesired behaviour is, it is a valuable form of managerial control. Management uses varying degrees of penalties when administering discipline according to the nature of the infraction. After a series of written reprimands for continually being late for work, the next step might be docking pay and then temporary suspension. Severe penalties, such as termination of employment, would be used for behaviours such as theft and sabotage. The objective is to achieve compliance with the organization's goals and standards through the least severe reprimand possible. See Figure 13.10.

Problems with Bureaucratic Control

All organizations make extensive use of bureaucratic control because rules and SOPs effectively control routine organizational activities. With a bureaucratic control system in place, managers can manage by exception and intervene and take corrective action only when necessary. However, managers need to be aware of a number of problems associated with bureaucratic control because these problems can reduce organizational effectiveness.[35]

First, establishing rules is always easier than discarding them. Organizations tend to become overly bureaucratic over time if managers do everything according to the rule book. When the amount of "red tape" becomes too great, decision making slows and managers react slowly to

Standardizing component parts and behaviour can lead to effective and efficient operations.

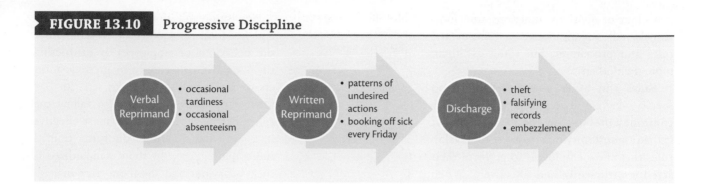

FIGURE 13.10 Progressive Discipline

changing conditions. This slowness can harm an organization's survival if quicker new competitors emerge.

Second, because rules constrain and standardize behaviour and lead people to behave in predictable ways, people may become so used to automatically following rules that they stop thinking for themselves. By definition, new ideas do not come from blindly following standardized procedures. Similarly, the pursuit of innovation implies a commitment by managers to discover new ways of doing things; innovation, however, is incompatible with the use of extensive bureaucratic control.

Managers must therefore be sensitive about the way they use bureaucratic control. It is most useful when organizational activities are routine and well understood and employees are making programmed decisions such as in mass-production settings or in a routine service setting—for example, in restaurants and stores such as Tim Hortons, Canadian Tire, and Midas Muffler. Bureaucratic control is not nearly as useful in situations where nonprogrammed decisions have to be made and

managers have to react quickly to changes in the organizational environment.

To use output control and behaviour control, managers must be able to identify the outcomes they want to achieve and the behaviours they want employees to perform to achieve these outcomes. For many of the most important organizational activities, output control and behaviour control are inappropriate for several reasons:

- Not all employees can be observed on a day-to-day basis.
- Rules and SOPs are of little use in crisis situations or in situations requiring innovation.
- Output controls can be a very crude measure of the quality of performance and could, in fact, harm performance in some instances.

Clan Control

Professionals such as scientists, engineers, doctors, and professors often have jobs that are relatively ambiguous in terms of standard operating procedures and which may require individualized response based on the situation.

How can managers try to control and regulate the behaviour of their subordinates when personal supervision is of little use, when rules cannot be developed to tell employees what to do, and when outputs and goals cannot be measured at all or can be measured usefully only over long periods? One source of control increasingly being used by organizations is *clan control,* which relies on a strong organizational culture. This form of control is also increasingly being used in organizations that value innovation and want to empower their employees.

How Clan Control Works

As we discussed in Chapter 7, *organizational culture* is the shared set of beliefs, expectations, values, norms, and work routines that influences how members of an organization relate to one another and work together to achieve

Tips **FOR MANAGERS**

Control

1. Making lists of "must-do" items that need to be done before the next task can be completed is an activity that boosts efficiency.

2. Making lists of "must-do" items and who will do them boosts effectiveness.

3. Involve employees in training programs that not only will help them do a better job but also will meet your control targets (e.g., safety, better financial reporting, etc.).

4. Finding the right balance of control for your organization works better with an open and inclusive culture.

clan control Control exerted on individuals and groups in an organization by shared values, norms, standards of behaviour, and expectations.

organizational goals. William Ouchi used the term **clan control** to describe the control exerted on individuals and groups in an organization by shared values, norms, standards of behaviour, and expectations. The control arising from clan control is not an externally imposed system of constraints, such as direct supervision or rules and procedures, but constraints that come from organizational culture. Rather, employees internalize organizational values and norms and then let these values and norms guide their decisions and actions. Just as people in society at large generally behave in accordance with socially acceptable values and norms—such as the norm that people should line up at the checkout counters in supermarkets—so are individuals in an organizational setting mindful of the force of organizational values and norms.

Clan control is an important source of control for two reasons. First, it makes control possible in situations where managers cannot use output or behaviour control. Second, and more importantly, when a strong and cohesive set of organizational values and norms is in place, employees focus on thinking about what is best for the organization in the long run—all their decisions and actions become oriented toward helping the organization perform well. For example, a teacher spends personal time after school coaching and counselling students; an R&D scientist works 80 hours a week, evenings and weekends, to help speed up a late project; a sales clerk at a department store runs after a customer who left a credit card at the cash register. Many researchers and managers believe that employees of some organizations go out of their way to help their organization because the organization has a strong and cohesive organizational culture—a culture that controls employee attitudes and behaviours. Strong bureaucratic control is

less likely to foster positive attitudes and behaviours that encourage employees to go above and beyond.

Explain how *innovative* and *conservative* cultures control managerial action.   **LO5**

How Culture Controls Managerial Action

The way in which organizational culture shapes and controls behaviour is evident in the way managers perform their four main functions—planning, organizing, leading, and controlling—when they work in different types of organizations (see Table 13.2). As we consider these functions, we continue to distinguish between two kinds of top managers: (1) those who create organizational values and norms that encourage creative, *innovative* and adaptive behaviour and (2) those who encourage a *conservative*, cautious approach in their subordinates. We noted earlier that both kinds of values and norms may be appropriate in different situations.

Planning

Top managers in an organization with an *innovative* culture are likely to encourage lower-level managers to take part in the planning process and develop a flexible approach to planning. They are likely to be willing to listen to new ideas and to take risks involving the development of new products.

In contrast, top managers in an organization with *conservative* values are likely to emphasize formal top-down planning. Suggestions from lower-level managers are likely to be subjected to a formal review, which can significantly slow down decision making. Although this deliberate approach may improve the quality of decision making in a nuclear power plant, it also can have unintended consequences. At conservative IBM, for example,

> **TABLE 13.2**   How Culture Controls Managerial Functions

Managerial Function	Type of Organization	
	Conservative	**Innovative**
Planning	Formal, top-down planning	All managers encouraged to participate in decision making
Organizing	Well-defined hierarchy of authority and clear reporting relationships	Organic, flexible structure
Leading	Rigid MBO and constant monitoring	Managers lead by example Encourage risk-taking
Controlling	Bureaucratic control Closed door corporate governance	Clan control Transparent corporate governance

before its more recent turnaround the planning process became so formalized that managers spent most of their time assembling complex slide shows and overheads to defend their current positions rather than thinking about what they should be doing to keep IBM abreast of the changes taking place in the computer industry.

Organizing

Valuing creativity, managers in an *innovative* culture are likely to try to create an organic structure, one that is flat, with few levels in the hierarchy, and in which authority is decentralized so that employees are encouraged to work together to find solutions to ongoing problems. A product team structure may be very suitable for an organization with an innovative culture.

In contrast, managers in a *conservative* culture are likely to create a well-defined hierarchy of authority and establish clear reporting relationships so that employees know exactly whom to report to and how to react to any problems that arise.

Leading

In an *innovative* culture, managers are likely to lead by example, encouraging employees to take risks and experiment. They are supportive regardless of employees succeeding or failing.

In contrast, managers in a conservative culture are likely to develop a rigid management by objectives system and to constantly monitor subordinates' progress toward goals, overseeing their every move.

Controlling

As this chapter makes clear, there are many control systems that managers can adopt to shape and influence employee behaviour. The control systems managers choose reflect how they want to motivate organizational members and keep them focused on organizational goals. Managers who want to encourage the development of *innovative* values and norms that encourage risk-taking choose output and behaviour controls that match this objective. They are likely to choose output controls that measure performance over the long run and develop a flexible MBO system suited to the long and uncertain process of innovation.

In contrast, managers who want to encourage the development of conservative values choose the opposite combination of output and behaviour controls. They rely heavily on direct supervision, bureaucratic rules and regulations that keep subordinates in check, based on fear of punishment and discipline. Sometimes managers who are hired by a company do not fit into the existing culture. Calgary-based WestJet fired CEO Steve Smith, who was far more controlling than the company's culture warranted. WestJet's founders sent a strong message to the employees by firing Smith in a year when the company had done very well financially.

The values and norms of an organization's culture strongly affect the way managers perform their management functions. The extent to which managers buy into the values and norms of their organization shapes their view of the world and their actions and decisions in particular circumstances.[36] In turn, the actions that managers take can have an impact on the performance of the organization. Thus, organizational culture, managerial action, and organizational performance are linked together.

Although organizational culture can give rise to managerial actions that ultimately benefit the organization, this is not always the case. Recall from Chapter 7 that sometimes culture can become so much a part of the organization that it becomes difficult to effect change and improve performance.[37] For example, Wayne Sales, the former CEO of Canadian Tire, tried desperately to revitalize customer service in the company's stores. Canadians had become so used to poor service that employees did not see the need to change. However, with increased competition from Home Depot Canada, RONA, Home Hardware, and Lowe's Canada, lack of customer service is a big issue. Sales set out to "drive away the chain's 'crappy tire' image" by changing the control systems to encourage employees to be more customer-focused.[38]

Summary and Review

LO1 What Is Organizational Control? Controlling is the process that managers use to monitor and evaluate how efficiently and effectively an organization and its members are performing the activities necessary to reach organizational goals. When goals are not met, managers can take corrective action to get back on track. Control processes allow managers to assess how *efficiently* the organization is producing goods and services, how *responsive* they are to customer needs, how *innovative* is the culture and how to increase the *quality* of goods and services produced to gain a competitive advantage. Organizational control is important because it helps managers *adapt to change and uncertainty, discover irregularities and errors, reduce costs, increase productivity, or add value, detect opportunities, deal with complexity,* and *decentralize decision making and facilitate teamwork.*

LO2 Steps in the Control Process Controlling is a four-step process: (1) establishing performance standards, (2) measuring actual performance, (3) comparing actual performance against performance standards, and (4) evaluating the results and taking corrective action if needed.

LO3 Control Systems and Operations Management Control systems set targets, monitor and evaluate performance, and help managers make sure the organization is working effectively and efficiently to reach its goals. Three systems of control are used by operations and supply chain managers: *feedforward* control used to control inputs; *concurrent* control, used during the conversion stage; and *feedback* control, used to provide information to managers in the post-production stage.

LO4 Types of Control to Coordinate and Motivate Employees *Output controls* and *behavioural controls* are used to coordinate and motivate employees. The main mechanisms to monitor output are financial measures of performance, organizational goals, and operating budgets. *Corporate governance practices* control managerial behaviour, while the main mechanisms to shape employee behaviour and induce them to work toward achieving organizational goals are *direct supervision, management by objectives,* and *bureaucratic control* based on standard operating procedures. *Clan control* operates on strong organizational culture where individuals and groups share values, norms, standards of behaviour, and expectations.

LO5 How Culture Controls Managerial Action Managers in organizations with *innovative cultures* carry out the managerial functions of planning, leading, organizing, and controlling very differently from managers in organizations with *conservative cultures*. In the former, clan control measures take precedence over bureaucratic and direct supervision forms of control.

McGraw Hill connect

KEY TERMS

benchmarking
bureaucratic control
clan control
concurrent control
control systems
controlling
corporate governance

discipline
feedback control
feedforward control
management by objectives
operating budget
operations management
operations managers

production system
productivity
Six Sigma
standard operating
   procedures (SOPs)
total quality management
   (TQM)

WRAP-UP TO   OPENING CASE

A Husky Solution for Organizational Control

One company that has become a poster child for innovative control measures and progressive employee management is Husky Injection Moldings of Aurora, Ontario. Reflecting the personal values of the company's founder and ex-president and CEO Robert Schad, the company has constructed a culture of innovation and proactively addresses issues of control in the workplace. After having read and understood the concepts in this chapter, you should be able to answer the following question:

1. *What is Husky doing to create organizational control?*

   ANSWER: Controlling is the process that managers use to monitor and evaluate how efficiently and effectively an organization and its members are achieving organizational goals and taking action to maintain or improve performance. As a global player in the plastics industry, Husky Injection Moldings Systems offers a diverse range of software that is designed for predictive, preventative, and proactive maintenance, as well as productivity and process monitoring. This provides customers with real-time solutions that maximize productivity, more accurately monitor factory processes, and better identify and resolve equipment problems to reduce downtime. Because the software can predict when maintenance is necessary, it is a feedforward control measure. The software anticipates the problems before they occur and communicates this information to the clients in real time, so that managers can take corrective action immediately.

   Husky also takes proactive measures to ensure a safe and healthy workplace for employees, which allows them to achieve organizational goals. The company provides on-site child care, subsidized healthy food, subsidized health and drug plans and fitness classes for employees. These feedforward control measures have resulted in Husky having a rate of absenteeism that is 40 percent below the national average and Workers' Compensation Board claims at 1.35 percent for every 200 000 hours of operation, compared with the average 5.5 percent.

Management in Action

TOPICS FOR DISCUSSION AND ACTION

LEVEL 1 Knowledge & Comprehension

1. Define organizational control and how it contributes to competitiveness. Why it is important to overall organizational performance?
2. Describe the four steps in the process of control.
3. Describe three systems of control managers use in operations management.

LEVEL 2 Application & Analysis

4. Identify the main methods of output and behaviour control, and discuss their advantages and disadvantages as means of coordinating and motivating employees.
5. Why is it important to involve subordinates in the control process?
6. What is clan control and how does it affect the way employees behave?

LEVEL 3 Synthesis & Evaluation

7. What types of controls would you expect to find most used in (a) a hospital, (b) the Armed Forces, and (c) a city police force? Why?
8. Watch the following video or a similar one on YouTube at www.youtube.com/watch?v=aOZhbOhEunY. Describe the culture at Google. What types of control measures are evident in these videos? What kinds of green initiatives make up the culture at Google?
9. Explain how *innovative* and *conservative* cultures control managerial action.

SELF-REFLECTION EXERCISE

Your parents have indicated that they are expecting a big party for their 25th wedding anniversary and that you are in charge of planning it. Develop a timeline for carrying out the project, and then identify ways to monitor progress in planning for the party. How will you know that your plans have been successful? At what critical points do you need to examine your plans to make sure that everything is on track?

SMALL GROUP BREAKOUT EXERCISE

How Best to Control the Sales Force?

Form groups of three or four, and appoint one member as the spokesperson who will communicate your findings to the whole class when called on by the instructor. Then discuss the following scenario:

You are the regional sales manager of an organization that supplies high-quality windows and doors to building supply centres nationwide. Over the last three years, the rate of sales growth has slackened. There is increasing evidence that to make their jobs easier, salespeople are primarily servicing large customer accounts and ignoring small accounts.

In addition, the salespeople are not dealing promptly with customer questions and complaints, and this inattention has resulted in a drop in after-sales service. You have talked about these problems, and you are meeting to design a control system to increase both the amount of sales and the quality of customer service.

1. What type of control do you think will best motivate the salespeople to achieve these goals?

2. What relative importance do you put on (1) output control, (2) behaviour control, and (3) organizational culture in this design?

BUSINESS PLANNING EXERCISE

Your professor may ask you to write a business plan for a new venture or a strategic plan for an existing venture. At the end of every chapter, you will have an opportunity to apply managerial and organizational concepts to the exercise of writing a business plan. Refer to Appendix A.

You and your team realize that you must use a variety of control measures in your venture to monitor and evaluate the use of resources and make sure the goals of the organization are being met. In order to complete the financial plan component of your business plan, you know you must use output control techniques, including the financial ratios and equations in the text, to forecast the cash flow for one year and the break-even point. Angel investors or any bank will want to see the bottom-line numbers on your expenses and expected revenues to determine if their ROI will be worthwhile. For the financial plan, you must create a pro forma cash flow, income statement, opening balance sheet, and break-even analysis.

1. **Cash flow projections for year one:** At which points over the year will your expenses exceed your revenue? How will you make up the shortfall? Subtract all expenses in the cost of goods sold from all revenues to project a net gain or loss for one year. This is your Pro Forma Income Statement.

2. **Opening balance sheet:** Are the assets and liabilities equal to the shareholders' equity?

3. **Break-even analysis:** When will the revenues exceed the expenses of the venture?

4. Identify the assumptions you will need to make to complete the financial plan section of your business plan such as interest rates, taxation rates, and other details on which to base your financial projections. These should be clearly stated with reference to the specific line item on the spreadsheet.

MANAGING ETHICALLY EXERCISE

You are a manager of a group of 10 employees in their twenties. They are very innovative and are not accustomed to tight rules and regulations. Managers at the company want order and control on every front. Your team is fighting the rules and regulations, which is creating an ethical dilemma for you. They are being very productive and innovative but clearly not in the way top management wants things run. You have been asked to bring more order to your team. You really like your team and think they are effective but will leave if they are forced to conform. And the company needs their expertise and energy to remain competitive in the high-tech world. What would you do?

MANAGEMENT CHALLENGE EXERCISE

Save the Children Project

Assume your professor has asked you to consult and manage the design of a special "Save the Children" innovative program that 10 teams of five students in your course will be working on. Save the Children Canada will be acting as final judge on the winning program submitted by different colleges and universities. You must manage 10 teams; because of the shortness of time for this request, the innovative program will need aspects designed by each team, as no one team can do it all. Hence, all 10 teams will have contributed to the finished product. Your professor will be grading you on how well you actually manage, motivate, and put into action controls to help each team function at optimal levels.

1. What is your plan to control the operations of the teams in such a way that they function optimally?

MANAGEMENT PORTFOLIO PROJECT

Answer the following questions about the organization you have chosen to follow:

1. What are the main types of control used by management to monitor and evaluate the performance of the organization and employees?

2. Are these methods of control appropriate, given the organization's strategy and culture?

3. What recommendations would you make with respect to the organizational control of this enterprise?

VIDEO MANAGEMENT CASE

Keeping Older Workers Safe on the Job

Ian Howcroft, vice-president of the Canadian Manufacturers and Exporters, discusses what employers can do to ensure the safety of workers as they age.

1. What type of control measures is Ian Howcroft recommending to ensure the safety of older workers when he suggests starting with a workplace assessment of special needs?

2. How should managers deal with older workers who can no longer perform the task they used to do?

3. What feedforward control measures are recommended by Howcroft for managers to make jobs fit older workers?

Management Case

3M Canada Company Fined $55 000 After Worker Injured

3M Canada Company was fined $55 000 for a violation of the *Occupational Health and Safety Act* after a worker was injured.[39]

On September 24, 2009, a worker at 3M's manufacturing facility in Perth was operating a production line. The worker was notified of a defect in the product coming out of the line. To fix the problem, the worker attempted to wipe a blade in the line. The blade was attached to a pair of rollers that guided the product through the line. The worker's hand was drawn into the machine by these rollers. The worker suffered a hand injury.

A Ministry of Labour investigation found that the blade and rollers were not guarded. 3M Canada Company pleaded guilty to failing to ensure that the machine was guarded to prevent access to the pinch point.

The fine was imposed by Justice of the Peace Raymond J. Switzer. In addition to the fine, the court imposed a 25 percent victim fine surcharge, as required by the *Provincial Offences Act*. The surcharge is credited to a special provincial government fund to assist victims of crime.

1. What kind of control system was used to determine there was a defect coming off the line?
2. When the worker attempted to wipe the blade on the line to correct the problem, what form of control measure was being used?
3. What kind of feedforward control measures could 3M Canada have used to prevent this injury?

connect

Connect allows you to practise important concepts at your own pace and on your own schedule, with 24/7 online access to an eBook, practice quizzes, video cases, interactive exercises, study tools, and more.

End of Part VI: Continuing Case

CARROT TOPS: CONTROLLING OPERATIONS

When Mel decided to start selling his own Carrot Tops brand-name products, he decided to outsource the production. Finding a reliable source of fresh produce from local organic farmers and producers has been a stumbling block to his success, even though he hired Janet Khan to head up produce procurement and logistics. When suppliers deliver organic produce to the store, Janet has to check every box for quality and quantity. If it meets her approval, it then gets stored in the walk-in refrigerators until it is ready to be put out for consumers. When the produce has been out for a while, one of Janet's employees goes around and cuts back the dead and dying leaves to present the produce in the best, most appealing manner. The employees must log their activity on the floor. Janet makes sure the produce is up to par by observing her employees while they work and reviews their logs. If employees fail to meet the standards Janet sets, their hours could be cut. Janet doesn't tolerate laziness. Occasionally, a customer will return some produce, claiming it was not fresh enough. Janet tries to avoid these complaints before they happen. Hiring the right people in the first place and training them well is where she begins.

Drawing on all segments of this case:

1. What are some of the pros and cons of outsourcing that Mel might encounter?

2. How are feedforward, concurrent, and feedback controls illustrated by Janet?

3. How could Janet use MIS and fair trade principles to better manage relations with suppliers?

4. How could Mel use MBO to control Janet's performance?

5. Would you describe Janet as an innovative or conservative manager?

A

Developing a Business Plan

The Business Plan as an Exercise in the Processes of Management[1]

Writing a business plan may never be a more important exercise than in the context of today's rapidly changing environment. Even if you are not an entrepreneur and do not wish to develop a new original idea and bring it to market, developing a business plan is still a valuable exercise in practising the management processes. It provides a crucial foundation for managing an organization. In this section of the text, we will treat developing a business plan as an exercise in the management processes of planning, organizing, leading, and controlling. By doing the exercises at the end of each chapter, you will have the foundation to put together a plan that will help you develop as a manager. The experience you will gain is valid for profit and not-for-profit organizations as well as new and existing ventures. Writing a business plan gives you practice in thinking about managing activities such as:

- Developing an idea to solve a problem

- Tapping into opportunities and countering threats in competitive conditions

- Organizing resources to achieve goals

- Targeting potential customers with promotional opportunities

- Designing an effective organizational structure

- Securing sources of finance

- Controlling for risk

What Is a Business Plan?

A business plan is a recognized management tool used to document the organization's objectives and to set out how these objectives will be achieved within a specific timeframe. It is a written document that describes who you are, what you intend to accomplish, how you will organize resources to attain your goals, and how you will overcome the risks involved to provide the anticipated returns. In general, a business plan comprises several elements, each giving the reader a piece of the overall picture of the project you are undertaking, and provides convincing reasons why you will be successful in this undertaking.

Managers and entrepreneurs use a business plan to seek support and financing to expand an existing business or to finance a new venture.

Putting It All Together

Throughout this course, you may have been asked to complete the end-of-chapter exercises on developing a business plan. Now is the time to start to put all the pieces together to create your comprehensive plan. Draw on the work that you have already done to write the major components of the business plan. See Table A.1.

At this point, you should familiarize yourself with a business planning software. There are several on the market. Your professor will instruct you as to which is appropriate for your course.[2] The software will help you compile the main elements in your plan and calculate the financial statements.

1. Nondisclosure Statement

A nondisclosure agreement is optional in a business plan. When used, it usually states that the information in the plan is proprietary and not to be shared, copied, or disclosed. The agreement should have a unique "copy number" that is the same as a number on the title page of the plan and a place for the recipient's signature. The agreement should be either a loose-leaf page or a page that can be torn out of the plan and retained by you. See the following example[3]:

Copy Number _____ 123 _____

FFP Consulting Inc.'s business plan is confidential, containing information proprietary to FFP Consulting Inc. None of the information contained in this plan may be reproduced or disclosed to any person under any circumstances without express written permission of FFP Consulting Inc. I have accepted and will protect the confidentiality of this business plan.

_____

Recipient's signature

---

2. Executive Summary

The executive summary is the first thing, besides the Table of Contents and Title page, that the reader will view, but it is generally the last thing the writer creates. The executive summary is a maximum one-page précis of your business plan. It is probably the most important part of your plan because readers will use it to make a judgment as to whether or not they want to continue

TABLE A.1	Major Business Plan Components
	Check off and date when completed and add any notes of interest
1. Nondisclosure Statement	❑
2. Executive Summary	❑
3. Profile of the Organization	❑
4. Profile of the Industry or Sector	❑
5. Profile of the Product or Service	❑
6. Marketing Plan	❑
7. Organizational Plan	❑
8. Operating and Control Systems Plan	❑
9. Financial Plan	❑
10. Appendices	❑

to examine your plan. The executive summary tells the reader the following information:

- Who you are and what your company/organization does

- The products and/or services that you provide or intend to provide

- Your target markets; that is, who are or will be your customers

- How you will promote your product/service to your customers

- What your financial projections are for a given period

- How you will achieve your goals; that is, your strategy for gaining a competitive advantage

- The strengths of your management team and why the reader should believe you can do what you are proposing

- Identify the major risks you expect and your solutions to minimize these threats

The executive summary should be no longer than one page.

3. Profile of the Organization

This section of the business plan tells the reader your vision, mission, and goals for the organization. Consider the following questions when preparing this section.

- What is the name of your company/organization?

- What is the legal structure and form of ownership?

- What are your reasons for going into business?

- What problem does your product or service solve, or what needs gap does it fill?

- What experience do you have that would enable you to pursue this venture successfully?

- Who makes up your management team, and what roles and responsibilities will they have?

Vision Statement

The vision for your company/organization is set out in a written statement telling the reader what direction or dream you wish your company to pursue for the next three to five years. Write this statement in the future tense. As stated in Chapter 5, Bill Gates's vision for Microsoft when it first began was to have "a computer on every desk, in every home, and in every office." The vision of the TD Bank is, simply, "to be the better bank."[4] The vision of the Australian company The Body Shop is "to be operating and recognised as the benchmark Company for the integration of Economic Success, Stakeholder Fulfillment, and Social and Environmental Change."[5] Cara Operations Ltd., founded by the Phelan family in 1883, is a privately owned Canadian company and the largest operator of full-service restaurants and the leading caterer to the travel industry in Canada. Cara's vision is "to be Canada's leading integrated restaurant company."[6] The vision of Renée's, a Canadian gourmet food products company, is "to be the market leader in developing and delivering superior-quality, innovative fresh food products."[7]

For additional examples, refer to Chapter 5: Managing Planning and Strategy.

Refer to the exercise you did for Chapter 5: Managing Planning and Strategy. Write the vision statement for your venture. Keep it short and sweet.

Mission Statement

The mission statement tells the reader what the purpose of your company/organization is. Refer to the mission statement of Canadian Tire outlined below (see Table A.2).[8] Ask yourself what the essence of your business is. What will the business really be doing? Why does it exist? What values is it premised on? Every noun, adjective, and verb in the statement is important and should explain the problem that will be solved or the need that will be fulfilled if your plan is implemented. Your mission statement should reflect your basic beliefs, values, and principles.

- Refer to the value statement and code of ethics you created for the exercise you did for Chapter 3: Managing Ethics, Social Responsibility, and Diversity. Incorporate these values and principles into your mission statement.

- Refer to the mission statement you wrote for the exercise you did for Chapter 5: Managing Planning and Strategy.

Write the mission statement for your venture. Keep it to 150 words or less.

Organizational Goals

Organizational goals must be made for the business as a whole and for each functional area. Organizationwide goals are longer term and are strategic in nature, while functional-level goals are shorter term and are more operational in nature. For example, corporate and divisional-level goals are generally made in the areas of market share, profitability, and return on investment. Functional-level goals include how departments will add value for the customer and reduce costs in the production of a good or service. Goals and objectives are statements of the level of performance desired within a certain timeframe. Goals must be formulated so that they are S.M.A.R.T plus C:

- **S**pecific

- **M**easurable

- **A**ttainable

- **R**ealistic, within a

- **T**imeframe

  plus **C**ommunicated to the relevant stakeholders.

An example of a SMART goal relating to market share might look like the following:

> *"By the end of the first year of operation, ABC company will have a 20-percent market share for its product XYZ."*

Mountain Equipment Co-op might formulate the goal of . . .

> *"giving 5 percent of gross profits to the major charitable organizations in the environmental movement by the year 2020."*

> **TABLE A.2**	**Mission Statement of Canadian Tire (in part)**
"Canadian Tire is a growing network of interrelated businesses... Canadian Tire continuously strives to meet the needs of its customers for total value by offering a unique package of location, price, service and assortment."	

This goal is consistent with the company's mission and strategic vision as stated above. Once goals are developed, plans must be formulated to achieve the objectives. These plans are generally referred to as strategies. The formulation of strategies depends upon the opportunities and threats facing your company from the forces in the organizational environment. You will formulate your strategy after doing an analysis of the current situation. The competitive analysis and strategy is analyzed in the context of the industry as a whole and detailed in the Marketing Plan component of the business plan.

Formulate the major goal for the venture as a whole, using a one-year timeframe.

Form of Ownership

If you are writing a business plan for an existing organization, the legal entity has no doubt been established already; however, it may make sense to consider a separate legal entity for the new product/service. If you are an entrepreneur or a group of entrepreneurs, you must decide what form of legal entity (form of ownership) will best suit the nature of the business, the competitive strategy, and the organizational structure of the business. Will you need a partner? Should you incorporate or simply operate as a sole proprietor? What advantages, if any, would there be in forming a cooperative structure? Refresh your memory about the advantages and disadvantages of each legal structure by reviewing an introductory business textbook. Now that you have developed your ideas and business plan up to this point, describe the legal form of your organization.

Which legal structure do you think is most appropriate, and why?

The Management Team

At the beginning of a new venture, the principal person who writes the business plan generally has overriding authority over the other members of the management team, if a team exists at all. In the case that several people are involved in the management team, the positions they will hold and roles they will play should be described and justified on the basis of their experience and expertise.

Provide a brief biography[9] of each member of the management team, and describe their roles and responsibilities in the venture.

4. Profile of the Industry or Sector

Industries are classified and coded according to specific criteria that are common across North America. The North American Industrial Classification System (NAICS)[10] (pronounced "Nakes") is used to codify industries and sectors. It is useful to know which NAICS code, and hence which industrial group, applies to your venture to research the changing trends from the forces acting in its organizational environment (Chapter 2). For example, if your business plan is to start a family restaurant, you would find that this type of venture is part of the Accommodation and Food Services Industry, NAICS 72211. From there, you can research the active forces within the industry that are providing opportunities for growth or proving to be a threat to your venture. Use *Porter's Five Forces Model* to analyze the threats to profitability within the industry (Chapter 5). Information on changing industrial trends can be found from Statistics Canada[11] and industry associations. For our family restaurant example, we could go to the Canadian Restaurant and Food Services Association website to learn about industry trends.[12] From this site, we learn that "the average Canadian household spent $2017 on food and alcoholic beverages served from restaurants and licensed establishments in 2007, a $99—or 5.2 percent—increase over 2006. Household spending on food purchased from restaurants rose by $81 to $1715." This indicates that consumers are increasing the amount of their income spent on food and alcohol from establishments similar to what you are proposing. However, additional research indicates that Food Service sales were projected to drop by 1.4 percent in the recession of 2009. Statistics on post-recession spending on food and alcoholic beverages either support your business plan or tell the reader the type and severity of the risks involved in investing in this industry. If the trend in the industry is toward contraction, rather than expansion, you have to tell the reader how you intend to deal with the risks.

Describe the trends in the industry and whether or not they pose an opportunity for growth or a threat to the profitability of your venture.

State how you will minimize the potential risks.

5. Profile of the Product/Service

This part of the business plan provides the reader with a complete overview of all the products and services you will offer.

Product or Service Description

It is important to stress to the reader the uniqueness of your offering. What will you provide or do that is different from your competitors? Why would consumers purchase your product or service over someone else's?

> **Describe in as much detail as possible the uniqueness of the product or service you will be offering.**

Regulations, Licences, and Permits

All businesses in Canada are subject to regulations at various levels of government. Consult BizPal,[13] a website designed to help businesspeople figure out all the regulations they must comply with and the permits and licences that are necessary to operate the venture. If you have developed a prototype of an original product or a modification of an existing product, you should apply for a patent and/or protection of your intellectual property. This can be done online at http://strategis.ic.gc.ca/sc_mrksv/cipo/welcome/welcom-e.html.

> **Describe the permits and licences that are required for your venture. Factor the costs into your financial plan projections.**

Future Product Development/Innovation

In this section, tell the reader how you expect your product or service offering to change in the future. Do you have plans for expansion? Will you bring new products and services on board, and when? How will you sustain your growth once the business reaches maturity? Give the reader a sense of how you will end the venture. Do you intend to sell the venture, franchise, or dissolve the company?

> **Describe your future product development and exit strategies.**

6. Marketing Plan

This part of the business plan includes an analysis of your venture's strengths and weaknesses relative to your competition (SWOT) as well as an analysis of the four Ps in the marketing mix: product, place (distribution channels), price, and promotion. Detailed research must be gathered on who will buy the product or service; what the potential size of the market is and whether there is potential for growth; the prices that should be charged; the distribution channel and the most effective promotion strategy to reach the target market.

SWOT Analysis

Referring to the SWOT analysis you did in Chapter 5, identify your strengths and weaknesses relative to one major competitor. Direct competitors can be found by searching the Yellow Pages and the websites of associations, trade magazines, chambers of commerce, and Statistics Canada. Things to compare might include:

Strengths	Weaknesses
• Resources (assets/people)	• Gaps in capabilities
• Experience	• Reputation
• Diversity	• Poor customer responsiveness
• Location	• Resources (assets/people)
• Sustainability strategy	• Inexperience
• Quality of product/service	• Lack of quality

Opportunities	Threats
• Market demand/changing trends	• Legal /political
• Competitors' vulnerabilities	• Demographic trends
• Partnerships	• Competitive advantages
• Innovation	• Barriers to entry
• Competitive advantages	• Suppliers

Strategies for a Competitive Advantage

After completing the SWOT analysis relative to your competition and remembering the analysis of the industry you did in section 4, you are now ready to articulate the kind of strategy that will gain you a competitive advantage. Refer to Chapter 5. Will you adopt a cost-leadership or a differentiation strategy? How will you focus that strategy?

> **Describe the business-level strategy you intend to use to gain a competitive advantage.**

Target Market Profile(s)

Which segment of the market will buy your product or service? Demographic characteristics such as age, income, geographic location, and buyer behaviour need to be researched and documented. This is usually done through conducting focus groups, giving surveys, interviewing potential market segments, and through observing and recording pre- and postpurchase behavioural habits of customers. Association websites and Statistics Canada[14] are good sources of data, including the 2011 census.

For each market segment, create a customer profile by researching the following:

• Demographic questions

• Customer attitudes on price and quality

• Where customers currently buy the product/service

• Where customers wish to buy the product/service

• The influence of advertising

- How much of the product/service the customer buys and how often

- Why the customer buys this product/service

Characteristics of the Customer	Customer Profile for Your Venture's Product/ Service/ Offering	Potential for Growth/ Trends	Source
Demographic information			
Frequency of purchase			
No. of units purchased yearly			
Price sensitivity			
Lifestyle/personality			
Advertising influences			
Motivation			
Buying decisions based on:			
Other			

Describe your target market(s).

Pricing

Before setting the price of your product or service, you must evaluate your costs per unit, what the markup should be, and what the competition charges for a similar product/service. Cost of goods should include material and labour overhead (utilities, rent, insurance, salaries), and costs from suppliers. You must add up the costs based on an estimate of the volume of sales. Markups or margins in your industry can be found by reading a trade journal or by asking the suppliers. The markup usually includes a degree of profit that represents the industry standard. Industry standards can be found from Statistic Canada, association websites, and organizations such as Dun & Bradstreet.[15]

If you plan to increase market penetration by using pricing specials or volume discounts, you should describe them. Before deciding to discount in order to undercut the competition and gain market share, you should consider that the competition could also lower its prices and therefore reduce the profit margins for everyone.

If you adopt a differentiation business-level strategy for your product/service, you may be able to justify charging more than the competition. To do this, you will offer customers a product or service that is unique and/or of better quality such that people will pay the higher price relative to the competition.

Describe your pricing strategy and how that compares with the competition.

Distribution (Place)

How will you make it convenient for your customers to access your product/service? The market conditions, attributes of the product/service, cost benefits, and characteristics of the venture should all be considered when deciding on a channel of distribution. It may be appropriate to sell directly to the customer or to a retailer if the target market is concentrated in a particular geographic area. If not, it may be appropriate to use a distributor or wholesaler. If the product is large, bulky, perishable, hazardous, or expensive, the rule of thumb is to channel the product through direct sales. If the cost of indirect sales (using a middle person such as a retailer or wholesaler) is minimal and the benefit is great in terms of reaching a dispersed market, it may be more appropriate to channel indirectly. And finally, if the venture has great financial strength, multiple channels may be considered.

If you intend to use dealers or distributors, discounts or commissions will be required and should be described.

Describe your distribution strategy.

When deciding on a *location* for your facilities, you must consider how much space you will need for the operation and whether or not the facility will be accessible to the consumer (direct sales). If you are considering purchasing or renting a building, further criteria may become relevant: Is it zoned for commercial use? Is it in need of renovation? Is there potential for expansion? Is there ample parking? What is the cost per square foot? How many competitors are in the area? Other criteria may be relevant to your location decision. Compare two or three sites against your criteria to come up with the best location for your venture.

Criteria	Site X	Site Y	Site Z
Cost per square foot			
Parking			
Accessibility			
History of the building			
Number of competitors in the area			
Zoning laws			
Potential for expansion			
Features of the area (specify)			
Other (specify)			

Describe the location of your venture.

Promotion

The success of your venture will largely depend on your promotional plan. Advertising, public relations, and

Internet marketing are common ways of promoting your organization to your target market. Consider that each market segment may require different promotional activities. Also consider the degree to which your target market is influenced by advertising. Would a slogan be appropriate to capture the vision of your organization or capitalize on the uniqueness of your product/service?

Develop a slogan and/or logo that promotes the image you want to project about your organization/ product/service.

Decide whether you will "pull" or "push" your promotions. Things to consider include:

- The pull strategy requires direct contact with the customer. This requires a major commitment to advertising. The objective is to attract the customers to every channel outlet for your product/service. If enough customers demand your product, the channels will want to carry it. The price and quality of your product is important here.

- The push strategy requires less investment in advertising. The push strategy maximizes the use of all available channels of distribution to "push" the offering into the marketplace, usually by giving large discounts or commissions as incentives to the channels to promote the offering. Research must be done into the channel discount requirements and the relationship that the competition has with the channel.

Create a list of public relations, Internet activities, and types of advertising that you can undertake to generate

Promotional Activity	Date and Contact Person	Cost and Length of Run	Expected Returns
Send a press kit with your company's profile, pictures, and press releases to newspapers and trade journals			
Host an open house			
Go to a trade show			
Write letters to the editors of various papers			
Develop a company website			
Blog			
Register with search engines			
Banner ads			
Billboard ads			
Radio/TV ads			
Other			

awareness of your venture in your target market(s). Expected returns include the audience reached and how this exposure will benefit you. Include the costs of the promotion plan in the financial plan section of the business plan.

Write your promotional strategy for each market segment.

7. Organizational Plan

This section provides a description of the organizational structure, culture, and human resources plan for your venture.

Organizational Structure

When designing the *organizational structure,* some things to consider are:

- How should similar jobs be grouped together into units or departments?

- Who should be accountable to whom to ensure the coordination of activities?

- How many levels of authority are needed?

The relationships that jobs have with one another are depicted in an organizational chart. The organizational chart shows the positions of all members. Refer to the business planning exercise you did for Chapter 6.

Draw an organizational chart for year one of your venture.

Organizational Culture

The organizational structure creates the foundation for the coordination of work that needs to be done. But finding the right mix of people to assume the responsibilities outlined in the structure is just as critical to the success of the organization as having a marketable product.

When building *organizational culture,* the founder and management team will foster the values and principles embodied in your vision and mission statements. The desired culture must be consistently role-modelled for employees. It must be deliberately embodied in the symbols and practices of the organization if it is to be successful. Revisit the value statement you wrote in Chapter 3.

Describe the values, principles, and norms that underlie your organizational culture.

Human Resources Management Plan

The objective of human resources planning is to match the right people to the right job at the right time. This section of the business plan provides the reader with a job analysis of the key positions and how the management will recruit, select, train, appraise, and compensate employees. Things to consider are:

- What kinds of labour (specifications) are needed to fulfill the duties of the positions (descriptions)?

- How will they be recruited?

- What selection techniques will be used to determine the best candidates?

- What kind of training and development will be offered?

- How will you know if they have learned the jobs?

- What levels of pay and pay structures will you offer that are consistent with the strategy of the venture?

Job Analysis

In conducting a job analysis for the venture, consult Chapter 11 as well as industry and association websites to determine what you need to include for each position. Consider the degree of enrichment you build into each job as a motivating factor.

For each position in the organizational chart, research and write a job description and a set of job specifications.

Recruitment

Where will you find the employees you need for your venture? Is there a need for highly specialized/qualified human resources? If so, determine if there will be a shortage in supply for those positions in the first year of operation.

Make a list of the external sources of potential applicants for each position.

Selection

What methods will you use to pick the most qualified and best-suited applicant for a position? The techniques you use, such as interviews, ability testing, background checks and so on must be valid and reliable.

Describe the selection techniques you will use to hire new employees and why they are valid and reliable.

Training and Development

Once you have offered a candidate a job, you must orient and train them in the roles and responsibilities of the position. Referring to Chapter 11, determine what types of training and development programs are suitable for each position.

Describe the types of training you will provide for each position.

Performance Appraisals

In order to determine if the employee has learned how to do the job, their performance levels must be appraised by management. The Human Resources Plan section of the business plan should describe how performance appraisals will be conducted and in what timeframe.

How will employee performance appraisals be conducted and feedback given?

Pay and Compensation

Research the pay levels and structures for the types of occupations you need for your venture. Industry standards can be found from Statistics Canada.[16] The amount of pay you offer should be consistent with the *strategy* you have adopted. For example, if our family restaurant intends to differentiate itself from the competition by focusing on high-income households as a target market, it makes sense that it can pay its waitstaff higher wages than if it adopted a cost-leadership strategy focusing on low-income households. Generally, if the competitive advantage is derived from superior quality, customer service, and innovation, higher than industry wages can be paid. If, on the other hand, the competitive advantage is derived from efficiency, lower than standard industry wages generally will be paid.

Will you offer wages at, above, or below the industry standards? Justify your answer in terms of the strategy of the venture.

8. Operating and Control Systems Plan

This section of the business plan describes the flow of goods and services from the input stage, through the conversion stage, and in the postproduction stage. Standards must be set for the use of resources at every stage and control measures implemented to ensure that the standards are being met. This involves an analysis of the whole supply chain. In particular, a supplier analysis, an inventory control analysis, and an assessment of how the goods will flow to the customer must be considered, whether the venture is a retail operation, a service provider, or a manufacturer.

Retail Operation or Service Provider

If your venture is a retail operation or a service provider, you should consider the following questions:

1. From whom will merchandise be purchased?

- Consider the supplier's reputation, past record, prices versus other suppliers, delivery methods, whether or not it supplies your competitors, and how important your business is to it.

2. How will the inventory and quality control system operate?

- Consider how you will inspect the goods received and what you will do if materials are defective.

- What are your storage and processing space needs?

- What is your ordering materials process?

3. How will the goods flow to the customer?

- What steps are involved in a business transaction?

- What technology (debit machines, scanners) will you need to serve customers effectively?

Create standards for each phase of the operation, and describe what methods of control you will use to ensure they are met.

	Standard/ Goal	Control Measures
Supplier analysis		
Inventory and quality control		
Flow of goods to customers		
Customer satisfaction		

Manufacturing Operation

If you are proposing a manufacturing operation, you should describe the complete operations management process. Some of the issues will be the same as above, but some will be different. In the *supplier analysis* area, you would include how much, if any, of the manufacturing process is subcontracted out to another firm. Who will perform such work, and how will you decide what to outsource and what operations to keep in-house? What specialized machinery and equipment is needed, and who will supply this? What are the capital equipment needs and expenditures? Include the costs in your financial plan and a full list of equipment in the appendices. In analyzing the *flow of goods,* illustrate the layout and all the steps in the production process.

Both service providers and manufacturers should have standards set for being responsive to customers. For example, a goal for customer service might be, "100-percent satisfaction or your money back guaranteed!" Enterprises must build in feedback control measures that allow customers to complain and praise the service and/or products, such as questionnaires and surveys.

Describe the risks that could arise in managing the operations of the venture and how you can minimize them.

9. Financial Plan

The financial plan tells the reader what level of potential investment commitment is needed and whether or not the business plan is feasible. It details the needed capital requirements for starting the venture, or new strategy, the forecast sales, and the expenses incurred in selling the product/service over a number of months and years.

Anyone reading your financial projections will want to know what assumptions went into the creation of the projections. This includes assumptions about, for example, the size of the market and your ability to penetrate it, staffing plans, management salaries, inventory turnover, receivables and payables periods, and expectations for investment or loans.

Refer to the exercise you did for Chapter 13: Managing Control and Operations and an accounting textbook to help you calculate the financial statements for your venture for a period of two years. Or simply follow the instructions in a business planning software program. This will create the spreadsheets for your plan.

Pro Forma Income Statement

The income statement subtracts all the costs incurred to operate your enterprise from the amounts received from selling goods and services. The result is a net income or a net loss for the year. You will be asked to enter revenue and expenses for each month of the first year, for each quarter of the second year.

Cash Flow Projections

The cash flow statement will show the amount of cash you have available at any given time during your business plan. If a negative cash balance occurs, you will have to examine your revenue and expense projections. To address the negative cash balance, you will have to increase revenues, decrease expenses, or arrange to get cash through a loan or capital investment. Cash flow is projected for each month of the first year and for each quarter of the second year.

Pro Forma Balance Sheet

The balance sheet is divided into two sections: assets and liabilities plus shareholders' equity. The two sections must always be in balance. A dollar amount or a "balance" represents each asset, liability, and component of shareholders' equity reported in the balance sheet. The balance sheet is projected for each month of the first year and for each quarter of the second year.

Break-Even Analysis

The projection of when the revenue will surpass the expenses of the venture is called the break-even point and is generally depicted graphically.

Alternative Scenarios

When presenting your business plan to an investor or to your management, it is of value to show projections for revenues and expenses that represent the best possible case and the worst possible case. It is recommended you provide some explanation for the circumstances that might precipitate either the best or worst case in the financial assumptions section.

Create a pro forma income statement, a cash flow statement, a balance sheet, and a break-even analysis for your business plan.

10. Appendices

The appendix of the business plan generally contains all the documents that are referenced in the plan itself and any backup material that is not necessary in the text of the document. You might consider including the following:

- Product/service samples
- Market research data
- Legal forms and documents
- Leases or contracts
- Price lists from suppliers, if applicable
- Promotional material examples
- Résumés of the management team
- Other backup material

Glossary

Chapter 1

CONCEPTUAL SKILLS The ability to analyze and diagnose a situation and to distinguish between cause and effect.

CONTROLLING Evaluating how well an organization is achieving its goals and taking action to maintain or improve performance; one of the four principal functions of management.

DEPARTMENT A group of people who work together and possess similar skills or use the same knowledge, tools, or techniques to perform their jobs; a group composed of subordinates who report to the same supervisor.

EFFECTIVENESS A measure of the appropriateness of the goals an organization is pursuing and of the degree to which the organization achieves those goals.

EFFICIENCY A measure of how well or productively resources are used to achieve a goal.

EMPOWERMENT The expansion of employees' knowledge, tasks, and decision-making responsibilities.

FIRST-LINE MANAGERS Managers who are responsible for the daily supervision and coordination of nonmanagerial employees.

HUMAN SKILLS The ability to understand, alter, lead, and control the behaviour of other individuals and groups.

LEADING Articulating a clear vision and energizing and empowering organizational members so that everyone understands his or her individual role in achieving organizational goals; one of the four principal functions of management.

MANAGEMENT The planning, organizing, leading, and controlling of resources to achieve organizational goals effectively and efficiently.

MANAGER A person who is responsible for supervising the use of an organization's resources to achieve its goals.

MIDDLE MANAGERS Managers who supervise first-line managers and are responsible for finding the best way to use resources to achieve organizational goals.

ORGANIZATIONAL PERFORMANCE A measure of how efficiently and effectively a manager uses resources to satisfy customers and achieve organizational goals.

ORGANIZATIONAL STRUCTURE A formal system of task and reporting relationships that coordinates and motivates organizational members so that they work together to reach organizational goals.

ORGANIZATIONS Collections of people who work together and coordinate their actions to achieve goals and desired future outcomes.

ORGANIZING Structuring workplace relationships so organizational members work together to achieve organizational goals; one of the four principal functions of management.

OUTSOURCING Contracting with another company, usually abroad, to have it perform an activity the organization previously performed itself.

PLANNING Identifying and selecting appropriate goals and courses of action; one of the four principal functions of management.

RESOURCES Assets such as people, machinery, raw materials, information, skills, and financial capital.

RESTRUCTURING Downsizing an organization by eliminating the jobs of large numbers of top, middle, and first-line managers and nonmanagerial employees.

ROLE The specific tasks that a person is expected to perform because of the position he or she holds in an organization.

SELF-MANAGED TEAMS Groups of employees who supervise their own activities and monitor the quality of the goods and services they provide.

SOCIAL ECONOMY A bridging concept for organizations that have social objectives central to their mission and their practice, and either have explicit economic objectives or generate some economic value through the services they provide and purchases that they undertake.

STRATEGY A cluster of decisions about what goals to pursue, what actions to take, and how to use resources to achieve goals.

TECHNICAL SKILLS Job-specific knowledge and techniques that are required to perform an organizational role.

TOP MANAGERS Managers who establish organizational goals, decide how departments should interact, and monitor the performance of middle managers.

TOP-MANAGEMENT TEAM A group composed of the CEO, the president, and the heads of the most important departments.

Chapter 2

ACHIEVEMENT ORIENTATION A worldview that values assertiveness, performance, success, and competition.

BARRIERS TO ENTRY Factors that make it difficult and costly for an organization to enter a particular task environment or industry.

BRAND LOYALTY Customers' preference for the products of organizations that currently exist in the task environment.

CERTAINTY The state of environmental forces that is stable enough to predict possible outcomes of decisions.

COLLECTIVISM A worldview that values subordination of the individual to the goals of the group and adherence to the principle that people should be judged by their contribution to the group.

COMPETITIVE ADVANTAGE The ability of one organization to outperform other organizations because it produces desired goods or services more efficiently and effectively than competitors do.

COMPETITORS Organizations that produce goods and services that are similar to a particular organization's goods and services.

CUSTOMERS Individuals and groups that buy the goods and services that an organization produces.

DEMOGRAPHIC FORCES Outcomes of changes in, or changing attitudes toward, the characteristics of a population, such as age, gender, ethnic origin, race, sexual orientation, and social class.

DISTRIBUTORS Organizations that help other organizations sell their goods or services to customers.

ECONOMIC FORCES Interest rates, inflation, unemployment, economic growth, and other factors that affect the general health and well-being of a nation or the regional economy of an organization.

ECONOMIES OF SCALE Cost advantages associated with large operations.

ENVIRONMENTAL CHANGE The degree to which forces in the task and general environments change and evolve over time.

EXTERNAL ENVIRONMENT The forces operating outside an organization that affect how the organization functions.

GENERAL ENVIRONMENT The economic, technological, socio-cultural, demographic, political and legal, and global forces that affect an organization and its task environment.

GLOBAL FORCES Outcomes of changes in international relationships; changes in nations' economic, political, and legal systems; and

changes in technology, such as falling trade barriers, the growth of representative democracies, and reliable and instantaneous communication.

GLOBAL ORGANIZATIONS Organizations that operate and compete in more than one country.

GLOBALIZATION The set of specific and general forces that work together to integrate and connect economic, political, and social systems across countries, cultures, or geographic regions so that nations become increasingly interdependent and similar.

INDIVIDUALISM A worldview that values individual freedom and self-expression and adherence to the principle that people should be judged by their individual achievements rather than by their social background.

INNOVATION The process of creating new goods and services or developing better ways to produce or provide goods and services; the implementation of creative ideas in an organization.

INTERNAL ENVIRONMENT The forces operating within an organization and stemming from the organization's structure and culture.

LONG-TERM ORIENTATION A worldview that values thrift and persistence in achieving goals.

NATIONAL CULTURE The set of values that a society considers important and the norms of behaviour that are approved or sanctioned in that society.

NURTURING ORIENTATION A worldview that values the quality of life, warm personal friendships, and services and care for the weak.

ORGANIZATIONAL ENVIRONMENT The set of forces and conditions that can affect the way an organization operates.

POLITICAL AND LEGAL FORCES Outcomes of changes in laws and regulations, such as the deregulation

of industries, the privatization of organizations, and increased emphasis on environmental protection.

POWER DISTANCE The degree to which societies accept the idea of inequalities in the power and well-being of their citizens are due to differences in individuals' physical and intellectual capabilities and heritage.

SHORT-TERM ORIENTATION A worldview that values personal stability or happiness and living for the present.

SOCIAL STRUCTURE The arrangement of relationships between individuals and groups in a society.

SOCIO-CULTURAL FORCES Pressures emanating from the social structure of a country or society or from the national culture.

STAKEHOLDERS Persons, groups, and institutions directly affected by the activities and decisions of an organization.

SUPPLIERS Individuals and organizations that provide an organization with the input resources that it needs to produce goods and services.

TASK ENVIRONMENT The set of forces and conditions that start with suppliers, distributors, customers, and competitors and affect an organization's ability to obtain inputs and dispose of its outputs, because they influence managers on a daily basis.

TECHNOLOGICAL FORCES Outcomes of changes in the technology that managers use to design, produce, or distribute goods and services.

TECHNOLOGY The combination of skills and equipment that managers use in the design, production, and distribution of goods and services.

UNCERTAINTY The state of environmental forces that is so dynamic that managers cannot predict the probable outcomes of a course of action.

UNCERTAINTY AVOIDANCE The degree to which societies are willing to tolerate uncertainty and risk.

VALUES Ideas about what a society believes to be good, right, desirable, or beautiful; stable, long-lasting beliefs about what is important.

Chapter 3

ACCOMMODATIVE APPROACH Moderate commitment to social responsibility; willingness to do more than the law requires, if asked.

BIAS The systematic tendency to use information about others in ways that result in inaccurate perceptions.

CODES OF ETHICS Formal standards and rules, based on beliefs about right or wrong, that managers can use to make appropriate decisions in the best interests of their stakeholders.

DEFENSIVE APPROACH Minimal commitment to social responsibility; willingness to do what the law requires and no more.

DISTRIBUTIVE JUSTICE A moral principle calling for the distribution of pay raises, promotions, and other organizational resources to be based on meaningful contributions that individuals have made and not on personal characteristics over which they have no control.

DIVERSITY Differences among people in age, gender, race, ethnicity, ability, and sexual orientation.

ETHICAL DECISIONS Decisions that reasonable or typical stakeholders would find acceptable because they aid stakeholders, the organization, or society.

ETHICAL DILEMMA The quandary people find themselves in when they have to decide if they should act in a way that might help another person or group even though doing so might go against their own self-interest.

ETHICS Moral principles or beliefs about what is right or wrong.

ETHICS OMBUDSPERSON An ethics officer who monitors an organization's practices and procedures to ensure that they are ethical.

GENERATION Y Also known as *millennials;* people born between 1981 and 1992.

HOSTILE WORK ENVIRONMENT SEXUAL HARASSMENT Telling lewd jokes, displaying pornography, making sexually oriented remarks about someone's personal appearance, and other sex-related actions that make the work environment unpleasant.

IMPACT INVESTING Investments that seek to solve social or environmental problems and generate financial returns to the investor.

INDIVIDUAL ETHICS Personal standards that govern how individuals interact with other people.

JUSTICE MODEL An ethical decision is a decision that distributes benefits and harms among people and groups in a fair, equitable, or impartial way.

MORAL RIGHTS MODEL An ethical decision is one that best maintains and protects the fundamental or inalienable rights and privileges of the people affected by it.

OBSTRUCTIONIST APPROACH Disregard for social responsibility; willingness to engage in and cover up unethical and illegal behaviour.

ORGANIZATIONAL STAKEHOLDERS Shareholders, employees, customers, suppliers, and others who have an interest, claim, or stake in an organization and in what it does.

OVERT DISCRIMINATION Knowingly and willingly denying diverse individuals access to opportunities and outcomes in an organization.

PROACTIVE APPROACH Strong commitment to social responsibility; eagerness to do more than the law requires and to use organizational resources to promote the interests of all organizational stakeholders.

PROCEDURAL JUSTICE A moral principle calling for the use of fair procedures to determine how to distribute outcomes to organizational members.

PROFESSIONAL ETHICS Standards that govern how members of a profession make decisions when the way they should behave is not clear-cut.

QUID PRO QUO SEXUAL HARASSMENT Asking or forcing an employee to perform sexual favours in exchange for some reward or to avoid negative consequences.

REPUTATION The esteem or high repute that individuals or organizations gain when they behave ethically.

SEXUAL HARASSMENT Unwelcome behaviour of a sexual nature in the workplace that negatively affects the work environment or leads to adverse job-related consequences for the employee.

SOCIAL AUDIT A tool that allows managers to analyze the profitability and social returns of socially responsible actions.

SOCIAL RESPONSIBILITY A manager's duty or obligation to make decisions that promote the well-being of stakeholders and society as a whole.

SOCIETAL ETHICS Standards that govern how members of a society deal with each other on issues such as fairness, justice, poverty, and the rights of the individual.

STEREOTYPE Simplistic and often inaccurate beliefs about the typical characteristics of particular groups of people.

UNETHICAL DECISIONS Decisions that a manager would prefer to disguise or hide from other people because they enable a company or a particular individual to gain at the expense of society or other stakeholders.

UTILITARIAN MODEL An ethical decision is a decision that produces the greatest good for the greatest number of people.

WORKPLACE HARASSMENT Any behaviour directed toward an employee that is known to be or ought to be known to be offensive and unwelcome.

Chapter 4

ADMINISTRATIVE MODEL An approach to decision making that explains why decision making is an inherently uncertain and risky process and why managers usually make satisfactory rather than optimum decisions.

AMBIGUOUS INFORMATION Information that can be interpreted in multiple and often conflicting ways.

BOUNDED RATIONALITY Cognitive limitations that constrain one's ability to interpret, process, and act on information.

CLASSICAL MODEL A prescriptive approach to decision making based on the idea that the decision maker can identify and evaluate all possible alternatives and their consequences and rationally choose the most suitable course of action.

CLOUD COMPUTING Web-based services including everything from managing supply chains and human resources, to data storage and digital content creation.

CREATIVITY A decision maker's ability to discover original and novel ideas that lead to feasible alternative courses of action.

DATA Raw, unsummarized, and unanalyzed facts.

DECISION MAKING The process by which managers respond to opportunities and threats by analyzing options and making determinations about specific organizational goals and courses of action.

DECISION SUPPORT SYSTEM An interactive computer-based management information system with model-building capability that managers can use when they must make nonroutine decisions.

ESCALATING COMMITMENT A source of cognitive bias resulting from the tendency to commit additional resources to a project even if evidence shows that the project is failing.

EXPERT SYSTEM A management information system that employs human knowledge captured in a computer to solve problems that ordinarily require human expertise.

HEURISTICS Rules of thumb that simplify decision making.

ILLUSION OF CONTROL A source of cognitive bias resulting from the tendency to overestimate one's own ability to control activities and events.

INFORMATION Data that are organized in a meaningful fashion.

INFORMATION DISTORTION Changes in meaning that occur as information passes through a series of senders and receivers.

INFORMATION TECHNOLOGY The means by which information is acquired, organized, stored, manipulated, and transmitted.

INNOVATION The process of creating new goods and services or developing better ways to produce or provide goods and services; the implementation of creative ideas in an organization.

INTRAPRENEUR A manager, scientist, or researcher who works inside an organization and notices opportunities to develop new or improved products and better ways to make them; employees of existing organizations who notice opportunities for product or service improvements and are responsible for managing the development process.

INTUITION Ability to make sound decisions based on past experience and immediate feelings about the information at hand.

JUDGMENT Ability to develop a sound opinion based on one's evaluation of the importance of the information at hand.

LEARNING ORGANIZATION An organization in which managers try to maximize the ability of individuals and groups to think and behave creatively and thus maximize the potential for organizational learning to take place.

MANAGEMENT INFORMATION SYSTEMS (MIS) Electronic systems of interconnected components designed to collect, process, store, and disseminate information to facilitate management decision making, planning, and control.

NONPROGRAMMED DECISION MAKING Nonroutine decision making that occurs in response to unusual, unpredictable opportunities and threats.

OPERATIONS INFORMATION SYSTEM A management information system that gathers, organizes, and summarizes comprehensive data in a form that managers can use in their nonroutine coordinating, controlling, and decision-making tasks.

OPTIMUM DECISION The best decision in light of what managers believe to be the most desirable future consequences for their organization.

ORGANIZATIONAL LEARNING The process through which managers seek to improve employees' desire and ability to understand and manage the organization and its task environment.

PRIOR HYPOTHESIS BIAS A cognitive bias resulting from the tendency to base decisions on strong prior beliefs even if evidence shows that those beliefs are wrong.

PROGRAMMED DECISION MAKING Routine, virtually automatic decision making that follows established rules or guidelines.

REAL-TIME INFORMATION Frequently updated information that reflects current conditions.

REPRESENTATIVENESS BIAS A cognitive bias resulting from the tendency to generalize inappropriately from a small sample or from a single vivid case or episode.

SATISFICING Searching for and choosing acceptable, or satisfactory, ways to respond to problems and opportunities, rather than trying to make the best decision.

SUSTAINABILITY Decisions that protect the environment, promote social responsibility, respect cultural differences, and provide an economic benefit.

SYSTEMATIC ERRORS Errors that people make over and over again and that result in poor decision making.

TRANSACTION-PROCESSING SYSTEM A management information system designed to handle large volumes of routine, recurring transactions.

Chapter 5

BUSINESS-LEVEL PLAN Divisional managers' decisions relating to divisions' long-term goals, overall strategy, and structure.

BUSINESS-LEVEL STRATEGY A plan that indicates how a division intends to compete against its rivals in an industry.

CO-OPETITION Arrangements in which firms compete vigorously with one another, while also cooperating in specific areas to achieve economies of scale.

CORPORATE-LEVEL PLANS Top management's decisions relating to the organization's mission, overall strategy, and structure.

CORPORATE-LEVEL STRATEGY A plan that indicates the industries and national markets in which an organization intends to compete.

COST-LEADERSHIP STRATEGY Driving the organization's costs down below the costs of its rivals.

CRISIS MANAGEMENT PLANS Formulated to deal with possible future crises.

DIFFERENTIATION STRATEGY Distinguishing an organization's products from the products of competitors in dimensions such as

product design, quality, or after-sales service.

DIVERSIFICATION Expanding operations into a new business or industry and producing new goods or services.

DIVISION A business unit that has its own set of managers and functions or departments and competes in a distinct industry.

DIVISIONAL MANAGERS Managers who control the various divisions of an organization.

FOCUSED DIFFERENTIATION STRATEGY Serving only one segment of the overall market and trying to be the most differentiated organization serving that segment.

FOCUSED LOW-COST STRATEGY Serving only one segment of the overall market and being the lowest-cost organization serving that segment.

FUNCTIONAL MANAGERS Managers who supervise the various functions—such as manufacturing, accounting, and sales—within a division.

FUNCTIONAL-LEVEL PLAN Functional managers' decisions relating to the goals that they propose to pursue to help the division reach its business-level goals.

FUNCTIONAL-LEVEL STRATEGY A plan that indicates how a function intends to achieve its goals.

FUNCTIONS Units or departments in which people have the same skills or use the same resources to perform their jobs.

GANTT CHART A graphic bar chart managers use to schedule the tasks in a project showing what tasks need to be done, who will do them, and by what timeframe.

GLOBAL STRATEGY Selling the same standardized product and using the same basic marketing approach in each national market.

GOAL A desired future outcome that an organization strives to achieve within a specified timeframe.

MISSION STATEMENT A broad declaration of an organization's purpose that identifies the organization's products and customers and distinguishes the organization from its competitors.

MULTI-DOMESTIC STRATEGY Customizing products and marketing strategies to specific national conditions.

PLANNING Identifying and selecting appropriate goals and courses of action; one of the four principal functions of management.

POLICY A general guide to action.

PORTER'S FIVE FORCES MODEL A technique managers use to analyze the potential profitability of entertaining and competing in a particular industry.

RELATED DIVERSIFICATION Entering a new business or industry to create a competitive advantage in one or more of an organization's existing divisions or businesses.

RULE A formal, written guide to action.

SCENARIO PLANNING The generation of multiple forecasts of future conditions followed by an analysis of how to respond effectively to each of those conditions; also called *contingency planning*.

STANDARD OPERATING PROCEDURES (SOPs) Written instructions describing the exact series of actions that should be followed in a specific situation; rules and policies that standardize behaviours.

STRATEGIC LEADERSHIP The ability of the CEO and top managers to convey a compelling vision of what they want the organization to achieve to their subordinates.

STRATEGY A cluster of decisions about what goals to pursue, what actions to take, and how to use resources to achieve goals.

STRATEGY FORMULATION Analysis of an organization's current situation followed by the development of strategies to accomplish the organization's mission and achieve its goals.

SWOT ANALYSIS A planning exercise in which managers identify organizational strengths (S) and weaknesses (W), and environmental opportunities (O) and threats (T) relative to the competition.

SYNERGY Performance gains that result when individuals and departments coordinate their actions.

TIME HORIZON The intended duration of a plan.

UNRELATED DIVERSIFICATION Entering a new industry or buying a company in a new industry that is not related in any way to an organization's current businesses or industries.

VERTICAL INTEGRATION A strategy that allows an organization to create value by producing its own inputs or distributing and selling its own outputs.

VISION STATEMENT A broad declaration of the big picture of the organization and/or a statement of its dreams for the future.

Chapter 6

AUTHORITY The power to hold people accountable for their actions and to make decisions concerning the use of organizational resources.

BOUNDARYLESS ORGANIZATION An organization whose members are linked by computers, computer-aided design systems, and video teleconferencing, and who rarely, if ever, see one another face to face.

BUSINESS-TO-BUSINESS (B2B) NETWORKS A group of organizations that join together and use software to link themselves to potential global suppliers to increase efficiency and effectiveness.

CROSS-FUNCTIONAL TEAM A group of individuals from different departments brought together to perform organizational tasks.

DECENTRALIZING AUTHORITY Giving lower-level managers and nonmanagerial employees the right to make important decisions about how to use organizational resources.

DIVISION OF LABOUR The overall result of job design among employees in an organization; splitting the work to be performed into particular tasks and assigning tasks to individual workers.

DIVISIONAL STRUCTURE An organizational structure composed of separate business units within which are the functions that work together to produce a specific product for a specific customer.

FUNCTIONAL STRUCTURE An organizational structure composed of all the departments that an organization requires to produce its goods or services.

GEOGRAPHIC STRUCTURE An organizational structure in which each region of a country or area of the world is served by a self-contained division.

HIERARCHY OF AUTHORITY An organization's chain of command, specifying the relative authority of each manager.

HYBRID STRUCTURE The structure of a large organization that has many divisions and simultaneously uses many different organizational structures.

JOB DESIGN The process by which managers decide how to divide tasks into specific jobs.

JOB ENLARGEMENT Increasing the number of different tasks in a given job by changing the division of labour.

JOB ENRICHMENT Increasing the degree of responsibility a worker has over his or her job.

JOB SIMPLIFICATION Reducing the number of tasks that each worker performs.

LINE MANAGER Someone in the direct line or chain of command who has formal authority over people and resources at lower levels.

MARKET STRUCTURE An organizational structure in which each kind of customer is served by a self-contained division; also called *customer structure*.

MATRIX STRUCTURE An organizational structure that simultaneously groups people and resources by function and by product.

MECHANISTIC STRUCTURE An organizational structure in which authority is centralized at the top of the hierarchy, tasks and roles are clearly specified, and employees are closely supervised.

MINIMUM CHAIN OF COMMAND The idea that top managers should always construct a hierarchy with the fewest levels of authority necessary to efficiently and effectively use organizational resources.

NETWORK STRUCTURE A series of strategic alliances that an organization creates with suppliers, manufacturers, and/or distributors to produce and market a product.

ORGANIC STRUCTURE An organizational structure in which authority is decentralized to middle and first-line managers and tasks and roles are left ambiguous to encourage employees to cooperate and respond quickly to the unexpected.

ORGANIZATIONAL DESIGN The process by which managers make specific organizing choices that result in a particular kind of organizational structure.

ORGANIZATIONAL STRUCTURE A formal system of task and reporting relationships that coordinates and motivates organizational members so that they work together to reach organizational goals.

OUTSOURCING Contracting with another company, usually abroad, to have it perform an activity the organization previously performed itself.

PRODUCT STRUCTURE An organizational structure in which each product line or business is handled by a self-contained division.

PRODUCT TEAM STRUCTURE An organizational structure in which employees are permanently assigned to a cross-functional team and report only to the product team manager or to one of his or her direct subordinates.

SPAN OF CONTROL The number of subordinates who report directly to a manager.

STAFF MANAGER Someone responsible for managing a specialist function, such as finance or marketing.

STRATEGIC ALLIANCE A formal agreement that commits two or more companies to exchange or share their resources in order to produce and market a product.

Chapter 7

ARTIFACTS Aspects of an organization's culture that one sees, hears, and feels.

ASSUMPTIONS The taken-for-granted notions of how something should be in an organization.

BELIEFS The understandings of how objects and ideas relate to each other.

BENCHMARKING Comparing performance on specific dimensions with the performance of high-performing organizations.

BOTTOM-UP CHANGE Change that is introduced gradually and involves managers and employees at all levels of an organization.

COMPLEXITY THEORY Organizations respond best to change if they are not perfectly aligned with their environment.

CREATIVITY A person's ability to discover original and novel ideas that lead to innovation.

CULTURAL CHANGES A shift in the shared set of beliefs, expectations, values, norms, and work routines that influence how members of an organization relate to one another and work together to achieve organizational goals.

DRIVING FORCES Forces that direct behaviour away from the status quo.

E-BUSINESS Connecting suppliers, customers, employees, and other stakeholders using the Internet and intranet applications to facilitate commerce.

ENTREPRENEURS People who notice opportunities and take responsibility for mobilizing the resources necessary to produce new and improved goods and services.

ENTREPRENEURSHIP The mobilization of resources to take advantage of an opportunity to provide customers with new or improved goods and services.

IMPOSED CHANGE New institutional arrangements made to comply with regulations.

INDUCED CHANGE Planned new institutional arrangements made to gain a competitive advantage.

INNOVATION The process of creating new goods and services or developing better ways to produce or provide goods and services; the implementation of creative ideas in an organization.

INTRAPRENEURS Employees of existing organizations who notice opportunities for product or service improvements and are responsible for managing the development process.

NORMS Unwritten rules or guidelines for appropriate behaviour in particular situations.

ORGANIZATIONAL CHANGE The movement of an organization away from its present state and toward some desired future state to increase its efficiency and effectiveness.

ORGANIZATIONAL CULTURE The shared set of beliefs, expectations, values, norms, and work routines that influence how members of an organization relate to one another and work together to achieve organizational goals.

ORGANIZATIONAL SOCIALIZATION The process by which newcomers learn an organization's values and norms

and acquire the work behaviours necessary to perform jobs effectively.

PERFORMANCE GAP A disparity between desired and actual performance levels.

PRODUCT CHAMPION A manager who takes "ownership" of a project and provides the leadership and vision that take a product from the idea stage to the final customer.

PRODUCT CHANGES A change in the products and services offered by the organization.

RESTRAINING FORCES Forces that prevent movement away from the status quo.

SKUNKWORKS A group of intrapreneurs who are deliberately separated from the normal operation of an organization to encourage them to devote all their attention to developing new products.

SOCIAL ENTREPRENEURS Individuals who pursue initiatives and opportunities and mobilize resources to address social problems and needs in order to improve society and well-being through creative solutions.

SOCIAL INNOVATION Developing new ways of solving social problems.

STRUCTURAL CHANGES Any change in the design and management of an organization.

TECHNOLOGICAL CHANGES Changes that relate to an organization's operational processes.

TOP-DOWN CHANGE Change that is introduced quickly throughout an organization by upper-level managers.

VALUES Ideas about what a society believes to be good, right, desirable, or beautiful; stable, long-lasting beliefs about what is important.

Chapter 8

EMPLOYEE RECOGNITION PROGRAMS Management expressions of interest, approval and appreciation for a job well done by individuals or groups of employees.

EMPLOYEE STOCK OPTIONS Financial instruments that entitle the bearer to buy shares of an organization's stock at a certain price during a certain period of time or under certain conditions.

EQUITY The justice, impartiality, and fairness to which all organizational members are entitled.

EQUITY THEORY A theory of motivation that focuses on people's perceptions of the fairness of their work outcomes relative to their work inputs.

EXPECTANCY In expectancy theory, a perception about the extent to which effort will result in a certain level of performance.

EXPECTANCY THEORY The theory that motivation will be high when employees believe that high levels of effort will lead to high performance and that high performance will lead to the attainment of desired outcomes.

EXTINCTION Stopping the performance of dysfunctional behaviours by eliminating whatever is reinforcing them.

EXTRINSICALLY MOTIVATED BEHAVIOUR Behaviour that is performed to acquire material or social rewards or to avoid punishment.

GOAL-SETTING THEORY A theory that focuses on identifying the types of goals that are most effective in producing high levels of motivation and performance and explaining why goals have these effects.

HERZBERG'S MOTIVATOR-HYGIENE THEORY A need theory that distinguishes between motivator needs (related to the nature of the work itself) and hygiene needs (related to the physical and psychological context in which the work is performed). Herzberg proposed that motivator needs must be met in order for motivation and job satisfaction to be high; also known as the *two-factor theory*.

INEQUITY Lack of fairness.

INPUT Anything a person contributes to his or her job or organization.

INSTRUMENTALITY In expectancy theory, a perception about the extent to which performance will result in the attainment of outcomes.

INTRINSICALLY MOTIVATED BEHAVIOUR Behaviour that is performed for its own sake.

LEARNING A relatively permanent change in knowledge or behaviour that results from practice or experience.

LEARNING THEORIES Theories that focus on increasing employee motivation and performance by linking the outcomes that employees receive to the performance of desired behaviours and the attainment of goals.

MASLOW'S HIERARCHY OF NEEDS An arrangement of five basic needs that, according to Maslow, motivate behaviour. Maslow proposed that the lowest level of unmet needs is the prime motivator and that only one level of needs is motivational at a time.

MERIT PAY PLAN A compensation plan that bases pay on performance.

MOTIVATION Psychological forces that determine the direction of a person's behaviour in an organization, level of effort, and level of persistence.

NEED A requirement or necessity for survival and well-being.

NEED FOR ACHIEVEMENT The extent to which an individual has a strong desire to perform challenging tasks well and to meet personal standards for excellence.

NEED FOR AFFILIATION The extent to which an individual is concerned about establishing and maintaining good interpersonal relations, being liked, and having the people around him or her get along with each other.

NEED FOR POWER The extent to which an individual desires to control or influence others.

NEED THEORIES Theories of motivation that focus on what needs people are trying to satisfy at work and what outcomes will satisfy those needs.

NEGATIVE REINFORCEMENT Eliminating or removing undesired outcomes once people have performed organizationally functional behaviours.

OPERANT CONDITIONING THEORY The theory that people learn to perform behaviours that lead to desired consequences and learn not to perform behaviours that lead to undesired consequences.

OUTCOME Anything a person gets from a job or organization.

OVERPAYMENT INEQUITY Inequity that exists when a person perceives that his or her own outcome/input ratio is greater than the ratio of a referent.

POSITIVE REINFORCEMENT Giving people outcomes they desire when they perform organizationally functional behaviours.

PROCESS THEORIES Theories that explain the processes by which employee behaviour can be aroused and then directed.

PROSOCIALLY MOTIVATED BEHAVIOUR Behaviour that is performed to benefit or help others.

PUNISHMENT Administering an undesired or negative consequence when dysfunctional behaviour occurs.

REINFORCER Any stimulus that causes a given behaviour to be repeated.

SELF-EFFICACY A person's belief about his or her ability to perform a behaviour successfully.

SELF-REINFORCER Any desired or attractive outcome or reward that a person gives to himself or herself for good performance.

SOCIAL LEARNING THEORY A theory that takes into account how learning and motivation are influenced by people's thoughts and beliefs and their observations of other people's behaviour.

TOTAL REWARD STRATEGY Encompasses both intrinsically and extrinsically motivating factors.

UNDERPAYMENT INEQUITY Inequity that exists when a person perceives that his or her own outcome/input ratio is less than the ratio of a referent.

VALENCE In expectancy theory, how desirable each of the outcomes available from a job or organization is to a person.

VICARIOUS LEARNING Learning that occurs when the learner becomes motivated to perform a behaviour by watching another person perform it and be reinforced for doing so; also called *observational learning*.

Chapter 9

CHARISMATIC LEADERS Enthusiastic, self-confident leaders who are able to communicate clearly their vision of how good things could be.

COERCIVE POWER The ability to persuade someone to do something that he or she otherwise would not.

CONSIDERATION OR EMPLOYEE-CENTRED BEHAVIOUR Behaviour indicating that a manager trusts, respects, and cares about subordinates.

CONTINGENCY MODELS OF LEADERSHIP Models of leadership that take into account the variables in the situation or context in which leadership occurs.

DEVELOPMENTAL CONSIDERATION Behaviour a leader engages in to support and encourage followers and help them develop and grow on the job.

EMOTIONAL INTELLIGENCE The ability to understand and manage one's moods and emotions and the moods and emotions of other people.

EMPOWERMENT The expansion of employees' knowledge, tasks, and decision-making responsibilities.

EXPERT POWER Power that is based in the special knowledge, skills, and expertise that a leader possesses.

INITIATING STRUCTURE OR TASK-ORIENTED BEHAVIOURS Behaviours that managers engage in to ensure that work gets done, subordinates perform their jobs acceptably, and the organization is efficient and effective.

INTELLECTUAL STIMULATION Behaviour a leader engages in to

make followers aware of problems and view these problems in new ways, consistent with the leader's vision.

LEADER An individual who is able to exert influence over other people to help achieve group or organizational goals.

LEADER–MEMBER RELATIONS The extent to which followers like, trust, and are loyal to their leader; can be good or poor.

LEADER SUBSTITUTE Characteristics of subordinates or characteristics of a situation or context that act in place of the influence of a leader and make leadership unnecessary.

LEADERSHIP The process by which an individual exerts influence over other people and inspires, motivates, and directs their activities to help achieve group or organizational goals.

LEGITIMATE POWER The authority that a manager has by virtue of his or her position in an organization's hierarchy.

PATH-GOAL THEORY A contingency model of leadership proposing that leaders can motivate subordinates by identifying their desired outcomes, rewarding them for high performance and the attainment of work goals with these desired outcomes, and clarifying for them the paths leading to the attainment of work goals.

PERSONAL LEADERSHIP STYLE The ways a manager chooses to influence others and how they approach planning, organizing, and controlling.

POSITION POWER The amount of legitimate, reward, and coercive power that a leader has by virtue of his or her position in an organization; can be strong or weak.

REFERENT POWER Power that comes from subordinates' and coworkers' respect, admiration, and loyalty.

REWARD POWER The ability of a manager to give or withhold tangible and intangible rewards.

SITUATIONAL LEADERSHIP THEORY (SLT) A contingency model of leadership that focuses on the followers' readiness.

TASK STRUCTURE The extent to which the work to be performed is clear-cut so that a leader's subordinates know what needs to be accomplished and how to go about doing it; can be high or low.

TRANSACTIONAL LEADERSHIP Leaders who guide their subordinates toward expected goals by rewarding them for high performance and reprimanding them for low performance, with no expectation of exceeding expected behaviour.

TRANSFORMATIONAL LEADERSHIP Leadership that makes subordinates aware of the importance of their jobs and performance to the organization and aware of their own needs for personal growth, and that motivates subordinates to work for the good of the organization.

Chapter 10

BRAINSTORMING A group problem-solving technique in which individuals meet face to face to generate and debate a wide variety of alternatives from which to make a decision.

CROSS-FUNCTIONAL TEAMS Groups of individuals from different departments brought together to perform organizational tasks.

DELPHI TECHNIQUE A decision-making technique in which group members do not meet face to face but respond in writing to questions posed by the group leader.

DEPARTMENT A group of people who work together and possess similar skills or use the same knowledge, tools, or techniques to perform their jobs; a group composed of subordinates who report to the same supervisor.

DEVIL'S ADVOCACY Critical analysis of a preferred alternative, made by a group member who plays the role of devil's advocate to defend unpopular or opposing alternatives for the sake of argument.

DIVISION OF LABOUR The overall result of job design among employees in an organization; splitting the work to be performed into particular tasks and assigning tasks to individual workers.

FORMAL GROUPS Groups that managers establish to achieve organizational goals.

FRIENDSHIP GROUPS Informal groups composed of employees who enjoy one another's company and socialize with one another.

GROUP Two or more people who interact with each other to reach certain goals or meet certain needs.

GROUP COHESIVENESS The degree to which members are attracted or loyal to a group.

GROUP DYNAMICS The ways in which group members interact determines their effectiveness.

GROUP NORMS Shared guidelines or rules of behaviour that most group members follow.

GROUP ROLE A set of behaviours and tasks that a member of a group is expected to perform because of his or her position in the group.

GROUPTHINK A pattern of faulty and biased decision making that occurs in groups whose members strive for agreement among themselves at the expense of accurately assessing information relevant to a decision.

INFORMAL GROUPS Groups that managers or nonmanagerial employees form to help achieve their own goals or meet their own needs.

INTEREST GROUPS Informal groups composed of employees seeking to achieve a common goal related to their membership in an organization.

MAINTENANCE ROLES Roles performed by group members to make sure there are good relationships among group members.

NOMINAL GROUP TECHNIQUE A decision-making technique in which group members write down ideas and solutions, read their suggestions to the whole group, and discuss and then rank the alternatives.

PRODUCTION BLOCKING A loss of productivity in brainstorming sessions due to the unstructured nature of brainstorming.

RELATIONSHIP CONFLICT Members of the group perceive each other's attitudes as a problem.

RESEARCH AND DEVELOPMENT TEAMS Teams whose members have the expertise and experience needed to develop new products.

ROLE MAKING Taking the initiative to modify an assigned role by taking on extra responsibilities.

SELF-MANAGED (OR SELF-DIRECTED) WORK TEAMS Groups of employees who supervise their own activities and monitor the quality of the goods and services they provide.

SOCIAL LOAFING The tendency of individuals to put forth less effort when they work in groups than when they work alone.

STANDING COMMITTEES Relatively permanent task forces charged with addressing long-term, enduring problems or issues facing an organization.

SYNERGY Performance gains that result when individuals and departments coordinate their actions.

TASK FORCES Cross-functional teams charged with solving a specific problem or addressing a specific issue within a fixed timeframe.

TASK-ORIENTED ROLES Roles performed by group members to make sure the task gets done.

TASK-RELATED CONFLICT Members of the group perceive a problem or have a disagreement about the nature of the task or project.

TEAM A group whose members work intensely with each other to achieve a specific common goal or objective.

TOP-MANAGEMENT TEAM A group composed of the CEO, the president, and the heads of the most important departments.

VIRTUAL TEAMS Teams whose members rarely or never meet face to face and interact by using various forms of information technology such as email, computer networks, telephones, faxes, and video conferences.

Chapter 11

ABILITY TESTS Assess the skills necessary to perform the job well.

BEHAVIOURAL INTERVIEW QUESTIONS Ask candidates how they dealt with a situation they encountered on the job.

CAFETERIA-STYLE BENEFIT PLANS Plans from which employees can choose the benefits that they want.

COLLECTIVE AGREEMENT A mutually agreed upon set of provisions that govern working conditions between a union and an employer for a set period of time.

COLLECTIVE BARGAINING Negotiations between labour unions and managers to resolve conflicts and disputes about issues such as working hours, wages, benefits, working conditions, and job security.

DEVELOPMENT Building the knowledge and skills of organizational members so that they will be prepared to take on new responsibilities and challenges.

FORMAL APPRAISALS Appraisals conducted at a set time during the year and based on performance dimensions and measures that were specified in advance.

HUMAN RESOURCE MANAGEMENT (HRM) Activities that managers engage in to attract and retain employees and to ensure that they perform at a high level and contribute to the accomplishment of organizational goals.

HUMAN RESOURCE PLANNING Activities that managers use to forecast their current and future needs for human resources.

INFORMAL APPRAISALS Unscheduled appraisals of ongoing progress and areas for improvement.

INTENTIONAL DISCRIMINATION The illegal practice of deliberately using prohibited grounds, such as race, religion, and sex, when making employment decisions.

JOB ANALYSIS Identifying the tasks, duties, and responsibilities that make up a job and the knowledge, skills, and abilities needed to perform the job.

LABOUR RELATIONS The activities that managers engage in to ensure that they have effective working relationships with the labour unions that represent their employees' interests.

LATERAL MOVES Job changes that entails no major changes in responsibility or authority levels.

NEEDS ASSESSMENT An assessment to determine which employees need training or development and what type of skills or knowledge they need to acquire.

OBJECTIVE APPRAISAL An appraisal that is based on facts and is likely to be numerical.

ON-THE-JOB TRAINING Training that takes place in the work setting as employees perform their job tasks.

OUTSOURCE To use outside suppliers and manufacturers to produce goods and services.

PAY LEVEL The relative position of an organization's pay incentives in comparison with those of other organizations in the same industry employing similar kinds of workers.

PAY STRUCTURE The arrangement of jobs into categories that reflect their relative importance to the organization and its goals, levels of skill required, and other characteristics.

PERFORMANCE APPRAISAL The evaluation of employees' job performance and contributions to their organization.

PERFORMANCE FEEDBACK The process through which managers share performance appraisal information with subordinates, give subordinates an opportunity to reflect on their own performance, and develop, with subordinates, plans for the future.

PERFORMANCE TESTS Measure the candidate's ability to perform actual job tasks.

PERSONALITY TESTS Measure personality traits and characteristics relevant to job performance.

PERSONNEL REPLACEMENT CHARTS A graphic illustration of current positions, who holds them, and whether they have the skills and qualifications necessary for succession planning.

PHYSICAL ABILITY TESTS Measure physical strength and stamina.

REALISTIC JOB PREVIEW (RJP) Communicating the good and bad aspects of a job to a candidate to prevent mismatched expectations and high turnover.

RECRUITMENT Activities that managers use to develop a pool of qualified candidates for open positions.

RELIABLE SELECTION TECHNIQUE A test or tool that yields consistent results when repeated.

SELECTION The process that managers use to determine the relative qualifications of job applicants and the individuals' potential for performing well in a particular job.

SITUATIONAL INTERVIEW QUESTIONS Ask candidates how they would deal with a situation they might encounter on the job.

STRATEGIC HUMAN RESOURCE MANAGEMENT The process by which managers design the components of a human resource management system to be consistent with each other, with other elements of organizational architecture, and with the organization's strategy and goals.

STRUCTURED INTERVIEW Formal questions asked in a set sequence.

SUBJECTIVE APPRAISAL An appraisal that is based on perceptions of traits, behaviours, or results.

360-DEGREE APPRAISAL A performance appraisal by peers, subordinates, superiors, and sometimes clients who are in a position to evaluate a manager's performance.

TRAINING Teaching organizational members how to perform their current jobs and helping them acquire the knowledge and skills they need to be effective performers.

UNINTENTIONAL DISCRIMINATION Unfair practices and policies that have an adverse impact on specific groups for reasons unrelated to the job.

UNSTRUCTURED INTERVIEW Unplanned questions asked as points of interest arise in the conversation.

VALID SELECTION TECHNIQUE A test or tool that measures the candidates' likely success or failure of performing the job.

Chapter 12

APPLICATIONS SOFTWARE Software designed for a specific task or use.

ARTIFICIAL INTELLIGENCE Behaviour performed by a machine that would be called intelligent if performed by a human being.

COMMUNICATION The sharing of information between two or more individuals or groups to reach a common understanding.

DECODING Interpreting and trying to make sense of a message.

DISTRIBUTIVE NEGOTIATION Adversarial negotiation in which the parties in conflict compete to win the most resources while conceding as little as possible.

ENCODING Translating a message into understandable symbols or language.

FILTERING Withholding part of a message out of the mistaken belief that the receiver does not need or will not want the information.

GRAPEVINE An informal communication network among people in organizations.

INFORMATION DISTORTION Changes in the meaning of a message as the message passes through a series of senders and receivers.

INFORMATION OVERLOAD A superabundance of information that increases the likelihood that important information is ignored or overlooked and tangential information receives attention.

INFORMATION RICHNESS The amount of information that a

communication medium can carry and the extent to which the medium enables sender and receiver to reach a common understanding.

INTEGRATIVE BARGAINING Cooperative negotiation in which the parties in conflict work together to achieve a resolution that is good for them all.

JARGON Specialized language that members of an occupation, group, or organization develop to facilitate communication among themselves.

MANAGEMENT BY WANDERING AROUND (MBWA) A face-to-face communication technique in which a manager walks around a work area and talks informally with employees about issues and concerns.

MEDIUM The pathway through which an encoded message is transmitted to a receiver.

MESSAGE The information that a sender wants to share.

NEGOTIATION A method of conflict resolution in which the parties in conflict consider various alternative ways to allocate resources to each other in order to come up with a solution acceptable to them all.

NETWORKING The exchange of information through a group or network of interlinked computers.

NOISE Anything that hampers any stage of the communication process.

NONVERBAL COMMUNICATION The encoding of messages by means of facial expressions, body language, and styles of dressing.

OPERATING SYSTEM SOFTWARE Software that tells computer hardware how to run.

ORGANIZATIONAL CONFLICT The discord that arises when the goals, interests, or values of different individuals or groups are incompatible and those individuals or groups block or thwart each other's attempts to achieve their objectives.

PERCEPTION The process through which people select, organize, and interpret sensory input to give meaning and order to the world around them.

RECEIVER The person or group for whom a message is intended.

RUMOURS Unofficial pieces of information of interest to organizational members but with no identifiable source.

SENDER The person or group wishing to share information.

STEREOTYPES Simplistic and often inaccurate beliefs about the typical characteristics of particular groups of people.

VERBAL COMMUNICATION The encoding of messages into words, either written or spoken.

Chapter 13

BENCHMARKING Comparing performance on specific dimensions with the performance of high-performing organizations.

BUREAUCRATIC CONTROL Control of behaviour by means of a comprehensive system of rules and standard operating procedures.

CLAN CONTROL Control exerted on individuals and groups in an organization by shared values, norms, standards of behaviour, and expectations.

CONCURRENT CONTROL Control that gives managers immediate feedback on how efficiently inputs are being transformed into outputs so that managers can correct problems as they arise.

CONTROL SYSTEMS Formal target-setting, monitoring, evaluation, and feedback systems that provide managers with information about how well the organization's strategy and structure are working.

CONTROLLING The process of monitoring and evaluating how well an organization is achieving its goals and taking action to maintain or improve performance; one of the four principal functions of management.

CORPORATE GOVERNANCE The processes companies use to be accountable to stakeholders, including investors, employees, the environment, and communities.

DISCIPLINE Managerial control through administering punishment when undesired workplace behaviours, such as absenteeism, lack of punctuality, and low performance, are exhibited, in an attempt to decrease their frequency.

FEEDBACK CONTROL Control that gives managers information about customers' reactions to goods and services so that corrective action can be taken if necessary.

FEEDFORWARD CONTROL Control that allows managers to anticipate and deal with potential problems.

MANAGEMENT BY OBJECTIVES A system of evaluating subordinates for their ability to achieve specific organizational goals or performance standards.

OPERATING BUDGET A budget that states how managers intend to use organizational resources to achieve organizational goals.

OPERATIONS MANAGEMENT The process of managing the use of materials and other resources in producing an organization's goods and services.

OPERATIONS MANAGERS Managers who are responsible for managing an organization's production system.

PRODUCTION SYSTEM The system that an organization uses to acquire inputs, convert the inputs into outputs, and dispose of the outputs.

PRODUCTIVITY The output of goods and services relative to the inputs.

SIX SIGMA A technique for improving performance based on error-free production and service provision.

STANDARD OPERATING PROCEDURES (SOPs) Written instructions describing the exact series of actions that should be followed in a specific situation; rules and policies that standardize behaviours.

TOTAL QUALITY MANAGEMENT (TQM) An approach to continuous improvements in quality at every stage of production.

Endnotes

Chapter 1

1. http://micro.newswire.ca/release.cgi? rkey=1610012435&view=51711-0& Start=0. Accessed November 1, 2008.

2. http://www.torontocfa.ca/imis15/ Content/Site_Navigation/Events ___Courses/Event_Detail.aspx?title= 11BRICK. Accessed Sept 21, 2011.

3. http://micro.newswire.ca/release. cgi?rkey=1610012435&view= 51711-0&Start=0. Accessed November 1, 2008.

4. G.R. Jones, *Organizational Theory* (Reading, MA: Addison-Wesley, 1995).

5. Jack Quarter, Laurie Mook, and Ann Armstrong, *Understanding the Social Economy: A Canadian Perspective* (Toronto: University of Toronto Press, 2009).

6. Ibid, p. 4.

7. Imagine Canada and Canadian Policy Research Networks, 2006. "Building Blocks for Strong Communities—Key Findings and Recommendations." Accessed May 20, 2012.

8. Adapted from http://www.marsdd. com/dmsassets/reports/Social_ entrepreneurship_Mars_series1.pdf. Accessed November 22, 2011.

9. Brick Brewing Company, http://www .newswire.ca/en/releases/archive/ March2011/17/c3677.html. Accessed March 18, 2011.

10. P. Drucker, *Management: Tasks, Responsibilities, Practices* (New York: Harper and Row, 1974).

11. J.P. Campbell, "On the Nature of Organizational Effectiveness," in P.S. Goodman, J.M. Pennings, and Associates, *New Perspectives on Organizational Effectiveness* (San Francisco: Jossey-Bass, 1977).

12. M. J. Provitera, "What Management Is: How It Works and Why It's Everyone's Business," *Academy of Management Executive* 17 (August 2003), 152–54.

13. "CEO Salaries," *Toronto Star,* http://www.thestar.com/ staticcontent/917086. Accessed September 21, 2011.

14. J. McGuire and E. Matta, "CEO Stock Options: The Silent Dimension of Ownership," *Academy of Management Journal* 46 (April 2003), 255–66.

15. J. G. Combs and M. S. Skill, "Managerialist and Human Capital Explanations for Key Executive Pay Premium: A Contingency Perspective," *Academy of Management Journal* 46 (February 2003), 63–74.

16. G.R. Jones, *Organizational Theory* (Reading, MA: Addison-Wesley, 1995).

17. P.F. Drucker, *Management Tasks, Responsibilities, and Practices* (New York: Harper and Row, 1974).

18. G. Dixon, "Clock Ticking for New CEOs," *The Globe and Mail,* May 8, 2001.

19. http://www.newswire.ca/en/releases/ archive/May2011/12/c3818.html. Accessed September 21, 2011.

20. http://www2.brickbeer.com/. Accessed September 21, 2011.

21. Adapted from Gordon Pitts, "As Tough as Her Father? Some Say Even Tougher," *The Globe and Mail*, Monday, August 13, 2007, B1, 8.

22. J. Kotter, *The General Managers* (New York: Free Press, 1992).

23. C.P. Hales, "What Do Managers Do? A Critical Review of the Evidence," *Journal of Management Studies,* January 1986, pp. 88–115; A.I. Kraul, P.R. Pedigo, D.D. McKenna, and M.D. Dunnette, "The Role of the Manager: What's Really Important in Different Management Jobs," *Academy of Management Executive,* November 1989, pp. 286–293.

24. A.K. Gupta, "Contingency Perspectives on Strategic Leadership," in D.C. Hambrick (ed.), *The Executive Effect: Concepts and Methods for Studying Top Managers* (Greenwich, CT: JAI Press, 1988), pp.147–178.

25. D.G. Ancona, "Top Management Teams: Preparing for the Revolution," in J.S. Carroll (ed.), *Applied Social Psychology and Organizational Settings* (Hillsdale, NJ: Erlbaum, 1990); D.C. Hambrick and P.A. Mason, "Upper Echelons: The Organization

as a Reflection of Its Top Managers," *Academy of Management Journal,* 9, 1984, pp. 193–206.

26. T.A. Mahony, T.H. Jerdee, and S.J. Carroll, "The Jobs of Management," *Industrial Relations,* 4, 1965, pp. 97–110; L. Gomez-Mejia, J. McCann, and R.C. Page, "The Structure of Managerial Behaviours and Rewards," *Industrial Relations,* 24, 1985, pp. 147–154.

27. K. Labich, "Making Over Middle Managers," *Fortune,* May 8, 1989, 58–64.

28. B. Wysocki, "Some Companies Cut Costs Too Far, Suffer from Corporate Anorexia," *The Wall Street Journal,* July 5, 1995, A1.

29. www.dell.com, 2008.

30. http://www.goodwill.org/about-us/. Accessed November 22, 2011.

31. Anthony Grnak, John Hughes and Douglas Hunter, *Building the Best, Lessons from Inside Canada's Best Managed Companies* (Toronto: Viking Canada, 2006), p. 91.

32. R.L. Katz, "Skills of an Effective Administrator," *Harvard Business Review,* September–October 1974, pp. 90–102.

33. Ibid.

34. P. Tharenou, "Going Up? Do Traits and Informal Social Processes Predict Advancing in Management?" *Academy of Management Journal* 44 (October 2001), 1005–18.

35. C. J. Collins and K. D. Clark, "Strategic Human Resource Practices, Top Management Team Social Networks, and Firm Performance: The Role of Human Resource Practices in Creating Organizational Competitive Advantage," *Academy of Management Journal* 46 (December 2003), 740–52.

36. H. Mintzberg, "The Manager's Job: Folklore and Fact," *Harvard Business Review,* July–August 1975, pp. 56–62.

37. H. Mintzberg, *The Nature of Managerial Work* (New York: Harper and Row, 1973).

38. Ibid.

39. Adapted from: Mark Kozak-Holland, "Plan for the Unthinkable," *Financial Post*, Monday, October 18, 2004, p. FE9.

40. The official Titanic site by Paramount Pictures and Twentieth Century Fox: www.titanicmovie.com.

41. Marcy Zitz, "The Anniversary of the Titanic Disaster: The Date the Titanic Sank," website: http://familyinternet. about.com/cs/entertainment/a/ aatitanic.htm.

42. Principles of Management Video DVD: Volume 2, number 6.

43. Chris Atchison, "Secrets of Canada's Best Bosses," *Profit Magazine,* February 16, 2011. http://www. profitguide.com/article/10103– secrets-of-Canada-s-best-bosses--page3. Accessed Sept. 22, 2012.

Chapter 2

1. "IKEA: How the Swedish Retailer Became a Global Cult Brand," *BusinessWeek,* November 14, 2005. Cover Story. http://www.businessweek.com/ magazine/content/05_46/b3959001. htm. Accessed September 27, 2011.

2. L.J. Bourgeois, "Strategy and Environment: A Conceptual Integration," *Academy of Management Review*, 5, 1985, pp. 25–39.

3. "Business: Link in the Global Chain," *The Economist,* June 2, 2001, 62–63.

4. "IKEA: How the Swedish Retailer Became a Global Cult Brand," *BusinessWeek,* November 14, 2005. Cover Story. http://www.businessweek.com/ magazine/content/05_46/b3959001. htm. Accessed September 27, 2011.

5. M. E. Porter, *Competitive Advantage* (New York: Free Press, 1985).

6. "IKEA: How the Swedish Retailer Became a Global Cult Brand," *BusinessWeek,* November 14, 2005. Cover Story. http://www.businessweek.com/ magazine/content/05_46/b3959001. htm. Accessed September 27, 2011.

7. "Researching Your Competition," StatsLink Canada, © John White, GDSourcing—Research & Retrieval 2006. Website: www.stats-link-canada. com/Industry-Competitors.html. Accessed May 15, 2008.

8. "IKEA: How the Swedish Retailer Became a Global Cult Brand," *BusinessWeek,* November 14, 2005. Cover Story. http://www.businessweek.com/

magazine/content/05_46/b3959001. htm. Accessed September 27, 2011.

9. For views on barriers to entry from an economics perspective, see M.E. Porter, *Competitive Strategy* (New York: Free Press, 1980). For the sociological perspective, see J. Pfeffer and G.R. Salancik, *The External Control of Organization: A Resource Dependence Perspective* (New York: Harper and Row, 1978).

10. M.E. Porter, *Competitive Strategy* (New York: Free Press, 1980); J.E. Bain, *Barriers to New Competition* (Cambridge, MA: Harvard University Press, 1956); R.J. Gilbert, "Mobility Barriers and the Value of Incumbency," in R. Schmalensee and R.D. Willig (eds.), *Handbook of Industrial Organization,* vol. 1 (Amsterdam: North Holland, 1989).

11. Brent Jang, "Leblanc on Sorrow, Remorse and His Little 'White Lie'" *The Globe and Mail*, Friday, March 18, 2005, pp. B1, 2.

12. C.W.L. Hill, "The Computer Industry: The New Industry of Industries," in C.W.L. Hill and G.R. Jones, *Strategic Management: An Integrated Approach,* 3rd ed. (Boston: Houghton Mifflin, 1995).

13. "IKEA: How the Swedish Retailer Became a Global Cult Brand," *BusinessWeek,* November 14, 2005. Cover Story. http://www.businessweek.com/ magazine/content/05_46/b3959001. htm. Accessed September 27, 2011.

14. J. Bhagwati, *Protectionism* (Cambridge, MA: MIT Press, 1988).

15. "When Fortune Frowned: A Special Report on the World Economy," *The Economist*, October 11, 2008, p. 3.

16. World Economic Forum.

17. www.canada.com/topics/news/story. html?id=c3a67e3b-1aef-4daf-a768- a54eedb80185. Accessed October 11, 2008.

18. J. Schumpeter, *Capitalism, Socialism and Democracy* (London: Macmillan, 1950), p. 68. Also see R.R. Winter and S.G. Winter, *An Evolutionary Theory of Economic Change* (Cambridge, MA: Harvard University Press, 1982).

19. "Demographic Time Bomb: Mitigating the Effects of Demographic Change in Canada," Report of the Standing Senate Committee on Banking, Trade

and Commerce, June 2006. Website: www.parl.gc.ca/39/1/parlbus/ commbus/senate/Com-e/bank-e/ rep-e/rep03jun06-e.htm. Accessed May 15, 2008.

20. Wallace Immen, "The Way We Will Be," *The Globe and Mail*, October 1, 2007. Website: www.wrien.com/ documents/TheWayWeWillBe.pdf. Accessed May 15, 2008.

21. "Women in Management in Canada," *Catalyst,* March 2011. http://www. catalyst.org/publication/247/women- in-management-in-canada. Accessed September 28, 2011.

22. "Women Matter 2010," McKinsey & Company. http://www.mckinsey.com/ locations/paris/home/womenmatter. asp. Accessed October 1, 2011

23. "Report on the Demographic Situation in Canada: Age and Sex Structure, 2010." Statistics Canada Demographic and Projections Section, July 2011. http://www.statcan.gc.ca/pub/91- 209-x/2011001/article/11511-eng.pdf. Accessed Sept. 28, 2011.

24. "Long-Term Global Demographic Trends: Reshaping the Geopolitical Landscape," Central Intelligence Agency, July 2001, p. 5. https:// www.cia.gov/library/reports/general- reports-1/Demo_Trends_For_Web. pdf. Accessed September 28, 2011.

25. N. Goodman, *An Introduction to Sociology* (New York: HarperCollins, 1991); C. Nakane, *Japanese Society* (Berkeley: University of California Press, 1970).

26. For a detailed discussion of the importance of the structure of law as a factor explaining economic change and growth, see D.C. North, *Institutions, Institutional Change and Economic Performance* (Cambridge: Cambridge University Press, 1990).

27. Barbara Shecter, "Cineplex Snaps Up Rival," *Financial Post,* Tuesday, June 14, 2005, pp. FP1, 6. See also Richard Blackwell, "Movie Marriage Promises Blockbuster Savings," *The Globe and Mail,* Wednesday, June 22, 2005, p. B3; and Gayle MacDonald, "Movie Boss Has Best Seat in the House," *The Globe and Mail,* Wednesday, June 15, 2005, pp. B1, 4.

28. R.B. Reich, *The Work of Nations* (New York: Knopf, 1991).

29. Jagdish Bhagwati, *Protectionism* (Cambridge, MA: MIT Press, 1988).

30. NAFTA Rules of Origin: Regional Content Rules. http://medey.com/pdf/ NAFTA%20Rules%20of%20Origin;%20 Regional%20Value%20Content.pdf. Accessed September 30, 2011.

31. E. B. Tylor, *Primitive Culture* (London: Murray, 1971).

32. Karl Moore, "Great Global Managers: They Don't Come From Great Powers. Here's Where to Look." www. conference-board.org/articles/atb_article. cfm?id=200. Accessed January 17, 2009.

33. Ibid.

34. R. Bellah, *Habits of the Heart: Individualism and Commitment in American Life* (Berkeley: University of California Press, 1985).

35. Adapted from G.H. Hofstede, *Culture's Consequences: International Differences in Work-Related Values* (Beverly Hills, CA: Sage Publications, 1984).

36. R. Bellah, *The Tokugawa Religion* (New York: Free Press, 1957).

37. C. Nakane, *Japanese Society* (Berkeley: University of California Press, 1970).

38. Karl Moore, "Great Global Managers: They Don't Come From Great Powers. Here's Where to Look." www. conference-board.org/articles/atb_article. cfm?id=200. Accessed January 17, 2009.

39. Ibid.

40. G. Hofstede, "The Cultural Relativity of Organizational Practices and Theories," *Journal of International Business Studies,* Fall 1983, 75–89.

41. G. Hofstede, B. Neuijen, D. D. Ohayv, and G. Sanders, "Measuring Organizational Cultures: A Qualitative and Quantitative Study across Twenty Cases," *Administrative Science Quarterly* 35 (1990), 286–316.

42. http://www.ethnicitycatering.ca/. Accessed November 22, 2011.

43. "In Praise of the Stateless Multinational," *The Economist,* September 20, 2008, p. 20.

44. "Roll-up-Rim Contest Wasteful, Critics Say," *The London Free Press,* March 2, 2005. www.canoe.ca/NewsStand /LondonFreePress/News/2005/ 03/02/946850-sun.html.

45. Bill Mah, "Tim Hortons Contest a Litterbug, Critics Say: Roll Up the Rim Begins," *National Post,* March 1, 2005.

46. R.B. Duncan, "Characteristics of Organization Environment and Perceived Environment," *Administrative Science Quarterly,* 17, 1972, pp. 313–327.

47. See "McDonald's USA Food Allergens and Sensitivities Listing." www. mcdonalds.com/app_controller. nutrition.categories.allergens.index.html.

48. Not everyone agrees with this assessment. Some argue that organizations and individual managers have little impact on the environment. See M.T. Hannan and J. Freeman, "Structural Inertia and Organizational Change," *American Sociological Review,* 49, 1984, pp. 149–164.

49. "Foreign Investment in Canada, Lie Back and Forget the Maple Leaf," *The Economist,* April 5, 2008, p. 42.

50. A. Shama, "Management Under Fire: The Transformation of Management in the Soviet Union and Eastern Europe," *Academy of Management Executive,* 1993, pp. 22–35.

51. Anthony Grnak, John Hughes, and Douglas Hunter, *Building the Best, Lessons from Inside Canada's Best Managed Companies* (Toronto: Viking Canada, 2006), p. 86.

52. Ibid, p. 37.

53. Michael Rachlis, "Medicare Made Easy," *The Globe and Mail,* Monday, April 26, 2004, p. A13.

54. "IKEA: How the Swedish Retailer Became a Global Cult Brand," *BusinessWeek,* November 14, 2005. Cover Story. http://www.businessweek.com/ magazine/content/05_46/b3959001. htm. Accessed September 27, 2011.

55. K. Seiders and L.L. Berry, "Service Fairness: What It Is and Why It Matters," *Academy of Management Executive,* 12, 1998, pp. 8–20.

56. Anthony Grnak, John Hughes, and Douglas Hunter, *Building the Best, Lessons from Inside Canada's Best Managed Companies* (Toronto: Viking Canada, 2006).

57. C. Anderson, "Values-Based Management," *Academy of Management Executive,* 11, 1997, pp. 25–46.

58. W.H. Shaw and V. Barry, *Moral Issues in Business,* 6th ed. (Belmont, CA: Wadsworth, 1995); and T. Donaldson, *Corporations and Morality* (Englewood Cliffs, NJ: Prentice-Hall, 1982).

59. D.R. Tobin, *The Knowledge Enabled Organization* (New York: AMACOM, 1998).

60. Adapted from "Impersonal Approach Hurts Business, Study Says," *The Globe and Mail,* Wednesday, August 20, 2003, C3.

61. Human Resource Management Video DVD Volume 2, number 3, 2010.

62. *The Economist.* February 4, 2012, p. 8.

Chapter 3

1. MEC website. http://www. mec.ca/AST/ContentPrimary/ AboutMEC/AboutOurCoOp. jsp?CONTENT%3C%3Ecnt_ id=10134198673220379. Accessed October 6, 2011.

2. T.L. Beauchamp and N.E. Bowie (eds.), *Ethical Theory and Business* (Englewood Cliffs, NJ: Prentice-Hall, 1979); and A. Macintyre, *After Virtue* (South Bend, IN: University of Notre Dame Press, 1981).

3. R.E. Goodin, "How to Determine Who Should Get What," *Ethics,* July 1975, pp. 310–321,

4. "Medical Marijuana Growth Rules to Change," The Canadian Press, CBC News, June 16, 2011. http://www.cbc. ca/news/health/story/2011/06/16/ marijuana-medical.html. Accessed October 7, 2011.

5. J.A. Pearce, "The Company Mission as a Strategic Tool," *Sloan Management Review,* Spring 1982, pp. 15–24.

6. C.I. Barnard, *The Functions of the Executive* (Cambridge, MA: Harvard University Press, 1948).

7. J. A. Pearce, "The Company Mission as a Strategic Tool," *Sloan Management Review,* Spring 1982, 15–24.

8. C. I. Barnard, *The Functions of the Executive* (Cambridge, MA: Harvard University Press, 1948).

9. R. E. Freeman, *Strategic Management: A Stakeholder Approach* (Marshfield, MA: Pitman, 1984).

10. P. S. Adler, "Corporate Scandals: It's Time for Reflection in Business Schools," *Academy of Management Executive* 16 (August 2002), 148–50.

11. "Richest CEOs Earn 189 Times Average Canadian." CBC News, January 3, 2012. http://www.cbc.ca/news/canada/ story/2012/01/03/business-ceo-pay. html. Accessed February 11, 2012.

12. E. P. Kelly, "A Better Way to Think about Business" (book review), *Academy of Management Executive* 14 (May 2000), 127–29.

13. T.M. Jones, "Ethical Decision Making by Individuals in Organizations: An Issue Contingent Model," *Academy of Management Journal,* 16, 1991, pp. 366–395; and G.F. Cavanaugh, D.J. Moberg, and M. Velasquez, "The Ethics of Organizational Politics," *Academy of Management Review,* 6, 1981, pp. 363–374.

14. T. M. Jones, "Instrumental Stakeholder Theory: A Synthesis of Ethics and Economics," *Academy of Management Review* 20 (1995), 404–37.

15. L.K. Trevino, "Ethical Decision Making in Organizations: A Person–Situation Interactionist Model," *Academy of Management Review,* 11, 1986, pp. 601–617; and W.H. Shaw and V. Barry, *Moral Issues in Business,* 6th ed. (Belmont, CA: Wadsworth, 1995)

16. S. W. Gellerman, "Why Good Managers Make Bad Decisions," in K. R. Andrews, ed., *Ethics in Practice: Managing the Moral Corporation* (Boston: Harvard Business School Press, 1989).

17. A.S. Waterman, "On the Uses of Psychological Theory and Research in the Process of Ethical Inquiry," *Psychological Bulletin,* 103, no. 3, 1988, pp. 283–298.

18. M. S. Frankel, "Professional Codes: Why, How, and with What Impact?" *Ethics* 8 (1989): 109–15.

19. J. Van Maanen and S. R. Barley, "Occupational Communities: Culture and Control in Organizations," in B. Staw and L. Cummings, eds., *Research in Organizational Behavior,* vol. 6 (Greenwich, CT: JAI Press, 1984), 287–365.

20. Jones, "Ethical Decision Making by Individuals in Organizations."

21. G. R. Jones, *Organizational Theory: Text and Cases* (Reading, MA: Addison-Wesley, 1997).

22. P. E. Murphy, "Creating Ethical Corporate Structure," *Sloan Management Review* (Winter 1989), 81–87.

23. "When It Comes to Ethics, Canadian Companies Are All Talk and Little Action, A Survey Shows," *Canadian Press Newswire,* February 17, 2000.

24. "India IT Boss Quits Over Scandal." http://news.bbc.co.uk/2/hi/business/7815031.stm. Accessed January 7, 2009.

25. E. Gatewood and A.B. Carroll, "The Anatomy of Corporate Social Response," *Business Horizons,* September–October 1981, pp. 9–16.

26. M. Friedman, "A Friedman Doctrine: The Social Responsibility of Business Is to Increase Its Profits," *New York Times Magazine,* September 13, 1970, p. 33.

27. Quoted in "CSR—Milton Friedman was Right," http://www.bathconsultancygroup.com/documents/CSR%20-%20Milton%20Friedman%20was%20right.pdf. Accessed October 7, 2011.

28. "Mining Could Be More Resourceful," *The Economist,* August 16, 2008, p. 64.

29. "Wal-Mart Canada Says Imports From Myanmar Ended in Spring," *Canadian Press Newswire,* July 18, 2000.

30. Danielle Sacks, "Working with the Enemy," *Fast Company*, September 2007, 74–81. Website: www.fastcompany.com/magazine/118/working-with-the-enemy.html.

31. "Environmental Sustainability Report: Wal-Mart Canada," http://admin.csrwire.com/system/report_pdfs/805/original/1239375228_Canada.pdf. Accessed October 7, 2011.

32. Ibid.

33. W.G. Ouchi, *Theory Z: How American Business Can Meet the Japanese Challenge* (Reading, MA: Addison-Wesley, 1981).

34. J.B. McGuire, A. Sundgren, and T. Schneewis, "Corporate Social Responsibility and Firm Financial Performance," *Academy of Management Review,* 31, 1988, pp. 854–872.

35. "Ecosystems and Human Well-Being: A Report of the Millennium Ecosystem Assessment (MA)," Business and Industry Synthesis Team, 2005. http://www.maweb.org/documents/document.353.aspx.pdf. Accessed October 10, 2011, p. 4.

36. J. Jedras, "Social Workers," *Silicon Valley NORTH,* July 30, 2001, p. 1.

37. M. Friedman, "A Friedman Doctrine: The Social Responsibility of Business Is to Increase Its Profits," *New York Times Magazine,* September 13, 1970, pp. 32, 33, 122, 124, 126.

38. Yasemin Saltuk, Amit Bouri, and Giselle Leung, *Insight into the Impact Investment Market: An In-Depth Analysis of Investor Perspectives and Over 2,200 Transactions,* 12/14/2011. Accessed December 15, 2011.

39. E.D. Bowman, "Corporate Social Responsibility and the Investor," *Journal of Contemporary Business,* Winter 1973, pp. 49–58.

40. Gardenswartz, L. & Rowe, A. (1994). Cited on http://www.collaborativejourneys.com/diversity-a-pathway-to-connection-common-ground-and-innovation/. Accessed May 20, 2012.

41. Ethnic Origin and Visible Minorities, Release no. 7, April 2, 2008. Website: www12.statcan.ca/census-recensement/2006/rt-td/eth-eng.cfm. Accessed October 25, 2008.

42. "Near Half in GTA Minorities," *Toronto Star*, April 2, 2008. Website: www.thestar.com/News/Canada/article/409112. Accessed May 18, 2008.

43. Colin Perkel, "Highly Educated Immigrants Still Lag in Earnings," *Toronto Star,* May 1, 2008. www.thestar.com/Canada/Census/article/420336. Accessed May 18, 2008.

44. Calgary Economic Development, "The Changing Profile of Calgary's Workforce Labour Force Profile," *CalgaryWorks,* June 2006, p. 32. Website: www.calgaryeconomicdevelopment.com/files/CED%20reports/LabourForce_SP04.pdf. Accessed May 18, 2008; see also Derek Sankey, "The Many Faces of Diversity," *National Post,* FP WORKING, Wednesday, April 9, 2009, WK3.

45. R. Folger and M.A. Konovsky, "Effects of Procedural and Distributive Justice on Reactions to Pay Raise Decisions," *Academy of Management Journal,* 32, 1989, pp. 115–130; and J. Greenberg, "Organizational Justice: Yesterday, Today, and Tomorrow," *Journal of Management,* 16, 1990, pp. 399–402.

46. Taken from "Employers Access to Support and Employees." Website: www.toronto.ca/yep/ease/myths.htm. Accessed August 22, 2008.

47. Website: www.canadastop100.com/diversity/chapters/Enbridge.pdf. Accessed October 25, 2008.

48. J. Greenberg, "Organizational Justice: Yesterday, Today, and Tomorrow," *Journal of Management,* 16, 1990, pp. 399–402.

49. Website: www.newagecanada.com/
eventmarketing.html. Accessed January
17, 2009.

50. G. Robinson and K. Dechant, "Building
a Case for Business Diversity," *Academy
of Management Executive,* 1997, pp. 3,
32–47.

51. Anthony Grnak, John Hughes, and
Douglas Hunter, *Building the Best,
Lessons from Inside Canada's Best
Managed Companies* (Toronto: Viking
Canada, 2006).

52. http://www.enterprisingnonprofits.ca/
resources/justwork-economic-initiative-
social-enterprise-profile. Accessed
November 22, 2011.

53. K. Kalawsky, "US Group Wants
Royal's Centura Buy Delayed: Alleges
Takeover Target Discriminates Against
Minorities," *Financial Post (National
Post),* April 10, 2001, p. C4.

54. Stefan Christoff, "Racism and
Reasonable Accommodation in
Quebec: The Debate is A Farce,"
Website: www.nationalpost.com/news/
story.html?id=d39d491c-f74c-4409-
8e4a-e04798faaca9&k=1284. Accessed
July 14, 2009.

55. Marina Strauss, *The Globe and
Mail* Update, July 24, 2009.
Website: www.theglobeandmail.
com/report-on-business/
loblaw-buys-asian-grocery-chain/
article1229762/.

56. H. Branswell, "When Nestlé Canada
Said Last Month It Would No Longer
Be Making Chocolate Bars in a Nut-
Free Facility, Thousands Wrote in to
Protest," *Canadian Press Newswire,*
May 14, 2001.

57. Ibid.

58. A.P. Carnevale and S.C. Stone,
"Diversity: Beyond the Golden Rule,"
Training & Development, October
1994, pp. 22–39.

59. "Selling Equity," *Financial Post
Magazine,* September 1994, pp. 20–25.

60. "Study Shows Women Who Are
Unhappy with Corporate Life Plan
to Start Own Businesses," *Women in
Management,* December–January 1999,
pp. 1–3.

61. Website: www.canadastop100.com/
diversity/. Accessed October 25, 2008.

62. Website: www.servicecanada.gc.ca/eng/
cs/fas/as/contracting/harass_policy.
shtml. Accessed July 13, 2009.

63. Ibid.

64. Website: www.safety-council.org/info/
OSH/bullies.html. Accessed July 13,
2009.

65. "Vic Toews Promises New RCMP
Discipline Legislation: Government
Promises to Help RCMP Deal with
Problem Officers," CBC News. http://
www.cbc.ca/news/canada/british-
columbia/story/2012/05/29/bc-rcmp-
discipline-law.html. Accessed May 30,
2012.

66. B. Carton, "Muscled Out? At Jenny
Craig, Men Are Ones Who Claim
Sex Discrimination," *The Wall Street
Journal,* November 29, 1994,
pp. A1, A7.

67. R.L. Paetzold and A.M. O'Leary-Kelly,
"Organizational Communication and
the Legal Dimensions of Hostile Work
Environment Sexual Harassment," in
G.L. Kreps (ed.), *Sexual Harassment:
Communication Implications* (Cresskill,
NJ: Hampton Press, 1993).

68. M. Galen, J. Weber, and A.Z. Cuneo,
"Sexual Harassment: Out of the
Shadows," *Fortune,* October 28, 1991,
pp. 30–31.

69. "Employers Underestimate Extent of
Sexual Harassment, Report Says," *The
Vancouver Sun,* March 8, 2001, p. D6.

70. A.M. O'Leary-Kelly, R.L. Paetzold, and
R.W. Griffin, "Sexual Harassment as
Aggressive Action: A Framework for
Understanding Sexual Harassment,"
paper presented at the annual meeting
of the Academy of Management,
Vancouver, August 1995.

71. "Employers Underestimate Extent of
Sexual Harassment, Report Says," *The
Vancouver Sun,* March 8, 2001, p. D6.

72. Information in this paragraph based on
Ian Jack, "Magna Suit Spotlights Auto
Industry Practices," *The Financial Post
Daily,* September 10, 1997, p. 1.

73. "Sexual Harassment in the Workplace,"
Website: www.metrac.org/programs/
info/prevent/har_book.pdf. Accessed
May 18, 2008.

74. S.J. Bresler and R. Thacker, "Four-
Point Plan Helps Solve Harassment
Problems," *HR Magazine,* May 1993,
pp. 117–124.

75. Adapted from Howard Levitt,
"Spurning Lover or Workplace
Harasser?" *National Post,* Wednesday,
March 9, 2005, p. FP10.

Chapter 4

1. D. Sacks, "The Catalyst," *Fast Company,*
October 2006, 59–61.

2. About PUMA, http://about.puma.
com/EN/1/, February 13, 2008.

3. Sacks, "The Catalyst."

4. Ibid.

5. "PUMA Progress Update on
Greenpeace Detox Campaign," http://
about.puma.com/?page_id=10.
Accessed October 11, 2011

6. "Puma Expects 2008 Sales, Profits to
Rise—PPR CFO," January 24, 2008,
www.reuters.com/articlePrint?articleI
d=USL2491288920080124, February
13, 2008.

7. Sacks, "The Catalyst."

8. Ibid.

9. Ibid.

10. Ibid.; "Fashion in Motion Africa 2005,
Zuly Bet," www.vam.ac.uk/collections/
fashion/fashion_motion/africa_05/
index.html, February 14, 2008.

11. www.puma.com, April 18, 2009.

12. Sacks, "The Catalyst."

13. Company Structure, http://about.
puma.com/EN/1/9/9/, February 13,
2008

14. Sacks, "The Catalyst."

15. G. P. Huber, *Managerial Decision
Making* (Glenview, IL: Scott, Foresman,
1993).

16. Sacks, "The Catalyst."

17. "What Steve Jobs Taught Me by
Kicking My Butt," *Canadian Business,*
October 10, 2011, p. 17.

18. H.A. Simon, *The New Science of
Management* (Englewood Cliffs, NJ:
Prentice-Hall, 1977).

19. D. Kahneman, "Maps of Bounded
Rationality: A Perspective on Intuitive
Judgment and Choice," Prize Lecture,
December 8, 2002; E. Jaffe, "What Was
I Thinking? Kahneman Explains How
Intuition Leads Us Astray," *American
Psychological Society* 17, no. 5 (May
2004), 23–26.

20. Alan Kearns, "The Big Career
Decisions," *National Post,* Wednesday,
May 4, 2005, p. FP9. See also the
website: www.econlib.org/library/Enc/
bios/Simon.html.

21. H.A. Simon, *Administrative Behavior*
(New York: Macmillan, 1947), p. 79.

22. H.A. Simon, *Models of Man* (New York: Wiley, 1957).

23. K.J. Arrow, *Aspects of the Theory of Risk Bearing* (Helsinki: Yrjo Johnssonis Saatio, 1965).

24. R.L. Daft and R.H. Lengel, "Organizational Information Requirements, Media Richness and Structural Design," *Management Science*, 32, 1986, pp. 554–571.

25. R. Cyert and J. March, *Behavioral Theory of the Firm* (Englewood Cliffs, NJ: Prentice-Hall, 1963).

26. J.G. March and H.A. Simon, *Organizations* (New York: Wiley, 1958).

27. H.A. Simon, "Making Management Decisions: The Role of Intuition and Emotion," *Academy of Management Executive*, 1, 1987, pp. 57–64.

28. M. H. Bazerman, *Judgment in Managerial Decision Making* (New York: Wiley, 1986). Also see Simon, *Administrative Behavior*.

29. M.H. Bazerman, *Judgment in Managerial Decision Making* (New York: Wiley, 1986); G.P. Huber, *Managerial Decision Making* (Glenview, IL: Scott, Foresman, 1993); and J.E. Russo and P.J. Schoemaker, *Decision Traps* (New York: Simon and Schuster, 1989).

30. M.D. Cohen, J.G. March, and J.P. Olsen, "A Garbage Can Model of Organizational Choice," *Administrative Science Quarterly*, 17, 1972, pp. 1–25.

31. Ibid.

32. P.C. Nutt, *Why Decisions Fail: Avoiding the Blunders and Traps That Lead to Debacles* (San Francisco: Berrett-Koehler Publishers, 2002); and M.H. Bazerman, *Judgment in Managerial Decision Making* (New York: Wiley, 1986).

33. J.E. Russo and P.J. Schoemaker, *Decision Traps* (New York: Simon and Schuster, 1989).

34. M.H. Bazerman, *Judgment in Managerial Decision Making* (New York: Wiley, 1986).

35. B. Berger, "NASA: One Year after *Columbia*—Bush's New Vision Changes Agency's Course Midstream," *Space News Business Report*, January 26, 2004, www.space.com/spacenews/businessmonday_040126. html.

36. J. Glanz and J. Schwartz, "Dogged Engineer's Effort to Assess Shuttle Damage," *The New York Times*, September 26, 2003, A1.

37. M. L. Wald and J. Schwartz, "NASA Chief Promises a Shift in Attitude," *The New York Times*, August 28, 2003, A23.

38. P.C. Nutt, *Why Decisions Fail: Avoiding the Blunders and Traps That Lead to Debacles* (San Francisco: Berrett-Koehler Publishers, 2002).

39. J.E. Russo and P.J. Schoemaker, *Decision Traps* (New York: Simon and Schuster, 1989).

40. D. Kahneman and A. Tversky, "Judgment Under Scrutiny: Heuristics and Biases," *Science*, 185, 1974, pp. 1124–1131.

41. C.R. Schwenk, "Cognitive Simplification Processes in Strategic Decision Making," *Strategic Management Journal*, 5, 1984, pp. 111–128.

42. An interesting example of the illusion of control is Richard Roll's hubris hypothesis of takeovers. See R. Roll, "The Hubris Hypothesis of Corporate Takeovers," *Journal of Business*, 59, 1986, pp. 197–216.

43. "What Steve Jobs Taught Me by Kicking My Butt," *Canadian Business*, October 10, 2011, p. 17.

44. B.M. Staw, "The Escalation of Commitment to a Course of Action," *Academy of Management Review*, 6, 1981, pp. 577–587.

45. John C. Edwards, "Self-Fulfilling Prophecy and Escalating Commitment," *The Journal of Applied Behavioral Science*, 37, no. 3, 2001, pp. 343–360. Website: http://jab.sagepub.com/cgi/content/abstract/37/3/343. Accessed May 22, 2008. See also Marc Street and Vera L. Street, "The Effects of Escalating Commitment on Ethical Decision-Making," *Journal of Business Ethics*, 64, 2006, pp. 343–356. Website: www.springerlink.com/content/g0u1r47kv975w272/. Accessed May 22, 2008.

46. "Really Bad Advice," *Maclean's*, September 19, 2011, p. 43.

47. J.E. Russo and P.J. Schoemaker, *Decision Traps* (New York: Simon and Schuster, 1989).

48. Ibid.

49. Website: www.crestaurant.com.

50. Website: www.vanaqua.org/oceanwise/ Jack MacDonald, CEO Compass Food Canada, Press Release May 9, 2008. Compass Group Canada takes leading role in sustainable seafood purchasing.

51. Website: www.compass-canada.com/home/media/sustainability_purchasing.pdf.

52. Website: www.imc2.com/Documents/StateOfSustainabilityCommunications.pdf. Accessed November 5, 2008.

53. Website: www.justmeans.com/index.php?action=viewcompanyprofile&id=122&sublinkid=33. Accessed November 5, 2008

54. See P. Senge, *The Fifth Discipline: The Art and Practice of the Learning Organization* (New York: Doubleday, 1990).

55. http://www.torontoenterprisefund.ca/_bin/resources/Featured_enterprise/Print.cfm. Accessed November 22, 2011.

56. T.A. Stewart, "3M Fights Back," *Fortune*, February 5, 1996, pp. 94–99; and T.D. Schellhardt, "David in Goliath," *The Wall Street Journal*, May 23, 1996, p. R14.

57. C. Salter, "FAST 50: The World's Most Innovative Companies," *Fast Company*, March 2008, 73–117.

58. M. Ullmann, "Creativity Cubed: Burntsand Has Found a Novel Program to Motivate Its Most Creative Employees. Can It Work for You?" *SVN Canada*, February 2001, pp. B22–B23.

59. N.B. Macintosh, *The Social Software of Accounting Information Systems* (New York: Wiley, 1995).

60. R.I. Benjamin and J. Blunt, "Critical IT Issues: The Next Ten Years," *Sloan Management Review*, Summer 1992, pp. 7–19; W.H. Davidow and M.S. Malone, *The Virtual Corporation* (New York: Harper Business, 1992).

61. C.A. O'Reilly, "Variations in Decision Makers' Use of Information: The Impact of Quality and Accessibility," *Academy of Management Journal*, 25, 1982, pp. 756–771.

62. G. Stalk and T.H. Hout, *Competing Against Time* (New York: Free Press, 1990).

63. R. Cyert and J. March, *Behavioral Theory of the Firm* (Englewood Cliffs, NJ: Prentice-Hall, 1963).

64. C. W. L. Hill and J. F. Pickering, "Divisionalization, Decentralization, and Performance of Large United Kingdom Companies," *Journal of Management Studies* 23 (1986), 26–50.

65. O. E. Williamson, *Markets and Hierarchies: Analysis and*

Anti-Trust Implications (New York: Free Press, 1975).

66. www.fedex.com, 2009.

67. E. Turban, *Decision Support and Expert Systems* (New York: Macmillan, 1988).

68. Ibid., 346.

69. E. Rich, *Artificial Intelligence* (New York: McGraw-Hill, 1983).

70. "A Special Report on Corporate IT," *The Economist,* October 25–31, 2008, p. 10.

71. Ibid., p. 4.

72. EMC2 Corporate Social Responsibility, Website: www.imc2.com/AboutUs/PR50.aspx. Accessed November 6, 2008.

73. Jennifer Newman and Darryl Grigg, "Managers Struggle with Ethical Questions," *Vancouver Sun,* June 21, 2008.

74. Website: www.cbc.ca.thehour. Accessed November 12, 2008.

75. http://www.canadianbusiness.com/article/48828–an-even-better-choice. Accessed October 11, 2011.

Chapter 5

1. Annual Report 2010. http://phx.corporate-ir.net/External.File?item=UGFyZW50SUQ9OTA4OTN8Q2hpbGRJRD0tMXxUeXBlPTM=&t=1ir.net/External.File?item=UGFyZW50SUQ9OTA4OTN8Q2hpbGRJRD0tMXxUeXBlPTM=&t=1. Accessed October 17, 2011.

2. "Amazon: The Kindle Tablet." *The New York Times,* October 17, 2011. http://topics.nytimes.com/top/news/business/companies/amazon_inc/index.html. Accessed October 19, 2011.

3. Poornima Gupta and Jim Finkle, "Problems Plague Apple iCloud, iOS Launch," Thomson Reuters, October 13, 2011.

4. Brad Stone, "Amazon, the Company That Ate the World," *BusinessWeek,* September 28, 2011. http://www.businessweek.com/magazine/the-omnivore-09282011.html. Accessed October 12, 2011.

5. A. Chandler, *Strategy and Structure: Chapters in the History of the American Enterprise* (Cambridge, MA: MIT Press, 1962).

6. F.J. Aguilar, "General Electric: Reg Jones and Jack Welch," in *General Managers in Action* (Oxford: Oxford University Press, 1992).

7. Ibid.

8. C.W. Hofer and D. Schendel, *Strategy Formulation: Analytical Concepts* (St. Paul, MN: West, 1978).

9. H. Fayol, *General and Industrial Management* (New York: IEEE Press, 1984). Fayol's work was first published in 1916.

10. Ibid., p. 18.

11. R. Phelps, C. Chan, S.C. Kapsalis, "Does Scenario Planning Affect Firm Performance?" *Journal of Business Research,* March 2001, pp. 223–232.

12. George Day and Paul Schoemaker, *Peripheral Vision* (Cambridge, MA: Harvard Business School Press).

13. Paul J. H. Schoemaker, "Are You Ready for Global Turmoil?" *BusinessWeek,* April 25, 2008. Website: www.businessweek.com/print/managing/content/apr2008/ca20080429_312634.htm.

14. Hill and McShane, *Principles of Management* (New York: McGraw-Hill/Irwin, 2008), p. 111.

15. "How Maple Leaf Foods Is Handling the Listeria Outbreak." Website: www.cbc.ca/money/story/2008/08/27/f-crisisresponse.html. Accessed November 13, 2008.

16. Ibid.

17. J. A. Pearce, "The Company Mission as a Strategic Tool," *Sloan Management Review,* Spring 1992, 15–24.

18. A. Chandler, *Strategy and Structure: Chapters in the History of the American Enterprise* (Cambridge, MA: MIT Press, 1962).

19. P.C. Nutt and R.W. Backoff, "Crafting Vision," *Journal of Management Inquiry,* December 1997, p. 309.

20. M. Ingram, "Our Job Is to Be Better," *The Globe and Mail,* May 12, 2001, p. F3.

21. Amazon.com, FAQs. http://phx.corporate-ir.net/phoenix.zhtml?c=97664&p=irol-faq#14296. Accessed October 14, 2011.

22. D.F. Abell, *Defining the Business: The Starting Point of Strategic Planning* (Englewood Cliffs, NJ: Prentice-Hall, 1980).

23. Amazon.com, FAQs.

24. G. Hamel and C. K. Prahalad, "Strategic Intent," *Harvard Business Review,* May–June 1989, 63–73.

25. D. I. Jung and B. J. Avolio, "Opening the Black Box: An Experimental Investigation of the Mediating Effects of Trust and Value Congruence on Transformational and Transactional Leadership," *Journal of Organizational Behavior,* December 2000, 949–64; B. M. Bass and B. J. Avolio, "Transformational and Transactional Leadership: 1992 and Beyond," *Journal of European Industrial Training,* January 1990, 20–35.

26. J. Porras and J. Collins, *Built to Last: Successful Habits of Visionary Companies* (New York: HarperCollins, 1994).

27. George T. Doran. "There's a S.M.A.R.T. Way to Write Management's Goals and Objectives," *Management Review (AMA Forum),* November 1981, pp. 35–36.

28. K.R. Andrews, *The Concept of Corporate Strategy* (Homewood, IL: Irwin, 1971).

29. Annual Report 2010. http://phx.corporate-ir.net/External.File?item=UGFyZW50SUQ9OTA4OTN8Q2hpbGRJRD0tMXxUeXBlPTM=&t=1. Accessed October 17, 2011.

30. Peter Drucker, "The Next Society," *The Economist*, 2001.

31. Cited in *The Economist*, "Dealing with the Downturn: Make Love—and War," August 9, 2008, p. 57; Adam M. Brandenburger and Barry J. Nalebuff, *Co-opetition: A Revolution Mindset* (New York: Bantam Double Day) 1997.

32. *The Economist,* "Dealing with the Downturn: Make Love—and War," August 9, 2008, p. 57.

33. "Samsung, the Next Big Bet," *The Economist,* October 1, 2011. From the print edition. http://www.economist.com/node/21530976. Accessed October 19, 2011.

34. http://www.enterprisingnonprofits.ca/resources/prince-george-native-friendship-centre-social-enterprise-profile. Accessed November 22, 2011

35. Tom Peters and Robert H. Waterman, Jr., *In Search of Excellence. Lessons from America's Best-Run Companies* (Toronto: HarperCollins Canada, 2004).

36. Catherine McLean and Gordon Pitts, "Bell Adopts a New Party Line," *The Globe and Mail*, Saturday, May 14, 2005, B4.

37. www.hitachi.com, 2008.

38. E. Penrose, *The Theory of the Growth of the Firm* (Oxford: Oxford University Press, 1959).

39. M.E. Porter, "From Competitive Advantage to Corporate Strategy," *Harvard Business Review,* 65, 1987, pp. 43–59.

40. "Success Story," Electronic Data Systems Corporation, 2008. Website: www.eds.com/sites/success/coors.aspx.

41. G. Pitts, "Small Is Beautiful, Conglomerates Signal," *The Globe and Mail,* April 1, 2002, pp. B1, B4.

42. For a review of the evidence, see C.W.L. Hill and G.R. Jones, *Strategic Management: An Integrated Approach,* 3rd ed. (Boston: Houghton Mifflin, 2000), Ch. 10.

43. V. Ramanujam and P. Varadarajan, "Research on Corporate Diversification: A Synthesis," *Strategic Management Journal,* 10, 1989, pp. 523–551. Also see A. Shleifer and R.W. Vishny, "Takeovers in the 1960s and 1980s: Evidence and Implications," in R.P. Rumelt, D.E. Schendel, and D.J. Teece, *Fundamental Issues in Strategy* (Boston: Harvard Business School Press, 1994).

44. J.R. Williams, B.L. Paez, and L. Sanders, "Conglomerates Revisited," *Strategic Management Journal,* 9, 1988, pp. 403–414.

45. H. Shaw, "Fish, Dairy Units Sacrificed to Help Raise Cash for Baked Goods: Bestfoods Deal," *Financial Post (National Post),* February 20, 2001, pp. C1, C6.

46. Doug Krumrei, "Corporate Profiles: George Weston Bakeries, Inc.," *Milling & Baking News,* December 1, 2001.

47. Website: www.mhhe.com/business/management/thompson/11e/case/starbucks-2.html. Accessed December 29, 2008.

48. M.K. Perry, "Vertical Integration: Determinants and Effects," in R. Schmalensee and R.D. Willig, *Handbook of Industrial Organization,* vol. 1 (New York: Elsevier Science Publishing, 1989).

49. Website: www.mhhe.com/business/management/thompson/11e/case/starbucks-2.html. Accessed December 29, 2008.

50. About Sun Opta Inc. http://www.sunopta.com/corporate.aspx?id=556. Accessed October 19, 2011.

51. T. Muris, D. Scheffman, and P. Spiller, "Strategy and Transaction Costs: The Organization of Distribution in the Carbonated Soft Drink Industry," *Journal of Economics and Management Strategy,* 1, 1992, pp. 77–97.

52. "Matsushita Electric Industrial (MEI) in 1987," Harvard Business School Case #388-144.

53. P. Ghemawat, *Commitment: The Dynamic of Strategy* (New York: Free Press, 1991).

54. www.ibm.com, 2008.

55. C.A. Bartlett and S. Ghoshal, *Managing Across Borders* (Boston: Harvard Business School Press, 1989).

56. C.K. Prahalad and Y.L. Doz, *The Multinational Mission* (New York: Free Press, 1987).

57. IKEA: How the Swedish Retailer Became a Global Cult Brand, *BusinessWeek,* November 14, 2005. Cover Story. http://www.businessweek.com/magazine/content/05_46/b3959001.htm. Accessed September 27, 2011.

58. M.E. Porter, *Competitive Strategy* (New York: Free Press, 1980).

59. Gordon Pitts, "Ganong Boss Aims for Sweet Spot," *The Globe and Mail,* March 3, 2003, p. B4.

60. C.W.L. Hill, "Differentiation versus Low Cost or Differentiation and Low Cost: A Contingency Framework," *Academy of Management Review,* 13, 1988, pp. 401–412.

61. For details see J.P. Womack, D.T. Jones, and D. Roos, *The Machine That Changed the World* (New York: Rawson Associates, 1990).

62. M.E. Porter, *Competitive Strategy* (New York: Free Press, 1980).

63. www.cott.com, 2008.

64. C.W.L. Hill and G.R. Jones, *Strategic Management: An Integrated Approach,* 3rd ed. (Boston: Houghton Mifflin, 2000).

65. See D. Garvin, "What Does Product Quality Really Mean?" *Sloan Management Review,* 26, Fall 1984, pp. 25–44; P.B. Crosby, *Quality Is Free* (New York: Mentor Books, 1980); and A. Gabor, *The Man Who Discovered Quality* (New York: Times Books, 1990).

66. Nickels et al., *Understanding Canadian Business* (Toronto: McGraw-Hill Ryerson, 2005).

67. Tara Perkins, "Legacy at a Crossroads," *The Globe and Mail,* August 15, 2009, B1.

68. Carly Weeks, "Campbell's Adding Salt Back to Its Soups," *The Globe and Mail,* Last updated Friday, Jul. 15, 2011. http://www.theglobeandmail.com/life/health/new-health/health-news/Campbell's-adding-salt-back-to-its-soups/article2097659/. Accessed October 19, 2011.

69. Website: www.thegreendoor.ca/.

70. Website: http://web.ustpaul.uottawa.ca/en.

71. Website: www.ottawaplus.ca/portal/profile.do?profileID=45275.

72. G. Mulvihill, "Campbell Is Really Cooking," *San Diego Tribune.com,* August 5, 2004.

73. W. D. Crotty, "Campbell Soup Is Not So Hot," www.MotleyFool.com, May 24, 2004.

74. A. Halperin, "Chicken Soup for the Investor's Soul," *BusinessWeek Online,* May 25, 2006, www.businessweek.com.

75. A. Carter, "Lighting a Fire under Campbell, www.businessweek.com, December 4, 2006.

76. www.campbellsoupcompany.com, 2008.

77. "Campbell Completes $850M Godiva Sale," www.yahoo.com, March 18, 2008.

78. Carly Weeks, "Campbell's Adding Salt Back to Its Soups."

Chapter 6

1. "Samsung Electronics Appoints New Executive Leadership in Major Organizational Realignment," January 12, 2010. http://www.samsung.com/us/news/newsRead.do?news_seq=16596&page=1. Accessed October 22, 2011.

2. "Samsung Electronics Names New CEO," *Reuters,* Monday December 19, 2009, http://www.reuters.com/article/2009/12/15/us-samsungelec-ceo-idUSTRE5BE05T20091215. Accessed October 23, 2011.

3. Sea-Jin Chang, *Sony versus Samsung,* John Wiley and Sons, 2008, p. 128.

4. "Samsung and Its Attractions," *The Economist,* October 1, 2011. From the Print Edition. http://www.economist.com/node/21530984. Accessed October 22, 2011.

5. "Samsung, the Next Big Bet," *The Economist,* October 1, 2011. From the Print Edition. http://www.economist.com/node/21530976. Accessed October 22, 2011.

6. P. R. Lawrence and J. W. Lorsch, *Organization and Environment* (Boston: Graduate School of Business Administration, Harvard University, 1967).

7. G.R. Jones, *Organizational Theory: Text and Cases* (Reading, MA: Addison-Wesley, 1995).

8. J. Child, *Organization: A Guide for Managers and Administrators* (New York: Harper and Row, 1977).

9. F.W. Taylor, *The Principles of Scientific Management* (New York: Harper, 1911).

10. R.W. Griffin, *Task Design: An Integrative Approach* (Glenview, IL: Scott, Foresman, 1982).

11. Ibid.

12. J. R. Hackman and G. R. Oldham, *Work Redesign* (Reading, MA: Addison-Wesley, 1980).

13. J.R. Galbraith and R.K. Kazanjian, *Strategy Implementation: Structure, System, and Process,* 2nd ed. (St. Paul, MN: West, 1986).

14. P.R. Lawrence and J.W. Lorsch, *Organization and Environment* (Boston: Graduate School of Business Administration, Harvard University, 1967).

15. G.R. Jones, *Organizational Theory: Text and Cases* (Reading, MA: Addison-Wesley, 1995).

16. P.R. Lawrence and J.W. Lorsch, *Organization and Environment* (Boston: Graduate School of Business Administration, Harvard University, 1967).

17. R.H. Hall, *Organizations: Structure and Process* (Englewood Cliffs, NJ: Prentice-Hall, 1972); and R. Miles, *Macro Organizational Behaviour* (Santa Monica, CA: Goodyear, 1980).

18. A.D. Chandler, *Strategy and Structure* (Cambridge, MA: MIT Press, 1962).

19. G.R. Jones and C.W.L. Hill, "Transaction Cost Analysis of Strategy–Structure Choice," *Strategic Management Journal,* 9, 1988, pp. 159–172.

20. Kaya Morgan, "FRED SMITH—Federal Express Renegade." Website: www .islandconnections.com/edit/smith .htm. Accessed July 15, 2008.

21. http://www.enterprisingnonprofits. ca/resources/

common-thread-cooperative-social-enterprise-profile. Accessed November 22, 2011.

22. "Samsung Electronics Appoints New Executive Leadership in Major Organizational Realignment," January 12, 2010. http://www.samsung. com/us/news/newsRead.do?news_ seq=16596&page=1. Accessed October 22, 2011.

23. S.M. Davis and P.R. Lawrence, *Matrix* (Reading, MA: Addison-Wesley, 1977); and J.R. Galbraith, "Matrix Organization Designs: How to Combine Functional and Project Forms," *Business Horizons,* 14, 1971, pp. 29–40.

24. L.R. Burns, "Matrix Management in Hospitals: Testing Theories of Matrix Structure and Development," *Administrative Science Quarterly,* 34, 1989, pp. 349–368.

25. C.W.L. Hill, *International Business* (Homewood, IL: Irwin, 1997).

26. G.R. Jones, *Organizational Theory: Text and Cases* (Reading, MA: Addison-Wesley, 1995).

27. Michael Maccoby, "Knowledge Workers Need New Structures," *Research Technology Management,* Vol. 30, No. 3 January–February 1996, pp. 56–58. Website: www.maccoby. com/Articles/KnowledgeWorkers. html.

28. G. S. Capowski, "Designing a Corporate Identity," *Management Review,* June 1993, 37–38.

29. J. Marcia, "Just Doing It," *Distribution,* January 1995, 36–40.

30. "Nike Battles Backlash from Overseas Sweatshops," *Marketing News,* November 9, 1998, 14.

31. J. Laabs, "Nike Gives Indonesian Workers a Raise," *Workforce,* December 1998, 15–16.

32. W. Echikson, "It's Europe's Turn to Sweat about Sweatshops," *BusinessWeek,* July 19, 1999, 96.

33. Anthony Grnak, John Hughes, and Douglas Hunter, *Building the Best, Lessons from Inside Canada's Best Managed Companies* (Toronto: Viking Canada, 2006), p. 154.

34. Poonam Khanna, "CP Rail Jumps Aboard Outsourcing Train," *Computing Canada,* December 10, 2004, p. 30. For more on outsourcing,

visit www.ezgoal.com/outsourcing/c. asp?a=Canada&outsourcing.

35. Grant Buckler, "Economies of Scale a Big Hit for IT Managers," *Computing Canada,* February 15, 2002. Website: www.findarticles. com/p/articles/mi_m0CGC/is_4_28/ ai_83056527#continue.

36. Beth Ellyn Rosenthal, "Outsourcing Manages Risk While Transforming Processes for Canada's Central Bank," June 2007. Website: www.outsourcing-canada.com/canadian2.html. Accessed December 21, 2008.

37. J. Barthelemy and D. Adsit, "The Seven Deadly Sins of Outsourcing," *Academy of Management Executive,* 17, (2), 2003, pp. 87–100.

38. P. Blau, "A Formal Theory of Differentiation in Organizations," *American Sociological Review,* 35, 1970, pp. 684–695.

39. S. Grey, "McDonald's CEO Announces Shifts of Top Executives," *The Wall Street Journal,* July 16, 2004, A11.

40. www.mcdonalds.com, 2008.

41. J. Child, *Organization: A Guide for Managers and Administrators* (New York: Harper and Row, 1977).

42. Information about Ducks Unlimited from "Salute! Celebrating the Progressive Employer," advertising supplement, *Benefits Canada,* March 1999, p. Insert 1–23; and www .ducksunlimited.ca.

43. Ibid.

44. P.M. Blau and R.A. Schoenherr, *The Structure of Organizations* (New York: Basic Books, 1971).

45. P. R. Lawrence and J. W. Lorsch, *Organization and Environment* (Boston: Graduate School of Business Administration, Harvard University, 1967), 50–55.

46. G.R. Jones, *Organizational Theory: Text and Cases* (Reading, MA: Addison-Wesley, 1995).

47. Marina Strauss, "Leadership Secrets of the Invisible Man," *The Globe and Mail Report on Business,* May 2011, pp. 56–62.

48. T. Burns and G.M. Stalker, *The Management of Innovation* (London: Tavistock, 1961).

49. L.A. Perlow, G.A. Okhuysen, and N.P. Repenning, "The Speed

Trap: Exploring the Relationship Between Decision Making and Temporal Context, *Academy of Management Journal,* 45, 2002, pp.931–955.

50. P.R. Lawrence and J.W. Lorsch, *Organization and Environment* (Boston: Graduate School of Business Administration, Harvard University, 1967).

51. R. Duncan, "What Is the Right Organizational Design?" *Organizational Dynamics,* Winter 1979, pp. 59–80.

52. T. Burns and G.R. Stalker, *The Management of Innovation* (London: Tavistock, 1966).

53. Scott Peterson, "Good Leaders Empower People," *National Post,* Wednesday, May 18, 2005, p. FP9.

54. D. Miller, "Strategy Making and Structure: Analysis and Implications for Performance," *Academy of Management Journal,* 30, 1987, pp. 7–32.

55. A.D. Chandler, *Strategy and Structure* (Cambridge, MA: MIT Press, 1962).

56. J. Stopford and L. Wells, *Managing the Multinational Enterprise* (London: Longman, 1972).

57. J. Woodward, *Management and Technology* (London: Her Majesty's Stationery Office, 1958).

58. C. Perrow, *Organizational Analysis: A Sociological View* (Belmont, CA: Wadsworth, 1970).

59. Jones, Gareth, *Essentials of Contemporary Management* 2ce, McGraw-Hill Ryerson, 2007.

60. Andrew Couts, "Microsoft Moving Forward In Bid To Buy Yahoo: Report," *Digital Trends,* October 20, 2011. http://www.digitaltrends.com/web/microsoft-moving-forward-in-bid-to-buy-yahoo-report/. Accessed October 23, 2011.

61. Robert D. Hof, "Yahoo's Bartz Shows Who's Boss." *BusinessWeek online,* February 26, 2009.

62. Douglas MacMillan, Ian King, and Ari Levy, "Bartz Fired as Yahoo CEO Amid Plans for Strategic Review," *Businessweek,* September 7, 2011. http://www.businessweek.com/technology/bartz-fired-as-yahoo-ceo-amid-plans-for-strategic-review-09072011.html. Accessed October 23, 2011.

Chapter 7

1. www.ford.com, 2008.

2. D. Kiley, "The New Heat on Ford," www.businessweek.com, June 4, 2007.

3. Ibid.

4. www.ford.com, 2008.

5. Kipp Bodnar, "Manufacturing Industry Best Practices: Ford's Culture Shift," *Manufacturing Industry News,* February 15, 2011. http://manufacturing.hubspot.com/bid/25731/Manufacturing-Industry-Best-Practices-Ford-s-Culture-Shift. Accessed October 24, 2011.

6. T. Lonier, "Some Insights and Statistics on Working Solo," www.workingsolo.com.

7. I. N. Katsikis and L. P. Kyrgidou, "The Concept of Sustainable Entrepreneurship: A Conceptual Framework and Empirical Analysis," *Academy of Management Proceedings,* 2007, 1–6, 6p, web.ebscohost.com/ehost/delivery?vid=7&hid=102&sid=434afdf5-5ed9-45d4-993b-, January 24, 2008; "What Is a Social Entrepreneur?" http://ashoka.org/social entrepreneur, February 20, 2008; C. Hsu, "Entrepreneur for Social Change," October 31, 2005, *U.S.News.com,* www.usnews.com/usnews/news/articles/051031/31drayton.htm; D. M. Sullivan, "Stimulating Social Entrepreneurship: Can Support From Cities Make a Difference? *Academy of Management Perspectives,* February 2007, 78.

8. Ibid.

9. Muhammad Yunus, *Building Social Business: The New Kind of Capitalism That Serves Humanity's Most Pressing Needs* (New York: Public Affairs, 2010), p. xvii.

10. http://socialinnovation.ca/about. Accessed November 22, 2011.

11. Ibid.

12. See, for example, H.S. Becker, "Culture: A Sociological View," *Yale Review,* Summer 1982, pp. 513–527; and E.H. Schein, *Organizational Culture and Leadership* (San Francisco: Jossey-Bass, 1985), p. 168.

13. T.E. Deal and A.A. Kennedy, "Culture: A New Look Through Old Lenses," *Journal of Applied Behavioral Science,* November 1983, p. 501.

14. M. Rokeach, *The Nature of Human Values* (New York: Free Press, 1973).

15. Burke, W. W. *Organizational Development: A Process of Learning and Changing* (2nd ed.). (Reading, MA: Addison-Wesley, 1992), p. 10–11.

16. E.H. Schein, "Leadership and Organizational Culture," in F. Hesselbein, M. Goldsmith, and R. Beckhard (eds.), *The Leader of the Future* (San Francisco: Jossey-Bass, 1996), pp. 61–62.

17. J.B. Sorensen, "The Strength of Corporate Culture and the Reliability of Firm Performance," *Administrative Science Quarterly,* 47, no. 1, 2002, pp. 70–91.

18. D.C. Feldman, "The Development and Enforcement of Group Norms," *Academy of Management Review,* 9, 1984, pp. 47–53.

19. www.nokia.com, 2001.

20. P. de Bendern, "Quirky Culture Paves Nokia's Road to Fortune," www.yahoo.com, 2000.

21. K. E. Weick, *The Social Psychology of Organization* (Reading, MA: Addison-Wesley, 1979).

22. G.R. Jones, *Organizational Theory: Text and Cases* (Reading, MA: Addison-Wesley, 1995).

23. H. Schein, "The Role of the Founder in Creating Organizational Culture," *Organizational Dynamics,* 12, 1983, pp. 13–28.

24. Anthony Grnak, John Hughes, and Douglas Hunter, op. cit.

25. J.M. George, "Personality, Affect, and Behaviour in Groups," *Journal of Applied Psychology,* 75, 1990, pp. 107–116.

26. J. Van Maanen, "Police Socialization: A Longitudinal Examination of Job Attitudes in an Urban Police Department," *Administrative Science Quarterly,* 20, 1975, pp. 207–228.

27. P.L. Berger and T. Luckman, *The Social Construction of Reality* (Garden City, NY: Anchor Books, 1967).

28. H.M. Trice and J.M. Beyer, "Studying Organizational Culture Through Rites and Ceremonials," *Academy of Management Review,* 9, 1984, pp. 653–669.

29. "Bonding and Brutality: Hazing Survives as a Way of Forging Loyalty to Groups," *Maclean's,* January 30, 1995, p. 18.

30. Aaron Karp, "WestJet's Value Proposition," *Air Transport World,* January 1, 2011. http://atwonline.com/airline-finance-data/article/WestJet-s-value-proposition-1231. Accessed October 25, 2011.

31. B. Ortega, "Wal-Mart's Meeting Is a Reason to Party," *The Wall Street Journal,* June 3, 1994, p. A1.

32. Website: www.senecac.on.ca/.

33. D. Akin, "Big Blue Chills Out: A Canadian Executive Leads the Campaign to Turn IBM into Cool Blue," *Financial Post (National Post),* October 11, 1999, pp. C1, C6.

34. A. Rafaeli and M.G. Pratt, "Tailored Meanings: On the Meaning and Impact of Organizational Dress," *Academy of Management Review,* January 1993, pp. 32–55.

35. Website: www.EIU.com. Accessed July 22, 2009.

36. L. Brown, "Research Action: Organizational Feedback, Understanding and Change," *Journal of Applied Behavioral Research,* 8, 1972, pp. 697–711; P.A. Clark, *Action Research and Organizational Change* (New York: Harper and Row, 1972); and N. Margulies and A.P. Raia (eds.), *Conceptual Foundations of Organizational Development* (New York: McGraw-Hill, 1978).

37. W.L. French and C.H. Bell, *Organizational Development* (Englewood Cliffs, NJ: Prentice-Hall, 1990).

38. Economist Intelligence Unit, E-Business Transformation. Website: http://store.eiu.com/product/313436031.html. Accessed August 18, 2009.

39. W.L. French, "A Checklist for Organizing and Implementing an OD Effort," in W.L. French, C.H. Bell, and R.A. Zawacki (eds.), *Organizational Development and Transformation* (Homewood, IL: Irwin, 1994), pp. 484–495.

40. K. Lewin, *Field Theory in Social Science* (New York: Harper and Row, 1951).

41. Ian Turner, "Strategy, Complexity and Uncertainty." Website: www.poolonline.com/archive/iss1fea5.html. Accessed August 2, 2009. Based on Ralph Stace.

42. J.R. Stepp and T.J. Schneider, "Fostering Change in a Unionized Environment," *Canadian Business Review,* Summer 1995, pp. 13–16.

43. Ibid.

44. Adapted from "Impersonal Approach Hurts Business, Study Says," *The Globe and Mail*, Wednesday, August 20, 2003, p. C3.

45. Aaron Karp, "WestJet's Value Proposition," *Air Transport World,* January 1, 2011. http://atwonline.com/airline-finance-data/article/WestJet-s-value-proposition-1231. Accessed October 25, 2011.

Chapter 8

1. C. J. Loomis, *Fortune* editor at large, "The Big Surprise Is Enterprise: Quietly beating out rivals Hertz and Avis, this privately held outfit reigns as the No. 1 car-rental company in America, and the Taylor family aims to keep it on top," *Fortune,* July 14, 2006, http://cnnmoney.printthis.clickability.com/pt/cpt?action=cpt&title=Fortune%3A+The+big..., March 31, 2008; http://aboutus.enterprise.com/who we are.html, April 21, 2009.

2. Enterprise Holdings, http://www.enterpriseholdings.com/. Accessed October 27, 2011.

3. "Top Entry Level Employers." CollegeGrad.com, http://www.collegegrad.com/topemployers/2011_entry_level.php. Accessed October 27, 2011.

4. Loomis, "The Big Surprise Is Enterprise."

5. "Enterprise Rent-A-Car's Pam Nicholson Named to *Fortune's* 50 Most Powerful Women in Business 2007," October 1, 2007, www.erac.com/recruit/news_details.asp?navID=frontpage&RID=234, March 27, 2008.

6. "Enterprise Ranked in Top 10 of *BusinessWeek*'s 'Customer Service Champs'"; Gerdes, "The Best Places to Launch a Career."

7. "It's Running a Business . . . Not Doing a Job," *Enterprise Rent-A-Car Careers—Opportunities,* www.erac.com/recruit/opportunities.asp, March 27, 2008.

8. Loomis, "The Big Surprise Is Enterprise"; Lehman, "A Clear Road to the Top."

9. Ibid.

10. Lehman, "A Clear Road to the Top."

11. Loomis, "The Big Surprise Is Enterprise."

12. Ibid.; Lehman, "A Clear Road to the Top."

13. J. A. Taylor Kindle, "Enterprise: Why We Give Where We Give: For Enterprise Rent-A-Car, giving back is linked to the primary business. That means planting 50 million trees over 50 years, for starters," www.businessweek.com/print/investor/content/jun2007/pi20070628_339711.htm, March 28, 2008.

14. Ibid.

15. M. Gunther, senior writer, "Renting 'Green'? Not So Easy, Enterprise-Rent-A-Car Goes Green, with Limits," *CNNMoney.com,* January 17, 2008, http://cnnmoney.printthis.clickability.com/pt/cpt?action=cpt&title=Enterprise-Rent-A-Car..., March 3, 2008; "Enterprise Rent-A-Car Announces Most Comprehensive Environmental Platform in Its Industry, Wednesday, June 6, 2007, *Enterprise Rent-A-Car Careers—Enterprise In The News,* www.erac.com/ recruit/news_detail.asp?navID=frontpage&RID=221, March 27, 2008.

16. Loomis, "The Big Surprise Is Enterprise"; Lehman, "A Clear Road to the Top."

17. R. Kanfer, "Motivation Theory and Industrial and Organizational Psychology," in M.D. Dunnette and L.M. Hough (eds.), *Handbook of Industrial and Organizational Psychology,* 2nd ed., vol. 1 (Palo Alto, CA: Consulting Psychologists Press, 1990), pp. 75–170.

18. N. Nicholson, "How to Motivate Your Problem People," *Harvard Business Review,* January 2003, 57–65.

19. A. M. Grant, "Does Intrinsic Motivation Fuel the Prosocial Fire? Motivational Synergy in Predicting Persistence, Performance, and Productivity," *Journal of Applied Psychology* 93, no. 1 (2008), 48–58.

20. Ibid.; C. D. Batson, "Prosocial Motiviation: Is It Ever Truly Altruistic?" in L. Berkowitz, ed., *Advances in Experimental Social Psychology,* vol. 20 (New York: Academic Press, 1987), 65–122.

21. Antony Bugg-Levine and Jed Emerson, *Impacting Investing, Transforming How We Make Money While Making*

a Difference, San Francisco: Jossey-Bass, 2011, p.xii.

22. Grant, "Does Intrinsic Motivation Fuel the Prosocial Fire?"

23. http://www.torontoenterprisefund. ca/_bin/resources/Featured_ enterprise/Inspirations.cfm. Accessed November 22, 2011

24. A.H. Maslow, *Motivation and Personality* (New York: Harper and Row, 1954); and J.P. Campbell and R.D. Pritchard, "Motivation Theory in Industrial and Organizational Psychology," in M.D. Dunnette (ed.), *Handbook of Industrial and Organizational Psychology* (Chicago: Rand McNally, 1976), pp. 63–130.

25. R. Kanfer, "Motivation Theory and Industrial and Organizational Psychology," in M.D. Dunnette and L.M. Hough (eds.), *Handbook of Industrial and Organizational Psychology,* 2nd ed., vol. 1 (Palo Alto, CA: Consulting Psychologists Press, 1990), pp. 75–170.

26. S. Ronen, "An Underlying Structure of Motivational Need Taxonomies: A Cross-Cultural Confirmation," in H.C. Triandis, M.D. Dunnette, and L.M. Hough (eds.), *Handbook of Industrial and Organizational Psychology,* vol. 4 (Palo Alto, CA: Consulting Psychologists Press, 1994), pp. 241–269.

27. N.J. Adler, *International Dimensions of Organizational Behavior,* 2nd ed. (Boston: P.W.S.-Kent, 1991); G. Hofstede, "Motivation, Leadership and Organization: Do American Theories Apply Abroad?" *Organizational Dynamics,* Summer 1980, pp. 42–63.

28. F. Herzberg, *Work and the Nature of Man* (Cleveland: World, 1966).

29. N. King, "Clarification and Evaluation of the Two-Factor Theory of Job Satisfaction," *Psychological Bulletin,* 74, 1970, pp. 18–31; and E.A. Locke, "The Nature and Causes of Job Satisfaction," in M.D. Dunnette (ed.), *Handbook of Industrial and Organizational Psychology* (Chicago: Rand McNally, 1976), pp. 1297–1349.

30. D. C. McClelland, *Human Motivation* (Glenview, IL: Scott, Foresman, 1985); D. C. McClelland, "How Motives, Skills, and Values Determine What People Do," *American Psychologist* 40 (1985), 812–25; D. C. McClelland,

"Managing Motivation to Expand Human Freedom," *American Psychologist* 33 (1978), 201–10.

31. D. G. Winter, *The Power Motive* (New York: Free Press, 1973).

32. M. J. Stahl, "Achievement, Power, and Managerial Motivation: Selecting Managerial Talent with the Job Choice Exercise," *Personnel Psychology* 36 (1983), 775–89; D. C. McClelland and D. H. Burnham, "Power Is the Great Motivator," *Harvard Business Review* 54 (1976), 100–10.

33. R. J. House, W. D. Spangler, and J. Woycke, "Personality and Charisma in the U.S. Presidency: A Psychological Theory of Leader Effectiveness," *Administrative Science Quarterly* 36 (1991), 364–96.

34. G. H. Hines, "Achievement, Motivation, Occupations, and Labor Turnover in New Zealand," *Journal of Applied Psychology* 58 (1973), 313–17; P. S. Hundal, "A Study of Entrepreneurial Motivation: Comparison of Fast- and Slow-Progressing Small Scale Industrial Entrepreneurs in Punjab, India," *Journal of Applied Psychology* 55 (1971), 317–23.

35. R.A. Clay, "Green Is Good for You," *Monitor on Psychology,* April 2001, pp. 40–42.

36. T.R. Mitchell, "Expectancy-Value Models in Organizational Psychology," in N.T. Feather (ed.), *Expectations and Actions: Expectancy-Value Models in Psychology* (Hillsdale, NJ: Erlbaum, 1982), pp. 293–312; V.H. Vroom, *Work and Motivation* (New York: Wiley, 1964).

37. N. Shope Griffin, "Personalize Your Management Development," *Harvard Business Review* 8, no. 10 (2003), 113–119.

38. Kevin Cox, "Irving Oil Fuels Its Leaders," *The Globe and Mail,* Wednesday, April 21, 2004, C1, 3.

39. T. J. Maurer, E. M. Weiss, and F. G. Barbeite, "A Model of Involvement in Work-Related Learning and Development Activity: The Effects of Individual, Situational, Motivational, and Age Variables," *Journal of Applied Psychology* 88, no. 4 (2003), 707–24.

40. J. S. Adams, "Toward an Understanding of Inequity," *Journal of Abnormal and Social Psychology* 67 (1963), 422–36.

41. J.S. Adams, "Toward an Understanding of Inequity," *Journal of Abnormal and Social Psychology,* 67, 1963, pp. 422–436; J. Greenberg, "Approaching Equity and Avoiding Inequity in Groups and Organizations," in J. Greenberg and R.L. Cohen (eds.), *Equity and Justice in Social Behavior* (New York: Academic Press, 1982), pp. 389–435; J. Greenberg, "Equity and Workplace Status: A Field Experiment," *Journal of Applied Psychology,* 73, 1988, pp. 606–613; and R.T. Mowday, "Equity Theory Predictions of Behavior in Organizations," in R.M. Steers and L.W. Porter, (eds.), *Motivation and Work Behavior* (New York: McGraw-Hill, 1987), pp. 89–110.

42. E.A. Locke and G.P. Latham, *A Theory of Goal Setting and Task Performance* (Englewood Cliffs, NJ: Prentice-Hall, 1990).

43. E.A. Locke and G.P. Latham, *A Theory of Goal Setting and Task Performance* (Englewood Cliffs, NJ: Prentice-Hall, 1990); J.J. Donovan and D.J. Radosevich, "The Moderating Role of Goal Commitment on the Goal Difficulty–Performance Relationship: A Meta-Analytic Review and Critical Analysis," *Journal of Applied Psychology,* 83, 1998, pp. 308–315; and M.E. Tubbs, "Goal Setting: A Meta-Analytic Examination of the Empirical Evidence," *Journal of Applied Psychology,* 71, 1986, pp. 474–483.

44. E. A. Locke, K. N. Shaw, L. M. Saari, and G. P. Latham, "Goal Setting and Task Performance: 1969–1980," *Psychological Bulletin* 90 (1981), 125–52.

45. P. C. Earley, T. Connolly, and G. Ekegren, "Goals, Strategy Development, and Task Performance: Some Limits on the Efficacy of Goal Setting," *Journal of Applied Psychology* 74 (1989), 24–33; R. Kanfer and P. L. Ackerman, "Motivation and Cognitive Abilities: An Integrative/Aptitude-Treatment Interaction Approach to Skill Acquisition," *Journal of Applied Psychology* 74 (1989), 657–90.

46. W. C. Hamner, "Reinforcement Theory and Contingency Management in Organizational Settings," in H. Tosi and W. C. Hamner, eds., *Organizational Behavior and Management: A Contingency Approach* (Chicago: St. Clair Press, 1974).

47. B. F. Skinner, *Contingencies of Reinforcement* (New York: Appleton-Century-Crofts, 1969).

48. H. W. Weiss, "Learning Theory and Industrial and Organizational Psychology," in Dunnette and Hough, *Handbook of Industrial and Organizational Psychology,* 171–221.

49. Hamner, "Reinforcement Theory and Contingency Management."

50. A. Bandura, *Principles of Behavior Modification* (New York: Holt, Rinehart and Winston, 1969); A. Bandura, *Social Learning Theory* (Englewood Cliffs, NJ: Prentice Hall, 1977); T. R. V. Davis and F. Luthans, "A Social Learning Approach to Organizational Behavior," *Academy of Management Review* 5 (1980), 281–90.

51. A. P. Goldstein and M. Sorcher, *Changing Supervisor Behaviors* (New York: Pergamon Press, 1974); F. Luthans and R. Kreitner, *Organizational Behavior Modification and Beyond* (Glenview, IL: Scott, Foresman, 1985).

52. Bandura, *Social Learning Theory;* Davis and Luthans, "A Social Learning Approach to Organizational Behavior"; Luthans and Kreitner, *Organizational Behavior Modification and Beyond.*

53. A. Bandura, "Self-Reinforcement: Theoretical and Methodological Considerations," *Behaviorism* 4 (1976), 135–55.

54. Hammonds, "Growth Search."

55. B. Elgin, "Managing Google's Idea Factory," *BusinessWeek,* October 3, 2005, 88–90.

56. A. Bandura, *Self-Efficacy: The Exercise of Control* (New York: W.H. Freeman, 1997); J. B. Vancouver, K. M. More, and R. J. Yoder, "Self-Efficacy and Resource Allocation: Support for a Nonmonotonic, Discontinous Model," *Journal of Applied Psychology* 93, no. 1 (2008), 35–47.

57. A. Bandura, "Self-Efficacy Mechanism in Human Agency," *American Psychologist* 37 (1982), 122–27; M. E. Gist and T. R. Mitchell, "Self-Efficacy: A Theoretical Analysis of Its Determinants and Malleability," *Academy of Management Review* 17 (1992), 183–211.

58. Gallup Employee Engagement, Wednesday, October 26, 2011. http://www.gallup.com/consulting/52/Employee-Engagement.aspx?gclid=CLv4reDYhqwCFYLsKgodHFem9g. Accessed October 26, 2011.

59. "Development Opportunities Top Factor in Reward Fairness: Study," *HR Reporter,* July 25, 2011. http://www.hrreporter.com/articleview?&articleid=10847&headline=development-opportunities-top-factor-in-reward-fairness-study. Accessed October 26, 2011.

60. E.E. Lawler III, *Pay and Organization Development* (Reading, MA: Addison-Wesley, 1981).

61. Based on S.E. Gross and J.P. Bacher, "The New Variable Pay Programs: How Some Succeed, Why Some Don't," *Compensation & Benefits Review,* January–February 1993, p. 51; and J.R. Schuster and P.K. Zingheim, "The New Variable Pay: Key Design Issues," *Compensation & Benefits Review,* March–April 1993, p. 28.

62. Peter Brieger, "Variable Pay Packages Gain Favour: Signing Bonuses, Profit Sharing Taking Place of Salary Hikes," *Financial Post (National Post),* September 13, 2002, p. FP5.

63. E. Beauchesne, "Pay Bonuses Improve Productivity, Study Shows," *The Vancouver Sun,* September 13, 2002, p. D5.

64. "Hope for Higher Pay: The Squeeze on Incomes Is Gradually Easing Up," *Maclean's,* November 25, 1996, pp. 100–101.

65. Lawler, *Pay and Organization Development.*

66. Ibid.

67. Ibid.

68. "Stock Option," *Encarta World English Dictionary,* June 28, 2001, www.dictionary.msn.com; personal interview with Professor Bala Dharan, Jones Graduate School of Business, Rice University, June 28, 2001.

69. Personal interview with Professor Bala Dharan.

70. Ibid.

71. A. J. Michels, "Dallas Semiconductor," *Fortune,* May 16, 1994, 81.

72. M. Betts, "Big Things Come in Small Buttons," *Computerworld,* August 3, 1992, 30.

73. M. Boslet, "Metal Buttons Toted by Crop Pickers Act as Mini Databases," *The Wall Street Journal,* June 1, 1994, B3.

74. C. D. Fisher, L. F. Schoenfeldt, and J. B. Shaw, *Human Resource Management* (Boston: Houghton Mifflin, 1990); B. E. Graham-Moore and T. L. Ross, *Productivity Gainsharing* (Englewood Cliffs, NJ: Prentice Hall, 1983); A. J. Geare, "Productivity from Scanlon Type Plans," *Academy of Management Review* 1 (1976), 99–108.

75. J. Labate, "Deal Those Workers In," *Fortune,* April 19, 1993, 26.

76. K. Belson, " Japan's Net Generation," *BusinessWeek,* March 19, 2001 (*BusinessWeek* Archives, June 27, 2001).

77. K. Belson, "Taking a Hint from the Upstarts," *BusinessWeek,* March 19, 2001 (*BusinessWeek* Archives, June 27, 2001); "Going for the Gold," *BusinessWeek,* March 19, 2001 (*BusinessWeek* Archives, June 27, 2001); "What the Government Can Do to Promote a Flexible Workforce," *BusinessWeek,* March 19, 2001 (*BusinessWeek* Archives, June 27, 2001).

78. Enterprise Holdings, http://www.enterpriseholdings.com/. Accessed October 27, 2011.

79. Lululemon success builds founder's fortune, by *Calgary Herald,* October 7, 2011. http://www.calgaryherald.com/business/company/Lululemon/Lululemon+success+builds+founder+fortune/5517402/story.html. Accessed October 27, 2011.

80. Jacqueline Nelson, "Loco for Lulu," *Canadian Business,* May 9, 2011, pp. 28–32.

81. Lululemon Manifesto, http://www.lululemon.com/about/culture. Accessed November 1, 2011.

82. http://www.marketwatch.com/investing/stock/lll?countrycode=ca. Accessed June 3, 2012.

83. Lululemon Manifesto.

Chapter 9

1. Telecommunications visionary receives CBLA, http://www.business.ualberta.ca/People/Media/MediaReleasesAndStories/2011/02/CongratulationstoTELUSDarrenEntwistlethe2011CBLArecipient.aspx, March 3, 2011. Accessed Nov. 1, 2011.

2. Ibid.

3. "Top 5 Mixed-Play Healthcare ICT Companies," Branham 300. http://www.branham300.com/index.

php?year=2011&listing=13. Accessed Nov. 3, 2011.

4. "Darren Entwistle—Canadian Business Leader of the Year Award Recipient," March 7, 2011. http://abfiualberta. wordpress.com/2011/03/07/133/. Accessed November 1, 2011.

5. Eric Reguly, "Perfectly Unhappy," *The Globe and Mail,* Friday, October 27, 2006. http://www.theglobeandmail. com/report-on-business/perfectly-unhappy/article850573/page2/. Accessed November 3, 2011.

6. G. Yukl, *Leadership in Organizations,* 2nd ed. (New York: Academic Press, 1989); and R.M. Stogdill, *Handbook of Leadership: A Survey of the Literature* (New York: Free Press, 1974).

7. Henri Fayol, *General and Industrial Management* (Belmont CA: David S. Lake Publisher, 1987). First published in 1916.

8. Max Weber, "The Types of Authority and Imperative Coordination," *The Theory of Social and Economic Organization* (NY: Oxford University Press), translated by A.M. Henderson and Talcott Parsons, 1949.

9. Mary Parker Follett, "Giving of Orders and the Psychology of Control," in L. Urwick, ed., *Freedom and Coordination: Lectures in Business Organisation by Mary Parker Follett* (London Management Trust Publications Ltd., 1949). The lectures were delivered in January 1933 at the London School of Economics.

10. Fredrick W. Taylor, *The Principles of Scientific Management,* public domain from Project Gutenberg. First published in 1911.

11. H. Mintzberg, *Power in and Around Organizations* (Englewood Cliffs, NJ: Prentice-Hall, 1983); and J. Pfeffer, *Power in Organizations* (Marshfield, MA: Pitman, 1981).

12. R.P. French Jr. and B. Raven, "The Bases of Social Power," in D. Cartwright and A.F. Zander (eds.), *Group Dynamics* (Evanston, IL: Row, Peterson, 1960), pp. 607–623.

13. Rob Shaw, "Reward Employee Ideas–Literally," *The Globe and Mail*, Friday, August 19, 2005, C1, 2.

14. M. Loeb, "Jack Welch Lets Fly on Budgets, Bonuses, and Buddy Boards," *Fortune,* May 29, 1995, 146.

15. Sharda Prashad, "Fill Your Power Gap," *The Globe and Mail*, Wednesday, July 23, 2003, C3.

16. T.M. Burton, "Visionary's Reward: Combine 'Simple Ideas' and Some Failures; Result: Sweet Revenge," *The Wall Street Journal,* February 3, 1995, pp. A1, A5.

17. L. Nakarmi, "A Flying Leap Toward the 21st Century? Pressure from Competitors and Seoul May Transform the Chaebol," *Business Week,* March 20, 1995, pp. 78–80.

18. J. Schaubroeck, J.R. Jones, and J.L. Xie, "Individual Differences in Utilizing Control to Cope with Job Demands: Effects on Susceptibility to Infectious Disease," *Journal of Applied Psychology,* 86, no. 2, 2001, pp. 265–278; and A.M. Owens, "Empowerment Can Make You Ill, Study Says," *National Post,* April 30, 2001, pp. A1, A8.

19. "Delta Promotes Empowerment," *The Globe and Mail,* May 31, 1999, advertising supplement, p. C5.

20. "How Do I Manage a Mobile Workforce?" Special Feature to *National Post: BUSINESS SOLUTIONS.* Presented by CISCO. *National Post,* Business Solutions Advertisement, Monday, March 3, 2008, FP8. Website: www. financialpost.com/small_business/story. html?id=343859. Accessed July 4, 2008.

21. J.P. Kotter, "What Leaders Really Do," *Harvard Business Review,* May–June 1990, pp. 103–111.

22. R.N. Kanungo, "Leadership in Organizations: Looking Ahead to the 21st Century," *Canadian Psychology,* 39, no. 1–2, 1998, p. 77. For more evidence of this consensus, see N. Adler, *International Dimensions of Organizational Behavior,* 3rd ed., (Cincinnati, OH: South Western College Publishing), 1997; R.J. House, "Leadership in the Twenty-First Century," in A. Howard (ed.), *The Changing Nature of Work* (San Francisco: Jossey-Bass), 1995, pp. 411–450; R.N. Kanungo and M. Mendonca, *Ethical Dimensions of Leadership* (Thousand Oaks, CA: Sage Publications, 1996); and A. Zaleznik, "The Leadership Gap," *Academy of Management Executive,* 4, no. 1, 1990, pp. 7–22.

23. B.M. Bass, Bass and Stogdill's *Handbook of Leadership: Theory, Research, and Managerial Applications,* 3rd ed. (New York: Free Press, 1990); R.J. House and M.L. Baetz, "Leadership: Some Empirical Generalizations and New Research Directions," in B.M. Staw and L.L. Cummings (eds.), *Research in Organizational Behavior,* vol. 1 (Greenwich, CT: JAI Press, 1979), pp. 341–423; S.A. Kirpatrick and E.A. Locke, "Leadership: Do Traits Matter?" *Academy of Management Executive,* 5, no. 2, 1991, pp. 48–60; and G. Yukl, *Leadership in Organizations,* 2nd ed. (New York: Academic Press, 1989); and G. Yukl and D.D. Van Fleet, "Theory and Research on Leadership in Organizations," in M.D. Dunnette and L.M. Hough (eds.), *Handbook of Industrial and Organizational Psychology,* 2nd ed., vol. 3 (Palo Alto, CA: Consulting Psychologists Press, 1992), pp. 147–197.

24. E.A. Fleishman, "Performance Assessment Based on an Empirically Derived Task Taxonomy," *Human Factors,* 9, 1967, pp. 349–366; E.A. Fleishman, "The Description of Supervisory Behavior," *Personnel Psychology,* 37, 1953, pp. 1–6; A.W. Halpin and B.J. Winer, "A Factorial Study of the Leader Behavior Descriptions," in R.M. Stogdill and A.I. Coons (eds.), *Leader Behavior: Its Description and Measurement* (Columbus Bureau of Business Research, Ohio State University, 1957); and D. Tscheulin, "Leader Behavior Measurement in German Industry," *Journal of Applied Psychology,* 56, 1971, pp. 28–31.

25. R. Likert, *New Patterns of Management* (New York: McGraw-Hill, 1961); and N.C. Morse and E. Reimer, "The Experimental Change of a Major Organizational Variable," *Journal of Abnormal and Social Psychology,* 52, 1956, pp. 120–129.

26. R.R. Blake and J.S. Mouton, *The New Managerial Grid* (Houston: Gulf, 1978).

27. David Sirota, Louis A. Mischkind, and Michael Irwin Meltzer, "Nothing Beats an Enthusiastic Employee," *The Globe and Mail*, Friday, July 29, 2005, C1.

28. http://www.metowe.com/charity. Accessed June 9, 2012.

29. E.A. Fleishman and E.F. Harris, "Patterns of Leadership Behavior

Related to Employee Grievances and Turnover," *Personnel Psychology,* 15, 1962, pp. 43–56.

30. This graphic is taken from website: www.mindtools.com/pages/article/newLDR_73.htm. Accessed January 3, 2009.

31. F.E. Fiedler, *A Theory of Leadership Effectiveness* (New York: McGraw-Hill, 1967); and F.E. Fiedler, "The Contingency Model and the Dynamics of the Leadership Process," in L. Berkowitz (ed.), *Advances in Experimental Social Psychology* (New York: Academic Press, 1978).

32. R.J. House and M.L. Baetz, "Leadership: Some Empirical Generalizations and New Research Directions," in B.M. Staw and L.L. Cummings (eds.), *Research in Organizational Behavior,* vol. 1 (Greenwich, CT: JAI Press, 1979), pp. 341–423; L.H. Peters, D.D. Hartke, and J.T. Pohlmann, "Fiedler's Contingency Theory of Leadership: An Application of the Meta-Analysis Procedures of Schmidt and Hunter," *Psychological Bulletin,* 97, 1985, pp. 274–285; and C.A. Schriesheim, B.J. Tepper, and L.A. Tetrault, "Least Preferred Co-Worker Score, Situational Control, and Leadership Effectiveness: A Meta-Analysis of Contingency Model Performance Predictions," *Journal of Applied Psychology,* 79, 1994, pp. 561–573.

33. P. Hersey and K.H. Blanchard, "So You Want to Know Your Leadership Style?" *Training and Development Journal,* February 1974, pp. 1–15; and P. Hersey and K.H. Blanchard, *Management of Organizational Behavior: Utilizing Human Resources,* 6th ed. (Englewood Cliffs, NJ: Prentice-Hall, 1993).

34. Cited in C.F. Fernandez and R.P. Vecchio, "Situational Leadership Theory Revisited: A Test of an Across-Jobs Perspective," *Leadership Quarterly,* 8, no.1, 1997, p. 67.

35. M.G. Evans, "The Effects of Supervisory Behavior on the Path–Goal Relationship," *Organizational Behavior and Human Performance,* 5, 1970, pp. 277–298; M.G. Evans, "Leadership and Motivation: A Core Concept," *Academy of Management Journal,* 13, 1970, pp. 91–102; R.J. House, "A Path–Goal Theory of Leader Effectiveness," *Administrative Science Quarterly,* September 1971, pp. 321–338; R.J.

House and T.R. Mitchell, "Path–Goal Theory of Leadership," *Journal of Contemporary Business,* Autumn 1974, p. 86; M.G. Evans, "Leadership," in S. Kerr (ed.), *Organizational Behavior* (Columbus, OH: Grid Publishing, 1979); R.J. House, "Retrospective Comment," in L.E. Boone and D.D. Bowen (eds.), *The Great Writings in Management and Organizational Behavior,* 2nd ed. (New York: Random House, 1987), pp. 354–364; M.G. Evans, "Fuhrungstheorien, Weg-ziel-theorie" (trans. G. Reber), in A. Kieser, G. Reber, and R. Wunderer (eds). *Handworterbuch Der Fuhrung,* 2nd ed. (Stuttgart, Germany: Schaffer Poeschal Verlag, 1995), pp. 1075–1091; and J.C. Wofford and L.Z. Liska, "Path–Goal Theories of Leadership: A Meta-Analysis," *Journal of Management,* 19, 1993, pp. 857–876.

36. R. McQueen, "The Long Shadow of Tom Stephens: He Branded MacBlo's Crew as Losers, Then Made Them into Winners," *Financial Post (National Post),* June 22, 1999, pp. C1, C5.

37. S. Kerr and J.M. Jermier, "Substitutes for Leadership: Their Meaning and Measurement," *Organizational Behavior and Human Performance,* 22, 1978, pp. 375–403; P.M. Podsakoff, B.P. Niehoff, S.B. MacKenzie, and M.L. Williams, "Do Substitutes for Leadership Really Substitute for Leadership? An Empirical Examination of Kerr and Jermier's Situational Leadership Model," *Organizational Behavior and Human Decision Processes,* 54, 1993, pp. 1–44.

38. S. Kerr and J.M. Jermier, "Substitutes for Leadership: Their Meaning and Measurement," *Organizational Behavior and Human Performance,* 22, 1978, pp. 375–403; and P.M. Podsakoff, B.P. Niehoff, S.B. MacKenzie, and M.L. Williams, "Do Substitutes for Leadership Really Substitute for Leadership? An Empirical Examination of Kerr and Jermier's Situational Leadership Model," *Organizational Behavior and Human Decision Processes,* 54, 1993, pp. 1–44.

39. J.M. Howell and B.J. Avolio, "The Leverage of Leadership," in *Leadership: Achieving Exceptional Performance,* supplement prepared by the Richard Ivey School of Business, *The Globe and Mail,* May 15, 1998, pp. C1, C2.

40. Ibid.

41. V. Smith, "Leading Us On," *Report on Business Magazine,* April 1999, pp. 91–96.

42. A. Bryman, "Leadership in Organizations," in S.R. Clegg, C. Hardy, and W.R. Nord (eds.), *Handbook of Organization Studies* (London: Sage Publications, 1996), pp. 276–292.

43. B.M. Bass, *Leadership and Performance Beyond Expectations* (New York: Free Press, 1985); B.M. Bass, Bass and Stogdill's *Handbook of Leadership: Theory, Research, and Managerial Applications,* 3rd ed. (New York: Free Press, 1990); and G. Yukl and D.D. Van Fleet, "Theory and Research on Leadership in Organizations," in M.D. Dunnette and L.M. Hough (eds.), *Handbook of Industrial and Organizational Psychology,* 2nd ed., vol. 3 (Palo Alto, CA: Consulting Psychologists Press, 1992), pp. 147–97.

44. J.A. Conger and R.N. Kanungo, "Behavioral Dimensions of Charismatic Leadership," in J.A. Conger, R.N. Kanungo, and Associates, *Charismatic Leadership* (San Francisco: Jossey-Bass, 1988).

45. J.A. Conger and R.N. Kanungo, *Charismatic Leadership in Organizations* (Thousand Oaks, CA: Sage, 1998).

46. "Building a Better Boss," *Maclean's,* September 30, 1996, p. 41.

47. T. Dvir, D. Eden, B.J. Avolio, and B. Shamir, "Impact of Transformational Leadership on Follower Development and Performance: A Field Experiment," *Academy of Management Journal,* 45, no. 4, 2002, pp. 735–744; R.J. House, J. Woycke, and E.M. Fodor, "Charismatic and Noncharismatic Leaders: Differences in Behavior and Effectiveness," in J.A. Conger and R.N. Kanungo, *Charismatic Leadership in Organizations,* (Thousand Oaks, CA: Sage, 1998), pp. 103–104; D.A. Waldman, B.M. Bass, and F.J. Yammarino, "Adding to Contingent-Reward Behavior: The Augmenting Effect of Charismatic Leadership," *Group & Organization Studies,* December 1990, pp. 381–394; S.A. Kirkpatrick and E.A. Locke, "Direct and Indirect Effects of Three Core Charismatic Leadership Components on Performance and Attitudes," *Journal of Applied Psychology,* February

1996, pp. 36–51; and J.A. Conger, R.N. Kanungo, and S.T. Menon, "Charismatic Leadership and Follower Outcome Effects," paper presented at the 58th Annual Academy of Management Meetings, San Diego, CA, August 1998.

48. J.M. Howell and P.J. Frost, "A Laboratory Study of Charismatic Leadership," *Organizational Behavior & Human Decision Processes,* 43, no. 2, April 1989, pp. 243–269.

49. "Building a Better Boss," *Maclean's,* September 30, 1996, p. 41.

50. A. Elsner, "The Era of CEO as Superhero Ends Amid Corporate Scandals," globeandmail.com, July 10, 2002.

51. B.M. Bass, *Leadership and Performance Beyond Expectations* (New York: Free Press, 1985); B.M. Bass, Bass and Stogdill's *Handbook of Leadership: Theory, Research, and Managerial Applications,* 3rd ed. (New York: Free Press, 1990); and G. Yukl and D.D. Van Fleet, "Theory and Research on Leadership in Organizations," in M.D. Dunnette and L.M. Hough (eds.), *Handbook of Industrial and Organizational Psychology,* 2nd ed., vol. 3 (Palo Alto, CA: Consulting Psychologists Press, 1992), pp. 147–197.

52. Anthony Grnak, John Hughes, and Douglas Hunter, *op.cit.,* p. 195.

53. *Op cit.,* note 75.

54. Cited in B.M. Bass and B.J. Avolio, "Developing Transformational Leadership: 1992 and Beyond," *Journal of European Industrial Training,* January 1990, p. 23.

55. J.M. Howell and B.J. Avolio, "The Leverage of Leadership," in *Leadership: Achieving Exceptional Performance,* supplement prepared by the Richard Ivey School of Business, *The Globe and Mail,* May 15, 1998, p. C2.

56. B.M. Bass, Bass and Stogdill's *Handbook of Leadership;* B.M. Bass and B.J. Avolio, "Transformational Leadership: A Response to Critiques," in M.M. Chemers and R. Ayman (eds.), *Leadership Theory and Research: Perspectives and Directions* (San Diego: Academic Press, 1993), pp. 49–80; B.M. Bass, B.J. Avolio, and L. Goodheim, "Biography and the Assessment of Transformational Leadership at the World Class Level," *Journal of Management,* 13, 1987, pp. 7–20; J.J. Hater and B.M. Bass, "Supervisors' Evaluations and Subordinates' Perceptions of Transformational and Transactional Leadership," *Journal of Applied Psychology,* 73, 1988, pp. 695–702; R. Pillai, "Crisis and Emergence of Charismatic Leadership in Groups: An Experimental Investigation," *Journal of Applied Psychology,* 26, 1996, pp. 543–562; J. Seltzer and B.M. Bass, "Transformational Leadership: Beyond Initiation and Consideration," *Journal of Management,* 16, 1990, pp. 693–703; and D.A. Waldman, B.M. Bass, and W.O. Einstein, "Effort, Performance, Transformational Leadership in Industrial and Military Service," *Journal of Occupation Psychology,* 60, 1987, pp. 1–10.

57. R. Pillai, C.A. Schriesheim, and E.S. Williams, "Fairness Perceptions and Trust as Mediators of Transformational and Transactional Leadership: A Two-Sample Study," *Journal of Management,* 25, 1999, pp. 897–933.

58. Website: http://mutual-funds.us/magazines/fortune/fortune500/2008/womenceos/. Accessed January 3, 2009.

59. Website: www.canadianbusiness.com/rankings/w100/list.jsp?pageID=article&year=2006&content=overview&type=overview. Accessed January 3, 2009.

60. "Women CEOs of the Fortune 1000." *Catalyst,* Oct. 2011. http://www.catalyst.org/publication/271/women-ceos-of-the-fortune-1000. Accessed Nov. 3, 2011.

61. "Women CEOs and Heads of the Financial Post 500," *Catalyst.* November 2011. http://www.catalyst.org/publication/322/women-ceos-and-heads-of-the-financial-post-500. Accessed Nov. 3, 2011.

62. "Women in Senior Management—Strategies for Creating an Environment Where Women Thrive," The Conference Board of Canada, November 2011. http://www.conferenceboard.ca/e-library/abstract.aspx?did=4475. Accessed June 4, 2012.

63. Ibid.

64. A.H. Eagly and B.T. Johnson, "Gender and Leadership Style: A Meta-Analysis," *Psychological Bulletin,* 108, 1990, pp. 233–256.

65. Ibid.

66. *The Economist,* "Workers Resent Scoldings from Female Bosses," *Houston Chronicle,* August 19, 2000, 1C.

67. Eagly and Johnson, "Gender and Leadership Style: A Meta-Analysis."

68. Ibid.

69. Ibid.

70. A.H. Eagly, S.J. Karau, and M.G. Makhijani, "Gender and the Effectiveness of Leaders: A Meta-Analysis," *Psychological Bulletin,* 117, 1995, pp. 125–145.

71. Ibid.

72. R. Calori and B. Dufour, "Management European Style," *Academy of Management Executive,* 9, no. 3, 1995, pp. 61–70.

73. Ibid.

74. J.M. George and K. Bettenhausen, "Understanding Prosocial Behavior, Sales Performance, and Turnover: A Group-Level Analysis in a Service Context," *Journal of Applied Psychology,* 75, 1990, pp. 698–709.

75. T. Sy, S. Cote, and R. Saavedra, "The Contagious Leader: Impact of the Leader's Mood on the Mood of Group Members, Group Affective Tone, and Group Processes," *Journal of Applied Psychology* 90, no. 2 (2005), 295–305.

76. N.M. Ashkanasy and C.S. Daus, "Emotion in the Workplace: The New Challenge for Managers," *Academy of Management Executive,* 16, no. 1, 2002, pp. 76–86; and J.M. George, "Emotions and Leadership: The Role of Emotional Intelligence," *Human Relations,* 53, 2002, pp. 1027–1055.

77. J.M. George, "Emotions and Leadership: The Role of Emotional Intelligence," *Human Relations,* 53, 2000, pp. 1027–1055.

78. "The Brain and Emotional Intelligence: An Interview with Daniel Goleman," *Tricycle,* May 18, 2011. http://www.tricycle.com/blog/brain-and-emotional-intelligence-interview-daniel-goleman. Accessed June 4, 2012.

79. J. Zhou and J.M. George, "Awakening Employee Creativity: The Role of Leader Emotional Intelligence," *The Leadership Quarterly* 14, no. 45 (August–October 2003), 545–68.

80. Ibid.

81. Ibid.

82. Adapted from: Harvey Schachter, "Monday Morning Manager," *The Globe and Mail,* Monday, July 3, 2006, p. B2 and Amazon.com website: www.amazon.com/gp/product/078521285X/002-5716207-3409632?v=glance&n=283155

83. Jerry Manas. *Napoleon on Project Management: Timeless Lessons in Planning, Execution, and Leadership.* Toronto: Nelson Business, 2006, 288 pages.

84. http://www.hrreporter.com/videodisplay/237-assessing-leadership-judgment.

85. Tom Lowry, "Taking the Ted Out of Turner Broadcasting." Reprinted from May 4, 2009 issue of *BusinessWeek.*

Chapter 10

1. Richard Branson, *Canadian Business,* November 3, 2011. http://www.canadianbusiness.com/article/54597--people-are-your-biggest-asset-treat-them-like-it. Accessed November 8, 2011.

2. P. Booth, *Challenge and Change: Embracing the Team Concept, Report 123-94,* Conference Board of Canada, 1994.

3. Cited in C. Joinson, "Teams at Work," *HRMagazine,* May 1999, p. 30; and P. Strozniak, "Teams at Work," *Industry Week,* September 18, 2000, p. 47.

4. T.M. Mills, *The Sociology of Small Groups* (Englewood Cliffs, NJ: Prentice-Hall, 1967); M.E. Shaw, *Group Dynamics* (New York: McGraw-Hill, 1981).

5. R. S. Buday, "Reengineering One Firm's Product Development and Another's Service Delivery," *Planning Review,* March–April 1993, 14–19; J. M. Burcke, "Hallmark's Quest for Quality Is a Job Never Done," *Business Insurance,* April 26, 1993, 122; M. Hammer and J. Champy, *Reengineering the Corporation* (New York: HarperBusiness, 1993); T. A. Stewart, "The Search for the Organization of Tomorrow," *Fortune,* May 18, 1992, 92–98.

6. A. Deutschman, "Inside the Mind of Jeff Bezos," *Fast Company,* August 2004, 50–58; and "Amazon.com Digital Media Technology," http://media-server.amazon .com/jobs/jobs.html, June 19, 2006.

7. P. Willcocks, "Yours and Mine? Can the New Owner of the Once-Troubled Myra Falls Copper and Zinc Mine Near Campbell River Forge a New Relationship With Workers and Their Union to Create a True Partnership?" *BCBusiness Magazine,* September 2000, pp. 114–120.

8. Website: www.unmillenniumproject.org.

9. For additional research and papers on the topic of self-managed work teams, see *Conference Proceedings: Anniversary Collection: The Best of 1990–1994.* Center for Collaborative Organizations (Center for the Study of Work Teams), University of North Texas, Denton, Texas. Website: www.workteams.unt.edu/old/literature/proceedings/Anver-contents.htm.

10. J.A. Pearce II and E.C. Ravlin, "The Design and Activation of Self-Regulating Work Groups," *Human Relations,* 11, 1987, pp. 751–782.

11. P. Booth, *Challenge and Change: Embracing the Team Concept, Report 123–94,* Conference Board of Canada, 1994.

12. B. Dumaine, "Who Needs a Boss?" *Fortune,* May 7, 1990, pp. 52–60; and J.A. Pearce II and E.C. Ravlin, "The Design and Activation of Self-Regulating Work Groups," *Human Relations,* 11, 1987, pp. 751–782.

13. B. Dumaine, "Who Needs a Boss?" *Fortune,* May 7, 1990, pp. 52–60; and A.R. Montebello and V.R. Buzzotta, "Work Teams That Work," *Training & Development,* March 1993, pp. 59–64.

14. http://www.cpsc-ccsp.ca/Employee%20Retention/Canadian%20General%20Tower%20Limited.htm. Canadian General Tower Limited. Accessed June 9, 2012.

15. T.D. Wall, N.J. Kemp, P.R. Jackson, and C.W. Clegg, "Outcomes of Autonomous Work Groups: A Long-Term Field Experiment," *Academy of Management Journal,* 29, 1986, pp. 280–304.

16. W.R. Pape, "Group Insurance," *Inc.* (Inc. Technology Supplement), June 17, 1997, pp. 29–31; A.M. Townsend, S.M. DeMarie, and A.R. Hendrickson, "Are You Ready for Virtual Teams?" *HRMagazine,* September 1996, pp. 122–126; and A.M. Townsend, S.M. DeMarie, and A.M. Hendrickson, "Virtual Teams: Technology and the Workplace of the Future," *Academy of Management Executive,* 12, no. 3, 1998, pp. 17–29.

17. A.M. Townsend, S.M. DeMarie, and A.R. Hendrickson, "Are You Ready for Virtual Teams?" *HRMagazine,* September 1996, pp. 122–126.

18. W.R. Pape, "Group Insurance," *Inc.* (Inc. Technology Supplement), June 17, 1997, pp. 29–31; and A.M. Townsend, S.M. DeMarie, and A.R. Hendrickson, "Are You Ready for Virtual Teams?" *HRMagazine,* September 1996, pp. 122–126.

19. B. Geber, "Virtual Teams," *Training* 32, no. 4 (August 1995), 36–40; T. Finholt and L. S. Sproull, "Electronic Groups at Work," *Organization Science* 1 (1990), 41–64.

20. Geber, "Virtual Teams."

21. E. J. Hill, B. C. Miller, S. P. Weiner, and J. Colihan, "Influences of the Virtual Office on Aspects of Work and Work/Life Balance," *Personnel Psychology* 31 (1998), 667–83; S. G. Strauss, "Technology, Group Process, and Group Outcomes: Testing the Connections in Computer-Mediated and Face-to-Face Groups," *Human Computer Interaction* 12 (1997), 227–66; M. E. Warkentin, L. Sayeed, and R. Hightower, "Virtual Teams versus Face-to-Face Teams: An Exploratory Study of a Web-Based Conference System," *Decision Sciences* 28, no. 4 (Fall 1997), 975–96.

22. S. A. Furst, M. Reeves, B. Rosen, and R. S. Blackburn, "Managing the Life Cycle of Virtual Teams," *Academy of Management Executive* 18, no. 2 (May 2004), 6–20.

23. Ibid.

24. Gratton, "Working Together . . . When Apart."

25. Ibid.

26. Ibid.

27. Ibid.

28. http://www.edf.org/about/our-mission-and-history. Accessed February 20, 2012.

29. A. Deutschman, "The Managing Wisdom of High-Tech Superstars," *Fortune,* October 17, 1994, pp. 197–206.

30. Ibid.

31. J.S. Lublin, "My Colleague, My Boss," *The Wall Street Journal,* April 12, 1995, pp. R4, R12.

32. R. G. LeFauve and A. C. Hax, "Managerial and Technological Innovations at Saturn Corporation," *MIT Management,* Spring 1992, 8–19.

33. B.W. Tuckman, "Developmental Sequences in Small Groups," *Psychological Bulletin,* 63, 1965, pp. 384–399; and B.W. Tuckman and M.C. Jensen, "Stages of Small Group Development," *Group and Organizational Studies,* 2, 1977, pp. 419–427.

34. C.J.G. Gersick, "Time and Transition in Work Teams: Toward a New Model of Group Development," *Academy of Management Journal,* 31, March 1988, pp. 9–41; C.J.G. Gersick, "Marking Time: Predictable Transitions in Task Groups," *Academy of Management Journal,* 32, June 1989, pp. 274–309.

35. J.R. Hackman, "Group Influences on Individuals in Organizations," in M.D. Dunnette and L.M. Hough (eds.), *Handbook of Industrial and Organizational Psychology,* 2nd ed., vol. 3 (Palo Alto, CA: Consulting Psychologists Press, 1992), pp. 199–267.

36. Ibid.

37. Ibid.

38. J.S. Lublin, "My Colleague, My Boss."

39. L. Festinger, "Informal Social Communication," *Psychological Review,* 57, 1950, pp. 271–282; and M.E. Shaw, *Group Dynamics* (New York: McGraw-Hill, 1981).

40. J.R. Hackman, "Group Influences on Individuals in Organizations," in M.D. Dunnette and L.M. Hough (eds.), *Handbook of Industrial and Organizational Psychology,* 2nd ed., vol. 3 (Palo Alto, CA: Consulting Psychologists Press, 1992), pp. 199–267; and M.E. Shaw, *Group Dynamics* (New York: McGraw-Hill, 1981).

41. D. Cartwright, "The Nature of Group Cohesiveness," in D. Cartwright and A. Zander, eds., *Group Dynamics,* 3d ed. (New York: Harper & Row, 1968); L. Festinger, S. Schacter, and K. Black, *Social Pressures in Informal Groups* (New York: Harper & Row, 1950); Shaw, *Group Dynamics.*

42. Janis Irving, *Victims of Groupthink* (Boston: Houghton Mifflin, 1972). See also Janis Irving, *Groupthink: Psychological Studies of Policy Decisions and Fiascos,* 2nd ed. (Boston: Houghton Mifflin, 1982).

43. I.L. Janis, *Groupthink: Psychological Studies of Policy Decisions and Fiascoes,* 2nd ed. (Boston: Houghton Mifflin, 1982).

44. Ibid.

45. Robert Pear, "He Wrote the Book on Intelligence," *The New York Times,* Sunday, July 11, 2004, p. WK12.

46. J.N. Choi and M.U. Kim, "The Organizational Application of Groupthink and Its Limitations in Organizations," *Journal of Applied Psychology,* 84, 1999, pp. 297–306.

47. C. McCauley, "The Nature of Social Influence in Groupthink: Compliance and Internalization," *Journal of Personality and Social Psychology,* 57, 1989, pp. 250–260; P.E. Tetlock, R.S. Peterson, C. McGuire, S. Chang, and P. Feld, "Assessing Political Group Dynamics: A Test of the Groupthink Model," *Journal of Personality and Social Psychology,* 63, 1992, pp. 781–796; S. Graham, "A Review of Attribution Theory in Achievement Contexts," *Educational Psychology Review,* 3, 1991, pp. 5–39; and G. Moorhead and J.R. Montanari, "An Empirical Investigation of the Groupthink Phenomenon," *Human Relations,* 39, 1986, pp. 399–410.

48. J. Longley and D.G. Pruitt, "Groupthink: A Critique of Janis' Theory," in L. Wheeler (ed.), *Review of Personality and Social Psychology* (Newbury Park, CA: Sage, 1980), pp. 507–513; and J.A. Sniezek, "Groups Under Uncertainty: An Examination of Confidence in Group Decision Making," *Organizational Behavior and Human Decision Processes,* 52, 1992, pp. 124–155.

49. J.N. Choi and M.U. Kim, "The Organizational Application of Groupthink and Its Limitations in Organizations," *Journal of Applied Psychology,* 84, 1999, pp. 297–306.

50. See N.R.F. Maier, *Principles of Human Relations* (New York: Wiley, 1952); I.L. Janis, *Groupthink: Psychological Studies of Policy Decisions and Fiascoes,* 2nd ed. (Boston: Houghton Mifflin, 1982); and C.R. Leana, "A Partial Test of Janis' Groupthink Model: Effects of Group Cohesiveness and Leader Behavior on Defective Decision Making," *Journal of Management,* Spring 1985, pp. 5–17.

51. See R.O. Mason, "A Dialectic Approach to Strategic Planning," *Management Science,* 13, 1969, pp. 403–414; R.A. Cosier and J.C. Aplin, "A Critical View of Dialectic Inquiry in Strategic Planning," *Strategic Management Journal,* 1, 1980, pp. 343–356; I.I. Mitroff and R.O. Mason, "Structuring III—Structured Policy Issues: Further Explorations in a Methodology for Messy Problems," *Strategic Management Journal,* 1, 1980, pp. 331–342.

52. Mary C. Gentile, *Differences That Work: Organizational Excellence Through Diversity* (Boston: Harvard Business School Press, 1994).

53. T.J. Bouchard Jr., J. Barsaloux, and G. Drauden, "Brainstorming Procedure, Group Size, and Sex as Determinants of Problem Solving Effectiveness of Individuals and Groups," *Journal of Applied Psychology,* 59, 1974, pp. 135–138.

54. L. Thompson and L.F. Brajkovich, "Improving the Creativity of Organizational Work Groups," *Academy of Management Executive,* 17, no. 1, 2003, pp. 96–111, B. Mullen, C. Johnson, and E. Salas, "Productivity Loss in Brainstorming Groups: A Meta-Analytic Integration," *Basic and Applied Social Psychology,* 12, no. 1, 1991, pp. 3–23; and M. Diehl and W. Stroebe, "Productivity Loss in Brainstorming Groups: Towards the Solution of a Riddle," *Journal of Personality and Social Psychology,* 53, 1987, pp. 497–509.

55. D.H. Gustafson, R.K. Shulka, A. Delbecq, and W.G. Walster, "A Comparative Study of Differences in Subjective Likelihood Estimates Made by Individuals, Interacting Groups, Delphi Groups, and Nominal Groups," *Organizational Behavior and Human Performance,* 9, 1973, pp. 280–291.

56. N. Dalkey, *The Delphi Method: An Experimental Study of Group Decision Making* (Santa Monica, CA: Rand Corp., 1989).

57. Lublin, "My Colleague, My Boss."

58. P.C. Earley, "Social Loafing and Collectivism: A Comparison of the United States and the People's Republic of China," *Administrative Science Quarterly,* 34, 1989, pp. 565–581; J.M. George, "Extrinsic and Intrinsic Origins of Perceived Social Loafing in Organizations," *Academy of Management Journal,* 35, 1992, pp. 191–202; S.G. Harkins,

B. Latane, and K. Williams, "Social Loafing: Allocating Effort or Taking it Easy," *Journal of Experimental Social Psychology,* 16, 1980, pp. 457–465; B. Latane, K.D. Williams, and S. Harkins, "Many Hands Make Light the Work: The Causes and Consequences of Social Loafing," *Journal of Personality and Social Psychology,* 37, 1979, pp. 822–832; and J.A. Shepperd, "Productivity Loss in Performance Groups: A Motivation Analysis," *Psychological Bulletin,* 113, 1993, pp. 67–81.

59. George, "Extrinsic and Intrinsic Origins"; G. R. Jones, "Task Visibility, Free Riding, and Shirking: Explaining the Effect of Structure and Technology on Employee Behavior," *Academy of Management Review* 9 (1984), 684–95; K. Williams, S. Harkins, and B. Latane, "Identifiability as a Deterrent to Social Loafing: Two Cheering Experiments," *Journal of Personality and Social Psychology* 40 (1981), 303–11.

60. S. Harkins and J. Jackson, "The Role of Evaluation in Eliminating Social Loafing," *Personality and Social Psychology Bulletin* 11 (1985), 457–65; N. L. Kerr and S. E. Bruun, "Ringelman Revisited: Alternative Explanations for the Social Loafing Effect," *Personality and Social Psychology Bulletin* 7 (1981), 224–231; Williams et al., "Identifiability as a Deterrent to Social Loafing."

61. B. Latane, "Responsibility and Effort in Organizations," in P. S. Goodman, ed., *Designing Effective Work Groups* (San Francisco: Jossey-Bass, 1986); Latane et al., "Many Hands Make Light the Work"; I. D. Steiner, *Group Process and Productivity* (New York: Academic Press, 1972).

62. Adapted from the American Management Association, "How to Build High-Performance Teams," Self-Study Course. Website: www.amanet. org/selfstudy/b13759.htm.

63. Adapted from Jim Clemmer, "Team Spirit Built From the Top," *The Globe and Mail*, Friday, November 26, 2004, C1.

64. http://www.hrreporter.com/ videodisplay/234-how-canadian-tire-changed-its-staffing-processes.

65. "Nobody Has a Good Day in Space If the Team Has a Bad Day," by Sean Fine, *Business without Borders,* Tuesday, August 2, 2011. http://www.bwob.ca/ profiles/%E2%80%98nobody-has-a-good-day-in-space-if-the-team-has-a-bad-day. Accessed: November 8, 2012.

Chapter 11

1. J. M. O'Brien, "100 Best Companies to Work For—A Perfect Season," *Fortune,* February 4, 2008, 64–66; "Four Seasons Employees Name Company to *Fortune* '100 Best Companies to Work For' List," www.fourseasons.com/about_us/press_ release_280.html, February 22, 2008; "100 Best Companies to Work For 2009: Four Seasons Hotel," http://money.cnn.com/ magazines/fortune/bestcompanies/2009/ snapshots/92.html, May 20, 2009.

2. "Four Seasons Employees Name Company to *Fortune* '100 Best Companies to Work For' List."

3. O'Brien, "100 Best Companies to Work For—A Perfect Season."

4. Ibid.

5. Ibid; "Creating the Four Seasons Difference," www.businessweek.com/print/ innovate/content/jan2008/id20080122 _671354.htm, February 22, 2008.

6. O'Brien, "100 Best Companies to Work For—A Perfect Season"; "Creating the Four Seasons Difference."

7. Ibid.; "Four Seasons Employees Name Company to *Fortune* '100 Best Companies to Work For' List."

8. O'Brien, "100 Best Companies to Work For—A Perfect Season."

9. "Creating the Four Seasons Difference."

10. O'Brien, "100 Best Companies to Work For—A Perfect Season."

11. Ibid.

12. Ibid.

13. Ibid.

14. Ibid.

15. Ibid.; "Creating the Four Seasons Difference"; "Four Seasons Employees Name Company to *Fortune* '100 Best Companies to Work For' List."

16. Website: www.fedpubs.com/subject/ legis/clc.htm. Accessed August 31, 2009.

17. Website: www.hc-sc.gc.ca/ewh-semt/ occup-travail/whmis-simdut/index-eng. php. Accessed August 31, 2009.

18. See the various provincial and territorial documents.

19. Website: www.ccohs.ca/. Accessed August 31, 2009.

20. For example, website: www.gov.pe.ca/ law/statutes/pdf/o-01_01.pdf. Accessed August 31, 2009.

21. J.E. Butler, G.R. Ferris, and N.K. Napier, *Strategy and Human Resource Management* (Cincinnati, OH: South Western, 1991); P.M. Wright and G.C. McMahan, "Theoretical Perspectives for Strategic Human Resource Management," *Journal of Management,* 18, 1992, pp. 295–320.

22. E. Porter, "Send Jobs to India? U.S. Companies Say It's Not Always Best," *The New York Times,* April 28, 2004, A1, A7.

23. D. Wessel, "The Future of Jobs: New Ones Arise; Wage Gap Widens," *The Wall Street Journal,* April 2, 2004, A1, A5; "Relocating the Back Office," *The Economist,* December 13, 2003, 67–69.

24. Porter, "Send Jobs to India?"

25. Ibid.

26. "Learning to Live with Offshoring," *BusinessWeek,* January 30, 2006, 122.

27. M. Lewis, "BCE Appoints Alcan Recruit 'Chief Talent Officer,'" *Financial Post (National Post),* May 24, 2001, p. C11.

28. E.L. Levine, *Everything You Always Wanted to Know About Job Analysis: A Job Analysis Primer* (Tampa, FL: Mariner, 1983).

29. R.L. Mathis and J.H. Jackson, *Human Resource Management,* 7th ed. (St. Paul, MN: West, 1994).

30. C.D. Fisher, L.F. Schoenfeldt, and J.B. Shaw, *Human Resource Management* (Boston: Houghton Mifflin, 1990).

31. P.M. Wright and G.C. McMahan, "Theoretical Perspectives for Strategic Human Resource Management," *Journal of Management,* 18, 1992, pp. 295–320.

32. L. Baird and I. Meshoulam, "Managing Two Fits for Strategic Human Resource Management," *Academy of Management Review,* 14, 1989, pp. 116–128; J. Milliman, M. Von Glinow, and M. Nathan, "Organizational Life Cycles and Strategic International Human Resource Management in Multinational Companies: Implications for Congruence Theory," *Academy of Management Review,* 16, 1991, pp. 318–339; R.S. Schuler and S.E. Jackson, "Linking Competitive Strategies With Human Resource Management Practices," *Academy of Management Executive,* 1, 1987, pp. 207–219; P.M. Wright and S.A. Snell, "Toward an Integrative View of Strategic Human Resource Management," *Human Resource Management Review,* 1, 1991, pp. 203–225.

33. S.L. Rynes, "Recruitment, Job Choice, and Post-Hire Consequences: A Call for New Research Directions," in M.D. Dunnette and L.M. Hough (eds.), *Handbook of Industrial and Organizational Psychology,* vol. 2 (Palo Alto, CA: Consulting Psychologists Press, 1991), pp. 399–444.

34. Special Report, "The Battle for Brainpower: A Survey of Talent," *The Economist,* October 7, 2006, p. 1, 3–5, 8–9, 12–14, 16, 18, 20, 22–24.

35. "The Battle for Brainpower," *The Economist,* October 7, 2006, p. 3.

36. "Nightmare Scenarios," *The Economist,* October 7, 2006, p. 14.

37. R. Sharpe, "The Life of the Party? Can Jeff Taylor Keep the Good Times Rolling at Monster.com?" *BusinessWeek,* June 4, 2001 (*BusinessWeek* Archives); D. H. Freedman, "The Monster Dilemma," *Inc.* Magazine, May 2007, 77–78; P. Korkki, "So Easy to Apply, So Hard to Be Noticed," *The New York Times,* July 1, 2007, BU16.

38. www.monster.com, June 2001.

39. www.jobline.org, Jobline press releases, May 8, 2001, accessed June 20, 2001.

40. http://t1.gstatic.com/images?q=tbn:ANd9GcTha3tk8h6Y0uyANaE9VimnXmJMOG03wZiq2540CEz3T1I_AL1gEw.

41. Stephanie Rosenbloom, "Savvy Job Hunters Work the Web," *National Post,* FP WORKING, Wednesday, May 7, 2008, WK2.

42. http://www.enterprisingnonprofits.ca/resources/embers-staffing-solutions-social-enterprise-profile. Accessed November 22, 2011.

43. R.M. Guion, "Personnel Assessment, Selection, and Placement," in M.D. Dunnette and L.M. Hough (eds.), *Handbook of Industrial and Organizational Psychology,* vol. 2 (Palo Alto, CA: Consulting Psychologists Press, 1991), pp. 327–397.

44. T. Joyner, "Job Background Checks Surge," *Houston Chronicle,* May 2, 2005, D6.

45. Ibid.; "ADP News Releases: Employer Services: ADP Hiring Index Reveals Background Checks Performed More Than Tripled Since 1997," Automatic Data Processing, Inc., June 3, 2006, www.investquest.com/iq/a/aud/ne/news/adp042505background.htm.

46. R.A. Noe, J.R. Hollenbeck, B. Gerhart, and P.M. Wright, *Human Resource Management: Gaining a Competitive Advantage* (Burr Ridge, IL: Irwin, 1994); J.A. Wheeler and J.A. Gier, "Reliability and Validity of the Situational Interview for a Sales Position," *Journal of Applied Psychology,* 2, 1987, pp. 484–487.

47. R.A. Noe, J.R. Hollenbeck, B. Gerhart, and P.M. Wright, *Human Resource Management: Gaining a Competitive Advantage* (Burr Ridge, IL: Irwin, 1994).

48. J. Flint, "Can You Tell Applesauce from Pickles?" *Forbes,* October 9, 1995, 106–8.

49. Tavia Grant, "Colour Them Controversial," *The Globe and Mail,* Wednesday, May 21, 2008, C1, 4. See also Caitlin Crawshaw, "Questionnaires Test Job Seeker's Patience," *National Post,* Wednesday, May 14, 2008, FP15.

50. J. Flint, "Can You Tell Applesauce from Pickles?"

51. "Wanted: Middle Managers, Audition Required," *The Wall Street Journal,* December 28, 1995, p. A1.

52. I.L. Goldstein, "Training in Work Organizations," in M.D. Dunnette and L.M. Hough (eds.), *Handbook of Industrial and Organizational Psychology,* vol. 2 (Palo Alto, CA: Consulting Psychologists Press, 1991), pp. 507–619.

53. N. Banerjee, "For Mary Kay Sales Reps in Russia, Hottest Shade Is the Color of Money," *The Wall Street Journal,* August 30, 1995, A8.

54. T. D. Allen, L. T. Eby, M. L. Poteet, E. Lentz, and L. Lima, "Career Benefits Associated with Mentoring for Protégés: A Meta-Analysis," *Journal of Applied Psychology* 89, no. 1 (2004), 127–36.

55. P. Garfinkel, "Putting a Formal Stamp on Mentoring," *The New York Times,* January 18, 2004, BU10.

56. Ibid.

57. Allen et al., "Career Benefits Associated with Mentoring"; L. Levin, "Lesson Learned: Know Your Limits; Get Outside Help Sooner Rather Than Later," *BusinessWeek Online,* July 5, 2004, www.businessweek.com; "Family, Inc.," *BusinessWeek Online,* November 10, 2003, www.businessweek.com; J. Salamon, "A Year with a Mentor; Now Comes the Test," *The New York Times,* September 30, 2003, B1, B5; E. White, "Making Mentorships Work," *The Wall Street Journal,* October 23, 2007, B11.

58. Garfinkel, "Putting a Formal Stamp on Mentoring."

59. C.D. Fisher, L.F. Schoenfeldt, and J.B. Shaw, *Human Resource Management* (Boston: Houghton Mifflin, 1990).

60. Ibid.; G. P. Latham and K. N. Wexley, *Increasing Productivity through Performance Appraisal* (Reading, MA: Addison-Wesley, 1982).

61. M.A. Peiperl, "Getting 360° Feedback Right," *Harvard Business Review,* January 2001, pp. 142–147.

62. A. Harrington, "Workers of the World, Rate Your Boss!" *Fortune,* September 18, 2000, 340, 342; www.ImproveNow.com, June 2001.

63. J. Flynn and F. Nayeri, "Continental Divide over Executive Pay," *BusinessWeek,* July 3, 1995, 40–41.

64. J. A. Byrne, "How High Can CEO Pay Go?" *BusinessWeek,* April 22, 1996, 100–6.

65. A. Borrus, "A Battle Royal against Regal Paychecks," *BusinessWeek,* February 24, 2003, 127; "Too Many Turkeys," *The Economist,* November 26, 2005, 75–76; G. Morgenson, "How to Slow Runaway Executive Pay," *The New York Times,* October 23, 2005, 1, 4.

66. Dana Flavelle, "Highest-Paid Canadian CEOs Got 27 Per Cent Pay Hike," *Toronto Star,* January 2, 2012. http://www.thestar.com/business/article/1109514--highest-paid-canadian-ceos-got-27-per-cent-pay-hike. Accessed February 24, 2012.

67. "Executive Pay."

68. "Home Depot Chief's Pay in 2007 Could Reach $8.9m.," *The New York Times,* January 25, 2007, C7; E. Carr, "The Stockpot," *The Economist, A Special Report on Executive Pay,* January 20, 2007, 6–10; E. Porter, "More Than Ever, It Pays to Be the Top Executive," *The New York Times,* May 25, 2007, A1, C7.

69. http://www.hrsdc.gc.ca/eng/labour/labour_relations/info_analysis/work_stoppages/2011_jantodec.shtml. Accessed February 24, 2012.

70. Ishak Saporta, "Managers' and Workers' Attitudes Toward Unions in the U.S. and Canada." Relations Industrielles/

Industrial Relations. Website: http://findarticles.com/p/articles/mi_hb4388/is_n3_v50/ai_n28662583/. Accessed August 2, 2009.

71. "Union Membership and Public Attitudes Towards Unions Have Changed Dramatically in the Last 20 Years," James Ferrabee. Website: www.irpp.org/ferrabee/archive/0805.htm. Accessed August 2, 2009.

72. "Union Membership in Canada—2008, Strategic Policy, Analysis, and Workplace Information Directorate Labour Program," Human Resources and Skills Development Canada. Accessed August 2, 2009. Website: www.hrsdc.gc.ca/eng/labour/labour_relations/info_analysis/union_membership/index.shtml.

73. J. M. O'Brien, "100 Best Companies to Work For—A Perfect Season," *Fortune,* February 4, 2008, 64–66; "Four Seasons Employees Name Company to *Fortune* '100 Best Companies to Work For' List," www.fourseasons.com/about_us/press_release_280.html, February 22, 2008; "100 Best Companies to Work For 2009: Four Seasons Hotel," http://money.cnn.com/magazines/fortune/bestcompanies/2009/snapshots/92.html, May 20, 2009.

74. "Four Seasons Employees Name Company to *Fortune* '100 Best Companies to Work For' List."

75. O'Brien, "100 Best Companies to Work For—A Perfect Season."

76. Ibid.

77. Derek Sankey, "Boomers Aim to Fill the Gaps in Management Expertise," *FP EDGE, Financial Post,* Monday, May 10, 2004, FE3.

78. http://greyfox.ca/.

Chapter 12

1. "Canadian Drug Maker Goes Social to Help Supply Chain Crisis," by Sharon Gaudin, July 25, 2011. Used with permission of Computerworld Online. Copyright (c) 2012. All rights reserved. http://www.itworldcanada.com/News/canadian-drug-maker-goes-social-to-help-supply-chain-crisis/143614. Accessed May 14, 2012.

2. C.A. O'Reilly and L.R. Pondy, "Organizational Communication," in S. Kerr (ed.), *Organizational Behavior* (Columbus, OH: Grid, 1979).

3. E.M. Rogers and R. Agarwala-Rogers, *Communication in Organizations* (New York: Free Press, 1976).

4. Deena Waisberg, "Dress Code Still in Force Though It's Stinking Hot," *National Post,* Saturday, August 6, 2005, FW3.

5. Kamal Fatehi, *International Management* (Upper Saddle River, NJ: Prentice Hall, 1996).

6. R. Winslow, "Hospitals' Weak Systems Hurt Patients, Study Says," *The Wall Street Journal,* July 5, 1995, B1, B6.

7. Mary Teresa Bitti, "The New Face of Canadian Business," FP ENTREPRENEUR: Strategies for Small and Mid-Size Businesses, *National Post,* Monday, May 2, 2005, FP110

8. Ibid.

9. D.A. Adams, P.A. Todd, and R.R. Nelson, "A Comparative Evaluation of the Impact of Electronic and Voice Mail on Organizational Communication," *Information & Management,* 24, 1993, pp. 9–21.

10. R.L. Daft, R.H. Lengel, and L.K. Trevino, "Message Equivocality, Media Selection, and Manager Performance: Implications for Information Systems," *MIS Quarterly,* 11, 1987, pp. 355–366; R.L. Daft and R.H. Lengel, "Information Richness: A New Approach to Managerial Behavior and Organization Design," in B.M. Staw and L.L. Cummings (eds.), *Research in Organizational Behavior* (Greenwich, CT: JAI Press, 1984).

11. R.L. Daft, *Organization Theory and Design* (St. Paul, MN: West, 1992).

12. Ibid.

13. T. J. Peters and R. H. Waterman Jr., *In Search of Excellence* (New York: Harper and Row, 1982); T. Peters and N. Austin, *A Passion for Excellence: The Leadership Difference* (New York: Random House, 1985).

14. "Lights, Camera, Meeting: Teleconferencing Becomes a Time-Saving Tool," *The Wall Street Journal,* February 21, 1995, p. A1.

15. "E-Mail Abuse: Workers Discover High-Tech Ways to Cause Trouble in the Office," *The Wall Street Journal,* November 22, 1994, p. A1; and "E-Mail Alert: Companies Lag in Devising Policies on How It Should Be Used," *The Wall Street Journal,* December 29, 1994, p. A1.

16. J. Kay, "Someone Will Watch Over Me: Think Your Office E-Mails are Private?

Think Again," *National Post Business,* January 2001, pp. 59–64.

17. http://www.frameworkorg.org/index.html. Accessed November 22, 2011.

18. http://www.frameworkorg.org/timeraiser.html. Accessed November 22, 2011.

19. http://www.frameworkorg.org/civic-footprint.html. Accessed November 22, 2011.

20. http://it.timeraiser.ca/OpenArchITC. Accessed November 22, 2011.

21. E. Rich, *Artificial Intelligence* (New York: McGraw-Hill, 1983).

22. Brandt, "Agents and Artificial Life."

23. www.ibm.com, 2001.

24. G.R. Jones and J.M. George, *Essentials of Contemporary Management,* 4th ed. (New York: McGraw-Hill Irwin, 2011).

25. "On the Road," *Newsweek,* June 6, 1994, p. 8.

26. C.R. Mill, "Feedback: The Art of Giving and Receiving Help," in L. Porter and C.R. Mill (eds), *The Reading Book for Human Relations Training* (Bethel, ME: NTL Institute of Applied Behavioral Science, 1976), pp. 18–19.

27. Based on S.P. Robbins and P.L. Hunsaker, *Training in Interpersonal Skills: TIPS for Managing People at Work,* 2nd ed. Upper Saddle River, NJ: Prentice-Hall, 1996), Ch 3.

28. J.A. Litterer, "Conflict in Organizations: A Reexamination," *Academy of Management Journal,* 9, 1966, pp. 178–186; S.M. Schmidt and T.A. Kochan, "Conflict: Towards Conceptual Clarity," *Administrative Science Quarterly,* 13, 1972, pp. 359–370; and R.H. Miles, *Macro Organizational Behavior* (Santa Monica, CA: Goodyear, 1980).

29. S.P. Robbins, *Managing Organizational Conflict: A Nontraditional Approach* (Englewood Cliffs, NJ: Prentice-Hall, 1974); and L. Coser, *The Functions of Social Conflict* (New York: Free Press, 1956).

30. L.R. Pondy, "Organizational Conflict: Concepts and Models," *Administrative Science Quarterly,* 2, 1967, pp. 296–320; and R.E. Walton and J.M. Dutton, "The Management of Interdepartmental Conflict: A Model and Review," *Administrative Science Quarterly,* 14, 1969, pp. 62–73.

31. http://thinkexist.com/quotations/conflict/. Accessed February 25, 2012.

32. K.W. Thomas, "Conflict and Negotiation Processes in Organizations," in M.D. Dunnette and L.M. Hough (eds.), *Handbook of Industrial and Organizational Psychology*, 2nd ed., vol. 3 (Palo Alto, CA: Consulting Psychologists Press, 1992), pp. 651–717.

33. P.R. Lawrence, L.B. Barnes, and J.W. Lorsch, *Organizational Behavior and Administration* (Homewood, IL: Irwin, 1976).

34. R.J. Lewicki and J.R. Litterer, *Negotiation* (Homewood, IL: Irwin, 1985); G.B. Northcraft and M.A. Neale, *Organizational Behavior* (Fort Worth, TX: Dryden, 1994); J.Z. Rubin and B.R. Brown, *The Social Psychology of Bargaining and Negotiation* (New York: Academic Press, 1975).

35. L. Thompson and R. Hastie, "Social Perception in Negotiation," *Organizational Behavior and Human Decision Processes*, 47, 1990, pp. 98–123.

36. K.W. Thomas, "Conflict and Negotiation Processes in Organizations," in M.D. Dunnette and L.M. Hough (eds.), *Handbook of Industrial and Organizational Psychology*, 2nd ed., vol. 3 (Palo Alto, CA: Consulting Psychologists Press, 1992), pp. 651–717.

37. R.J. Lewicki, S.E. Weiss, and D. Lewin, "Models of Conflict, Negotiation and Third Party Intervention: A Review and Synthesis," *Journal of Organizational Behavior*, 13, 1992, pp. 209–252.

38. G.B. Northcraft and M.A. Neale, *Organizational Behavior* (Fort Worth, TX: Dryden, 1994).

39. R.J. Lewicki, S.E. Weiss, and D. Lewin, "Models of Conflict, Negotiation and Third Party Intervention"; G.B. Northcraft and M.A. Neale, *Organizational Behavior* (Fort Worth, TX: Dryden, 1994); and D.G. Pruitt, "Integrative Agreements: Nature and Consequences," in M.H. Bazerman and R.J. Lewicki (eds.), *Negotiating in Organizations* (Beverly Hills, CA: Sage, 1983).

40. R. Fischer and W. Ury, *Getting to Yes* (Boston: Houghton Mifflin, 1981); and G.B. Northcraft and M.A. Neale, *Organizational Behavior* (Fort Worth, TX: Dryden, 1994).

41. P.J. Carnevale and D.G. Pruitt, "Negotiation and Mediation," *Annual Review of Psychology*, 43, 1992, pp. 531–582.

42. *Canadian Business Journal*, July 2012.

Chapter 13

1. Slightly adapted from Dierdre McMurdy, "People Get Stress Relief Express-Style," *Financial Post*, Saturday, January 15, 2005, IN1, 2.

2. http://www.newmaterials.com/Customisation/Companies/Husky_Injection_Molding_Systems.asp. Accessed Dec. 6, 2011.

3. http://www.newmaterials.com/Customisation/News/Advanced_Composites/Injection_Molding_Equipment/Husky_introduces_Predictive_Maintenance_program.asp'. Accessed December 6, 2011.

4. W.G. Ouchi, "Markets, Bureaucracies, and Clans," *Administrative Science Quarterly*, 25, 1980, pp. 129–141.

5. L. Clifford, "Why You Can Safely Ignore Six Sigma," *Fortune*, January 22, 2001, 140.

6. A. Kinicki and B.K. Williams, *Management: A Practical Introduction* (Boston: McGraw-Hill Irwin, 2003).

7. E.E. Lawler III and J.G. Rhode, *Information and Control in Organizations* (Pacific Palisades, CA: Goodyear, 1976).

8. C.W.L. Hill and G.R. Jones, *Strategic Management: An Integrated Approach*, 4th ed. (Boston: Houghton Mifflin, 1997).

9. W.G. Ouchi, "The Transmission of Control Through Organizational Hierarchy," *Academy of Management Journal*, 21, 1978, pp. 173–192.

10. W.G. Ouchi, "The Relationship Between Organizational Structure and Organizational Control," *Administrative Science Quarterly*, 22, 1977, pp. 95–113.

11. W.G. Ouchi, "Markets, Bureaucracies, and Clans," *Administrative Science Quarterly*, 25, 1980, pp. 129–141.

12. W.H. Newman, *Constructive Control* (Englewood Cliffs, NJ: Prentice-Hall, 1975).

13. J.D. Thompson, *Organizations in Action* (New York: McGraw-Hill, 1967).

14. R.N. Anthony, *The Management Control Function* (Boston: Harvard Business School Press, 1988).

15. P. Lorange, M. Morton, and S. Ghoshal, *Strategic Control* (St. Paul, MN: West, 1986).

16. H. Koontz and R.W. Bradspies, "Managing Through Feedforward Control," *Business Horizons*, June 1972, pp. 25–36.

17. http://www.tenthousandvillages.ca/cgi-bin/category.cgi?item=pageAboutUs1&type=store. Accessed Nov. 22, 2011.

18. W.G. Ouchi, "Markets, Bureaucracies, and Clans," *Administrative Science Quarterly*, 25, 1980, pp. 129–141.

19. C.W.L. Hill and G.R. Jones, *Strategic Management: An Integrated Approach*, 4th ed. (Boston: Houghton Mifflin, 1997).

20. Andrea James, "Starbucks Profit Takes Bitter Shot for the Year," *Seattle P-I*, November 11, 2008. Website: http://seattlepi.nwsource.com/business/387203_sbuxearns11.html. Accessed November 15, 2008.

21. R. Simons, "Strategic Orientation and Top Management Attention to Control Systems," *Strategic Management Journal*, 12, 1991, pp. 49–62.

22. B. Woolridge and S.W. Floyd, "The Strategy Process, Middle Management Involvement, and Organizational Performance," *Strategic Management Journal* 11 (1990), 231–41.

23. J.A. Alexander, "Adaptive Changes in Corporate Control Practices," *Academy of Management Journal*, 34, 1991, pp. 162–193.

24. "RIM Provides Status Update and Reports on Results of Internal Review of Stock Option Grants by Special Committee." Website: http://press.rim.com/financial/release.jsp?id=1193. Accessed July 29, 2009.

25. Quoted in www.corpgov.net/. Accessed August 1, 2009.

26. "Global Principles of Accountable Corporate Governance." Website: www.calpers-governance.org/docs-sof/marketinitiatives/2009-04-01-corp-governance-pub20-final-glossy.pdf. Accessed August 1, 2009.

27. G.H.B. Ross, "Revolution in Management Control," *Management Accounting*, 72, 1992, pp. 23–27.

28. P. F. Drucker, *The Practice of Management* (New York: Harper & Row, 1954).

29. S. J. Carroll and H. L. Tosi, *Management by Objectives: Applications and Research* (New York: Macmillan, 1973).

30. R. Rodgers and J. E. Hunter, "Impact of Management by Objectives on Organizational Productivity," *Journal of Applied Psychology* 76 (1991), 322–26.

31. M. B. Gavin, S. G. Green, and G. T. Fairhurst, "Managerial Control Strategies for Poor Performance over Time and the Impact on Subordinate Reactions," *Organizational Behavior and Human Decision Processes* 63 (1995), 207–21.

32. www.cypress.com, 2001.

33. B. Dumaine, "The Bureaucracy Busters," *Fortune,* June 17, 1991, 46.

34. D.S. Pugh, D.J. Hickson, C.R. Hinings, and C. Turner, "Dimensions of Organizational Structure," *Administrative Science Quarterly,* 13, 1968, pp. 65–91.

35. P.M. Blau, *The Dynamics of Bureaucracy* (Chicago: University of Chicago Press, 1955).

36. S. Mcgee, "Garish Jackets Add to Clamor of Chicago Pits," *The Wall Street Journal,* July 31, 1995, p. C1.

37. K.E. Weick, *The Social Psychology of Organization* (Reading, MA: Addison-Wesley, 1979).

38. J. McCann, "Cutting the Crap," *National Post Business,* March 2001, pp. 47–57.

39. "3M Canada Company Fined $55,000 After Worker Injured." http://news.ontario.ca/mol/en/2011/03/3m-canada-company-fined-55000-after-worker-injured.html. Accessed December 7, 2011.

Appendix A

1. Written by J.W. Haddad, Professor, School of Business Management, Seneca College of Applied Arts and Technology, Toronto, Canada.

2. I suggest using *PlanWrite Business Plan Writer Deluxe 2006,* McGraw-Hill Irwin, ISBN-13: 978-0-07-328146-9, ISBN-10: 0-07-328146-8.

3. *PlanWrite Business Plan Writer Deluxe.*

4. TD Bank Financial Group, 150th Annual Report 2005, p. 4.

5. Website: www.thebodyshop.com.au/infopage.cfm?topicID=20.

6. Website: www.cara.com.

7. Website: www.renees.com/vision.asp.

8. Website: www.thebodyshop.com.au/infopage.cfm?pageID=53.

9. This is not a full résumé. The full résumés of the management team can be included in the Appendices. For this section of the business plan, simply state what experience and/or credentials make the manager suitable for the role they are taking on within the venture.

10. Website: www.statcan.gc.ca/subjects-sujets/standard-norme/naics-scian/2002/naics-scian02l-eng.htm.

11. Website: www.statcan.gc.ca.

12. Website: www.crfa.ca/research/statistics/.

13. Website: www.bizpal.ca/index_e.shtml.

14. Website: www.statcan.gc.ca/start-debut-eng.html.

15. Website: www.dnb.ca/default.htm.

16. Op. cit.

Photo Credits

Chapter 1

p. 3, Courtesy of Brick Brewing Co. Limited, www.brickbeer.com; p. 12, © Mtoumbev/Dreamstime.com/GetStock.com; p. 15, © Convisum/Dreamstime.com/GetStock.com; p. 17 (left), © Sean Lock/Getty Images; p. 17 (right), © Jose Luis Pelaez Inc./Blend Images, LLC.

Chapter 2

p. 29, © Inter IKEA Systems B.V.; p. 35, © cozyta/Shutterstock.com; p. 35, © Landov; p. 36, © Jeff Greenberg/Alamy; p. 37, © Monkey Business Images/Shutterstock.com; p. 38, © Beathan/Corbis; p. 39, © UN Photo/Yutaka Nagata; p. 48, © Inter IKEA Systems B.V.

Chapter 3

p. 59, Photo by Peter Jordan, Mountain Equipment Cooperative Blog, http://blog.mec.ca/2011/08/02/happy-birthday-mec/chrismcneill_first-store_bridge-river/; p. 62, © donskarpo/Shutterstock.com; p. 74, © livestockimages/Shutterstock.com; p. 77, © Photographer's Choice/Getty Images.

Chapter 4

p. 91, © Bernhard Classen/Alamy; p. 96, © Comstock Images/Jupiter Images; p. 100, © Christine Ferrari/Shutterstock.com; p. 101, © Drive Images/Alamy; p. 103, © Edmond Terakopian/Barcroft Media/Landov; p. 110, © Oleksiy Mark/Shutterstock.com.

Chapter 5

p. 121, © Geoffrey Robinson/Rex Features/The Canadian Press; p. 126 (left), © Rido/Shutterstock.com; p. 126 (right), Reprinted by permission of Harvard Business Review Press. From *Peripheral Vision: Detecting the Weak Signals that Will Make or Break Your Company*, by George S. Day and Paul J. H. Shoemaker. Boston, MA, 2006. Copyright © 2006 by Harvard Business Publishing Corporation. All rights reserved; p. 128, © Martin Barraud/OJO Images/Getty Images; p. 130, © Cmcderm1/Dreamstime.com/GetStock.com; p. 136, Courtesy of Bell; p. 137, © Jonathan Hayward/The Canadian Press; © F1 Online Digitale Bildagentur GmbH/Alamy; p. 141, Courtesy of Brick Brewing Co., Limited, www.brickbeer.com; p. 142, © 2012 Cott Corporation. All rights reserved. www.cott.com.

Chapter 6

p. 155, © Steve Marcus/Reuters/Landov; p. 160, © Mario Beauregard/CPI/The Canadian Press; p. 163, © Purestock/SuperStock; p. 169, © Martin Thomas Photography/Alamy; p. 174, © jijomathaidesigners/Shutterstock.com; p. 177, © Picsfive/Shutterstock.com; p. 178, © Digital Vision/Getty Images.

Chapter 7

p. 187, © Ford Motor Corporation; p. 193, © AP Photo/John Cogill/The Canadian Press; p. 194 (left), Lehtikuva, 2005. The Canadian Press All rights reserved; p. 194 (right), © AP Images; p. 196, © Blend Images/Shutterstock.com; p. 197 (left), Courtesy of WestJet; p. 197 (right), Courtesy of Husky Injection Molding Systems; p. 198 (left), © Georgia Straight Photo, www.straight.com; p. 198 (right), © Design Pics/Kristy-Anne Glubish; p. 205, © Peshkova/Shutterstock.com.

Chapter 8

p. 215, © AP Photo/James A. Finley/The Canadian Press; p. 218, © Blend Images/Getty Images; p. 224, © Henry Georgi/All Canada Photos; p. 227, © Comstock/Jupiterimages; p. 229, © Pixelbliss/Shutterstock.com; p. 230, © Tupungato/Dreamstime.com/GetStock.com; p. 232, © Marques/Shutterstock.com; p. 236, © Image Source/Getty Images; p. 244, © Ian Lindsay, *The Vancouver Sun*.

Chapter 9

p. 247, Courtesy of Telus. All rights reserved; p. 252, © Yuri Arcurs/Shutterstock.com; p. 256, © Stephen Aaron Rees/Shutterstock.com; p. 260, © Monkey Business Images/Shutterstock.com; p. 265, © John Robertson/Alamy; p. 266, © Dan Riedlhuber/Reuters/Landov.

Chapter 10

p. 279, © Dean Lewins/EPA/Landov; p. 282, © Lise Gagné/iStockphoto.com; p. 285, Lise Gagné/iStockphoto.com; p. 287, Environmental Defense Fund, "Our Mission and History." Copyright © 2011 Environmental Defense Fund. Used by permission. The original material is available at www.edf.org/about/our-mission-and-history. Accessed May 14, 2012; p. 289, © AVAVA/Shutterstock.com; p. 292, © Purestock/SuperStock; p. 299, © StockLife/Shutterstock.com; p. 300, © AVAVA/Shutterstock.com; p. 301, © Helder Almeida/Shutterstock.com.

Chapter 11

p. 311, Courtesy of Four Seasons. Photographer Robert Leon; p. 317, © Nagy-Bagoly Arpad/Shutterstock.com; p. 319, © John Lund/Sam Diephuis/Blend Images, LLC; p. 320, © Mishkaki/Dreamstime.com/GetStock.com; p. 321, © Andresr/Shutterstock.com; p. 331 (left), Powered by Light RF/Alamy; p. 331 (right), © Mike Cassese/Reuters/Landov; p. 332, © Mark Spowart/The Canadian Press.

Chapter 12

p. 343, © CTK/Alamy; p. 345, © Morgan Lane Studios/iStockphoto.com; p. 346, © Lise Gagné/iStockphoto.com; p. 347, © webphotographer/iStockphoto.com; p. 350, © SuperStock/Alamy; p. 358, © SuperStock/Alamy; p. 363, © Ariel Skelley/Getty Images.

Chapter 13

p. 373, Courtesy of Husky Molding Systems; p. 374, © Vicza/Dreamstime.com/GetStock.com; p. 375, © Jurisam/Dreamstime.com/GetStock.com; p. 376, © Scala/Art Resource, NY; p. 378, Courtesy of Husky Molding Systems; p. 379, © Heymo/Shutterstock.com; p. 384, © Perry Mastrovito/Corbis; p. 385, © Robbi/Shutterstock; p. 391, © Madlen/Shutterstock.com.

Index

Name/Company/URL

Subject